The Great Meat Cookbook

PORK TENDERLOIN STUFFED WITH PORCINI MUSHROOMS
WITH TOMATO SALSA VERDE (PAGE 324)

THE GREAT MEAT COOKBOOK

BRUCE AIDELLS

with **ANNE-MARIE RAMO**

PHOTOGRAPHS BY LUCA TROVATO

HOUGHTON MIFFLIN HARCOURT

BOSTON • NEW YORK • 2012

For information about permission to reproduce selections from this book, write to Permissions, Houghton Mifflin Harcourt Publishing Company, 215 Park Avenue South, New York, New York 10003.

www.hmhbooks.com

Library of Congress Cataloging-in-Publication Data is available.
ISBN 978-0-547-24141-8

Book design by George Restrepo, Rest Design
Food styling by Rori Trovato
Prop styling by Jennifer Barguiarena
Meats in photographs courtesy of Golden Gate Meat Company, San Francisco, California,
    and Preferred Meats, Oakland, California

Cover photograph: Standing Rib Roast with Porcini-Spinach Stuffing, Toasted Peppercorn and
    Whiskey Sauce, and Horseradish Cream, page 96

Printed in the United States of America
DOW 10 9 8 7 6 5 4 3 2 1

Illustrations on pages 41, 244, 458, and 548 © 1998 by Mary Newell DePalma.
Selected photographs on pages 50, 94, 161, and 186 are reprinted from *The Art of Beef Cutting: A Meat Professional's Guide to Butchering and Merchandising* by Kari Underly, used by permission of John Wiley & Sons, Inc.
Photographs of Angus beef on pages 44, 51, 162, and 186 courtesy of Certified Angus Beef® Brand. Used by permission.
All other beef and veal photographs courtesy of The Beef Checkoff, used by permission.
Photographs of country hams on page 346 courtesy of Edwards of Surry, Virginia. Used by permission.
Pork photographs courtesy of the National Pork Board, used by permission.
Lamb photographs courtesy of the American Lamb Board, used by permission.
Photographs on page 39 courtesy of USDA/AMS, used by permission.

Some of the recipes were previously published in slightly different form in the following magazines: *Bon Appétit, Cooking Pleasures, Cooking Light, Eating Well, Fine Cooking, Food & Wine, Gourmet,* and *Real Food.*

To my wife, Nancy Oakes,
who gets up each day to make her patrons happy
by striving to cook food to the highest standard.

You are my inspiration.

Contents

Introduction

In the sixteen-plus years that have passed since Denis Kelly and I wrote *The Complete Meat Cookbook,* the world of meat cookery has changed. Back then, we visited our local supermarket, selected the cut we needed, and into the basket it went. The conditions on the farm, the breed, and other such factors were rarely, if ever, a consideration. Maybe we paid attention to whether the meat was Prime or Choice and how tender it would be, and perhaps we thought about the price, but that was about it.

Today best-selling books, TV and movie exposés, and numerous magazine and newspaper articles have heightened our awareness. As a result, a growing number of food lovers have decided that they no longer want to buy meat produced in industrialized feedlots or other confinement systems and instead opt for sustainably raised meat. In addition to concerns about the detrimental effects that factory farming has on animals and the workers, as well as the environment, many people prefer to avoid meat from animals that have been pumped full of antibiotics and growth promotants. And others are simply looking for more choices in flavor and texture than commodity (i.e., supermarket) meat offers.

With the rising number of farmers who have returned to traditional methods and sell their meat at farmers' markets, through Community Supported Agriculture (CSA) programs, and over the Internet, a truly diverse supply is available to anyone willing to search it out. It's also led to a host of new terms: "heirloom breed," "pasture raised," "humanely raised," "grass fed," "grass finished," "grain finished," "raised without antibiotics or growth promotants," "natural," "USDA Certified Organic." What do these labels mean and how are they regulated? And how do we cook the meat displaying these claims? *The Great Meat Cookbook* will help you make sense of the confusion.

Whether you buy meat from a farmer or at the supermarket, you need to know how to choose great cuts and match them to the best cooking method. Lean beef and pork are still the norm in America, as they were when we wrote *The Complete Meat Cookbook*. But in addition to this commodity beef and pork, you'll now find lean grass-fed beef, bison, pasture-raised lamb, goat, and veal in the marketplace. The techniques and recipes in this book will give you delicious results no matter what meat you choose.

If you're like me, you're looking for new and exciting ways to spice up your meals. Grilled steaks with Spanish Sweet Pepper and Chorizo Butter (page 59),

Thai Green Curry–Marinated Beef Kebabs (page 129), and Pork Stew with Hard Cider, Baby Onions, and Potatoes (page 376) are just a few of the recipes in this collection that will bring excitement to your table. You will also find many recipes that pair small portions of meat with larger amounts of vegetables or grains.

The Great Meat Cookbook isn't just about common cuts. I've included lots of recipes for underappreciated parts of the animal—shoulder, shanks, neck, and leg, for example. Using these lower-priced cuts, you can make some of the world's great meat dishes without breaking the bank. And by so doing, you help the farmer who needs to sell every part of his or her animals.

I have also delved into the fine art of charcuterie and elegant classics like pâtés and cured meats. In addition, I've given you simple recipes for making your own bacon, ham, and corned beef.

Since turning leftovers into creative and delicious new dishes is also important when serving meat regularly and on a budget, you will find a multitude of ideas and recipes to make sure that leftovers will never be boring in your house.

Sustainable Meat

Buying Local. One way that we as consumers participate in sustainability is by buying meat locally, whether at a grocery store that carries local products or at a farmers' market.

You can also become a supporter of a meat CSA program. CSAs are ideal for purchasing grass-fed beef, bison, lamb, goat, heirloom pork, and pasture-raised veal—and they give you the opportunity to contribute to the success of a local farm. You pay a fee in advance and receive a weekly or monthly allotment of meat directly from the farmer. In this way, you're essentially investing in the farm and sharing some of the risks and benefits. The meat usually has been quick-frozen, and I provide you with tips on the best ways to thaw it safely so it remains juicy.

Pasture-Raised Beef, Bison, Lamb, Goats, and Veal. Inherent in sustainable meat production is the premise that cattle, bison, sheep, and goats are raised as nature intended—out in the pasture, where they are allowed to graze and forage. Because all grazing animals spend the first part of their weaned lives eating grass, it's important to verify that farmers making grass-fed claims actually keep their animals in pasture for their entire lives and finish them on pasture and forage only. Farmers who follow sustainable practices also should move their animals continuously from one pasture to another so the animals don't overgraze the land and so their natural fertilizer stimulates new growth and viable pasture, which readies the area for the next feeding rotation.

Meat producers who adhere to these practices may mention it on their labels or in their marketing materials, using such terms as "grass fed," "pasture raised," or "raised outdoors." Although all these words imply the practice of allowing animals continuous and unconfined access to pasture throughout their life cycle, only grass (forage) fed is verifiable by the USDA Agricultural Marketing Service.

Pasture-Raised Pork. Pigs need a variety of foods—grains (corn or barley), soy, nuts, acorns, and even milk products like whey—to provide ample nutrients. The terms "pasture raised" and "pastured" mean the animals are raised outdoors where they belong, not crammed into cement buildings on a CAFO (concentrated animal feeding operation) pig farm.

Using This Book

In this book I've tried to supply you with knowledge about all the major cuts no matter what type of meat you choose. Within each chapter, I've organized recipes by type (steaks, roasts) and by the basic cooking method, with dry-heat methods followed by the slower moist-heat methods.

Each recipe is tagged with key words to help you to quickly identify the one that fits your needs. You may be cooking for your family or for a crowd. Sometimes you're interested in comfort food; other times you want a recipe that's fit for company.

If you're in a hurry, you'll find recipes here that take 30 minutes or less. There are also recipes for dishes that keep well, rewarm well, freeze well, and make great leftovers. "Two-for-One" recipes are designed to turn leftovers into a completely different dish. Recipes labeled "Meat as a Condiment" use less than 3 ounces of meat per portion. Other recipes were developed specifically for heirloom breeds—particularly heirloom pork—or for lean grass-fed beef, bison, lamb, and pasture-raised veal. (See page 602 for lists of recipes by category.)

At the end of most recipes, brief notes give you ideas for flavorings or ingredients to substitute, serving suggestions, and occasionally, side dishes. Each recipe comes with alternative cuts that can be used instead of the one called for in the recipe.

And then there are the recipes that I call "Great Meat Dishes of the World"—important classics from various ethnic cuisines. Most of these are worthy of a special occasion and often include additional recipes for side dishes to make the experience complete. These—like all the recipes in this book—are a great way to share great meals with friends and family.

Buying, Storing, and Safe Handling

Seventy years ago—when our great-grandparents bought their meat at butcher shops—there would have been little need for a book telling them how to buy great meat. All they had to do was ask their butcher to recommend something good. If they weren't happy, they would let him know or they'd take their business down the street to another shop.

As supermarkets became the place where most meat was sold, the neighborhood butcher shop was driven almost to extinction. Recently, however, butcher shops are making a comeback. These are not the butcher shops of old: instead they cater to folks looking for more than they might find at their local grocery store. Many of them specialize in grass-fed beef and lamb, pasture-raised pork from heirloom breeds, and more exotic meats, like bison and goat. Some sell organically raised meats as well. The butchers who own these shops are often chef types who got into meat cutting more as a passion than a trade. Because there are so few master butchers to learn from, most are self-trained. Often referring to themselves as "artisans," they practice the time-honored ways of butchery, forming relationships with farmers and buying whole carcasses (especially pork and lamb). And though artisan shops are not the place to shop for budget packs of eight pork chops, you can ask these butchers for "something good," just as your great-grandma did.

At the supermarket, though, getting advice from a knowledgeable butcher is becoming increasingly difficult. That is where this book can really help.

Judging Meat Quality

Appearance. In general, meat should have a consistent color: no purplish spots, no blemishes, and no discolored areas. Keep in mind that many service butcher cases use lights that make meat look particularly good. Make your assessments when the meat is out of the case. It should be well trimmed. A ¼-inch layer of fat on steaks, chops, and roasts is just right. Excess liquid in the Styrofoam tray indicates that the meat may have been frozen and thawed or, in the case of pork, it could also mean that the animal was improperly processed. With pork and some beef, it may mean that the meat has been pumped with a saltwater-phosphate solution. Or the package may have been sitting around too long.

Read the Label. If the meat has a store label, check it. The label won't provide information about the grade, supplier, and other issues of quality, but it will help you to identify the cut and the area of the carcass, called a primal cut, that the piece of meat came from, so you can determine a suitable method of cooking.

It will also include the sell-by date. Do not buy meat beyond that date.

ABBREVIATIONS USED ON MEAT LABELS	
BI	Bone in
BNLS	Boneless
CNTRY	Country
DBLE	Double
LG	Large
LN	Loin
POT RST	Pot roast
RND	Round
SHLDR	Shoulder
SQ	Square
STK	Steak
TRM	Trim

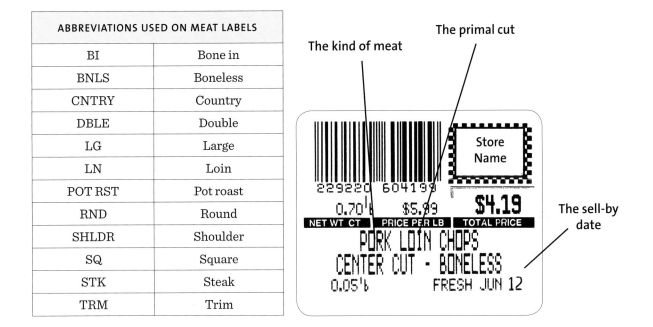

Smell. Smell is the most important indicator of freshness. Fresh meat should smell fresh, with only a mild aroma. Meat packaged in a vacuum-sealed bag will have a stronger smell when removed from the bag, but it should not have any ammonia odors.

Touch. Meat should be firm to the touch, not soft and flabby. Soft meat may mean that the muscle fibers were damaged by improper freezing and/or thawing and are leaking moisture.

Storing Meat

Meat is very perishable, and it must be kept cold (32°F to 40°F) at all times. Particularly critical is the time between dropping the meat into your shopping cart and getting it into the refrigerator at home. Meat should be the last thing you add to your shopping cart. If it will take more than 20 to 30 minutes to get it into your refrigerator, bring a cooler and ice.

Meat stored at 38°F will keep longer than that stored at 42°F (most home refrigerators operate at 38°F, which is fine). If meat and other perishables are spoiling frequently in your refrigerator, use a thermometer to measure the temperature and adjust your thermostat accordingly. The temperature in your refrigerator should not exceed 40°F.

Store meat in the meat compartment, in its original packaging, for no more than 2 to 4 days. Make sure it sits below raw foods like lettuce, so it doesn't drip on these foods.

Use meat that has been diced or ground—and organ meats like liver and sweetbreads—within 1 to 2 days. The sooner you cook the meat, the better. If you are not going to use the meat within these storage times, freeze it immediately.

Cooked meat will keep in the refrigerator for 3 to 4 days.

Thawing Meat

Meat purchased at farmers' markets, CSAs, over the Internet, or by mail-order is usually frozen. Keep it frozen until you're ready to use it. After thawing, cook steaks, chops, and roasts within 2 days; cook ground meat within 1 day.

Thawing at room temperature on a counter is not safe, nor is thawing meat in hot water. There is much too high a risk of bacteria proliferating on the surface before the interior is thawed.

The Refrigerator. Frozen meat should be thawed as slowly as possible—i.e., in the refrigerator—to minimize cell damage and loss of juices. This involves some advance planning.

Individually wrapped steaks, chops, ground meat, and ribs need about 24 hours to thaw.

Roasts (as well as steaks and chops packed in large packages) take longer: A 4-pound roast or package of meat will take about 2 days; a big 5-bone prime rib (about 12 pounds) will take 4 to 5 days.

If time does not allow for refrigerator thawing, there are two other ways to safely thaw meat.

Cold Water. You can thaw meat in cold water. Make sure it is in a leakproof container such as a sturdy zipper-lock bag. Immerse the meat in a lot of cold water (I use a sink) and change the water every 30 minutes so that it doesn't warm. With this method:

- A 1-pound steak or 1-pound package of ground meat will take about 1 hour to thaw.
- A 3- to 4-pound roast will take about 3 hours.
- For larger roasts—5 pounds and up—allow about 30 minutes per pound.

Meat thawed in cold water should be refrigerated immediately and cooked the day it is thawed.

The Microwave. You can thaw small packages of meat (under 2 pounds) in the microwave, but it will thaw unevenly and there will be areas that become warm or even start to cook. Before thawing in the microwave, remove the meat from its packaging and place it on a plate or in a microwavable container. Use the defrost function and check the meat frequently.

Meat thawed in a microwave should be cooked immediately.

Freezing Meat

The more quickly meat is frozen, the less chance there is that ice crystals will form, and less damage will be done to the muscle tissue.

Meat is frozen commercially in special "quick freezers" that maintain a temperature of -20°F to -40°F. Home freezers operate at about 0°F to 10°F, so they will never be as effective as commercial ones, but you can do a few things to freeze meat successfully at home:

- Remove the meat from its packaging.
- Put steaks, chops, and ribs in individual zipper-lock freezer bags, being sure to squeeze out as much air as possible, or seal them in vacuum bags. Airtight packages help prevent freezer burn. (Freezer burn is characterized by dry, brown, leathery patches on the meat's surface. The meat will not taste good and it should be discarded.)
- Label and date the packages.
- Don't stack the packages when you place them in the freezer. Ideally, each one should be on its own shelf, so the cold air can circulate around it, but in a pinch, you can put a new package on top of a frozen one. Once all the meat is frozen, you can stack the packages.

Meat does not last forever in the freezer. It will lose quality, and the fats will oxidize and taste rancid.

- Use frozen ground meats and raw sausages within 3 months.

- Use frozen steaks, chops, ribs, and other small pieces within 3 months.
- Use frozen roasts within 6 months.
- Use frozen ham, bacon, and smoked sausages within 3 months.
- Use frozen cooked meats within 3 months.

Refreezing Meat

You can refreeze meat that has been thawed in the refrigerator as long as it has been kept cold at all times and is refrozen within 2 days (preferably less) for solid meat, or within 1 day for ground meat. There will be a loss in the quality because some moisture will be purged from the meat fibers, but the meat will be safe to eat.

Cooking Frozen Meat

In a pinch, you can cook smaller pieces—such as steaks, chops, and pre-formed burger patties—from frozen, especially if you don't mind well-done meat. The outer edges of the meat will be very well done by the time the center thaws and begins to cook. And cooking times will be about 50 percent longer.

Don't try to cook larger pieces, like roasts, from the freezer.

Safe Handling

Because meat is perishable and can have bacteria on its surface, basic rules of cleanliness and hygiene should be observed.

Clean Your Work Surfaces. Bacteria left on surfaces that raw meat has touched can contaminate other foods you prepare (salad greens, for example), so always clean your work space after preparing meat. Get a separate cutting board that you use only for meat and that you scrub diligently after every use, or—better still—buy a cutting board that you can run through the dishwasher to sanitize after every use. Sponges and towels are great vehicles for spreading bacteria, so make sure they are well washed in hot soapy water after coming in contact with meat or the cutting board. I always run my sponges through the dishwasher, and I use paper towels to clean up meat juices and debris.

Your hands count as a surface, too; wash them well with soap and hot water before and after handling raw meat.

Cook Meat Thoroughly. The USDA defines a minimum safe internal temperature of 145°F for cooked steaks, chops, and roasts and 160°F for cooked ground meat. I don't always agree with this advice. At 145°F, meat is cooked to medium doneness, which not everyone, myself included, cares for.

If you let meat come to room temperature before cooking it—as I recommend in my recipes—surface bacteria can grow, but when you sear and brown it, any surface bacteria will be destroyed. However, if you prefer to err on the side of caution, you can cook the meat directly from the refrigerator.

Take Special Care When Cooking Ground Meat. This is another story. Here, each individual particle of meat and fat has been exposed to the germ-filled environment of the butcher shop or packinghouse where it was ground. While the surface bacteria on a steak is destroyed by cooking, bacteria in the interior of a hamburger can still be viable and dangerous. The USDA recommendation of 160°F internal temperature, or well-done, ensures safety.

If you are a fan of medium-rare burgers, grind your own meat (see page 132); it will reduce the risk of bacterial contamination.

Keep Cooked Food Hot. The danger zone is between 40°F and 140°F, so don't let cooked meat sit on a buffet for more than an hour. A better solution is to keep it in a chafing dish, where the temperature will exceed 140°F at all times. Don't take chances: When in doubt, throw it out. The damage done by spoilage bacteria is not reversible; reheating will not help.

Handle Marinades Safely. Many of my recipes use marinades to flavor the meat. Any bacteria present in the meat will transfer to the marinade as they sit together. You have two options if you want to use a marinade to baste meat or make a sauce:

- Set some of the marinade aside before it comes into contact with raw meat.
- Bring used marinade to a full boil before using it again.

Cooking Flavorful Meat

My guess is that you bought this book so you could learn to prepare flavorful meat dishes. My goal is not to disappoint you. In each chapter, you'll find recipes that use the full arsenal of cooking methods to achieve consistently tender and delicious meat dishes inspired by cuisines from all over the globe.

Dry-Heat Versus Moist-Heat Cooking

There are two basic ways to apply heat to meat: dry heat and moist heat.

Dry-heat cooking methods, in which heat is applied directly to the meat, include grilling (not barbecuing), broiling, pan-broiling, sautéing, panfrying, stir-frying, deep-frying, and roasting (including indirect grilling, which is also called grill-roasting, and spit-roasting).

Dry heat is the ideal way to cook tender cuts such as steaks, roasts, chops, and cutlets as well as burgers and sausages. Most of these come from the middle of the animal, although a few are found in the shoulder and hip (sirloin). Since water and fat get squeezed out of the muscle as it cooks, lean meats such as grass-fed beef, veal, bison, and commodity pork, will become drier and tougher as they become more well done.

Dry-heat cooking makes meat flavorful because it allows the surface to brown. The browning causes a series of chemical changes (called the Maillard reaction) to occur, adding robust, meaty flavors. To contribute even more flavor, the meat can be seasoned with a spice rub, spice paste, or marinade.

Moist-heat cooking methods include braising, stewing, pot-roasting, pressure-cooking, steaming, poaching, barbecuing, and slow-roasting. Moist-heat cooking is ideal for tougher cuts such as brisket, neck, shanks, ribs, and shoulder. Moisture in the form of steam or hot liquid softens tough collagen and turns it into soft gelatin. The softening begins at 160°F. At well-done temperatures, water is expelled from muscle tissue as well, and the meat can dry out unless there is ample intramuscular fat or connective tissue to provide a moist mouthfeel. Well-marbled cuts make for a juicier moist-heat-cooked dish than do lean cuts. However, some cuts that are rich in collagen but lack a lot of intramuscular fat—such as beef shanks or shoulder cuts of bison—can also yield tender and succulent results.

Although barbecuing and slow-roasting don't involve adding water, they are considered moist-heat cooking because the low temperatures (between 200°F and 250°F) keep the moisture within the meat itself, where it gently transforms the collagen to gelatin.

Moist-heat cooking doesn't allow for the surface of the meat to reach the temperature necessary for a full Maillard reaction, but there are other ways to create great taste. The meat is usually browned first, which does impart a deep flavor to the exterior. Then the meat is slowly cooked in a seasoned liquid, where its flavors commingle with the cooking liquid, resulting in dishes as subtle as veal ragù or as intense as lamb curry.

Grilling and Barbecuing

Today there are many great choices for both charcoal and gas-fired grills. Provided I have the time and energy, I prefer my trusty kettle-style charcoal grill, because I like the extra-smoky flavors that charcoal imparts. I always use hardwood charcoal rather than briquettes, because it burns hotter and longer. (Where I live, mesquite is the most common and popular hardwood.) But if I'm feeling lazy or am in a hurry, I fire up my gas grill, which works fine for chops, steaks, and burgers. The drippings hitting the flames provide adequate grilled flavors, and it's easy to regulate the heat source. Best of all, there are no ashes to clean out and dispose of. All the grilling recipes in this book can be made with either a charcoal or gas grill with excellent results.

How to Direct-Grill

On a Charcoal Grill

1 Create a fire of varying degrees of intensity by layering the coals once they are glowing. Areas that are two or three layers or more thick will have intense heat, while areas one layer thick will produce moderate heat. Leave an area with no coals to which you can move meat if flare-ups occur.

2 To test the intensity of the high-heat area, hold your hand just above the grate. You should be able to hold it there only to the count of 2. If the coals are not hot enough, wait for them to heat a bit more or pile on more coals.

3 Continue to heat until the grate is very hot, 3 to 4 minutes, then oil the grill by moistening a paper towel with vegetable oil and, using tongs to hold the towel, rub it all over the grate. Make sure the vents in the bottom and the lid of the grill are fully open. (You can grill directly without using the lid, but I prefer to use it, because it helps reduce the risk of flare-ups.)

4 Lay the meat over the high-heat area and immediately cover the grill. If flare-ups occur, close the vents in the top of the grill, which will cut off the airflow. If the flames continue, move the meat to an area with less-intense heat and wait for the flames to die down. Return the meat to the intense heat and

reopen the vents. Grill the meat for about 2 minutes per side, or until deeply brown but not charred. (If the meat begins to char before 2 minutes, flip it.) Check the internal temperature with an accurate thermometer (see page 15 for my recommendations). If the meat is not done to your liking, move it to a less-intense area and continue to grill until it reaches the desired temperature. Always let the meat rest so that the carry-over, or residual, heat completes the cooking and the juices are reabsorbed.

On a Gas Grill

For gas grills with three or four burners, preheat all the burners, then adjust them so you have one section at full heat, another at moderate heat, and a third with no heat. Follow the same method as for charcoal, moving the meat if it cooks too quickly and chars. After searing the meat, if it's not done, finish cooking it over moderate heat with the grill closed. For two-section grills, set up a high-heat section and a moderate-heat section and move the meat if flare-ups occur. If flare-ups continue, shut off one section and move the meat there. When the flames subside, move the meat back over the area of high heat to finish cooking.

How to Indirect-Grill (Grill-Roast)

On a Charcoal Grill

1   Spread two or three layers of hot coals over half of the grill. For smaller cuts, such as steaks or chops, sear the meat. (It is not necessary to sear large roasts, because the meat will be on the grill for long enough to brown.) Bank the coals on opposite sides of the grill and center a drip pan underneath (or between the coals). Place the meat over the drip pan, so that there is no fire directly under it. Insert a cable-type digital continuous-read meat thermometer (see page 15) into the center of the meat, making sure the cable is not over direct heat.

2   Cover the grill and follow the recipe for timing to your preferred level of doneness. You may have to add more coals for larger roasts. Control the temperature of the grill by opening and closing the bottom and top vents. During the roasting, add soaked wood chunks or chips to the fire to give the meat a smoky flavor if you wish. If the meat is to be glazed, move the coals so they cover half of the grill, brush on the glaze or sauce, place the meat directly over the fire, and sear until the sauce forms a bubbly glaze. For larger cuts, such as hams or a large roast, you can simply brush the glaze onto the meat for the last 15 to 20 minutes of its grill-roasting time.

MY TIPS FOR GRILLING

- Wear shoes, not sandals. Embers can pop through vents and burn your feet.
- Buy some welder's gloves; they're great for handling hot items.
- Invest in restaurant-quality spring-loaded tongs. I like the Rösle brand. (Avoid "Father's Day" grilling tool sets; they're too flimsy.)
- Build a fire with varying areas of heat intensity and move the meat if flare-ups occur.
- If the meat is cooking too fast, move it to an area with less intense heat. Turning and moving meat around is what grilling is all about. Burned meat is the hallmark of an inexperienced griller.
- Never judge doneness by color. Instead, measure the internal temperature with an accurate meat thermometer. Steaks thinner than ½ inch thick are too thin to reliably test with a thermometer, so make a little nick into them with your knife to check.
- Always let steaks rest for at least 5 minutes before serving.

On a Gas Grill

1 Indirect grilling is much easier on a gas grill than on a charcoal grill. Preheat all burners on high for about 15 minutes. For two-burner grills, shut off one of the burners. For three- or four-burner grills, leave the outer burners on and shut off the middle burner(s). Set smaller cuts, such as back ribs, rack of lamb, or tri-tip, directly over the fire and sear all over. Larger cuts don't need to be seared. Place the seared meat in a roasting pan and center it over the unlit section of the grill. Insert a cable-type digital continuous-read thermometer into the center of the meat, making sure the cable is not over direct heat, and close the grill. If you want a smoky flavor, add soaked hardwood chips to the smoke box if your grill has one; otherwise, place the chips in a clean tuna can and, using tongs, set the can over a burner. Replace the soaked chips periodically as they are used up. Adjust the burners so that the temperature of the grill is between 325°F and 375°F, or whatever the recipe specifies.

2 To glaze larger pieces of meat, such as ham or Boston butt, apply the sauce or glaze during the last 15 to 20 minutes of cooking and turn up the burners to create a grill temperature of 400°F. To glaze small pieces, such as a slab of back ribs or rack of lamb, apply the glaze and then cook the meat over direct heat until the glaze is bubbly and browned.

How to Barbecue

A slower form of indirect grilling, true barbecuing is actually a type of moist-heat cooking. Barbecuing is best done in the range of 200°F to 275°F: The internal temperature of the apparatus should not exceed 275°F. With gas grills, it may be difficult to maintain such a low temperature, so consult your owner's manual or test the grill by letting it run (without the meat) for an hour or more to see if you can keep the temperature that low.

If you plan to do a lot of barbecuing, I recommend purchasing an apparatus designed for low-temperature cooking. Good choices are a water smoker, Big Green Egg, or a Texas barbecue (see Sources), where the heat source is off to the side.

1 To use a kettle-style grill, set it up as you would for indirect grilling, but use only about 30 briquettes. Place a roasting pan between the two banks of coals and add 2 to 3 inches of water. Wrap 2 to 3 cups of soaked wood chips or chunks in aluminum foil, puncture the packet with lots of holes, and set over the coals. Put in the grate and set the meat over the drip pan.

2 Cover the grill. If your grill does not have a thermometer, place a dial-type instant-read thermometer (see page 16) in a partially closed vent hole. At first the internal temperature may be 300°F, but it should settle down to between 200°F and 250°F after 30 minutes. If it's still too hot, partially close the lower vents of the grill. As you barbecue, add more coals as needed and, when the smoke packet is used up, add two or three more packets, one at a time, depending on how smoky you want the meat. A slab of spareribs should take 3 to 4 hours, while a 6-pound Boston butt (pork shoulder butt) will take 8 to 10 hours.

Flavor Steps

The cooking method helps make meat flavorful, but it is the seasonings and marinades that give meat its unique taste profile and produce countless delicious dishes. Almost every recipe in this book begins with a flavor step. The most basic is a good sprinkling of kosher salt and freshly ground black pepper. Add more herbs and/or spices, and you have a dry rub. Moisten the seasoning with oil, lemon juice, wine, yogurt, or other liquid ingredients, and you've got a spice paste. Combine

WHEN SHOULD YOU SALT?

Some books say you shouldn't add salt to meat before cooking because salting it can draw out the juices. It's true that salting the meat and letting it sit for a day or so will eventually cause it to release moisture. But when you add salt just before cooking, it combines with the compounds produced when the meat is browned and helps highlight those wonderful savory flavors. Salting the meat after cooking it, on the other hand, has the effect of just adding a layer of salt, and the result is a less complex flavor profile.

spices, soy sauce, vinegar, olive oil, beer, fruit juice, or other liquids, and you have a marinade. Make a solution of water, salt, sugar, and other ingredients, and you have a flavor brine.

How to Judge When Meat Is Done

Knowing how to tell when meat is done to your liking is the most important lesson you can learn from this book. If you have been relying on time tables to determine when a piece of meat has reached your desired level of doneness, *Stop!* Time-based criteria for determining doneness are just plain unreliable.

Four factors determine how long it takes for a piece of meat to cook:
- The internal temperature of the meat when you begin cooking it.
- The vagaries of your heat source (ovens aren't reliable; just because you set your oven thermostat to 350°F doesn't mean the oven is in fact at 350°F).
- The shape of the piece of meat you are cooking (diameter is more important than length).
- The composition of the meat: lean meat cooks more quickly than fattier meat.

Doneness is accurately determined by one variant: the internal temperature of the meat you are cooking. To measure this, you need an accurate thermometer. There are many choices, and I have my favorites (see below). Some cost less than $10, while others can be more than $100. For $15 to $30, you can purchase a thermometer that will be more than adequate for getting the job done. But please, don't cheap out: You will regret it. All it takes to learn this lesson is to ruin one expensive Christmas prime rib.

Thermometers

Continuous-Read Thermometers

Often simply called meat thermometers, these are meant to be left in the meat as it roasts in the oven, continuously showing the internal temperature. One type is made of all metal and has a dial. Most are hopelessly inaccurate and don't even begin measuring temperature until 140°F, well beyond rare and medium-rare. Another type is made of glass; these are inaccurate, break easily, and get coated with burnt-on grease. If you have one of these, throw it away.

If I were to recommend only one thermometer, it would be a **digital continuous-read thermometer** with a wire cable that allows you to monitor the meat without opening the oven door. Sometimes these are called digital oven-cord thermometers. The thermometer allows you to preset the internal temperature you want. When it is reached, an alarm sounds. Some even have a remote unit you can carry with you so that you can hear the alarm in another room. Most of these include a timer as well. You can also use these thermometers outside the oven to check thinner pieces of meat. The probe needs to be inserted only ½ inch into the food. There are several brands, and most cost $30 or less.

A couple of caveats:

- The cable probes don't last forever and can break if they come in contact with direct heat (such as the flames of a gas or charcoal grill), so make sure to buy a couple of replacements.
- Some come programmed with settings for rare, medium-rare, and the like. These are based on USDA recommendations and should be ignored. Instead, use the temperatures I suggest in the recipes.
- These thermometers break easily if dropped.

Instant-Read Thermometers

Dial-type instant-read thermometers have a plastic cover and cannot be left in food while it cooks. They require 15 to 20 seconds to get a reading. The probe must be inserted 3 inches into the food, so they don't work well with thinner pieces of meat. They are not always accurate and may be off plus or minus 5°F. But they are inexpensive (about $8) and sturdy and usually survive being dropped.

Made of metal and plastic and battery-driven, **digital instant-read thermometers** cannot be left in food while it is cooking, either. They require only about 10 seconds to get a reading. The sensing thermistor is right at the tip of the probe, so it needs to penetrate only about ½ inch into food to get a reading, and it can be used for thin as well as thick cuts of meat. These thermometers do break easily if dropped, and some models require hard-to-find batteries. Look for models with an on/off switch.

MY FAVORITE MEAT THERMOMETERS

Thermapen by **ThermoWorks** (about $90): You can't beat this one. Although it costs more than most digital instant-reads, it is sturdy and won't break when dropped. Moisture resistant. Quicker and more accurate than other digital instant-reads.

ThermoWorks Original Cooking Thermometer/Timer (about $19): The heatproof cable allows you to leave this digital continuous-read thermometer in the meat throughout cooking. Holds up well and functions reliably.

Digital instant-read thermometer (about $15). I don't have a favorite brand, but the ThermoWorks pocket digital thermometer is reliable.

I prefer the digital instant-read to the dial-type instant-read thermometer because it's more versatile (can be used for thin and thick cuts of meat), easier to read, and usually more accurate. It costs only a few dollars more than the dial-type.

If you want a thermometer that works very quickly and gives great results, **thermocouple digital thermometers** are the way to go. These, too, have a plastic cover and cannot be left in food while cooking. They are very accurate and fast, requiring only 2 to 5 seconds to register a reading. They have a very thin probe right at the tip and so need to be inserted only ¼ inch into thin cuts. Because of their speed, they are ideal for checking the temperature in several locations to make sure food is cooked evenly, which is very useful for large cuts, such as rib roasts, pork legs, and legs of lamb. The drawbacks are that they are expensive and often very large. However, there are some pocket ones (see opposite page).

How to Use a Thermometer

Measure the temperature at the coolest part of the meat, which is at the center, or half the distance of the diameter. Avoid placing the probe next to the bones. For large roasts, take several readings along the central axis at various points. Check thin cuts, such as chops, steaks, and burgers, by pushing the probe through the side; you'll get much more reliable results. Lift the piece of meat out of the pan or off the grill so that you can stick the probe at least 2 to 3 inches into the meat without burning yourself.

If you are using a cable-type continuous-read thermometer, set it to the desired temperature. Insert the probe into the center of the roast and make sure it is not touching any bones. Once the alarm goes off, use the probe to check a couple other areas to make sure they have come up to temperature. The probe will be quite hot, so use insulated gloves or a pot holder to grab it.

LETTING MEAT COME TO ROOM TEMPERATURE

Many recipes for cooking meat with dry heat tell you to let the meat rest on the counter until it "comes to room temperature." I decided to see exactly what that means, because I too subscribe to letting meat warm to ensure even cooking and reduce cooking time. I compared two relatively small roasts, weighing 3.78 pounds and 2.24 pounds, allowing them to warm in a 70°F room after removing them from a 38°F refrigerator. After 3¾ hours, the smaller roast had reached an internal temperature of only 60°F—10 degrees less than room temperature.

Even though the meat will probably not warm up to room temperature, it's still very important to let it sit *at* room temperature. Follow the times that I've given in the recipes. The interior may warm to only 50°F or so, but the meat will cook more evenly and the cooking time will be shorter.

CONVECTION OVENS

Many new ovens come equipped with a convection option. Convection ovens have a fan in the back to move hot air around. As a result, they are more efficient at cooking food than radiant-heat (nonconvection) ovens set at the same temperature. Also, because the hot air is constantly moving, convection ovens heat food more evenly. All this is good news, especially for roasting. The truth is I almost never use anything but my convection oven for roasting. However, because there was no way for me to know if you have one in your home, I tested all the recipes in this book using a nonconvection oven.

ADAPTING MY RECIPES TO CONVECTION OVENS

Experts recommend that if using a convection oven, you lower the temperature by 25°F and expect things to be done a little faster. I don't do this.

- **For a small roast** (such as rack of lamb, tri-tip, and beef tenderloin), I roast at 400°F.
- **For a larger roast,** weighing 5 pounds or more (such as leg of lamb, prime rib, and top loin roast), I roast at 350°F for the entire time.
- **For a relatively lean roast** (such as pork loin, leg of pork, beef sirloin tip, cross-rib, and top sirloin), I roast at 325°F.
- **For low-temperature cooking** (200°F to 250°F), as in recipes intended to allow lean grass-fed beef and bison to cook evenly with a minimum of moisture loss, I cook at the recommended temperature and check for doneness sooner.
- **For pot roasts and other braises,** I cook at the temperature recommended in the recipe and check for doneness sooner.

In all cases, roasts are done more quickly in a convection oven. Since cooking times vary widely—from as little as 15 minutes for a rack of lamb to 2 to 3 hours for a large prime rib—I can't give you good advice for how much less time meat will take in a convection oven. I absolutely recommend that you invest in a cable-type digital continuous-read thermometer (see page 15) and set it to alert you when your roast is done. If you are using an instant-read thermometer, begin testing earlier than recommended in the recipe.

Letting Meat Rest and Heat Carryover

It is very important that meat be allowed to rest after being removed from the heat source. Two things happen: Juices are reabsorbed from the surface to the interior, and the carry-over heat causes the internal temperature to rise 5 to 20 degrees.

Large pieces of meat have greater carry-over heat because they hold their heat longer than smaller pieces of meat. Additionally, the hotter the heat source is when the meat is cooked, the hotter the surface of the meat will be and the greater the heat carryover. Meat cooked in a 250°F oven will have only 5°F or less heat carry-over, while meat cooked in a 450°F oven may have as much as 20°F of heat carry-over. If you roast in a convection oven, there will be more carry-over cooking.

The resting times suggested in each recipe allow for the cooking to be completed and the meat to be still hot when served. For large roasts (8 pounds or more), I recommend resting times of up to 40 minutes. These roasts will hold their heat even longer than that. So, if you are not quite done cooking the rest of the meal, just make sure your roast is tented with aluminum foil while you finish everything up, and it will still be sufficiently hot when you serve it.

About Ingredients

Fats

Oil. An inexpensive olive oil is fine for cooking and sautéing; a good extra-virgin is best for dressings and condiments. When it comes to vegetable oil for pan-frying and deep-frying, I prefer mild-flavored oils like peanut or canola.

Lard. Lard is excellent for panfrying and deep-frying. Never use hydrogenated or partially hydrogenated brands like Armour; hydrogenated fats are bad for you. Either make your own (see page 434) or buy nonhydrogenated lard, which you can find in ethnic markets (particularly Mexican markets that may even make their own) and farmers' markets.

Bacon Fat. Some of my recipes, such as those for braises and stews, call for you to reserve the bacon fat because it adds great flavor. You can also substitute bacon fat for lard or oil when browning meat. But because bacon fat has already been cooked at a high temperature, it isn't stable enough for deep-frying.

Butter. I prefer unsalted butter, because I like its taste. If you use salted butter, reduce the salt in the recipe. I never use margarine (I don't like the taste or the mouthfeel); you shouldn't either.

Herbs

Most of my recipes call for fresh herbs, which are now available year-round in most markets. I never use dried rosemary, parsley, cilantro, or chervil, because I don't like the taste. If you can't find them fresh, leave them out.

If you must substitute dried herbs like thyme, oregano, or marjoram, use half as much. Dried herbs lose most of their flavor in about a month, so it's best to purchase small quantities; store them in airtight jars and replace them frequently.

Salt

I cook with Diamond Crystal kosher salt, which is lighter by volume than Morton kosher salt or table salt. Here's how it plays out: 1 cup of Diamond Crystal weighs 5 ounces; 1 cup of Morton kosher salt weighs 8 ounces; and 1 cup of regular table salt weighs 10 ounces.

- If you use Morton kosher salt, reduce the recipe's amount by 25 percent.
- If you use table salt, reduce the recipe's amount by 50 percent.

Spices

Black Pepper. Ground black pepper loses its potency after a few hours. Always grind it fresh.

Other Spices. For best flavor, buy spices like cumin, coriander, allspice, and fennel whole and grind them fresh for each recipe. Once ground, most spices lose their flavor and potency quickly. Ground spices should be replaced after 2 to 3 months. I usually buy spices from a spice dealer (see Sources) or an Indian, Middle Eastern, or Mexican market that offers lots of spices and turns its inventory frequently.

Stocks and Broths

Homemade stocks are best. You'll find a recipe for Basic Meat Stock on page 168. If time doesn't permit you to make stock from scratch, use canned low-sodium chicken broth (Swanson works well). Canned stocks or broths all contain salt in varying amounts, so when making a sauce, don't add additional salt until the sauce has reduced and reached the correct viscosity; taste before adding.

Remember: Good cookin' is worth livin'!

Beef & Bison

Beef and Bison

R E C I P E S

STEAKS

ROASTS FOR SPECIAL OCCASIONS

ROASTS FOR EVERYDAY MEALS

KEBABS

GROUND BEEF AND BISON

Beef: The All-Time Favorite

"Beef. It's what's for dinner."

It's an old slogan but still relevant. When most Americans think of meat, beef comes to mind first. It's more than just food; beef is part of our national culture and folklore. And besides, beef tastes good.

Another reason beef remains popular is because it works so well with how we cook and entertain. Grilling is overwhelmingly popular, and beef offers easy and versatile grilling choices like burgers and steaks — but even roasts can be grill-roasted or spit-roasted. Beef is also the choice for holiday meals and special entertaining. Christmas dinner for many of us means a beautiful prime rib, and when guests are coming, a roast beef tenderloin marks the occasion as celebratory.

While tender cuts, like steaks and roasts, are expensive, underutilized cuts, like shanks, briskets, and various chuck cuts, are good buys and produce wonderful pot roasts, stews, and other braises, which are ideal for family meals and even for special occasions.

But many consumers are looking for more choices beyond the beef typically sold in supermarkets — choices related to how the cattle are raised and fed and how they affect the environment.

Changing Beef Choices

A growing number of beef lovers, influenced by best-selling books like *The Omnivore's Dilemma* by Michael Pollan and Eric Schlosser's *Fast Food Nation,* have concerns about cattle produced in the conventional way. The beef commonly sold in supermarkets comes from animals that spend the last part of their lives in CAFOs (concentrated animal feeding operations), crowded together in huge feedlots, fattened with an energy-rich diet of grains (usually corn). As Pollan and Schlosser document, a cow's digestive system is designed to thrive on grasses, and when the animal is fed concentrated nutrients like corn, it becomes stressed and unhealthy. On the feedlots, the cattle are given low doses of hormones and antibiotics (a practice called subtherapeutic use) not only to keep diseases in check but, more important, for a secondary effect, promoting growth. The result has been the evolution of antibiotic-resistant bacteria, which are bad for the health of the cattle and dangerous to humans as well. The development of new "superbug" strains of deadly E. coli and salmonella are a consequence of this indiscriminant use of antibiotics.

Among other issues of concern are the impact CAFOs, which release copious amounts of animal waste and liquid effluent containing hormones and antibiotics, have on the environment. These practices are contrary to the basic tenants of sustainable agriculture, and increasingly, many people have simply said no to beef produced in the conventional way. However, beef lovers do not need to give up great-tasting beef to stay true to their beliefs and commitments. There are choices: grass-fed beef, certified organic beef, and natural or naturally raised beef. What do these terms mean, and what are the guarantees that the terms really mean what they say they do?

Grass-Fed Beef

Eating grass-fed beef today is similar to the experience our grandparents or great-grandparents would have had. Before World War II, most American beef was not finished on grain but spent its entire life on pasture, eating grass. Other major beef-producing nations, such as Argentina, Uruguay, Brazil, and Australia, still produce cattle this way. In the United States, a growing number of ranchers are returning to traditional practices, raising and finishing their cattle solely on grass and forage. But they are not simply turning back the clock to the old ways. Contemporary ranchers are applying new knowledge of what types of grass and plants work best for their land and climate and what breeds and crossbreeds of cattle work best on the pasture in their locales. They have also adapted modern grazing methods to ensure that the cattle are always eating rich, nutritious grasses and other plants. By moving their herds frequently to fresh pasture and not allowing overgrazing, modern ranchers can produce cattle that thrive and grow.

Some of these ranchers choose popular breeds such as Black Angus, while others select heritage breeds that have been traditionally raised on grass. A few ranchers harvest their cattle younger than conventional commodity beef, which is slaughtered at eighteen to twenty-two months, but most let their animals graze to a slightly older age, because they grow more slowly on grass than those that gorge on corn in feedlots. Some ranchers, such as B N Ranch (see page 28), graze their animals until they are thirty months old, to allow them to fatten and develop more marbling in the meat.

I've had the pleasurable (and sometimes not so pleasurable) experience of tasting grass-finished beef from all over the world. For example, I have had grass-fed beef from Uruguay and Argentina (Estancia brand) and Australia (Greg Norman brand). Ranchers have sent me samples from many parts of the United States as well, and I've tasted grass-fed beef raised locally here in northern California. When I haven't enjoyed the meat, it's usually been because it was harvested from pastures that were not at their prime, such as during the summer months in northern California, when the weather is dry and grass is sparse.

While commodity (conventionally raised) beef is produced to taste consistent, grass-fed beef — just like fine wine — reflects its *terroir*, taking on the unique set of flavors from what the animals eat. The result is a range of beefy flavors, with more character than commodity beef. Many studies have indicated that grass-fed beef is lower in fat and has more vitamins and minerals and higher amounts of heart-healthy omega-3 fatty acids than grain-fed beef. If you are a meat lover, you owe it to yourself to sample and compare grass-fed beef from various sources.

If you have a supplier at your local farmers' market or one who sells direct from his or her ranch, give the meat a try. If you don't live in an area with lush grass and there are no producers of grass-fed beef, check out the Internet (see Sources), because most suppliers will sell directly from their websites. If you have questions about the cattle's diet (that is, is it supplemented with grain?), or whether hormones or antibiotics are administered, or what breed the rancher raises and what age the animals are when harvested, simply ask. At the farmers' markets I routinely visit, I rarely find a rancher who is not enthusiastic about what he or she does. Given the opportunity, these ranchers are overjoyed to share their enthusiasm with you — they may even arrange a ranch visit or invite you to lunch. (And if you want to share your experience with me, post a note on my Facebook page at www.facebook.com/MeatGuru telling me all about it.)

Defining Grass-Fed Beef

In 2007, after years of debate and discussion, the USDA set standards for what is meant by "grass (forage) fed" as it applies to cattle and other ruminants (bison, sheep, and goats). Essentially, 100 percent of the diet must come from forage (such as grass and legumes, as well as hay and silage) — never grain, never soybeans, never cottonseed meal. In states that have harsh winters, such as Montana and the Dakotas, some small ranchers may choose to house their cattle, while others do not,

MY IDEAL BEEF

My good friend Bill Niman, who has been called the "Guru of Happy Cows" by the *Los Angeles Times,* and his wife, Nicolette Hahn Niman, run the B N Ranch in Bolinas, California. Bill has chosen cattle that are ideally suited to the ranch's seaside location, and he raises them entirely on grass. They spend their lives in pasture and are never given hormones or antibiotics. Bill raises his cattle for a full thirty months, which he says makes all the difference in the meat, because it develops more marbling and taste.

Bill feels, as I do, that grass-fed beef is a seasonal product (he compares it to a great ripe tomato). In 2011 the cattle at BN Ranch reached their peak in the middle of May, when the grass was still green. Bill sent me some beautifully marbled New York strip steaks. I fired up the grill and cooked the steaks with just salt and pepper. I have to tell you, the steaks were amazingly tender, with true beef flavor, unmatched by commodity beef.

but in either case, the cattle must be fed harvested forage. During the growing season, however, to be deemed "grass fed," the animals must have *continuous* access to pasture.

Nothing in the grass-fed claim says that the animals are not administered antibiotics or hormones, but the cattle have less need for these because they're not crowded in feedlots or fed a digestively stressful diet of corn and other grains. Therefore, most of these producers don't administer them. If the farmers wish, they can go through an extensive application process and then state on the label that no antibiotics or hormones have been used.

Companies using the USDA "grass-fed" claim do so on a voluntary basis, but the claim must be supported by documentation. Other organizations have created standards that go beyond the requirements of the USDA grass-fed claim. For example, the American Grassfed Association requires that meat bearing its seal comes from cattle that live their entire lives on the pasture or range. Other certifying agencies that have created standards for sustainability or animal welfare include Food Alliance and Animal Welfare Approved. These standards can be complicated (Food Alliance, for example, certifies ranchers that meet certain animal welfare standards and environmental standards, as well as certain labor practices), but such certifications can be more powerful than label claims. They give the consumer a more comprehensive picture of how the animals were raised, and they require an auditor to visit to verify that the producer is, in fact, adhering to the standards. Because of its independent nature, however, third-party verification can be expensive.

Many grass-fed beef ranchers run small operations, and any fees would cut into their slim profit margins, so they may not apply for third-party verification. Nonetheless, you can learn how they raise their animals by using a good, old-fashioned method: Ask. This can be as simple as showing up at a farmers' market where beef is sold and having a conversation with the rancher.

Because raising beef entirely on grass is more expensive, expect the meat to be more costly than commodity or all-natural beef. In general, the meat will be leaner, although some grass-fed beef can be well marbled. Cuts may be smaller, because the cattle are typically smaller when they go to market (about 1,100 pounds, compared with the 1,250 to 1,400 pounds for grain-finished animals).

Meat from an animal (beef, bison, or lamb) raised and finished on grass and forage is seasonal. Grass-fed beef is at its peak when the grass the cattle feeds on is also at its peak, which in most climate zones is late spring and early summer. Here in northern California, the grass begins turning green when the rainy season starts in October and November and grows rapidly in the early spring months, peaking in March or April, depending on how long the rains last. This is the best time to harvest animals for market. The grass dies in the late spring, so May through October aren't great months for slaughtering beef in Northern California. For bison that live in the high prairies of Colorado or Montana, the summer rain means that September and October are the best times to harvest.

The smart rancher slaughters in peak months. They may then freeze some of the meat and sell it throughout the year, or they may sell all the meat fresh during the peak season and let customers freeze their own supply. It's much better to purchase grass-fed meat that was frozen at its seasonal peak than to buy fresh meat during the off-season. Trust me: Quickly frozen beef is excellent, provided that you thaw it slowly (see page 6). Don't be afraid to ask how long the beef has been frozen, and don't buy meat that has been frozen for two seasons or more.

You may consider "cow-pooling": going in with a group to purchase a side of beef directly from the producer. This is a great way to buy at the peak of season, and at lower prices than at farmers' markets or specialty stores. Find meat producers in your area who sell direct at LocalHarvest.org, or see Sources.

Some ranchers in the southern two thirds of the country (areas that don't have lots of snow) provide high-quality grass-fed beef year-round by planting pastures of different annual grasses and rotating the cows through the different fields. (This system, called a forage chain, is also used in Argentina.) Planting annual crops, however, increases the rancher's costs. Somewhat ironically, one of the best crops for this purpose is corn, which the cattle can easily digest when the plant is in its immature stage, before it forms ears.

USDA Certified Organic Beef

The USDA certifies organic beef producers who follow specific practices set forth in its National Organic Program. The producers' adherence must be documented on-site by approved third-party auditing organizations.

USDA Certified Organic beef must be fed only organic feed and cannot be administered antibiotics and hormones. The cattle must spend the entire growing season (or a minimum of 120 days) each year in pasture and actively graze on grass and other pasture forage. In addition, they must have access to the outdoors and not be continuously confined during the nongrazing season.

However, beef labeled USDA Certified Organic can still be given grain as a supplement. In fact, USDA Certified Organic beef can be finished on organic grain for up to 120 days—or one fifth of a cow's lifetime. Also, when it's not grazing season (or for up to 245 days), the cattle can be kept in a feedlot, as long as they have access to pasture. The feedlots must provide sufficient space and access to feed and meet environmental and animal health requirements—a striking difference from traditional commodity beef feedlots.

IS GRASS-FED BEEF CERTIFIED ORGANIC?

Grass-fed beef cannot be Certified Organic unless the cattle are fed grass from certified organic pastures. Some ranchers do raise grass-fed cattle on organic grasses and have the meat labeled Certified Organic (see Sources for some of the companies that sell this beef).

Just as some farmers raise vegetables that would be labeled Certified Organic if they paid for certification but choose not to incur the expense, small ranchers, such as those you might encounter at your local farmers' market, may not be certified, although they produce beef that would qualify. It's best to get to know the suppliers and ask for details about how they raise their cattle so you can determine if their beef is the type you're looking for.

The bottom line is that while certified organic cattle do spend time in pasture, they should not be confused with grass-fed beef.

Because of the added cost of third-party verification, expect to pay more for USDA Certified Organic beef and even more for USDA Certified Organic grass-fed beef. Depending on the specifics of how the animals are raised and finished, marbling, leanness, and the size of cuts — as well as tenderness and flavor — will vary.

Natural Beef

As the USDA defines the term "natural beef," the meat cannot contain any artificial flavorings, colorings, ingredients, or chemical preservatives, and it can be processed only minimally. Claiming that beef is "natural," however, is confusing and misleading, because typically nothing is done to beef other than butchering the meat into various cuts. In other words, by the USDA definition, *all* raw beef is "natural," but many consumers mistake the term to mean USDA Certified Organic or grass-fed. Allowing raw beef to be labeled "natural" is as meaningless as allowing bottled water to be labeled "cholesterol-free." Useless claims like this make us all question the legitimacy of USDA-approved labels.

Nonetheless, many companies use the terms "natural" and "all natural" for beef raised without antibiotics or hormones and on a diet with no animal byproducts. You should find out exactly what the company means by "natural." Some labels do state "raised without antibiotics or hormones and fed a vegetarian diet only."

Expect beef raised with no antibiotics or hormones and fed a 100-percent vegetarian diet to cost more than commodity beef. Usually the meat is branded; Country Natural Beef is one example. I recommend that you check out the websites (see Sources) for various all-natural beef companies or pick up their brochures to learn more about how their production practices differ from those of commodity beef companies. Often these practices are related to humane treatment and the type of feed given to the cattle during finishing.

The taste and tenderness of this meat will vary from brand to brand.

Naturally Raised Beef

Because of the confusion surrounding the terms "natural" and "all natural," the USDA has come up with a clearer term: "naturally raised." Beef bearing this claim comes from cattle raised entirely without hormones and antibiotics and never fed animal by-products. These cattle may have been finished on grain in feedlots or out on the pasture. Unfortunately, however, although many companies meet these criteria, the agency has not yet cleared the term for use on labels.

Commodity Beef

Commodity beef is the beef typically sold in supermarkets. It is all about consistency and reliability. It will taste the same whenever and wherever you buy it.

Cattle that are raised for commodity beef go through three distinct phases. During the first part of their lives, they stay with their mothers in the pasture, drinking milk and eating grass, until they're weaned, at about six to eight months. At this point, they may be sold to an intermediary operation, where they are gradually introduced to grain to acclimate them to the feedlot environment, or they may be kept on the same ranch in separate pastures from the newly weaned calves. During this phase, they eat grass, possibly supplemented with grains such as wheat and oats. They remain in this stocker phase, gaining up to 3 pounds a day, until they reach 750 to 900 pounds.

For the third phase, they're shipped to feedlots for finishing. There they are allowed to gorge on corn and other nutrients (you can assume it's not an all-vegetarian diet unless the meat is labeled as such) for four to six months or, on average, about 150 days. Because of the crowded conditions of the feedlots and the stress placed on their digestive systems by a grain diet designed to encourage weight gain, the cattle are continually administered low doses of antibiotics and hormones. They are allowed to reach a weight of 1,250 to 1,400 pounds and are slaughtered at eighteen to twenty-two months of age.

TERMS AT A GLANCE

Grass-Fed Beef
- Fed a lifetime diet of grass and forage
- Live primarily in pastures but may be temporarily housed during bad weather

USDA Certified Organic Beef
- Cannot be given antibiotics, hormones, or animal by-products
- Can be confined during nongrazing season, if with access to pasture
- Can be finished on organic grain in feedlots
- Must be verified by approved third-party auditors

Natural Beef with the label stating "raised without antibiotics or hormones and fed a vegetarian diet only"
- Cannot be given antibiotics, hormones, or animal by-products
- Can be finished on grain in feedlots or in pasture

Natural Beef with no other claims
- Essentially a term for commodity beef
- Diet may not be 100-percent vegetarian
- Can be given antibiotics and hormones
- Kept in feedlots for finishing on grain

Naturally Raised Beef
- Cannot be given antibiotics, hormones, or animal by-products
- Can be finished on grain in feedlots
- Term has not yet been approved for use

Commodity Beef
- Routinely given antibiotics, hormones, and animal by-products
- Always finished on grain in feedlots

Beef Breeds

Worldwide there are more than eight hundred breeds of cattle. In the United States, breeds of British origin dominate the beef industry, with Black Angus being the most common; Black Angus is often sold as a specific brand. Other popular breeds found in America are Hereford, Shorthorn, and Durham. Some ranchers may raise only specific breeds, but in general, beef producers crossbreed to develop animals that do well on their ranches. Producers of commodity beef also look to cattle that will easily gain weight when finished with grain in feedlots.

Different breeds have attributes that allow them to perform well under varied conditions. For example, ranchers in cold climates want breeds or crosses that

WAGYU BEEF

Wagyu is the Japanese word for "Japanese cow." This category of beef is made up of several breeds of cattle, all of which are likely to display dense marbling (usually marbled significantly beyond USDA Prime). The most famous is known as Kobe beef, and only a specific breed of cattle called Tajima-gyu — born and grown in the prefecture that surrounds the city of Kobe — can be called Kobe. Kobe is a registered trademark, and the brand is protected.

In the United States, a few cattle from some of the breeds that are collectively called Wagyu have been crossed with Black Angus cattle to produce American Wagyu beef. (Many producers call their meat American Kobe, which is misleading and violates the Japanese trademark.)

To produce this highly marbled meat, the cattle are fed for extended periods — 350 days or more — on a diet rich in grain. As with commodity beef, they are administered antibiotics and hormones, and their diet may include animal by-products. The result is juicy and supertender beef with a softer fat than regular beef. The meat is expensive, but it is so rich that a little goes a long way. Marbling occurs in all muscles, so even traditionally lean and dry cuts like eye of round and bottom round are well marbled and often tender and juicy. Seek out these cuts, which cost less than steaks cut from the loin and rib. Wagyu beef can be found online (see Sources) or at upscale specialty butchers.

Cooking Wagyu Beef

The softer intramuscular fat of Wagyu beef has a lower melting point than that of most other beef. Even when the meat is cooked rare, the fat will have mostly melted, leaving the meat rich and juicy. If you like your steaks very rare (less than 120°F), the meat may taste fatty. I recommend cooking Wagyu steaks and roasts to medium-rare, as this renders out some of the fat.

Fans of well-done meat will find that Wagyu cooked this way will still be tender and juicy. If you are going to cook the meat medium-well or well, use moderate heat (300°F to 325°F) so that you don't overcook the exterior (which would make it hard and tough) before the inside is cooked.

do well in harsh winters, while southern ranchers look for breeds that do well in warm, humid weather.

Ranchers wanting to produce larger, leaner animals may choose to cross the English breed Hereford with a European breed such as Charolais. Those wanting to produce superior grass-fed beef may look to breeds such as Kerry from Ireland, Galloway from Scotland, and Dexter from England—all put on weight and produce well-marbled meat when finished on grass in pasture.

Unusual breeds have also been appearing in the marketplace. One example is Randall, a rare breed that can produce deep, beefy steaks with yellow fat (it is being served in restaurants in the Washington, D.C., area). Highland cattle, long-haired shaggy beasts ideal for cold climates, are raised in several parts of the country—Maine and Napa, California, for example. The meat is well marbled, with a lovely beefy flavor, and it too is being sold to restaurants. Other specialty breeds you may come across are Chianina and Piedmontese from Italy, Limousin and Charolais from France, and Criollo from Spain.

If you're interested in exploring breed-specific meat, start by going to restaurants. Chefs are often the first to be offered new products. You can ask them where they buy their beef, and you can also start exploring the Internet.

Although fans of each breed claim superior taste, tenderness, and eating qualities, the breed is not the only factor that determines quality of the meat. That depends on many other factors, including the grazing conditions, how the cattle were finished, and their age at harvesting.

Bison (Buffalo)

"Bison" is the correct name for the magnificent beasts that Europeans first saw in North America and mistakenly thought were a species of water buffalo. It's estimated that in the 1600s, 30 million bison roamed the great prairies of this continent. There are now more than 200,000 head of bison raised in the United States and more than 250,000 in Canada. Unlike cattle, which are a domesticated livestock that have been genetically separated into specific breeds for centuries, bison are wild animals that are still genetically diverse, ensuring lots of variation in the meat produced.

Bison are predisposed to live and thrive on grass, like the tall grass prairies of old. Today's bison spend most of their lives grazing in pasture on grass and forage, but the majority are then shipped off to feedlots for finishing on grain. Grain-finishing allows the bison to put on weight more quickly—though the meat will not marble—so that they reach market size at a younger age. The lack of exercise from being confined in a feedlot also means the meat will be more tender. Producers believe that because many Americans prefer the flavor profile of grain-finished beef, they will favor grain-finished bison, but the meat loses some of its unique taste. Bison are wild animals that fear confinement, and in my opinion, the extreme stress placed on confined bison outweighs any benefits of the feedlot.

Ranchers who raise bison entirely on their traditional diet of grass usually label the meat "grass-fed" and advertise that practice on their websites and in their marketing material. Grass-fed bison tastes very similar to lean grass-fed beef, with a slightly sweeter, deeper flavor. I particularly like the tougher, gnarly cuts. Long moist-heat cooking makes these cuts tender and really highlights that bison flavor.

GRASS-FINISHED VERSUS GRAIN-FINISHED BISON

Grass-Finished Bison
- The meat has a unique flavor, but it can be tough.
- The meat is higher in omega-3s and other nutrients than grain-finished meat.
- You'll get the best meat when the grass is best, but there are variations based on geography and climate.
- The animals are raised in a natural manner, which is less stressful for them.
- Raising bison in pasture has less impact on the environment, and it can actually be beneficial, since the animals eat only selected vegetation.
- The animals can never be administered antibiotics.

Grain-Finished Bison
- It is illegal to give hormones to bison; it's legal but not common to administer antibiotics. Check the label to be sure these have not been used.
- The controlled diet means consistent quality and a familiar flavor profile, but the meat loses some of the unique bison taste.
- The meat is more tender than grass-finished bison due to the animals' lack of exercise in the feedlot and their younger age when sent to market.
- Because the process doesn't rely on grass, grain-finishing makes bison available year-round.
- Grain-finishing in feedlots puts huge stress on the animals.
- The process produces a great deal of waste, uses excessive water, and has a large negative impact on the environment.

The meat of grass-fed bison will have a darker purple color, and the fat may be yellowish. Grass-fed bison is also higher in omega-3s and other nutrients than grain-finished bison. Grain-finishing is rarely noted on the label, so you should ask. To find ranchers providing grass-fed bison, see Sources.

Like beef, grass-fed bison is best when the grass it eats is best, so, like beef, bison is a seasonal food. September and October, for example, are the optimal time for harvesting bison in Colorado, but check your own supplier to learn when pastures are at their prime. Buy bison fresh in season and frozen out of season.

How to Buy Beef

Start by choosing the right cut for the recipe you wish to make. Then check the sell-by date (see page 6 for details on storing meat in the refrigerator) and look at the package. Excessive liquid indicates that the beef was frozen and then thawed or — even worse — that it was "enhanced" (see page 38).

- The meat should be moist, with no brown spots, brown edges, or bloody clots.
- The fat should be white and creamy, with no brown edges (the fat on grass-fed beef may be slightly yellow).
- The texture of the muscle of most cuts should be fine grained (exceptions are cuts like flank steak, brisket, skirt steak, or bottom sirloin flap [*bavette*], which have a coarser texture).

Color is no indication of whether the beef is fresh. When beef is exposed to air, it oxidizes and begins to turn from cherry red to brownish red. Most consumers are turned off by this brownish color, so beef packers use airtight packages that contain high levels of oxygen to keep the meat bright red. Also, many butchers use a kind of lighting that makes the beef displayed in their cases look redder.

Some big-box retailers sell larger cuts of beef in vacuum bags (an economical and good way to purchase commodity beef). This meat will have a purplish color. When the bag is opened, the meat will return to its characteristic red color in a few minutes. Beef packed in a vacuum bag will exude some moisture, which may have a strong, slightly sour odor when the package is opened. The odor will dissipate quickly and should not be cause for alarm. Fresh beef smells fresh, with only a slight meaty smell.

- If your Styrofoam-packaged beef has stale, sour, or ammonialike odors, it has gone bad and should be returned to the store or thrown out.
- Spoiled beef will be sticky to the touch.

BEWARE "ENHANCED" BEEF

By pumping lean beef with a solution of water, salt, phosphates, and other chemicals and flavorings, meat processors prevent it from drying out and becoming tough if it's overcooked. The practice is also a great advantage to the producer, who gets to sell you a lower grade of beef — and water — at a higher price.

While the pumping does help to tenderize the meat, it produces a soft, spongy, and rubbery texture (especially when the meat is cooked beyond medium) and adds unwanted salt. If you're not sure if the beef sold at your store is "enhanced," look at the label for terms like "guaranteed tender," "tender and juicy," "flavor-enhanced," and "extra tender." Be sure to read the fine print, which must state the percentage of water pumped in and all the ingredients in the pumping solution.

Beef Grades

Most beef is slaughtered and processed in USDA-inspected plants (some small ranchers who sell directly to customers or through a local farmers' market use state- rather than federally inspected plants). After the meat is processed, the producer can decide to have it graded, but this step costs money, and many small retailers who sell directly to consumers skip the process for that reason. Often, when large producers know that the meat will not merit a Choice or Prime grade, they will spare themselves the inspector's grading fee. Ungraded beef is known as "no roll," so called because the rolling USDA stamp is not applied to the carcass.

Grading is not a reflection of the conditions under which the animals were raised or the conditions of the packinghouse; it is based on the amount of marbling (intramuscular fat). The age of the cow (it should be less than thirty months), the appearance of the leaner meat (it should have a nice, fine texture), and the color (not too dark red) are also considered. Generally speaking, the more highly marbled the carcass, the more tender, juicy, and flavorful the meat will be, and highly marbled beef commands a higher price.

While there are actually eight grades of beef, only the top three — Prime, Choice, and Select — find their way into supermarkets and butcher shops.

Prime. Only 2 to 3 percent of all graded beef is graded Prime, and most of that goes to restaurants and high-end supermarkets and butcher shops. The meat counters and butcher shops that do offer Prime usually sell only the deluxe cuts (steaks and tender roasts, such as standing rib and tenderloin). Less-luxurious cuts — such as flat-iron, bottom sirloin flap (*bavette*), short ribs, and top round — from Prime-grade animals will be well marbled and usually more tender than the same cuts of a lower grade. Ask the butcher if he or she can supply you with these, and you may save some money and end up with some very tender, juicy results.

Choice. There are three levels of marbling for beef that is labeled Choice. About 5 percent of beef from all grades will have moderate marbling (sometimes referred to as Top Choice); 15 percent will have modest marbling; and 37 percent will have small marbling.

Some stores may buy only Choice with small marbling, while others may have a mixture of levels. When choosing steaks and roasts, look for the pieces that have the most marbling. Some markets and butcher shops purchase only Top Choice. Expect to pay more for it, but the chances that the meat will be tender and juicy are higher.

Select. About 40 percent of all graded beef is labeled Select. Because Select and most ungraded beef have almost no marbling, even cuts like steaks and roasts cooked much beyond medium with dry heat will be tough and dry. Treat Select-graded beef like lean grass-fed beef and bison, taking care not to overcook it.

To save themselves the expense, producers of grass-fed beef rarely have their meat graded. Most would be graded Select, though some would be Choice or Prime.

Bison. Bison is never graded. It is leaner than USDA Select.

PRIME

Moderately
abundant marbling

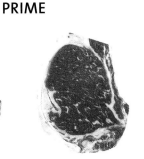

Slightly
abundant marbling

CHOICE

Moderate
marbling

Modest
marbling

SELECT

Slight marbling

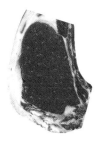

Small
marbling

PRIVATE LABELS AND STORE-BRANDED BEEF

Several major producers offer Top Choice brands nationally. Among them are Sterling Silver Premium Beef, Chairman's Reserve Certified Premium Beef, and Certified Angus Beef. Many other brands employ the term "Angus," implying that this is premium beef. However, information on the grades of these brands may not be available and so the term designates only the breed.

Many large supermarket chains offer their own brands. One national chain, Safeway, sells beef branded Rancher's Reserve, which is furnished by Cargill Meat Solutions. Safeway believes that tenderness is the most important criterion, and it actually guarantees that its beef is tender, though it does not advertise the grade.

Some cuts may be Choice and others Select; you'll never know. To ensure tenderness, proprietary procedures are used in the slaughter and processing of the beef, and samples are consistently tested in Safeway labs to ensure they meet the company's tenderness standards. As with any beef you purchase, it's up to you to decide whether you agree.

Unless other claims are made, store-branded beef is commodity beef. If you prefer beef produced from animals that were never administered antibiotics and hormones and were fed a 100-percent vegetarian diet, store-branded beef is not for you. Instead, search out brands that clearly state "no antibiotics or hormones" and "fed an all-vegetarian diet" on their labels (see page 33).

Primal Cuts of Beef and Bison

Knowing a little about the eight primal cuts — the basic sections into which a carcass is divided by the wholesaler — not only gives you an anatomical overview of where cuts come from but also helps you understand why certain cuts respond best to specific cooking methods.

In general, muscles that are more active, such as the **round** (hind leg), **chuck** (shoulder and neck), **brisket** (chest), **plate** (underbelly), and **shank** (lower leg), are going to be tougher, but they have loads of flavor. These cuts are best cooked using moist heat (braising, stewing, pot-roasting), because long, slow cooking turns tough collagen into soft, succulent gelatin.

Muscles that are mainly for support, such as those along the back, produce tender cuts. The best examples are the tenderloin, top loin, and rib eye, which come from the rib and loin primals. These cuts are ideal for dry-heat cooking methods, such as grilling, broiling, roasting, and panfrying.

Knowing a little about primals can also save you money by offering you options. The carcass is divided into primals at rather arbitrary points, not necessarily where one muscle ends and another begins, so you may find very similar meat in two primals. For example, steaks cut from the area of the chuck that is closest to the rib primal will be as good as rib steaks but cost considerably less.

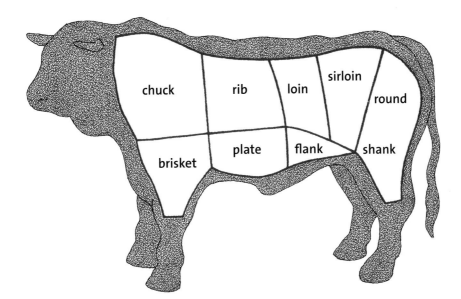

GOOD CHEAP CUTS

Sustainable ranchers — particularly those who sell at farmers' markets and through CSAs — have to sell every part of their animals to survive economically. The following list of underutilized cuts is great for all us who watch our budgets yet still want to put delicious beef dishes on the table. Check the index for recipes that use these cuts.

- **Sirloin tip steak, cross-rib steak, and chuck arm steak (ranch steak)**: If you can find well-marbled samples, these can be grilled or cooked with dry heat. Otherwise, I recommend braising.
- **Rump roast, bottom round roast, and cross-rib roast:** All these cuts are best braised for pot roast, especially if they have some marbling. A true rump roast can be roasted with dry heat.
- **Beef rib bones:** Although they don't have much meat, these are delicious grilled or roasted and make a satisfying meal.
- **Brisket, chuck roll, and chuck under blade roast:** These cuts make great pot roasts.
- **Shanks:** Because of the considerable collagen they contain, shanks turn soft and silky when cooked low and slow. They can be used for stews. A whole shank makes a spectacular presentation and can be cooked using any pot roast recipe.
- **Cheeks:** Both bison and beef cheeks will need to be special-ordered. They have a unique firm but tender texture when fully cooked. Stew these small (1-pound) cuts or make them into small pot roasts.
- **Tongue:** Because of most consumers' unfamiliarity with it, tongue is usually extremely well priced. It has great flavor and is delicious both fresh and pickled. The meat is very tender and is especially good in tacos (page 226).

BEEF AT A GLANCE

Look for

- Fine grain in most cuts (flank and brisket will be more coarse)
- White fat (the fat of grass-fed beef may be slightly yellow)
- Moist, firm meat
- A fresh, slightly beefy, smell (meat in vacuum bags will have a strong smell that should dissipate after the package is opened)

Avoid

- Meat that is browning or discolored or has bloody clots
- Meat with fat that is browning
- Meat that is sticky to the touch
- Meat that has stale, sour, or ammonialike odors
- Meat in packages with excessive liquid

Storage

- From 2 to 4 days in the refrigerator; up to 6 months in the freezer

Best Buys

- Shank, rib bones, brisket, chuck-eye steak, Denver steak, flat-iron steak, bottom sirloin flap (*bavette*), whole flat-iron, tongue
- With grass-fed beef, cuts from the chuck and round
- With Prime grade and Wagyu beef, cuts such as top round and sirloin tip

Luxury Treats

- Tenderloin, standing rib roast, rib-eye steak, top loin roast

Cooking Beef and Bison

- For all types of dry-heat cooking (grilling, broiling, frying, and roasting), always use an accurate thermometer to measure doneness (see page 15).
- Remove the meat from the heat when it's 5 to 20 degrees lower than the target final temperature recommended in the recipe. In general, let steaks and thinner cuts rest for 5 to 10 minutes (no longer, or they will begin to cool) and let larger roasts rest for 20 to 30 minutes. Consult the individual recipes for specific instructions.

- Cook lean cuts at gentle, low heat for tender and juicy results.
- Lean beef and bison cooked beyond medium-rare have a high risk of becoming dry and tough. If you prefer meat cooked to medium or medium-well, flavor-brine the meat first (see page 249) to introduce more moisture.
- If you like your beef or bison well-done, choose tougher cuts and use a moist-heat cooking method.

Beef and Bison Doneness

The key to tender, juicy meat is cooking it to the right temperature — no more, no less. The following charts, based on my experience, give what I believe to be the correct temperatures for all stages of doneness, from very rare to well-done. To the USDA, however, food safety, not deliciousness, is the paramount issue. To ensure the destruction of meat-borne pathogens such as E. coli H 157:N7, it recommends higher doneness temperatures than I do, stipulating that solid pieces of meat like steaks and roasts be cooked to 145°F and ground meat to 160°F. Unfortunately, these temperatures may render the meat tough and dry.

In roasts or steaks, the interior portion of the meat is essentially germ free. Only the surface of the meat can come in contact with bacteria, and only a minimal amount of the meat is exposed. In most cooking methods for these cuts, the heat at the surface will be high enough to kill bacteria, thus ensuring healthy eating no matter what the internal temperature. There is always some risk, albeit quite small, of bacterial contamination, so you must make up your own mind. You can follow the USDA's recommendations and be absolutely safe — or accept some risk and eat a porterhouse the way it was meant to be: rare and juicy.

Ground meat, however, is different because each particle of meat and fat has been exposed to the germ-filled environment of the butcher shop or packinghouse where it was ground. While the surface bacteria will be destroyed by cooking, bacteria in the interior of a hamburger can still be viable and dangerous. The USDA recommendation of 160°F internal temperature, or well-done, ensures safety. Exposure to a temperature of 155°F for 15 seconds will kill bacteria, and 1 minute at 150°F is also sufficient. The USDA recommendation thus allows for a margin of error. Anyone who is immunologically compromised or pregnant should err on the side of caution.

With moist-heat cooking (braising and stewing), meat is usually cooked to temperatures of 160°F to 190°F or more, at which point the collagen in the cut will have turned into gelatin and, together with the ample fat, will make for tender results. In this method of cooking, the best way to determine doneness is to see how easily a fork can penetrate the meat — or, better yet, taste it.

Because carryover heat will vary depending on the size of the piece of meat and the intensity of the heat source, consult the individual recipes to determine exactly what the internal temperature of the meat should be when it is removed from the heat, and follow the resting times given in the recipes.

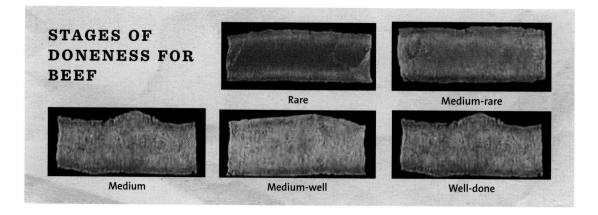

STAGES OF DONENESS FOR BEEF

Rare · Medium-rare · Medium · Medium-well · Well-done

Very Rare. The center of the meat will be soft and the same color as raw meat (cherry red for beef, purple-red for bison). The rest of the meat will be bright pink and juicy. When large roasts, such as prime rib, are removed from the oven at 105°F to 110°F, they will often reach a final temperature of 120°F or more after 45 minutes of rest and so may be considered rare rather than very rare. The final internal temperatures of very large roasts (8 pounds or more) that rest for 45 minutes may increase by 15 to 20 degrees. Consult the specific recipes for details.

MEAT	REMOVE FROM HEAT	IDEAL TEMPERATURE (AFTER RESTING)	USDA RECOMMENDATION
Beef and bison steaks	110°F to 115°F	115°F to 120°F	Does not recommend
Beef and bison roasts	105°F to 110°F	115°F to 125°F	Does not recommend

Rare. The meat will be fairly soft and bright pink to red in the center, not blood red as in very rare. Some blood-red areas may remain near the bones and in the very center of large roasts. The meat will be very juicy.

MEAT	REMOVE FROM HEAT	IDEAL TEMPERATURE (AFTER RESTING)	USDA RECOMMENDATION
Beef and bison steaks	120°F to 125°F	125°F to 130°F	Does not recommend
Beef and bison roasts	110°F to 115°F	125°F to 130°F	Does not recommend

Medium-Rare. Beef and bison can be reliably cooked to this degree of doneness. The meat will be quite pink in the center, with no blood-red areas, and will have begun to turn grayish around the edges. It will be firmer than rare but still quite juicy.

MEAT	REMOVE FROM HEAT	IDEAL TEMPERATURE (AFTER RESTING)	USDA RECOMMENDATION
Beef and bison steaks	125°F to 130°F	130°F to 135°F	145°F
Beef and bison roasts	120°F to 125°F	130°F to 135°F	145°F

Medium. This doneness is fine for well-marbled cuts of beef, such as prime rib or chuck-eye roast. The meat will be pink in the center and gray at the periphery, the texture quite firm, and the grain compact.

MEAT	REMOVE FROM HEAT	IDEAL TEMPERATURE (AFTER RESTING)	USDA RECOMMENDATION
Beef and bison steaks	130°F to 135°F	140°F to 145°F	N/A*
Beef and bison roasts	130°F to 135°F	140°F to 145°F	N/A*

Medium-Well. Use low heat (less than 250°F) to cook lean beef or bison to this range. The meat will usually be almost uniformly gray, with a pinkish tint near the bone. Fatty cuts, such as rib roast or beef chuck, will still be juicy, but lean beef may be dry. I do not recommend this degree of doneness for bison or lean grass-fed beef.

MEAT	REMOVE FROM HEAT	IDEAL TEMPERATURE (AFTER RESTING)	USDA RECOMMENDATION
Beef steaks	140°F to 145°F	150°F to 155°F	N/A*
Beef roasts	140°F to 150°F	150°F to 155°F	N/A*

Well-Done. Meat is overcooked at this stage unless it is fatty and naturally juicy, like prime rib roasts or well-marbled chuck eye. Use cuts suitable for moist-heat cooking, such as chuck steaks. I don't recommend this degree of doneness for bison or lean grass-fed beef.

MEAT	REMOVE FROM HEAT	IDEAL TEMPERATURE (AFTER RESTING)	USDA RECOMMENDATION
Beef steaks and roasts	150°F to 155°F	160°F to 165°F plus	N/A*

* The USDA does not provide temperatures for this degree of doneness.

Beef and Bison Steaks

In the palace of beef, steak is king.

Any slice of beef, no matter where on the carcass it comes from, can be called a steak, but different portions of the animal yield very different steaks, which vary in tenderness, juiciness, and depth of flavor. Not only does anatomy affect flavor, but other factors, such as breed, age, diet (grain-finished versus grass-fed), intramuscular fat (marbling), processing procedures, and aging, also have a huge impact on how great a steak will be. Some steaks are so tough that they must be cooked with moist heat, and even a great steak can be ruined if cooked to well-done.

Tenderness in Steaks

Because most people think the prime attribute of a good steak is tenderness, knowing how to choose a great tender steak will always be important. Serve a customer in a high-end restaurant a steak that requires a little chewing, and you are sure to get it returned to the kitchen. My wife learned this lesson with New York strip steak at her restaurant, Boulevard. Although this steak is a very popular cut with a high price, it does not rank as one of the most tender. Flat-iron, rib-eye, and Denver steaks are all more tender.

When thinking about steaks, a lot of folks don't consider something that is just as important as tenderness: intensity of flavor, which I call "beefiness." That's a shame, because there are many lesser-known steaks with rich, beefy flavor that are a better value than some of the supertender steaks.

Maybe you're scratching your head and wondering, Who says these steaks are so tender, anyway?

The answer is, meat scientists and trained sensory professionals. At the request of the National Cattlemen's Beef Association, they compared a wide range of beef muscles for tenderness and juiciness using such objective measures as the Warner-Brazier Shear Force Test (the more force required to tear apart a piece of cooked meat, the tougher the meat). To account for the actual perception of tenderness when eating meat, the objective results were compared to assessments by trained sensory professionals. Some clear winners emerged, as shown in the Steak Tenderness Comparisons chart that follows.

STEAK TENDERNESS COMPARISONS

Ultratender
- Fillet steak (tenderloin, filet mignon)

Very Tender
- *Flat-iron steak (top blade steak)
- Rib-eye cap steak

Tender
- *Denver steak (chuck flap steak, chuck under blade steak)
- *Petite tender steak (shoulder tender steak)
- Tri-tip steak
- Rib-eye steak, bone-in rib steak
- New York strip steak
- *Delmonico steak (chuck-eye steak)
- T-bone and porterhouse steaks (includes New York strip and tenderloin)

Moderately Tender/Can Be Chewy
Marinating or tenderizing — or both — these steaks can be helpful.
- Top sirloin steak (chateaubriand)
- *Bottom sirloin flap (*bavette*)
- *Flank steak
- *Top round steak (London broil)
- *Skirt steak
- *Ball tip steak
- Baseball steak
- Top sirloin cap steak (culotte steak)
- *Hanging tender steak (butcher's steak, *onglet*)
- Sirloin tip side steak
- Top round cap steak
- Clod steak (ranch steak)

*These steaks have great "beefy" flavor.

Continued on page 48

Tough

Use moist heat when cooking these steaks.

- Eye-of-round steak
- Mock tender steak (Scotch fillet steak, Jewish tender steak)
- 7-bone steak
- Chuck steak
- Shoulder steak
- Outside round steak
- Bottom round steak (Western griller)
- Chuck blade steak
- Arm steak
- Bone-in round steak

Tenderizing Steaks

Aging. Time in a cold refrigerator with controlled humidity allows natural enzymes in beef cells to break down the connective fibers, making the meat more tender. The beef may be packed in vacuum bags (wet-aging) or left unwrapped (dry-aging). Dry-aging also improves and concentrates flavor.

Only expensive cuts — such as the whole rib and short loin — of Prime or Top Choice beef are dry-aged. The process results in noticeable loss of moisture from evaporation, with a further loss in weight from trimming, so expect to pay a significant premium for dry-aged beef. But dry-aged beef has a rich and mellow flavor that I love.

I don't recommend aging beef at home. Your refrigerator won't be cold enough, nor will it have the right humidity for reliable aging.

Pounding. Pounding with a meat mallet or other pounder physically breaks down muscle fibers and connective tissue and results in very thin pieces of meat ideal for breading and frying (as for chicken-fried steak) or quick sautéing. Good cuts for this technique are top round steak, bottom round steak (Western griller), and sirloin tips.

I don't recommend pounding steaks thinner than ⅜ to ¾ inch. It destroys the texture and makes the steaks lose moisture.

Tenderizing with a Jaccard. A Jaccard is a tool with many sharp blades. At fifteen to twenty dollars, it is a great investment (see Sources). You press it into a steak, tenderizing the meat by cutting connective tissue and muscle fibers. It's often used in restaurants for moderately tender cuts, such as sirloin or New York strip, but I recommend it for grass-fed beef and bison, which tends to be lean and more chewy.

Tenderizing steaks with a Jaccard before marinating may also help the marinade penetrate more deeply into the meat. Stabbing a steak repeatedly with a fork will create a similar result, but it is not as effective.

Marinating. Marinades that contain acids — such as citrus, vinegar, yogurt, or wine — will tenderize only about the outer ¼ inch of the meat and will never tenderize a chewy cut, but they do add great flavor and are ideal for sirloin or cuts from the round that can use a flavor boost. Marinades that contain natural enzymes — pineapple, ginger, fig, papaya, or kiwi — will tenderize, but again, usually only the outer ¼ inch of the meat. Leaving meat in these marinades for long periods won't help in tenderizing; it just results in mushy meat.

Salt-based marinades (flavor brines) help tenderize the meat and improve its ability to hold moisture, resulting in juicier meat even when cooked beyond medium. I highly recommend using a flavor brine for really lean cuts (sirloin tip, sirloin, and top round) from lean grass-fed beef, bison, and Select-grade beef — and for any cut with minimal marbling that you plan to cook beyond medium.

Beef and Bison Steaks at a Glance

Because there's massive confusion when it comes to naming cuts, several years ago the commodity boards responsible for marketing meat came together to create a uniform standard for naming retail meat cuts and called it the Uniform Retail Meat Identity Standards (URMIS). Many of the large supermarket chains use this labeling system. It first identifies the animal (beef, pork, etc.), then the primal area (chuck, rib, and so on), and, finally, the specific cut (see page 5 for an example of a typical retail label).

When it comes to naming specific cuts, though, things can get very confusing. Not only are there regional differences (in New York City, for example, a New York strip is called a shell steak), but there's nothing to stop enterprising meat managers from coming up with their own names.

The chart that follows identifies each cut of steak by its URMIS name and gives as many alternative names as I could think of.

Because beef and bison have a similar anatomy, both animals are divided into the same primal areas and share the same names for various steak cuts. The main difference between the two is that bison yields fewer steaks, especially from the chuck and sirloin.

From the Rib

Rib-eye steak, bone in (beef rib steak, cowboy steak). This is my favorite steak (see page 61). Steaks cut from the small end of the rib (ribs 9 through 12) have fewer fat pockets than steaks cut from the large end ribs (ribs 6 through 9).

Rib-eye steak, boneless (Spencer steak, Delmonico steak, beauty steak, fillet steak, market steak). One inch thick is ideal for grilling. Goes well with dry rubs.

Rib-eye cap steak, boneless. Very tender and delicious; expensive. Considered by meat lovers to be the best steak, period.

Rib-eye fillet steak, boneless. Ideal for thick but smaller-portion steaks.

Frenched rib steak, bone in (cowboy steak). An elegant way to serve a rib steak on the bone. Expensive.

From the Chuck
(the shoulder, arm, and neck)

Chuck-eye steak, boneless (Delmonico steak, chuck fillet steak, chuck steak, bottom chuck steak). Same muscle as the rib eye, but with a little more fat and some gristle. Look for steaks as close to the rib primal as you can get. A bargain cut.

Top blade steak, boneless (flat-iron steak, book steak, top chuck steak). Cut across the top blade, this has a center line of gristle. Grill or braise. If the gristle has been removed (ask to be sure), it's the second most tender steak and ideal for grilling.

Petite tender steak, boneless (shoulder tender steak). Small tenderloin-shaped muscle weighing less than 1 pound. Tender and ideal for 2 people. Can be cut into medallions for quick cooking. Fifth most tender muscle (see page 48) and a good buy.

Shoulder steak, boneless (ranch steak, shoulder arm steak, chuck London broil, clod steak). Cut from the shoulder clod (arm section). Very beefy. Great alternative to sirloin.

Chuck under blade center steak, boneless (chuck under steak, chuck under blade steak, Denver steak chuck flap). Great beefy flavor, juicy, and fairly tender. The fourth most tender muscle (see page 47).

From the Short Loin
(the area between the rib and hip)

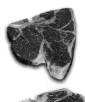

Porterhouse steak, bone in (his-and-hers steak). T-shaped bone with a section of New York strip and tenderloin. When cut thick, ideal for sharing. Expensive.

T-bone steak, bone in. Smaller eye of tenderloin than the porterhouse, more toward the head end.

Tenderloin steak, boneless (filet mignon, fillet steak, filet de boeuf, chateaubriand). The most tender muscle, but it does not have a strong beefy flavor. Ideal for sautéing. Very expensive.

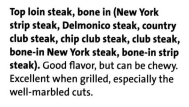

Top loin steak, bone in (New York strip steak, Delmonico steak, country club steak, chip club steak, club steak, bone-in New York steak, bone-in strip steak). Good flavor, but can be chewy. Excellent when grilled, especially the well-marbled cuts.

Top loin steak, boneless (New York steak, New York strip, strip loin steak, shell steak, strip steak, Kansas City steak, veiny steak, ambassador steak, club steak, hotel-style steak, sirloin strip steak, Manhattan fillet). Good flavor, but can be chewy. The most popular steak, especially at steak houses.

From the Top Sirloin
(the upper part of the hip)

Top sirloin cap steak, boneless (culotte steak, top sirloin cap). Depending on which part it's cut from, can be somewhat chewy, but has great flavor.

Top sirloin steak, boneless (shell sirloin steak, wedge sirloin steak, top sirloin butt center cut, sirloin butt, top sirloin butt, chateaubriand, London broil). Lean, but good flavor. Ideal for marinating.

Top sirloin butt center-cut steak, boneless (baseball steak, sirloin fillet steak). Ideal when marinated and tenderized. These steaks are cut 2 inches thick or more.

From the Bottom Sirloin
(the underside of the hip)

Tri-tip steak, boneless (triangle steak, California steak, Newport steak, boomerang steak; often mislabeled culotte). Best when marinated. Easy to cut for yourself from a whole tri-tip. Good value.

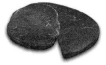

Flap-meat steak, boneless (sirloin tips, flap meat, *bavette*, bottom sirloin flap steak). Looks like a flank steak, but larger. Excellent flavor, especially when graded Prime or Top Choice. Marinate steaks from lower-graded meat.

Ball tip steak, boneless (bottom sirloin butt steak). Best marinated. Great value.

Bottom sirloin steak, boneless (sirloin tips). Best marinated and/or tenderized. Lean and chewy. Great value.

From the Round

Top round steak (London broil, inside round steak). Relatively tender; a great steak for marinating and grilling. Look for at least a 2-pound steak and serve cut into thick slices.

From the Plate
(the underside, below the rib section)

Skirt steak, boneless (fajitas, Philadelphia steak). Comes from the diaphragm or abdominal muscle. Best marinated and tenderized. Tough outer membrane must be removed.

From the Flank
(the lower abdomen)

Flank steak, boneless (London broil, jiffy steak, flank steak fillet). My favorite marinating steak.

Hanging tender steak, boneless (hanger steak, hanging tenderloin, butcher's steak, *onglet*). Only one per animal; it supports the diaphragm. Needs center line of gristle removed before grilling. Dry-rub or marinate. Very beefy.

STEAK HOUSE GRILLED RIB EYE WITH FLAVORED BUTTER

Fit for Company, Family Meal, Great Leftovers

Serves 4 to 6

Why is it that so often the steaks served in steak houses taste better than those we grill at home? The answer is not restaurateurs' access to USDA Prime beef, because, in fact, most of them serve USDA Choice, just like you can buy at any good supermarket. The secret lies in the correct seasoning, the grilling technique, and the final flavor enhancements. For a really great steak, cooked perfectly rare or medium-rare on the inside and nicely seared and deep brown on the outside, start with a thick steak, 2½ to 3 inches thick, and let it warm for 2 hours at room temperature before grilling. A thick steak ensures that the exterior has a chance to develop a beautifully brown crust before the interior becomes overcooked, and bringing the meat to room temperature makes for even cooking and a rosy hue throughout. Don't skimp on the salt and pepper when you season the steak before cooking. The robust flavor of beef calls for a good dose of both.

Grilling a thick steak requires a two-step process: searing it directly over the fire and finishing it in a covered grill away from the fire (indirect grilling or grill-roasting—basically the same as roasting). Once your steak is cooked, you must resist the urge to cut into it right away: Let it rest for 10 minutes with a few pats of flavored butter melting over it. As far as what cut to choose, I prefer a bone-in rib eye because of its great beefy flavor and the added enjoyment of a bone to gnaw on. If you prefer another favorite steakhouse cut—porterhouse, T-bone, New York strip, top sirloin, or fillet—see the directions for alternative cuts on page 54.

2 teaspoons extra-virgin olive oil

1 2½- to 3-inch-thick bone-in rib-eye steak
   (2½–3 pounds)

1½ teaspoons salt

1 teaspoon freshly ground black pepper

Flavored Butter (pages 58–59)

1 Rub the oil on both sides of the steak. Season generously with ¾ teaspoon of the salt and ½ teaspoon of the pepper on each side. Place the steak on a platter and let it rest at room temperature (66°F to 72°F) for 2 hours. The internal temperature of the steak should come up to 50°F to 60°F.

2   Set up a charcoal or gas grill for indirect grilling (see page 12).

3   Lightly oil the grill. Place the steak directly over the hot coals or fire and grill for 2 to 3 minutes, or until the steak is deep brown. If flare-ups arise, move the steak to the section of the grill with no fire and wait for the flare-ups to subside, then return the steak to the heat and continue searing it. Turn and sear the other side for 2 to 3 minutes, or until deeply brown but not burned.

4   Once the steak is nicely seared, move it to the section of the grill with no fire, with the bone facing the heat (this helps protect the steak from burning). Cover the grill and grill-roast for 10 to 15 minutes, or until the internal temperature reaches 120°F to 125°F for rare (my preference), 125°F to 130°F for medium-rare, or 130°F to 135°F for medium. Transfer the steak to a warm serving platter and let rest for 10 minutes, loosely covered with aluminum foil. After 5 minutes, place three ¼-inch-thick pats of the flavored butter on the meat. The temperature of the steak will rise 10 to 15 degrees as it rests.

5   Cut the meat from the bone and slice crosswise into ½-inch-thick slices. Serve at once, spooning some of the melted butter over the slices.

Alternative Cuts: The classic steak house cuts are porterhouse, T-bone, New York strip, top sirloin, and fillet. To serve 4 people, buy 2 to 3 pounds total: four 3-inch-thick fillet steaks, two 2-inch-thick New York strips, or one 2½- to 3-inch-thick porterhouse, T-bone, or top sirloin. Begin checking the internal temperature after about 10 minutes of covered grilling. Fillet steaks will take the least amount of time and porterhouse and T-bones the most.

Cook's Note
- Two hours may seem a long time to leave a piece of meat out at room temperature, but if you start with a refrigerated steak at 38°F and your kitchen has an ambient temperature of 68°F, the center of the meat will take quite a while to warm up. For more details, see page 17.

Re-creating the Steak House Experience at Home

No steak house experience would be complete without a crisp, cool iceberg lettuce wedge with a great blue cheese dressing, rich and cheesy twice-baked potatoes, and a green vegetable, such as broccolini.

ICEBERG WEDGES WITH BLUE CHEESE, BUTTERMILK, AND SCALLION DRESSING

Serves 4

½ pound blue cheese, coarsely chopped (I like Rogue Creamery Oregon Blue or Maytag Blue)

2 scallions, white and green parts, coarsely chopped, plus more scallion greens for garnish

½ cup mayonnaise

1 tablespoon red wine vinegar
Coarsely ground black pepper

¾ cup buttermilk, or more if needed

1 medium head iceberg lettuce, quartered and cored

1 Crumble about ½ cup of the blue cheese and set it aside.

2 With the motor running, drop the scallions through the feed tube of a small food processor. After 10 seconds, shut off the machine and scrape down the sides of the bowl. Add the remaining blue cheese and pulse a few times to chop the cheese. Add the mayonnaise, vinegar, and 2 teaspoons pepper. With the motor running, add the buttermilk. Stop and check the texture: If it's too thick, add enough additional buttermilk to produce a thick and creamy but pourable dressing.

3 To assemble the salad, lay each lettuce wedge cut side up on a salad plate. Spoon over about ¼ cup of the dressing, or more to your liking, sprinkle with some of the reserved blue cheese and some of the scallion greens, then add a few grindings of pepper, or let guests add their own. *(Leftover dressing will keep for a week in a sealed container in the refrigerator.)*

TWICE-BAKED POTATOES WITH SOUR CREAM AND PARMIGIANO FILLING

Serves 4

4 Yukon Gold or russet potatoes (about 12 ounces each), well scrubbed and dried

3 tablespoons butter

1 cup sour cream

½ cup thinly sliced fresh chives or scallions (white and light green parts)

½ cup freshly grated Parmigiano-Reggiano

2 teaspoons good balsamic vinegar

Salt and freshly ground black pepper

1 Preheat the oven to 350°F.

2 Place the potatoes directly on an oven rack. Bake for 30 minutes, then prick all over with a fork. Continue to bake the potatoes for 30 to 40 minutes more, or until soft when squeezed. Remove the potatoes from the oven and increase the temperature to 375°F.

3 While the potatoes are still hot, hold each one with a towel and cut off the top quarter lengthwise. Gently scoop out the flesh, making sure to leave enough flesh attached to the skin that the potato still holds its shape, and transfer the flesh to a bowl. Scrape the flesh from the tops and add to the bowl; discard the top skins or eat as a snack.

4 Using a fork, smash 2 tablespoons of the butter into the potato flesh until it is melted. Add the sour cream, chives, all but 2 tablespoons of the cheese, and the vinegar. Work in the ingredients and season to taste with salt and pepper. Don't overmix; it's okay if the mixture has a few lumps.

5 Spoon the filling back into the reserved shells, mounding it nicely and making sure the filled shells can stand upright. (*At this point, you can wrap each potato and refrigerate for several hours, or overnight, until ready for the final baking.*)

6 Remound the filling if you refrigerated the potatoes and it got flattened, and dot each potato with a little of the remaining 1 tablespoon butter. Sprinkle each potato with some of the remaining 2 tablespoons cheese. Place in a baking pan and bake for 20 minutes, or until the potatoes are warmed through and starting to nicely brown on the top. (If baking straight from the refrigerator, allow 10 to 15 minutes more to heat.) Serve hot.

BROCCOLINI WITH PECAN BROWN BUTTER

Serves 4

If you can't find broccolini, use broccoli florets.

2 bunches broccolini (about 1¼ pounds), washed and tough stems trimmed

3 tablespoons butter

1 tablespoon minced shallot

1 teaspoon minced garlic

¼ cup pecan halves, toasted (see Cook's Notes)

Salt and freshly ground black pepper

2 teaspoons fresh lemon juice, or to taste

1 Bring 6 quarts of salted water to a boil in a large pot. Add the broccolini and stir to separate the stems. When the water returns to a boil, adjust the heat to maintain a light boil and cook for 4 to 5 minutes. Taste a stem: the broccolini is done when it is crisp-tender. Drain and set aside, covered to keep warm.

2 Meanwhile, melt the butter in a medium skillet over medium heat. Add the shallot and garlic and stir for 2 to 3 minutes, or until softened. Add the pecans and a pinch each of salt and pepper. Increase the heat to medium-high and stir continuously until the butter has browned and the pecans have a toasted aroma. Remove from the heat and stir in the lemon juice. Toss the mixture with the broccolini and season to taste with salt and pepper. Serve at once.

Cook's Notes

- To toast the pecans, spread them on a small baking sheet and bake in the middle of a 350°F oven until nicely golden brown with a nutty aroma, 5 to 10 minutes. Transfer to a bowl to cool.

- Try the Pecan Brown Butter on other vegetables, such as asparagus or cauliflower.

Flavored Butters

CAESAR BUTTER

Makes enough for 4 to 6 steaks

2 tablespoons finely chopped fresh flat-leaf parsley	2 tablespoons freshly grated Parmigiano-Reggiano
1 teaspoon Dijon mustard	1 teaspoon minced garlic
¼ teaspoon Worcestershire sauce	¼ teaspoon salt
1 anchovy fillet, minced	1 teaspoon freshly ground black pepper
1 teaspoon finely grated lemon zest	8 tablespoons (1 stick) butter, softened

1 Combine the parsley, mustard, Worcestershire, anchovy, lemon zest, cheese, garlic, salt, and pepper in a small bowl. Cut up the butter and stir it in until the mixture is well blended.

2 Spread a 12-x-18-inch sheet of plastic wrap on a work surface and scrape the butter onto the plastic wrap. Shape and roll the mixture into a log 1½ to 2 inches in diameter. Seal in the plastic and refrigerate until firm, at least 1 hour, or until ready to use. *(Any leftover butter can be rewrapped and refrigerated for up to 1 week or frozen for up to 2 months.)*

HERB AND SHALLOT BUTTER

Makes enough for 4 to 6 steaks

8 tablespoons (1 stick) butter, softened	2 teaspoons Dijon mustard
2 tablespoons finely chopped shallots	½ teaspoon Worcestershire sauce
1 tablespoon chopped fresh flat-leaf parsley	1 teaspoon minced garlic
1 teaspoon chopped fresh basil	½ teaspoon salt
1 teaspoon chopped fresh rosemary	1 teaspoon freshly ground black pepper
1 teaspoon fennel pollen (see Sources) or ground fennel seeds	

1 Melt 2 teaspoons of the butter in a small skillet over medium heat. Add the shallots and cook, stirring, for 2 minutes, or until soft. Scrape into a bowl and set aside to cool.

2 Cut the remaining butter into ½-inch cubes. Scoop the butter into a food processor.

Add the shallots and the remaining ingredients and pulse several times to form a homogenous mixture.

3 Spread a 12-x-18-inch sheet of plastic wrap on a work surface and scrape the butter onto the plastic wrap. Shape and roll the mixture into a log 1½ to 2 inches in diameter. Seal in the plastic and refrigerate until firm, at least 1 hour, or until ready to use. *(Any leftover butter can be rewrapped and refrigerated for up to 1 week or frozen for up to 2 months.)*

SPANISH SWEET PEPPER AND CHORIZO BUTTER

Makes enough for 4 to 6 steaks

2 garlic cloves, peeled	1 tablespoon chopped fresh flat-leaf parsley
¼ cup diced Spanish chorizo (I use the softer *semicurado*; see page 414), linguica, or Cajun andouille	½ teaspoon freshly ground black pepper
	¼ teaspoon Worcestershire sauce
¼ cup jarred Spanish piquillo peppers or fire-roasted red bell peppers	8 tablespoons (1 stick) butter, softened

1 With the motor running, drop the garlic cloves through the feed tube of a food processor. Scrape down the sides of the bowl and add the sausage, piquillo peppers, and parsley. Pulse a few times to finely chop. Add the remaining ingredients and pulse to blend.

2 Spread a 12-x-18-inch sheet of plastic wrap on a work surface and scrape the butter onto the plastic wrap. Shape and roll the butter into a log 1½ to 2 inches in diameter. Seal in the plastic and refrigerate until firm, at least 1 hour, or until ready to use. *(Any leftover butter can be rewrapped and refrigerated for 1 week or frozen for up to 2 months.)*

Cook's Note
- The sausage gives the butter a great meaty flavor, but if you can't find it, go ahead and leave it out; add ½ teaspoon salt to the recipe.

OTHER FLAVORED BUTTERS SUITABLE FOR STEAKS
- Cornichon Butter (page 258)
- Tomato–Blue Cheese Butter (page 555)

Grilling Marinated or Spice-Rubbed Steaks

When I am fortunate enough to have a nicely marbled steak, all I do is season it with a little salt and pepper so that I don't detract from the great beefy flavor. But steaks that meet this criterion, such as grass-fed or USDA Prime rib eye, New York strip, porterhouse, and fillet, are expensive.

Other steaks cuts from less-tender parts of the animal can benefit from marinades, dry rubs, and spice pastes that improve both their flavor and texture. Select the flavoring you're in the mood for from the choices on page 63, then choose the appropriate grilling technique for the cut you are using from the list that follows. (For more on grilling, see page 11.)

The Cuts

Steaks from the sirloin, chuck, round, and flank are ideal for marinating or rubbing with a spice paste or rub and grilling. For information on each steak, see pages 50–51.

Flank Steak: For a ¾-inch-thick flank steak, 1¼ to 1½ pounds

If it was marinated, remove the steak from the marinade and pat dry. Otherwise, leave the dry rub or spice paste that coats the meat. Let the steak rest at room temperature for 30 to 45 minutes. Grill over medium-hot coals or, if using a gas grill, over a medium-hot flame for 2 to 3 minutes per side for medium-rare, to an internal temperature of 125°F to 130°F. Let rest for 5 minutes, then cut across the grain into ¼-inch-thick diagonal slices. *Serves 4*

Skirt Steak: For 1½ pounds skirt steak (2 or 3 pieces), about ½ inch thick

If they were marinated, remove the steaks from the marinade and pat dry. Otherwise, leave the dry rub or spice paste that coats the meat. Let the steaks rest at room temperature for 20 to 30 minutes. Grill over medium-hot coals or, if using a gas grill, over a medium-hot flame for 2 to 3 minutes per side for medium-rare. Cut into a piece to make sure it is cooked to your liking. (A ½-inch-thick steak is too thin to measure accurately with an instant-read thermometer.) Let rest for 5 minutes, then cut across the grain into ¼-inch-thick diagonal slices. *Serves 4*

Top Round Steak (often sold as London broil): For a 2-inch-thick steak, 2 to 2½ pounds

If it was marinated, remove the steak from the marinade and pat dry. Otherwise, leave the dry rub or spice paste that coats the meat. Let the steak rest at room temperature for 1½ hours. Set up a charcoal or gas grill for indirect grilling (see page 12). Grill over the hot coals or hot flame for 2 to 3 minutes, or until seared a deep brown. Flip and sear the other side for 2 to 3 minutes. Move the steak to the section of the grill with no fire, cover, and cook for 10 minutes, or until the internal temperature reaches 125°F to 130°F for medium-rare. Let rest for 10 minutes, then cut across the grain into ½-inch-thick diagonal slices. *Serves 4 to 6, with leftovers*

Top Sirloin Steak (sometimes labeled London broil or chateaubriand): For a 1¼- to 1½-inch-thick steak, about 2 pounds
If it was marinated, remove the steak from the marinade and pat dry. Otherwise, leave the dry rub or spice paste that coats the meat. Let the steak rest at room temperature for 40 to 60 minutes. Grill over medium-hot coals or, if using a gas grill, a medium-hot flame for 3 to 4 minutes per side. If it has reached an internal temperature of 125°F to 130°F, it's medium-rare. If not, move the steak to a less-intense part of the grill and cook for a minute or two more, until the correct internal temperature is reached. Let rest for 5 minutes, then cut across the grain into ½-inch-thick diagonal slices. *Serves 4*

Bottom Sirloin Steak: For four 1-inch-thick steaks
The bottom sirloin consists of three well-marbled cuts called tri-tip, ball tip, and flap-meat steaks (*bavette*). They are great dry-rubbed or marinated. Grill as for flat-iron steak (see page 62). *Serves 4*

Baseball Steak: For four 2- to 3-inch-thick steaks
This steak gets its name from the fact that when grilled, it swells up to resemble a baseball. There are only two of these delicious steaks per carcass. They're cut from

MY FAVORITE STEAKS

I love gnawing on steak bones. And I like thick steaks with a rich, beefy flavor.

That's why my favorite steak is a bone-in rib eye. Because a 2-inch-thick rib eye weighs in at around 2 pounds, I need two or three friends to share it. So I serve this steak when we have company, slicing the meat and keeping the bone for myself.

When it comes to a smaller boneless steak, my first choice is boneless rib eye; at about 1 inch thick, it's the right size for me. For an inexpensive but beefy steak, I choose a Denver steak (from the chuck), which is pretty tender and very beefy and juicy.

If I plan to marinate a steak — another thing I love to do — my favorite is flank steak, but I also look to a skirt (from the plate), tri-tip (from the bottom sirloin), or hanging tender. All of these steaks are full of beefy flavor, which holds up even with strongly flavored marinades containing soy, chiles, ginger, or garlic.

the tip of the ball to the top sirloin and are 2 to 3 inches thick. Marinate overnight and grill as for top round steak (see page 60). *Serves 4*

Flat-Iron Steak: For four 1-inch-thick flat-iron steaks cut by the butcher to remove the center line of gristle, 1½ to 2 pounds total

If they were marinated, remove the steaks from the marinade and pat dry. Otherwise, leave the dry rub or spice paste that coats the meat. Let the steaks rest at room temperature for 30 to 45 minutes. Grill over medium-hot coals or, if using a gas grill, a medium-hot flame for 3 to 4 minutes per side for medium-rare, or until they reach an internal temperature of 125°F to 130°F. Let rest for 5 minutes, then cut across the grain into ½-inch-thick diagonal slices. *Serves 4*

Culotte Steak (also called top sirloin cap): For four 1-inch-thick steaks

Marinate and grill as for flat-iron steak (above). *Serves 4*

Chuck Steak: For all varieties of boneless chuck steak; 2 pounds (2 to 4 steaks, depending on the cut), 1 inch thick

These are best marinated overnight. Remove the steaks from the marinade and pat dry. Let rest at room temperature for 40 to 60 minutes. Grill over medium-hot coals or, if using a gas grill, a medium-hot flame for 3 to 4 minutes, or until nicely browned. Turn the steaks and grill for 3 to 4 minutes more. Move to a less-intense part of the grill, cover, and cook for 2 to 3 minutes more, or until the internal temperature reaches 125°F to 130°F for medium-rare. Let rest for 5 to 10 minutes. If using 2 steaks, cut each one in half. *Serves 4*

GRILLING THIN STEAKS

Some steaks — skirt steak, flat-iron steak, and flank steak, among others — are less than 1 inch thick. I recommend quick grilling for these babies.

- Season or marinate the steaks and let them sit at room temperature for 45 minutes to 1 hour.
- Set up a charcoal or gas grill for direct grilling (see page 11).
- Place the steaks over the heat and grill for 1½ to 2 minutes. Flip and grill for 1½ to 2 minutes more. If flare-ups occur, move the steaks to an area of the grill with no fire; when the flare-ups subside, return the meat to the heat and continue searing.
- It's very difficult to measure the internal temperature of thin steaks, so you will have to test by cutting a small nick with a knife to peek inside. Transfer to a warm platter and let rest for 5 minutes.

Marinades, Spice Rubs, and Spice Pastes for Steaks

Marinades for Steaks

MUSHROOM MARINADE

Makes enough for 4 large steaks or 6 to 8 small steaks

1 ounce dried mushrooms, such as porcini, morels, or shiitakes	6 garlic cloves, sliced
	1 teaspoon dried mint
1½ cups boiling water	2 tablespoons balsamic vinegar
⅓ cup soy sauce	2 teaspoons freshly ground black pepper
½ cup Guinness or other stout	2 tablespoons canola oil

1 Place the mushrooms in a small bowl and cover with the boiling water. Let soak for at least 45 minutes, or up to several hours. Remove the mushrooms with a slotted spoon and reserve for another use. Pour the soaking liquid into a medium bowl, leaving any grit behind. Cool the liquid in the freezer for 10 minutes.

2 Stir the remaining ingredients into the mushroom liquid.

3 Place the steaks of your choice in a large zipper-lock bag. Pour over the marinade, seal the bag, and turn and shake it to ensure the steaks are coated with the marinade. Marinate for 2 hours at room temperature or, better still, refrigerate overnight. Turn the bag from time to time to redistribute the marinade. Let the steaks sit at room temperature for 2 hours and pat dry before grilling.

Cook's Notes

- Save the marinade to make a simple mushroom sauce: Bring the liquid to a boil. Chop the reserved mushrooms and add them to the liquid. Stir in 1 teaspoon cornstarch combined with 1 tablespoon cold water and boil for 1 minute to thicken. Season to taste with salt and pepper.

- For an Asian variation, use shiitake mushrooms; omit the mint and add ½ teaspoon Chinese five-spice powder. Use 1 tablespoon sesame oil instead of the canola oil and Chinese black vinegar instead of the balsamic.

BASIC OLIVE OIL AND FRESH HERB MARINADE

Makes enough for 2 large steaks or 4 small steaks

This is an ideal marinade for tender cuts such as porterhouse, New York strip, Denver, sirloin, rib-eye, and flat-iron steaks.

½ cup extra-virgin olive oil

1 tablespoon red wine vinegar

6 garlic cloves, sliced

2 teaspoons salt

2 teaspoons freshly ground black pepper

1 tablespoon chopped fresh rosemary

2 teaspoons chopped fresh sage

2 teaspoons fennel pollen (see Sources) or ground fennel seeds

1 Place the olive oil in a small bowl, add the remaining ingredients, and stir well.

2 Place the steaks of your choice in a large zipper-lock bag. Pour in the marinade, seal the bag, and turn to ensure the steaks are coated with the marinade. Marinate for 2 hours at room temperature or, better still, refrigerate overnight. Turn the bag from time to time to redistribute the marinade. Let the steaks sit at room temperature for 2 hours and pat dry before grilling.

MEXICAN BEER, CHILE, AND CILANTRO MARINADE

Makes enough for 2 to 3 pounds of steak

This marinade is ideal for skirt, flank, chuck, and bottom sirloin flap (*bavette*) steaks.

1 12-ounce bottle Mexican beer

¼ cup soy sauce

¼ cup fresh lime juice

1 teaspoon Tabasco or other hot sauce

2 tablespoons chile powder, such as ancho, California, or New Mexico

2 teaspoons ground cumin

3 tablespoons minced white onion

1 cup finely chopped fresh cilantro

6 garlic cloves, sliced

2 teaspoons dried oregano (I use Mexican)

1 teaspoon salt

2 teaspoons unsulfured molasses

2 teaspoons freshly ground black pepper

¼ cup canola oil

1 Pour the beer into a medium bowl and stir in the remaining ingredients.

2 Place the steaks of your choice in a large zipper-lock bag. Pour in the marinade, seal the bag, and turn to ensure the steaks are coated with the marinade. Marinate for 2 hours at room temperature or, better still, refrigerate overnight. Turn the bag from time to time to redistribute the marinade. Let the steaks sit at room temperature for 2 hours and pat dry before grilling.

MUSTARDY MARINADE

Makes enough for 2 to 3 pounds of steak

Ideal for beefy steaks such as flank, flat-iron, skirt, top round, ball tip, bottom sirloin flap (*bavette*), or hanger.

½ cup Dijon mustard	2 teaspoons minced garlic
¼ cup coarse-grain mustard	4 teaspoons Worcestershire sauce
¼ cup soy sauce	2 tablespoons balsamic vinegar
2 tablespoons chopped fresh rosemary	1 teaspoon Tabasco or other hot sauce
2 tablespoons minced shallots	¼ cup olive oil

1 Place the mustards in a small bowl, add the remaining ingredients, and stir to combine.

2 Place the steaks of your choice in a large zipper-lock bag. Pour in the marinade, seal the bag, and turn to ensure the steaks are coated with the marinade. Marinate for 2 hours at room temperature or, better still, refrigerate overnight. Turn the bag from time to time to redistribute the marinade. Let the steaks sit at room temperature for 2 hours and pat dry before grilling.

COFFEE MARINADE

Makes enough for 2 large steaks

The bitter undertones of coffee are an ideal complement to the smoky flavors of grilled beef. This marinade is particularly good with bone-in rib-eye and bone-in chuck steaks.

1 cup strong coffee (I use espresso), cooled	1 teaspoon ground cumin
3 tablespoons balsamic vinegar	3 tablespoons soy sauce
2 tablespoons minced white onion	2 teaspoons Worcestershire sauce
2 tablespoons minced garlic	2 teaspoons dark brown sugar
1 chipotle chile in adobo (I use Herdez brand), finely chopped	2 teaspoons Tabasco or other hot sauce
2 teaspoons chopped fresh sage	2 teaspoons freshly ground black pepper
	¼ cup canola oil

1 Pour the coffee into a small bowl and stir in the remaining ingredients.

2 Place the steaks of your choice in a large zipper-lock bag. Pour in the marinade, seal the bag, and turn to ensure the steaks are coated with the marinade. Marinate for 2 hours at room temperature or, better still, refrigerate overnight. (*For a 2- to 3-inch-thick bone-in steak, it's best to marinate overnight.*) Turn the bag from time to time to redistribute the marinade. Let the steaks sit at room temperature for 2 hours and pat dry before grilling.

OTHER MARINADE RECIPES SUITABLE FOR STEAKS

- Carne Asada Marinade (page 70)
- Guinness Marinade (page 75)
- Beer Marinade (page 80)
- Tagliata Marinade (page 84)
- Herb Marinade (page 90)
- Garlic-Herb Marinade (page 119)
- Thai Green Curry Marinade (page 129)
- Fresh Plum Marinade (page 266)
- Malaysian Marinade (page 268)
- Caribbean Pineapple Marinade (page 291)
- Bun Cha Hanoi Marinade (page 308)
- Pomegranate Marinade (page 395)
- Smoky Chile Marinade (page 398)
- Asian Tamarind Marinade (page 539)

Spice Rubs for Steaks

Each of these rubs makes enough for 2 rib-eye, porterhouse, or sirloin steaks or 4 smaller steaks.

STAR ANISE AND ROSEMARY DRY RUB

4 teaspoons salt

1 teaspoon freshly ground black pepper

1 teaspoon ground star anise or ½ teaspoon Chinese five-spice powder

1 tablespoon chopped fresh rosemary

Olive oil for brushing

Combine all the ingredients except the oil in a small bowl. Brush the steaks of your choice with olive oil and sprinkle the rub generously all over them. Cover and let stand for 2 hours at room temperature or, better still, refrigerate overnight.

MUSTARD HERB RUB

4 teaspoons salt

1 teaspoon freshly ground black pepper

1 teaspoon dry mustard powder (I use Colman's)

2 teaspoons chopped mixed fresh herbs, such as savory, rosemary, thyme, marjoram, oregano, sage, and tarragon

2 teaspoons sweet Hungarian paprika or Spanish paprika (*pimentón de la Vera*; see Sources)

½ teaspoon ground caraway seeds

Follow the directions for Star Anise and Rosemary Dry Rub (above).

MOROCCAN RUB

4 teaspoons salt

1 teaspoon freshly ground black pepper

1½ teaspoons ras el hanout (see Sources) or ½ teaspoon each ground ginger, coriander, and allspice

½ teaspoon turmeric

½ teaspoon ground cumin

2 teaspoons sweet Hungarian paprika

1 teaspoon finely grated lemon zest or finely chopped salt-pickled lemons (see Preserved Lemons, page 499, or Sources)

Follow the directions for Star Anise and Rosemary Dry Rub (page 66).

MEXICAN RUB

4 teaspoons salt

½ teaspoon freshly ground black pepper

½ teaspoon ground cumin

½ teaspoon ground coriander

1 teaspoon garlic powder

½ teaspoon dried oregano (I use Mexican)

2 teaspoons ancho or New Mexico chile powder

1 teaspoon light brown sugar

½ teaspoon cayenne pepper

Follow the directions for Star Anise and Rosemary Dry Rub (page 66).

COFFEE AND CHOCOLATE RUB

4 teaspoons salt

2 teaspoons freshly ground black pepper

1 tablespoon finely ground espresso beans

1 teaspoon unsweetened cocoa powder

1 teaspoon garlic powder

½ teaspoon ground cumin

½ teaspoon raw sugar or dark brown sugar

½ teaspoon ground ginger

⅛ teaspoon ground allspice

1 tablespoon ancho or New Mexico chile powder

Follow the directions for Star Anise and Rosemary Dry Rub (page 66).

Cook's Note

- This rub is great with fattier cuts such as rib-eye, chuck, and skirt steaks and well-marbled New York strip.

PORCINI SPICE RUB

4 teaspoons salt	½ teaspoon dried mint
2 tablespoons porcini powder (see Cook's Notes, page 79)	⅛ teaspoon freshly grated nutmeg
1 teaspoon garlic powder	2 teaspoons freshly ground black pepper
2 teaspoons chopped fresh thyme	

Follow the directions for Star Anise and Rosemary Dry Rub (page 66).

Spice Pastes for Steaks

A spice paste is somewhere between a dry rub and a marinade. Because the seasonings are highly concentrated, they can flavor meat in as little as 2 hours, more quickly than a liquid marinade. However, I like to leave my spice paste–rubbed steaks in the refrigerator overnight. I leave most of the paste on before grilling, so it can continue to flavor the steaks and form a crusty exterior.

Each of these pastes makes enough for 2 large steaks, such as porterhouse or rib eye, or 4 smaller steaks.

SPANISH-STYLE SPICE PASTE

4 teaspoons salt	1 teaspoon chopped fresh marjoram
2 teaspoons minced garlic	2 teaspoons freshly ground black pepper
2 tablespoons Spanish paprika (*pimentón de la Vera*; see Sources)	1 teaspoon chopped fresh thyme
Pinch of saffron threads	2 teaspoons sherry vinegar
	2 tablespoons extra-virgin olive oil

Combine all the ingredients in a small bowl and whisk well. Smear over the steaks of your choice. Place in a nonreactive dish, cover with plastic wrap, and marinate for 2 hours at room temperature or, better still, overnight in the refrigerator.

ORANGE AND SHALLOT SPICE PASTE

3 teaspoons salt

¼ cup orange juice

1 tablespoon minced shallot

1 teaspoon red miso or 2 teaspoons soy sauce

1 teaspoon minced garlic

1 teaspoon finely grated orange zest

1 teaspoon chopped fresh rosemary

2 teaspoons freshly ground black pepper

1 tablespoon olive oil

Follow the directions for Spanish-Style Spice Paste (page 68).

MUSTARD AND SAGE SPICE PASTE

2 teaspoons salt

2 teaspoons freshly ground black pepper

2 tablespoons Dijon mustard

2 teaspoons finely chopped fresh sage

2 tablespoons finely chopped Chinese fermented black beans

2 teaspoons minced garlic

1 tablespoon olive oil

Follow the directions for Spanish-Style Spice Paste (page 68).

SMOKY BACON SPICE PASTE

3 teaspoons salt

2 teaspoons Dijon mustard

½ teaspoon dark brown sugar

1 teaspoon finely chopped chipotle chile in adobo (I use Herdez brand)

1 teaspoon minced garlic

1 teaspoon Worcestershire sauce

2 teaspoons freshly ground black pepper

2 tablespoons melted bacon fat

Follow the directions for Spanish-Style Spice Paste (page 68).

OTHER RUBS AND PASTES SUITABLE FOR STEAKS

- Porcini and Rosemary Rub (page 78)
- Herb Rub (page 86)
- Spanish Adobo Rub (page 116)
- New Mexico Chile Spice Rub (page 165)
- Aleppo Pepper Spice Rub (page 272)
- Red Chile Paste (page 286)
- Fennel and Herb Rub (page 294)
- Spanish Spice Paste (page 329)
- Pancetta-Herb Paste (page 332)
- Aromatic Spice Rub (page 371)
- Sage and Thyme Rub (page 378)
- Lemon Confit Rub (page 400)
- Herbes de Provence Rub (page 430)

FLANK STEAK CARNE ASADA PADILLA

Fit for Company, Great Leftovers
Serves 4

Because I live in an area with a large Mexican community, I often shop in Latino markets. Naturally, I always check out the butcher area, where there are trays of beef cut very thin and covered with various marinades, all labeled *carne asada* (grilled meat). While I can't always identify the cut, I know that it is often bottom sirloin flap (*bavette*) cut very thin (about ⅛ inch), skirt steak, or, sometimes, butterflied flank steak. Since flap is hard to find in non-Hispanic markets and can sometimes be tough, my preferred cut is flank steak.

This recipe comes from Alex Padilla, who hails from Honduras. He started working for my wife, Nancy Oakes, at age nineteen and eventually worked his way up to executive sous chef. His mother was a hotel chef in Honduras before moving to the United States. His secret ingredient in this marinade is the fat produced from cooking Mexican chorizo.

Carne Asada Marinade

- ¼ cup melted chorizo drippings or bacon fat or olive oil
- ¼ cup fresh lime juice
- 2 tablespoons cider vinegar
- 3 tablespoons soy sauce
- 3 tablespoons ground annatto seeds (achiote; see Sources), annatto paste, or ancho chile powder
- 1 tablespoon minced garlic
- ½ cup peeled, seeded, and diced ripe Roma tomato
- ½ cup chopped fresh cilantro
- ½ cup chopped fresh flat-leaf parsley
- 1 teaspoon salt
- 1 teaspoon freshly ground black pepper
- 1 teaspoon ground cumin

- 1 1- to 1½-pound flank steak

1. **Marinade:** Place all the ingredients except the steak in a blender and blend well to form a homogenous paste.

2. Pierce the steak all over with a sharp fork or skewer. Place in a large zipper-lock bag and pour over the marinade. Turn and shake the bag to distribute the marinade and place in a bowl. Marinate for 2 hours at room temperature or, better still, overnight in the refrigerator, turning and shaking the bag from time to time.

3. Remove the steak from the marinade. If the steak has been refrigerated, let it sit at room temperature for 1 hour.

4   **To broil the steak:** Preheat the broiler. Pat the steak dry, place on the broiler pan, and broil about 3 inches from the heating element for 3 to 4 minutes. Flip and broil for 3 to 4 minutes more. This should yield medium-rare meat.

Alternatively, to grill the steak: Set up a charcoal or gas grill for medium-high heat (see page 11 for more on grilling). Pat the steak dry and grill for 3 to 4 minutes. Flip and grill for 3 to 4 minutes more. This should yield medium-rare meat.

5   Let the steak rest, loosely covered with aluminum foil, for 5 to 10 minutes, then cut across the grain into ¼-inch-thick diagonal slices.

Alternative Cuts: Skirt steak or bottom sirloin flap steak (*bavette*); culotte steak, cut ½ inch thick; tri-tip steak, cut ½ inch thick.

Cook's Notes
- The steak can also be marinated using any of the suggested steak marinades, spice rubs, and pastes on pages 63–69).
- For a simple taco meal, serve the sliced steak with warm tortillas, salsas, shredded cheese, and Pico de Gallo (page 259).
- If you want to be traditional, slice the flank horizontally in half (as if you were butterflying it, but cut all the way through) to produce 2 thin steaks, about ¼ inch thick, and proceed with the recipe. Reduce the cooking time to 2 to 3 minutes per side; the meat will come out medium to well-done. This is how *carne asada* is cooked at most traditional Mexican tacquerías.

Leftovers
- Serve leftover *carne asada* as a tostada salad. Buy some premade tostada shells, and toss finely shredded cabbage with mayonnaise and lime juice until well dressed. Spoon the cabbage into the shells, then top with the meat, Pico de Gallo (page 259), and some crumbled queso fresco.
- You can gently rewarm the sliced meat in a microwave or over low heat in a covered pan, then use it to fill tacos or to make a sandwich called a Mexican *torta* (page 302).

STEAK SANDWICH WITH CAESAR MAYO

Family Meal, In a Hurry

Serves 4

While it is good when made with cold steak, this sandwich is even more special with steak that is freshly grilled. The sandwich is a great way to add flavor and excitement if you are using a nonpremium cut, such as sirloin, flank, bottom sirloin flap (*bavette*), or top round.

Adjust the thickness of your slices depending on how tender the meat is. With tender cuts like fillet, New York strip, or flat-iron, I like to cut the steak into slices about ¼ inch thick; for tougher steaks, cut ⅛-inch-thick slices. You can also make these sandwiches with leftover roast beef, thinly sliced and piled on the rolls.

While I prefer to toast the mayonnaise-slathered rolls under the broiler, you can skip this step if you are in a hurry.

Caesar Mayonnaise

1 cup mayonnaise

1 garlic clove, finely chopped

2 anchovy fillets, finely chopped

2 teaspoons Dijon mustard

2 teaspoons finely grated lemon zest

1 teaspoon Worcestershire sauce

⅓ cup freshly grated Parmigiano-Reggiano

2 teaspoons freshly ground black pepper

1 tablespoon finely chopped fresh flat-leaf parsley

1 tablespoon sweet Hungarian paprika

4 crusty sandwich rolls, split

1½ pounds leftover grilled or pan-seared steak, cut into slices (see headnote)

8 large leaves from romaine lettuce hearts

1 **Mayonnaise:** Place all the mayonnaise ingredients in a food processor and pulse to combine. For the best flavor, let sit for 20 to 30 minutes before using; or scrape into a container and refrigerate for up to 1 week. (Makes 1½ cups; enough for 6 to 8 sandwiches.)

2 Preheat the broiler. Slather some of the mayonnaise on the cut sides of the sandwich rolls. Broil about 4 inches from the heat source for 3 to 4 minutes, or until the mayonnaise begins to brown and bubble.

3   To assemble the sandwiches, divide the meat into 4 portions and lay over the bottom halves of the rolls. Lay the lettuce leaves over the meat and cover with the top halves of the rolls. Cut the sandwiches in half and serve.

Alternative Cuts: Grilled sweet Italian sausages, split in half; grilled hamburger patties.

Leftovers

- The Caesar Mayonnaise recipe makes extra, which you can use as a condiment for other sandwiches. It is good with veal, pork, grilled fish, or chicken.

Bison Steaks

All the bison steaks suitable for dry-heat cooking come from the middle of the animal and are almost always sold boneless. Most bison lovers, including me, consider steaks cut from the rib area to be the best. They're deeply flavored and tender, and they have more fat than the other steaks. Other steaks available are the top loin (New York strip), tenderloin (the most tender, but very expensive), top sirloin, and flank. I don't recommend steaks cut from the chuck or round, which are tough.

Don't overcook bison steaks. They're ideal rare to medium-rare. If you want steaks cooked to medium, use a Jaccard (see page 49) and a flavor brine (page 249) to help tenderize the meat and retain moisture.

GRILLING LEAN BEEF AND BISON STEAKS

Lean beef (some grass-fed, Select grade, or no-roll) and bison need special attention when you're grilling.

- Choose steaks that are at least 1½ inches thick; up to 3 inches thick is even better. Season or marinate as instructed in the individual recipe and allow the meat to sit at room temperature (65°F to 72°F) for 2 hours.

- Prepare the coals, and when they're ready, spread them over half the grill. Or, if using gas, heat all the burners to medium-high; when the grill is hot, leave one section on and turn off all the others. (See page 11 for more on grilling.)

- Lay the steaks directly over the heat and sear until browned nicely, 2 to 3 minutes. Flip and sear the other side for 2 to 3 minutes more. If flare-ups occur, move the meat to an area of the grill with no fire; when the flare-ups subside, return the meat to the heat and continue searing.

- Once the steaks are seared, move them to an area of the grill with no fire. If you have a cable-type digital continuous-read thermometer, insert it into the center of the steak — through the side — and set it for 10 degrees lower than your desired degree of doneness (make sure the cable isn't over any flame). Cover the grill and try to maintain a temperature of 275°F to 300°F. If you're using an instant-read thermometer, begin monitoring the internal temperature after 10 minutes. When the steaks are 10 degrees less than the desired degree of doneness, transfer them to a heated platter and let rest for 10 minutes (15 minutes for a 3-inch steak). If you want, smear on a flavored butter (pages 58–59). Cut into ½-inch-thick slices and serve.

GUINNESS-MARINATED BISON RIB-EYE STEAK SANDWICHES WITH MUSHROOMS AND GRILLED ONIONS

Grass-Fed Beef

Serves 4

The dark ales called stout are great served with bison or beef. They also work well as a flavor base for marinating. Guinness is one of the best-known stouts and the most readily available, but any favorite stout will work fine. Rib eyes are the best-tasting bison steaks, but they must be cut at least 1½ inches thick so that you can sear and brown the outside without overcooking the inside. Because bison is so lean, the steaks should be cooked to no more than medium-rare.

Guinness Marinade

- 1 cup Guinness or other stout
- 2 teaspoons freshly ground black pepper
- ⅓ cup soy sauce
- 2 tablespoons mild molasses
- 1 tablespoon chopped fresh thyme
- 1 tablespoon minced garlic
- ½ cup finely chopped red onion
- ½ teaspoon Worcestershire sauce

- 1 1½- to 2-inch-thick boneless bison rib-eye steak (1½–2 pounds)
- 24 large cremini mushrooms, stems removed
- 1 large red onion, cut into ½-inch-thick slices
- 2–3 tablespoons olive oil
  Salt and freshly ground black pepper
- 4 ½- to ¾-inch-thick slices rye bread

1. **Marinade:** Combine all the ingredients in a small bowl. Place the steak in a zipper-lock bag. Pour in the marinade, seal the bag, and turn and shake the bag to distribute the marinade. Place the bag in a bowl and refrigerate overnight, turning and shaking the bag from time to time.

2. Set up a charcoal or gas grill for indirect grilling (see page 11 for more on grilling).

3. Remove the steak from the marinade and pat dry. Reserve the marinade if desired (see Cook's Notes). Brush the mushroom caps and onion slices with the olive oil and sprinkle with salt and pepper to taste. Place the vegetables in a grilling basket (see Cook's Notes). Grill the steak for 2 to 3 minutes, until nicely browned. Flip and grill for 2 to 3 minutes more. Transfer the steak to an area of the grill with no fire and cover the grill. Check the internal temperature after 10 minutes: The steak is done when

cooked to an internal temperature of 125°F to 130°F for medium-rare. Transfer the steak to a platter and let rest while you cook the vegetables.

4   Grill the vegetables for 4 to 6 minutes, turning the basket occasionally, until soft and beginning to brown.

5   Meanwhile, briefly grill the bread or toast in a toaster. Take care not to burn it.

6   Lay a piece of toast on each plate. Lay a slice or two of grilled onion over it. Slice the steak ½ inch thick and arrange the slices over the onions. Scatter 6 mushrooms over the meat on each plate. Pour any meat juices over the open-faced sandwiches and serve.

Alternative Cuts: Any 1½- to 2-inch-thick boneless bison steak or lean, grass-fed beef steak, such as New York strip, fillet, or sirloin.

Cook's Notes

- If you don't have a grill basket, skewer the mushrooms so that the skewer is parallel to the flat side of the mushroom caps. Skewer the onions as well, with the skewer parallel to the cut side of the onions; I use two skewers, which keep the onions from falling apart and ending up in the fire.

- You can use the leftover marinade as a dipping sauce. After removing the steak from the marinade, pour the marinade into a small pan and bring to a boil. Simmer for 2 to 3 minutes. Drizzle a little of the heated marinade over the steak sandwiches and pour the rest into individual small bowls that diners can dip their meat and vegetables into.

- You can smear any of the flavored butters from pages 58–59 over the steak while it's resting. Smear some of the butter on the hot toast as well.

PAN-SEARED GRASS-FED PORTERHOUSE WITH PORCINI AND ROSEMARY RUB

Grass-Fed Beef, Fit for Company

Serves 4

Using porcini powder in rubs for steaks helps to enhance the natural beefy (bisony) flavor. It also gives the steak a beautiful rich brown exterior and delightful aroma.

Powdered dried porcini mushrooms are loaded with umami, which experts say is one of the tongue's five tastes, along with sweet, sour, salty, and bitter. It's characterized as savory or meaty, and foods such as mushrooms, meats, and aged cheeses are rich in this flavor component. In a way, the mushroom powder acts as a natural MSG (monosodium glutamate), helping to accent and enhance flavors, especially in meat.

Don't attempt to pan-sear steaks less than ¾ inch thick, because by the time they are nicely browned, they will be overcooked.

2 1-inch-thick grass-fed porterhouse steaks (about 2 pounds total)	**Porcini and Rosemary Rub**
4 garlic cloves, smashed	2 tablespoons porcini powder (see Cook's Notes)
½ cup soy sauce	1 tablespoon finely chopped fresh rosemary
	2 teaspoons coarsely ground black pepper
	1 tablespoon olive oil

1 Place the steaks in a zipper-lock bag. Combine the garlic and soy sauce and pour over the steaks. Seal the bag and turn and shake until the steaks are well coated. Lay the bag flat in a pan and marinate at room temperature for 2 hours, turning the steaks from time to time.

2 **Rub:** Combine the porcini powder, rosemary, and pepper in a small bowl. Mix well.

3 Preheat the oven to 275°F.

4 Remove the steaks from the marinade and shake off the excess. Scrape off any garlic. Pat dry. Generously sprinkle the rub over the steaks so that both sides are completely coated.

5 Heat the oil in a 12-inch cast-iron skillet over high heat. Swirl to completely coat the bottom of the pan. Add one steak and cook for 2 minutes. Flip and cook for 2 minutes more. The steak should have a deep brown exterior. If not, sear for a minute more per side. Transfer the steak to a baking sheet or roasting pan. Repeat with the second steak and place it next to the first steak.

6 Place the steaks in the oven and, after 10 minutes, check the internal temperature. They're done when the temperature reaches 125°F to 130°F for medium-rare. Remove the steaks from the oven, cover loosely with aluminum foil, and let rest for 5 minutes.

7 Cut around the T-shaped bone to remove the meat, then cut into ½-inch-thick slices and serve.

Alternative Cuts: Any tender lean beef or bison steak, such as rib eye, sirloin, New York strip, or fillet of similar thickness; also works for lean USDA Select–grade beef.

Cook's Notes
- Porcini powder can be purchased from specialty stores such as Penzey's (see Sources), or you can make your own by grinding 3 or 4 dried porcini mushroom slices in a spice grinder.

- You can also grill the steaks. Set up a charcoal or gas grill for indirect grilling (see page 12). Sear the steaks over a medium-hot fire for 2 minutes per side, then move them to the section of the grill with no fire and grill-roast until medium-rare, about 10 minutes.

PAN-BROILED BEER-MARINATED HANGER STEAK

Cheap Eats

Serves 4

No self-respecting bistro can call itself such without *steak frites* (steak and French fries) on the menu. More often than not, the steak of choice is hanger steak, called *onglet* in French. Its popularity is due to its deep beefy flavor and quick preparation time. Unfortunately, there is only one hanger steak per animal, and traditionally it was usually taken home by the butcher for his family, which is why it's sometimes called butcher steak. The hanger steak hangs off the interior of a suspended beef carcass (hence its name), just below the tenderloin on the left side of the steer. It helps to support the diaphragm and consists of two lobes of loosely grained meat separated by a strip of gristle; it weighs about 2 pounds untrimmed. If the butcher hasn't trimmed it, cut out the gristle by cutting along either side of the strip to yield two uneven 1-pound steaks. To ensure quick cooking, butterfly each steak so that you end up with pieces ¾ to 1 inch thick. Because this steak is somewhat chewy, it's very important to slice it across the grain. The grain is clearly visible, because the muscle striations are loose; the fibers run diagonal to the long axis of the steak and are easier to slice across if you cut each steak crosswise into two pieces.

Because hanger steak has a nice robust flavor, it's ideal for marinating (see pages 63–66 for other marinade ideas). It's also quite tasty when coated with a dry rub or spice paste (pages 66–69). It's best cooked to medium-rare, and never more than medium (pink), because this lean steak can easily dry out.

Beer Marinade

- 2 teaspoons Dijon mustard
- 2 tablespoons olive oil
- 2 tablespoons malt vinegar
- ¼ cup soy sauce
- 1 tablespoon minced garlic
- 2 teaspoons chopped fresh rosemary
- 2 teaspoons Worcestershire sauce
- ½ cup beer (I use an amber ale)
- 2 teaspoons freshly ground black pepper

- 1 hanger steak (about 2 pounds), divided into 2 lobes and butterflied (see headnote)
  Salt and freshly ground black pepper
  Vegetable oil

1 **Marinade:** Whisk together the mustard and oil in a small bowl. Whisk in the vinegar, soy sauce, garlic, and rosemary, then whisk in the Worcestershire, beer, and 2 teaspoons pepper. Place the steaks in a zipper-lock bag. Pour the marinade over the

steaks, seal the bag, and turn and shake to distribute the marinade. Place the bag in a bowl and refrigerate overnight, or for up to 24 hours, turning the bag from time to time.

2   Remove the steaks from the marinade (discard the marinade), and pat the steaks dry. Let rest at room temperature for 40 to 60 minutes.

3   Lightly season the steaks with salt and pepper. Heat a heavy ridged grill pan or cast-iron skillet over high heat and brush with a thin coating of vegetable oil. Lay the steaks in the pan and grill for 2 to 3 minutes, or until nicely browned. Turn and grill for 2 to 3 minutes more, or until the internal temperature registers 125°F to 130°F for medium-rare. Transfer the steaks to a carving board, cover loosely with aluminum foil, and let rest for 5 minutes before carving.

4   Cut each steak in half, then cut across the grain into ¼-inch-thick slices.

Alternative Cuts: Skirt steak has a flavor and loose grain similar to hanger and is about the same thickness as a butterflied hanger steak. Flank steak is also a good choice, but it lacks the beefiness of hanger steak. Flat-iron steak also works well and has a robust flavor. Bottom sirloin flap steak (*bavette*) is similar in flavor and is tender and flavorful if you can find a Prime-grade or well-marbled Choice-grade steak.

Cook's Notes

- Since hanger steak can be hard to find, you may need to ask your butcher to order it. Have him trim the gristle and butterfly it for you.

- If you have well-marbled steaks, omit the marinade and simply season them generously with salt and pepper.

- If you'd prefer to cook the steak on a charcoal or gas grill, leave it whole and don't butterfly it. Follow the directions for grilling top round (see page 60).

TWO-STEP PAN-BROILED DOUBLE-THICK STEAK

In a Hurry, Wood-Fired Oven

Serves 4 to 6

To cook a thick steak, you'll need a good heavy pan (I prefer cast iron) and a two-step cooking process, followed by an ample rest to complete the cooking and redistribute the juices. Step 1 is searing over high heat for 2 to 3 minutes per side in a skillet. Step 2 is finishing the steak in a 425°F oven. A wood-fired oven is even better and gives the meat a great flavor. The other key is generously seasoning the meat: ¾ teaspoon salt per side and the same amount of freshly ground pepper. I like to serve these steaks Tuscan-style, with a generous drizzle of good extra-virgin olive oil. If you can find a new-harvest oil, all the better.

1 2½- to 3-inch-thick bone-in rib-eye, T-bone, or porterhouse steak (about 3 pounds)	1½ teaspoons salt
1–2 tablespoons extra-virgin olive oil, plus (optional) more for drizzling	1½ teaspoons freshly ground black pepper
	½ teaspoon ground coriander

1   Coat the steak with the oil. Combine the salt, pepper, and coriander in a small bowl and sprinkle half of the mixture on each side of the steak. Wrap the steak in plastic wrap and let rest at room temperature for 2 hours or refrigerate overnight.

2   If the steak has been refrigerated, let rest at room temperature for 2 hours.

3   Preheat the oven to 425°F.

4   Heat a 12-inch ovenproof skillet, such as cast iron, over high heat (make sure your exhaust fan is on). When the pan begins to smoke and an edge of the steak sizzles when touched against it, add the steak. Sear for 2 to 3 minutes, or until deep brown. Turn and sear for 2 to 3 minutes more, then pop the pan into the oven. Roast for 10 to 15 minutes, or until the internal temperature reaches 120°F to 125°F for rare or 125°F to 130°F for medium-rare. Transfer the steak to a cutting board and let rest, tented loosely with aluminum foil, for 10 minutes.

5   To serve, cut between the bone and the meat to release the meat, then cut the meat crosswise into ½-inch-thick slices. Arrange on plates and drizzle generously with extra-virgin olive oil (if using).

Alternative Cuts: London broil (top round), top sirloin (chateaubriand), fillet, New York strip, chuck-eye (Delmonico), or baseball steak.

Cook's Notes

- This method works well with any tender, marbled cut of beef, bone-in or boneless, at least 2½ inches thick.

- You can use any of the dry rubs or marinades on pages 63–68 instead of the salt and pepper rub. I particularly like the Coffee and Chocolate Rub (page 67).

- This steak is also good with a flavored butter of your choice (pages 58–59).

- If using the two-step method for grass-fed beef or bison, place in a slow (275°F) oven after searing to maintain juiciness, and begin checking the internal temperature after 15 minutes.

BEEF FILLET PAILLARDS WITH ARUGULA, MUSHROOMS, AND PARMESAN (STEAK TAGLIATA)

In a Hurry, Grass-Fed Beef

Serves 4

This recipe is an embellished version of steak *tagliata* (meaning "sliced"), which I've eaten all over Italy. The basic version is a thin steak, seared and served with a pile of olive-oil-and-lemon-dressed arugula over the top and garnished with shaved Parmigiano-Reggiano. I've added mushrooms to the salad. If you try this recipe with grass-fed beef, be very careful to sear the meat for no more than 30 seconds per side; just a few seconds more can make the lean beef dry.

Tagliata Marinade

- ½ cup extra-virgin olive oil
- 1 tablespoon minced garlic
- 2 teaspoons finely chopped fresh rosemary

- 4 ¾-inch-thick fillet steaks, gently pounded to a thickness of ⅜ inch

Dressing

- 1 teaspoon finely grated lemon zest
- 2 teaspoons fresh lemon juice, or more to taste
- 2 teaspoons mayonnaise
- 2 tablespoons extra-virgin olive oil
  Salt and freshly ground black pepper

- 2 teaspoons salt
- 1 teaspoon freshly ground black pepper
- 2 cups arugula
- 1 cup thinly sliced cremini or white button mushrooms (I use a mandoline)
- ¼ pound chunk Parmigiano-Reggiano

1. **Marinade:** Mix together all the ingredients in a small bowl. Place the steaks in a large zipper-lock bag. Pour the marinade over the steaks, seal the bag, and turn and shake to make sure the steaks are coated. Marinate for 1 hour at room temperature or up to 24 hours in the refrigerator. Let sit at room temperature for 2 hours before cooking.

2. **Dressing:** Whisk the lemon zest and juice into the mayonnaise, then whisk in the oil. Add more lemon juice and salt and pepper to suit your taste. Set aside.

3. Heat a ridged grill pan or heavy cast-iron skillet over high heat until hot. Remove the steak from the marinade, pat dry, and sprinkle lightly with the salt and pepper. Sear 1

or 2 paillards at a time, taking care not to overcrowd the pan, for 30 seconds. Turn and sear the other side for 30 seconds. Place each paillard on a warm plate. (It's okay to serve this dish less than piping hot.) Top each paillard with one quarter of the arugula, one quarter of the mushrooms, and 6 to 8 shavings of cheese (use a vegetable peeler). Drizzle the dressing over the salads, and serve.

Alternative Cuts: Boneless New York strip steaks, cut in half crosswise, then pounded. For grass-fed beef, use either the fillet or the more fatty boneless rib-eye steak; for regular beef, boneless culotte, tri-tip, top sirloin, or top round steaks.

PAN-SEARED FILLET STEAKS WITH IRISH WHISKEY AND CREAM PAN SAUCE

Fit for Company

Serves 4

There is a good reason this famous dish prepared table-side in fancy French restaurants has been around so long. The buttery, tender fillet steaks are the perfect foil to the zesty sauce.

4 1- to 1¼-inch-thick fillet steaks (6–8 ounces each)	½ cup homemade beef stock (see page 168) or canned low-sodium chicken broth
Salt and freshly ground black pepper	½ teaspoon Worcestershire sauce
1 tablespoon butter	2 teaspoons Dijon mustard
3 tablespoons finely chopped shallots	½ cup heavy cream
¼ cup Irish whiskey or brandy	Fresh lemon juice

1. Season each steak generously with salt and pepper. Heat a heavy skillet, large enough to hold all 4 steaks, over medium-high heat. Add the butter, and when it begins to foam, add the steaks. Cook for about 3 minutes, or until the bottoms are nicely browned. Flip the steaks and cook for 3 minutes more, or until the internal temperature reaches 120°F to 125°F for rare. Transfer to a warm platter and tent with aluminum foil while you make the sauce.

2. To make the pan sauce, reduce the heat to medium and add the shallots to the pan. Cook, stirring, for 1 minute. Remove from the heat, add the whiskey, and scrape up any browned bits from the bottom of the pan. Return to the heat, add the stock and Worcestershire, and bring to a boil. Whisk in the mustard, then the cream, and simmer, whisking, until the sauce is reduced to a syrupy consistency, 2 to 3 minutes. Season to taste with lemon juice, salt, and pepper. Return the steaks to the pan, spoon some sauce over the steaks, and rewarm them for about 1 minute. Serve at once.

Alternative Cuts: Boneless New York strip steaks, cut in half; boneless sirloin, culotte, rib-eye, baseball, petite tender, flat-iron, or rib-eye cap steaks.

Cook's Note
- This is a perfect dish to serve for a romantic dinner. Serve with oven-roasted potatoes and start with a green salad.

STEAK WITH PORCINI-SHALLOT SAUCE

Fit for Company

Serves 4

My coauthor, Anne-marie Ramo, likes to serve this recipe when she entertains on weeknights and doesn't have a lot of time but wants something decadent. An elegant presentation of a simple sautéed steak and a quick pan sauce, it's suitable for any dried mushroom you may have in your pantry: morels, portobellos, or shiitakes, or a wild mushroom blend.

The key to getting the shallots crispy is making sure they're very dry before adding them to the oil. Give them a quick blot on a paper towel before cooking.

1 ounce dried porcini mushrooms

1 cup boiling water

Fried Shallots

¼ cup grapeseed or peanut oil

2 large shallots, very thinly sliced (about ½ cup)

4 1- to 1½-inch-thick boneless steaks
(6–8 ounces each; see Pan-Seared Fillet
Steaks, page 86, for choices)
Salt and freshly ground black pepper

1 tablespoon butter

Sauce

2 shallots, finely chopped

¼ cup dry Madeira

¼ cup dry red wine

½ cup homemade beef stock (see page 168)
or canned low-sodium chicken broth

2 tablespoons cold butter, cut into 2 pieces
Salt and freshly ground black pepper

1 Place the porcini in a small bowl and cover with the boiling water. Soak for at least 45 minutes, or up to several hours, until soft.

2 Remove the porcini from the soaking liquid with a slotted spoon. Chop and set aside. Strain the soaking liquid, leaving behind any grit in the bottom of the bowl, and reserve.

3 **Fried shallots:** Heat the oil in a small skillet over medium-high heat. Add the shallots and fry, stirring frequently, until crispy, about 5 minutes. Reduce the heat if the shallots begin to brown too quickly. Transfer to paper towels to drain.

4 Season the steaks with salt and pepper. Sauté them in the butter, following the directions for Pan-Seared Fillet Steaks (page 86). Keep warm while you make the sauce.

5   **Sauce:** Drain all but about 1 tablespoon of the fat from the pan. Reduce the heat to medium, add the chopped shallots, and sauté until translucent, about 3 minutes. Add the mushrooms and sauté for 1 minute more. Add the reserved mushroom soaking liquid, the Madeira, red wine, and stock and cook, stirring and scraping up any browned bits from the bottom of the pan, until reduced to about 1 cup, about 10 minutes. Remove from the heat and stir in the butter, 1 tablespoon at a time, until incorporated. Season to taste with salt and pepper.

6   Return the steaks to the pan, set over medium heat, and warm through, about 1 minute.

7   To serve, place each steak on a dinner plate. Spoon the sauce over the steak and top with the fried shallots.

Alternative Cuts: Ball tip, bottom sirloin flap (*bavette*), tri-tip, petite tender, cut into 1-inch medallions, or Denver.

Cook's Note
- Grapeseed and peanut oil are ideal for frying the shallots because of their high smoke point, but any vegetable oil, such as canola, will do.

SAUTÉED STEAK WITH "ROCKEFELLER" PAN SAUCE

In a Hurry

Serves 4

Oysters Rockefeller, a perennial favorite, was the inspiration for this spinach-and-anise–flavored pan sauce. It can be made with or without oysters, but either way, the sauce goes well with sautéed steak.

4 1- to 1¼-inch thick boneless steaks (6–8 ounces each; see Pan-Seared Fillet Steaks, page 86, for choices)
   Salt and freshly ground black pepper
½ teaspoon fennel pollen (see Sources) or ground fennel seeds
2 tablespoons butter

Sauce

4 scallions, white and light green parts separated and thinly sliced
2 teaspoons minced garlic
¼ cup Herbsaint, Pernod, Absente, or other anise-flavored liqueur
½ cup canned low-sodium chicken broth or a mixture of chicken broth and oyster liquor
2 cups cooked spinach, squeezed dry and chopped (about 2 pounds)
½ cup finely chopped celery leaves
½ cup loosely packed watercress, chopped
1 teaspoon chopped fresh tarragon
2 tablespoons chopped fresh flat-leaf parsley
12–16 small oysters, shucked (optional)
3 tablespoons cold butter, cut into 3 pieces
   Salt and freshly ground black pepper
   Tabasco or other hot sauce

1   Season the steaks with salt, pepper, and the fennel pollen and sauté in the butter, following the directions for Pan-Seared Fillet Steaks (page 86). Keep warm.

2   **Sauce:** Reduce the heat to medium, add the scallion whites to the pan, and sauté for 30 seconds. Add the garlic and sauté for 30 seconds more. Remove the pan from the heat and pour in the liqueur. Return to high heat and cook, stirring and scraping any browned bits from the bottom of the pan, until the liquid has almost evaporated. (If you are using a gas stove, the alcohol may flame; shake the pan until the flames subside.) Add the broth, spinach, celery leaves, watercress, and tarragon and cook, stirring, until the liquid just becomes syrupy, about 5 minutes.

3   Add the parsley and scallion greens. If using the oysters, add them and cook for 1 minute, or until just plump. Gently stir in the butter, 1 tablespoon at a time, to produce a velvety sauce. Remove from the heat and season to taste with salt, pepper, and Tabasco. Spoon the sauce over the steaks and serve.

WOOD OVEN–ROASTED STEAK

Wood-Fired Oven, Fit for Company
Serves 4 to 6

The high temperature of a wood-fired oven, combined with an herb marinade, gives these steaks an exceptional flavor. For best results, choose steaks on the bone that are at least 2½ inches thick. (Thinner steaks will overcook before the exterior is nicely browned.) Marinate the steaks overnight and let them come to room temperature before roasting. If you don't have a wood-fired oven, you can grill-roast these steaks with excellent results (see Cook's Notes).

Herb Marinade
- ½ cup extra-virgin olive oil
- 4–6 garlic cloves, thinly sliced
- 2 tablespoons chopped fresh rosemary
- 1 tablespoon fresh thyme leaves

- 1 2½- to 3-inch-thick porterhouse or bone-in rib-eye steak (about 3 pounds)
- 2 teaspoons salt
- 1½ teaspoons coarsely ground black pepper

1 **Marinade:** The day before cooking the steak, heat the oil in a small saucepan over low heat. Add the garlic and cook until soft but not colored, about 5 minutes. Stir in the rosemary and thyme and cook for 1 minute more. Allow to cool to room temperature.

2 Generously sprinkle all sides of the steak with 1½ teaspoons of the salt and 1 teaspoon of the pepper and place in a zipper-lock bag. Pour the marinade over the steak, seal the bag, and turn and shake the bag to coat the steak. Place the bag in a bowl and refrigerate overnight.

3 The next day, remove the steak from the marinade, shake off the excess, and remove any garlic, leaving the rosemary and thyme on the meat. Let rest at room temperature for 2 hours while you fire up a wood oven.

4 When the oven floor reaches 550°F to 600°F, it's time to roast the steak. Place the steak in a cast-iron skillet and place in the oven. After about 10 minutes, flip over the steak. It should have begun to brown nicely. About 5 minutes later, begin checking the steak for doneness with an instant-read thermometer inserted into the thickest part of the steak. For rare, remove the steak when it's 105°F to 110°F; for medium-rare, 115°F to 120°F. Place the steak on a carving board and let rest, loosely covered with aluminum foil, for 10 to 15 minutes. The internal temperature will rise 15 to 20 degrees.

5 To carve, separate the meat from the bone and cut into ½-inch-thick slices. Arrange the meat on a platter and sprinkle it with the remaining ½ teaspoon salt and ½ teaspoon pepper. (Serve the bone to any serious bone-gnawing carnivores or, better still, reserve it for yourself.)

Alternative Cuts: Any 2½- to 3-inch-thick tender steak works well, including sirloin cuts, a whole tri-tip roast, a whole culotte, a boneless New York strip, or a 3-pound section of tenderloin roast. This recipe works well with a wide range of beef, from lean grass-fed to ultramarbled Wagyu. If using grass-fed, aim for rare and reduce the cooking time to about 7 minutes per side. For Wagyu, use the same general cooking times, but if you like medium to well-done meat, remove it from the oven when the internal temperature reaches 120°F to 125°F. It will still be juicy, due to its abundant marbling.

Cook's Notes

- To grill-roast the steak, set up a charcoal or gas grill for indirect heat (see page 12). Lay the steak over a medium-hot fire and sear it for 2 to 3 minutes per side, until nicely browned. Place a roasting pan or cast-iron skillet over the area of the grill that has no heat and add the steak. Cover the grill and grill-roast for 10 minutes, then begin monitoring the internal temperature. Remove the steak from the grill when the internal temperature is 120°F to 125°F for rare or 125°F to 130°F for medium-rare. (The steak will have less carryover heat than one cooked in a wood-fired oven.) Transfer to a platter, cover loosely with aluminum foil, and let sit for 10 to 15 minutes before slicing and serving.

- For an extra-garlicky treat, make one and a half times the marinade recipe and reserve ¼ cup (before marinating). Drizzle the reserved marinade over the sliced beef.

- You can embellish the steak with any of the flavored butters (pages 58–59), which are particularly nice with grass-fed beef. Place the butter on the steak while it is resting, then spoon the melted butter over the sliced beef, omitting the final seasoning with salt and pepper.

Leftovers

- Sliced cold leftovers make great sandwiches (see page 72).

Beef and Bison Roasts

Preparing a beef roast for dinner couldn't be easier, and a roast is often the choice for both special-occasion meals and simple family dinners. When it comes to a great roast, juiciness and flavor are important, but for most folks—just as with steaks—tenderness is the most important attribute when choosing a chunk of meat.

Beef and Bison Roasts at a Glance

You can expect to find as many regional differences with the names of roasts as you do with steaks—maybe more so. This chart identifies each roast by the Uniform Retail Meat Identity Standards name (which is used by many large supermarket chains) and then gives many alternative names.

From the Rib

Rib-eye roast, small end, bone in (standing rib roast, prime rib). My favorite beef roast when cost doesn't matter. Rich, with good beef flavor. Okay even when cooked to medium or medium-well. From the rear of the animal, ribs 9 through 12. Has less fat and is more expensive than the large-end roast.

Rib roast, large end, bone in (large-end roast). From ribs 6 to 9, the section that adjoins the chuck. Has more fat than the small-end roast.

Rib-eye roast, boneless (prime rib, rib-eye roast, rib eye, rib-eye roll, regular roll roast, Spencer roast, Delmonico roast). Easier to carve than bone in, but then there are no bones to chew on. The best-tasting bison roast.

From the Short Loin
(the area of the loin between the rib and the hip area, called the sirloin)

Top loin roast, boneless (strip loin roast, sirloin strip roast, New York strip roast, shell roast, club roast). Fairly tender and juicy. Roasts quickly and is easy to carve. At 10 to 14 pounds for a whole roast, it's ideal for a party for 15 to 20 people. Not as flavorful as rib eye, and it can dry out when cooked beyond medium. Smaller pieces are ideal to grill-roast for summer entertaining. Very expensive.

Tenderloin roast, boneless (whole fillet, tenderloin tip roasts, filet mignon roast, chateaubriand roast). Very tender. Roasts very quickly and can easily be butterflied and stuffed (see Rosa di Parma, page 106). Will impress guests. Mild flavored and can be quite dry if roasted beyond medium. Best for grill-roasting. Most expensive roast.

Continued on page 94

From the Top Sirloin
(the upper part of the hip)

Top sirloin roast, boneless (top butt, top sirloin butt, center-cut sirloin roast, chateaubriand). Usually sold as a thick 3-pound or larger slice. Lean, and will dry out if overcooked.

Top sirloin cap roast, boneless (culotte). When marbled, has good flavor. Some areas closer to the round are chewy; the area closer to the loin is more tender.

From the Bottom Sirloin
(the underside of the hip)

Tri-tip roast, boneless (triangle roast, California roast, Newport roast, boomerang roast). The direction of the grain changes from one side of the meat to the other side. Great flavor, and tender when cut across the grain. At around 2 pounds, an ideal roast for 4 people. Easy to grill.

Ball tip roast, boneless (tip roast, butcher's heart). Fairly lean and can be tough. See instructions for oven-roasting lean beef on page 120, or use as a pot roast.

Bottom sirloin butt, flap roast, boneless (rolled sirloin flap roast, *bavette* roast). Can have great flavor, but tenderness will vary depending on the grade. Must be rolled and tied. If tender, roast in a hot oven; lean grass-fed beef and bison should be roasted at a low temperature (see instructions for oven-roasting lean beef on page 120) or braised.

From the Round (the hind leg)

Rump roast, boneless (wedge cut, Western market roast, melon roast, diamond-cut roast, round tip roast). Comes from the area where the hip meets the leg and contains ends of muscles from both the sirloin and round. Part of the rump ends in the bottom round, which can be confusing, since many butchers simply cut the bottom round into several 3- to 5-pound roasts and simply label them as "rump roast"; these may be too tough and lean to roast and are better braised (see page 160).

Top round roast, boneless (inside roast). A solid chunk ideal for roast beef. Leftovers make great sandwiches.

Tip roast, cap off, boneless (ball tip roast, cap-off roast, sirloin tip roast, peeled knuckle roast). This solid-muscle roast is an extension of the bottom sirloin ball tip, which is cut when the round primal is separated from the sirloin primal. It's lean but relatively tender and is best not overcooked (medium-rare is good). Thinly cut cold leftovers make great roast beef sandwiches.

Sirloin tip center roast, boneless (sirloin tip roast, knuckle roast). The tip roast is separated into two muscle groups. The center muscle is fairly tender and can be roasted nicely to medium-rare.

From the Chuck
(the shoulder, arm, and neck)

All chuck roasts can also be braised for pot roast.

Cross-rib roast, boneless (rolled cross-rib roast, Boston-cut roast, English-cut roast, English roll, shoulder clod roast, Diamond Jim roast). Rolled and tied; good beefy flavor. Makes a good inexpensive beef roast that may have some gristle running through it. When cold and thinly sliced, it makes great sandwiches.

Chuck-eye roast, boneless (inside chuck roll, chuck roll, mock rib eye, chuck fillet, chuck wagon roast). A low-priced roast that has several muscles, including the continuation of the rib eye. Other muscles may contain some gristle and be chewier but have great flavor. A poor man's rib-eye roast.

From the Flank

Flank steak, boneless (beef flank roll). Can be rolled and tied to make a small roast. Great flavor. Its small size (1½ to 2½ pounds) makes this a good cut to roast for small groups. Easy to stuff. Reasonably priced and easy to grill-roast. Also good when braised.

From the Plate (the underside, below the rib section)

Skirt steak. Can be rolled and tied to make a small roast. Make sure the tough surface membrane has been removed. Easy to stuff and has great flavor. Also good when braised.

Beef Roasts for Special Occasions

Special occasions usually mean a luxury cut—which will come with a luxury price. This group includes the rib eye (bone in or boneless), the boneless top loin, and the boneless tenderloin. These roasts work for meals of all sizes. For a small group, you can purchase a few pounds of top loin or tenderloin. For a large group, you'll need to spring for a whole top loin or a 7-bone standing rib roast.

SHOPPING FOR A BONE-IN BEEF RIB ROAST

A whole rib roast has seven ribs. The end closest to the chuck (shoulder and neck) is called the large end, and the end closest to the short loin is called the small end.

- Rib roasts from the small end have less waste, with fewer pockets of fat, and may be more expensive per pound than large-end roasts. Since this section is next to the top loin strip, it will have similar taste and eating qualities.
- A roast from the large end has more fat and several muscle groups. Because it's near the chuck, it has a more beefy flavor.

Unless you are serving a very small group, buy at least a 3-bone roast. I allot about 1 pound per person for bone-in roasts, with some leftovers.

- A 3-bone small-end roast weighs 6 to 8 pounds and should feed 6 to 8 people.
- A 3-bone large-end roast weighs 7 to 9 pounds; it will feed about 8 people.
- A 5-bone roast weighs 10 to 12 pounds and will easily feed 12 people.
- For a larger group or family of serious meat eaters, buy a 7-bone rib roast, which weighs 15 to 20 pounds. Don't worry about leftovers; they'll make great sandwiches or roast beef hash.

STANDING RIB ROAST WITH PORCINI-SPINACH STUFFING, TOASTED PEPPERCORN AND WHISKEY SAUCE, AND HORSERADISH CREAM

Fit for Company, Fit for a Crowd, Great Leftovers, Grass-Fed

Serves 8, with plenty of leftovers

Buy the best slab of beef you can afford and roast it to your liking. The sauce made from the pan juices was inspired by the French dish steak *au poivre,* with Irish whiskey, which stands up to the deep beefy flavors of rib roast, replacing the brandy. You can also use a blended scotch if you like a slightly smoky flavor. This is an excellent recipe for grass-fed beef, because the stuffing adds rich flavor to the lean meat. You can also serve this roast with Scallion and Parmesan Yorkshire Puddings (page 105).

1 4-bone standing rib-eye roast (about 8 pounds), chine bone removed and fat trimmed to ¼ inch	3 tablespoons finely chopped fresh rosemary
	1 tablespoon crushed fennel seeds
Porcini-Spinach Stuffing (recipe follows)	2 tablespoons olive oil
2 tablespoons minced garlic	Toasted Peppercorn and Whiskey Sauce (recipe follows)
1½ tablespoons salt	Horseradish Cream (recipe follows)
1 tablespoon freshly ground black pepper	

1   Allow the roast to stand at room temperature for 4 hours.

2   Preheat the oven to 450°F, with a rack in the lower third of the oven.

3   Using a long sharp knife, cut the roast between the bones and the meat so that the rack of ribs is almost severed from the meat, leaving about ¾ inch of the meat attached to the bones. Place the roast on a flat surface so that you are looking down into the crevices between the bones and meat. Spread the stuffing into each crevice, using a rubber spatula to pack it in. Tie the bones back in place with a couple of loops of butcher's twine to keep the stuffing inside.

4   Combine the garlic, salt, pepper, rosemary, fennel seeds, and oil in a small bowl. Generously rub the mixture over the top and sides of the roast and bones. Place a large

V-shape roasting rack in a roasting pan and nestle the roast on the rack so that the bones are sticking straight up. Wrap the bone tips in aluminum foil to prevent burning.

5   If you have a cable-type digital continuous-read thermometer, insert it into the center of the roast and set it for 110°F to 115°F for rare or 120°F to 125°F for medium-rare. Roast for 20 minutes, then turn down the oven to 350°F. If you are not using a continuous-read thermometer, begin monitoring the internal temperature with an instant-read thermometer after 45 minutes, checking the temperature every 15 minutes. When the roast is done (usually 1¼ to 2 hours), set aside, covered loosely with aluminum foil, to rest for at least 20 minutes and up to 45 minutes before carving and serving. The final temperature will rise 10 to 15 degrees. While the roast is resting, finish the Toasted Peppercorn and Whiskey Sauce.

6   To carve and serve, remove the twine from the roast. Place the roast on a cutting board so that the bones are vertical. Sever the strip of meat attached to the bones and spoon the stuffing into a serving bowl. Set the bones aside, and turn the roast so the bone side lies flat. Cut the roast into ¼- to ½-inch-thick slices and arrange in an overlapping row on a serving platter. Slice between the bones to separate them and add to the platter. Pour any carving juices into the sauce. Serve with the sauce and the Horseradish Cream on the side.

Alternative Cuts: Ask your butcher for a New York strip with the bones attached. A rack of pork or veal would also work. Adjust roasting times and temperatures appropriately: Pork roasts take 45 minutes to 1 hour to reach an internal temperature of 135°F to 140°F. Veal roasts take about 45 minutes to reach an internal temperature of 125°F to 135°F (medium-rare to medium).

Cook's Notes

- If you want to make this meal really special, purchase a well-marbled Wagyu standing rib roast, which is best cooked to medium-rare or even medium.

- At the opposite end of the marbling spectrum is a grass-fed beef or bison rib roast. After 20 minutes, turn the oven down to 275°F and allow extra time for cooking. Serve rare to medium-rare, so that it does not dry out.

PORCINI-SPINACH STUFFING

Makes about 3 cups

1 ounce dried porcini mushrooms

1 cup boiling water

2 mild Italian sausages, homemade (page 410) or store-bought, removed from the casings

½ cup chopped shallots

1 tablespoon chopped garlic

2 cups ¼-inch bread cubes, roughly cut from day-old coarse bread (don't use store-bought dried bread cubes)

1 teaspoon chopped fresh rosemary

1 cup cooked spinach, squeezed dry and chopped (frozen is okay)

1 large egg, lightly beaten

Salt and freshly ground black pepper

1 Place the porcini in a small bowl and cover with the boiling water. Soak for at least 45 minutes, or up to several hours, until soft.

2 Remove the porcini from the liquid with a slotted spoon. Chop and set aside. Strain the soaking liquid, leaving behind any grit in the bottom of the bowl, and reserve.

3 Heat a large skillet over medium heat. Add the sausages and cook for about 5 minutes, breaking the meat apart with a fork as it browns. Add the mushrooms, shallots, and garlic, cover, and cook for about 5 minutes more, stirring from time to time, until the vegetables are tender.

4 Transfer the mixture to a large bowl. Stir in the bread cubes, rosemary, spinach, and egg and mix well. Moisten with ¼ cup of the reserved mushroom liquid. The stuffing should be slightly moist, but not wet. (Save any leftover mushroom liquid for the Toasted Peppercorn and Whiskey Sauce.) Season to taste with salt and pepper and refrigerate until cool. (*The stuffing is best made a day ahead and refrigerated, but don't stuff the meat ahead, as spoilage can easily occur.*) Stuff the roast as directed on page 96 and continue with the recipe.

Cook's Note

• If you have extra stuffing, bake it in a buttered casserole dish for 30 minutes.

TOASTED PEPPERCORN AND WHISKEY SAUCE

Makes 3 to 4 cups

1 tablespoon cracked black peppercorns

1 tablespoon olive oil

½ cup finely chopped shallots

2 teaspoons minced garlic

1 cup Irish whiskey or scotch

3 cups dry red wine

4 cups homemade beef stock (see page 168) or canned low-sodium chicken broth

Reserved mushroom soaking liquid from stuffing

2 tablespoons Dijon mustard

1 cup heavy cream

2 teaspoons chopped fresh rosemary, or more to taste

Salt

1 Scatter the cracked peppercorns in a small heavy skillet and toast over medium heat until fragrant, 3 to 5 minutes. Transfer to a small bowl and set aside.

2 Heat the oil in a large saucepan over medium heat. Add the shallots and cook, stirring, until soft, 2 to 3 minutes. Add the garlic and cook for 1 minute more. Remove from the heat and pour in ½ cup of the whiskey, then return to the heat and cook until the alcohol is burned off. Add the red wine, bring to a boil, and boil until reduced to about 1 cup, 7 to 10 minutes. Add 3 cups of the stock and the mushroom soaking liquid and boil until reduced to about 3 cups. Whisk together the mustard and cream and whisk into the sauce. Continue to boil until the sauce becomes syrupy, 10 to 15 minutes. Cover and set aside.

3 While the roast is resting, pour off all the fat from the roasting pan, leaving the juices in the pan. Place the pan over two burners on medium heat, add the remaining ½ cup whiskey and 1 cup stock, and bring to a boil, scraping up any browned bits from the bottom of the roasting pan. Strain the pan liquid into the sauce and cook until the sauce develops a rich, meaty flavor and is just turning syrupy again, about 5 minutes. Add 2 teaspoons of the toasted peppercorns and the rosemary, then add more peppercorns and/or rosemary and salt to taste. Serve the sauce at once.

HORSERADISH CREAM

Makes 2¼ cups

1½ cups sour cream

½ cup prepared horseradish, drained

1 teaspoon fresh lemon juice

3 tablespoons thinly sliced scallion greens

1 tablespoon finely chopped fresh flat-leaf parsley

Salt and freshly ground black pepper

Combine the sour cream, horseradish, lemon juice, scallions, and parsley in a small bowl and season to taste with salt and pepper. Cover and set aside in the refrigerator for at least 30 minutes to allow the flavors to develop. (*You can make the cream up to several hours ahead.*)

STANDING RIB ROAST WITH BACON AND ROSEMARY JUS AND YORKSHIRE PUDDINGS

Fit for Company, Fit for a Crowd, Great Leftovers

Serves 12, with plenty of leftovers for sandwiches (page 72)

When it comes to the great holiday tradition of roast beef and Yorkshire pudding, I bow to our English cousins across the Atlantic, who invented the dish. Inspired by my wife, Nancy Oakes, I have eschewed the traditional flour-based gravy and opted for a lighter sauce, called a jus. This is simply a pan sauce naturally thickened by reduction. You can leave it out and serve the roast as is, but a little of this intensely flavored sauce drizzled over the meat and Yorkshire pudding sure is tasty. You may also want to serve some Horseradish Cream (page 101) on the side.

6 garlic cloves, peeled	1 5-bone standing rib-eye roast (about
3 tablespoons fresh thyme leaves	12 pounds), chine bone removed and fat
2½ tablespoons salt	trimmed to ¼ inch (save the fat for
1 tablespoon freshly ground black pepper	Yorkshire pudding)
2½ tablespoons olive oil	Bacon and Rosemary Jus (recipe follows)
	Scallion and Parmesan Yorkshire Puddings
	(recipe follows)

1   With the motor running, drop the garlic through the feed tube of a small food processor. Stop and scrape the sides of the bowl. Add the thyme, salt, pepper, and oil and pulse to form a paste.

2   Pat the roast dry with paper towels. Place the roast bone side down on a cutting board and cut ten to twelve 2-inch-long gashes through the fat, taking care not to cut into the meat itself. Press some of the garlic-herb mixture into each gash and smear the rest over the top, sides, and ends of the roast. Let sit for 4 hours at room temperature.

3   Preheat the oven to 450°F, with a rack in the lower third of the oven.

4   Place the roast bone side down in a roasting pan, or, if you have a large roasting rack, fit the rack into the pan and place the roast on the rack. If you have a cable-type digital continuous-read thermometer, insert it into the center of the roast and set it for

110°F to 115°F for rare or 120°F to 125°F for medium-rare. Roast for 20 minutes, then turn down the oven to 350°F and continue to roast until it has reached the desired temperature. If you are not using a continuous-read thermometer, begin monitoring the internal temperature with an instant-read thermometer after 1 hour, checking the temperature every 15 minutes. When the roast is done, set it aside, loosely covered with aluminum foil, to rest for at least 20 minutes, and up to 45 minutes, before carving and serving. The final temperature will rise 10 to 15 degrees. While the roast is resting, finish the Bacon and Rosemary Jus.

5   To carve and serve, place the roast on a carving board so that the bones are vertical. Run a carving knife between the bones and the meat to sever the rack from the meat. Set the bones aside and turn the roast so that the bone side lies flat. Cut the roast into ¼- to ½-inch-thick slices and arrange the slices in an overlapping row on a serving platter. Slice between the bones and add to the platter. Stir any carving juices into the jus. Serve with the jus and the Yorkshire puddings.

Alternative Cuts: Boneless rib-eye roast, New York strip roast, or 2 whole beef tenderloins (begin checking beef tenderloin for doneness 20 minutes after reducing the oven temperature to 350°F).

Cook's Notes

- Buy the best beef you can afford — USDA Choice or, if you can find it, USDA Prime. If you are really feeling flush, purchase a pricey but delicious Wagyu rib roast.

- I often season the roast ahead, wrap it in plastic wrap, and refrigerate it overnight, or for up to 36 hours, to allow the seasonings to penetrate the meat. (Let the roast stand for 4 hours at room temperature before roasting.)

- If you make this roast with grass-fed beef or bison, cook the roast to 110°F for rare. After 20 minutes, reduce the oven temperature to 275°F and allow extra time for cooking.

- I like to roast red beets or big chunks of celery root and parsnips to serve with our holiday roast. Broccolini with Pecan Brown Butter (page 57), spinach, or asparagus is also nice.

BACON AND ROSEMARY JUS

Makes 2 to 3 cups

2 ounces dried porcini mushrooms	1 750-ml bottle fruity red wine, such as Zinfandel
2 cups boiling water	
¼ pound thick-sliced bacon, cut into ½-inch-wide strips	5 cups homemade beef stock (see page 168) or canned low-sodium chicken broth
½ cup thinly sliced shallots	1 fresh rosemary sprig
3 tablespoons thinly sliced garlic	Salt and freshly ground black pepper
½ pound white or cremini mushrooms, thinly sliced	4 tablespoons (½ stick) butter, cut into 4 pieces

1 Place the porcini in a small bowl and cover with the boiling water. Soak for at least 45 minutes, or up to several hours, until soft.

2 Remove the porcini from the liquid with a slotted spoon. Chop and set aside. Strain the soaking liquid, leaving behind any grit in the bottom of the bowl, and reserve.

3 Heat a large saucepan over medium heat. Fry the bacon until golden but not quite crisp. Leave about 2 tablespoons of the fat in the pan with the bacon; save the rest of the fat for another purpose or discard.

4 Add the shallots and garlic to the pan, cover, and cook until soft, stirring from time to time, about 3 minutes. Stir in the fresh mushrooms and cook until soft, 5 to 7 minutes, scraping up any browned bits from the bottom of the pan. Add the porcini and red wine, bring to a boil, and boil until reduced to about 1 cup, about 15 minutes. Add the porcini soaking liquid and the stock and continue to boil until the sauce is reduced to 5 cups, about 30 minutes. Skim off any fat or scum from the surface of the sauce, add the rosemary, and cook for 3 minutes more. Remove the rosemary, cover, and set the sauce aside.

5 While the roast is resting, pour off all the fat from the roasting pan, leaving the juices in the pan. Place the pan over two burners on medium heat and add the sauce. Bring to a boil, scraping up any browned bits from the bottom of the roasting pan. Pour the sauce back into the saucepan and boil until the sauce develops a rich, meaty flavor and is just turning syrupy. There should be about 3 cups of jus. Season to taste with salt and pepper. Whisk in the butter 1 tablespoon at a time just until it is melted and the sauce becomes velvety. Serve at once.

SCALLION AND PARMESAN YORKSHIRE PUDDINGS

Serves 12

Yorkshire pudding and popovers are essentially the same; I prefer individual Yorkshire puddings (i.e., popovers) because the presentation is more dramatic. These airy puddings can be tricky. If you want perfection every time, use only whole milk (not low-fat). Also, you must whisk the batter by hand, because an electric mixer will overbeat the batter and it will not puff and rise. Use heavy pottery custard cups, large-hole cast-iron muffin pans, or popover pans.

11 tablespoons butter, melted, or ½ cup plus 3 tablespoons melted beef fat (see Cook's Notes), or a combination

1 cup freshly grated Parmigiano-Reggiano

8 large eggs

2⅔ cups whole milk

2⅔ cups all-purpose flour

½ teaspoon salt

½ cup finely chopped scallions, white and light green parts

1 Preheat the oven to 375°F, with a rack in the lower third.

2 Brush 12 custard cups or large muffin or popover molds (¾-cup capacity) with 3 tablespoons of the butter. Dust each cup or mold with some of the cheese and shake out any excess to use in the batter. Set aside.

3 Beat the eggs in a large bowl, then beat in the milk until well blended. In another bowl, combine the flour and salt. Using a fork or pastry blender, stir the remaining ½ cup butter into the flour. Gradually add the flour and butter mixture to the egg mixture, blending well with a whisk (no electric mixer); a few lumps are okay. Whisk in the remaining cheese and the scallions. Fill each cup with ½ to ⅔ cup of the batter.

4 Bake until the puddings are brown and puffy and give off a wonderful cheesy aroma, 55 to 60 minutes. Remove the puddings and serve at once.

Cook's Notes

- If you want to use beef fat in the recipe, trim and save the fat from the roast, or get the butcher to supply some extra trimmed fat. Cut into ¼-inch dice (you will need about 1½ cups) and spread in a small ovenproof skillet. Roast at 350°F until the fat has rendered and only little bits of solid fat remain, about 20 minutes. Strain and reserve the melted fat. This should yield about ¾ cup melted fat.

- For fresh variation, pull the top off each Yorkshire pudding and fill the cavity with cooked sweet peas (frozen are fine) and a pat of butter. Replace the tops and serve.

ROSA DI PARMA (WHOLE BEEF FILLET STUFFED WITH PROSCIUTTO AND PARMIGIANO-REGGIANO)

Fit for Company, Fit for a Crowd, Great Leftovers

Serves 12

Mama Rosa Musi is the quintessential Italian grandmother: old enough to be believable as a grandmother but still young and vibrant enough to make a multicourse meal for forty in a tiny kitchen. Her warmth, graciousness, and generosity make you feel like a family member within the first half hour of meeting her.

I arrived at her house in the village of Reverberi in the hills outside Parma as a guest of the *consorzio* that makes and markets Parmigiano-Reggiano. That afternoon, with the aid of her daughters, Lucia and Maria, Mama Rosa showed me how to make the stuffed pasta squares called *tortelli,* filled with ricotta (from the local dairy), chard, and Parmigiano-Reggiano. For the pièce de résistance, I learned to make rosa di Parma, a whole fillet butterflied and stuffed with prosciutto and Parmigiano-Reggiano, rolled, tied, rubbed with fresh sage, rosemary, and garlic, and roasted.

Whole fillet is not cheap, nor are the ingredients used to give it flavor here. It's a royal dish, worthy of the most elegant of dinner parties or special celebrations. The fact that its name, Rosa, matched our hostess's was an appropriate coincidence.

This menu makes for a very festive holiday dinner for a dozen guests. If you are serving fewer people, reduce the size of the roast accordingly. You can ask the butcher to double-butterfly the fillet or do it yourself, as described below.

1 4- to 5-pound trimmed whole beef fillet (beef tenderloin) roast (6 pounds untrimmed)	**Herb Rub**
6–8 thin slices prosciutto	1 tablespoon salt
2 cups freshly grated Parmigiano-Reggiano	1½ teaspoons freshly ground black pepper
2 tablespoons olive oil	1½ tablespoons minced garlic
	1 tablespoon finely chopped fresh sage
	1 tablespoon finely chopped fresh rosemary

1 If it's still attached, cut away the side strip of meat from the fillet (save for a stir-fry). Trim away most of the external fat and any of the underlying membrane, called the silver skin. To double-butterfly the fillet, place it on a cutting board with a short end toward you. Keeping your knife parallel to the board, make a cut along one long side of

the roast, about two thirds of the way down from the top of the fillet, cutting to about 1 inch from the other side. (Do not cut all the way through.) Flip over the fillet and turn it around so the other short end is toward you. Repeat the cut on the uncut side, once again cutting along the long side of the roast, about two thirds of the way down from the top, stopping about 1 inch from the other side. Open both cuts so you have a large rectangle and turn the meat fat side down. Use the heel of your hand to press the fillet open into an even thickness. (Tenderloin is so tender that you won't need to pound it.)

2   Cover the meat with a layer of prosciutto slices (it's okay if the slices overlap). Spread the Parmigiano-Reggiano over the prosciutto to make an even layer, covering all of it except for a 1-inch border. Starting from a long side, roll up the meat jelly roll style. Tie the roast at 2-inch intervals with butcher's twine. Let it rest at room temperature for 1 hour.

3   Preheat the oven to 450°F.

4   Lightly brush the roast all over with the olive oil. Combine all the herb rub ingredients in a small bowl, then coat the roast all over with the rub. Place the roast on a rack in a shallow roasting pan and roast for 25 minutes, or until an instant-read thermometer inserted in the center registers 110°F to 115°F for rare, 120°F to 125°F for medium-rare, or 130°F to 135°F for medium. Remove from the oven, cover loosely with aluminum foil, and let rest for 15 to 20 minutes before slicing.

5   To serve, remove the twine and cut the roast into ½-inch-thick slices.

Alternative Cuts: Butterflied flank steak (you may need to increase the amount of prosciutto and cheese), butterflied boneless bottom sirloin flap roast (*bavette*), boneless New York strip roast, cut in half lengthwise and butterflied. These cuts may serve fewer depending on which one you buy; figure on 4 to 5 ounces per serving.

SPINACH AND RICOTTA DUMPLINGS

Serves 12

These are a lot easier to make than *tortelli* because they have no pasta wrappers.

3 bunches spinach (2–3 pounds), washed	¼ teaspoon freshly grated nutmeg
2 pounds whole-milk ricotta cheese	½ cup chopped fresh flat-leaf parsley
3 cups freshly grated Parmigiano-Reggiano, plus more for serving	4 large eggs, lightly beaten
Salt and freshly ground black pepper	12 tablespoons (1½ sticks) butter
	20 fresh sage leaves, coarsely chopped

1   Cook the spinach in a large pot of boiling salted water until wilted, about 30 seconds. With a large skimmer, remove the spinach and drain; keep the water on the stove for cooking the dumplings. Let the spinach cool slightly, then squeeze until quite dry and finely chop.

2   Transfer the spinach to a large bowl, add the ricotta, 2 cups of the Parmigiano, 1½ teaspoons salt, 1 teaspoon pepper, the nutmeg, parsley, and eggs, and beat well to combine. Cover and refrigerate until ready to make the dumplings. (*The spinach mixture can be refrigerated for 1 day.*)

3   To make the dumplings, scoop tablespoons of the mixture onto a lightly floured surface and roll each one under your palms to form a cylinder about 1½ inches long and ½ inch in diameter. Arrange on a floured tray or sheet. (*The dumplings can be covered with a dish towel and refrigerated for up to 6 hours before cooking.*)

4 Bring the spinach water back to a boil. Reduce to a simmer, add the dumplings in batches, and cook until they rise to the surface, 5 to 7 minutes. Remove with a skimmer, drain well, and place on a platter.

5 Meanwhile, heat 6 tablespoons of the butter and half of the sage in a large nonstick skillet over medium heat until the butter is melted and the sage is fragrant, 2 to 3 minutes. Add half of the cooked dumplings and toss in the butter for 1 to 2 minutes to heat through, then add ½ cup of the remaining cheese and toss and shake until well coated. Transfer to a warm serving platter and repeat with the remaining cooked dumplings, 6 tablespoons butter, sage, and ½ cup cheese. Taste for salt and pepper and serve at once, with more grated Parmigiano-Reggiano alongside.

Cook's Note

- If you are a skilled *tortelli* maker, then by all means use the dumpling mixture as the filling. In Emilia-Romagna, *tortelli* are usually made in 2-inch squares. If making *tortelli*, leave the eggs out of the dumpling mixture, and serve as above with butter, sage, and Parmigiano-Reggiano.

ESCAROLE AND WHITE BEAN GRATIN

Serves 12

Italians frequently combine beans and various greens to make a hearty side dish. Besides escarole, you can use kale, collard greens, or broccoli rabe.

¼ pound pancetta, diced	2 teaspoons chopped fresh thyme
1 cup finely chopped onions	2 teaspoons chopped fresh sage
½ cup finely chopped celery	4 cups cooked white beans, baby limas,
3 tablespoons minced garlic	cannellini beans, or Italian butter beans
2 large heads escarole, cored, leaves separated,	Salt and freshly ground black pepper
washed, and coarsely chopped	Extra-virgin olive oil
2 cups homemade chicken stock or canned	2 cups fresh bread crumbs
low-sodium chicken broth	2 cups freshly grated Parmigiano-Reggiano

1 Preheat the oven to 350°F.

2 Heat a large Dutch oven over medium heat. Add the pancetta and cook until all the fat has rendered and the pancetta is lightly crisped. Add the onions and celery, cover, and cook until soft, about 5 minutes. Add the garlic and cook for 2 minutes more. Add the escarole and toss with the vegetables until well coated, then add the stock, thyme, and sage, cover, and cook until the escarole is tender, about 10 minutes.

3 Stir in the beans and cook for 10 minutes more. Season to taste with salt and pepper.

4 Lightly oil a large shallow baking dish or gratin dish with some olive oil. Scrape in the bean mixture and level the top. Combine the bread crumbs, cheese, and 3 tablespoons oil in a medium bowl and mix until the crumbs are lightly moistened, adding more oil if needed. Sprinkle the crumbs evenly over the bean mixture. Bake for 45 minutes, or until bubbly and the crumbs begin to lightly brown. Serve from the dish.

Cook's Note

- Have some good extra-virgin olive oil on the table for guests to sprinkle over their beans. If you can find new-harvest olive oil, even better.

PARMIGIANO-REGGIANO AND AGED BALSAMICO FOR DESSERT

Serves 12

Parmigiano-Reggiano is enjoyed as a dessert in Emilia-Romagna. Using a wedge-shaped cheese knife or a paring knife, chip off chunks from a 1½-pound chunk of cheese. Arrange the pieces on a platter and drizzle with the best aged balsamic vinegar you can afford. The finest is *extra vecchio* from the Consorzio Aceto Balsamico di Modena or Aceto Balsamico Tradizionale di Reggio Emilia. It's not cheap, but a little goes a long way. If you don't have aged balsamic vinegar, serve the cheese on its own.

HERB-SALTED NEW YORK STRIP ROAST WITH MOREL SAUCE

Fit for Company, Fit for a Crowd, Great Leftovers

Serves 16

For this festive and impressive roast, I cook the meat in a salt crust that deeply seasons it and creates a gentle cooking environment. The crust is not meant to be eaten, but it drives the flavors of the fresh herbs and garlic inward.

Herb and Salt Crust

- 4 cups kosher or coarse sea salt
- 2 large egg whites
- 2 cups water
- 5 tablespoons chopped fresh thyme
- 2 tablespoons chopped fresh flat-leaf parsley
- 2 tablespoons chopped juniper berries
- 3 tablespoons freshly ground black pepper
- ¼ cup chopped garlic
- 4–5 cups all-purpose flour

- 1 8- to 10-pound New York strip roast, fat trimmed to ¼ inch
  Salt and freshly ground black pepper
  Morel Sauce (recipe follows)

1. **Crust:** Combine the salt, egg whites, water, thyme, parsley, juniper berries, pepper, and garlic in a large bowl and mix with an electric mixer on medium speed. Add 4 cups of the flour and mix until the dough is firm and feels slightly dry and stiff, like Play-Doh, adding more flour if needed. Continue to mix for 2 minutes, or until the dough is smooth and firm but not sticky. Wrap the dough in plastic wrap and refrigerate for at least 2 hours, and up to 6 hours.

2. Three hours before roasting, remove the roast from the refrigerator and let stand at room temperature.

3. Preheat the oven to 350°F.

4. Season the roast all over with salt and pepper. Heat a large heavy roasting pan over two burners on medium-high heat. Add the roast, fat side down, and sear until browned, about 5 minutes. Flip and brown the other side, about 5 minutes more. Remove from the heat.

5. Roll out the dough to about ¼ inch thick on a lightly floured surface. Drape the dough over the roast, tucking it around the sides. Roast for about 1½ hours, or until the meat registers 120°F to 125°F for medium-rare on an instant-read thermometer. Remove the roast from the oven and let rest for 20 minutes.

6　Tear open and remove the crust. Brush off any visible salt. (*At this point, the roast can rest for up to 20 minutes more.*) Present the roast to your guests whole, then slice and serve with the Morel Sauce.

Alternative Cuts: Whole tenderloin — reduce the crust recipe by half and roast for 45 to 60 minutes, or until the meat reaches 120°F. Boneless rib-eye roast (weighing up to 10 pounds) — it may take an extra 30 minutes to roast to the desired temperature of 120°F to 125°F.

Cook's Notes

- The surest way to ruin this dish is to remove the crust before the allotted resting time of 20 minutes. It's very important that the meat is allowed to sit to reabsorb its juices and to heighten the aroma of the herbs.

- You can omit the salt crust. Season the roast generously with salt and freshly ground black pepper and roast following the directions above. If you wish, sprinkle 2 tablespoons chopped fresh thyme and/or 2 teaspoons chopped juniper berries on the surface of the roast once it's browned. Add the defatted pan juices to the Morel Sauce.

MOREL SAUCE

Makes 3 to 4 cups

Dried morels are one of my favorite splurges. In truth, I prefer dried to fresh ones for this luxurious sauce. Besides having a more intense flavor, they hold their shape better as the sauce reduces, and the sauce clings to their unusual crenellated surfaces.

3 cups boiling water

2 ounces small dried morel mushrooms, picked over to clean

½ cup minced shallots

4½ tablespoons butter

2 large garlic cloves, minced

2 cups dry marsala or cream sherry

2 cups heavy cream

2 tablespoons fresh lemon juice

2 tablespoons minced fresh chives

3 teaspoons chopped fresh thyme or tarragon

Salt and freshly ground black pepper

1 Pour the boiling water over the morels in a medium bowl. Soak until soft, at least 45 minutes, or up to several hours.

2 Lift out the morels with a slotted spoon, squeeze dry, and reserve. Strain the soaking liquid into a small saucepan, leaving behind any dirt or debris in the bottom of the bowl. Bring to a boil and boil until reduced to about ½ cup, about 10 minutes. Set aside.

3 Sauté the shallots in the butter in a medium saucepan over medium heat until soft and golden brown, 3 to 5 minutes. Add the garlic and cook for 1 minute, then add the morels and cook over low heat for 3 minutes more, stirring often. Add the marsala, increase the heat to a low boil, and cook for 10 minutes, or until the mixture just starts to dry out. Add the reduced mushroom liquid and the cream, bring to a simmer, and simmer until the sauce has the thickness of heavy cream. (*The sauce can be kept warm for up to 30 minutes before serving.*)

4 Add the lemon juice, chives, and thyme to the sauce and season to taste with salt and pepper. Serve.

Cook's Note

- If you are roasting the meat without the salt crust, pour off any fat from the roasting pan, add 1 cup of the marsala to the pan, and scrape up any browned bits from the bottom of the pan. Add to the sauce when adding the reduced mushroom soaking liquid.

Beef and Bison Roasts for Everyday Meals

For everyday cooking, you want a relatively inexpensive roast that is small enough to cook in a short amount of time yet large enough to feed a family of 4 to 6. If there happens to be some meat left over for sandwiches, all the better.

My favorite cut for everyday roast beef dinners is tri-tip. When nicely marbled, the meat is tender, juicy, and flavorful, and it lends itself both to oven and grill-roasting. It also takes well to flavor boosts like rubs and marinades. When I'm feeding extra guests, I'll often roast two tri-tips instead of looking for a large roast that may be less flavorful.

Another good choice is a roast cut from the top sirloin. The whole top sirloin can be cut into two roasts — top sirloin butt and top sirloin cap roast (also called culotte) — and both are good choices. Culotte is often cut into steaks, so ask the butcher to sell you a whole or partial piece to roast.

Other good roasts come from the round. My first choice is top round, but, sadly, most butchers cut it into steaks and call them London broil. If you can get the butcher to sell you a 3- to 4-pound chunk and tie or net it, it will make an excellent roast; otherwise, you can roast a 2- to 3-inch steak. Sirloin tip, sometimes called knuckle roast — which is actually from the round, not from the sirloin (butchers seem to love to mislead us with names) — is a common cut. If it's adequately marbled, it can be roasted nicely to medium-rare.

The chuck provides a cross-rib roast from the shoulder clod, a solid muscle with no fatty pockets. This was roast beef in my house when I was growing up. When marinated and slow-roasted, this cut will be impressive; slice the leftovers thin, and you have the start of a superlative sandwich. Flat cuts, such as flank steak, can be stuffed, rolled, and tied to make excellent roasts.

Despite what you may read in other books or magazines, don't buy eye of round or bottom round for roast beef unless you can get these cuts in a well-marbled Prime grade. Even when cooked in a low oven (200°F to 250°F), which keeps the juices in, these cuts will be tough and tasteless unless they are Prime or Wagyu.

GRILL- OR OVEN-ROASTED TRI-TIP WITH SPANISH ADOBO RUB

Family Meal, Great Leftovers, Grass-Fed Beef

Serves 4 to 6

Small cuts of beef such as tri-tip and culotte are ideal for grilling over indirect heat. They are a perfect choice for an everyday family roast beef meal. Both relatively inexpensive, tri-tip and culotte can be roasted in well under an hour and lend themselves to many different flavor profiles simply by varying the flavor step (see Cook's Note).

Adobo is found throughout the Spanish-speaking world and refers to a mixture of vinegar or citrus and various spices that is rubbed over the food or used as part of the sauce. This recipe can be given a "south of the border" twist by substituting cumin for the marjoram, chile powder for the paprika, and fresh lime juice for the vinegar; garnish with cilantro and serve with tortillas. As with most marinades and pastes, the flavor is improved by letting the roast marinate overnight in the refrigerator.

Spanish Adobo Rub

- 3 garlic cloves, peeled
- 2 teaspoons chopped fresh marjoram
- 2 teaspoons salt
- 1 teaspoon freshly ground black pepper
- 3 tablespoons Spanish paprika (*pimentón de la Vera*; see Sources) or sweet Hungarian paprika

- ¼ cup sherry vinegar
- 1 tablespoon olive oil

- 1 1½- to 2½-pound tri-tip roast, fat trimmed to about ¼ inch

1 **Rub:** With the motor running, drop the garlic through the feed tube of a food processor. Scrape down the sides of the bowl, add the remaining ingredients, and process to form a thick red paste. Rub the paste all over the meat. *(The meat can be wrapped in plastic wrap and refrigerated overnight.)*

2 Let the roast sit for 1 to 2 hours at room temperature. Scrape some of the spice rub off the meat leaving a little to form a nice crust.

3 **To grill-roast:** Set up a charcoal or gas grill for indirect grilling (see page 12 for more on grilling). Sear the roast for 2 to 3 minutes on each side over direct heat, then move to the area of the grill with no heat. If you have a cable-type digital continuous-read thermometer, insert it into the meat and set it for 110°F to 115°F for rare or 120°F to 125°F for medium-rare. Cover the grill. If you don't have a continuous-read thermometer, begin checking the temperature with an instant-read thermometer after 15

minutes, checking every 10 minutes until the meat reaches your desired degree of doneness.

To oven-roast: Preheat the oven to 450°F. Set the roast in a roasting pan, fat side up, and roast for 15 minutes, or until it reaches 110°F to 115°F for rare or 120°F to 125°F for medium-rare.

4   Let the roast rest, loosely covered with aluminum foil, for 10 to 15 minutes. Cut across the grain into ¼-inch-thick slices and serve.

Alternative Cuts: Whole culotte, tenderloin of an equivalent weight, New York strip of an equivalent weight, boneless rib-eye roast (which will take longer because it's thicker), or any other sirloin roast you can find such as top sirloin butt or ball tip from the round.

Cook's Note
- You can flavor the tri-tip with any of the marinade, spice rub, or spice paste recipes for steaks (pages 63–69)

GRILLING ROASTS FROM LEAN GRASS-FED BEEF AND BISON

The best cuts for grilling are tri-tip, fillet, small boneless rib-eye, sirloin, sirloin tip, chuck-eye, and New York strip roast.

- Season the roast as described in the recipe, then let it rest at room temperature for 2 to 3 hours.
- Prepare the coals, and when they're ready, spread them over half the grill. Or, if using gas, heat all the burners to medium-high, then leave one section on and turn off all the others. (See page 11 for more on grilling.)
- Lay the roast directly over the heat and sear on all sides, which may take 10 minutes total. If flare-ups occur, move the meat to an area of the grill with no fire; when the flare-ups subside, return the meat to the heat and continue searing.

- Once the roast is seared, set it fat side up in a roasting pan or skillet just large enough to hold it, and place it on the part of the grill with no heat. If you have a cable-type digital continuous-read thermometer, insert it into the center of the roast and set it for 10 degrees lower than your desired degree of doneness (make sure the cable isn't over any flame). Cover the grill and try to maintain a temperature of 275°F to 300°F. If you're using an instant-read thermometer, begin monitoring the internal temperature after 15 minutes for small roasts, such as tri-tips or tenderloins, and after 40 minutes for larger roasts.
- When the roast is done, transfer to a platter and allow it to rest, tented with aluminum foil, for 15 to 20 minutes before slicing and serving.

BEEF CROSS-RIB ROAST WITH GARLIC-HERB MARINADE

Cheap Eats, Family Meal, Great Leftovers, Grass-Fed Beef

Serves 4 to 6

Most cross-rib roasts tend to be lean and a bit chewy. This recipe improves both flavor and juiciness by relying on slow-roasting to keep the juices in the meat and gently cook the muscle fibers so they don't shrink and force out moisture. My wife, Nancy Oakes, who started her cooking career making cold sandwiches in an Irish bar, always used cross-rib roasts for her popular roast beef sandwiches with Russian Dressing (page 136). The trick is to slice the beef as thin as possible, which helps make the meat more tender. Since most of us don't have an electric slicing machine, chill the meat well (place it in the freezer for 15 minutes) and use your sharpest knife or an electric knife.

Garlic-Herb Marinade

- 1 cup olive oil
- 12 garlic cloves, peeled
- 1 tablespoon chopped fresh winter savory or rosemary
- 1 tablespoon chopped fresh thyme
- 2 tablespoons chopped fresh sage

- 2 teaspoons salt
- 2 teaspoons freshly ground black pepper

- 1 4- to 5-pound boneless cross-rib roast, rolled and tied
- Salt and freshly ground black pepper

1. **Marinade:** Heat the oil in a small saucepan over low heat. Add the garlic cloves and cook, stirring, for 3 to 5 minutes, or until the garlic softens but does not begin to color. Remove the pan from the heat and stir in the remaining ingredients. Let cool for 10 minutes.

2. Place the roast in a large zipper-lock bag. Pour in the marinade, seal the bag, and turn the bag so that the roast is well coated. Marinate at room temperature for 2 to 3 hours or refrigerate overnight.

3. If the roast has been refrigerated, let sit at room temperature for 2 to 3 hours before cooking.

4. Preheat the oven to 450°F.

5. Remove the roast from the marinade. Scrape off the garlic but leave any herbs on the surface of the roast. Place fat side up on a V-shape roasting rack in a roasting pan. If

you have a cable-type digital continuous-read thermometer, insert it into the center of the roast and set it for 120°F for medium-rare. Roast for 15 minutes, then reduce the oven temperature to 250°F. If you don't have a continuous-read thermometer, start testing the roast with an instant-read thermometer after 45 minutes, and remove the roast at 120°F to 125°F. Let the roast rest for 15 minutes. The final temperature will rise 5 to 10 degrees.

6 Remove the string. Slice the roast into ⅛- to ¼-inch-thick slices and serve.

Alternative Cuts: Rump roast — the true cut from the ass end, not from the bottom round; sirloin tip; top round; chuck-eye; ball tip; culotte; or sirloin butt roast. Avoid bottom round roasts and eye-of-round roasts unless they come from an animal graded Prime and/or show some marbling.

Cook's Note
- The roast will be uniformly light red all the way across when sliced, with no gray ring. This is the result of the lower-temperature roasting and of letting the meat warm to room temperature before roasting.

OVEN-ROASTING LEAN BEEF AND BISON

This method is designed for roasting all cuts of lean grass-fed beef, no-roll beef, and bison, as well as tougher lean Choice-grade roasts, such as sirloin tip, rump, cross-rib, sirloin, and top round.

If you wish to cook your roast beyond medium-rare, consider flavor-brining the roast first (see page 249). If you want well-done meat, make a pot roast.

- Season the roast as described in the recipe, then let it sit at room temperature for 3 to 4 hours.
- Preheat the oven to 250°F.
- While the oven is preheating, heat a slick of olive oil or vegetable oil in a large skillet over medium-high heat. Add the roast and brown it nicely on all sides, 2 to 3 minutes per side. Reduce the heat if the roast begins to brown too quickly.
- Once the roast is browned, place it fat side up on a rack set in a roasting pan. Insert a cable-type digital continuous-read thermometer into the meat and set it to about 5 degrees lower than the desired degree of doneness. Place the pan in the oven. Depending on how large the roast is, it may take 2 hours or more, so plan accordingly (a 5-pound sirloin tip takes 2 hours to reach 120°F in my oven). If you're using an instant-read thermometer, start testing a 5-pound roast after 1½ hours.
- Let the roast rest, tented with aluminum foil, for 20 to 30 minutes, then slice and serve. For tougher roasts — such as sirloin tip — slice the meat as thin as possible (an electric knife works well).

SPINACH AND GORGONZOLA–STUFFED FLANK STEAK

Fit for Company, Family Meal, Great Leftovers
Serves 6

When stuffed, rolled, and tied, a flank steak can serve as a roast. A relatively low-cost cut, flank gains points for elegance when stuffed with a flavorful cheese and spinach filling. When the meat is sliced, the pretty pinwheels make a great presentation. This is easy enough to put together on a weeknight or for quick entertaining. The recipe is from my coauthor, Anne-marie Ramo.

Besides Gorgonzola, you can use any full-flavored blue cheese; my favorite is Rogue River Blue from Rogue Creamery. Or use goat cheese or any other soft cheese that suits your fancy.

Ask your butcher to butterfly the steak for you, or do it yourself following the instructions below. Or, if your steak is already very thin, use a meat mallet to pound it thinner.

1 1½- to 2½-pound flank steak, trimmed	1 cup fresh bread crumbs
3 tablespoons olive oil	½ pound Gorgonzola or other blue cheese, crumbled
1 shallot, finely chopped	
1 pound spinach, washed, stemmed, and chopped	Salt and freshly ground black pepper

1   Preheat the oven to 375°F.

2   To butterfly the steak: Using a long sharp knife, holding it parallel to the work surface, cut through one long side of the steak, stopping about ½ inch from the opposite side. Open up the steak as you would a book. (Don't worry if you made a hole or two in the meat, because it will be concealed when you roll up the steak.) Or, if the steak is already thin, don't butterfly it; just pound it with a meat mallet to ¼ to ½ inch thick. Set aside.

3   Heat a large skillet over medium heat and add 1 tablespoon of the olive oil. Add the shallot and sauté until soft, about 3 minutes. Add the spinach and cook until just wilted, about 3 minutes. Transfer to a strainer.

4   When it is cool enough to handle, squeeze out all of the moisture from the spinach. You should have about 1 cup of spinach. Transfer to a medium bowl and stir in the bread crumbs and cheese. Season to taste with salt and pepper.

5 Place the steak on a sheet of plastic wrap with a long side of the steak facing you. Smear the spinach mixture evenly over the steak, leaving a 1-inch border along the edge farthest from you. Beginning with the side nearest you and using the plastic wrap as an aid, roll up the steak, gently pressing on the filling, then tie the rolled steak with butcher's twine at 2- to 3-inch intervals. Season the outside with salt and pepper to taste.

6 Heat the remaining 2 tablespoons olive oil in a large roasting pan or ovenproof skillet over medium-high heat. Sear the roast on all sides, about 3 minutes per side. Place in the oven and roast for 25 minutes, or until an instant-read thermometer inserted into the center of the roast reads 120°F to 125°F for medium-rare. Transfer to a cutting board, tent with aluminum foil, and allow to rest for 10 to 15 minutes.

7 To serve, remove the string from the steak and cut into ½- to ¾-inch-thick slices.

Alternative Cuts: Double-butterflied fillet (see page 106 for method); bottom sirloin flap steak (*bavette*), butterflied and pounded to about ½ inch thick; or grass-fed flank steak or double-butterflied grass-fed tenderloin.

Cook's Notes
- Be sure to choose a flank steak that is of even thickness throughout to ensure consistent cooking.
- Do not tie the roast too tightly. The twine should hold the roast together but not constrict it.
- This is a great recipe for grass-fed flank steak, because the stuffing supplies richness and moisture.

ROAST BISON SIRLOIN

Family Meal, Great Leftovers, Grass-Fed Beef
Serves 6 to 8, with leftovers

This low-temperature roasting method is ideal for all lean roasts, including bison and grass-fed beef. Because the oven temperature is too low to brown the meat, it's best to brown it in a skillet first. For even cooking, it's very important that you let the roast sit at room temperature for at least 2, and up to 4, hours before roasting.

1   5- to 6-pound boneless bison sirloin roast
3   tablespoons olive oil
    Salt and freshly ground black pepper

2–3   tablespoons chopped fresh herbs, such as thyme, sage, rosemary, summer or winter savory, and/or fennel fronds, or 2–3 tablespoons spice rub of your choice (pages 66–68)

1   Remove the roast from the refrigerator and let it sit at room temperature for 2 to 4 hours. (Ideally, the center of the roast should come to 50°F to 55°F.)

2   Preheat the oven to 200°F.

3   Smear the surface of the meat with 1 tablespoon of the oil and season generously with salt and pepper. Heat a large heavy ovenproof skillet over medium-high heat. Add the remaining 2 tablespoons oil and brown the roast on all sides, about 10 minutes. Remove from the heat and coat the roast with the herbs or spice rub.

4   Place the skillet in the oven and roast until the internal temperature of the roast reaches 120°F to 125°F for medium-rare, 2½ to 4 hours, depending on the temperature of the meat when it went into the oven and how well your oven holds a steady temperature. Remove the roast from the oven and let rest, loosely covered with aluminum foil, for 20 minutes. Cut across the grain into ¼-inch-thick slices and serve.

Alternative Cuts: Bison rib-eye, loin, or tenderloin roast. Grass-fed beef loin, rib eye, sirloin, or cross-rib roast or sirloin tip. Select-grade beef sirloin tip or cross-rib, top round, or sirloin roast.

Leftovers
- Don't try to rewarm a bison roast — it will dry out and toughen. Instead, slice it thin and use in sandwiches. It's particularly nice with rye bread and Russian Dressing (page 136).

ROASTED GINGER-ORANGE-GLAZED PRIME RIB BONES

Cheap Eats, Family Meal
Serves 4 to 6

The increased popularity of boneless rib-eye steak and roasts has created a glut of rib back bones, or prime rib bones. Some butchers save them in their freezers and then offer them at bargain prices for the summer grilling season. Even though they come from the same ribs that make short ribs, there is little meat on these bones, but what is there is succulent and tasty because there is plenty of fat interspersed. The bones are ideal for long roasting and are best served well-done, which also allows some of the fat to render out. This recipe uses the oven and broiler, but you can also cook the ribs in an outdoor grill over indirect heat and then glaze them over direct heat (see page 11 for more on grilling).

Dry Rub

- 4 teaspoons salt
- 2 teaspoons freshly ground black pepper
- 1 teaspoon dark brown sugar
- 1 teaspoon ground cumin
- ½ teaspoon ground ginger
- 1 teaspoon dry mustard powder (I use Colman's)
- 2 teaspoons Hungarian paprika

- 4–5 pounds prime rib bones (also called beef rib back bones), trimmed of external fat

Ginger-Orange Glaze

- 2 tablespoons peanut oil
- 1½ cups finely chopped red onions
- 1 tablespoon minced garlic
- 1 tablespoon minced fresh ginger
- 1 cup fresh orange juice
- ½ cup orange marmalade
- 3 tablespoons soy sauce
- ½ cup bottled chili sauce (I use Heinz)
- ¼ cup fresh lemon juice
- ¼ teaspoon Chinese five-spice powder
- ½ teaspoon Tabasco or other hot sauce
- 1 teaspoon Worcestershire sauce

Garnish

- Asian sesame oil
- 3 tablespoons toasted sesame seeds (see Cook's Notes)

1. Preheat the oven to 350°F. Line the broiler pan with aluminum foil.

2. **Rub:** Combine the rub ingredients and sprinkle all over the ribs. (*At this point, you can wrap the ribs in plastic wrap and refrigerate them overnight.*)

3   **Glaze:** Heat the oil in a medium saucepan over medium-high heat. Add the red onions and cook until soft, about 5 minutes, stirring frequently. Stir in the garlic and ginger and cook for 1 minute more. Whisk in the remaining glaze ingredients and bring to a boil, then reduce the heat and simmer until the glaze is thick and syrupy, 5 to 10 minutes. Set aside. (*You can make the glaze ahead and store it covered in the refrigerator for up to 2 to 3 weeks. Rewarm before using; you may have to add a few drops of water or orange juice to thin it out.*)

4   Lay the ribs on the broiler pan, meat side up, and roast in the oven for 45 to 60 minutes, or until tender. Remove from the oven and turn on the broiler.

5   Brush the ribs with some of the glaze and position the broiler pan 2 to 3 inches from the heat. Broil for 2 minutes, or until the glaze is shiny and bubbly. Turn over the ribs, brush with glaze, and broil until shiny and bubbly.

6   Arrange the ribs on a platter and brush them one more time with the glaze, then drizzle with sesame oil and sprinkle with the sesame seeds. (*Store any remaining glaze in the refrigerator and use to glaze grilled pork chops, spareribs, or chicken.*)

Alternative Cuts: English-cut or flanken-style short ribs, but they will take longer to cook, 1½ to 2 hours. Korean-style short ribs, which should be roasted for about 20 minutes. Pork chops and any cut of pork rib also work well.

Cook's Notes

- To toast sesame seeds, place the seeds in a small skillet over medium heat and stir and shake until they begin to lightly brown and give off a toasty aroma, 3 to 5 minutes. Immediately transfer the seeds to a bowl, or they will burn.

- The rib bones can also be prepared using any of the marinade or rub recipes for pork ribs (pages 395–402). Because they're small and tender the ribs can be cooked over direct heat (see page 11 for more on grilling). If the marinade or rub contains sugar, use a moderate fire and turn the ribs often so that they don't burn.

Beef Kebabs

Just about every culture in the world has a traditional kebab, and there are good reasons for the kebab's popularity. Kebabs make use of a variety of cuts, as well as bits and pieces. They cook quickly, so only a little fuel is consumed. They also allow the cook to serve small portions of meat that pack a whole lot of flavor. Beef kebabs are particularly appealing because the meat can be complemented by a host of different flavorings — from soy, curry, and chile to citrus and sweet glazes.

Although just about any tender or semitender cut can be turned into a kebab, my favorite cuts are from areas that are slightly chewy yet rich in flavor and have adequate marbling so that the meat doesn't dry out, even if it's overcooked. Ideally, I like to cook kebabs medium-rare to medium, but it's difficult to control doneness with little pieces of meat. If you are a lover of rare meat, choose an ultratender cut, and don't overmarinate it in an acidic marinade. If using acidic ingredients such as citrus or vinegar, 2 hours at room temperature is ideal, or up to 6 hours in the refrigerator.

Kebabs can be served as a first course or a main dish, and when you wrap them in warm flatbread or toasty rolls, they make great sandwiches. Not all kebabs are made with cubed meat: Some are thin strips of meat threaded onto skewers — think Indonesian satay or Japanese yakitori — that are ideal to serve as a passed hors d'oeuvre or as part of a multicourse Asian meal.

GREAT CUTS FOR KEBABS

Avoid ready-cut kebab meat. You have no idea where these pieces came from, and you will probably pay a premium price for cubes cut from the tough and chewy bottom round or eye of round.

For cubes

When cutting the meat into cubes, aim for about 1½ inches (you may want ¾-inch cubes if you'll be serving them as a passed hors d'oeuvre). Make sure to trim any gristle and excess fat.

- My first choice is well-marbled tri-tip, followed by Denver steak, then top sirloin (which can be a bit pricey). If you are not looking to save money, New York strip makes great kebabs.
- Other good choices that are a bit chewier, but ideal if you are using an acidic marinade, are top round, chuck-eye steaks, cross-rib steaks, and ball tip steaks.
- Tender cuts for rare kebabs are tenderloin, rib eye, rib-eye cap, and flat-iron steaks.

For strips

- Ideal cuts are skirt, flank, bottom sirloin flap (*bavette*), and flat-iron steak. Cut each of these across the grain into ¼-inch-thick by 1- to 1½-inch wide strips. Skirt steak and flank steak should be cut on the bias.

THAI GREEN CURRY–MARINATED BEEF KEBABS

Cheap Eats
Serves 6

For these spicy kebabs, I like to use full-flavored cuts of beef, my first choice being those from the chuck. Good choices are flat-iron, Denver, or chuck-eye steaks (from the rib-eye area of the chuck), and cross-rib steaks if they show marbling. I also like the tri-tip and the sirloin butt if they're well marbled.

Thai Green Curry Marinade
- 1 tablespoon Thai green curry paste
- 2 tablespoons soy sauce
- 1 tablespoon Asian fish sauce
- 2 tablespoons fresh lime juice
- 2 teaspoons light brown sugar
- 1 teaspoon minced fresh ginger
- 2 teaspoons minced garlic
- ¼ cup chopped fresh cilantro
- 2 tablespoons peanut oil

- 2 pounds boneless beef (see headnote), cut into 1½-inch cubes
- 24 2-inch-wide white mushrooms
- 1 large red onion, cut into 1-inch wedges
- 1 large red bell pepper, cored, seeded, and cut into 1-inch squares
- 1 tablespoon chopped fresh basil (I use Thai basil)
- 1 tablespoon chopped fresh mint
  Fresh Plum Sambal (optional; page 263)
  12 metal skewers

1. **Marinade:** Whisk all the ingredients together in a small bowl. Place the meat in a large zipper-lock bag. Pour over the marinade, seal the bag, and turn and shake the bag to coat the meat. Place in a bowl to catch any leaks. Marinate in the refrigerator for at least 6 hours, or, better yet, overnight, turning the bag from time to time to redistribute the marinade.

2. At least 30 minutes and up to 1 hour before cooking, remove the meat from the marinade and set aside. Pour the marinade into a small saucepan and bring to a boil, then transfer to a small bowl and set aside.

3. Set up a charcoal or gas grill for medium-high heat (see page 11 for more on grilling).

4. Thread the meat onto skewers. Thread the mushrooms onto separate skewers, and alternate pieces of red onion and bell pepper on the remaining skewers. Brush all the vegetables with some of the reserved marinade.

5   Grill the kebabs and vegetables, turning them frequently and basting with some of the reserved marinade each time they're turned: The beef will take 4 to 5 minutes for rare or 5 to 6 minutes for medium-rare. The mushrooms will take 2 to 3 minutes (or until they're soft), and the bell peppers and onions will take 6 to 8 minutes.

6   Give the kebabs a final brushing with the marinade, then transfer all of the goodies from the skewers onto a platter. Sprinkle with the basil and mint and serve with the Plum Sambal on the side (if using).

Alternative Cuts: Besides the choices in the headnote, cubes of New York strip, boneless rib-eye, or top round steaks.

Cook's Notes

- For a different flavor profile, use Thai red curry paste instead of green.

- If you like your kebabs extra spicy, add 2 to 3 tablespoons of Sriracha sauce to the marinade, to suit your taste.

- If you wish to serve these skewers as an hors d'oeuvre, cut the meat into ½- to ¾-inch chunks. Use 6-inch skewers and reduce the cooking time to 2 to 3 minutes. Omit the vegetables.

- This recipe also works well with beef cut into strips. Cut skirt, flank, or bottom sirloin flap steaks (*bavette*) into strips ¼ to ⅜ inch thick, 1 to 1½ inches wide, and 4 to 6 inches long. Thread them onto skewers and grill as directed above.

Ground Beef and Bison

The ground beef you find in the supermarket will have a label that tells you its percentage of lean meat and percentage of fat. My favorite for burgers is labeled "Ground Beef 80/20," meaning it's 80 percent lean meat and 20 percent fat. Lean ground beef will be labeled "90/10"; extralean will be labeled "95/5." Most ground bison will be "95/5." The definitions of lean and extra lean can vary from store to store, so always check the percentage.

If a specific primal cut is mentioned on the label — "Ground Beef Sirloin 90/10," for example — then the meat must come from cuts and trimmings of that primal. But if the label reads "Ground Beef," then the meat can come from any part of the carcass.

The best way to know what's in your ground beef is to grind it yourself (see below). Or, if you have a butcher who will grind meat for you, ask him or her to grind a combination of cuts — say a mix of chuck roast and sirloin.

GRINDING MEAT AT HOME

Plan to grind meat the day that you purchase it so that it's at maximum freshness. If you want to be extra cautious, follow the advice of the food science writer Harold McGee. To kill surface bacteria, he brings a pot of water to a boil and blanches the large chunk of meat for 30 to 60 seconds. He immediately transfers the meat to an ice bath, then drains it and pats it dry. Otherwise, simply use freshly purchased meat directly from the refrigerator.

- To keep the fat firm and the meat cold during chopping, place the clean food processor bowl and the blade in the freezer for 30 minutes before you begin.
- Cut the meat into ¾-inch cubes. If you are not grinding the meat immediately, refrigerate it.
- Place no more than ¾ pound meat at a time in the food processor. Use the pulse switch in 2-second bursts to produce ⅛- to ¼-inch pieces of meat. Don't overprocess, or you'll end up with meat slurry.
- You can also use a meat grinder fitted with the ¼-inch plate.
- Use the ground meat immediately, or wrap it and freeze (see page 7) for up to 2 months.

BARBECUE SAUCE–GLAZED MEAT LOAF

Cheap Eats, Family Meal, Great Leftovers

Serves 4 to 6

My coauthor, Anne-marie Ramo, admits that she was never a big fan of meat loaf until she met her husband, who loves it. In the quest for marital bliss, she set to work on a recipe she could love. Known for her killer barbecued meats, she found a way to sneak in barbecue flavor, and added a handful of chopped bacon to the mix as well. The resulting recipe made her a convert, and her husband is happy to report it's the best he's ever tasted. Anne-marie uses her own homemade barbecue sauce, but you can use any sauce you like, homemade or bottled. In the summertime, you can grill-roast this dish outside; see Cook's Notes.

½ cup chili sauce (I use Heinz)

½ cup Easy Barbecue Sauce (recipe follows) or store-bought barbecue sauce

1 cup fresh bread crumbs made from rustic bread

½ cup buttermilk

2 tablespoons melted bacon fat or olive oil

2 cups finely chopped onions

½ cup finely chopped peeled carrots

2 garlic cloves, minced

½ cup grated extra-sharp cheddar cheese

¼ cup chopped fresh flat-leaf parsley

2 teaspoons chopped fresh sage or ½ teaspoon dried

1 teaspoon chopped fresh thyme or ½ teaspoon dried

1½ pounds ground beef (80% lean), home-ground (see page 132) or store-bought

½ pound lean ground veal or turkey

¼ pound bacon, finely chopped

2 large eggs, lightly beaten

1½ teaspoons salt

1 teaspoon freshly ground black pepper

1 Preheat the oven to 350°F. Grease an 8½-x-4½-inch glass loaf pan.

2 Combine the chili sauce and barbecue sauce in a small bowl, and set aside.

3 Place the bread crumbs in a small bowl and add the buttermilk. Set aside.

4 Heat the bacon fat in a medium skillet over medium-high heat. Add the onions and carrots, cover, and cook until the vegetables soften, about 10 minutes, stirring occasionally. Add the garlic and cook for 1 minute more. Transfer the mixture to a large bowl.

5 Squeeze the buttermilk from the bread and add the bread, ½ cup of the barbecue sauce mixture, the cheese, parsley, sage, thyme, beef, veal, bacon, eggs, salt, and pepper to the

onion mixture. Using your hands, knead and squeeze the mixture until well blended, but don't overmix.

6 Pack the meat mixture into the loaf pan. Gently knock the pan a few times on the work surface to remove air bubbles and pack the meat down, then mound the top of the loaf. Bake for 1 hour, or until the internal temperature reaches 130°F to 135°F. Brush a generous amount of the remaining barbecue sauce mixture over the top and bake for 10 minutes more. Brush one more time with the remaining barbecue sauce mixture and bake for 10 minutes more, or until the internal temperature reaches 150°F.

7 Let the meat loaf rest for 10 minutes, then remove from the pan, slice into ¾-inch-thick slices, and serve.

Alternative Cuts: Ground bison or grass-fed beef; use an additional ¼ pound bacon, finely chopped.

Cook's Notes

- If you use a metal loaf pan instead of glass, the meat loaf may take 10 to 15 minutes longer to reach 150°F.

- You can also form the mixture into a free-form log shape (about 10 x 4 x 4 inches) on a baking sheet.

- If you like, lay some bacon strips in a crisscross pattern over the top of the loaf before popping it into the oven.

- To grill-roast, set up a gas grill for indirect heat (see page 12), then bring it to 350°F. Cover a metal pan with aluminum foil, place on the side of the grill with no fire, and cook for 1 hour, monitoring the temperature of the grill to maintain a constant 350°F. Remove the foil and finish the cooking, following the directions above for basting with barbecue sauce.

Leftovers

- For a great meat loaf sandwich, combine mayonnaise with some barbecue sauce and slather it onto toasted whole-grain bread, top with the meat loaf, and serve with slices of dill pickle.

- Also see The Ultimate Meat Loaf Sandwich (page 136).

EASY BARBECUE SAUCE

Makes about 5 cups

4 cups canned tomato sauce

1 cup cider vinegar

2 cups firmly packed dark brown sugar

½ cup coarse brown mustard

¼ cup Worcestershire sauce

2 small onions, finely chopped

6 garlic cloves, finely chopped

2 teaspoons hickory liquid smoke

1 teaspoon finely ground coffee beans (I use espresso beans)

½ teaspoon chipotle chile powder (optional)

¼ teaspoon ground allspice

Salt and freshly ground black pepper

Combine all the ingredients except the salt and pepper in a large saucepan and bring to a boil. Lower the heat and simmer for 30 to 45 minutes, or until thick. Season to taste with salt and pepper. (*The sauce can be cooled and stored in a covered container in the refrigerator for up to 2 weeks.*)

THE ULTIMATE MEAT LOAF SANDWICH

In a Hurry, Comfort Food

Makes 4 sandwiches

I love cold meat loaf even more than hot, and if you start with a great recipe (page 133), it doesn't take much to make a terrific sandwich. My choice for bread is toasted rye or bakery-made coarse-grain whole wheat. Then all you need are some juicy slices of vine-ripened heirloom tomatoes (I use Brandywines), a generous slathering of homemade Russian dressing, and perhaps some superthin slices of sweet onion. On the side, I serve a kosher dill pickle, sliced into quarters.

Russian Dressing
- 1 cup mayonnaise
- 1 tablespoon finely chopped scallion greens
- 2 tablespoons finely chopped fresh flat-leaf parsley
- 1 tablespoon prepared horseradish, drained
- 1 teaspoon Dijon mustard
- ½ teaspoon Worcestershire sauce
- 3 tablespoons ketchup

- 8 slices good rye or whole wheat bread, toasted
- 1 cup finely shredded iceberg lettuce (optional)
- 8 ¼-inch-thick slices cold meat loaf
- ½ cup shaved sweet onions (optional)
- 8 ⅛-inch-thick slices large ripe tomato (I use heirloom)

Kosher dill pickles, quartered lengthwise

1 **Dressing:** Whisk together all the ingredients in a small bowl until well combined.

2 Smear each slice of toast with some of the dressing, and cover 4 of the slices with the lettuce (if using). Place 2 slices of meat loaf on top and spread some more dressing on the meat loaf. Scatter on the onions (if using) and lay a slice of tomato on top of each sandwich. Assemble the sandwiches, cut in half, and serve with dill pickle spears.

Cook's Note
- For a variation, use the Russian Dressing to make a simple coleslaw: Combine 2 cups finely shredded cabbage with ¼ cup finely chopped sweet onion, 1 teaspoon sugar, 1 tablespoon fresh lemon juice, and ¼ cup of the dressing. Pile the coleslaw on the sandwiches in the place of the tomato, lettuce, and onion.

Leftovers
- Store extra Russian Dressing in a sealed container in the refrigerator for up to 1 week. It is great on roast beef sandwiches, too.

SPICY MIDDLE EASTERN BISON MEATBALLS WITH CILANTRO-YOGURT SAUCE

Fit for Company, Family Meal

Makes about 25 hors d'oeuvre–sized meatballs or serves 4 as a main course

Normally meatballs made with lean ground meat are a recipe for disaster. Not so here: The yogurt adds lightness and juiciness — but be sure to use whole-milk or at least 2% fat Greek yogurt.

For hors d'oeuvres, 1-inch-diameter meatballs are ideal; form 1½-inch-diameter meatballs for a main course. Instead of panfrying the meatballs, you can skewer and grill them. Or shape them into oval patties and fry or grill them — patties are great for stuffing pita bread.

Spicy Meatballs

- ½ cup fresh bread crumbs
- 1 tablespoon milk, or more if needed
- 1 teaspoon coriander seeds
- 1 teaspoon fennel seeds
- 1 teaspoon cumin seeds
- 3 tablespoons olive oil
- 1 cup chopped onions
- 2 tablespoons chopped garlic
- 2–3 tablespoons seeded chopped jalapeño chile (about 1 small jalapeño)
- 2 tablespoons plain Greek yogurt (whole-milk or 2%)
- 1¼ pounds ground bison (85%–95% lean), home-ground (see page 132) or store-bought
- 1 large egg, lightly beaten
- ¼ cup chopped fresh cilantro
- 1 teaspoon chopped fresh sage
- ¼ teaspoon ground allspice
- 1 teaspoon salt
- ½ teaspoon freshly ground black pepper

Cilantro-Yogurt Sauce

- ½ cup plain Greek yogurt (whole-milk or 2%)
- 1 teaspoon reserved toasted seed powder
- 1 teaspoon sugar
- 3 scallions, white and light green parts, chopped
- 2 tablespoons chopped fresh mint
- 1 teaspoon chopped fresh sage
- 1½ cups chopped fresh cilantro (about 1 bunch)
- 1 tablespoon fresh lemon juice
- 1 tablespoon olive oil
- Salt and freshly ground black pepper

1 **Meatballs:** Combine the bread crumbs and milk in a small bowl and stir until the bread is moist; add more milk if needed. Set aside.

2 Heat a medium skillet over medium heat. Sprinkle in the coriander, fennel, and cumin seeds and shake the pan until the seeds are lightly toasted and fragrant, 3 to 5 minutes. Remove from the heat and grind to a powder with a mortar and a pestle or a spice grinder. Reserve 1 teaspoon of the powder for the Cilantro-Yogurt Sauce.

3 Heat the same pan over medium heat and add 1 tablespoon of the oil. Add the onions and garlic, cover, and cook until the onions are soft but not colored, about 5 minutes, stirring from time to time. Transfer to a plate and refrigerate to cool for 10 minutes.

4 Dump the onions, soaked bread, and 2 teaspoons of the toasted seed powder into a food processor. Add the jalapeño and yogurt and pulse to form a puree. Scrape this mixture into a large bowl and add the bison, egg, cilantro, sage, allspice, salt, and pepper. Using clean hands, squeeze and toss the mixture until everything is well blended; do not overmix. (*You can cover and refrigerate the mixture for up to 6 hours.*)

5 When ready to cook, moisten your hands and roll the bison mixture into 1-inch balls for hors d'oeuvres or into 1½-inch balls for a main dish. Heat the remaining 2 tablespoons oil in a large nonstick skillet over medium heat. Working in 2 or 3 batches, cook the meatballs, turning occasionally, until lightly browned on all sides and cooked through, 7 to 10 minutes per batch. When each batch is done, transfer to a warm platter.

6 **Sauce:** Dump all the ingredients except the salt and pepper into a blender and blend to form a smooth mixture. Season to taste with salt and pepper. (*You can make the sauce up to a day ahead and refrigerate it.*)

7 To serve, drizzle the sauce over the meatballs, or serve the sauce separately. If serving as a main dish, give diners their own little bowls of sauce and let them go at it as they please.

Alternative Cuts: Ground lamb, goat, or grass-fed beef, or two or more ground meats combined.

Cook's Note

- If grilling the meatballs, use flat skewers so that the balls don't roll around when you turn them. Grill over medium heat for about 10 minutes, turning the skewers frequently, until the meatballs are nicely browned and firm to the touch.

Leftovers

- Gently warm leftover meatballs, covered, in a microwavable dish, then stuff them into warm pita bread. Garnish with Cilantro-Yogurt Sauce, thinly sliced tomatoes, diced cucumbers, and thinly sliced sweet onions.

ITALIAN WEDDING SOUP
(ITALIAN MEATBALL SOUP)

Fit for Company, Cheap Eats, Rewarms Well
Serves 4 to 6

Italian wedding soup, or *minestra maritata,* doesn't really have much to do with weddings at all. It's said to get its name from the "marriage" of the ingredients — meat, greens, and noodles or eggs. Recipes range from the simple, like the one Anne-marie Ramo provides here, to the complex, requiring days and many ingredients to prepare.

Although Anne-marie is of Italian descent, this recipe didn't come from that side of her family. She remembers making it first with her maternal grandfather, Virgil Olsen, when she was a little girl — swirling the stock when it was time to add the eggs and eating it in a big mug on a chilly day. Her grandpa didn't add meatballs, but the meatballs make this dish a little more substantial without being too fussy.

Meatballs

- ½ cup finely chopped onion
- ⅓ cup chopped fresh flat-leaf parsley
- 1 large egg, lightly beaten
- 1 teaspoon minced garlic
- 1 teaspoon salt
- ½ teaspoon freshly ground black pepper
- 1 cup fresh bread crumbs made from rustic white bread
- ½ cup freshly grated Parmigiano-Reggiano
- 6 ounces ground beef (85% lean), home-ground (see page 132) or store-bought
- 6 ounces ground pork or Italian sausages, removed from the casings
- ¼ pound ground veal or turkey

Soup

- 3 quarts homemade chicken stock or best-quality canned low-sodium chicken broth
- 1 pound escarole, spinach, chard, or curly endive, washed and coarsely chopped
- 2 large eggs
- 2 tablespoons freshly grated Parmigiano-Reggiano, plus more for garnish
- Salt and freshly ground black pepper
- Chopped fresh flat-leaf parsley

1 **Meatballs:** Combine all the ingredients in a large bowl, mixing quickly and gently. Do not overmix, or the meatballs will be rubbery. Roll the mixture into 1-inch balls. (You should have 22 to 24 meatballs.)

2 **Soup:** Bring the stock to a boil in a large pot over medium-high heat. Add the meatballs and escarole, reduce the heat to a simmer, and cook until the meatballs are cooked through and the escarole is tender, 5 to 8 minutes.

3   While the meatballs and escarole are cooking, whisk the eggs and cheese in a medium bowl to blend. Turn off the heat and, stirring the soup in one direction, drizzle in the egg mixture to form thin ribbons of egg. Season to taste with salt and pepper.

4   To serve, ladle the soup into bowls, dividing the meatballs evenly. Garnish each serving with more cheese and some parsley.

Alternative Cuts: Any combination of ground meat you like — all beef, all pork, or all turkey; beef and pork; beef and turkey; etc.; a nice blend is half beef and half homemade Italian sausage (page 410). Grass-fed beef or bison; or add a little lamb or goat to the mix.

Cook's Notes

- For a richer cheese flavor, add 2 to 4 ounces Parmigiano-Reggiano cheese rinds to the stock and simmer for 10 minutes before adding the meatballs to the soup. Remove and discard the rinds before serving.

- These are great all-purpose meatballs. Panfry or bake them and serve as is or in tomato sauce. Make them as little or as big as you like.

TURKISH PASTA WITH BISON SAUCE

Cheap Eats, Grass-Fed Beef

Serves 4

Turkish cooking styles have influenced the food of most of the eastern and southern Mediterranean—lands that were once part of the vast territories ruled by the Ottoman Turks and their empire. The Turks use a wide array of spices, including sweet aromatics such as cinnamon, allspice, and cloves. The spices marry well with lamb and goat, both of which are commonly used in Turkish cooking. They also go well with bison.

2 tablespoons olive oil

1½ cups finely chopped onions

1 cup finely chopped peeled carrots

½ cup finely chopped celery

1 tablespoon minced garlic

3 tablespoons Baharat (page 536, or see Cook's Note)

Salt and freshly ground black pepper

1 pound ground bison, home-ground (see page 132) or store-bought

½ cup pomegranate juice

1½ cups canned diced tomatoes (I use Muir Glen)

1 tablespoon fresh lemon juice, plus more to taste

1 tablespoon chopped fresh mint

1 cup chopped fresh cilantro

¾ pound wide dried pasta, such as pappardelle or narrow lasagna noodles

½ cup plain Greek yogurt (whole-milk or 2%)

1. Heat the oil in a large deep skillet or Dutch oven over medium heat. Add the onions, carrots, and celery and cook, covered, for 10 minutes, or until softened, stirring from time to time. Add the garlic and cook for 1 minute more. Add the baharat, 1 teaspoon salt, and 1 teaspoon pepper and stir until the vegetables are well coated and the spices are fragrant, about 45 seconds.

2. Turn up the heat to medium-high, add the bison, and cook, breaking up the meat with a fork, until no longer pink. Add the pomegranate juice and scrape any browned bits from the bottom of the pan.

3. Stir in the tomatoes and their juices, the lemon juice, mint, and ¾ cup of the cilantro. Bring to a simmer and cook, uncovered, for 20 minutes, adding a little water if the sauce becomes too thick or, if it's too watery, increase the heat and boil for a few minutes to concentrate slightly. Season to taste with salt, pepper, and lemon juice.

4. Meanwhile, cook the pasta in a large pot of boiling salted water until al dente. Drain.

5   Divide the noodles among four shallow serving bowls. Spoon over the bison sauce, garnish with dollops of yogurt, and sprinkle over the remaining ¼ cup cilantro.

Alternative Cuts: Ground lamb, ground goat, ground beef, or a combination of ground lamb or goat and ground bison or beef.

Cook's Note

- To substitute for Baharat, combine 2 tablespoons sweet Hungarian paprika, ¼ teaspoon ground cinnamon, 1 teaspoon ground coriander, ½ teaspoon ground cumin, ¼ teaspoon ground allspice, and 1 teaspoon dried mint.

VALETTE FAMILY STUFFED WHOLE CABBAGE

Cheap Eats, Family Meal, Fit for Company, Fit for a Crowd
Serves 8 to 10

My good friend and accomplished amateur cook Jean-Michel Valette speaks fondly of his childhood days in France, when he often visited his grandmother, who lived in Vouvray in the Loire Valley. The dish he loved best was her stuffed whole cabbage. When I pressed him for details, all he could remember is that she used a lot of butter. Through trial and error and the help of Julia Child's *Mastering the Art of French Cooking, Volume Two,* we came up with something close that makes Jean-Michel very happy. Julia's ingenious contribution is to use a mixing bowl to re-form the individual leaves into the shape of a whole head. Unmolded, this makes an impressive presentation, which is then cut into wedges and served. A much simpler method is simply to layer the leaves and stuffing in a deep casserole dish or Dutch oven. (You'll find instructions in the Cook's Notes.) Use crinkly-leafed savoy cabbage, which is much easier to separate into individual leaves than the ordinary tight-headed green cabbage. I always use the chicken livers, which give a creamy texture to the stuffing but add very little liver flavor. This is a long recipe, perfect to make on a cold weekend day. But check the Filling Options on page 149 for an easy stuffing using leftover braised meat from pot roasts or other braises.

Beef, Ham, and Sausage Stuffing

- 4 tablespoons (½ stick) butter
- 1½ cups finely chopped onions
- ½ cup finely chopped shallots
- 1 cup chopped leeks, white and pale green parts
- ½ cup finely chopped peeled carrots
- ½ cup finely chopped celery
- 1 tablespoon chopped fresh thyme
- 1 tablespoon minced garlic
  Salt and freshly ground black pepper
- 2 cups fresh bread crumbs
- ½ cup plain whole-milk Greek yogurt or sour cream

- 1 pound ground beef (80% lean), home-ground (see page 132) or store-bought
- ¼ pound ground veal or pork
- ½ pound mild ham, such as jambon de Paris, or smoked ham, cut into ⅜-inch dice
- ½ pound mild Italian fennel sausages, homemade (page 410) or store-bought, removed from the casings
- ½ pound chicken livers, finely chopped (optional)
- 8 large chard leaves, stems removed, blanched in boiling water until wilted, squeezed dry, and chopped
- 2 large eggs

1 large head savoy cabbage (at least 8 inches in diameter and about 2½ pounds)
  Butter
4 bay leaves
3–4 thick-cut bacon slices, cut in half crosswise
2–3 cups homemade beef stock (see page 168) or canned low-sodium chicken broth, plus more if needed

1 cup dry white wine (I use Vouvray)
1 cup canned crushed or pureed Italian plum tomatoes
1 teaspoon chopped fresh thyme
½ cup crème fraîche or sour cream (optional)

1 **Stuffing:** Melt the butter in a large skillet over medium heat. Add the onions, shallots, leeks, carrots, celery, thyme, and garlic and season to taste with salt and pepper. Cover and cook until the vegetables are soft and just beginning to color, stirring occasionally, about 15 minutes.

2 Meanwhile, combine the bread crumbs and yogurt in a large bowl.

3 When the vegetables are done, scrape them and any juices into the bowl. Add the beef, veal, ham, sausages, livers (if using), chard, eggs, 2 teaspoons salt, and 1 teaspoon pepper. Using a wooden spoon or, better still, your hands, mix the mixture until well blended. (You should have about 8 cups filling.) Fry up a small patty, taste, and adjust the seasonings. Set aside in the refrigerator while you prepare the cabbage.

4 Bring a large pot of lightly salted water to a boil. Cut an angled circle around the core of the cabbage and remove the core. Discard any outer leaves that are browned or damaged. Peel off the leaves one at a time until you get to the heart. Drop the heart into the boiling water, add several individual leaves to the pot, and blanch until the leaves are soft and pliable, 2 to 3 minutes. Remove the individual leaves and drain, then continue until all the leaves are blanched. Remove the heart, which should now be fully cooked. Finely chop the cabbage heart and mix it into the stuffing.

5 Preheat the oven to 350°F.

6 To assemble the stuffed cabbage, generously butter a 4-quart deep stainless steel bowl or rounded casserole (it should be 8 to 9 inches in diameter). Arrange the bay leaves in a four-leaf-clover pattern in the bottom of the bowl. Arrange the 3 or 4 largest cabbage leaves, overlapping, so that they line the bowl, with the core ends at the rim of the bowl. Spoon in enough stuffing to cover the lower third of the leaves. Lay more cabbage leaves over the stuffing, ensuring that the leaves totally cover the sides of the bowl, and then place more stuffing over the new layer of leaves. Continue the layering process until the stuffing is used up and/or you are within ½ inch of the rim of the bowl. Fold in any cabbage leaves overhanging the edges of the bowl, then cover the top of the stuffing with enough overlapping cabbage leaves to seal in the stuffing, tucking

the leaves down the sides of the bowl. Lay the strips of bacon on top of the cabbage in a pinwheel pattern.

7   Combine 2 cups of the stock and the white wine and pour enough of this mixture down the sides of the bowl to come to about an inch from the top of the cabbage, adding more stock if needed. (*At this point, you can cover and refrigerate the cabbage overnight. You will need to add 20 minutes to the baking time.*)

8   Heat the bowl over medium heat until the liquid begins to simmer. Remove from the heat, lay a circle of parchment paper over the cabbage, and seal the bowl with aluminum foil. Place the bowl in a baking pan in case any juices spill over. Bake for 2 to 2½ hours, making sure the liquid maintains a simmer; adjust the oven temperature if the heat is too low or too intense. Baste the top of the cabbage with the liquid from time to time and add more stock if needed so that the liquid remains at least halfway up the sides of the bowl. The cabbage is done when the internal temperature reaches 160°F.

9   To make the sauce, remove the foil and parchment from the cabbage. Handling the bowl with oven mitts or pot holders, pour all the braising liquid into a saucepan and set the cabbage aside to rest for 15 to 20 minutes. Degrease the surface of the liquid. You should have at least 2 cups. If not, add more stock. Stir in the tomatoes, bring to a simmer, and cook for 5 minutes. Remove from the heat, then add the thyme and crème fraîche (if using).

10   To unmold the cabbage, remove the bacon, chop it, and add to the sauce. Drain any additional liquid into the sauce. Place a large deep platter upside down over the bowl and flip the bowl over to unmold the cabbage. Pour any liquid from the platter into the sauce. Cut the cabbage into wedges with a sharp knife and serve with the sauce on the side.

Alternative Cuts: All ground pork, a pork and sausage mixture, or a veal and pork mixture.

Cook's Notes
- If the savoy cabbage leaves don't come off easily or you use a standard green cabbage, soften the leaves by blanching the whole head to start. Place the head in the boiling water, core side down, and simmer for 10 minutes. Spear the core with a large sturdy fork, remove the cabbage from the water, and cool under cold running water. Gently peel off as many leaves as you can, one at a time, without tearing them, or if need be, cut them away at the core end to free them. Repeat the process until you get down to the small inner leaves at the heart of the cabbage.

- For a less spectacular but equally tasty presentation, here's a much simpler method for layering the cabbage: Arrange 4 of the largest cabbage leaves on the bottom of a greased 6- to 8-quart Dutch oven or casserole. Spread the leaves with a third of the stuffing, then cover the stuffing with 4 or 5 more leaves and another third of the stuffing. Repeat one last time, then cover the top layer with 4 to 6 more leaves. Arrange the bacon on top and place the bay leaves over the bacon. Pour in the stock-wine mixture up to about an inch from the top. Cover the top with a round of parchment paper, cover with the lid or aluminum foil, and bake for 1 hour. Remove the lid or foil and the parchment and bake until the center reaches 160°F, 30 to 60 minutes more. Pour off the liquid and use to make the sauce as above. Let the casserole rest for 15 to 20 minutes, then cut into wedges and serve with the sauce.

Leftovers
- Cut the cabbage into serving-sized wedges, cover, and microwave for 3 to 5 minutes, or until hot. Gently rewarm the sauce on the stove top and serve with the cabbage.

Filling Options for Stuffed Cabbage

Here's a recipe for a stuffing made with leftover braised meat from pot roasts, short ribs, or stews: Use 3 to 4 cups diced braised meat. Add ½ cup leftover braising sauce, 1 cup freshly grated Parmigiano-Reggiano, and 4 chopped chard leaves. Add 2 cups bread crumbs and 2 large eggs and stir to combine. Fry up a small patty, taste, and adjust the seasonings. Assemble as described in step 6 of the recipe above, pouring in the stock and wine before baking. Leftovers from the following recipes are fantastic:

- Jeff's Daube (Provençal Beef Stew; page 190)
- Italian-Inspired Braised Oxtails with Fried Capers and Sage Leaves (page 215)
- Peposo alla Fornacina (Baker's Peppery Beef Shanks; page 218)
- Friuli-Style Braised Beef Cheeks (page 220)
- Pork Stew with Fennel and Butternut Squash (page 371)
- Wine and Vinegar–Braised Picnic Shoulder (page 378)
- Stinco (Braised and Roasted Pork Shanks) (page 385)
- Veal Breast Stuffed with Mushrooms, Chard, and Parmesan (page 580)
- Provençal-Style Braised Veal Breast Ragù (page 583)
- Jeff's Osso Buco with Artichokes (page 585)

JAMAICAN BEEF PATTIES
(SPICY BEEF TURNOVERS)

Cheap Eats, Freezes Well

Makes 12 turnovers

These turnovers are the Jamaican version of the somewhat bland Cornish pasty. Jamaicans spice up the dish and give it a nice golden hue by adding a little turmeric to the crust. Patties are served throughout the day as snacks, at lunch, and at dinner, paired with vegetables and other dishes to round out the meal. Some say that the patty is to the Jamaican culture what the hamburger is to America. There are many recipes, using all types of meat and all levels of spice. This one falls in the medium-hot range, but you can easily increase or decrease the heat level by adding more or less minced chile. Scotch bonnets can be hard to find, but habanero chiles are fine substitutes. You can also use the common jalapeño.

Pastry

- 2 cups all-purpose flour
- ½ teaspoon turmeric
- ¼ teaspoon salt
- ¼ cup lard (preferably homemade; see page 434)
- 4 tablespoons (½ stick) unsalted butter
- ⅓ cup cold water

Filling

- 2 tablespoons butter
- 1 onion, finely chopped
- ½ teaspoon stemmed, seeded, and minced Scotch bonnet or habanero chile or 1 tablespoon minced jalapeño chile, or more to taste

- ¼ cup finely chopped scallion whites
- ½ pound ground beef (85% lean), home-ground (see page 132) or store-bought
  Salt and freshly ground black pepper
- 1 teaspoon curry powder, homemade (page 526) or store-bought
- ½ teaspoon ground allspice
- 1 teaspoon chopped fresh thyme
- ¼ cup fresh bread crumbs
- ¼ cup homemade beef stock (see page 168) or canned low-sodium chicken broth
- ¼ cup finely chopped scallion greens

- 1 large egg, beaten with 2 tablespoons water for egg wash

1 **Pastry:** Combine the flour, turmeric, and salt in a large bowl. Cut in the lard and butter until crumbly. Add the cold water and stir to make a stiff dough. Lightly flour your work surface and roll out the dough to ⅛ inch thick. Try not to roll the dough too thin, or it will be too delicate to hold the filling. Cut the dough into twelve 6-inch circles (use a plate or pan lid as a guide). Cover with wax paper or a damp cloth until

ready to use. (*You can place the pastry circles in a single layer on a baking sheet, wrap in plastic wrap, and refrigerate for up to 1 day.*)

2   **Filling:** Melt the butter in a large heavy skillet over medium heat. Sauté the onion and chile until soft, about 5 minutes. Add the scallion whites and cook for 1 minute more. Add the ground beef, 1 teaspoon salt, 1 teaspoon pepper, the curry powder, allspice, and thyme and mix well. Cook, stirring occasionally, until the meat is no longer pink. Stir in the bread crumbs and stock, cover, and simmer until the liquid has almost evaporated, 10 to 15 minutes. The filling should be moist but not soupy. Stir in the scallion greens. Season to taste with salt, pepper, and more hot chile, if desired. Remove from the heat and cool. (*You can make the filling a day in advance, cover, and refrigerate.*)

3   Preheat the oven to 400°F. Lightly grease a baking sheet.

4   Place 2 to 3 tablespoons of the filling on one half of each pastry circle. Moisten the edges of the dough with water and fold the dough over the meat filling, creating a half-moon shape. Crimp the edges closed with a fork.

5   Transfer the pastries to the baking sheet. Lightly brush with the egg wash. Bake for 30 to 40 minutes, or until the pastries are golden brown. Serve warm or at room temperature.

Alternative Cuts: Ground pork, goat, or lamb; grass-fed beef or bison, but add 2 more tablespoons of butter to the filling. Or combine two or more ground meats: Beef and goat are especially tasty.

Cook's Notes

- Scotch bonnet and habanero chiles are hot enough to cause skin irritation. Wear vinyl or latex gloves when you stem, seed, and chop the chiles.

- You can make the patties in advance and freeze them. Place the unbaked patties on a baking sheet. Freeze until firm, then transfer to a zipper-lock bag. When ready to serve, bake the still-frozen patties, adding about 15 minutes to the cooking time.

- These are great for lunch or a light dinner with a salad, coleslaw, or light soup.

- To make appetizer-sized patties, cut the dough into 4-inch rounds and use about 1 tablespoon filling for each. (Makes about 24 turnovers.)

Ground Beef and Bison Sandwiches

Tips for Making Burgers

The Meat. When I grind my own meat, or when I buy it from a butcher who grinds meat to order, I know what I'm getting and I feel comfortable eating that burger medium-rare without worrying about bacterial contamination.

- For great beefy flavor, my favorite cut for hamburgers is boneless short rib. Boneless chuck, with a little of the outer fat attached, is also good.
- If you're using lean grass-fed beef or bison (which is often 95 percent lean), add ¼ pound bacon or trimmed fat, finely chopped, to every pound of ground meat.
- If you buy preground meat, choose 80 percent lean and 20 percent fat.

Seasoning. Season ground meat before you shape the patties so the seasoning works its way all through the meat.

- Use 1 teaspoon kosher salt and ½ teaspoon freshly ground black pepper (plus any additional seasonings) for each pound of meat.
- Use a fork to toss the meat and seasonings together until well blended. Don't overmix the meat, or the burgers will be tough.

Forming the Patties

- Use about ⅓ pound meat per patty.
- Shape the meat gently into patties about ¾ inch thick. Don't pack the meat tightly; it will make the burgers dense and rubbery.
- To keep the patties from swelling up when you cook them, use your thumb to make an indentation about ¼ inch deep in the center of each one.

COOKING BURGERS SAFELY

With a solid piece of meat, only the exterior is exposed to the environment. That's not the case with ground meat. Every particle of it is exposed to whatever nasty bugs lurk about. And the burger meat that's sold in many stores has been ground in huge facilities where there may be the risk of bacterial contamination.

The USDA recommends cooking store-bought ground meat to 160°F. This is prudent thinking, and you should follow this recommendation — particularly if you are pregnant or immunologically weakened.

However, some of us like our burgers pink, or even medium-rare. The solution here is to buy a solid piece of meat and grind it at home (see page 132).

In every case, follow these rules:

- Keep ground meat chilled at all times.
- Wash your hands well with soap and hot water before and after handling ground meat.
- Clean all surfaces that come into contact with ground meat.

SMOKY BISON CHEESEBURGER

Family Meal, Grass-Fed Beef

Serves 4

Lean ground bison meat has a slightly sweet, beefy flavor that is ideal for a smoky-tasting burger. If you can't find bison, substitute 85% or 90% lean ground beef. Because ground bison is so lean, I add moisture and texture by mixing wild rice and smoky cheese with the meat. Use any leftover dressing on salad, cold meat loaf sandwiches, or other meat sandwiches.

Burgers

- 1 pound ground bison (90% lean), home-ground (see page 132) or store-bought
- ½ cup cooked wild rice
- 1 teaspoon minced garlic
- 1 tablespoon sweet Hungarian paprika or Spanish paprika (*pimentón de la Vera*; see Sources)
- 1 cup grated smoked cheese, such as cheddar, Gouda, or mozzarella
- ½ teaspoon salt
- ¾ teaspoon freshly ground black pepper
- 1 tablespoon smoky barbecue sauce (I use KC Masterpiece or Bull's-Eye, or see Anne-marie's Easy Barbecue Sauce, page 135)
- 2 teaspoons Dijon mustard

Thousand Island Barbecue Dressing

- 1 cup mayonnaise
- ¼ cup chili sauce (I use Heinz)
- 2 tablespoons smoky barbecue sauce (see above)
- 1 tablespoon sweet pickle relish
- 1 teaspoon Worcestershire sauce

- 4 whole-grain hamburger buns, toasted
  Tomato slices
  Thinly sliced sweet onions
  Romaine or iceberg lettuce leaves
  Dill pickle slices

1 Set up a charcoal or gas grill for medium-high heat (see page 11 for more on grilling).

2 **Burgers:** Using a fork, lightly toss the bison and rice with the remaining burger ingredients in a medium bowl until well mixed; don't overmix. Form the bison mixture into 4 patties, ¾ to 1 inch thick. Press your thumb into the center of each patty to create a depression.

3 **Dressing:** Combine all the ingredients in a small bowl and mix well. Set aside. (*The dressing can be made ahead and stored, covered, in the refrigerator for up to 3 weeks.*)

4.   Lightly oil the grill rack. Grill the burgers for 3 to 4 minutes per side, or until medium-rare to medium; do not cook longer, or they will dry out.

5.   To serve, generously slather barbecue dressing on each half of the toasted buns. Place a burger on each bottom half and top with a tomato slice, some onion slices, lettuce, and pickles. Assemble the burgers, cut in half, and serve immediately.

Alternative Cuts: Grass-fed ground beef, 90% lean ground beef, or ground goat.

Cook's Note

- If you can find only 95% lean ground bison, you can increase the fat percentage and the smoky flavor by adding 3 to 4 ounces bacon, finely chopped, per pound of meat. If you want to cook the burgers beyond medium, it's best to add the bacon to prevent the meat from drying out.

WHAT'S THE DIFFERENCE BETWEEN "HAMBURGER" AND "GROUND BEEF"?

According to the USDA, no water, phosphates, extenders, or binders can be added to either "ground beef" or "hamburger." Both can contain seasonings, and both can contain up to 30 percent fat.

The difference is in the kind of fat. Hamburger can contain subcutaneous fat and various trimmings that have been exposed to the environment of the packinghouse and are thus very susceptible to contamination. And it may have been treated with ammonia hydroxide gas to destroy pathogens. The mixture is called "pink slime" by critics. Hamburger is usually cheaper than ground beef, but I wouldn't buy it.

CALABRESE BURGERS

In a Hurry, Fit for Company

Serves 4

The cooking of Calabria in southern Italy can be quite spicy, relying on both fresh and dried chiles for flavor and heat. The amount of red pepper flakes in this recipe produces burgers of only moderate heat. If you like more chile flavor and heat in your food, increase the pepper flakes in ½-teaspoon increments, using up to 2 teaspoons. For the accompanying mayonnaise, you can add Tabasco or other hot pepper sauce to suit your taste. If you like your burgers cooked beyond medium be sure to purchase fattier meat (80% lean).

Burgers

- 1½ pounds ground beef (80% to 85% lean), home-ground (see page 132) or store-bought
- ½ cup finely chopped red or sweet onion
- 2 tablespoons finely chopped capers
- 2 tablespoons extra-virgin olive oil
- 1 tablespoon finely grated lemon zest
- 2 teaspoons chopped fresh oregano
- 1 tablespoon tomato paste
- 1 teaspoon salt
- 1 teaspoon freshly ground black pepper
- ½ teaspoon crushed red pepper flakes, or more to taste

Sun-Dried Tomato Mayonnaise

- 4 oil-packed sun-dried tomatoes, drained
- 2 teaspoons drained capers
- ½ cup mayonnaise
- 2 teaspoons fresh lemon juice
- 1 teaspoon chopped fresh oregano
  A few drops of Tabasco or other hot sauce (optional)

Olive-Tomato Garnish

- 3 ripe tomatoes, diced
- 2 tablespoons chopped pitted Italian green olives
- 1 tablespoon finely chopped sweet onion
  Pinch of salt

- 4 ¼-inch-thick slices mozzarella or Monterey Jack cheese
- 4 ciabatta rolls or large French or Italian rolls, split and toasted

1 Set up a charcoal or gas grill for medium-high heat (see page 11 for more on grilling).

2 **Burgers:** Using a fork, lightly toss the meat with the remaining ingredients in a medium bowl until well mixed; don't overmix. Shape the beef mixture into 4 oval patties, ¾ to 1 inch thick.

3   **Mayonnaise:** With the motor running, drop the tomatoes and capers through the feed tube of a food processor and process until chopped. Scrape down the sides of the bowl. Add the remaining ingredients and pulse several times to blend. Set aside.

4   **Garnish:** Stir together all the ingredients in a medium bowl. Set aside.

5   Lightly oil the grill rack. Grill the burgers for 3 to 4 minutes per side, or until just firm to the touch. Top with the mozzarella, cover the grill, and cook for 1 to 2 minutes more, or until the cheese is melted. This will yield medium-rare to medium burgers.

6   Slather both sides of the rolls with the mayonnaise and place a burger on the bottom half of each one. Top with the Olive-Tomato Garnish, close the sandwiches, cut in half, and serve immediately.

Alternative Cuts: Grass-fed beef, ground bison, or ground goat or lamb, or a combination.

Cook's Note
- You can also use these burgers for Italian Burger Subs (page 158).

ITALIAN BURGER SUBS

In a Hurry, Fit for Company

Serves 4

These burgers were inspired by the submarine, or hero, sandwiches served up in Italian delis, with a beef patty replacing the traditional cold cuts. There's no need to serve the sandwich piping hot: mildly warm is my favorite, or you can let it cool to room temperature. For a large gathering (think Super Bowl party), make a giant sub using an entire loaf of French or Italian bread (1½ to 2 feet long is perfect). Then cut the loaf into sections, figuring 4 to 6 servings per loaf. Don't bother to toast the whole loaf, but be sure to buy really fresh bread baked the same day.

Burgers

¼ pound pancetta, diced

1¼ pounds ground beef (80%–85% lean), home-ground (see page 132) or store-bought

½ cup freshly grated Parmigiano-Reggiano

1 teaspoon minced garlic

½ teaspoon salt

1 teaspoon freshly ground black pepper

2 teaspoons ground fennel seeds

1 tablespoon olive oil

4 ⅛-inch-thick slices fontina or provolone cheese, large enough to cover the burger patties

4 6-inch Italian or sourdough rolls, split

¼ cup olive oil

2 tablespoons red wine vinegar

1 teaspoon dried basil or 2 teaspoons chopped fresh

Strips of bottled fire-roasted red bell peppers or other sweet peppers

Shredded lettuce

Peperoncini, stems removed (optional)

Thinly sliced sweet onion (optional)

1 Set up a charcoal or gas grill for medium-high heat (see page 11 for more on grilling).

2 **Burgers:** Pulse the pancetta in a food processor until finely ground; don't puree. Using a fork, lightly toss the pancetta with the remaining ingredients in a medium bowl until well mixed; don't overmix. Form the meat mixture into 4 oval patties, ¾ inch thick.

3 Lightly oil the grill rack. Grill the burgers for 3 to 4 minutes. Flip and grill for 2 to 3 minutes more for medium-rare to medium, 125°F to 135°F. Place a slice of cheese on top of each burger, cover the grill, and cook for 2 minutes more, or until the cheese is melted.

4 While the burgers are grilling, toast the rolls. Whisk together the oil, vinegar, and basil and brush the dressing on the cut surfaces of the rolls.

5   Place the burgers on the bottom halves of the rolls and cover with the fire-roasted peppers and lettuce. Place some peperoncini and onions (if using) over the lettuce and close the sandwiches. Cut in half and serve immediately.

Alternative Cuts: Ground pork or a mixture of one half beef, one quarter pork, and one quarter veal.

Cook's Note
- If serving the burgers at room temperature, cook to a final temperature of 130°F to 140°F for medium-rare to medium and just layer the cheese over the meat instead of melting it.

Beef and Bison Pot Roasts and Braising Steaks

Pot roasts and braising steaks are cooked with moist heat. Most braising steak cuts are simply thinner versions of the pot roast cut. That means that recipes for braising steaks and pot roasts are interchangeable. You'll just need to decrease the cooking time when using a braising steak in a pot roast recipe — and vice versa.

The best candidates for this moist-heat cooking method are cuts that have ample fat and/or plenty of connective tissue. As the meat cooks, its connective tissue turns to gelatin, becoming soft and resulting in tender and juicy meat. Cuts with these attributes come from the chuck, brisket, and shank.

In my opinion, the best pot roasts and braising steaks come from the chuck, which includes the entire shoulder and upper arm area. The chuck is divided into three large sections: the arm; the upper shoulder, called the blade (which includes the blade bone and some of the upper rib); and the neck. Labels for some chuck cuts will include the portion of the chuck from which they came: for example, the chuck arm pot roast or chuck neck pot roast. All roasts cut from the chuck make good pot roasts and can be used more or less interchangeably.

Many so-called meat experts swear by the bottom round (often mislabeled rump roast) as a great cut for pot-roasting, but I have had success only when I find bottom round roasts that display adequate marbling. In general, if you can purchase the piece of bottom round next to the rump of the steer and it's marbled, it will make a fine pot roast (see Rump Roast Braised in Ale, page 177).

Cooking Lean Grass-Fed Beef and Bison with Moist Heat

Making a pot roast is a great way to introduce yourself to the pleasures of bison and lean grass-fed beef. When many folks start cooking these leaner meats, they fire up the grill for a hamburger or a steak, and then if the steak is tough, they give up. No such worries with pot roast.

Start with brisket or cuts from the chuck. Even though these cuts will have less marbling than similar cuts of commodity beef, they have the all-important connective tissue that — when cooked long and slow in a moist environment — becomes soft and silky and produces a delicious, tender pot roast with little fat. An added plus is that the stronger beefy flavors of grass-fed beef and bison become more subtle and harmonious as they mingle with the braising liquid. To me, these pot roasts are usually superior to those made with commodity beef. A great recipe to start with is Pot-Roasted Grass-Fed Beef Chuck with Winter Root Vegetables (page 174).

Braising is the ideal method for some tougher steaks from grass-fed beef and bison too. Although the meat may lack the marbling found in Choice-grade commodity beef, the tougher cuts from the upper shoulder and neck are richer in collagen than supermarket beef. When the meat is cooked long and slow, this collagen turns into soft gelatin, which adds moist mouthfeel and a succulent texture to the roast.

Pot Roasts and Braising Steaks at a Glance

From the Round (the hind leg)

Rump roast, boneless (wedge cut, Western market roast, melon roast, diamond cut roast, round tip roast). This roast comes from the hip area and contains muscles from both the top and bottom rounds. Better marbled and with better flavor than rump that is labeled "bottom round rump roast."

Bottom round rump roast, boneless (round tip roast, back of rump roast). Should come from the tip of the bottom round closest to the hip area, where the true rump roast is, an extension of the rump into the bottom round. Unfortunately, many meat departments cut up the entire bottom round and label the pieces "bottom round rump roast." Has more marbling than the rear areas of the bottom round and can yield a reasonably juicy pot roast.

Bottom round roast/steak, boneless (bottom round rump roast, outside roast, bottom round pot roast, Yankee roast, round roast, bottom round oven roast). Can be very lean and often makes for a stringy, dry, and inferior pot roast. Look for meat with adequate marbling, or don't buy it.

Eye-round roast, boneless (round-eye pot roast, eye-of-round roast). A very lean and somewhat tough cut. Will produce a very dry pot roast unless there is some marbling. Some say it can be dry-roasted, but I don't agree.

Heel-of-the-round roast/steak, boneless (Pike's Peak roast, diamond cut roast, Denver pot roast, horseshoe roast, heel pot roast). Tough, but can yield an okay pot roast because the ample collagen will turn soft.

Tip roast/steak, boneless (face round roast, tip sirloin roast, sirloin tip roast, crescent roast, knuckle roast). Very lean, but can make a reasonable pot roast or braised steak. Look for better-marbled examples.

Round steak, bone in or boneless. Cross section of the round, containing parts of the bottom and top round and eye of round. May include a bit of round bone. Look for better-marbled examples, because cuts lacking marbling will become dry and stringy.

From the Brisket (the chest, under the neck) and Foreshank

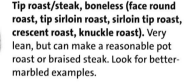

Whole brisket, boneless (fresh beef brisket, whole brisket, brisket). One of my favorite pot roasts, because it includes both the fattier "point" section and the leaner "flat" cut (see below). Yields succulent pot roast that is easy to slice and rewarms well. Can also be used for stews.

Brisket, point cut, boneless (brisket front cut, brisket thick cut, brisket nose cut). This fatty cut, called point because this part of the roast has a pointed end, is cheaper than the leaner flat cut and ideal for folks who like a fattier but more flavorful pot roast.

Brisket, flat cut, boneless (brisket, first cut, thin cut). Though a leaner cut than the point, the flat has ample fat to yield moist pot roast and is easier to slice.

From the Chuck
(the shoulder, arm, and neck)

Arm pot roast/steak, bone in (arm chuck arm roast, chuck round-bone pot roast, round-bone roast). Juicy, with good beef flavor.

Cross-rib roast, boneless (rolled cross-rib roast, Boston-cut roast, English-cut roast, English roll, Diamond Jim roast). Not too fatty and easy to slice. Has the great flavor of short ribs with fewer fat pockets. Look for netted or tied roasts, which will stay together better. When cut into thick steaks, can be used for braised steak.

Shoulder roast/steak, bone in (English steak, shoulder steak, honey cut). Cut from the arm section of the chuck, often referred to as the clod. The steaks are sometimes called clod steaks, and the roasts shoulder clod roasts.

Chuck pot roast, boneless (chuck roast). May come from any area of the chuck, which may or may not be specified. Good flavor and makes a tender and juicy pot roast. One of my favorite pot roast cuts.

7-bone chuck roast/steak, bone in (center-cut pot roast, chuck roast, center-cut roast, 7-bone roast). Cut from the blade area; made up of several muscle groups, including the flat-iron and mock tender, under blade, and rib eye. I like this pot roast because all sections offer great flavor and texture. The bones result in a rich sauce.

Chuck blade roast/steak, boneless (chuck roast blade cut, chuck roast first cut). Cut from the same area as the 7-bone pot roast, but with the rib and blade bones, top blade, and mock tender removed.

Top blade roast, boneless (flat-iron roast, lifter roast). Great flavor with uniform texture; easy to slice. A center line of connective tissue holds it together and turns soft when cooked until tender.

Mock tender roast, boneless (medallion pot roast, Scotch tender, Jewish tender). Misnamed, because this cut is not tender, but it makes an okay pot roast. Make sure there is some marbling, because it can dry out otherwise.

Chuck-eye roast, boneless (inside chuck roll, chuck fillet pot roast). While the 4- to 6-inch section closest to the rib primal is tender enough to dry-roast, the chuck eye also makes a great pot roast. Buy a netted or tied roast so that it won't fall apart during cooking.

CURRY AND GUINNESS-BRAISED CHUCK STEAK

Family Meal, Rewarms Well, Great Leftovers

Serves 4, with leftovers

This recipe might have been invented by a homesick Irish soldier stationed in India during the British Raj. Having his daily ration of Guinness on hand, plenty of curry spice, and a precious bit of tough beef, he may have asked the battalion cook to throw together a steak with those ingredients. Truth is, I made up this dish, and although I'm not Irish and did not serve in India, the result is a slow-simmered piece of beef with some really great gravy, the curry spices and Guinness blending into a delicious sauce. I like to serve the dish with steamed basmati rice or bulgur wheat and Fresh Plum Sambal (page 263), or if time does not allow, an assortment of bottled chutneys and Indian pickles. Oh, a mug of Guinness is mandatory.

Salt and freshly ground black pepper

4 teaspoons Bruce's Curry Powder (page 526)

1 1½- to 2-inch-thick boneless chuck steak (2 pounds) or a 7-bone chuck steak (3 pounds)

2 teaspoons olive oil

4 cups finely chopped onions

½ cup ¼-inch-diced peeled carrots

½ cup ¼-inch-diced celery

1 teaspoon dark brown sugar, or more to taste

1 cup homemade beef stock (see page 168) or canned low-sodium chicken broth

2 bay leaves

1 12-ounce bottle Guinness or other stout

1 tablespoon malt vinegar or cider vinegar, or more to taste

2 teaspoons minced garlic

1 pound cremini mushrooms, sliced

½ cup sour cream (optional)

1 Combine 1 teaspoon salt, ½ teaspoon pepper, and 1 teaspoon of the curry powder in a small bowl. Season the meat generously all over with the mixture.

2 Heat the oil in a heavy lidded skillet, sauté pan, or Dutch oven over medium-high heat. Add the steak and sear until nicely browned, about 5 minutes. Turn and sear the other side for 5 minutes more. Set aside.

3 Pour off all but about 2 tablespoons fat from the pan and reduce the heat to medium. Add the onions, carrots, and celery, cover, and cook for 10 minutes, or until the vegetables are soft and the onions are beginning to color, stirring occasionally. Stir in the remaining 1 tablespoon curry powder and cook for 1 minute more.

4   Add the brown sugar and stock, stirring and scraping any browned bits from the bottom of the pan. Add the bay leaves, stout, vinegar, and steak. Bring to a boil, reduce to a simmer, cover, and cook for 1½ hours, turning every ½ hour. The steak is done when it is fork-tender. Stir in the garlic and mushrooms, cover, and cook for 5 minutes more.

5   Remove the steak to a warm platter. Discard the bay leaves. Degrease the sauce, then cook over high heat until it begins to thicken and becomes syrupy. Season to taste with salt, pepper, brown sugar, and/or vinegar; the sauce should be mildly sweet and sour. Remove from the heat and whisk in the sour cream (if using).

6   Cut the steak into slices or chunks, pour the sauce over the steak, and serve.

Alternative Cuts: Any variety of chuck steak, such as shoulder clod, flat-iron, or chuck arm steak. Also good with rump, top round steak (London broil), sirloin tip, or bottom round steak, if there is enough marbling.

Cook's Note
- To turn this into a pot roast that will feed 6 to 8, buy a 4- to 5-pound chuck pot roast. It will take about ½ hour longer. You don't need to double the recipe, but do increase the stock to 1 cup, the mushrooms to 2 pounds, and the sour cream (if using) to 2 cups.

BRAISED BEEF STEAK WITH TEQUILA, TOMATO, AND ORANGE

Family Meal, Rewarms Well, Great Leftovers

Serves 4, with leftovers

This decidedly Mexican-influenced braised steak has a subtle tropical flavor from the tequila and fresh orange and lime juices. You can make it even more tropical by replacing the orange juice with pineapple juice. The recipe makes a superb pot roast: Simply double the size of the chunk of meat and the amount of seasonings in the rub.

The recipe uses the oven for braising, but it can also be done on the stove top at a low simmer. It's also ideal for slow cookers.

Once the meat is cooked, serve it with lots of warm tortillas and Mexican rice. Any leftovers can be shredded to make a great filling for burritos or enchiladas.

New Mexico Chile Spice Rub

- 1 teaspoon ground cumin
- 1 teaspoon ground coriander
- 2 teaspoons New Mexico or California chile powder
- ⅛ teaspoon ground cinnamon
- 1 teaspoon salt
- 1 teaspoon freshly ground black pepper

- 1 1-inch-thick boneless chuck steak (1½ pounds), 7-bone chuck steak (about 2 pounds), or round-bone steak (1½–2 pounds)
- 2 tablespoons olive oil
- 2 cups thinly sliced onions
- 2 tablespoons minced garlic
- 1 cup tequila

- 1 14.5-ounce can diced tomatoes (I use Muir Glen), drained
- 3 chipotle chiles in adobo (I use Herdez brand), chopped
- ½ cup fresh orange juice
- ¼ cup fresh lime juice, plus more to taste
- 1 cup homemade beef stock (see page 168) or canned low-sodium chicken broth
- 2 bay leaves
- Salt and freshly ground black pepper

Garnish

- Orange slices
- Chopped fresh cilantro
- Finely chopped red onions
- Pico de Gallo (page 259)

1 **Rub:** Combine all the ingredients in a small bowl. Sprinkle all over the meat; reserve any leftover rub to add to the braising liquid.

2 Preheat the oven to 325°F.

3 Heat the oil in a large Dutch oven over medium-high heat. Sear the meat until all sides are nicely browned, about 5 minutes per side. Transfer the meat to a platter. Pour off

all but 2 tablespoons fat from the pot and add the onions. Cover and cook until the onions are soft and just beginning to color, about 10 minutes, stirring from time to time. Stir in the garlic and cook for 1 minute more.

4   Pour in the tequila and stir, scraping up any browned bits from the bottom of the pot. Bring to a boil and reduce the tequila by about half, about 5 minutes. Add the tomatoes, chipotle chiles, orange juice, lime juice, stock, bay leaves, and any leftover spice rub and bring to a boil. Add the steak, reduce the heat to a simmer, cover, and transfer to the oven. Braise until the meat is fork-tender, 1½ to 2 hours, turning every 45 minutes.

5   Transfer the pot to the stove top. Remove the meat and discard the bay leaf. Degrease the liquid, then boil until it just becomes syrupy, about 10 minutes. Season to taste with salt, pepper, and lime juice.

6   Return the meat to the pot and cook for 2 to 3 minutes more to reheat. Slice or cut into chunks and serve with the garnishes.

Alternative Cuts: Any chuck steak cut, rump steak, sirloin tip steak, top round steak (London broil), or well-marbled bottom round steak.

Cook's Notes
- If you replace the orange juice with fresh pineapple juice, instead of garnishing with orange slices, garnish with half-slices of fresh pineapple.
- This dish is great made a day ahead, but wait to adjust the lime juice until just before serving. Let cool and refrigerate overnight, then remove any congealed surface fat before gently rewarming the dish.

BASIC MEAT STOCK

Makes about 6 cups

You can use this recipe to make beef, veal, bison, pork, or lamb stock. Simply use any meaty bones available to you, making sure they're in 3- to 4-inch pieces. "Meaty" means there is meat attached to the bones; don't use naked bones.

4 pounds beef, veal, bison, pork, or lamb shanks, necks, and/or other meaty bones, cut into 3- to 4-inch pieces

Salt and freshly ground black pepper

1 cup water

1 large onion, not peeled, quartered

2 celery stalks, cut into 2-inch pieces

2 large carrots, peeled and cut into 2-inch pieces

1 bay leaf

2 fresh thyme sprigs

1 Preheat the oven to 475°F.

2 Put the bones in a large roasting pan and sprinkle lightly with salt and pepper. Roast until golden brown, about 45 minutes, turning the bones once or twice so that they brown evenly.

3 Transfer the bones to a large pot and cover with water by about 2 inches. Remove and discard the fat from the roasting pan. Add the 1 cup water to the roasting pan and bring to a boil over medium heat, scraping up the browned bits from the bottom of the pan. Pour this deglazing liquid into the pot and bring to a boil, then reduce the heat to a simmer. Skim and discard the fat and scum accumulated on the surface. Add the onion, celery, carrots, bay leaf, and thyme and simmer, uncovered, skimming often, for 2 hours, adding water as necessary to keep the bones covered.

4 Strain the stock through a fine-mesh sieve into a storage container; discard the solids. Set aside to cool completely. (*The stock can be covered and refrigerated for up to 5 days or frozen for up to 3 months. Freeze it in smaller containers so you always have some at the ready.*)

SPANISH-STYLE BRAISED BISON OR GRASS-FED BEEF BRISKET

Family Meal, Rewarms Well, Great Leftovers, Grass-Fed Beef

Serves 6 to 8

Bison is a little tougher than beef brisket, but when slowly braised, either one becomes tender and flavorful, suitable for any holiday table and a special treat for Hanukkah. This dish is best when made a day ahead; see Cook's Note.

2 tablespoons Spanish paprika (*pimentón de la Vera*; see Sources)

2 teaspoons salt

2 teaspoons freshly ground black pepper

1 6- to 8-pound bison or grass-fed beef brisket with the deckle (fatty edge) left on

2 tablespoons extra-virgin olive oil

3 large onions, thinly sliced (about 6 cups)

2 tablespoons chopped garlic

2 cups dry Spanish sherry

2 cups homemade beef stock (see page 168) or canned low-sodium chicken broth

1 14.5-ounce can diced tomatoes (I use Muir Glen)

2 bay leaves
  Pinch of saffron threads

2 teaspoons fresh thyme leaves

2 tablespoons sherry vinegar, or more to taste

½ cup pitted Spanish green olives
  Salt and freshly ground black pepper

1 Preheat the oven to 325°F.

2 Combine the paprika, salt, and pepper in a small bowl and sprinkle it all over the meat.

3 Heat the oil in a large Dutch oven over medium-high heat. Brown the brisket on both sides, 3 to 4 minutes per side. Remove the meat and pour off all but 1 tablespoon of fat from the pot. Reduce the heat to medium, add the onions and garlic, and cook until the onions are soft, about 10 minutes. Add the sherry, stock, tomatoes, bay leaves, saffron, thyme, and vinegar and bring to a boil, scraping up any browned bits from the bottom of the pot.

4 Return the brisket to the pot and spoon some of the onions and tomatoes over the top. Cover the pot, transfer the brisket to the oven, and bake for 1½ hours.

5 Turn over the brisket and add the olives. Cover and cook for 1½ to 2 hours more, or until fork-tender: Bison will take 3½ to 4 hours; beef, 3 to 3½ hours.

6   Remove the meat to a platter and cover loosely with aluminum foil to keep warm. Discard the bay leaves. If the sauce is too thin, bring to a boil to concentrate the flavors. Degrease the sauce and season to taste with salt, pepper, and vinegar, if necessary.

7   To serve, cut the meat into ⅜-inch-thick slices, arrange on plates, and nap with the sauce.

Alternative Cuts: Conventional beef brisket. Bison or grass-fed chuck pot roast: cook bison for 2½ to 3 hours, beef for 2 hours. Bison hump, which may take 6 hours to cook.

Cook's Note
- This is best made a day ahead so that the sauce thickens and the meat absorbs its flavors. Let cool, then place the brisket and the sauce in separate containers and refrigerate, tightly covered. Before serving, remove any congealed fat. Slice the meat and reheat gently in the sauce on the stove or in the microwave.

MY FAVORITE POT ROAST CUTS

My favorite cut is a **7-bone chuck roast**, because it's composed of several flavorful muscles, including the tender flat-iron and rib eye, as well as full-flavored tougher muscles such as the under blade. The cut includes the area of the shoulder-blade bone whose ridges give it a shape like a number seven.

The boneless chuck **cross-rib roast** comes rolled and tied, and it has the same great flavor as short ribs. When it's adequately marbled, it produces a juicy and succulent pot roast. Its even shape makes it easy to slice and present in nice round slices. Sometimes it's sold simply as chuck shoulder pot roast.

It's pretty hard to beat a **brisket**, which is always sold boneless, for pot roast. I like a whole brisket with the fattier point cut attached; it makes for a more succulent result. However, most stores sell brisket with the point cut removed and call it the flat cut, or first-cut brisket. Since this is a leaner cut, don't overcook it or it will become stringy.

The **top blade roast** is quite tender except for a line of gristle in the center, but it has enough marbling to withstand long, slow cooking, and braising will tenderize the gristle. Its uniform shape means you'll have good-looking slices when you serve it. It's a flavorful but somewhat pricey cut for a pot roast.

If you can find a true **bottom round rump roast** — one that is actually cut from the lower hip area — and it has some marbling, it will make an excellent pot roast.

MUSTARD AND BOURBON–GLAZED POT ROAST

Cheap Eats, Rewarms Well, Great Leftovers

Serves 6, with leftovers

When fresh and aromatic, paprika adds a sweet and pungent flavor to sauces. Too often, however, it's not fresh, lacks aroma, and is but a shadow of its potential. To judge how fresh your paprika is, smell it: It should have a fruity and pungent sweet chile aroma. Instead of less-than-fresh paprika, I turn to my local spice blender for California chile powder, ground fresh from a mild variety of whole dried red chiles.

For the best flavor, season the roast ahead and refrigerate overnight before cooking. Glazing the roast with mustard adds a crusty layer of flavor and an appetizing appearance, but you can leave this final step out.

You can also use a 7-bone roast, which tends to separate during cooking but is fine served as chunks.

Mustard-Spice Rub

- 2 teaspoons chopped fresh thyme
- 2 teaspoons chopped fresh rosemary
- 1 teaspoon dry mustard powder (I use Colman's)
- 2 teaspoons paprika or California chile powder
- 2 teaspoons freshly ground black pepper
- 2 teaspoons salt

- 1 4-pound boneless chuck-eye roast, tied, or 4-pound flat-cut brisket
- ½ cup homemade beef stock (see page 168), canned low-sodium chicken broth, or water, plus more if needed

- ½ cup bourbon
- 2 teaspoons unsulfured molasses
- 1 tablespoon coarse-grain mustard
- 2 large onions, halved and thinly sliced (about 4 cups)
- 4 garlic cloves, peeled
  Salt and freshly ground black pepper

Mustard Glaze

- ¼ cup Dijon mustard
- 2 teaspoons chopped fresh rosemary

1 **Rub:** Combine all the ingredients in a small bowl. If using brisket, to keep its flat shape and ensure that it does not break apart during cooking, tie several loops of butcher's twine around the diameter and the length of the roast. Sprinkle the rub generously over both sides of the roast. (*If time allows, wrap the roast in plastic wrap and refrigerate overnight.*)

2   Set up a gas or charcoal grill for indirect grilling (see page 12). Lightly oil the grill rack.

3   Sear the roast on the grill over medium-high heat until nicely browned, 3 to 5 minutes per side. Transfer the roast to a large Dutch oven. Whisk together the stock, bourbon, molasses, and mustard in a small bowl and pour over the meat. Scatter the onions and garlic on top. Place the pot over the area of the grill with no fire. Cover the pot, close the grill lid, and cook for 1 hour. (If your grill has a thermometer, it should read about 350°F.)

4   Turn over the roast, so that the onions are now on the bottom, and add more stock or water if needed. Continue to cook, uncovered, for 1 hour, checking every 20 to 30 minutes to make sure there is still liquid in the pot and to stir the onions so that they brown evenly; add more stock or water if needed.

5   Replace the lid on the pot and cook for 1 hour more if using chuck, 1½ to 2 hours if using brisket, or until the meat is tender; check every 30 minutes. (*For best results, let cool, then remove the meat, wrap in plastic wrap, and refrigerate overnight; refrigerate the sauce separately.*)

6   Heat the grill to medium. Meanwhile, remove the meat from the cooking liquid (if you have not already done so). Scrape any onions adhering to the meat into the cooking liquid. Remove the twine and pat the meat dry. Discard the fat from the cooking liquid.

7   **Glaze:** Combine ¼ cup of the cooking liquid and onions, the mustard, and rosemary in a food processor or a blender and puree. Brush some glaze over one side of the meat and place glaze side down on the grill. Brush the top of the roast with more glaze. When the glaze turns brown, turn over the meat and brown the other side.

8   Meanwhile, reheat the cooking liquid and season to taste with salt and pepper. Remove the twine if necessary, slice the meat into ½-inch-thick slices, ladle over the cooking liquid, and serve.

Alternative Cuts: Rolled and tied roasts from the chuck: whole mock tender roast, chuck roll, whole flat-iron, chuck arm, or cross-rib roast. Well-marbled rump, bottom round, or eye of round roasts.

Cook's Note

- To braise the meat in the oven instead of grilling, follow the directions for Pot-Roasted Grass-Fed Beef Chuck with Winter Root Vegetables (page 174).

Leftovers

- Use leftovers to make a Sloppy Bruce Sandwich: Coarsely chop the meat, combine it with the sauce, and reheat. Toast some rye bread; or, if you have any leftover glaze, brush it over the bread and broil for a few minutes. Spoon the meat and sauce over the bread and eat open-faced with a knife and fork.

- If using brisket, for a wonderful French dip sandwich, cut the leftovers into ¼-inch-thick slices and gently rewarm the sauce. Dip French rolls into the sauce, and pile on the meat. Garnish with prepared horseradish.

GRILL-BRAISING

It's the middle of summer and you've got a hankering for pot roast or slow-cooked short ribs, but you don't want to heat up your kitchen. No problem: Your trusty grill will come to the rescue. When your grill is covered, it functions more like an oven, so it's a great tool for braising.

The grill even has advantages over the oven. First, the fire adds a lovely grilled taste to the meat during the initial searing. Second, you can finish your braised meat by glazing it directly over the fire, adding great caramelized flavor as well.

This is an ideal technique for a gas grill. If you're cooking with charcoal, and the charcoal burns out or the heat is too low, you'll need to replenish it (see page 11 for more on grilling).

Once you've mastered grill-braising, you can adapt it to any braising recipe in the book. Here are the simple steps:

- Flavor the meat. Do this ahead, perhaps even the night before.

- Prepare the coals, and when they're ready, spread them over half the grill. Or, if using gas, heat all the burners to medium-high; when the grill is hot, leave one section on and turn off all the others.

- Sear the meat over direct heat on all sides. Set it aside.

- Prepare the braising sauce in a heavy pot with a lid. Add the meat, cover the pot, and move it to the side of the grill with no heat. Cover the grill and cook slowly.

- When the meat is done, make a glaze (which will likely use the braising sauce as a base). Brush it on the meat and cook the meat over direct heat until the glaze is bubbly.

Check out these other grill-braise recipes:
- Grill-Braised Vietnamese Short Ribs with Sweet Vinegar Glaze (page 206)
- Grill-Braised Moroccan Lamb Shanks with Honey Glaze (page 528)

POT-ROASTED GRASS-FED BEEF CHUCK WITH WINTER ROOT VEGETABLES

**Grass-Fed Beef, Family Meal, Rewarms Well,
Great Leftovers**

Serves 6

A good pot roast, when properly cooked, is as appealing as any roast prime rib. This recipe, a complete meal cooked in one pot, uses a method for oven pot-roasting developed by my good friend and former coauthor Lisa Weiss. It always produces great results with little worry. For the best flavor, season the roast and refrigerate overnight before cooking.

Mustard and Paprika Rub

- 2 teaspoons chopped fresh thyme
- 2 teaspoons sweet Hungarian paprika
- 1 teaspoon dry mustard powder (I use Colman's)
- 1 teaspoon light brown sugar
- 2 teaspoons salt
- 2 teaspoons freshly ground black pepper

- 1 4-pound boneless grass-fed beef chuck roast, tied
- 6 ounces slab bacon, cut into 1 x ½-inch-thick strips (lardons)
- 2 cups dry red wine

- ½ cup homemade beef stock (see page 168), canned low-sodium chicken broth, or water, plus more if needed
- 3 bay leaves
- 4 cups thinly sliced onions (about 2 large)
- 12 garlic cloves, peeled
- 12 small shallots, peeled
- 4 large carrots, peeled and cut into 1-inch chunks
- 3 medium parsnips, peeled and cut into 1-inch chunks
- 1 small celery root, peeled and cut into 1-inch chunks

  Salt and freshly ground black pepper

1 **Rub:** Combine all the ingredients in a small bowl. Rub thoroughly over all sides of the meat. (*If time allows, wrap the roast in plastic wrap and refrigerate overnight.*)

2 Preheat the oven to 325°F.

3 Heat a large Dutch oven over medium heat. Add the bacon and cook, stirring from time to time, until browned and lightly crisped. Remove with a slotted spoon and leave about 2 tablespoons of fat in the pot. Increase the heat to medium-high, add the roast, and sear on all sides until nicely browned, about 7 minutes total. Remove the meat.

4 Pour the red wine into the pot, bring to a boil, scraping any browned bits from the bottom of the pot, and reduce to ½ cup, about 10 minutes. Add the stock, reserved bacon,

and bay leaves, and lay in the roast. Scatter the onions and garlic over and around the meat, cover, and bake for 1 hour.

5   Remove the lid, turn over the meat so that it is on top of the onions, and bake for 1 hour more, checking after 30 minutes to make sure there is still liquid in the pot and to stir the onions so that they brown evenly; add more stock or water if necessary.

6   Remove the roast and add the shallots, carrots, parsnips, and celery root to the pot with the onions. Return the meat to the pot, cover, and bake for 1 hour more, or until the roast is fork-tender and the vegetables are soft. If the roast is not done, continue to bake, checking every 20 minutes.

7   Remove the meat and vegetables, discarding the bay leaves. Cover loosely with aluminum foil and set aside while you complete the sauce. Degrease the cooking liquid, and boil briefly to concentrate, if desired. Season to taste with salt and pepper. (*You can refrigerate the roast and sauce separately overnight and reheat to serve the next day, discarding any congealed fat on the top of the sauce.*)

8   To serve, remove the twine, slice the meat into thick slices or chunks, and ladle the sauce over the meat and vegetables.

Alternative Cuts: Grass-fed beef brisket or bison brisket. Whole beef shank. Bison chuck roast cuts, such as flat-iron or cross-rib roasts. Grass-fed beef 7-bone chuck roast.

Cook's Note
- If using bison, a whole flat-iron roast is my preferred cut for pot roast. Bison chuck may take 30 to 60 minutes longer to become tender.

Leftovers
- Dice the meat, chop the vegetables, and cover with a biscuit crust for a great beef potpie.
- Use the diced meat and chopped vegetables as a pasta sauce.

RUMP ROAST BRAISED IN ALE

Family Meal, Rewarms Well, Great Leftovers
Serves 6 to 8

This slightly sweet pot roast is inspired by both the classic Belgian beef carbonnade and the German pot roast called sauerbraten. It's best served with a full-flavored dark beer, such as porter or German bock. Choose a rump roast with as much marbling as you can find.

Herb and Dry Mustard Rub

2 teaspoons chopped fresh sage

2 teaspoons chopped fresh thyme

½ teaspoon ground coriander

2 teaspoons dry mustard powder (I use Colman's)

1 teaspoon dark brown sugar

1 tablespoon salt

2 teaspoons freshly ground black pepper

1 4-pound rump roast, tied

3 strips thick-cut bacon, cut into ¼-inch-wide pieces

2 cups homemade beef stock (see page 168) or canned low-sodium chicken broth, plus more if needed

1 12-ounce bottle porter or bock beer

1 teaspoon dark brown sugar, or more to taste

6 pitted prunes

1 teaspoon caraway seeds

4 bay leaves

6 cups thinly sliced onions (2½–3 pounds)

8 garlic cloves

2 cups peeled carrot chunks

1 pound cremini mushrooms, sliced

2 tablespoons coarse-grain mustard

1 tablespoon malt vinegar, or more to taste

Salt and freshly ground black pepper

1   Preheat the oven to 350°F.

2   **Rub:** Combine all the ingredients in a small bowl and rub all over the roast. If there's extra rub, save it to add to the braising sauce.

3   Heat a large Dutch oven over medium-high heat. Add the bacon and fry until brown. Remove from the pot, drain on paper towels, and set aside. Add the roast to the pot and sear for 4 to 5 minutes on one side, or until nicely browned. Flip over the meat and sear for 4 to 5 minutes more, or until the other side is nicely browned. Remove the meat and pour off all but 3 tablespoons of fat.

4   Pour the stock into the pot, scraping up any browned bits from the bottom of the pot. Stir in the beer, brown sugar, and any extra rub. Return the meat to the pot, fat side

up, and scatter the reserved bacon, the prunes, caraway, bay leaves, onions, and garlic over it. Cover the pot and bake for 1 hour. Remove the lid and turn over the roast so that the onions fall into the liquid. Bake, uncovered, for 30 minutes more, stirring the onions and adding stock or water if it evaporates.

5   Cover and bake for 30 minutes more. Lift up the meat and add the carrots and mushrooms to the liquid in the pot. Cover and bake for 15 to 20 minutes more, or until the meat and carrots are tender. (*You can refrigerate the meat in the sauce overnight. The next day, remove the meat and congealed fat. Finish the sauce by adding the mustard and vinegar. Slice the cold meat and rewarm in the sauce.*)

6   To finish the sauce, remove the solids from the pot and keep warm, covered with aluminum foil. Discard the bay leaves. Remove any fat from the surface of the sauce and, if desired, boil the sauce to concentrate it. Whisk in the mustard and vinegar and season to taste with salt, pepper, additional vinegar, and/or brown sugar. To serve, remove the twine and slice the meat, then spoon the sauce, prunes, and vegetables over.

Alternative Cuts: Brisket (increase the cooking time by 1 hour). Sirloin tip, eye of round, and bottom round — look for roasts with some marbling. Any rolled and tied roast from the chuck — cross-rib works well, as does chuck-eye roast.

Cook's Notes
- If you're not a beer drinker, this dish can be made with the same amount of a slightly sweet Riesling.

- If you don't have malt vinegar, use cider vinegar.

- To add more body to the sauce, puree all the prunes and ½ cup of the cooked onions in a food processor and add back into the sauce.

Leftovers
- For a real German treat, serve slices of rewarmed roast over egg noodles tossed with some sauce, carrots, and mushrooms and garnished with a dollop of sour cream.

- Leftovers make great Reuben-type sandwiches: Cook some sauerkraut in the leftover braising sauce. Slather toasted rye bread with mustard, then layer on rewarmed slices of meat, some sauerkraut, and slices of Swiss cheese.

IRISH CORNED BEEF AND VEGETABLES WITH DILL PICKLE–HORSERADISH CREAM AND GUINNESS-MUSTARD SAUCE

Family Meal, Fit for Company, Great Leftovers

Serves 6, with plenty of leftovers

Using a little beer to boil corned beef provides a pleasant malty flavor. Choose a dark beer, such as Guinness or other stout or, for a hint of sweetness, try a porter. Dark German beer, called Dunkel, is also good. Don't throw away the stock: Save it for a cabbage or other winter vegetable soup. I use a whole corned beef brisket, which includes both the fattier point cut and the lean first cut.

1 6- to 8-pound whole corned beef brisket, homemade (page 446) or store-bought	4 medium onions, halved through the roots
1 12-ounce bottle Guinness or other stout, porter, or dark German beer	6 small turnips, peeled and halved, or 2 medium rutabagas, peeled and quartered
1 tablespoon coriander seeds	2 parsnips, peeled and cut into 2-inch chunks
4 bay leaves	6 medium carrots, peeled
1 dried chile, such as cayenne	1 2-pound green cabbage, cored and quartered
2 allspice berries	Dill Pickle–Horseradish Cream (recipe follows)
8 medium boiling potatoes, scrubbed	Guinness-Mustard Sauce (recipe follows)

1 Place the corned beef in a Dutch oven. Pour in the beer and enough water to cover the meat by 1 to 2 inches. Wrap the coriander seeds, bay leaves, chile, and allspice in a square of cheesecloth, tie with butcher's twine, and throw the spices into the pot. Bring to a boil, then reduce the heat to a simmer, cover the pot, and cook for 2 hours. Check the beef by inserting a knife into the thickest part. If it shows no resistance, the meat is tender. To make sure, cut off a bit and taste it. If it is not tender, continue to cook, checking every 30 minutes. Remove the beef from the pot and cover loosely with aluminum foil to keep warm.

2 Add the potatoes, onions, turnips, parsnips, carrots, and cabbage to the pot, cover, and cook at a slow boil for 20 minutes, or until tender. Return the beef to the pot to rewarm for 2 to 3 minutes. Discard the spice bag. Cut the meat across the grain into

¼-inch-thick slices and arrange on a platter with the vegetables. Serve with the Dill Pickle–Horseradish Cream and Guinness-Mustard Sauce.

Alternative Cuts: If you can't find a whole corned beef, use two first-cut pieces for a total of 6 to 8 pounds. Also try this with home-cured bison or Petit Salé Pork (page 447).

Cook's Notes
- The horseradish cream is also great with roast veal, baked ham, boiled beef, and tongue.
- Use the mustard sauce for corned beef sandwiches, such as my Toasted Corned Beef and Fontina Sandwiches (page 184).

Leftovers
- Use in Hash Cakes with Poached Eggs (page 182).
- Also great in Reuben-type sandwiches (see page 178).

DILL PICKLE–HORSERADISH CREAM

Makes about 1½ cups

1 cup sour cream

1 tablespoon chopped fresh chives or scallion greens

6 tablespoons prepared horseradish, drained

1 tablespoon finely chopped dill pickle

Combine the ingredients in a small bowl. Cover and refrigerate for at least 2 hours, or up to 2 days.

GUINNESS-MUSTARD SAUCE

Makes about ¾ cup

½ cup coarse-grain mustard

2 tablespoons Guinness or other stout

2 tablespoons Dijon mustard

½ teaspoon light brown sugar

1 tablespoon finely chopped shallot

Combine the ingredients in a small bowl. Cover and refrigerate for at least 2 hours, or up to 4 days.

HASH CAKES WITH POACHED EGGS

Cheap Eats

Serves 4 to 6

This is great breakfast fare, nice and crisp. Two cakes with eggs is a generous serving.

¼ cup finely chopped fat from leftover Irish Corned Beef (page 179) or finely chopped bacon

⅔ cup finely chopped red onion

½ cup chopped leftover cabbage from corned beef

½ cup diced leftover root vegetables (a mixture of carrots, turnips, and parsnips) from corned beef

2 cups (about 1 pound) finely chopped leftover corned beef

2 cups diced leftover boiled potatoes from corned beef

Salt and freshly ground black pepper

2 large eggs, lightly beaten

2–3 tablespoons bacon fat, butter, or olive oil

8–12 poached eggs for serving

1 Heat a 12-inch heavy nonstick skillet over medium heat. Add the corned beef fat and cook until the fat has melted and the remaining solids are light brown. Add the onion and cook until soft, about 5 minutes. Add the cabbage and root vegetables and cook, stirring, for 5 minutes.

2 Scrape the mixture into a large bowl, add the chopped meat and potatoes, and mix well. Season to taste with salt and pepper, then stir in the beaten eggs. Form the mixture into 8 to 12 cakes about ¾ inch thick and 3 to 4 inches in diameter. Place on a platter, cover with plastic wrap, and refrigerate for at least 1 hour, and up to 4 hours.

3 To fry, heat 2 tablespoons of the bacon fat in a large nonstick skillet over medium-high heat and cook 3 or 4 cakes at a time until the bottoms are nicely browned, 3 to 5 minutes. Flip the cakes and brown the other sides, 3 to 5 minutes. Remove and keep the cakes warm while you cook the remaining cakes, adding more fat if necessary.

4 To serve, place a poached egg on top of each cake.

TOASTED CORNED BEEF AND FONTINA SANDWICHES
Fit for Company, Comfort Food

Serves 4

Serve these sandwiches with real kosher dill pickles and lots of coleslaw. I use the best Italian fontina from Val d'Aosta, but the less expensive Danish fontina works well.

Dijon mustard

8 slices Jewish-style rye bread

1 pound thinly sliced leftover Irish Corned Beef
(page 179)

4–6 ¼-inch-thick slices fontina cheese

½ sweet onion, thinly sliced (optional)

4 tablespoons (½ stick) butter, softened

Kosher dill pickles

Coleslaw, store-bought or homemade
(see below)

1   Spread the mustard on the bread. Divide the corned beef into 8 portions and lay over the slices of mustard-slathered bread. Cover half with the cheese and the other half with some onion slices (if using). Press the two halves of each sandwich together. Spread the butter on both sides of each sandwich.

2   Heat a 12-inch heavy nonstick skillet over medium heat. Add 2 sandwiches, cover the skillet, and cook until nicely golden. Flip and cook until the other side is golden and the cheese is melted. Repeat with the remaining 2 sandwiches. Serve with dill pickles and coleslaw.

Alternative Cuts: Leftover ham or pickled tongue.

Cook's Notes

- My favorite coleslaw to serve with this sandwich is one made with Russian Dressing (page 136).

- Substitute Comté, Cantal, Gruyère, or Emmenthaler for the fontina.

- Turn this sandwich into a Reuben by replacing the (optional) onions with a layer of sauerkraut and using Russian dressing instead of mustard.

Beef and Bison Stew Meat, Short Ribs, and Other Gnarly Cuts

Short ribs, shanks, cheeks, and oxtails — these cuts are all rich with collagen. Cook them long and slow in a moist environment and you'll be rewarded with silky, succulent deliciousness. They're often braised on the bone, but cut the meat into chunks and you have the start of a terrific stew. The long cooking times for these dishes make them great candidates for the slow cooker. You can also make them a day or two ahead, and they're even better reheated.

Stew meat. The best cuts for stew meat have ample fat and connective tissue, or collagen, so that when the meat becomes tender, it holds together and remains juicy. Choose any cut of boneless chuck or brisket, or use short ribs, cheek meat, or shanks. Don't purchase meat labeled "stew meat" because you won't know which cut it comes from (most likely, it will be bottom round or eye of round, which the butcher is trying to get rid of).

A fork should easily penetrate the meat when it's done, but you can also take a bite from time to time as it cooks to check.

Short ribs. These used to be a bargain, but then restaurants started serving them, and now folks love them so much that demand has pushed the price up a bit. They're still a good buy, however. Short ribs are cut from all twelve ribs of the cow, but exactly where they come from is usually not indicated on the label. If you can find a butcher who cuts his or her own, ask for short ribs from the chuck, which are a bit leaner and have great beefy flavor.

Short ribs come two ways: When cut between the rib bones, they're called **English-cut short ribs** or, simply, beef short ribs. These short ribs, the most common in supermarkets, are also sold boneless. When cut into strips across two to four adjacent rib bones, they're called **flanken-style short ribs**. Thin strips of flanken short ribs are sold as Korean-style short ribs and are usually marinated and grilled. When cut thinly into crosswise slices, the normally chewy short ribs become tender enough to grill. Thickly cut flanken short ribs and English-cut short ribs need moist heat to become tender.

Meat from the chuck eye is sometimes cut into thick strips and sold as **country-style beef ribs**; use them as you would short ribs.

Short ribs from lean grass-fed beef and bison provide some of the best eating from these animals. The short ribs are usually leaner than those from commodity beef (which often have large pockets of unpleasant fat), but they have enough fat and collagen to cook up into a succulent and tender delight. They may take a little longer to cook than supermarket short ribs, so make sure to taste them to determine when they're tender.

Beef shanks, beef cheeks, and oxtails. These are tough cuts loaded with collagen and take a long time to cook, but the results are well worth the effort.

The Gnarly Cuts at a Glance

Short Ribs

Short ribs, bone in (braising ribs, barbecue ribs, English-cut ribs, fancy ribs). These consist of single rib bones cut between the ribs; they can be cut to various lengths from 3 to 5 inches. May be from the chuck or plate but usually are not differentiated on the label; often just labeled "short ribs."

Flanken-style short ribs, bone in (kosher ribs, braising ribs, barbecue ribs, Hawaiian-style ribs, Korean-style ribs). Cut across 2 or more ribs, usually in 1- to 2-inch-thick slices. From the chuck or plate. When cut really thin (about ¼ inch) they are called Hawaiian-style or Korean-style ribs and are usually marinated and grilled.

Short ribs, boneless. Cut from various areas of the chuck or plate and may be sold as English-cut or flanken-style ribs.

Country-style ribs, boneless. Cut from the center-cut blade area or the shoulder clod (arm), these thick strips of beef can be cooked like short ribs.

Other Gnarly Cuts

Crosscut beef shank, bone in (center-cut beef shank, beef shank, beef shinbone, foreshank for soup). Soft and silky when cooked long and slow. Can be cut into chunks for stew. Has great flavor and produces a rich, gelatinous sauce.

Beef cheeks, boneless. This muscle does lots of work and is interlaced with collagen, which turns soft after long moist-heat cooking. Rich meat with a silky and firm texture. Great for stews and as a miniature pot roast for 2 to 3 people.

Oxtails, bone in. A beef tail cut into round sections between the joints. Makes for luxurious braises, soft and unctuous, with rich gravy. One of my favorite braising cuts.

HUNGARIAN GOULASH

Family Meal

Serves 6

In America, any stewlike dish that contains a bit of paprika and/or tomato may be called goulash by the less-than-accurate cook. I remember being served a thick reddish concoction at Boy Scout camp that was distinguished only by being slightly more palatable than the other common camp dish, mystery meat.

Traditional goulash as made in Hungary is not thickened and doesn't contain flour; many recipes don't even have paprika. However, my recipe has both hot and sweet paprika. I always use the real stuff from Hungary — as fresh as I can find. If spicy food is not your thing, leave out the hot paprika. To make this stew a more substantial one-pot meal, I've added potatoes and carrots. You can serve the goulash over dumplings, egg noodles, or spätzle.

Garnishing goulash with a dollop of sour cream isn't traditionally Hungarian, but I love sour cream.

2 tablespoons bacon fat, lard, or olive oil

3 cups chopped onions

2 garlic cloves, minced

3 tablespoons sweet Hungarian paprika

2 teaspoons hot Hungarian paprika (optional)

3 pounds boneless chuck roast (any cut), cut into 1½-inch cubes

Salt and freshly ground black pepper

4 cups homemade beef stock (see page 168) or canned low-sodium chicken broth

2 teaspoons caraway seeds, ground

2 cups ½-inch-diced peeled Yukon Gold, red, or white boiling potatoes

2 cups ½-inch-diced peeled carrots

1 large red bell pepper, cored, seeded, and diced

3 medium tomatoes, peeled, seeded, and diced, or ⅔ cup drained, chopped canned tomatoes

Egg Dumplings (recipe follows)

Sour cream (optional)

2 tablespoons chopped fresh marjoram

1   Heat the fat in a large Dutch oven over medium heat. Add the onions and garlic and cook, stirring occasionally, until softened and golden brown, about 20 minutes.

2   Add the sweet paprika and hot paprika (if using) and stir until the onions are well coated, 1 to 2 minutes. Stir in the meat, a little salt, and a few grinds of pepper. Add ½ cup of the stock, increase the heat to medium-high, and cook until the liquid is almost evaporated. Add the remaining 3½ cups stock and the caraway and bring to a boil, then reduce the heat to maintain a simmer and cook, covered, for 1 hour, or until the meat is almost tender. Skim the liquid and discard the fat.

3   Add the potatoes, carrots, bell pepper, and tomatoes. Cook for 20 minutes, or until the potatoes are tender. Degrease the surface. You can serve the goulash as is, with a souplike consistency, or you can reduce it until it just turns syrupy. To do so, strain all the solids from the soup and set aside. Bring to a boil and reduce the liquid, then add back the solids. Season the goulash to taste with salt and pepper.

4   To serve, ladle the dumplings into warmed soup bowls and spoon in the goulash. Garnish with sour cream (if using) and a sprinkling of the marjoram.

Alternative Cuts: Boneless short ribs, nicely marbled rump roast, beef shank removed from the bone, or brisket (beef shank and brisket will require a cooking time of 30 minutes longer or more).

Cook's Note

- Goulash, which is traditionally served somewhat on the soupy side, is best eaten with a spoon.

EGG DUMPLINGS

Serves 6

---

1   large egg, lightly beaten
1   tablespoon melted lard, bacon fat, or butter
⅓   cup water

1   teaspoon salt
1½   cups all-purpose flour

1   Mix together the egg, lard, water, and salt in a medium bowl. Stir in the flour just until a soft dough forms, being careful not to overmix.

2   Drop tablespoonfuls of dough (it's okay if they're a little uneven and rustically misshapen) into a large pot of boiling salted water. The dumplings are done when they rise to the surface, about 10 minutes. Remove them with a slotted spoon and drain. If you make these ahead, add to the goulash and reheat right before serving.

JEFF'S DAUBE (PROVENÇAL BEEF STEW)

Fit for Company, Rewarms Well, Great Leftovers
Serves 6 to 8

Seattle is one of my favorite cities, and although there are many excellent restaurants, the highlight for me is a meal at my friend Jeff Bergman's house. For several years, he cooked professionally, and he has continued to perfect his craft, becoming one of the greatest cooks I know, professional or amateur. His recipes take some time, but they are well worth the effort. An example is this daube, a red wine–based beef stew from Provence. Jeff's is one of the best I've had, here or in France.

Because of the time and effort involved, this is a dish to make when important company is coming over, but don't fear, it's not a difficult recipe. Jeff says that daube greatly benefits from being made the day before so that the braising juices can saturate the tender meat. He serves the daube with rice, gnocchi, cooked egg pasta such as pappardelle, or his favorite choice, a creamy mixed-root puree of potatoes, celery root, parsnips, and Jerusalem artichokes.

Bouquet Garni

- 10 fresh flat-leaf parsley sprigs
- 10 fresh thyme sprigs
- 4 fresh summer savory sprigs
- 4 bay leaves
- 1 1-inch-wide strip orange peel

- 2 750-ml bottles dry red wine, such as Côtes du Rhône, Shiraz, California Syrah, or Petite Syrah
- ¼ cup cognac
- ½ cup all-purpose flour
  Salt and freshly ground black pepper
- 3 pounds trimmed beef shank meat, cut into 2-inch chunks and dried with paper towels
- 3 pounds trimmed boneless beef short ribs, cut into 2-inch pieces and dried with paper towels
- 6 tablespoons extra-virgin olive oil

- 2 quarts homemade beef stock (see page 168) or canned low-sodium chicken broth
- 2 large carrots, peeled and cut into 1-inch pieces
- 2 medium leeks, white and pale green parts, cut into 1-inch pieces
- 1 celery stalk, cut into 1-inch pieces
- 1 large onion, cut into 1-inch wedges
- 6 large shallots, cut into quarters
- 12 garlic cloves, peeled
- 2 tablespoons tomato paste
- 2 tablespoons red wine vinegar

Garnish

- ¼ pound slab bacon, cut into 1-x-½-inch-thick strips (lardons)
- 3 tablespoons minced fresh flat-leaf parsley

1   Preheat the oven to 325°F.

2   **Bouquet garni:** Tie all the herbs and the orange peel into a bundle with butcher's twine. Set aside.

3   Place the wine in a large saucepan, bring to a boil, and boil until reduced by half, about 20 minutes. Set aside.

4   Meanwhile, place the cognac in a small saucepan and bring to a boil over high heat. As soon as it comes to a boil, remove from the heat, carefully ignite the cognac with a long match or butane fire starter, and return to the heat to burn off the alcohol. Set aside.

5   In a small bowl, combine the flour with 2 teaspoons each salt and pepper. Sprinkle the beef pieces with the seasoned flour. Heat 2 tablespoons of the oil in a large Dutch oven over medium-high heat. Add the beef to the pot, being careful not to overcrowd (you may have to brown it in batches). Cook the beef for 3 to 4 minutes per side, until a dark brown crust forms. Adjust the heat if the pot becomes too hot: The meat should sizzle gently. Remove the browned pieces to a platter and continue until all the meat is nicely browned, adding 2 tablespoons more of the oil as needed. Pour off any fat in the pot and discard. Add 1 cup of the stock and bring to a boil, scraping up all the browned bits from the bottom of the pot. Add the deglazing juices to the reserved wine. Wipe the pot dry with paper towels.

6   Add the remaining 2 tablespoons oil to the pot and heat over medium-high heat until hot. Add the carrots, leeks, celery, onion, shallots, and garlic and sauté for 6 to 8 minutes, or until slightly softened and lightly browned. Add the tomato paste, stir to coat the vegetables, and cook for 1 minute. Add the bouquet garni, then add the reduced wine, reduced cognac, the remaining 7 cups stock, and the vinegar and stir to combine.

7   Add the browned beef and any juices and stir again. Bring the daube to a boil, cover, place in the oven, and cook for 2 hours. Check the beef for tenderness with the point of a knife. If the blade is easily inserted into the meat with no resistance, the daube is done. If not, continue to cook, checking every 20 minutes, until tender. Remove from the oven. (*At this point, you can let the daube cool and refrigerate overnight.*)

8   Degrease the surface of the daube. (If it's been refrigerated, reheat over medium heat.) Carefully remove the meat to a platter (it's tender and will break apart easily). Pour the braising liquid through a fine-mesh strainer and discard the vegetables and bouquet garni. Return the braising liquid to the pot, bring to a boil, and reduce until slightly thickened and syrupy.

9 Meanwhile, place the bacon strips in a small skillet and cook over medium heat until lightly brown and beginning to crisp. Drain on paper towels.

10 Add the beef and bacon strips to the liquid, carefully tossing to coat them. Warm through for 5 minutes, then season to taste with salt and pepper.

11 To serve, place the meat on a large platter, spoon the sauce over it, and sprinkle with the parsley.

Alternative Cuts: Boneless chuck of any cut or rump roast (reduce the cooking time by about 30 minutes), brisket, beef cheeks (increase the cooking time by 30 minutes).

Cook's Note

- Instead of using meat cut into pieces, make this as a pot roast. Buy chuck, brisket, or rump roast for pot-roasting and begin checking for doneness after 2 hours.

Leftovers

- Serve any leftovers over your favorite pasta, or use leftover daube instead of bison to make Cottage Pie (page 196); you will need about 4 cups daube.

- Substitute 4 to 6 cups daube for the filling in Irish Beef-Cheek Pie with Stout (page 222).

GREAT BEEF CUTS FOR STEW

Don't cut your chunks of stew meat too small; 2-inch cubes are ideal. And if you buy any bone-in cut, remove the bones, season them, brown them, and cook them in the stew to add extra flavor. You can discard the bones later or give them to your dog.

- My first choice is **short ribs**. I usually cut my own chunks off the bone, but boneless short ribs work equally well.

- I like **chuck blade pot roast**, but any bone-in or boneless pot roast from the chuck works well for stew and will have ample fat. Some stores cut the under blade area of the chuck into thick strips and sell them as **beef country-style ribs**. These work great for stew.

- **Brisket** has a rich, beefy flavor and makes good stew. Don't overcook it, or it will become stringy.

- **Beef shanks** are pretty lean, but they have loads of collagen and make great stew meat.

- If you can find them, **beef cheeks** are also loaded with collagen, so they turn soft and silky when tender and make especially nice stews. They have a texture similar to shank meat.

FEIJOADA (BRAZILIAN BLACK BEAN STEW)

Fit for Company, Fit for a Crowd, Rewarms Well
Serves 10 to 12

Like other dishes with peasant roots and a national identity, feijoada comes in many variations. Brazil's national dish varies not only from region to region but from family to family. My version was inspired by a recipe from the book *Real Stew* by Clifford Wright, whose recipe in turn was inspired by one from Margarette de Andrade, a friend of his. I have made a few changes, leaving out such hard-to-find items as pigs' ears, feet, and tails. In Brazil, feijoada is often made with a dried jerkylike beef called *carne seca*. It is not sold in the United States, so I have replaced it with pastrami. Traditionally the meats are separated from the beans, cut into slices, and served on their own. I prefer to present everything together, which is a simpler and more rustic presentation. I do like feijoada with toasted farina or manioc root powder.

4 cups dried black beans, picked over and rinsed

1 smoked beef tongue (about 1½ pounds) or 2 meaty smoked ham hocks

4 quarts water

4 bay leaves

1 pound pastrami, cut from the brisket or navel (don't use bottom-round pastrami)

1 pound semicured Spanish chorizo, homemade (page 414) or store-bought

1 2-pound boneless chuck roast (any cut), rolled and tied

2 large onions, chopped

6 garlic cloves, chopped

1 bunch cilantro, stems finely chopped, leaves coarsely chopped (1½ cups total)

Grated zest of ½ orange

1 pound linguica, cut into ½-inch-thick rounds

3 navel oranges, halved through the stem end and cut into ¼-inch-thick slices

½ cup farina (Cream of Wheat) or manioc flour (see Sources)

2 tablespoons vegetable oil

Salt and freshly ground black pepper

1   Soak the beans overnight in cold water to cover by about 3 inches.

2   Place the tongue or ham hocks in a large pot with the water and 2 of the bay leaves. Bring to a boil over high heat, reduce the heat, and cook at a low boil until the skin of the tongue can be easily removed or the meat of the hocks is tender and almost falling off the bone, 1½ to 2½ hours. Remove the meat, discarding the bay leaves and reserving the cooking liquid. When the tongue is cool enough to handle, peel off the skin and discard; or, if you are using ham hocks, remove the skin and fat, pull the meat from the bones, and chop. (*You can do this step up to a day ahead and refrigerate the meat and liquid separately.*)

3   Drain the beans, place them in a large Dutch oven, and pour over 2 quarts of the reserved cooking liquid; save the remaining liquid to add later. Bring to a slow boil over medium heat. Add the pastrami, ½ pound of the chorizo, the peeled tongue (if using), the chuck roast, the remaining 2 bay leaves, the onions, garlic, cilantro stems, and orange zest. Make sure everything is covered with liquid; add more cooking liquid or water if necessary. Cover and simmer until the meats are tender and the beans are soft, 1½ to 2 hours or more. Add more liquid if the stew begins to dry out. (*The feijoada can be made a day ahead, covered and refrigerated.*)

4   Meanwhile, about 20 minutes before the meats are tender, slice the remaining ½ pound chorizo. Add it to the stew, along with the linguica, chopped ham hocks (if using), and orange slices. Stir in more cooking liquid or water if the stew becomes too dry.

5   While the feijoada finishes cooking, toast the farina or manioc flour in the oil in a small nonstick skillet over medium-low heat until golden brown and gives off a nutty aroma. Set aside.

6   Remove the tongue (if using), chuck roast, pastrami, and whole piece of chorizo to a cutting board. Remove and discard the string from the roast. Cut the tongue and roast into 1-inch chunks, shred or dice the pastrami, and cut the chorizo into ½-inch-thick rounds. Add everything back into the stew. Season to taste with salt and pepper.

7   To serve, ladle each portion into a shallow soup bowl and garnish with a sprinkling of the toasted farina or manioc and cilantro leaves.

Alternative Cuts: Choices are many here. You can use slab bacon or smoked pork loin, beef shin, brisket, corned beef, pork ribs, Petit Salé Pork (page 447), pigs' feet, ham, pigs' tails, pig skin, pork shin, bacon rind, oxtails — basically any cheap cuts of beef and/or pork that require long, moist cooking you can find.

Cook's Notes
- To find Spanish and Portuguese sausages, see Sources.
- To serve feijoada in the traditional Brazilian style, remove the meats and cut them into serving-size chunks, arrange on a platter, and garnish with some of the cilantro leaves. Place the beans in a deep serving bowl or tureen and garnish with orange slices and more cilantro. Let guests garnish their own portions with the toasted farina or manioc flour. Serve buffet style.

BISON COTTAGE PIE

**Fit for Company, Family Meal, Rewarms Well,
Grass-Fed Beef**

Serves 6

A truly great cottage pie, made with long-braised diced meats in a rich sauce with lots of root vegetables and a light, fluffy, and cheesy potato crust, is a dish worthy of a place on any table. I prefer to use bison because of its rich flavor. It's tougher than beef, but with lots of collagen that softens to tenderness and adds body to the gravy. If you can't find bison, substitute grass-fed beef chuck or boneless short ribs.

⅓ cup all-purpose flour

1 tablespoon sweet Hungarian paprika

Salt and freshly ground black pepper

2½ pounds boneless bison chuck roast, boneless short ribs, or brisket, cut into ¾-inch cubes

⅓ pound thick-sliced bacon, cut crosswise into ½-inch-wide pieces

2 tablespoons olive oil, or more if needed

1 cup chopped onions

½ cup chopped peeled carrots

½ cup chopped celery

1 tablespoon chopped garlic

2 cups full-bodied dry red wine, such as Syrah or Zinfandel

1 cup canned crushed tomatoes

2½ cups homemade beef stock (see page 168) or canned low-sodium chicken broth

2 bay leaves

1 teaspoon chopped fresh thyme

1 teaspoon chopped fresh sage

10 ounces pearl onions, not peeled

1½ cups 1-inch pieces peeled parsnips

1 cup trimmed baby turnips

Mashed Potato Crust

2 pounds russet potatoes, peeled and quartered

8 tablespoons (1 stick) butter

¾ cup whole milk

⅓ cup heavy cream

1 teaspoon salt

½ teaspoon freshly ground black pepper

2 large eggs

1 tablespoon water

1 cup freshly grated Parmigiano-Reggiano

1 Combine the flour, paprika, 1½ teaspoons salt, and 1 teaspoon pepper in a large shallow bowl. Add the bison and toss to coat all over. Set aside.

2 Heat a large Dutch oven over medium heat. Add the bacon and cook, stirring, until nicely browned and just crisp. Remove with a slotted spoon and set aside. Leave the fat in the pot.

3 Turn up the heat to medium-high, add the oil, and sear the bison until nicely brown all over, about 10 minutes; remove and set aside. (You may have to do this in batches, adding more oil as needed.) Pour off all but 2 tablespoons fat. Reduce the heat to medium

and stir in the chopped onions, carrots, celery, and garlic. Cover and cook, stirring, until the vegetables begin to soften, about 5 minutes. Pour in the red wine, scrape up any browned bits from the bottom of the pot, and bring to a boil. Add the bison, bacon, tomatoes, stock, bay leaves, thyme, and sage. Reduce the heat to a simmer, cover, and cook for 2 hours, or until the bison is tender.

4   While the bison is cooking, blanch the pearl onions in a 2-quart saucepan half filled with boiling salted water for 2 minutes. Transfer to a bowl of ice water. Drain, trim off any root ends, and slip off the skins.

5   When the bison is done, add the parsnips and turnips and cook for 10 to 15 minutes, until softened. Discard the bay leaves. Add the pearl onions and cook for 5 minutes more, or until the vegetables are tender. Season to taste with salt and pepper. Cool (or, better still, refrigerate the bison filling overnight).

6   Preheat the oven to 400°F.

7   **Crust:** Boil the potatoes in salted water to cover by at least 1 inch for 18 to 20 minutes, or until tender when pierced with a fork. Drain.

8   Heat the butter, milk, and cream in a saucepan to almost a boil. Push the potatoes through a ricer into a large bowl and whisk in the heated milk mixture, salt, and pepper. Continue to whisk to cool the mashed potatoes a bit, but don't overmix. Lightly beat 1 of the eggs and whisk in.

9   Skim the fat from the bison filling and spoon the filling into a 13-x-9-inch baking dish. Cover with the mashed potatoes and use a fork to create a streaked pattern on the top. Beat together the remaining egg and water, then brush the potatoes with the mixture. Sprinkle the cheese over the top. Bake for 30 to 40 minutes, or until the crust is nicely browned and the filling is warmed through (it should be 125°F when tested with an instant-read thermometer). Let rest for 10 minutes and serve.

Alternative Cuts: Grass-fed or conventional beef chuck roast, boneless short ribs, brisket, or boneless shank; cooking time will be about 30 minutes less.

Cook's Notes
- You can assemble the pie ahead, cover with plastic wrap, and refrigerate overnight. Add 20 minutes to the baking time.
- This deceptively humble dish is ideal for company and warrants a fine wine to go with it. My preference would be a Hermitage from Jean-Louis Chave or a Côtes du Rhône or California Syrah from Radio-Coteau.

MEXICAN BEEF BRISKET AND WINTER SQUASH CHILI

Family Meal, Fit for Company, Fit for a Crowd, Great Leftovers

Serves 8 to 10, with leftovers

Chili con carne has its origins in the slow-cooked stews of Mexico. One such dish, chili Colorado, was no doubt made in clay pots cooked long and slow over small fires or in bakers' ovens. No need for multiple steps here: Just combine all the ingredients and cook (if you have a slow cooker, this is an ideal recipe, but do brown the bacon first). Enjoy in warmed bowls with the garnishes of your choice; roll up the warm tortillas and dip them into the juices. If there are leftovers, wrap them in tortillas for tacos, burritos, or enchiladas or, if you're feeling ambitious, use as a filling for tamales.

6 dried ancho chiles

2 cups boiling water

6 ounces bacon, diced

4 cups chopped onions

5 pounds first-cut beef brisket, cut into 3-inch chunks

Salt and freshly ground black pepper

2 jalapeño chiles, stemmed, seeded, and chopped (optional)

6 garlic cloves, peeled

2 teaspoons cumin seeds

1 teaspoon dried oregano (I use Mexican)

1 teaspoon ground coriander

2 tablespoons chili powder (I use Gebhardt; see Sources)

1 14.5-ounce can diced fire-roasted tomatoes with green chiles (I use Muir Glen)

1 12-ounce bottle Mexican beer, plus more if needed

1 bunch cilantro, stems chopped, leaves saved for garnish (1½ cups total)

4 fire-roasted mild green chiles (see page 284), such as Anaheim, peeled, seeded, and diced, or one 7-ounce can diced fire-roasted green chiles

3 cups 2-inch chunks peeled and seeded butternut or banana squash

Garnish

Fresh cilantro leaves (from above)

Finely chopped onions

Peeled, seeded, and sliced avocados

Shredded Monterey Jack cheese

Warm corn or flour tortillas

1   Tear the dried ancho chiles apart, discard the seeds and stems, and place in a small bowl. Pour over the boiling water and soak until soft, at least 30 minutes, or up to several hours.

2   Preheat the oven to 325°F.

3   Fry the bacon in a large Dutch oven over medium heat until it begins to brown. Add the onions and cook, covered, for 5 minutes. Season the beef with salt and pepper. Remove the pot from the heat and stir in the beef.

4   Place the soaked chiles and about ½ cup of the soaking liquid in a blender (save the remaining liquid to add to the pot later if needed). Add the jalapeños (if using), garlic, cumin, oregano, coriander, chili powder, and 2 teaspoons salt. Blend to form a puree, then add to the pot along with the tomatoes, beer, cilantro stems, and green chiles. Stir well, cover, place in the oven, and bake for 2 hours. If the chili becomes too dry during cooking, add some of the reserved chile-soaking liquid or more beer. The meat is done when it's fork-tender. If the meat is not yet fork-tender, return the covered pot to the oven and check it every 20 to 30 minutes. Stir in the squash and bake for 20 minutes more, or until the squash is tender.

5   Remove the pot from the oven. Degrease the chili (or, better still, cool, refrigerate overnight, and then remove the congealed fat; reheat to serve). Season to taste with salt and pepper. Serve in bowls with the garnishes on the side, and the warmed tortillas to roll and dip.

Alternative Cuts: Any cut of chuck roast, rump roast, bottom sirloin flap (*bavette*), or short ribs (reduce the cooking time for these cuts by 30 minutes, then start checking for doneness). Beef cheeks, oxtails, or shank (you may need to increase the cooking time by an hour or so). You can also use sirloin tip or a bottom round or eye-of-round roast if the meat has at least moderate marbling. Also good with equivalent cuts of bison.

Cook's Note
- Other good dried chiles to use are guajillo, mulato, California, and New Mexico.

Leftovers
- For a delightful summer soup, dilute leftover chili with beef or chicken stock, then add cooked pinto beans or kidney beans, diced carrots, fresh corn, and green beans.

- Turn leftover chili into a hearty winter soup by diluting it with beef or chicken stock, then adding cooked kidney or pinto beans and cubed carrots, turnips, potatoes, celery, and rutabaga.

- Also see the recommendations in the headnote.

BRAISED MONTANA COFFEE-MARINATED BISON SHORT RIBS

Fit for Company, Rewarms Well, Freezes Well, Grass-Fed Beef

Serves 4 to 6

With its huge forequarter, a bison produces lots of short ribs. That's great news, because short ribs are some of the tastiest parts of the beast and bison short ribs are plentiful enough to be reasonably priced. Montana has some of the largest herds of bison, and I imagine cowboys cooking up a mess of ribs with some leftover coffee and a bit of bacon—the shallots and soy sauce here, however, may not have been part of the chuck wagon larder. These are some tasty ribs.

Coffee-Maple Marinade/Brine

- 4 cups water
- 3 cups chilled strong coffee
- ½ cup Diamond Crystal kosher salt or ¼ cup table salt
- 3 tablespoons dark brown sugar
- ¼ cup real maple syrup
- 2 tablespoons chopped fresh rosemary
- 2 tablespoons Worcestershire sauce
- 2 cups ice cubes

- 4 pounds bone-in English-cut bison short ribs

Montana Coffee Sauce

- ¼ cup diced bacon
- 2 cups chopped onions
- ½ cup chopped shallots
- 2 tablespoons chopped garlic
- 1 small jalapeño chile, stemmed, seeded, and chopped
- 1 cup strong coffee
- 1 cup homemade beef stock (see page 168) or canned low-sodium chicken broth
- ¼ cup chili sauce (I use Heinz) or ketchup
- 1 teaspoon Worcestershire sauce
- 2 tablespoons Dijon mustard
- 2 teaspoons dark brown sugar, or more to taste
- 2 tablespoons soy sauce
- 2 tablespoons cider vinegar, or more to taste
  Salt and freshly ground black pepper

1   **Marinade/Brine:** Combine the water, coffee, salt, and brown sugar in a large plastic tub or stainless steel bowl and stir until the salt and sugar are dissolved. Stir in the maple syrup, rosemary, and Worcestershire. Chill the brine by stirring in the ice until it melts; the brine should be very cold, about 45°F, before the meat is added. Add the ribs, weigh them down with a plate, and refrigerate for 4 to 6 hours.

2   Remove the ribs from the brine and pat them dry. Discard the brine. (*At this point, the ribs can be wrapped in plastic and refrigerated for up to 2 days.*)

3   Preheat the oven to 325°F.

4   **Sauce:** Cook the bacon in a large Dutch oven over medium heat until browned and beginning to crisp. Remove the bacon with a slotted spoon, drain on paper towels, and set aside. Increase the heat to medium-high and, working in batches, add the ribs to the pot and lightly brown on all sides, about 7 minutes per batch. Remove to a plate and set aside.

5   Add the onions, shallots, garlic, and jalapeño to the pot and reduce the heat to medium. Cover and cook, stirring from time to time, until the vegetables are soft, about 10 minutes. Stir in the coffee and stock and scrape up any browned bits from the bottom of the pot. Stir in the remaining sauce ingredients and bring to a boil.

6   Add the bacon and short ribs, and when the pot returns to a boil, cover and pop into the oven. Cook for 2 hours, or until the ribs are fork-tender. If not done, cover and continue cooking, checking every 30 minutes.

7   When the ribs are done, remove from the oven and degrease any surface fat. If the sauce is too thin, remove the ribs and boil down to a syrupy consistency. You should have 2 to 3 cups sauce. Taste the sauce and add more vinegar and brown sugar, and season with salt and pepper to suit your taste. If necessary, return the ribs to the sauce and reheat before serving.

Alternative Cuts: Bison back ribs (use 6 to 8 pounds), grass-fed beef back ribs (check them after 1½ hours; they may take less time to cook), or beef oxtails (they will take 3 to 4 hours to cook).

Cook's Notes
- This dish is best when made up to 2 days ahead and refrigerated. The gelatin from the meat thickens the sauce nicely after a day or so of refrigeration. Remove the congealed fat and rewarm.

- Bison short ribs are much leaner than beef ribs, but they still have enough fat to yield soft and juicy meat. Just be sure to cook them long and slow.

- If there is any sauce left over, use it to glaze grilled steaks or pork chops.

- The Coffee-Maple Marinade/Brine is a great way to add juiciness to lean roasts. Try it with grass-fed cuts such as sirloin tip, top round, cross-rib, and lean cuts of pork such as loin or leg.

LAZY MAN'S SHORT RIBS

Family Meal, Rewarms Well, Great Leftovers

Serves 6

This recipe is lazy not because it relies on a convenience food, but because it's so simple and foolproof. It's perfect when you want to put a warm and comforting meal on the table and don't have time or energy for a lot of cooking steps. It does take a couple of hours to complete the cooking, but this can be done while you are doing something else, or even a day or two ahead. When you are ready to serve, simply pull the short ribs from the fridge, remove the congealed fat, and rewarm.

2 teaspoons chopped fresh rosemary	2 tablespoons chopped garlic
2 teaspoons chopped fresh thyme	1 cup dry red wine, plus more if needed
Salt and freshly ground black pepper	1 cup homemade beef stock (see page 168)
4 pounds bone-in English-cut beef short ribs	or canned low-sodium chicken broth,
4 cups diced onions	plus more if needed
1 cup diced celery	2 bay leaves
1 cup diced peeled carrots	

1 Preheat the oven to 350°F.

2 Combine the rosemary, thyme, 2 teaspoons salt, and 1 teaspoon pepper in a large bowl. Toss with the short ribs and arrange the ribs in a large Dutch oven. Spread the onions, celery, carrots, and garlic over the meat, then pour in the red wine and stock and add the bay leaves. Cover and bake for 1 hour.

3 Remove the lid, stir so that most of the meat is on top of the vegetables, and bake, uncovered, for 30 minutes. Stir and turn the short ribs to help everything brown evenly, and check to make sure there is still liquid in the pot. If not, add more wine or stock. Replace the lid and bake for 30 minutes more, or until the meat is fork-tender. If not tender, continue to cook, covered, checking every 20 minutes.

4 Remove the meat and arrange on a platter. Discard the bay leaves and degrease the sauce. Boil the sauce to reduce if it's too thin. Season to taste with salt and pepper, spoon the vegetables and sauce over the meat, and serve.

Alternative Cuts: Any chuck roast that you can cut into chunks or brisket, cut into chunks. This method is also excellent with tougher cuts of beef or lamb, such as oxtails, lamb neck, beef neck bones, or lamb or beef shanks. If using neck, increase the amount to 6 pounds. Allow 1 shank per person for lamb and about ¾ pound beef shank per person. Beef shanks and oxtails will take 1 hour or more additional cooking time.

Cook's Notes

- You can easily adapt this recipe for a slow cooker. Brown the short ribs first in olive oil, and then brown the vegetables in the fat. Place everything in the slow cooker and follow the manufacturer's instructions for the correct time and temperature for beef stew.

- Serve this dish with steamed bulgur or brown rice.

GRILL-BRAISED VIETNAMESE SHORT RIBS WITH SWEET VINEGAR GLAZE

Fit for Company
Serves 4

Five-spice powder, a Chinese flavoring, is also popular in Vietnamese cooking. Star anise, which gives five-spice powder its characteristic licorice flavor, is also used whole in this braise. See page 173 for more on grill-braising.

Five-Spice Rub

- 1 teaspoon Chinese five-spice powder
- 1 tablespoon mild chile powder, such as New Mexico or California, or sweet Hungarian paprika
- 2 teaspoons salt
- 1 teaspoon freshly ground black pepper
- 1 teaspoon dark brown sugar

- 8 flanken-style beef short ribs (about 4 pounds)
- 2 tablespoons peanut oil
- 2 cups chopped onions
- 1 tablespoon minced garlic
- 2 teaspoons minced fresh ginger

- 3 cups homemade beef stock (see page 168) or canned low-sodium chicken broth
- 2 tablespoons Asian fish sauce
- ¼ cup plus 2 teaspoons rice vinegar
- 1 tablespoon soy sauce
- 3 tablespoons dark brown sugar
- 1 whole star anise
- ½ pound thick fresh Asian rice noodles or cooked dried linguine

Garnish

- 2 cups bean sprouts
- Thinly sliced scallions
- Fresh cilantro sprigs

1. **Rub:** Combine all the ingredients in a small bowl and sprinkle generously all over the ribs. For the best flavor, place the ribs on a platter, wrap in plastic wrap, and let rest for at least 2 hours at room temperature, or refrigerate overnight.

2. Set up a gas grill for indirect cooking. Sear the ribs over medium-high heat for 1 to 2 minutes per side, turning, until all sides are nicely browned but not charred. Set aside. Once the ribs are cool enough to handle, tie the meat to the bones with butcher's twine.

3. Heat a large Dutch oven over medium heat on the stovetop. When it is hot, add the oil. Add the onions and cook until soft, about 5 minutes. Stir in the garlic and ginger and cook, stirring, for 1 minute more. Add the stock, fish sauce, ¼ cup of the rice vinegar, the soy sauce, 1 tablespoon of the brown sugar, and the star anise and bring to a boil. Add the short ribs.

4   Place the pot over the area of the grill with no fire. Cover the pot, close the grill lid, and cook for 30 minutes. (If your grill has a thermometer, it should read about 350°F.) Check, and if all the ribs are not submerged in the simmering liquid, move them around so that the uncovered ones spend time in the liquid. Cover the pot and adjust the heat if necessary to maintain a slow simmer. Check again 30 minutes later, move the ribs around if necessary, and cover the pot. After another 30 minutes, check the ribs for tenderness. You should just be able to pierce them with a fork, but they should not be falling apart. If not tender enough, continue to cook, covered, checking every 15 minutes. Remove the ribs and set aside.

5   Degrease the sauce and taste: It should have a nice rich flavor. If it is too thin, return the sauce to direct heat and reduce until flavorful. Set the pot aside. (*At this point, you can cover and refrigerate the sauce and meat overnight.*)

6   To make the sweet vinegar glaze, pour 1 cup of the sauce into a small saucepan and stir in the remaining 2 teaspoons rice vinegar and 2 tablespoons brown sugar. Place over high heat and boil the glaze until it becomes syrupy, about 5 minutes. Brush the glaze over one side of each rib and place the ribs on the grill over medium-high heat. Grill until the glaze begins to bubble and darken slightly. Turn the ribs and brush with the glaze. Continue to brush and glaze, turning frequently, until all sides are nicely glazed. Transfer the ribs to a warm pan or platter and drizzle the remaining glaze over them.

7   Meanwhile, bring a pot of water to a boil. Cook the noodles for 3 to 5 minutes, or until tender; drain. To serve, divide the noodles among four large shallow soup bowls. Ladle over the sauce. Mound the bean sprouts over the top. Remove any remaining twine from the ribs and place 2 ribs, and any juices, on top of the noodles in each bowl. Sprinkle with scallions and a few sprigs of cilantro.

Alternative Cuts: Boneless short ribs. English-cut short ribs. Any boneless chuck roast, cut into 3-inch chunks; beef country-style ribs; or brisket, cut into 3-inch chunks. Beef shank or oxtails (increase the cooking time by at least 1 hour).

Cook's Note
- This recipe is a more concentrated version of the classic Vietnamese soup pho. To turn it into pho, use 6 cups chicken stock and ¼ cup fish sauce and don't reduce the sauce. To serve 8, allow 1 short rib per person.

Leftovers
- Serve the more concentrated dish one night, then add stock and serve as a soup another day for lunch.

COCIDO FROM CASTILLA–LA MANCHA

Fit for Company, Rewarms Well, Great Leftovers, Grass-Fed Beef

Serves 6 to 8

Despite the fact that paella is ubiquitous in restaurants all over Spain, it's not the national dish. That title goes to *cocido*. *Cocido* is a boiled dinner made up of chickpeas, broth, fresh and cured meats, and various vegetables. It can be served in one bowl, or its components can be divided into courses: a soup course, a bean course, and a meat course. It may include condiments, or it may not. Every region has its own variation. One of the most famous versions is *cocido Madrileño,* from Madrid. It's such a revered dish that many restaurants there specialize in just *cocido*. In fact, in the narrow streets behind the palace, there is a whole neighborhood of *cocido Madrileño* restaurants. Sunday lunch seems to be the time for families to pursue *cocido.*

One restaurant, named Lhardy, is so popular that a line usually stretches down the stairs and onto the street. And it produces so much extra broth that passers-by are invited to wander in, fill up a cup, and stand around, perhaps purchasing some warm meat-filled turnovers to accompany it. My recipe is an amalgam of two or three versions I had in Madrid and in a neighboring region, Castilla–La Mancha.

2 cups (1 pound) dried chickpeas, picked over and rinsed	Freshly ground black pepper
4 quarts homemade beef stock (see page 168) or canned low-sodium chicken broth	1 pound semicured Spanish chorizo, homemade (see page 414) or store-bought
1 serrano ham bone (optional; see Cook's Notes)	1 pound Spanish blood sausages (*morcillas*; see Sources)
½ pound fatty serrano ham trimmings, including bits of skin, fat, and lean meat (see Cook's Notes)	6 chicken leg quarters, legs and thighs separated
1 ½-pound chunk pancetta or salt pork	6 carrots, peeled and cut in half
3 pounds bone-in beef short ribs, brisket, or shanks	3 tablespoons chopped garlic
	3 medium onions
2 teaspoons Spanish paprika (*pimentón de la Vera*; see Sources)	4 medium leeks, white and pale green parts
½ teaspoon Spanish saffron threads or ⅛ teaspoon powdered saffron	2 small heads green cabbage, each cored and cut into 6 wedges
2 bay leaves	12 small red potatoes, scrubbed
	Salt
	¼ cup chopped fresh flat-leaf parsley

1   Soak the chickpeas in cold water to cover overnight; drain.

2   Combine the stock, chickpeas, ham bone (if using), ham trimmings, pancetta, beef, paprika, saffron, bay leaves, and 1 teaspoon pepper in a large Dutch oven and bring to a boil over medium-high heat. Turn down the heat and simmer for 1 to 1½ hours, or until the chickpeas and beef are almost tender.

3   Add the chorizo, blood sausages, chicken, carrots, garlic, onions, leeks, cabbage, and potatoes and simmer for 30 minutes, or until everything is tender and the chicken is fully cooked. Season to taste with salt and pepper.

4   Remove the meats and set aside. Remove the vegetables to a platter. Discard the bay leaves, ham bone, and skin. Cut the beef into chunks and discard the bones. Cut the sausages into 1-inch chunks. Slice the pancetta thickly. Arrange the meat on the platter with the vegetables and garnish with the parsley. Strain the broth and serve the broth and chickpeas separately.

Alternative Cuts: Tough, gristly cuts of bison, while not traditional, are ideal for this dish. Use shank, short ribs, or neck, and increase the cooking time before adding the sausages, vegetables, and chicken. Other beef choices include any boneless chuck pot roast cuts or rump, bottom round, or eye-of-round roast. You could also use a rolled and tied flank steak, skirt steak, or bottom sirloin flap steak (*bavette*). Sirloin tip and chuck cross-rib roast are other good choices. Veal, beef, or pork tongue is also excellent in *cocido*. Or consider making it with tough cuts from grass-fed beef, such as shank, brisket, short ribs, and neck.

Cook's Notes

- Instead of a serrano ham bone, use a bone from any ham or throw in a ham hock.
- If you don't have serrano ham scraps, increase the pancetta to ¾ pound.
- I use Spanish paprika and saffron in this dish because of their rich taste.

CHINESE-STYLE BRAISED OXTAILS WITH BABY BOK CHOY

Fit for Company, Two-for-One, Rewarms Well, Great Leftovers

Serves 6

I've always been drawn to Chinese cooking because of the large range of exotic flavors and the frequent use of underappreciated fattier cuts such as pork belly, pork shoulder, and oxtails. My dear friend and talented home cook Edy Young often invites me to enjoy her Chinese cooking. Braised oxtails are a frequent dish on her table, and she shared this recipe with me. Licorice-flavored star anise gives the meat its characteristic flavor. You can use oxtails from traditional grain-finished beef or grass-fed beef, which, though leaner, will have ample fat. This dish is best made ahead.

4 pounds oxtails, most external fat trimmed

2 cups homemade beef stock (see page 168), canned low-sodium chicken broth, or water

2 whole star anise

6 ¼-inch rounds fresh ginger

2 cups halved and sliced onions

8 garlic cloves, sliced

½ cup soy sauce

3 tablespoons dark brown sugar

1 tablespoon Chinese brown bean paste (also called ground bean paste)

12 baby bok choy, washed

½ cup thinly sliced scallions (white and light green parts)

Steamed rice (I use jasmine rice), for serving

1   Arrange the oxtails in a large Dutch oven. Add the stock, star anise, ginger, onions, garlic, soy sauce, brown sugar, and bean paste, making sure the oxtails are covered in liquid; if necessary, add water to cover. Bring to a boil, then reduce to a simmer and cook, partially covered, for 3 hours, or until the meat is almost falling off the bone. If not tender, continue to cook, checking every 30 minutes. The oxtails are best if cooled and refrigerated in their liquid for up to 3 days so that the surface fat congeals and the meat develops a rich, savory flavor.

2   When ready to serve, remove the congealed fat and bring the oxtails to a simmer. Heat for 10 minutes. If the sauce is thin, remove the oxtails and boil the sauce to reduce until it becomes flavorful. Don't overreduce, or the sauce will become too salty. Discard the star anise and ginger. Return the oxtails to the pot and rewarm while you cook the bok choy.

3   Bring a pot of salted water to a boil. Add the bok choy and cook for 3 to 4 minutes, or until tender. Drain.

4   To serve, place 2 bok choy in each of six shallow soup bowls. Ladle over the oxtails and sauce and sprinkle generously with the scallions. Serve steamed rice on the side.

Alternative Cuts: Beef or bison shanks.

Cook's Note

- Substitute snow peas, sugar snap peas, Napa cabbage cut into 6 wedges, Chinese broccoli (*gai lan*), regular broccoli, shiitake mushrooms, or Chinese mustard greens for the baby bok choy. Snow peas and sugar snap peas need only 1 to 2 minutes of cooking, while broccoli will need 5 to 6 minutes.

Leftovers

- Turn leftovers into chow mein: Remove the meat from the bones and cut into chunks or shred. Cook Chinese egg noodles until just tender. Toss the noodles with the meat, some scallion pieces, and slivers of yellow onion in a little oil in a wok or large skillet, moisten the noodles with just enough braising sauce to create a light sauce, and heat through. Garnish with thinly sliced scallions and serve.

ITALIAN-INSPIRED BRAISED OXTAILS WITH FRIED CAPERS AND SAGE LEAVES

Family Meal, Two-for-One, Freezes Well

Serves 6, with leftovers

I'm going to encourage you to serve this braised oxtail dish as Italians do, in courses. For a *primo* (first course), toss some of the braising sauce with your favorite pasta, such as linguine, spaghetti, or fettuccine, or, if you are so inclined, with homemade egg pasta cut into the wide noodles called pappardelle. There should be just enough sauce to generously coat the noodles: They should never be swimming in sauce. Add a sprinkling of freshly grated Parmigiano-Reggiano and dig in.

Then serve the oxtails napped with some braising sauce and garnished with the fried capers and sage, accompanied by oven-roasted cauliflower or fennel or an oven-roasted root vegetable, such as parsnips, celery root, turnips, or carrots. Another nice presentation is to serve the oxtails in a shallow bowl on top of some pureed celery root or mashed rutabaga.

5–6 pounds oxtails

2 tablespoons chopped fresh sage

Salt and freshly ground black pepper

3 tablespoons olive oil

1 large onion, chopped

1 large carrot, peeled and chopped

2 leeks, white and pale green parts, split and thinly sliced

2 celery stalks, chopped

3 anchovy fillets, minced

4 garlic cloves, minced

2 cups dry red wine (I use Italian)

¼ cup grappa, kirsch, or brandy (optional)

4 cups homemade beef stock (see page 168) or canned low-sodium chicken broth, plus more if needed

Zest of 1 lemon, removed in long strips with a vegetable peeler

2 bay leaves

6 fresh or canned plum tomatoes, chopped

3 tablespoons chopped fresh basil

Pasta of your choice (see headnote; 1 pound dried or 1½ pounds fresh)

Freshly grated Parmigiano-Reggiano

Garnish

3 tablespoons olive oil

30 fresh sage leaves

3 tablespoons capers, drained and patted dry on paper towels

1   Preheat the oven to 325°F.

2   Trim any external fat from the oxtails and sprinkle them all over with the chopped sage and salt and pepper. Heat a large Dutch oven over medium-high heat and add the oil. Fry the oxtails in batches, 2 to 3 minutes per side. Remove to a platter and set aside.

3   Pour off all but about 3 tablespoons of fat from the pot and add the onion, carrot, leeks, celery, and anchovies. Reduce the heat to medium, cover, and cook until the vegetables are soft and beginning to color, stirring occasionally, about 10 minutes. Stir in the garlic and cook for 1 minute more. Pour in the red wine and grappa (if using) and bring to a boil, scraping up any browned bits from the bottom of the pot. Boil until reduced to about ½ cup, 10 to 15 minutes.

4   Add the stock, lemon zest, bay leaves, and tomatoes. Return the oxtails and any juices to the pot, in layers if needed so that they're tightly packed. Cover, place in the oven, and cook for 3 hours, or until the meat is tender and almost falling off the bone. If not done, cover and cook longer, checking every 30 minutes. During the cooking, check the pot every hour or so to make sure there is sufficient liquid, adding stock if necessary. When the oxtails are tender, stir in the basil. (*At this point, you can cool the oxtails and sauce and then refrigerate separately overnight. The next day, remove all the congealed fat from the surface and continue with the recipe.*)

5   If you didn't refrigerate the dish, remove the oxtails and degrease the sauce. (If you did refrigerate it, reheat the sauce.) Discard the bay leaves and lemon zest. If the sauce is thin, boil to reduce it until just syrupy; don't reduce it too much, or the gelatin released from the oxtails will make the sauce very sticky. Season to taste with salt and pepper.

6   Bring a pot of salted water to a boil and cook the pasta. Meanwhile, prepare the garnish by heating the oil in a small nonstick skillet over medium-high heat. Add the sage leaves and cook, stirring, for about 1 minute, or until crisp and starting to brown. Remove with a slotted spoon to a paper towel and set aside. Add the capers to the pan and fry them for 1 to 3 minutes, or until they turn grayish brown and begin to crisp. Transfer the capers to a paper towel; save the oil.

7   When the pasta is done, toss with enough sauce to adequately coat it and serve as a first course with the cheese. While enjoying the pasta course, gently rewarm the oxtails in the remaining sauce.

8   To serve, place the oxtails and sauce in shallow serving bowls, top each with a few sage leaves and capers, and drizzle with some of the frying oil.

Alternative Cuts: Use only collagen-laden tough cuts. Good choices are beef shank, neck, cheeks, or tongue. Many cuts of bison are suitable because bison is generally tougher than beef, with more collagen. Besides the equivalent cuts mentioned above, you can use any bison chuck cut, especially hump or neck meat. Bison short ribs and brisket, cut into chunks, are good choices as well. This stew is also delicious made with veal shank, veal cheeks, or breast of veal, cut into pieces.

Cook's Notes

- Oxtails are typically sold as one whole tail that is cut between each joint, yielding rounds of meat in decreasingly smaller diameter from the rump end to the tip. Tails weigh 2½ to 3 pounds each, so you'll need 2 tails' worth of oxtails. Since the pieces near the tip of the tail are mostly bone, allow 1 large piece and 2 or 3 small pieces per serving.

- You can remove the meat from the bone before serving. Use a sharp paring knife to tease the meat from each section of bone, leaving it in small chunks. Don't bother trying to remove what little meat there is from the tip sections; serve them to those who like sucking on the bones.

Leftovers

- Remove the meat from the bones and combine it with the sauce. Serve the next day over polenta, pasta, or rice. Or make a baked pasta by tossing the meat and sauce with cooked penne, elbow macaroni, rigatoni, or another tube-shape pasta. Stir in 2 cups ricotta cheese and 1 cup freshly grated Parmigiano-Reggiano or pecorino cheese, spread in a baking dish, and bake until bubbly and browning on the surface, about 40 minutes.

PEPOSO ALLA FORNACINA
(BAKER'S PEPPERY BEEF SHANKS)

Family Meal, Rewarms Well, Great Leftovers
Serves 6

Going to Portland, Oregon, is always a pleasure for me. Not only is it a lovely and friendly city, but I know I will eat well because I always have at least two meals at Nostrana restaurant—and, if I am lucky, a meal at the owner-chef Cathy Whims's house. Cathy and I have frequently traveled in Italy as part of a food research group led by the Italian food writer Faith Willinger. This recipe from Tuscany has decidedly peasant origins and relies on very few ingredients. Most of the flavor comes from the large amounts of garlic and black pepper and a whole bottle of red wine.

It's best to make this a day ahead.

4–5 pounds beef shank (6 shank rounds), sliced across the bone into 1½-inch-thick slices	4 4-inch-long fresh rosemary sprigs
2 garlic heads, separated into cloves and peeled	1 tablespoon tomato paste
Salt and freshly ground black pepper	1 750-ml bottle red wine (I use Chianti), or more if needed

1 Preheat the oven to 300°F.

2 Combine the beef, garlic, 1½ teaspoons salt, 2½ tablespoons pepper, and the rosemary in a large Dutch oven. Place the tomato paste in a small bowl and whisk in some red wine to thin it out. Add the tomato mixture and the rest of the wine to the pot. The liquid should cover the meat; add more wine if needed. Bring to a boil, cover, and place the pot in the oven. Cook for 2½ to 3 hours, checking every 30 minutes, until the meat is tender and falling off the bone. Discard the rosemary sprigs. Cool, cover, and refrigerate overnight.

3 Remove the fat from the surface of the cooking liquid. The meat can be served on the bone, but Cathy likes to pull it off the bone in big pieces, then serve each diner a marrowbone. Rewarm the *peposo*. If the sauce is not concentrated enough, boil to reduce it to a slightly syrupy consistency. Season to taste with salt and more pepper.

Alternative Cuts: Boneless beef chuck roast or brisket, cut into 2-inch chunks; oxtails; or beef cheeks.

Cook's Note

- Cathy likes to serve this dish on garlic bruschetta. Cut Italian or French bread into 1-inch-thick slices and toast on a grill or under the broiler. Rub with a cut clove of garlic and brush with good extra-virgin olive oil.

Leftovers

- Remove the meat from the bones, chop, and serve with the sauce over fresh pasta, such as pappardelle or linguine, or soft polenta.

- Make a savory pie by substituting 4 to 6 cups chopped or shredded *peposo* meat for the filling in Irish Beef-Cheek Pie with Stout (page 222). Use only the crust part of the recipe.

FRIULI-STYLE BRAISED BEEF CHEEKS

Family Meal, Fit for Company, Great Leftovers

Serves 4

Leave it to the Italians to make the most of these truly delicious morsels. Beef cheeks, when cooked long and slow, transform from tough to beautifully flavored and unctuously silky meat. That's because the abundant collagen in this heavily used muscle turns into gelatin, giving the meat great texture. Other tough cuts, such as shank and neck, will do, but they are not quite as tender as cheeks.

The idea for this recipe came from several trips to Friuli, a region of Italy that borders Austria and Slovenia. The paprika and juniper show the influence of the neighboring Austro-Hungarian region. Speck is a smoked form of prosciutto popular in Friuli and other areas of Italy bordering Austria. If you can't find it, use Westphalian ham, the German smoked ham, or a lean smoky bacon.

3 tablespoons all-purpose flour	2 tablespoons minced garlic
Salt and freshly ground black pepper	½ ounce sun-dried tomatoes (not oil-packed),
1 teaspoon ground sage	soaked in hot water for 30 minutes, drained,
1 tablespoon sweet Hungarian paprika	and sliced
4 beef cheeks (about 4 pounds), trimmed	½ cup grappa, kirsch, or brandy
5 tablespoons olive oil	2 cups homemade beef stock (see page 168)
1 cup dry white wine	or canned low-sodium chicken broth,
¼ pound speck (see Sources), Westphalian ham,	plus more if needed
or lean smoky bacon, chopped	¼ cup Dijon mustard
1 cup thinly sliced shallots	8 juniper berries, crushed
⅓ cup chopped celery	4 teaspoons chopped fresh rosemary
¼ cup chopped peeled carrot	1 tablespoon chopped fresh sage

1   Preheat the oven to 325°F.

2   Combine the flour, 1 tablespoon salt, 2 teaspoons pepper, the ground sage, and paprika in a shallow bowl. Dredge the cheeks in the mixture, shaking off any excess flour.

3   Heat a large Dutch oven over medium-high heat. Add 3 tablespoons of the oil and brown the cheeks on all sides, about 7 minutes. (You may need to do this in batches.) Remove the cheeks from the pot and set aside. Pour off all but 2 tablespoons of the fat. Pour in the white wine, stir, and bring to a boil, scraping up any browned bits from the bottom of the pot. Pour the wine into a bowl and reserve.

4   Reduce the heat to medium. Add the remaining 2 tablespoons oil and the speck to the pot and cook for 1 to 2 minutes. Add the shallots, celery, carrot, garlic, and sun-dried tomatoes and cook, stirring, for about 5 minutes. Add the grappa and stock and stir, scraping up any browned bits from the bottom of the pot. Stir in the reserved wine, mustard, juniper berries, 2 teaspoons of the rosemary, and the fresh sage and return the cheeks to the pot. Bring to a boil, cover, and place in the oven. Cook for 2 to 3 hours, or until the beef is very tender, turning over the cheeks every hour and adding more stock if needed.

5   Remove the pot from the oven and degrease the sauce. If it's too thin, remove the cheeks from the sauce and bring to a boil to concentrate the flavors.

6   Stir in the remaining 2 teaspoons rosemary and season the sauce with salt and pepper. Cut the meat into large chunks, and rewarm if necessary. Serve with plenty of sauce.

Alternative Cuts: Beef shank, short ribs, brisket, or any pot roast cut from the chuck. These cuts will take less time to cook than beef cheeks.

Cook's Notes

- With this dish, unlike most braised dishes, it's best to degrease the sauce while it's still hot. So much gelatin is released from the cheeks during cooking that the fat will emulsify into the sauce as it cools.

- Serve with oven-roasted root vegetables, such as parsnips, carrots, rutabaga, and boiling onions. This is also nice with a celery root puree, or you can simply serve the cheeks over mashed potatoes.

Leftovers

- Dice any leftover cheek meat and toss with fresh pasta, or combine with cooked penne, sprinkle with a diced smoked cheese, such as smoked mozzarella, and bake until hot.

IRISH BEEF-CHEEK PIE WITH STOUT

Family Meal, Comfort Food, Great Leftovers
Serves 4 to 6

This is Anne-marie Ramo's modern-day upgrade of the Irish pub standard, steak and kidney pie. Cooking the beef cheeks slowly melts the fat and softens the collagen, creating a silky sauce with succulent bites of meat. The sauce gets a boost of flavor from richly flavored stout, vinegar, and Worcestershire. This hearty one-dish meal needs only a salad and maybe some Irish soda bread for soaking up the sauce.

¼ cup all-purpose flour
Salt and freshly ground black pepper
2 teaspoons sweet Hungarian paprika
1 tablespoon chopped fresh thyme
3 slices thick-cut bacon (about ¼ pound), cut crosswise into ½-inch-wide strips
2½ pounds beef cheeks, trimmed and cut into 1-inch pieces
1 red onion, thinly sliced
½ cup sliced shallots
2 cups thinly sliced leeks (white and pale green parts)
1 pound mushrooms, sliced
1 12-ounce bottle Guinness or other stout or porter
¼ cup malt vinegar or cider vinegar

2 teaspoons Worcestershire sauce
2 bay leaves
3 fresh thyme sprigs
2 cups homemade beef stock (see page 168) or canned low-sodium chicken broth

Pie Dough
1½ cups self-rising flour
½ teaspoon salt
¼ teaspoon freshly ground black pepper
½ cup lard (preferably homemade; see page 434) or nonhydrogenated vegetable shortening
2–4 tablespoons cold water
1 large egg yolk, mixed with 1 teaspoon milk

1. Combine the all-purpose flour, 1 tablespoon salt, 2 teaspoons pepper, the paprika, and chopped thyme in a shallow bowl; set aside.

2. Cook the bacon in a large Dutch oven over medium heat until just brown and crisp. Remove with a slotted spoon and set aside. Dredge the beef cheeks in the seasoned flour, shaking off any excess, and brown on all sides in the bacon fat, 5 to 10 minutes. (You may need to do this in batches.) Remove the meat from the pot and set aside.

3. Drain all but 2 tablespoons of fat from the pot. Add the red onion, shallots, and leeks and cook until soft and beginning to brown, about 10 minutes. Return the bacon and the beef to the pot and add the mushrooms, stout, vinegar, Worcestershire, bay leaves,

thyme sprigs, and stock. Bring to a simmer, scraping up any browned bits from the bottom of the pot. Cover and simmer for 2 to 3 hours, or until the meat is tender.

4   Remove the pot from the heat. Discard the bay leaves and thyme sprigs. If the sauce is too thin, remove the solids and boil to slightly thicken. Degrease the sauce, then season to taste with salt and pepper. Return the solids to the pot and reheat, then transfer to a 10-inch deep-dish pie plate or an 8-cup casserole dish and allow to cool, or cover and refrigerate overnight.

5   Preheat the oven to 400°F.

6   **Dough:** Place the self-rising flour in a large bowl and add the salt and pepper. Cut in the lard until it is in pea-sized pieces. Sprinkle with 2 tablespoons water and mix. Add more water if needed to form a soft dough. Cover with a towel and let rest for 10 minutes.

7   On a lightly floured surface, roll out the dough ⅛ inch thick with a diameter 2 inches greater than your pie dish. Cut a 2-inch round from the exterior of the pastry circle and lay it around the rim of the pie dish. Dampen it with water, then put the pastry lid in place. Trim and crimp the edges. Cut a few small steam holes in the center of the crust with a sharp paring knife and brush with the egg yolk mixture.

8   Bake for 15 minutes, then lower the oven temperature to 350°F and bake until the crust is golden, 30 to 45 minutes more. Serve each guest a chunk of crust and some of the filling.

Alternative Cuts: Any cut of beef chuck, short ribs, brisket, or shank meat cut from the bone. Adjust the cooking time accordingly, testing after 2 hours. This recipe works very well with tough cuts of bison or grass-fed beef, also.

Cook's Notes

- If you are looking for a more traditional steak and kidney pie, substitute 2 pounds cubed boneless chuck roast and ½ pound cubed beef kidneys for the beef cheeks (reduce the cooking time to 1½ to 2 hours).

- The dough is excellent for any savory pastry, such as homemade potpie or meat-filled pasties or turnovers. Make a double or triple recipe, divide, shape into disks, and freeze the extra dough for quick use when you have leftover roasted or braised meat to convert into another meal.

Beef Tongue and Liver

I love tongue. There's no meat on the animal that is as soft and unctuous.

In the late-nineteenth and early-twentieth centuries, tongue was a sought-after luxury cut, prized for its great texture and flavor. Today, even though there is only one tongue per animal, it's still a bargain cut. It reheats well, it's a classic filling for tacos, and it makes a great sandwich too. I like pairing it with a good sharp mustard and horseradish, but there are those who opt for coleslaw, Russian dressing, and rye bread.

Tongue is very perishable, so freshness is important. Buy it from a store that sells a lot of it — Mexican, kosher, and Eastern European butchers are a good bet — or special-order it.

Beef liver, too, has its rewards at the table. Cook it properly — it should remain pink in the center — and it will be tender and succulent.

Good liver should smell fresh, with no sour or off odors. It doesn't freeze well, so don't buy frozen. The butcher will usually get rid of the membrane that encases the liver, but if not, remove it, along with any veins or sinews, yourself.

MEXICAN-STYLE POACHED BEEF TONGUE TACOS

Two-for-One, Rewarms Well

Serves 4 or 5, with leftover tongue

I am lucky to have the Vega family, who originally hail from the Mexican state of Michoacán, as neighbors. Elvia Vega grew up in a family of good cooks who love to entertain, and she seizes upon every occasion to have a fiesta: christenings, birthdays, engagement parties, the first day of spring. When it comes to the food, it's always tacos with all the trimmings — rice, beans, salsas, pickled vegetables — and lots of cold beer. My favorite is her poached beef tongue taco. I always go home with leftovers to rewarm for lunch the next day.

Tongue has a soft and succulent texture, yet it does not fall apart even when it is cooked to very tender. Its taste is mildly beefy, not unlike poached brisket. The meat is rich, so a little goes a long way.

While this tongue is great diced as a filling for tacos, it also makes a great main course with salsa verde, some Mexican-style rice, and freshly cooked pinto beans.

1 whole beef tongue, 1½ to 2½ pounds	**Taco Fixings**
2 bay leaves	12–15 corn tortillas
4 cloves	Salsa Verde, homemade (page 260)
4 black peppercorns	or store-bought
4 allspice berries	Pico de Gallo, homemade (page 259)
1 medium onion	or store-bought
1 garlic head	Mexican Pickled Vegetables (recipe follows)
3 dried ancho, mulato, or guajillo chiles,	Finely chopped sweet onions
or a combination	Chopped fresh cilantro
Salt and freshly ground black pepper	Lime wedges
	Tabasco or other hot sauce

1   Cut the tongue in half lengthwise. Place it in a large pot and add the bay leaves, cloves, peppercorns, allspice, onion, garlic, chiles, 2 tablespoons salt, and water to cover by about 2 inches. Bring to a boil, reduce the heat to a low boil, and cook for 3 to 4 hours, or until the tongue is very tender. (Taste a bit to be sure.) Transfer the tongue to a plate, strain the broth, and reserve.

2 When the tongue is cool enough to handle, use one hand to hold the tongue and peel off the tough outer skin with the other (this is easiest to do while the tongue is still warm). Trim away any loose gristle, bone, or fat. Keep warm.

3 Preheat the oven to 350°F.

4 Warm the tortillas by wrapping them in aluminum foil and placing them in the oven for 10 to 15 minutes.

5 Cut the tongue into ½-inch cubes, transfer to a serving bowl, and season to taste with salt and pepper. Fill each tortilla with some of the tongue and arrange on a platter. Let guests add their own "fixings" at the table.

Alternative Cuts: Brisket, short ribs, cross-rib roast, or rump roast. Beef shanks and beef cheeks have a similar texture to tongue when cooked to very tender. The time for cooking all these meats will vary; test after 2 hours. For a real treat, try bison tongue. You can also use veal or pork tongue in an equivalent amount; they will take less time to cook.

Cook's Note
- Use the leftover cooking broth to cook beans or to make bean or vegetable soup.

MEXICAN PICKLED VEGETABLES

Makes 3 quarts

One of the joys of visiting a taco stand is the self-service salsa bar. Besides an array of salsas, there is always a container of pickled vegetables consisting mainly of whole or sliced jalapeño chiles, a few sliced carrots, and sliced onions. These are eaten alongside the taco or sometimes as a garnish. For me, the jalapeños are usually too hot, but I do love eating the less-spicy carrots and onions. My neighbor Elvia Vega likes to pickle vegetables, but she uses bell peppers, cauliflower, and carrots, with a little heat from some sliced jalapeños. It's like a Mexican version of Italian giardiniera, and I love it with any sandwich or burger as well.

This recipe makes a large batch, but it keeps well in the refrigerator. Packed into glass jars, it's a nice gift.

When refrigerated, the olive oil will congeal, so let the mixture come to room temperature before stirring the oil and serving.

2 cups extra-virgin olive oil

1 medium onion, sliced

5 garlic cloves, peeled

1 cauliflower, cored and broken into small florets

3 carrots, peeled and cut into ¼-inch-thick rounds

1 pound small boiling onions, peeled

1 red or yellow bell pepper, cored, seeded, and sliced into ¼-inch-wide strips

8 jalapeño chiles, stemmed, seeded, and thinly sliced

2½ cups white vinegar

1 teaspoon cloves

2 teaspoons allspice berries

2 teaspoons coriander seeds

1 teaspoon cumin seeds

1 tablespoon black peppercorns

2 tablespoons dried oregano (I use Mexican)

6 bay leaves

Salt

1 Heat the oil in a Dutch oven over medium heat. Add the sliced onion and the garlic and cook for 5 minutes, or until the onion is soft. Add the cauliflower, carrots, boiling onions, bell pepper, and jalapeños. Cover and cook until the vegetables are crisp-tender, about 7 minutes. Add the vinegar, cloves, allspice, coriander, cumin, peppercorns, oregano, bay leaves, and 1 tablespoon salt. Bring to a boil and boil for 2 minutes. Taste a piece and add more salt if needed.

2 Pack, while still hot, into clean hot canning jars or storage tubs. Seal with the lids, then allow to cool to room temperature before refrigerating. (*The vegetables keep in the refrigerator for up to 2 months.*)

BEEF LIVER WITH CHORIZO, FRESH PIMIENTOS, AND SHERRY

Cheap Eats, In a Hurry
Serves 4

Fresh pimientos have a rich, deep sweet pepper flavor. They're in season at the end of summer and can often be found at farmers' markets. If they're not available in your area, use red bell peppers. Some Spanish-style chorizo is sold fully cured; it is firm and dry and is best eaten as is. Others, called *semicurado* (semicured), are dried for only a week or so and are still soft to the touch; these are best used for cooking, sliced or whole. You can make your own semicured chorizo (see page 414) or buy it from Spanish food suppliers (see Sources).

¼ cup olive oil

2 links semicured Spanish chorizo (see headnote), cut into ¼-inch-thick rounds

2 fresh pimientos or 1 large red bell pepper, cored, seeded, and cut into ¼-inch-wide strips

2 cups thinly sliced onions
Salt and freshly ground black pepper

¼ teaspoon ground allspice

2 teaspoons Spanish paprika (*pimentón de la Vera*; see Sources)

¼ teaspoon ground ginger

1¼ pounds beef liver, membrane removed, cut into ¼-inch-thick slices, then cut crosswise into ½-inch-wide strips

1 cup dry Spanish sherry

1 tablespoon sherry vinegar

2 teaspoons chopped fresh sage
Lemon wedges

1 Heat 1 tablespoon of the oil in a large heavy skillet over medium heat. Add the chorizo and fry, turning once or twice, until just beginning to brown on both sides, 3 to 5 minutes. Remove with a slotted spoon and set aside.

2 Add the pimientos, cover, and cook until soft and fragrant, stirring from time to time, about 10 minutes. Stir in the onions, cover, and cook, stirring occasionally, for 10 minutes, or until the onions are soft and just beginning to color. Remove the vegetables and set aside.

3 Combine 1 teaspoon salt, ½ teaspoon pepper, the allspice, paprika, and ginger in a small bowl and sprinkle over the liver slices to fully coat. Add the remaining 3 tablespoons oil to the pan and heat over medium-high heat. Add the liver and cook, stirring, until firm but still pink when cut into, 3 to 4 minutes. Remove and set aside.

4   Pour off any excess fat from the pan. Add the sherry and vinegar and bring to a boil, scraping up any browned bits from the bottom of the pan. Boil to reduce the liquid by half, about 5 minutes. Add the chorizo, vegetables, and sage and simmer for 5 minutes.

5   Return the liver to the pan and cook for 2 minutes more to warm through. Season to taste with salt and pepper. Serve with lemon wedges.

Alternative Cuts: Calf's liver or lamb's liver. If you are not a liver fan, use flank steak, New York strip steak, or fillet steak, cut into ½-inch-wide strips.

Cook's Notes
- You can use linguica or andouille instead of chorizo.
- Instead of fresh pimientos or bell peppers, you can use canned piquillo peppers, cut into strips. Add to the pan along with the vegetables in step 4.

Pork

Pork

RECITES

PORK CHOPS, STEAKS, CUTLETS, AND MEDALLIONS

PORK KEBABS

GROUND PORK, CHOPPED PORK, AND PORK SAUSAGES

PORK ROASTS

HAM

HAM LEFTOVERS

PORK STEWS, POT ROASTS, AND OTHER BRAISES

PORK RIBS

The Versatile Pig

It was a happy day indeed when the first wild pig wandered into the encampments of neolithic farmers some eight or nine thousand years ago. This early embodiment of what we now call a pig was an omnivorous opportunist and found easy pickings among the scraps of these less-than-tidy early farmers. But it wasn't long before the primitive agrarians began eating the pigs, then domesticating them and keeping herds.

The modern pig is still an omnivore, but most often it is fed a sustainable diet of grains, vegetables, and protein-rich soy. Nothing goes to waste, because every part of the pig can be consumed. No farm animal gives us more.

We are all familiar with the chop, the tenderloin, the slab of ribs. Maybe a roast when we entertain. But the entire pig offers many options for delicious dining — shanks, fresh ham, picnic shoulder, and pork belly, to name but a few parts. Even for the harried home cook, these cuts are easily approachable. In this chapter, and in the following chapter on preserved meats, you will find recipes for just about every cut currently available.

Changing Pork Choices

Essentially, all breeds of pigs fall into two categories: lard or bacon type.

Most American breeds are lard-type pigs, with stout legs and large, fat bodies. They put on weight easily and early, and the meat is abundantly interspersed with fat — which makes it very tasty. Berkshire, Duroc, Hampshire, and Gloucestershire Old Spot are all lard-type breeds.

Bacon-type pigs are lean and muscular and are popular because they produce lean bellies that are ideal for bacon. Only a few American breeds — such as Yorkshire and Tamworth (both of English origin) — are considered true bacon-type pigs.

In the years before World War II, lard was an essential part of the American diet, as well as an industrial lubricant and a component in munitions. Pigs were therefore raised to yield significant amounts of lard, and they grew to three hundred pounds or more before they were sent to market. But then things changed. After the war, industry substituted petrochemicals for lard, and by the 1980s, pigs were bred to have less body fat and leaner meat. Instead of embracing the diversity offered by the many distinct breeds, conventional pork producers began to select and crossbreed pigs to adapt to the industrialized growing conditions of large indoor pens and a diet of mostly corn and soybeans. Although individual producers may raise different crossbreeds based on their desired characteristics (ability to adapt to weather, litter size, and other preferences that the farmer may have), the goal is always the same: to produce uniform and consistent pork. The result is a

MY IDEAL PORK

The pork I love best comes from a breed or crossbreed that is raised for its flavor, not its ability to be raised in confinement. The meat is well marbled, juicy (even when cooked to well-done), and boasts a distinct "porky" flavor.

Some friends raised a pig as a gift for my sixtieth birthday. It was a Hampshire, and it had lived a pampered life, fed on scraps from the restaurant Terra in the Napa Valley. No one named the pig; we just referred to it as "Dinner." Dinner was slaughtered at 350 pounds, and twenty chefs gathered for a pig-processing day. There was a portable barbecue for cooking the fresh cuts, and I led the team that preserved all the other parts. We made hams, sausages, salami, bacon, *lardo* (the utterly delicious Tuscan cured and aged fat), and head cheese, using the feet for extra gelatin. And we feasted on the best pork I've ever eaten — moist, succulent meat packed with porky flavor.

pig that grows quickly and efficiently to produce lean meat (31 percent leaner than pork before 1980), with a mild flavor — the "Other White Meat."

Heirloom Pork

"Heirloom pork" is an overall term that refers to old breeds that fell out of favor because they were less adaptable to industrial farming methods. Unlike commodity pork — whose characteristics are uniformity and consistency — heirloom pork is about diversity and variation. I buy heirloom pork because it tastes so much better than commodity pork, and I enjoy comparing the tastes and textural variations of the different breeds.

Now that more consumers want pork with great flavor and juiciness, the demand for heirloom breeds is growing. The following are a few of the heirloom breeds you may find at specialty grocers, farmers' markets, and on the Internet.

Berkshire. In comparative tastings of pork chops from several pig breeds, Berkshire comes in first. This lard-type pig has been known since around the mid-1600s, but in the last ten years or so, discerning consumers and chefs have shown an enthusiastic interest in it, and now Berkshire is the most common variety of heirloom breed sold. Many small operations that sell their meat at farmers' markets and on websites (see Sources) offer Berkshires raised in pasture, and some even sell USDA Certified Organic Berkshires (see page 240). This breed is also sold under the Japanese name Kurobuta, which translates as "black pig."

Duroc. This breed produces superior fresh meat, and it's also especially suited for making high-quality ham and bacon. It has a belly with just the right ratio of fat to lean and legs that are large and well marbled, without too much external fat. It does well in both pasture and CAFOs (concentrated animal feeding operations). Some producers, such as Vande Rose Farms (see Sources), sell Duroc nationally.

Gloucestershire Old Spot. This breed produces superior meat because of its ample body fat. It is known as an orchard pig, because it can be let loose to eat fallen fruit. Its ability to withstand harsh weather and rough conditions has made it popular with farmers that raise pigs in pasture.

Tamworth. This bacon-type pig produces excellent meat and superb bacon and ham. A forager, it has fans among pasture-raising pork farmers. It does well in forests and under rugged conditions.

Ossabaw Island. Recently developed from wild pigs that originated on an isolated island off the coast of Georgia, this breed is thought to be descended from pigs first brought to the New World by Spanish explorers and may be related to the Spanish breed Ibérico. Ossabaw are being raised in various parts of the country and produce delicious meat.

Mangalitsa. This unique breed — called the Wooly Pig because of its coat — originated in Austria-Hungary in the nineteenth century. It produces more subcutaneous back fat than any other breed. It also gives well-marbled, great-tasting meat at a very dear price — unless you have use for lots of lard.

Other breeds making a comeback include Red Wattle, Chester White, Choctaw, Yorkshire, Poland China, Large Black, Guinea Hog, Mulefoot, and Hereford. Each has its fans.

Some farmers cross two or more pure heirloom breeds to yield progeny with characteristics from each contributor breed. Plenty of excellent pork comes from crossbreeds.

Breed alone doesn't determine the taste and texture of heirloom pork. Other important factors include climate, feed, and whether the pigs are raised in pasture or in confinement buildings. So you need to look around and taste what's available to find what you prefer.

I recommend that you begin your adventure locally. If you are fortunate enough to live near a farmers' market where local pork farmers offer their meat, give it a try (check out www.eatwild.com for local sources). Query the farmer about what breed or crossbreed he or she raises. Ask what makes the pork special. If it's important to you, ask if the pigs are raised outdoors or in confinement.

Many small farms now offer their meat on websites (see Sources), and they are a great source for cooks who don't have access to heirloom pork where they live or for those who want to try many different heirloom breeds. Some sites, such as www.heritagefoodsusa.com, represent several small heirloom-breed farms, and their websites have lots of information about specific farms and farmers.

Pasture-Raised Pork

Farmers choosing to produce pasture-raised pork allow the hogs to live outdoors most of the year or, in areas of the country that have severe winters, in large open-hoop barns. Small houses of varying design allow sows to farrow and nurse their young on deep straw bedding that provides comfort and warmth. There is mud for pigs to wallow in and to keep themselves cool and their skin healthy. Famers who use the term "pasture raised" on labels are not prohibited from administering antibiotics in the feed, but most producers don't, because they are not needed. For the USDA to approve the label "no antibiotics administered," no subtherapeutic antibiotics can be given. If a sick pig needs antibiotic medication, the pig must be marked as such and sold into the ordinary commodity market.

Pasture-raised pigs are free to forage. When a farmer has forested land, the pigs can roam the woods, eating some of their favorite foods, such as acorns and other tree nuts, succulent roots, and wild mushrooms. Other farmers allow pigs to wander in fruit orchards, eating fallen fruits such as apples and pears. Foraging does not provide enough nutrition to maintain growth, so the pigs' diet is supplemented with grains, soy, nuts, vegetables, field crops, dairy products, and other foods, depending on the practices of the individual farmer. Some farms even plant crops such as corn and squash and let the pigs wander through, feeding themselves while fertilizing the soil with their manure. The result of raising hogs that spend their entire lives outdoors in pasture is that when the animals go to market, they are loaded with more porky goodness, with a higher pH so there will be less loss of moisture in cooking (see page 242), and the redder color that nature intended for pork. The animals are usually older and larger than commodity pigs, which means they have been given the time to develop more marbling and richer flavor.

Some extremely specialized farms, such as Becker Lane Organic Farm in Iowa (see Sources), finish some of their Berkshire pigs on acorns to produce highly marbled meat. In Oregon, a farm called Tails and Trotters (see Sources) finishes its

ABOUT THE COST

Pork from heirloom breeds — indeed, all specialty pork — costs more than commodity pork for several reasons: The pigs take longer to reach market weight; they may require a better quality of feed; they may produce smaller litters with a lower survival rate; and they don't thrive in the factory CAFO environment. Heirloom pigs do best when raised in pasture, and they require more attention and care from the farmer.

pigs on hazelnuts. I have eaten pork from both of these farms and can say that the meat was as good as that from the famed acorn-fed Ibérico pigs of Spain, equally succulent and rich in flavor.

USDA Certified Organic Pork

USDA Certified Organic pork comes from pigs that throughout their lives are fed only organic food — be it corn, soybeans, or any other feed. Pork labeled "USDA Certified Organic" can be from animals raised primarily indoors if the pigs have access to pasture, or from pigs raised entirely outdoors. Certified Organic pigs cannot be given any growth promotants or antibiotics. If antibiotics must be administered to a sick pig, the animal cannot be sold as USDA Certified Organic. The farms must be inspected through third-party audits; a number of organizations perform this task.

No specific breeds are required for pork to be USDA Certified Organic, but several Certified Organic producers have chosen to raise heirloom breeds (see Sources), and they usually state this on their labels and marketing materials.

Natural Pork

The USDA sets certain requirements for label claims. "Natural" refers to meat that is minimally processed: no added flavorings or coloring, no chemical preservatives, and no artificial or synthetic ingredients. But because the term refers only to how the meat is processed, not how the animals are raised, any raw pork meets these criteria, and therefore "natural" essentially means nothing.

A better term than "natural" would be "naturally raised," meaning that the pigs have not been given any antibiotics, growth promotants, animal by-products, or hormones. In fact, it is illegal to give hormones to any pig; nonetheless, you will see pork labeled "no hormones" (a practice that borders on deception because it implies that other pork may contain hormones). As with beef, so far the USDA has not granted permission to use "naturally raised" as a label term for any pork product.

Commodity Pork

"Commodity" pork by definition implies no identifying characteristics, so there will be little or no information available on a label about the breed, where the pork comes from, what the animal's living conditions were, or what it ate. Commodity pork producers typically administer four doses of antibiotics in the feed to stimulate growth, and the pigs are raised in CAFOs. The goal is uniformity and consistency. The pork chop you buy in the supermarket this week is pretty much the same as the one you bought last week, last month, or last year. This standardization is possible only with industrialized production. In most cases, the meat tastes fine, as long as you don't overcook lean cuts such as chops or loins.

TERMS AT A GLANCE

Pasture-Raised Pork
- Rarely given antibiotics (never given hormones, which are illegal for all pork)
- Raised outdoors during mild months and on deep bedding in open-hoop barns in the winter, with continuous access to pasture
- Farrowing (breeding) houses with deep straw bedding are provided
- Diet of corn, soy, whey, and other foodstuffs

USDA Certified Organic Pork
- No antibiotics (or hormones, which are illegal) are administered
- 100-percent organic diet of corn, soy, and other feed
- Can be raised indoors but must have access to pasture and spend some time outdoors
- Claim must be verified by approved third-party auditors

Natural Pork with label stating "raised without antibiotics"
- Cannot be administered antibiotics (or hormones, which are illegal)
- May be raised outdoors, but this is not required

Natural Pork with no other claims
- Essentially a term for commodity pork
- Diet may include animal by-products
- Can be given antibiotics (but not hormones, which are illegal)
- Can be raised completely indoors on CAFOs

Naturally Raised Pork
- Antibiotics (or hormones, which are illegal) cannot be administered
- May or may not spend its entire life indoors
- Term has not yet been approved for use

Commodity Pork
- Spends its entire life indoors in CAFOs
- Antibiotics are administered (but not hormones, which are illegal)
- Fed corn, soy, and other feed

How to Buy Pork

Pork isn't graded, as beef is, according to how well the meat is marbled. Most of the pork you'll find in the supermarket or at a conventional butcher shop will be lean. But there's no reason you can't look for pork with more marbling, even for leaner cuts like loin.

Another very important criterion in determining pork quality is its pH (a measure of acidity). In fact, pH is so important that some pork producers boast of a higher pH as a selling point when marketing their "premium" brand. The lower the pH, the more acidic the pork, and the more likely it will be to lose moisture and become hard and dry when overcooked. Of course there is no way for us to measure pH at the supermarket, but color is a good indicator. Basically, the redder the pork, the higher the pH. When you are perusing the meat case, look for pork with a deeper reddish hue, or select the meat that is the rosiest of the bunch.

Farmers' markets and more specialized butchers offer "specialty pork," which is a term that includes heirloom pork, antibiotic-free pork, USDA Certified Organic pork, pasture-raised pork, and unspecified breeds sold directly by small farmers. You have to rely on the seller to tell you about what you are buying, because there is no real way to tell one category from another once the meat is in the meat case. Remember, too, that some mighty fine pork may not have a fancy name. Your local farmer may not have a herd of pedigreed hogs, but if he or she raises the hogs with care, they'll produce well-marbled and delicious pork.

What to Look For

The best fresh pork will possess the following qualities:

- No blemishes or dark spots.
- No dried edges.
- Creamy white fat (not brownish or yellow). On chops and loin roasts, the fat should have been trimmed to about ¼ inch.
- Flecks of fat (marbling) running through the meat. Lean cuts (even from some heirloom breeds) from the loin, tenderloin, sirloin, and leg will have little or no marbling.
- A light red to reddish hue. Look for the reddest example of the cut you're buying. Keep in mind that color varies: cuts from the shoulder will be redder than cuts from the loin.
- A tight, fine grain (not coarse and stringy).
- For bone-in cuts, moist bones with streaks of light red running through them.
- Firm meat that springs back when pressed with a finger.
- No odor, except perhaps a faint porky aroma.

PALE, SOFT, AND EXUDATIVE (PSE) PORK

You bought a piece of pork that was sitting in a puddle on its Styrofoam tray. It was very pale, and it stayed squished when you poked it. Then you cooked it, and it was dry, tough, and tasteless.

This is pale, soft, and exudative (PSE) pork. PSE is caused by abnormal muscle metabolism, and it's the result of stress-ful handling of the pig before processing. In some breeds, when the animal is agitated, it releases lactic acid, resulting in acidic pork. The lower pH diminishes the ability of the muscle fibers to retain moisture, which slowly oozes from the pale meat.

PSE pork is not common, but a small percentage of it does reach the market. Now that you know how to recognize this flawed and inedible meat, don't buy it.

If the pork you buy is mushy, weepy, or sticky, or if it has a sour or ammonia-like odor, return it or throw it away.

Storing Pork

Fresh pork will keep for 2 to 4 days in the refrigerator and for 4 to 6 months in the freezer.

Cured pork — such as bacon, ham, and smoked sausage — will keep for 5 to 7 days in the refrigerator and 2 to 3 months in the freezer.

Primal Cuts of Pork

The compact pig is broken down into four primal cuts (see diagram, page 244):

- The **ham primal** (back leg and hip) gives us hams, sirloin, shanks, ham hocks, and pig's feet.
- The **loin primal** (most of the meat along the backbone) is typically cut into loin and rib chops and roasts; it also contains the tenderloin. These cuts fetch the highest prices. You can save a little money by buying the whole primal and getting the butcher to remove the spine (chine bone). Then you can easily cut it into smaller roasts and chops.
- The **belly primal** is usually turned into bacon and spareribs. Fresh belly is becoming very popular, and can be braised or roasted.
- The **shoulder primal,** which includes the upper shoulder, neck, and fore-leg, is divided into the arm portion — called the picnic — and the upper shoulder — called the Boston butt or pork shoulder butt. It also provides shanks and pig's feet. This primal offers the best-priced and most versatile meat.

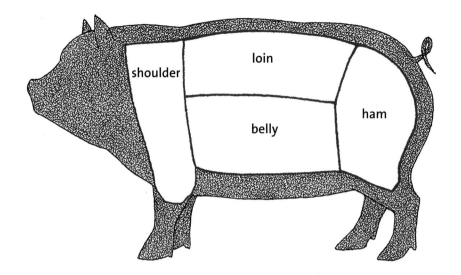

Good Cheap Cuts

Most of these cuts come from larger muscles on the pig, so there is a more ample supply available, and as a bonus, they are friendly to your wallet. Check the index to locate recipes for each of these cuts.

Pork Shanks (Pork Hocks or Pork Shin)

From the shoulder or ham primal, shanks appear most often in the market cured and smoked, and they are sold as ham hocks. In fact, your local producer may turn all shanks into ham hocks. If you can find them fresh, shanks are quite delicious. Because they are tough, with lots of sinew, they require long and slow braising to turn the collagenous sinew into unctuous gelatin, resulting in meat with a soft, silky texture. Shanks are also ideal for soups and stocks. Cooked until tender, the meat can be used in recipes as a substitute for leftover baked ham.

Pig's Feet (Pig's Trotters)

You won't find much meat on the feet, which come from the shoulder and ham primals, but they are great for flavoring stews and bean dishes. Because of their skin and gristle, they produce lots of gelatin, which adds body to sauces and stocks. Often brined or pickled in vinegar, pig's feet are enjoyed the world over, especially by the Germans, Mexicans, British, and Chinese. Some folks love the texture of the skin.

BEWARE "GUARANTEED TENDER" AND "ENHANCED" PORK

Cooking today's lean commodity pork can be tricky, and clinging to the old standard of cooking leaner cuts to temperatures of 160°F and above produces dry, hard, and altogether inedible results. What have many of our large commodity pork producers done to help us out with this dilemma? They "enhance" their pork by pumping a solution of salt, water, and phosphates directly into the meat.

This pumped pork is often labeled with such terms as "flavor enhanced," "extra tender," "marinated," or other equally misleading descriptions. The only real enhancement here is the bottom line of the packer, who is selling you at least 10 percent water at the price of pork. To my taste, this "enhanced" meat is soft and spongy (similar to the texture of most water-added hams). Furthermore, I don't need the extra salt, and I think phosphates give the meat a bitter, acrid taste.

I prefer to flavor-brine pork myself (see page 249), so that I can control the salt and added flavors. However, brining "enhanced" pork is pointless. Pay special attention when buying pork in the supermarket and look at the fine print under the name of the cut. If you see any of the phrases mentioned above relating to "tenderness" and "juiciness," leave the meat in the store. Also, you cannot use "enhanced" pork for any preserved meat recipes that call for brining or curing.

Fresh Ham (Leg of Pork)

Cut from the ham primal, the legs, which make up 20 to 25 percent of the total meat on a pig, should be at the top of your meat-buying list. Meat from the leg is quite versatile: It can be roasted whole, broken down into smaller roasts, sliced for cutlets and steaks, and home-cured for hams (see page 444). Individual roasts cut from the leg, such as the top round (inside) and bottom round (outside), as well as the knuckle and sirloin, can be substituted for pork loin roast in most recipes. Leftover roasted pork leg can be used for sandwiches (see page 302). Diced meat can be used in stir-fries. Ground meat can be used in burgers, meat loaves, sausages, and pâtés. You may need to add a bit of extra fat.

Because fresh ham can be hard to find in the supermarket, you may need to special-order it. Individual leg roasts can be found at warehouse stores like Costco. Farmers' markets and websites are also good sources.

Pork Belly (Fresh Bacon)

From the belly primal, the pork belly with the ribs attached makes up 10 to 15 percent of the total meat of the pig. Some of the more talented small suppliers turn their bellies into smoked bacon, while others offer the belly only raw and uncured at farmers' markets and via the Internet. Making your own smoked bacon is pretty easy, so have a go (see page 438). Restaurant chefs have discovered fresh pork belly in a big way, and it is featured as a flavoring ingredient and a main course on many menus. There is reason for its popularity: It is very rich and has great flavor. It's usually braised, which contributes flavor and tenderizes the meat, then crisped by searing it on the stove top or in a very hot oven. You can substitute pork belly in many roast recipes that use Boston butt, picnic shoulder, and blade-end loin roast for slow-roasting or pot roasts. You can also substitute pork belly in recipes for stews using country-style ribs. You'll probably need to special-order pork belly. Suppliers at farmers' markets often sell it, and if you buy a whole or half pig, it will be included — that's reason enough to buy pork this way!

Pork Cheeks

Pork cheeks are used in stews and pasta sauces. They can also be substituted for shoulder meat or country-style ribs, and they can be used in any stew recipe; cooking times should be increased. Rich tasting and succulent, these are well worth searching out. Special-order them, ask your farmers' market supplier to save them for you, or order them on the Internet.

Boston Butt (Pork Shoulder Butt)

The shoulder, from the primal cut of the same name, is made up of the Boston butt and the picnic shoulder and accounts for about 20 percent of the meat on a pig. The Boston butt is usually very inexpensive and is the more versatile cut. Best of all, it has some of the tastiest meat on the pig. One of my favorite cuts, it's ideal for pot-roasting, stewing, slow-roasting, barbecuing, and preserving as confit. Cubes can be skewered; thin strips can be stir-fried. Sliced into steaks, strips, or country-style ribs, Boston butt can be grilled. It is the first choice for fresh sausages and salamis. It can be cured and smoked for shoulder hams and shoulder bacon (see page 442).

Cut into strips, Boston butt can be substituted in any recipe calling for country-style ribs. It can also be used in any roast pork recipe (cooking times will need to be increased) and in any pork pot roast recipe. Boston butt is the best cut to grind for any recipe using ground pork.

Picnic Shoulder Roast

The other half of the shoulder primal, the picnic shoulder is inexpensive, but it has less meat and more bone, skin, and sinew than the Boston butt. It still can be very tasty and takes well to braising, slow-roasting, and stewing. Broken down and trimmed of sinew and cartilage, the meat and fat can be used for making sausage.

Because of the nice amount of bone, the picnic shoulder is ideal for making soups and stocks. Cured in brine (*petit salé,* see page 447), it can be used to make a boiled dinner with cabbage and other root vegetables.

Pork Neck

There's not a lot of meat on the bones of the neck, which is from the shoulder primal, but what there is is great for flavoring stews, beans, and sauces. In some areas, pork necks may be sold brined and smoked. Some farmers' market suppliers use them to make pork stock to bottle and sell. You can use neck bones in stews; replace each ½ pound boneless meat with 1½ pounds neck bones.

Pork Liver

Pork liver is very inexpensive, yet when turned into a pâté or terrine, it becomes a luxury item. Because the liver is a filter organ, the better raised and fed the pig, the better tasting the liver. So seek out liver from small pork farmers — particularly from those who raise heirloom breeds of pigs organically in pasture.

Cooking Today's Pork

After years of telling cooks that all pork must be cooked to 160°F — which produced dried-out and inedible pork chops, tenderloins, and roasts — the USDA has relented. It has finally agreed with those of us who write recipes and tell our readers to cook pork to a much lower temperature. The agency now recommends cooking lean and tender cuts to an internal temperature of 145°F, followed by a 3-minute rest, which will cause the temperature to rise farther. This is a vast improvement over the old recommendation, and the results will be more palatable.

While well-marbled heirloom pork can be cooked to 145°F and still produce juicy chops, roasts, and tenderloins, I prefer to remove these cuts at 135°F to 140°F and give chops and tenderloins a 5-minute rest and roasts a 10- to 15-minute rest. The final internal temperature will rise to 140°F to 150°F. While the USDA says that pork cooked to 145°F is medium-rare, I consider that medium, which means the interior is faintly rosy pink. By the way, if you are worried about trichinosis, fear not: The spores are killed when pork reaches 138°F and is held there for just a few minutes.

And that old slogan of the National Pork Board, "The Other White Meat"? Gone. In general, most parts of today's pork are tender and can be used with dry-heat cooking methods, such as grilling, roasting, and broiling.

With moist-heat cooking (braising and stewing), meat is usually cooked to temperatures of 160°F to 190°F or more. These methods rely on the collagen turning into gelatin, as well as the ample fat in the meat, to produce tender and juicy results. Here the best way to determine doneness is to see how easily a fork can penetrate the meat — or to taste it.

Pork Doneness

The following charts are based on what I believe will give the best cooking results. The temperatures are slightly lower than what the USDA recommends. Those who are immunologically compromised or pregnant should cook pork to 160°F, as the USDA recommends. This is the safest temperature to destroy food-borne bacteria.

Use these temperatures for dry-heat methods. Because carry-over heat will vary depending on the size of the piece of meat and the intensity of the heat source, consult the individual recipes to determine exactly what internal temperature the meat should be when removed from the heat source, and follow the resting times given in the recipes.

Medium. This is an ideal range for lean tenderloin, loin cuts, and leg roasts. Fattier pork cuts, such as Boston butt, need a higher level of doneness for the best flavor.

MEAT	REMOVE FROM HEAT	IDEAL TEMPERATURE (AFTER RESTING)	USDA RECOMMENDS
Pork chops	135°F to 140°F	140°F to 145°F	145°F
Pork roasts	135°F to 140°F	140°F to 150°F	145°F

Medium-Well. The meat will usually be almost uniformly gray, with a pinkish tint near the bone. Fattier pork, such as Boston butt, is best cooked to this temperature or higher; the juices may be faintly pink. Well-marbled loin cuts from heirloom pork, such as the blade end of the loin, can be cooked to these temperatures.

MEAT	REMOVE FROM HEAT	IDEAL TEMPERATURE (AFTER RESTING)	USDA RECOMMENDS
Pork chops	145°F to 150°F	150°F to 155°F	N/A*
Pork roasts	145°F to 150°F	150°F to 160°F	N/A*

Well-Done. Meat is overcooked at this stage unless it is fatty and naturally juicy — cuts such as spareribs or Boston butt. Use cuts suitable for moist-heat cooking, such as blade pork chops. I do not recommend this degree of doneness for lean pork unless it has been flavor-brined.

MEAT	REMOVE FROM HEAT	IDEAL TEMPERATURE (AFTER RESTING)	USDA RECOMMENDS
Pork roasts and flavor-brined pork chops and roasts	155°F to 160°F	165°F to 170°F	N/A*

* The USDA does not provide temperatures for this degree of doneness.

Flavor-Brining

Those of you who are familiar with my recipes know that I love to flavor-brine meat. Flavor-brining ensures moist and tender pork, and it can also be used for lean cuts of beef and bison. Flavor-brining is the simple method of soaking the meat in a bath of salted, flavored water for a period of time prior to cooking. Through osmosis and diffusion, this liquid is transferred into the meat cells and helps tenderize the meat from within.

If you buy commodity pork, I recommend that you take the time to flavor-brine any lean cuts of pork from the loin, tenderloin, sirloin, and leg that you plan to cook with dry heat. (Be sure that the pork is not labeled "tender" or "enhanced," meaning that it already has been injected with brine; see page 245.)

Keep in mind a few simple rules when flavor-brining:

- Cool the flavor brine to at least 45°F before adding the meat.
- Always refrigerate meat while it is brining.
- Follow the recommended brining times. Large pieces of meat can take an overnight soak or longer, while small pieces, such as chops, need only 3 to 6 hours. It is possible to overbrine, which will cause the meat to become too salty.
- If you are not using one of my recipes, watch the salt. Saltier flavor brines take less time to work but are much more difficult to control and can easily result in oversalted meat.

BRINING TIMES

CUT AND THICKNESS	BRINING TIME
Kebabs, ¾- to 1-inch cubes	1 hour
Kebabs, 1½-inch cubes	2 hours
Pork chops, ½ to ¾ inch thick	2 hours
Pork chops, ¾ to 1 inch thick	3 hours
Pork chops, 1¼ to 2 inches thick	4 to 6 hours
Pork tenderloin	4 to 6 hours
Pork tenderloin, butterflied	2 hours
Boneless pork loin roast	24 hours
Bone-in pork loin roast	48 hours
Pork knuckle roast	24 hours
Boneless sirloin roast	24 to 36 hours
Boneless pork leg roast, rolled and tied	24 to 36 hours
Bone-in butt or shank-half pork leg	2 to 3 days
Whole bone-in pork leg	3 days

Flavor Brines for Pork Chops

These recipes make enough for 4 pork chops. For larger cuts, such as pork loin roasts, double or triple the recipe.

I use Diamond Crystal brand kosher salt in my flavor brine recipes. If you use Morton brand kosher salt, cut the amount by one quarter; if you use table salt, cut the amount by half.

Technique

1 Stir together the water (and any other liquid ingredients), salt, and sugar until dissolved. Stir in the ice and any other flavorings and cool the brine to 45°F or lower.

2 Place 4 pork chops in a zipper-lock bag. Pour in the flavor brine and seal the bag. Place the bag in a bowl in case it leaks and refrigerate for 2 to 6 hours, depending on the thickness of the chops (see Brining Times, above). Remove the chops, discard the flavor brine, and pat the chops dry. Proceed with the recipe, or wrap the chops in plastic wrap and refrigerate until ready to cook, up to 2 days.

BASIC FLAVOR BRINE

- 3 cups water
- ¼ cup salt (I use Diamond Crystal kosher salt)
- ¼ cup firmly packed light brown sugar
- 2 cups ice cubes

CARIBBEAN FLAVOR BRINE

- 2½ cups water
- ½ cup dark rum
- 3 tablespoons soy sauce
- 3 tablespoons salt (I use Diamond Crystal kosher salt)
- 3 tablespoons dark brown sugar
- 1½ tablespoons unsulfured molasses
- 1 tablespoon Worcestershire sauce
- 1 teaspoon ground allspice
- 1 tablespoon minced fresh ginger
- ½ teaspoon ground cinnamon
- 2 cups ice cubes

KENTUCKY FLAVOR BRINE

- 2¾ cups water
- ¼ cup bourbon
- ¼ cup salt (I use Diamond Crystal kosher salt)
- 3 tablespoons dark brown sugar
- 2 tablespoons sorghum molasses, Steen's Pure Cane Syrup, or unsulfured molasses
- 1 teaspoon Worcestershire sauce
- 2 teaspoons pure vanilla extract
- 2 cups ice cubes

STOUT AND MALT FLAVOR BRINE

- 2½ cups water
- ½ cup Guinness or other stout
- ¼ cup salt (I use Diamond Crystal kosher salt)
- 3 tablespoons malt syrup (see Sources) or real maple syrup
- 1 tablespoon A.1. Steak Sauce
- 2 cups ice cubes

TURKISH FLAVOR BRINE

3 cups water	1 tablespoon ground cumin
¼ cup salt (I use Diamond Crystal kosher salt)	¼ cup minced onion
2 tablespoons light brown sugar	2 tablespoons finely grated lemon zest
¼ cup pomegranate molasses (see Sources) or cherry syrup	2 tablespoons minced garlic
¼ cup chopped fresh mint	2 cups ice cubes

OTHER FLAVOR BRINE RECIPES

- Coffee-Maple Marinade/Brine (page 202)
- Cider Flavor Brine (page 278)

Pork Chops, Steaks, Cutlets, and Medallions

The versatile chop is by far the most popular cut of fresh pork. It can be cooked successfully with any type of dry heat: grilling, broiling, panfrying, deep-frying, sautéing, stir-frying, and baking. It pairs well with a host of flavors and ingredients.

My favorite chops, which are from the Berkshire breed, have ample marbling and a rich, porky flavor, but most specialty pork has enough marbling to provide flavorful, moist, and tender meat, even when it's cooked beyond 150°F. Commodity pork is quite lean, so don't overcook it; it benefits greatly from flavor-brining (see page 249).

What are usually labeled "chops" come from the loin. Slices cut from the shoulder, sirloin, and leg are usually called steaks. But when it comes to pork, "chops" and "steaks" are often used interchangeably. "Cutlet" usually refers to thin slices of tender boneless pork cut from the loin, leg, or sirloin. "Medallions" are thick slices cut from boneless cuts that have a small diameter, such as tenderloins.

Pork Chops, Steaks, and Cutlets at a Glance

From the Loin

Center-cut rib chop, bone in (rib-cut chop, rib end chop, rib chop). One of my top choices, with just enough fat and juicy meat. Has a great bone for gnawing. Should be 1 inch thick or more.

Top loin chop, boneless (strip chop, center-cut loin chop). Ask for chops from the rib area or look for ones with the most marbling. Often sold labeled only as "boneless pork loin chops"; also sold as America's Cut.

Blade chop, bone in (blade-end pork loin chop, pork chop end cut, blade steak). Composed of several muscles, this has more intramuscular fat and connective tissue than the rest of the loin. Very tasty and suitable for both dry-heat cooking and braising. Can be a little chewy, but has a great price.

Top loin chop, bone in (T-bone loin chop, strip chop, loin chop, center-cut loin chop, loin end chop, center loin chop). Has a characteristic T-shape bone and contains parts of the tenderloin and the top loin. Can be very lean and will dry out when overcooked. Buy at least 1¼ to 2 inches thick. Flavor-brine it unless well marbled.

Sirloin chop, bone in (sirloin steak, sirloin end chop). From the hip end of the loin; made up of several muscles and can contain part of the hip bone. Best when cut thick. Quite lean, so best flavor-brined; not suitable for cooking with long, moist heat. Can be a fairly inexpensive way to enjoy heirloom pork.

Sirloin, boneless (sirloin cutlet). See bone-in sirloin chops above. Can be pounded or tenderized for cutlets and schnitzel.

From the Shoulder

Blade steak, bone in or boneless (pork steak, shoulder steak, pork 7-rib cut, Boston butt steak). See blade chop.

From the Leg

Pork leg (fresh ham) steak, boneless (pork leg cutlets, top steak, bottom steak, tip steak, eye steak). When cut into thin slices, makes excellent scallops or thin cutlets.

MY FAVORITE PORK CHOPS

I'll make no bones about it; I like my pork chops on the bone. I love **blade-end pork chops** — the ones cut closest to the shoulder — because they have more fat. They can be a bit chewy, and yes, there are pockets of fat between the several muscle groups that must be trimmed away while eating. Blade chops can be hard to find, because most butchers cut them up into country-style ribs, but, boy, are they good.

I also love chops from the rib area, the porcine equivalent of beef prime rib. **Center-cut rib chops** from the loin can be grilled, panfried, broiled, or baked. If you can find an heirloom variety, such as Berkshire or Duroc, you won't need to flavor-brine them. For best results, choose chops cut 1¼ to 1½ inches thick; for grilling or baking, buy chops 2 to 2½ inches thick.

GRILLING PORK CHOPS

There is no better cooking method to complement the great flavor of Berkshire, Tamworth, Duroc, and other heirloom pigs than grilling. This simple method allows the porkiness of the meat to shine, with nothing but a little bit of smoke to accentuate it.

If you are grilling commodity chops from the supermarket, I recommend flavor-brining first (see page 249). Then the chops can be grilled as is or can be seasoned with a dry rub or spice paste (see pages 66–69). If you take care not to overcook the chops, you can use a marinade (see pages 63–66) instead of flavor-brining.

For best results, I recommend grilling bone-in chops that are cut 1½ to 2 inches thick, and allowing them to rest at room temperature for 1 hour before grilling.

Once you've mastered this simple technique, the only thing that makes each variation different is how you choose to add flavor to the chops. For any given recipe, you can choose from one or more flavor steps.

You can add flavors:

- Before you cook, with stuffings, marinades, flavor brines, dry rubs, and/or spice pastes.
- During cooking, by smoking, basting, and/or glazing.
- After the chops are cooked, with sauces, condiments (such as salsas, relishes, and chutneys), compound butters, and/or garnishes (such as lime or lemon wedges).

Tips for Grilling Pork Chops

THE FIRE

- Grill over a fire that is not too hot: medium-high is best.
- Layer the coals so that you have three degrees of heat: medium-high, medium, and no fire at all. Or, if you are using a gas grill, adjust the burners accordingly.
- To determine the heat intensity of each area of the grill, hold your hand about 2 inches above the grate. If you can keep your hand there for a count of 2 to 3, you have medium-high heat; a count of 4 to 6 is medium heat.

METHOD

- To sear the chops, place them over the hottest area of the grill. If using a charcoal grill, open the top and bottom vents. Cover and grill for 2 to 3 minutes per side.
- Once seared, move the chops to the area of medium heat, close the lid, and continue grilling.
- If there are sweet ingredients in the marinade or spice rub, take extra care that the chops don't burn.

- If flare-ups occur, immediately move the chops to an area of less-intense heat or no heat at all and cover the grill until the flames die down.
- Medium-thick chops (1 to 1¾ inches) will take 3 to 5 minutes per side.
- For thick chops (2 inches or more), sear them for 2 minutes per side, then move them to the area with no heat, cover the grill, and cook for an additional 5 to 8 minutes, or until they reach the correct internal temperature.
- Apply any sauce or glaze 1 to 2 minutes before the meat is done. Don't let the sauce or glaze burn.
- Monitor doneness with an instant-read thermometer. The chops are done when they reach an internal temperature of 135°F to 140°F.
- Transfer the finished chops to a warm platter and cover loosely with aluminum foil. Make sure all the chops rest for at least 5 minutes — 10 minutes for thick chops — before serving.

DRY RUBS AND SPICE PASTES FOR GRILLING PORK

- New Mexico Chile Spice Rub (page 165)
- Aleppo Pepper Spice Rub (page 272)
- Spicy Herb Rub with Espelette Pepper (page 274)
- Fresh Thyme and Rosemary Rub (page 276)
- Red Chile Paste (page 286)
- Fennel and Herb Rub (page 294)
- Spanish Spice Paste (page 329)
- Sage and Thyme Rub (page 378)
- Ancho Chile Spice Rub (page 382)
- Lemon Confit Rub (page 400)
- Herbes de Provence Rub (page 430)

MUSTARD AND SAVORY–MARINATED PORK CHOPS WITH CORNICHON BUTTER

Family Meal, Heirloom Pork

Serves 4

This simple but delicious grilled pork chop comes from one of the best cooks I know and a fellow lover of all things porky, Jeff Bergman. A meal at Jeff's Seattle home is better than one at most restaurants. This recipe adds flavor before cooking using a marinade and after with a compound butter made with chopped cornichons. Jeff prefers to use heirloom pork chops, his favorite breed being Duroc, but as long as you remove the chops from the grill when they reach 135°F to 140°F, you can use pork from your favorite market. See Tips for Grilling Pork Chops (page 254).

Marinade

- 3 small garlic cloves, minced
- 3 tablespoons dry vermouth
- 1 tablespoon coarse-grain mustard
- 1 tablespoon chopped fresh summer savory or rosemary
- 1 tablespoon chopped fresh thyme
- ½ teaspoon salt
- ½ teaspoon freshly ground black pepper
- 3 tablespoons extra-virgin olive oil

- 4 1½- to 2-inch-thick bone-in center-cut rib pork chops
- 1½ teaspoons salt
- ½ teaspoon freshly ground black pepper

Cornichon Butter (recipe follows)

1 **Marinade:** Whisk together the garlic, vermouth, mustard, savory, thyme, salt, and pepper in a small bowl. Whisk in the olive oil. Place the marinade in a shallow dish large enough to hold the chops snugly.

2 Pierce each pork chop all over with a fork. Add the chops to the marinade and turn to coat on all sides. Cover and refrigerate for 6 to 8 hours, or overnight.

3 Remove the chops from the marinade, shaking off the excess. Let stand at room temperature for 1 hour before grilling.

4 Set up a charcoal or gas grill for indirect grilling (see page 12).

5 Season the chops with the salt and pepper. Place on the grill and cook for 2 minutes, taking care not to burn them and moving them if flare-ups occur. Turn and grill on the other side for 2 minutes. Move to the part of the grill with no heat, cover the grill, and cook for 5 to 10 minutes more, or until the chops are firm to the touch, with a faint pink color remaining, and an instant-read thermometer registers 135°F to 140°F close to the bone. Remove from the grill and top each chop with a tablespoon of the Cornichon Butter. Let rest, loosely covered with aluminum foil, for 5 to 10 minutes before serving.

Alternative Cuts: Blade-end pork loin chops, T-bone (center-cut) loin chops, or boneless chops; veal rib chops, beef steaks, or goat chops.

Cook's Notes

- If your store doesn't have chops 1½ to 2 inches thick, ask the butcher to cut some for you. Make sure you tell him or her to cut between the bones so that each chop has a whole rib bone. If your store can't cut you thick chops, buy ones that are at least 1 inch thick and grill over the indirect heat for only 4 to 5 minutes per side.

- If you like your chops well-done, eliminate the marinade and use a flavor brine instead (pages 250–52). Once the chops are flavor-brined, season them with freshly ground black pepper and chopped fresh savory and thyme.

Leftovers

- Toss strips of leftover pork with a mustardy vinaigrette and serve over frisée.

- Use leftover Cornichon Butter as a spread for ham, cold beef, or veal sandwiches or to top grilled steaks, veal chops, or burgers.

CORNICHON BUTTER

Makes about 1 cup

2 tablespoons minced shallots

1 tablespoon dry white wine or vermouth

8 tablespoons (1 stick) butter, softened

2 tablespoons Dijon mustard

3 tablespoons chopped cornichons

¾ teaspoon salt

¾ teaspoon freshly ground black pepper

1 Mix the shallots and white wine in a medium bowl and set aside to macerate for 10 minutes. Meanwhile, pulse the butter and mustard in a food processor until well combined.

2 Transfer the butter mixture to the bowl with the shallots, add the cornichons, salt, and pepper, and blend with a rubber spatula until well combined.

3 Spread a 12-inch-long piece of plastic wrap on your work surface and scrape the butter onto the plastic wrap. Shape and roll the butter into a rough log, 1½ to 2 inches in diameter, leaving about 2 inches at either end of the wrap. Twist the ends to seal, and refrigerate for at least 3 hours before use. (*The butter will keep for about 1 week in the refrigerator or 3 to 4 months in the freezer.*)

Salsas, Chutneys, and Sambals

FIRE-ROASTED SALSA

Makes about 1½ cups

4 ripe medium tomatoes

2 large jalapeño chiles

2 small garlic cloves, chopped

Salt

1 Preheat the broiler. Place the tomatoes and jalapeños about 4 inches from the heat and broil for 3 to 5 minutes. Turn and continue to broil, turning occasionally, until charred on all sides. Let cool.

2 Core the tomatoes and stem the jalapeños. Place in a blender with the garlic and 1 teaspoon salt and pulse to form a chunky mixture. Add more salt to taste. (*The salsa can be made 2 to 3 days ahead and refrigerated.*)

PICO DE GALLO

Makes about 2 cups

3 ripe medium tomatoes, diced

1 medium red onion, finely chopped

1–3 jalapeño chiles, stemmed, seeded, and finely chopped, to taste

1 teaspoon sugar

Finely grated zest and juice of 1 lime

1 cup chopped fresh cilantro

Salt and freshly ground black pepper

Place the tomatoes, red onion, jalapeños, sugar, lime zest and juice, and cilantro in a bowl and stir to combine. Season to taste with salt and pepper. (*The Pico de Gallo can be made 1 day ahead and refrigerated.*)

Cook's Note

• You can add 1 cup diced fresh fruit, such as plums, pineapple, mango, peaches, nectarines, or any citrus fruit, to the Pico de Gallo.

SALSA VERDE

Makes about 2 cups

10 medium tomatillos, husks discarded, rinsed, and chopped

1–3 jalapeño chiles, stemmed, seeded, and coarsely chopped, to taste

2 small garlic cloves, peeled
Salt

1 Place the tomatillos in a small saucepan, along with the jalapeños, bring to a boil, and cook for 5 to 10 minutes, or until soft. Let cool.

2 Place the tomatillos, jalapeños, garlic, and 1 teaspoon salt in a blender and blend until smooth. Add more salt to taste if necessary. (*The salsa can be made up to 2 days ahead and refrigerated.*)

Cook's Note
• If you can't find fresh tomatillos, use canned. Drain them, and don't boil.

TANGERINE CHUTNEY

Makes about 2 cups

This is also delicious with leftover ham and hot biscuits. For the best flavor, look for a red pepper jelly that contains ancho or chipotle chiles.

1 cup red pepper jelly

½ cup tangerine, orange, or lemon marmalade

¼ cup chopped scallions

2 teaspoons dry mustard powder (I use Colman's)

¼ teaspoon salt

2 tablespoons red wine vinegar

2 tablespoons finely grated tangerine zest

6–8 tangerines, seedless mandarin oranges, or tangelos

1 Stir together the red pepper jelly, marmalade, and scallions in a medium bowl. In a small bowl, dissolve the mustard powder and salt in the vinegar. Add to the marmalade mixture along with the tangerine zest.

2 Cut the peel and white pith off the tangerines with a sharp paring knife, following the contour of the fruit, just deep enough to expose the flesh. Working over a strainer set over a bowl, cut between the membranes to remove the segments. Allow the fruit to drain in the strainer for at least 10 minutes or up to 8 hours. Drink the juice and stir the segments into the jelly right before serving.

RHUBARB-DRIED CHERRY CHUTNEY

Makes about 6 cups

2 pounds rhubarb, trimmed and cut into ½-inch pieces

2 cups coarsely chopped onions

1½ cups sun-dried tart cherries

1½ cups sugar

4 garlic cloves, minced

1 tablespoon salt

2 teaspoons brown mustard seeds

1 teaspoon ground allspice

1 teaspoon ground coriander

½ jalapeño chile, stemmed, seeded, and minced

¼ teaspoon ground cinnamon

¼ teaspoon ground ginger

¼ teaspoon ground cloves

2 teaspoons finely grated orange zest

2 cups cider vinegar

¼ cup Lyle's Golden Syrup (see Cook's Notes)

1 Combine all the ingredients in a large heavy saucepan. Bring to a boil, reduce the heat to medium-low, partially cover the pan, and simmer, stirring occasionally, until the chutney has the consistency of thick applesauce, about 25 minutes. It should lightly mound on the spoon.

2 Put the chutney into storage jars and refrigerate for at least 2 days before using. (*The chutney will keep, refrigerated, for about a month.*)

Cook's Notes

- Lyle's Golden Syrup comes from England and has a mild molasses flavor. You can substitute Steen's Pure Cane Syrup or dark corn syrup or a mixture of 3 tablespoons honey plus 1 tablespoon unsulfured molasses.
- Serve this chutney with grilled or baked pork chops, ribs, or roasts, or even your Thanksgiving turkey.

FRESH PLUM SAMBAL

Makes about 2½ cups

To make this sambal, use a firm-fleshed plum with yellow flesh. Serve at once, so it does not get too watery as it stands.

½ cup finely chopped red onion

½ teaspoon salt

1½ tablespoons fresh lime juice, or more to taste

4–6 firm yellow-fleshed plums, split, pitted, and diced (about 2 cups)

1 tablespoon finely chopped fresh lemongrass (inner tender leaves)

1 tablespoon chopped fresh mint

1 tablespoon chopped fresh basil

1 jalapeño chile, stemmed, seeded, and finely chopped (optional)

1 teaspoon sugar, or more to taste

1 Place the red onion in a small bowl and toss with the salt and lime juice. Let sit at room temperature for 30 minutes to lightly pickle.

2 Just before serving, add the remaining ingredients to the red onion and toss to mix. Taste and add more sugar and/or lime, if desired.

GRILLED BONELESS PORK CHOPS STUFFED WITH FONTINA, SUN-DRIED TOMATOES, AND PROSCIUTTO

Fit for Company, In a Hurry

Serves 4

These pork chops stuffed with an intense sun-dried tomato and prosciutto filling ooze with cheese flavors in each bite. It's easiest to cut a pocket for the stuffing into boneless chops, but bone-in rib chops also work well. Use chops about 1¼ inches thick; thicker chops will get *too* thick once stuffed.

4 1¼-inch-thick boneless pork rib chops (6–8 ounces each)

4 ⅛-inch-thick slices fontina cheese (I use fontina from Val d'Aosta), about the size of the pork chops

4 thin slices prosciutto (I use prosciutto di Parma or domestic prosciutto from La Quercia; see Sources), about the size of the pork chops

8 oil-packed sun-dried tomatoes, drained

2 teaspoons salt

2 teaspoons freshly ground black pepper

2 teaspoons chopped fresh sage

2 tablespoons olive oil

Garlic-Tomato Oil

¼ cup extra-virgin olive oil

2 garlic cloves, sliced

1 oil-packed sun-dried tomato, cut into thin strips

1 To butterfly the chops: Lay each chop on a flat surface and, with the knife parallel to the work surface, cut into the chop midway, ending the cut about ¼ inch from the opposite edge. Open each chop like a book and lay a slice of cheese, a slice of prosciutto, and 2 sun-dried tomatoes on one side. Re-form the chops and seal the edges with toothpicks. (*You can stuff the chops a day ahead. Wrap in plastic wrap and refrigerate.*)

2 Combine the salt, pepper, and sage in a small bowl. Brush each chop all over with the oil and then sprinkle with the sage mixture. Let the chops stand at room temperature for 1 hour before grilling.

3 **Garlic-Tomato Oil:** Heat a small saucepan over medium heat. Add the oil, garlic, and sun-dried tomato strips and cook for 1 to 2 minutes, or until the garlic has softened but has not begun to color. Set aside.

4   Set up a charcoal or gas grill for indirect grilling and grill the chops as directed in the recipe for Mustard and Savory–Marinated Pork Chops (page 256). When the chops are done, remove them from the grill and brush generously with the Garlic-Tomato Oil. Let rest for 5 minutes.

5   Flip the chops and brush again with the oil right before serving.

Alternative Cuts: Bone-in loin pork chops, bone-in rib chops, butterflied tenderloin (see the directions for grilling stuffed pork tenderloin, page 322), or pounded cutlets (stuffed and formed into rolls or folded over the stuffing).

Cook's Note

- To vary the filling, use Gruyère cheese and Westphalian ham; young Manchego cheese and serrano ham; mozzarella, fresh basil, and sliced Italian green olives; cheddar cheese and piquillo peppers; cheddar cheese and sliced pickled pearl onions; fire-roasted green chiles and Monterey Jack cheese with pickled jalapeños; and so on.

Leftovers

- For a great sandwich, cut the cold chops crosswise into slices. Slather toasted buns or French rolls with mayonnaise mixed with some chopped sun-dried tomatoes and chopped fresh basil. Assemble and gently heat the sandwich to warm the cheese (this makes a great panini as well).

PLUM-MARINATED PORK T-BONE LOIN CHOPS

Heirloom Pork

Serves 4

Sometimes a marinade is more than a marinade and becomes the base for a great sauce. Fresh plums smack of summer's bounty and are great with pork. Use a sweet, red-fleshed plum such as Santa Rosa, which has good color and rich fruit flavor. Because T-bone loin chops tend to be lean, make sure not to overcook them. Better still, use well-marbled chops from heirloom pork, such as Berkshire, if you can find them. You can also use pork tenderloin with this recipe. Note that the pork must marinate overnight.

Fresh Plum Marinade

½ cup finely chopped red onion

1 teaspoon minced fresh ginger

1 teaspoon minced garlic

1 cup pitted and diced red-fleshed plums, such as Santa Rosa

½ cup prune juice

¼ cup pomegranate juice

2 tablespoons soy sauce

3 tablespoons peanut oil

4 1½- to 2-inch-thick pork T-bone loin chops

Plum Sauce

Reserved marinade

¼ cup plum preserves

2 teaspoons Asian sesame oil

¼ cup chopped fresh cilantro

1 **Marinade:** Combine all the ingredients in a small bowl. Place the chops in a large zipper-lock bag and pour in the marinade. Seal the bag, place in a bowl to catch any leaks, and marinate the chops overnight in the refrigerator, turning them a few times to redistribute the marinade.

2 Remove the chops from the marinade, shaking off the excess. Set the marinade aside for the sauce. Let the chops stand at room temperature for 1 hour before grilling.

3 Set up a charcoal or gas grill for indirect grilling and grill the chops as directed in the recipe for Mustard and Savory–Marinated Pork Chops (page 256).

4 **Sauce:** Meanwhile, pour the reserved marinade into a small saucepan. Whisk in the plum preserves and bring to a boil, continuing to whisk, until the preserves have

melted and the sauce just becomes syrupy. Set aside until the chops are done. If the sauce cools, gently rewarm.

5 To serve, place the chops on a platter and ladle the sauce over the top. Drizzle with the sesame oil and sprinkle with the cilantro.

Alternative Cuts: Any bone-in or boneless pork chop, pork tenderloin (whole or butterflied; see directions for grill-roasting, page 322), or back ribs (see Roasting the Perfect Slab of Ribs, page 394).

Cook's Note
- When you don't feel like firing up the grill, you can cook these chops under the broiler for 3 to 4 minutes per side. Make the sauce before you broil the chops. Just before they are done, brush on some of the sauce and broil for about 1 minute, until the sauce begins to bubble, then flip the chops and do the same on the other side. Take care not to burn the glaze. Serve with the remaining sauce.

MALAYSIAN MARINATED BLADE-END PORK CHOPS WITH GREEN PAPAYA SALAD

Cheap Eats

Serves 6

Malaysia is primarily a Muslim country, and the majority of the population does not eat pork, but a large non-Muslim ethnic minority called the Baba-Nyonya revere it. Their cooking shows a strong influence from their Chinese ancestors, who were originally brought to Malaysia to work on the rubber plantations. This marinade is also great on pork back ribs and spareribs, which can then be roasted on the grill (see page 394) or baked. The marinade is equally tasty with lamb breast, lamb shoulder chops, or prime rib bones (beef rib back bones). If you'd like, turn the marinade into a sauce; see Cook's Notes.

The chops are best marinated overnight.

Malaysian Marinade

- 1 tablespoon fennel seeds
- 2 teaspoons coriander seeds
- 1 teaspoon cumin seeds
- 8 macadamia nuts
- 1 jalapeño chile, stemmed, seeded, and finely chopped (optional)
- 1 fresh lemongrass stalk, tender inner leaves only, minced
- 1 cup chopped white onions
- 3 garlic cloves, peeled
- 2 teaspoons finely grated lime zest
- 2 tablespoons fresh lime juice
- 1 tablespoon chopped fresh ginger or galangal (see Cook's Notes)

- 1 tablespoon dark brown sugar
- 1 teaspoon *belacan* (see Cook's Notes) or 2 anchovy fillets
- ⅓ cup soy sauce
- 1 tablespoon Sriracha sauce
- 1 cup unsweetened coconut milk, stirred well

- 6 1½-inch-thick bone-in blade-end pork loin chops (3–4 pounds total)

Garnish

Lime wedges

Green Papaya Salad (recipe follows)

1 **Marinade:** Heat a small skillet over medium heat and sprinkle in the fennel, coriander, and cumin seeds. Shaking the pan continuously, toast the seeds until they are fragrant and just begin to smoke, about 2 minutes. Transfer to a mortar and grind with a pestle into a powder. Add the nuts and continue to grind until the mixture forms a

dry paste. Scrape the nut mixture into a blender and add the remaining ingredients. Blend by pulsing until the mixture becomes smooth and homogenous.

2   Place the chops in a large zipper-lock bag and pour in the marinade. Seal the bag, place the bag in a bowl to catch leaks, and refrigerate overnight, turning and shaking the bag from time to time to redistribute the marinade.

3   Remove the chops from the marinade, shaking off the excess. Save the marinade if you wish to make a sauce. Let the chops stand at room temperature for 1 hour before grilling.

4   Set up a charcoal or gas grill for indirect grilling and grill the chops as directed in the recipe for Mustard and Savory–Marinated Pork Chops (page 256). Serve with lime wedges and Green Papaya Salad.

Alternative Cuts: Bone-in country-style ribs, blade-end pork loin chops, boneless country-style ribs, or bone-in rib chops; back ribs or spareribs (see headnote); lamb breast, lamb shoulder chops, beef prime rib bones (beef rib back bones).

Cook's Notes

- Fresh galangal looks like ginger but has a distinct taste. It can be found in Asian specialty stores.

- *Belacan,* made from fermented shrimp, is used in Malaysian and Indonesian cooking. It is known as *terasi* in Indonesia and *mam ruoc* in Vietnam. While it has a strong odor and taste, it provides an essential, subtle background flavor in a marinade or sauce. It keeps well in the refrigerator. Anchovies are an adequate substitute.

- To turn the marinade into a sauce, pour it into a small saucepan, add 1 cup canned low-sodium chicken broth, bring to a boil, and reduce until syrupy.

Leftovers

- If you make the marinade sauce, dice the leftover meat and warm it in the sauce to serve over rice. You can extend the recipe by adding some mushrooms, diced zucchini, broccoli florets, or cooked carrots to the meat.

GREEN PAPAYA SALAD

Serves 6

1½ tablespoons dark brown sugar or crushed palm sugar (see Sources), or more to taste

3 tablespoons Asian fish sauce

3 tablespoons fresh lime juice, or more to taste

1 teaspoon dried shrimp (see Sources) or ½ teaspoon minced anchovy

1 garlic clove, peeled

1 bird's-eye or serrano chile, stemmed, seeded, and chopped

2 cups long julienne strips peeled green papaya

6 green beans, sliced into diagonal slivers

8 cherry tomatoes, quartered

¼ cup dry-roasted peanuts

Salt

1 Place the brown sugar in a small bowl, add the fish sauce and lime juice, and stir until dissolved. Pound the shrimp in a mortar with a pestle; add the garlic and continue to pound until a paste forms. Add the chile and pound to bruise, but don't turn it into a paste. Scrape into the fish sauce mixture and stir to combine. Set the dressing aside.

2 Toss together the papaya, green beans, and tomatoes in a medium bowl. Stir in the peanuts and dressing until well mixed, then check for seasonings: The salad should be spicy, sour, salty, and sweet, in that order. Adjust to taste with lime juice, salt, and/or sugar. Transfer to a large shallow bowl or deep platter and serve immediately. (This salad gets soggy easily, so don't put it together until just before serving.)

Cook's Notes

- If spicy isn't your thing, leave the chile out or use less.
- Hand-slicing the green papaya into julienne strips is best, but if you have a sharp shredding blade on your food processor, you can use it. Do not use a hand shredder, which will give soggy results.

BAKED PORK CHOPS WITH BACON, POMEGRANATE, AND PINE NUT RELISH

In a Hurry, Comfort Food, Heirloom Pork

Serves 4

The simplicity of this old-fashioned recipe is ideal for well-marbled heirloom pork, especially from the Berkshire breed, but any well-marbled chop will do. Normally I wouldn't consider baking today's lean pork chops without flavor-brining them first, but the fat and high pH of the Berkshire variety make for juicy results, even if the meat is slightly overcooked. If you use store-bought commodity pork, it must be flavor-brined (see Cook's Notes).

Aleppo Pepper Spice Rub

- 1 tablespoon Aleppo pepper (see Cook's Notes)
- 1 tablespoon sweet Hungarian paprika
- 2 teaspoons chopped fresh sage
- 2 teaspoons freshly ground black pepper
- 2 teaspoons salt

- 4 1½- to 2-inch-thick bone-in pork rib chops (I use Berkshire breed), about 3 pounds total
- 3 tablespoons olive oil
- All-purpose flour for dredging

Braised Bacon, Pomegranate, and Pine Nut Relish

- ½ pound slab bacon, cut into ½-inch dice
- 2 cups homemade pork stock (see page 168) or canned low-sodium chicken broth
- 3 tablespoons pomegranate molasses (see Sources) or cherry syrup
- ⅓ cup pomegranate seeds
- ¼ cup toasted pine nuts (see Cook's Notes)
- 8 cardamom pods, seeds removed and toasted (see Cook's Notes)
- Freshly ground black pepper

1 Preheat the oven to 400°F.

2 **Rub:** Combine all the rub ingredients in a small bowl. Brush the chops with a tablespoon of the oil and sprinkle generously with the rub. Dredge each chop in the flour, shaking off any excess. Let the chops stand at room temperature for 1 hour.

3 Heat a 12-inch heavy, nonstick, ovenproof skillet over medium-high heat. Add the remaining 2 tablespoons oil, then add the chops and sear for 3 minutes, or until nicely brown. Turn over the chops and brown for 3 minutes more.

4 Transfer the skillet to the oven and bake the chops for about 15 minutes, until they are firm to the touch and register 135°F to 140°F on an instant-read thermometer

inserted into the center of a chop. Transfer the chops to a warm platter and let rest for 5 minutes.

5   **Relish:** Meanwhile, blanch the bacon in boiling water for 1 minute and drain. Heat a medium saucepan over medium heat, add the bacon and stock, and bring to a simmer. Reduce the heat and gently simmer, watching carefully, until the stock has reduced to a glaze, about 5 minutes. Degrease the glaze and stir in the pomegranate molasses, pomegranate seeds, pine nuts, and toasted cardamom seeds. Season with pepper to taste and heat through.

6   Serve the chops with the relish on the side.

Alternative Cuts: Rib, T-bone loin, sirloin, or blade-end chops from other heirloom pork breeds; supermarket pork chops of any cut but preferably blade-end chops, at least 1½ inches and up to 2 inches thick (flavor-brine them first). Thick-cut smoked pork chops are also great and don't require flavor-brining; omit the salt from the rub.

Cook's Notes
- Aleppo pepper is a deeply flavored red pepper originally from Syria (see Sources). If you can't find the ground pepper, substitute 1 tablespoon California or New Mexico chile powder or add another tablespoon of Hungarian paprika.
- If substituting commodity pork, use the Basic Flavor Brine (page 251) or the Stout and Malt Flavor Brine (page 251).
- To toast pine nuts, heat a small skillet over medium-low heat. Sprinkle in the nuts and shake the pan continuously until the nuts begin to turn golden brown. Transfer immediately to a bowl to stop the nuts from overbrowning. Toast the cardamom seeds in the same way just until fragrant, about 2 minutes.
- The relish is also a great condiment for roast pork, beef, or veal.

BAKING PORK CHOPS
- Your best choice is old-fashioned pork like Berkshire or other heirloom breed.
- If you're using commodity pork from the supermarket, buy thick chops — 1½ to 2 inches thick — and flavor-brine them first.
- Coat the chops with a breading to protect the meat and seal in the juices.
- Brown the chops nicely on both sides in an ovenproof skillet.
- Bake the chops until they reach an internal temperature of 135°F to 140°F on an instant-read thermometer (the temperature will rise 5 to 10 degrees while resting).
- Let rest for 5 minutes before serving.

PANFRIED PORK CHOPS STUFFED WITH PRUNES AND WESTPHALIAN HAM

In a Hurry, Family Meal

Serves 4

This is the simplest and quickest way to prepare stuffed pork chops. What makes them particularly delicious is the spice rub. For even more flavor, stuff and season the chops the day before you cook them, wrap them in plastic wrap, and refrigerate so that the flavors of the spices and filling have an opportunity to penetrate the meat. To add a touch more smoky flavor, I like to fry the chops in bacon fat, but good olive oil will work fine. Bone-in rib chops are my first choice, but you can use boneless loin chops, especially if they are cut from the rib section.

4   pitted prunes

2   thin slices Westphalian ham (see Cook's Notes) or prosciutto

4   1¼-inch-thick bone-in or boneless pork chops (preferably cut from the rib section of the loin)

Spicy Herb Rub with Espelette Pepper

1   teaspoon salt

1   teaspoon freshly ground black pepper

½   teaspoon Espelette pepper (see Cook's Notes) or crushed red pepper flakes

2   teaspoons chopped fresh sage

2   teaspoons fennel seeds, crushed

1   teaspoon chopped fresh rosemary

2   teaspoons sweet Hungarian paprika

2   tablespoons bacon fat or olive oil

2   teaspoons balsamic vinegar

2   teaspoons unsulfured molasses

    Tabasco or other hot sauce

1   Soak the prunes in boiling water to cover for 5 minutes. Drain and cut each prune in half lengthwise. Cut the ham into strips as wide as the prune pieces and wrap several strips around each prune.

2   Holding the knife parallel to the work surface, cut a horizontal pocket large enough to hold 2 prune halves side by side in each pork chop. Set aside.

3   **Rub:** Combine all the ingredients and sprinkle generously over the chops and into each pocket. Insert the ham-wrapped prune halves into the chops, placing 2 side by side in each pocket. (*At this point, you can wrap the chops in plastic wrap and refrigerate overnight.*) Let the chops stand at room temperature for 1 hour.

4   Heat the bacon fat in a large heavy skillet over medium-high heat. Add the chops and cook for 2 to 3 minutes, or until nicely browned on the bottom. Flip the chops, cover the pan, and cook for 3 to 4 minutes more, or until the chops are firm to the touch and the internal temperature reaches 135°F to 140°F on an instant-read thermometer.

5   Transfer the chops to a warm platter. Combine the vinegar, molasses, and Tabasco to taste in a small bowl and brush generously over the chops. Let rest for 5 minutes before serving.

Alternative Cuts: Boneless loin chops; T-bone loin chops; smoked rib chops (omit the ham and stuff with just prunes); or 2-inch-thick medallions cut from the tenderloin (cut a pocket and use only 1 ham-wrapped prune half per medallion).

Cook's Notes

- Westphalian ham is a smoky dry ham from Germany. If you can't find it, you can use prosciutto, Italian or domestic speck (see Sources), or serrano ham.

- Espelette is a mildly hot chile pepper from the Basque country. It is sweet, aromatic, and slightly smoky. The ground dried pepper (see Sources) is also expensive. You can substitute red pepper flakes, hot Hungarian paprika, Spanish paprika (*pimentón de la Vera*; see Sources), or ground New Mexico chile.

- Instead of brushing on the balsamic mixture, you can make a simple pan sauce: Pour off any fat and add ½ cup canned low-sodium chicken broth to the pan after you remove the chops. Stir and scrape up any browned bits stuck to the bottom of the pan. Add 1 tablespoon balsamic vinegar, 1 tablespoon Dijon mustard, and 1 tablespoon real maple syrup, bring to a simmer, and reduce until the sauce just turns syrupy. Pour over the chops.

- You can leave out the prune-and-ham stuffing if you are in a hurry, but the salty-sweet stuffing adds flavor to the interior of the chop and offers up a little surprise when you bite into it.

PORK CHOPS WITH LEEKS IN MUSTARD SAUCE

In a Hurry, Family Meal

Serves 4

You can flavor-brine these chops using one of the recipes on pages 251–52. Or season the chops, wrap them in plastic wrap, and refrigerate for up to 24 hours; the salt in the seasoning will help make the chops juicy.

4   1½- to 2-inch-thick bone-in pork rib chops (2½–3 pounds total)

Fresh Thyme and Rosemary Rub

2   teaspoons salt

1   teaspoon freshly ground black pepper

2   teaspoons chopped fresh thyme

1   teaspoon chopped fresh rosemary

2   slices thick-cut bacon, cut crosswise into ¼-inch-wide strips

4   cups thinly sliced leeks (white and pale green parts)

2   teaspoons chopped garlic

¼   cup brandy

1   cup homemade pork stock (see page 168) or canned low-sodium chicken broth

2   teaspoons chopped fresh sage

2   tablespoons Dijon mustard

⅓   cup crème fraîche or sour cream

    Salt and freshly ground black pepper

1   Pat the chops dry with paper towels.

2   **Rub:** Combine all the ingredients and sprinkle generously over both sides of the chops. (*For more flavor and juiciness, wrap the chops in plastic wrap and refrigerate overnight.*) Let the chops stand at room temperature for 1 hour.

3   Heat a large heavy skillet over medium heat. Add the bacon and cook, stirring, until lightly crisp. Remove the bacon and set aside. Increase the heat to medium-high, add the chops, and sear until nicely browned on the first side, 3 to 4 minutes. Flip and brown the other side, 3 to 4 minutes more. Remove the chops and set aside.

4   Pour off all but 2 to 3 tablespoons of the fat from the pan, add the leeks, and cook, stirring, until softened, about 7 minutes. Stir in the garlic and cook for 1 minute more. Add the brandy and stock and scrape up any browned bits from the bottom of the pan.

5   Add the bacon and sage, then bury the chops in the leeks and add any accumulated juices. Reduce the heat to a simmer, cover, and cook for 3 to 5 minutes. Turn over

the chops, cover, and cook for 3 to 5 minutes more, or until the internal temperature reaches 135°F to 140°F on an instant-read thermometer. Transfer the chops to a warm platter and set aside while you finish the pan sauce.

6   Skim off any surface fat and, if there is still liquid in the pan, reduce until it is just about evaporated. Whisk in the mustard until well incorporated with the leeks. Stir in the crème fraîche and simmer for 2 to 3 minutes, or until lightly thickened. Season to taste with salt and pepper. Spoon the sauce over the chops and serve.

Alternative Cuts: Pork T-bone loin chops, boneless loin chops, tenderloin medallions, sirloin chops, or blade-end loin chops, all cut 1½ to 2 inches thick.

Cook's Note
- You can substitute thinly sliced yellow or red onions or a mixture of onions and shallots for the leeks.

SEARED PORK T-BONE LOIN CHOPS WITH SAUTÉED APPLE

In a Hurry, Family Meal, Heirloom Pork

Serves 4

There's a good reason pork is paired with apples so often: They taste darn good together. This recipe gives you good apple flavor that isn't overly sweet, and once the chops are flavor-brined, they are very quick to prepare.

Cider Flavor Brine
- 1 cup water
- 2 cups apple cider or apple juice
- ¼ cup salt (I use Diamond Crystal kosher salt)
- ¼ cup honey or real maple syrup
- ⅛ teaspoon ground cinnamon
- 2 cups ice cubes

- 4 1¼-inch-thick pork T-bone loin chops (about 10 ounces each)
- 1 teaspoon chopped fresh sage
- 1 teaspoon freshly ground black pepper
- ⅛ teaspoon ground ginger
- 2 teaspoons olive oil

Sautéed Apple
- 3 tablespoons butter
- ½ cup sliced onion
- ½ cup hard apple cider or dry white wine
- 1 tart apple, such as Pippin or Granny Smith, cored, peeled, and thinly sliced
- ½ cup homemade pork stock (see page 168) or canned low-sodium chicken broth
- ½ cup apple cider or apple juice
- ⅛ teaspoon ground ginger
- Salt and freshly ground black pepper
- Light brown sugar

1 **Brine:** Pour the water and cider into a medium bowl and stir in the salt until dissolved; stir in the honey and cinnamon. Stir in the ice to chill the mixture to 45°F or less. Place the chops in a large zipper-lock bag, pour over the flavor brine, and seal the bag. Place the bag in a bowl in case of leaks, and refrigerate for at least 4 hours or up to 6 hours.

2 Remove the chops from the flavor brine and pat dry. (*You can wrap the chops in plastic wrap and refrigerate for up to 2 days.*) Let the chops stand at room temperature for 1 hour.

3 Combine the sage, pepper, and ginger in a small bowl and sprinkle over both sides of each chop. Heat a large heavy skillet over medium-high heat, add the oil, and heat until hot. Add the chops and sear for 2 to 3 minutes, or until lightly browned on the

first side. Turn over the chops and brown the other side for 2 to 3 minutes more. (You may need to do this in 2 batches.) Transfer the chops to a plate.

4 **Apple:** Pour off any fat from the pan, reduce the heat to medium, and add 1 tablespoon of the butter. Add the onion, cover, and cook until translucent, about 5 minutes. Add the hard cider and stir, scraping up any browned bits from the bottom of the pan. Cook for a minute to boil off some of the alcohol. Add the apple, stock, apple cider, and ginger and bring to a boil.

5 Add the chops, reduce the heat to a simmer, cover, and cook for 3 minutes. Turn the chops, cover, and cook for 3 minutes more, or until the internal temperature reaches 135°F to 140°F on an instant-read thermometer. Transfer the chops to a warm platter and cover loosely with aluminum foil.

6 Bring the cooking liquid to a boil and cook until the sauce is syrupy and the apple is tender, about 5 minutes. Stir in the remaining 2 tablespoons butter, then season with salt, pepper, and brown sugar to taste.

7 Spoon the sauce and apple mixture over the chops and serve.

Alternative Cuts: Pork rib chops, sirloin chops, boneless loin chops, or any pork chops that make you happy, as long as they are plenty thick. I particularly love this with well-marbled pork from the farmers' market and with heirloom varieties that I purchase at my specialty butcher; heirloom varieties have a strong flavor that complements the apple.

Cook's Note
- Instead of sweet apple cider, you can use hard cider in the flavor brine.

PORK CUTLETS WITH PEAR AND SHERRY VINEGAR PAN SAUCE

In a Hurry, Family Meal

Serves 4

Many types of fruits — prunes, sour cherries, quince, figs, and dried apricots — go well with pork. Firm ripe pears, especially the Bosc variety, which hold their shape when cooked, are tasty, too, as are Asian pears.

8 ½- to ¾-inch-thick boneless pork chops, pounded to ¼ inch thickness	3 tablespoons finely chopped shallots
Salt and freshly ground black pepper	3 tablespoons sherry vinegar or cider vinegar
1 firm ripe pear (I use Bosc)	⅔ cup homemade pork stock (see page 168) or canned low-sodium chicken broth
1 tablespoon light brown sugar	1 tablespoon finely chopped fresh mint or flat-leaf parsley
1 tablespoon butter, plus more as needed	
½ tablespoon olive oil, plus more as needed	

1. Sprinkle both sides of the pork with salt and pepper to taste. Let stand at room temperature for 30 minutes.

2. Peel and core the pear, then cut it lengthwise into quarters. Thinly slice the quarters crosswise and toss the slices in a small bowl with the brown sugar.

3. Heat a large skillet over medium-high heat and add 1 tablespoon butter and ½ tablespoon oil. When the butter has melted, sear the pork cutlets, in batches, for 30 seconds per side, adding more butter and oil as needed. Do not overcook the pork. Remove the cutlets and set aside.

4. Add the shallots to the fat remaining in the pan and cook, stirring, for 3 minutes, or until softened. Add the pear and any juice and cook, stirring constantly, for 3 minutes, or until the pear begins to color. Add the vinegar and stock, bring to a simmer, and cook until the liquid becomes syrupy, about 6 minutes. Season to taste with salt and pepper.

5. Push the pear to one side of the skillet and return the pork, along with any juices, to the pan. Spoon some of the pear over the pork and cook for 1 minute to warm through. Place the cutlets on a warm platter with the pear and sauce spooned over. Sprinkle with the mint and serve.

Alternative Cuts: Pork tenderloin cut into medallions, slices cut from boneless sirloin, or cutlets from the pork leg inside (top round). Or use ½-inch-thick slices of boneless smoked pork loin, also called Canadian bacon (page 441, or see Sources), but don't pound them; serve 2 slices per person.

Cook's Note

- This recipe also makes a great pan sauce for seared pork chops (page 278) or pork tenderloin medallions (page 283). If using chops or medallions, sear them for 2 to 3 minutes per side.

COOKING PORK CHOPS, STEAKS, AND CUTLETS ON THE STOVE TOP

Cooking pork chops in a skillet is simple, fast, and an easy way to get a pork dinner on the table. Most recipes for sautéing pork chops can be grouped into one of two categories: those for lean chops and those for fattier ones.

Ideal Methods for Lean and Tender Chops, Steaks, and Cutlets

The challenge is to create a nicely browned exterior without overcooking the meat. The best chops for these methods are center-cut rib chops, T-bone (center-cut) chops, and sirloin chops. Cutlets from the leg, boneless sirloin, tenderloin cut into medallions, and boneless loin are also good candidates. Chops should be no less than ¾ inch thick (1 to 1¼ inches thick is better). Cutlets are often only ¼ inch thick; in order not to overcook them, you may have to sacrifice the browned exterior. Flouring chops and cutlets first helps to protect the meat and also provides a nice brown exterior.

- Cook fully in a skillet and serve alone or with a condiment.
- Cook fully in a skillet, then use the browned bits on the bottom of the pan as a base for a pan sauce.
- For a quick pan braise, sear in a skillet, use the browned bits to make a pan sauce, and then finish cooking (6 to 8 minutes) in the sauce.

Ideal Method for Fattier Chops and Steaks

The best cuts for longer pan-braising are blade-end loin chops, country-style ribs, and shoulder steaks (also called Boston butt steaks or blade steaks). These cuts tend to be chewier and will take longer to become tender, with the meat almost falling off the bone. Smoked pork chops (especially from the rib area) and ham steaks can also braise for longer times.

- Sear quickly in a skillet, use the browned bits to make a pan sauce, and then finish cooking (up to 45 minutes or even 1 hour) in the sauce.

PORK TENDERLOIN MEDALLIONS WITH ROASTED PEPPER AND CHERRY PEPPER PAN SAUCE

In a Hurry

Serves 4

The region of Campania, whose capital city is Naples, has some of my favorite food in all of Italy, which is why I visit it often. How can you not love an area that produces wood-fired pizza, great seafood, and lusty pasta sauces based on the locally grown tomatoes? Oh, and did I mention mozzarella di bufala and sausages infused with fennel and garlic? But it is the hospitality of the folks who have fed me this food that attracts me most. Bernardino Lombardo, owner of La Caveja, unassumingly opens his farm to both friends and strangers. Bernardino raises apples and pears; a large flock of capons, which he sells to restaurants in the area; and Cinta Senese pigs, a native variety that he lets grow to six hundred pounds or more. The meat of these pigs is heavily marbled, producing revered hams, cured back fat (*lardo*), and salamis. One night Bernardino panfried some tenderloin medallions in his own olive oil and dressed them with peppers from his garden and pickled cherry peppers from last year's crop.

2 teaspoons chopped fresh sage	2 teaspoons vinegar from the cherry peppers (see below)
2 teaspoons salt	
1 teaspoon freshly ground black pepper	1–1½ cups ½-inch-wide strips fire-roasted red or yellow bell peppers (store-bought or homemade; see Cook's Note)
12 1½-inch-thick slices pork tenderloin (about 1½ pounds total)	
2 tablespoons olive oil	6 bottled cherry peppers, stemmed, quartered, and seeded
1 tablespoon chopped garlic	
½ cup dry white wine	2 tablespoons finely chopped scallions

1   Combine the sage, salt, and pepper in a small bowl and sprinkle over both sides of the medallions. Let stand at room temperature for 30 minutes.

2   Heat a large heavy skillet over medium-high heat and add 1 tablespoon of the oil. Cook the medallions in 2 batches, adding more oil as needed, until lightly browned on both sides, 2 to 3 minutes per side. Set the medallions aside.

3 Pour off all but 1 tablespoon of the fat in the pan and reduce the heat to medium. Add the garlic and cook, stirring, for 1 minute. Add the white wine and pepper vinegar, bring to a boil, scraping up any browned bits from the bottom of the pan. Boil to reduce the sauce until it just begins to thicken. Reduce the heat to medium, add the peppers, and cook for 2 minutes more. Return the medallions to the pan and cook for 1 minute more to warm them through.

4 Serve immediately, garnished with the scallions.

Alternative Cuts: An equivalent weight of scaloppine cut from the loin or sirloin.

Cook's Note

- **To fire-roast peppers:** Char them over an open gas flame or under the broiler, turning, until blackened. Place in a paper or plastic bag for 10 minutes, then scrape off the skin, cut open the pepper, and remove the seeds. Pat dry.

CARLOS'S GRILLED CHILE-MARINATED THIN-CUT PORK SOFT TACOS

Fit for Company, Cheap Eats, Great Leftovers

Serves 6

Carlos P. Hernandez lives in Bakersfield, California, but he comes from the village of Tingüindín in the Mexican state of Michoacán. Before emigrating to California, he expressed his entrepreneurial spirit with a small taco stand that he set up in the center of his village on market days. Soon he garnered a strong local following and a reputation for the best tacos in the area. Today he no longer sells his tacos, but he is the cook when his large family gathers for celebrations, which is often. I was able to get him to share his recipe for marinating thin slices of pork, which he quickly grills and coarsely chops as a filling for warm soft corn tortilla tacos. Carlos's preferred cut is Boston butt cut into ¼-inch-thick slices, but he confessed that some diet-conscious family members insist that he also marinate leaner boneless pork loin chops (see Cook's Notes).

Red Chile Paste

- 6 dried ancho chiles, stemmed, seeded, and torn
- 1 guajillo chile, stemmed, seeded, and torn
- 1 tablespoon minced fresh ginger
- 1 tablespoon minced garlic
- 1 teaspoon cumin seeds
- 10 black peppercorns
- 6 cloves
- 2 bay leaves
- ¼ teaspoon ground cinnamon
- 2 teaspoons dried oregano (I use Mexican)
- 1 tablespoon chopped Mexican chocolate or unsweetened chocolate

- ¼ cup red wine vinegar
- 2 teaspoons salt

- 2 pounds boneless Boston butt (pork shoulder butt), cut into ¼-inch-thick cutlets
- 18 corn tortillas
  Pico de Gallo (page 259)
  Salsa Verde (page 260)
  Diced grilled pineapple (see Cook's Notes)
  Finely chopped red onion
  Lime wedges
  Chopped fresh cilantro
  Tabasco or other hot sauce

1 **Paste:** Place the chiles in a small bowl and pour boiling water over to cover. Soak for at least 30 minutes, or until the chiles are soft. Drain the chiles, reserving the soaking liquid, and place in a blender along with the ginger and garlic.

2 Drop the cumin seeds, peppercorns, cloves, and bay leaves into a spice grinder and pulse to grind to a powder. Add to the blender, along with the cinnamon, oregano, chocolate, vinegar, and salt. Blend to a soft paste, adding some of the chile-soaking liquid if needed.

3 Smear the paste all over the pork slices, transfer to a large zipper-lock bag, and seal. Marinate at room temperature for 2 hours, or in the refrigerator overnight, turning and shaking the bag from time to time to redistribute the contents.

4 Set up a charcoal or gas grill for medium-high heat (see page 11 for more on grilling). Preheat the oven to 350°F.

5 Remove the pork from the bag, but don't scrape off the marinade paste. Grill for 1 to 2 minutes per side, or until the meat is just faintly pink on the interior. You may have to cook the meat in batches. Place on a cutting board and chop into ½-inch pieces, then transfer to a large serving bowl.

6 While the meat is cooking, wrap the tortillas in aluminum foil and heat in the oven for 10 to 15 minutes. Remove the foil, and wrap the tortillas in a kitchen towel to keep warm.

7 Let guests make their own tacos with the pork, tortillas, and various accompaniments.

Alternative Cuts: Blade-end pork loin chops; boneless country-style ribs cut lengthwise into ½-inch-wide strips; sirloin pork chops; or butterflied and pounded whole pork tenderloin. Take care not to overcook sirloin and tenderloin.

Cook's Notes

- To make the tacos with leaner boneless pork loin chops, cut the meat into ¼-inch-thick slices and grill for 1 minute per side, or until faintly pink but still juicy. Let rest for 3 to 5 minutes before chopping into ½-inch chunks.

- At his taco cart, Carlos would cook his pork stacked on a vertical spit (called *al pastor*), slicing off pieces as he filled orders. The top of the spit was decorated with a skinned pineapple and, if you requested, he would slice you off a chunk. To replicate this at home, smear ¾-inch-thick slices of fresh pineapple with some of the marinade. Grill the slices and serve with the tacos.

GRILLING THIN CHOPS, STEAKS, OR CUTLETS

Grilling any thin slice of pork can be tricky, because an error of a minute or less can yield dry or overcooked meat. Here are a few tips:

- If you have the time, flavor-brine before grilling.

- Use a spice paste. It not only adds flavor but protects the meat as well.

- Grill thin cuts quickly on a well-oiled grill: 1 minute per side for ¼-inch-thick pieces and about 2 minutes per side for ½-inch-thick pieces. A 3- to 5-minute rest — on a warm platter and covered with aluminum foil — should be sufficient.

SOFT TACOS
Family Meal, Fit for Company, Fit for a Crowd

Making soft tacos is not really about a recipe but more about the fixings. At most taco stands, the plate is garnished with spicy pickled vegetables, pickled jalapeños, and sliced radishes. The easiest way to present soft tacos is to have all the fixings arranged in bowls and a stack of hot corn tortillas wrapped in a towel and let guests go at it. Simply lay a hot tortilla on a plate, spoon up whatever meat or meats are offered, and garnish with salsa and/or pico de gallo. Figure on about ¼ cup of chopped meat per taco. A smart strategy when you make any of the following dishes is to be sure you have leftovers so that you can make some tacos the next day.

FILLINGS

Beef and Bison
- Grilled steak rubbed with Mexican Rub (page 67)
- Flank Steak Carne Asada Padilla (page 70)
- Steak marinated in Mexican Beer, Chile, and Cilantro Marinade (page 64)
- Braised Beef Steak with Tequila, Tomato, and Orange (page 165)
- Mexican Beef Brisket and Winter Squash Chili (page 199)
- Mexican-Style Poached Beef Tongue (page 226)

Pork
- Carlos's Grilled Chile-Marinated Thin-Cut Pork (page 286)
- Beer and Tequila Carnitas (page 380)
- Chile-Braised Pork Belly (page 382)
- Grilled Back Ribs in Smoky Chile Marinade (page 398)

Goat
- Mexican Braised Goat with Chiles (Birria de Chivo; page 515)

Salsas and Garnishes
- Fire-Roasted Salsa (page 259)
- Pico de Gallo (page 259)
- Salsa Verde (page 260)
- My Guacamole (page 304)
- Shredded iceberg lettuce
- Finely chopped red or sweet onion
- Chopped fresh cilantro
- Chopped scallions
- Shredded cabbage
- Grated Monterey Jack, cheddar, or queso Oaxaca
- Mexican crema or sour cream

On the Side
- Mexican Pickled Vegetables (page 228)

Cook's Note
- If burritos are your thing, provide large, warm flour tortillas and add refried beans (homemade or canned) and Mexican rice to the list of fillings above.

Pork Kebabs

Spearing morsels of succulent pork on lances of metal or wood and then grilling them is a great way to liven up a meal with only small quantities of meat. And it's a practice you'll find the world over. Marinating pork chunks in a soy- or fish sauce–based marinade is popular throughout Asia, while marinades of citrus, olive oil, and herbs are common in the Mediterranean. In Mexico and other countries in South America, spicy pastes are the flavorings of choice.

Because most pork is tender, kebabs can be made from all sorts of cuts, including tenderloin, loin, leg, shoulder, even belly. Lean pork can be improved with rubs, marinades, or flavor brines, but take care not to overmarinate lean and very tender cuts like tenderloin or loin. Marinades that contain acidic ingredients can begin to turn small pieces of pork to mush if the meat sits for too long. For most marinade recipes, an overnight soak in the refrigerator (12 to 16 hours) should be sufficient. Try the marinades in the recipes I've provided in this chapter, but also feel free to use any of the marinades or flavor brines in the book. Use the brining times on page 250.

When it comes to putting together combinations of ingredients to make up your skewers, pork pairs well with eggplant, tomato, bell pepper, onion, mushroom, fennel, and summer squash. It's also delicious with fruit such as pineapple, peach, fig, plum, date, prune, and apple. You can also combine pork with seafood, such as shrimp and lobster, or firm fish, such as shark or monkfish. Plus, you can embellish your skewers with cubes of bacon, pancetta, or ham.

Kebabs make wonderful hors d'oeuvres, especially for cocktail parties. For easy eating, cut the pork into ¾-inch cubes. For main dishes, cut the pork into 1½-inch cubes; they're less likely to dry out.

TIPS FOR GRILLING KEBABS

- Use flat metal skewers if possible.
- If your only option is round skewers, use two of them, running them parallel to each other through the meat and vegetables so that the ingredients won't slip when you turn them.
- Soak wooden skewers in cold water for 30 minutes before grilling to prevent burning.
- Ingredients on the same skewer should be about the same size and density so that they cook at the same rate. Quick-cooking vegetables, such as cherry tomatoes, summer squash, and mushrooms, should go on their own skewers. The same goes for bread, which would burn long before the meat was cooked.
- If you are using a glaze that has sweet ingredients, apply it toward the end of cooking so that it doesn't burn.

CARIBBEAN PORK KEBABS WITH SWEET POTATO AND PECAN RELISH

Fit for Company

Serves 6

Priscilla Yee from Concord, California, is a talented cook and recipe writer who has won numerous prestigious recipe contests, including the Pillsbury Bake-Off and the National Beef Cook-Off. She has a knack for creating the kind of recipes people love: quick, precise, and easy to make. She often incorporates ethnic touches that reflect the diversity of the San Francisco Bay Area. Inspired by the flavors of Jamaica, this recipe is one of Priscilla's winners. If you wish, you can turn the marinade into a dipping sauce to serve alongside these skewers.

Caribbean Pineapple Marinade

- 2 teaspoons minced garlic
- 2 teaspoons minced fresh ginger
- 1 teaspoon ground allspice
- 2 teaspoons curry powder, homemade (page 526) or store-bought
- ½ teaspoon cayenne pepper
- ¼ teaspoon ground cinnamon
- ⅓ cup dark rum
- ¼ cup soy sauce
- ½ cup pineapple juice
- 2 tablespoons Worcestershire sauce
- 1 tablespoon dark brown sugar

- 2 pounds pork tenderloin, cut into 1½-inch cubes
- 1 red onion, cut into 1-inch pieces
- 1 cup 1-inch cubes fresh pineapple
  Sweet Potato and Pecan Relish (recipe follows)

- 9 12-inch flat metal skewers, or twelve 9-inch bamboo skewers soaked in water for 30 minutes

1. **Marinade:** Combine all the ingredients in a medium bowl. Put the pork cubes in a large zipper-lock bag and pour over the marinade. Seal the bag and place in a bowl to catch any leaks. Marinate for 2 hours at room temperature or overnight in the refrigerator, turning and shaking the bag occasionally to redistribute the marinade.

2. Set up a charcoal or gas grill for medium-high heat (see page 11 for more on grilling).

3. Remove the meat from the marinade; save the marinade to boil for a dipping sauce (see Cook's Notes) or discard it. Pat the meat dry and thread onto skewers, alternating with the red onion and pineapple.

4 Grill until the pork is firm to the touch, turning the skewers frequently to prevent burning, about 10 minutes. Serve with the Sweet Potato and Pecan Relish alongside.

Alternative Cuts: Boneless country-style ribs, pork loin, leg meat, or sirloin.

Cook's Notes

- For a real treat, use cubed fresh pork belly, increasing the cooking time to 15 minutes. Take care to turn the skewers frequently.

- The marinade is also great with 1¼-inch-thick pork chops.

- To turn the marinade into a dipping sauce, pour into a small saucepan, bring to a boil, then reduce the heat and simmer for 5 minutes. Combine 1 teaspoon cornstarch with 2 tablespoons cold water and stir into the sauce. Boil for 30 seconds to a consistency of light syrup. Serve in individual small bowls for dipping.

SWEET POTATO AND PECAN RELISH

Makes about 4 cups

This relish also goes well with grilled or baked pork chops or ham.

2 large sweet potatoes (about 2 pounds), peeled and cut into ½-inch cubes

6 tablespoons olive oil

1 tablespoon chopped fresh rosemary

2 garlic cloves, chopped

1 red bell pepper, fire-roasted (see page 284), peeled, seeded, and cut into ¼-inch dice

1 Anaheim chile, fire-roasted (see page 284), peeled, seeded, and diced

1 small red onion, cut into ¼-inch dice

½ cup toasted pecans (see Step 2, page 354), coarsely chopped

2 tablespoons real maple syrup

¼ cup red wine vinegar

Salt and freshly ground black pepper

1 Preheat the oven to 375°F.

2 Toss the sweet potatoes with 2 tablespoons of the oil, the rosemary, and garlic in a medium bowl. Transfer to a baking sheet or roasting pan. Roast until the potatoes are just tender, 15 to 20 minutes. Remove from the oven and set aside to cool.

3 Put the bell pepper, chile, red onion, and pecans in a medium bowl. Add the cooled sweet potatoes and toss to combine. In a small bowl, whisk together the maple syrup, vinegar, the remaining ¼ cup oil, and salt and pepper to taste. Toss the sweet potato mixture with the vinaigrette. (*The relish keeps in the refrigerator for up to 24 hours. Let come to room temperature before serving.*)

GRILLED SCALLIONS WRAPPED IN PORK BELLY

In a Hurry, Cheap Eats

Serves 6 as part of a mixed grill or as an appetizer

La Tenuta Rocchetta, a farm near the ancient Greek temple ruins of Selinunte on the southern coast of Sicily, produces some of Italy's best olive oil. What makes owner Pierluigi Crescimanno's oil so special, besides the superior olives, is the attention he pays to every detail of the production. Once when the harvest crush was winding down, my friend the Italian food writer Faith Willinger brought me to the farm to visit the orchards and partake of the annual family feast. First came Pierluigi's mama's legendary chickpea soup, drizzled with the freshly pressed and yet-to-be bottled oil, then plates of pasta, and finally platters of grilled pork from the family's prized pigs. Every dish was delicious, but what stayed with me were the large scallions wrapped in fresh bacon, seasoned with local herbs, and basted with the freshly pressed oil. Since pork belly is rich, serve these skewers as part of a mixed grill, along with chops or kebabs of lean pork seasoned with the same rub used on the belly or as an appetizer. Make sure to get the thickest scallions you can find — ½ inch is ideal. Look for new-harvest extra-virgin olive oil to brush on the kebabs as well.

Fennel and Herb Rub

- 2 tablespoons salt
- 1 tablespoon freshly ground black pepper
- 1 tablespoon chopped fresh oregano
- 1 tablespoon chopped fresh sage
- 2 teaspoons fennel pollen (see Sources) or ground fennel seeds

- 12 large scallions, trimmed to 8 inches long
- 12 ⅛-inch-thick slices skinless pork belly
- Good extra-virgin olive oil

- Wooden skewers, soaked in warm water for at least 30 minutes

1. **Rub:** Combine all the ingredients in a small bowl.

2. Set up a charcoal or gas grill for medium-high heat (see page 11 for more on grilling). Starting at the root end of each scallion, wrap a slice of pork belly around the scallion to resemble a barber's pole. Secure with skewers at both ends. Brush with olive oil and sprinkle generously with the rub. (Save any extra rub to season kebabs or pork chops.)

3   Grill, turning frequently, until the belly begins to brown nicely, moving the scallions to the cool parts of the grill if flare-ups occur. Remove from the grill, brush again with olive oil, and serve immediately.

Alternative Cuts: Thick slices of pancetta or smoked bacon, but omit the salt from the rub recipe.

Cook's Notes
- Fresh pork belly from the heirloom breeds Duroc or Tamworth is particularly good because it is relatively lean and not too chewy.
- If you can get a bottle of unfiltered *olio nuovo,* the current year's freshly harvested and pressed olive oil from Italian olives, all the better. This fresh, new pressing is an experience not to be missed (for La Tenuta Rocchetta olive oil, see Sources).

Ground Pork, Chopped Pork, and Pork Sausages

You can purchase pork already ground, but the best cut for grinding, chopping, or shredding is the Boston butt (pork shoulder butt). It has just about the right ratio of lean to fat when you grind it. When cut into thin slices, Boston butt is tender enough for a quick stir-fry, and it won't dry out when it's diced or shredded or cooked long and slow in a ragú or stew.

Adding herbs, spices, and other flavorings to ground pork turns it into a sausage mixture to be used as is or to stuff into a casing. Details for grinding pork and making your own sausages can be found in the next chapter (page 407). Sausage mixtures are packed with flavor, so they're a logical and delicious component of pasta dishes and stuffing.

Ground pork is used as the basis for a filling in the many varieties of Asian and Eastern European dumplings (see Pork and Apple Dumplings, page 305). Coarsely chopped, diced, or shredded pork can also be used as a foundation for rustic ragùs to serve over pasta or for Hispanic dishes such as green chile stews and chili Colorado.

SPANISH-STYLE PORK BURGERS

In a Hurry, Family Meal
Serves 4

Spain produces some of the best olives in the world. It is also known for its superb paprika, called *pimentón de la Vera,* which has a smoky flavor; for its intensely flavored pimientos, called piquillo peppers; and for many fine varieties of chorizo sausages. If you can't find piquillo peppers, substitute good canned whole pimientos; if necessary, substitute provolone cheese for the Manchego.

1 tablespoon extra-virgin olive oil (I use Spanish)

1 large Spanish or red onion, thinly sliced (about 3 cups)

Salt and freshly ground black pepper

1¼ pounds ground pork (85% lean)

¼ pound Spanish chorizo (*semicurado*; see Cook's Notes), homemade (page 414) or store-bought, finely chopped

¼ cup Spanish green olives, such as manzanilla, pitted and finely chopped

2 teaspoons Spanish paprika (*pimentón de la Vera*; see Sources) or sweet Hungarian paprika

2 teaspoons minced garlic

⅓ cup mayonnaise

2 teaspoons finely grated lemon zest

1 tablespoon fresh lemon juice

Pinch of saffron threads (I use Spanish)

4 hamburger buns, toasted

½ cup grated young Manchego cheese (optional)

4 whole piquillo peppers (see Sources), cut lengthwise in half

1 Heat the oil in a large skillet over medium heat. Add the onion, season with a little salt and pepper, cover, and cook until soft and translucent, stirring from time to time, about 10 minutes. Divide the onions into 2 equal parts and let cool. Finely chop half the onions.

2 Combine the ground pork, chorizo, chopped onions, olives, paprika, garlic, ½ teaspoon salt, and ¾ teaspoon pepper in a medium bowl. Mix well with your hands and form into 4 equal patties, about ¾ inch thick. Using your thumb, create a depression in the center of each patty.

3 Combine the mayonnaise, lemon zest, lemon juice, and saffron in a small bowl. Mix well and set aside.

4   Set up a charcoal or gas grill for medium-high heat (see page 11 for more on grilling).

5   Grill the burgers until done to medium to medium-well, 4 to 5 minutes per side. Cut into a patty to check; it should be just faintly pink.

6   Slather each side of the toasted buns with some of the mayonnaise mixture. Place a patty on each bottom half and top with the cheese (if using), then some of the reserved onions and a piece of piquillo pepper. Finally, top with the other bun half. Serve immediately.

Alternative Cuts: Ground beef of any type (85% lean), ground veal (85% lean), or ground goat meat.

Cook's Notes

- If you can't find lean ground pork (85% lean), it's easy to grind your own. Purchase 1¼ pounds boneless Boston butt and follow the instructions for grinding pork on page 407.

- If you can't find semicured chorizo and don't want to make your own, you can leave it out or replace it with an equivalent weight of andouille sausage or additional ground pork with an additional tablespoon of Spanish paprika.

VIETNAMESE PORK SANDWICHES
(BANH MI THIT)

In a Hurry

Serves 4

You can use leftover pork and sausage from Hanoi Rice Noodles and Grilled Pork or, better still, marinate extra pork to cook fresh for these sandwiches at a later time.

Pickled Vegetables

2 medium carrots, peeled and julienned

1 3-inch section daikon radish, peeled and julienned

¼ cup rice vinegar

1 tablespoon sugar

Pinch of salt

½ pound leftover pork and/or sausages from Hanoi Rice Noodles and Grilled Pork (page 308), sliced ¼ inch thick, plus leftover dipping sauce, or freshly marinated Boston butt (see headnote), thinly sliced

4 6-inch-long French rolls or pieces of baguette

Mayonnaise

Sriracha sauce (optional)

1 6-inch piece English cucumber, cut lengthwise into 8 very thin slices

1 jalapeño chile, stemmed and thinly sliced on the bias (optional)

12 fresh cilantro sprigs

12 large fresh basil leaves (I use Thai or purple)

1 **Vegetables:** Toss together the carrots, daikon, rice vinegar, sugar, and salt in a medium bowl. Let the vegetables pickle at room temperature for 1 hour.

2 Preheat the oven to 300°F.

3 Rewarm the leftover pork and sliced sausage in the dipping sauce, or grill the marinated pork as directed in Hanoi Rice Noodles and Grilled Pork (page 308). Set aside.

4 Warm the rolls in the oven to crisp up the crust and warm the inside, about 5 minutes.

5 To assemble the sandwiches, cut the rolls in half. Slather each cut side with mayonnaise and drizzle over a little Sriracha (if using). Layer a cucumber slice on each side of each roll, then pile one quarter of the meat on one side. Top with the pickled vegetables (make sure to use tongs or a slotted spoon so as not to get too much liquid). Finally, place some of the sliced jalapeño (if using), 3 cilantro sprigs, and 3 basil leaves on one side of each sandwich. Put the rolls together, cut the sandwiches in half, and serve.

MEXICAN TORTAS

Family Meal

Serves 4

My neighborhood is filled with taquerías, both free-standing and mobile. Besides turning out freshly made soft tacos, burritos, and crispy tostadas, they usually offer an assortment of tortas, Mexican sandwiches made on soft rolls called *bolillos*. What makes the sandwiches special are the various condiments on them. At one of my favorite stands, La Fondita in Santa Rosa, California, the sandwiches are dressed with a spicy mayonnaise and stuffed with tomatoes, avocados, shredded cabbage, and sweet onions. The meat filling is sprinkled with a healthy dose of spicy salsa.

Usually the choices of filling for tortas are the same choices offered for tacos and burritos (see page 289). Use leftovers from any of those recipes, either chopped into cubes or thinly sliced, then briefly heated to warm through. You can also make tortas with leftover beef roast, beef pot roast, pork roast, or lamb roast.

Serve the tortas with homemade Mexican Pickled Vegetables (page 228) and lots of napkins (or wear a bib).

Lime Mayonnaise

- ⅓ cup mayonnaise
- 1 tablespoon fresh lime juice
- 1 tablespoon finely chopped pickled jalapeño chile (optional)
- ½ cup chopped fresh cilantro

- 2–3 cups diced or chopped meat (see headnote) or 1 pound sliced ham or sliced leftover roasted or pot-roasted meat
- 4 soft French rolls or Mexican *bolillos*, split and toasted

- 1 cup shredded Monterey Jack cheese
- 4 Anaheim chiles, fire-roasted (see page 284) and cut into strips, or one 7-ounce can fire-roasted green chiles
- 8 thin slices ripe tomato
- 1 cup shredded cabbage
- 1 avocado, halved, seeded, peeled, and cut lengthwise into thin slices, or My Guacamole (recipe follows)
- 4 slices red onion

1 **Mayonnaise:** Combine all the ingredients in a small bowl and mix until well blended. Set aside.

2 For diced, chopped, or pot-roasted meat, gently heat in a skillet to warm; leave ham or roasted meat cold.

3 To assemble the tortas, generously slather lime mayonnaise on each cut side of the rolls. Spoon or layer the meat over one half of each roll, sprinkle with the cheese, and

top with the roasted chiles, tomato, cabbage, avocado (or guacamole), and red onion. Put the top half of each roll on top, cut the sandwich in half, and serve.

Cook's Note

• If you'd like a little more spice, spoon or sprinkle a salsa (pages 259–60) or bottled hot sauce over the meat before closing the sandwiches.

MY GUACAMOLE

Makes 1½ cups

1 large ripe Hass avocado, halved, seeded, and peeled	¼ cup chopped fresh cilantro
¼ cup diced ripe tomato	2 teaspoons finely chopped stemmed and seeded jalapeño chile (optional)
¼ cup finely chopped red onion	Salt and freshly ground black pepper

Coarsely mash the avocado with a fork or potato masher in a medium bowl. Do not over-mash; the texture should be quite lumpy. Stir in the tomato, red onion, cilantro, jalapeño (if using), ½ teaspoon salt, and ½ teaspoon pepper. Taste and adjust the seasonings. Serve immediately.

PORK AND APPLE DUMPLINGS (PIEROGI)

Cheap Eats, Comfort Food, Great Leftovers, Freezes Well

Serves 4 to 6 (makes about 30 dumplings)

Michelle Aaron, who worked with me at Aidells Sausage Company, grew up in Canada in an area settled by Eastern European immigrants. One of her favorite foods was the popular Polish dumpling called pierogi. Usually filled with potatoes, mild cheese, or sauerkraut, pierogi are eaten as a main course alongside cabbage and apples. When Michelle moved to the Bay Area, she missed her pierogi and began to experiment with flavors. This pork and apple filling is one of her stellar combinations.

Both Michelle and I love these pierogi for breakfast, topped with sour cream, but you could also serve them as lunch or dinner. Drizzle the pierogi with melted butter and top with sauerkraut in the Polish style, or serve with crisp lardons of bacon — just don't skip the sour cream.

These dumplings freeze well and can be plopped into boiling water straight from the freezer (allow an extra minute or two to cook through). Keep some in the freezer, and you always have some ready for a speedy breakfast or unexpected guests. Pierogi are also wonderful as hors d'oeuvres.

Dumpling Dough

- 3 cups all-purpose flour, plus more if needed
- 2 teaspoons salt
- 1 large egg
- ¾ cup water
- ¼ cup canola oil

Pork and Apple Filling

- 1 tablespoon butter
- ½ cup finely chopped onion
- 6 ounces ground pork (80%–85% lean)
- ½ cup peeled, finely diced apple, such as Granny Smith or Pippin
- ⅛ teaspoon ground cinnamon
- Pinch of freshly grated nutmeg
- Salt and freshly ground black pepper

- Sour cream and/or melted butter
- Sauerkraut

1 **Dough:** Combine the flour and salt in a large bowl. In another bowl, whisk together the egg, water, and oil, then stir into the flour until it forms a shaggy mass. Turn out onto a floured work surface and knead until the dough comes together and is soft but not sticky, adding more flour if necessary. If the dough is too dry, add water 1 tablespoon at a time. Cut the dough in half, form into 2 disks, and wrap each with plastic wrap. Let rest in the refrigerator for 1 hour.

2 **Filling:** Meanwhile, heat the butter in a medium skillet over medium heat. Add the onion and cook, stirring frequently, until soft, about 5 minutes. Remove from the heat and let cool.

3 Combine the pork, apple, cinnamon, nutmeg, and the cooled onion in a large bowl. Stir in ½ teaspoon salt and ½ teaspoon pepper. In a small skillet, cook a small patty, then taste, and add more salt or pepper to the filling if needed. Form the filling into

teaspoon-sized meatballs and roll each one gently between your hands to elongate slightly. Put the meatballs aside, covered, while you roll out the dough.

4   Put one of the dough disks on a lightly floured work surface. Roll out to about $\frac{1}{16}$ inch thick. Using a 3-inch round biscuit cutter, cut out about 15 circles. Place a meatball in the center of one of the circles and, with your finger, lightly moisten the circumference of the circle with water. Fold over the dough to make a half-moon shape, pressing the edges together to seal. Put the dumpling on a baking sheet and cover with a damp towel. Repeat filling and shaping the remaining dough circles. Roll out the other dough disk and fill and form the remaining dumplings.

5   Bring a large pot of generously salted water to a boil. Add the dumplings and bring back to a boil. Cook for 4 to 6 minutes, or until the dumplings are tender and float to the surface. Drain well and serve topped with sour cream and sauerkraut.

Alternative Cuts: Ground beef, a mixture of ground beef and pork, ground veal, or a mixture of ground veal and pork.

Cook's Notes
- For a slightly smoky variation, replace 2 ounces of the ground pork with 2 ounces finely chopped ham or bacon.

- Replace the apple with $\frac{1}{2}$ cup cooked sweet corn.

- Add $\frac{1}{2}$ cup rinsed, drained, and chopped sauerkraut to the filling.

- Once you've mastered the dumpling dough, the sky's the limit on stuffing possibilities. Besides the three suggestions above, you can combine other meat, chopped onion, and a cheese such as hoop cheese or farmer's cheese. If you have any leftover pot roast or stew, you can chop it finely and mix with just enough gravy to moisten and use that. You can also mix leftover pot roast or stew with a bit of mashed potatoes.

- Instead of serving pierogi as they are, you can add them to chicken broth for a great soup.

HANOI RICE NOODLES AND GRILLED PORK (BUN CHA HANOI)

Meat as a Condiment, Cheap Eats
Serves 4 to 6

A few years ago, my wife, Nancy, and I visited Vietnam as part of a group of culinarians led by the Vietnamese cookbook author Mai Pham. One of our most memorable meals was a mixed grill of pork served at a Hanoi restaurant called Bun Cha Hang Manh. Grilled thin slices of pork shoulder and pork sausage patties were accompanied by rice vermicelli and the ever-present Vietnamese table salad of herbs and greens. This recipe is adapted from *Pleasures of the Vietnamese Table* by Mai Pham.

Bun Cha Hanoi Marinade

- 3 scallions, sliced into thin rings
- 2 shallots, minced
- 1½ tablespoons Asian fish sauce
- 1½ teaspoons light brown sugar
- ½ teaspoon salt
- 1 teaspoon freshly ground black pepper
- 1 tablespoon vegetable oil

- ¾ pound boneless Boston butt (pork shoulder butt), sliced across the grain then cut into 1-inch-long-x-¼-inch-wide strips
- ¾ pound ground pork
- ⅓ cup finely chopped onion
- ⅔ pound dried Vietnamese rice vermicelli *(bun)*

Table Salad

- 2 heads red leaf lettuce, leaves separated and washed
- ½ cucumber, julienned
- 2 cups bean sprouts
- 12 fresh mint sprigs
- 12 fresh basil sprigs (preferably Thai)
- 6 fresh purple or green basil sprigs
- 24 fresh cilantro sprigs

Vietnamese Dipping Sauce

- 6 fresh Thai bird chiles or 2 serrano chiles, stemmed, or to taste
- 2 garlic cloves, sliced
- 6 tablespoons sugar
- 1 cup warm water
- 3 tablespoons fresh lime juice
- ⅔ cup Asian fish sauce
- ¼ cup finely shredded peeled carrot

1 **Marinade:** Combine the scallions, shallots, fish sauce, brown sugar, salt, and pepper in a medium bowl and stir to blend. Divide the marinade equally between two bowls. Add the oil and pork strips to one bowl, toss the strips to evenly coat, and marinate at

room temperature for 30 minutes, or up to 2 hours. In the second bowl, combine the marinade with the ground pork and onion and mix well. Shape the mixture into patties about 2 inches wide and ½ inch thick. Set them aside in the refrigerator until ready to cook. (*You can make the patties up to 1 day ahead and refrigerate them wrapped in plastic wrap.*)

2   Set up a charcoal or gas grill or broiler for medium-high heat (see page 11 for more on grilling), or preheat the broiler. (You can also fry the meat in a skillet.) Grill or broil the pork slices and pork patties until the meat is cooked through and the edges of the pork slices are nicely charred, 2 minutes per side for slices and 3 minutes per side for patties. Transfer to a serving plate.

3   Meanwhile, bring a large pot of water to a boil. Cook the vermicelli until al dente, 4 to 5 minutes. Drain, rinse, and cool.

4   **Salad:** Arrange all the ingredients in attractive rows on a large platter.

5   **Sauce:** Cut the chiles into thin rings. Set one third of the chiles aside. Place the remaining chiles, the garlic, and sugar in a mortar and, with the pestle, pound into a coarse, wet paste. (If you don't have a mortar, chop with a knife.) Transfer to a small bowl and add the water, lime juice, and fish sauce. Stir well to dissolve the sugar. Add the reserved chiles and the carrots. Set aside for 10 minutes to mellow.

6   Set the table with a platter of the cold rice noodles, the table salad, and a bowl of half the dipping sauce. Divide the remaining dipping sauce among four to six small bowls. Serve each guest a small bowl of dipping sauce, and each a bowl to eat from.

7   Slice the patties. To serve, invite guests to place a few slices of pork and the sliced pork patties in their dipping sauce and let soak for a few minutes, then place some noodles, salad, and meat in their bowls and drizzle some of the remaining sauce on top.

Alternative Cuts: For leaner but less tasty cuts, you can use thin-sliced pork loin strips or blade-end loin or country-style ribs, cut into thin strips. For a more succulent treat, use thin slices of fresh pork belly, cut into strips.

Cook's Notes
- If you can't find Thai basil, use regular basil.
- Another way to eat *bun cha Hanoi* is to place some noodles in the center of a lettuce leaf. Top with meat, herbs, and a drizzle of sauce. Wrap and eat out of hand, dipping the end of the roll into the dipping sauce, if desired.

THAI PORK SALAD (LAAB)

Meat as a Condiment, Family Meal

Serves 4

Every time I visit my favorite neighborhood Thai eatery, I order *laab*, a spicy, tangy salad of minced pork, fresh herbs, and shredded vegetables. One of the best versions I have ever had was at Saffron Thai Grilled Chicken, a modest but authentic restaurant in San Diego run by cookbook author and Thai food expert Su-Mei Yu, who makes *laab* with roast duck and other meats. The appeal of this salad is its contrasting textures, from crunchy to soft. It is decidedly spicy.

Dressing

- 2 tablespoons boiling water
- 1 tablespoon dark brown sugar, or more to taste
- ¼ cup fresh lime juice
- 2 tablespoons Asian fish sauce
- 1 garlic clove, minced
- 2 fresh Thai bird or serrano chiles, stemmed, seeded, and minced
- Salt (optional)

- 1 tablespoon peanut oil
- 1 pound ground pork (85% lean)
- 2 teaspoons minced fresh ginger
- 1 teaspoon minced garlic
- 1 tablespoon Asian fish sauce
- 2 tablespoons fresh lime juice, or more to taste

- Salt
- 3 tablespoons minced shallots
- 2 tablespoons finely chopped scallions
- 3 kaffir lime leaves (fresh or frozen; see Sources), shredded, or 1 teaspoon finely grated lime zest
- 1 teaspoon Sriracha sauce, or more to taste (optional)
- ¼ cup chopped fresh cilantro
- 12 fresh mint leaves, torn
- 3 cups shredded iceberg lettuce
- 10 cherry tomatoes, cut in half
- 12 green beans, cut into thirds on the diagonal
- 10 arugula leaves or watercress sprigs
- ½ cup julienned English cucumber
- ½ cup dry-roasted salted peanuts

1. **Dressing:** Combine the boiling water and brown sugar in a small bowl and stir until the sugar is mostly dissolved. Stir in the lime juice and fish sauce and stir until the sugar is completely dissolved. Cool, then stir in the garlic and chiles. Taste and add salt if needed.

2. Heat the oil in a large skillet over medium-high heat. Add the pork, ginger, and garlic and cook, mashing the meat with a fork to break it up into small pieces. When the meat is just going from pink to gray, stir in the fish sauce and lime juice and cook for 1 minute more. Add salt to taste.

3   Transfer the meat to a medium bowl and stir in the shallots, scallions, and kaffir lime leaves. Add 2 tablespoons of the dressing and the Sriracha (if using). Taste the mixture. It should be sweet, sour, spicy, and salty. If not, adjust the flavors with brown sugar, lime juice, Sriracha, and/or salt. Toss in the cilantro and mint.

4   Spread the lettuce on a platter, then scatter on the tomatoes, green beans, arugula, and cucumber. Drizzle with the remaining dressing and spoon on the meat. Garnish with the peanuts and serve immediately.

Alternative Cuts: Ground beef or ground lamb; grilled rare beef steak, finely diced; or grilled pork tenderloin, finely diced.

Cook's Note

- This salad will get soggy almost immediately, so make it right before serving.

ALL-PORK CASSOULET

Fit for Company, Fit for a Crowd, Great Leftovers, Freezes Well

Serves 12, with leftovers

As a sausage maker, I was drawn to cassoulet, a glorified version of pork and beans. I scrutinized several recipes and decided that Julia Child's version in *Mastering the Art of French Cooking* was the definitive one. At the time, I was the chef at Poulet, a poultry-centric charcuterie in Berkeley, California. It took me close to a week to make the cassoulet. First I had to salt and cure the duck legs for duck confit, then prepare at least two kinds of pork sausage, a mild Toulouse and a smoky French country sausage. Then there was the lamb ragú and the initial cooking of the beans. Finally, everything was combined and baked for several hours, forming a rich bread crumb crust on top. Was it delicious? Of course! Would I spend five days to make that recipe again? Probably not.

A few years ago I had the chance to visit Gascony, the home of cassoulet, and sampled several versions. My favorite was made with all pork. When I got home, I came up with a recipe using pork confit and sausage. My version is less time-consuming than Julia's, and I love its lovely fresh flavor from the homemade tomato sauce.

My preferred beans are French heirloom beans called Tarbais, Italian butter beans, or White Emergo beans, but you can substitute more available varieties.

Leftover cassoulet tastes even better reheated the next day.

Beans

- 2 pounds (about 5 cups) dried white beans (see Cook's Notes), picked over and rinsed
- 1 ½-pound piece pancetta
- 1 onion, not peeled
- 1 garlic head, not peeled
- 4 bay leaves
- 6 fresh thyme sprigs
- ½ bunch fresh flat-leaf parsley
- 2 teaspoons salt
- 2 teaspoons freshly ground black pepper

Sauce

- 4 tablespoons olive oil or 2 tablespoons fat from Pork Confit (see below)
- 3 pounds boneless country-style ribs, cut into 2-inch cubes (if you haven't made Pork Confit)

  Salt and freshly ground black pepper
- 2 cups chopped onions
- 2 cups dry white wine
- 2 cups homemade pork stock (see page 168), canned low-sodium chicken broth, juices from the Pork Confit, or a combination

4 cups Gary's Heirloom Tomato Sauce (recipe follows)

3 pounds sweet Italian sausage, homemade (page 410; see Cook's Notes) or store-bought

2½ pounds Pork Confit (page 430), or use boneless country-style ribs (see above)

2 cups coarse fresh bread crumbs

¼ cup olive oil or melted fat from Pork Confit

1 **Beans:** Bring 4 quarts water to a boil in a large heavy casserole or saucepan. Add the beans, return to a boil, and cook for 3 minutes. Remove from the heat and let the beans soak for 1 hour.

2 Drain the beans, discard the liquid, and return the beans to the pot. Add another 4 quarts water and the pancetta, onion, and garlic. Using butcher's twine, wrap the bay leaves, thyme, and parsley in a bundle (or put them in a little cheesecloth bag) and add to the pot, along with the salt and pepper. Bring to a boil, then reduce the heat to a simmer and cook until the beans are just tender but not falling apart. (Begin sampling the beans after 20 minutes of cooking.) Drain and reserve the liquid. Discard the herb bundle, onion, and garlic. Remove the pancetta and set aside the beans.

3 **Meanwhile, make the sauce:** If you are using Pork Confit, go to step 4. If using ribs, heat 2 tablespoons olive oil in a 3-quart casserole or Dutch oven over medium-high heat. Sprinkle the ribs with salt and pepper and brown them on all sides, 7 to 10 minutes. Transfer the meat to a plate with a slotted spoon and set aside.

4 If using Pork Confit, heat the 2 tablespoons fat in a heavy 3-quart casserole or Dutch oven over medium-high heat. If using ribs, heat the remaining 2 tablespoons olive oil. Add the onions and cook for 5 minutes, stirring frequently. Add the white wine and boil until reduced by half, 5 to 10 minutes. Add the stock and bring to a boil. Reduce the heat to a simmer. If using Pork Confit, cook the sauce for 15 minutes. Or, if using ribs, return them to the pot and cook with the sauce for 45 minutes.

5 Remove the ribs with a slotted spoon and set aside. Cut the pancetta into ½-inch cubes. Cook in a medium skillet over medium heat until lightly browned. Drain, then add to the sauce. Stir in the tomato sauce and season lightly with salt and pepper (the cassoulet will absorb salt from the sausage and Pork Confit).

6 Preheat the oven to 350°F.

7 Heat a large skillet over medium heat and add the sausages. (They will release fat, so none needs to be added.) Cook until nicely browned on all sides, about 7 minutes. Remove from the heat and, when the sausages are cool enough to handle, cut them into 2-inch pieces. Set aside, adding any juices to the sauce.

8   Spoon one third of the beans into an 8-quart casserole or heavy Dutch oven and add half of the ribs or confit and half of the sausages. Pour over one third of the sauce. Spoon over another third of the beans and arrange the remaining ribs or confit and sausages on top. Pour over a third of the sauce, then add the final layer of beans and the rest of the sauce. If there is not enough sauce to immerse the beans, pour over some of the reserved bean cooking liquid (saving the rest to use in bean soup). Sprinkle the bread crumbs evenly over the surface, then drizzle with the olive oil or the fat.

9   Bake the cassoulet for 30 minutes. Using the back of a large spoon, push some of the crispy crumbs down into the beans. Cook for another 30 minutes, until the bread crumbs have become golden and crispy. If not yet crispy, increase the oven temperature to 450°F and cook for 15 minutes more or crisp the bread crumbs under the broiler for 2 to 3 minutes. Serve.

Alternative Cuts: Country-style ribs; Boston butt; or assorted fresh and smoked sausages, such as sweet Italian, andouille, smoked country sausage, and garlic sausage.

Cook's Notes

- While store-bought Great Northern white beans are perfectly acceptable, the better the bean, the better the cassoulet. No matter what you buy, look for beans from the current year's crop. Better still, buy beans from a specialty bean purveyor, such as Rancho Gordo or Phipps Country Store and Farm (see Sources).

- Cooking times for different types of bean will vary, so sample the beans often as they cook. The freshness of the bean will also have an effect on cooking time.

- If you've made Pork Confit, there will be a layer of melted fat on top and a layer of congealed juices beneath. Pour the juices (about 2 cups) into a bowl and use them in the cassoulet.

- Use any combination of mild sausages you desire. If you are making your own, there is no need to stuff the meat into casings; simply form it into small patties. Good choices are Maple and Sage Pork Sausage Patties (page 408), Sweet Italian Sausage (page 410), and Kale and Garlic Sausage (page 412).

- Cooked cassoulet can be reheated, covered, in a preheated 375°F oven for 20 minutes, or until warmed through. Portioned into ovenproof casseroles, it can be frozen for up to 2 months and cooked straight from the freezer until the center reaches 130°F on an instant-read thermometer.

GARY'S HEIRLOOM TOMATO SAUCE

Makes 2 quarts

My wife and I have been gathering for Christmas dinner at Gary and Julie Wagner's house in the Napa Valley for the past twenty years. An accomplished cook in his own right, Gary loves to help when his professional chef friends come to cook in his kitchen. He makes tons of his famous tomato sauce every year when tomatoes are in season and freezes it so his lucky friends get to have some year-round.

If you don't have access to heirloom tomatoes or vine-ripened garden tomatoes, use whatever you can find that are ripe and sweet, or substitute canned. You'll be sorely disappointed if you use the mealy, pale supermarket things that pass for tomatoes. Gary doesn't skin his tomatoes, which saves time and works just fine.

1 cup good extra-virgin olive oil	A handful of fresh rosemary sprigs, tied together with butcher's twine
5 pounds heirloom tomatoes (very ripe, various sizes and colors), cored and cut into chunks	3 bay leaves
2 onions, coarsely chopped	2 anchovy fillets
1 red onion, coarsely chopped	1 tablespoon sweet Hungarian paprika or Spanish paprika (*pimentón de la Vera*; see Sources)
1 garlic head, not peeled	Salt and freshly ground black pepper
A large handful of fresh basil leaves, torn	
A handful of fresh thyme sprigs, tied together with butcher's twine	

1 Heat the oil in an 8-quart saucepan or Dutch oven over medium heat. Add the remaining ingredients plus 1 tablespoon salt and 2 teaspoons pepper, and stir until well combined. Bring to a boil, reduce the heat to a simmer, and cook, uncovered, for 2 hours, stirring occasionally. Add water if the sauce becomes too thick. Season to taste with additional salt and pepper if desired.

2 Remove the garlic, thyme bundle, rosemary bundle, and bay leaves, and discard. Put the sauce through a food mill fitted with a large-holed disk to separate out the skins. Or, if you don't own a food mill, put the sauce into a blender in batches and blend to a smooth sauce. If the sauce is too thin, return it to the pot and reduce it over high heat until lightly thickened. (For the cassoulet, you want it fairly thin so that the beans will absorb the liquid. If you're using the sauce for pasta, you'll want it fairly thick.) Cool. (*Freeze excess sauce in plastic 1-pint containers, leaving a 1-inch space at the top. The sauce will keep for 1 year in the freezer.*)

MY NEAPOLITAN CABBIE'S BAKED ZITI WITH BROCCOLI RABE AND HOT ITALIAN SAUSAGE

Meat as a Condiment, Great Leftovers, Family Meal, Fit for Company, Rewarms Well

Serves 6

No law-abiding American driver could survive the chaos that rules Neapolitan streets. As a tourist, you must take cabs. Besides being brave and courageous drivers, the cabbies are a wealth of culinary information. (Italians spend almost as much time talking about food as they do eating it.) On a drive to the National Museum of San Martino on the hill overlooking Naples, a well-fed cabbie rapturously described the baked ziti with hot sausage, bitter greens, and provola (a local buffalo cheese) that his family was famous for. Given our language barrier, I was unable to get an exact recipe, but I played around with the ingredients and came up with something I think he would have enjoyed.

Salt

1 pound broccoli rabe

1 pound ziti, rigatoni, or penne

2 tablespoons extra-virgin olive oil

1 pound hot Italian sausage, homemade (see Cook's Note, page 410) or store-bought, casings removed

2 cups canned chopped or diced tomatoes (I use San Marzano) or Gary's Heirloom Tomato Sauce (page 316)

1 teaspoon dried basil (if using canned tomatoes)

2 cups shredded provola, provolone, or pecorino cheese

Freshly ground black pepper

1   Bring 4 quarts water to a boil in a large pot and add 1 tablespoon salt and the broccoli rabe. Boil for 3 to 5 minutes, or until the broccoli rabe is tender. Drain, coarsely chop, and set aside.

2   Preheat the oven to 400°F. Oil a 13-x-9-inch baking dish.

3   In another large pot, bring 4 to 6 quarts water to a boil. Add 3 tablespoons salt and the pasta and cook for 10 to 12 minutes, or just until al dente. Drain.

4   Meanwhile, heat the oil in a large skillet over medium-high heat. Add the sausage and cook for 5 minutes, breaking it up with a slotted spoon or fork. Add the tomatoes and basil (if using), reduce the heat to a simmer, and cook until the sauce just thickens. Or, if using the premade sauce, add it to the sausages and heat through. Stir the broccoli rabe into the sauce and remove the pan from the heat.

5   In a large bowl, mix together the cooked pasta, sauce, and 1 cup of the cheese. Season to taste with salt and pepper. Spoon the pasta mixture into the baking dish, sprinkle the top with the remaining 1 cup cheese, and bake until the cheese is golden brown, 15 to 20 minutes. Serve.

Alternative Cuts: Any Italian sausage of your choice, store-bought or homemade (see page 410 for a recipe).

Cook's Note
- This is an ideal dish for potlucks and for when you have to feed a big group. It can be served warm and not piping hot. It rewarms well covered in aluminum foil.

Pork Roasts

The most common and popular roasts come from the center-cut pork loin, sold bone in or boneless, in various size pieces. **Loin** (particularly from commodity pork) can be lean, so if you plan to cook beyond my recommended temperatures of 135°F to 140°F, I recommend flavor-brining first to preserve juiciness. However, heirloom breeds and pasture-raised pigs raised on smaller farms often produce better-marbled loins and can be roasted with excellent results without flavor-brining.

Roasts from the **blade end** of the loin and the **Boston butt** have more fat and make excellent candidates for the oven. They can be roasted—long and slow—until well-done and produce succulent results.

For small groups, **pork tenderloin** makes a nice roast, as does the small boneless sirloin roast. If you have purchased commodity pork, flavor-brine it first.

For large groups and special occasions, look to **fresh hams** (leg of pork), bought whole or in halves. The flavor of leg meat is excellent. Some purveyors provide roasts made from boned-out individual leg muscles; these make great alternatives to the more common loin roasts when you're cooking for a smaller group.

Pork Roasts at a Glance

From the Loin

Center rib roast, bone in (pork loin rib half, center-cut roast, rack of pork, standing rib roast of pork). Good flavor and easy to serve if you make sure to have the butcher remove the chine bone.

Center loin roast, bone in (pork roast, center-cut loin roast, center-cut roast, T-bone loin roast, loin roast). The loin end is leaner than the rib end; it is more difficult to carve and can dry out. Best flavor-brined.

Blade roast, bone in (blade-end pork loin roast, pork blade roast). Has ample fat and good flavor. Can be roasted or braised. A good value.

Blade roast, boneless (chef's prime roast). Because the blade end of the loin has more fat, this cut makes a nice juicy roast and is usually affordably priced.

Top loin roast, boneless (pork loin roast, center-cut pork loin roast). Quick to cook and easy to slice. You can purchase any size piece to accommodate your needs. Usually not distinguished by what part of the loin it comes from; the blade area should be less lean. Best flavor-brined unless well marbled.

Tenderloin. Usually sold two to a package. The pieces can be tied together to make a 2- to 2½-pound roast, which can also be stuffed. Easy to grill-roast but very lean. Best to flavor-brine. Expensive but no waste.

Top loin double roast, boneless (double pork loin roast, boneless pork roast). This bigger pork loin roast is ideal for larger groups, and you can place a stuffing between the two sections.

Sirloin roast, boneless (sirloin end roast). This small, lean roast is ideal for family meals. Best to flavor-brine.

From the Shoulder

Blade Boston butt roast, bone in (pork shoulder butt, fresh pork butt, Boston butt, Boston shoulder, pork butt roast, Boston-style butt). My favorite for an old-fashioned long, slow-cooked roast. Can be roasted, braised, or barbecued. Juicy, flavorful, and a great buy.

Blade Boston roast, boneless (boneless Boston Butt, boneless pork shoulder roast, rolled butt roast, butt roast, Boston roast). See bone-in blade Boston roast, above. Sold as whole, half, or in pieces. Should be tied or netted.

Arm picnic, bone in (fresh picnic, picnic shoulder, picnic). The upper arm portion of the foreleg. Must be roasted or barbecued long and slow to almost falling off the bone. Ideal for braising, but has lots of bone, gristle, skin, and fat. Very inexpensive with great flavor.

Arm picnic, boneless (boneless fresh picnic, boneless picnic, picnic shoulder). See arm picnic, bone in. A great roast to cut up for stew.

From the Leg

Pork leg (fresh ham), whole, bone in (whole leg of pork). Weighing 15 to 20 pounds, this makes a spectacular roast for large groups. Inexpensive, with great meaty flavor. May need to be special-ordered.

Pork leg (fresh ham), boneless. Sold whole or half. It's easier to slice than a bone-in leg but the slices do separate into sections. Ideal for buffets or roasts for larger groups. May need to be special-ordered.

Pork leg (fresh ham), rump half, bone in (butt half fresh ham, pork leg sirloin half, pork leg butt, fresh ham butt). Weighs 7 to 10 pounds. May need to be special-ordered.

Pork leg (fresh ham), shank half, bone in (shank half, shank roast, shank end half, shank end of fresh ham, leg roast shank half). Weighs 7 to 10 pounds. Easier to carve than the rump half (above). May need to be special-ordered.

Pork leg (fresh ham), top roast, boneless (pork inside roast, pork top round roast). Lean but tender. At 3 to 5 pounds, a great roast for 4 to 8 people. Should be tied or netted.

Pork leg (fresh ham), bottom roast, boneless (pork outside roast, pork bottom round). At 4 to 6 pounds, a great roast for 6 to 9 people. A little leaner than the top (inside) roast. Should be tied or netted.

Pork leg (fresh ham), tip roast, boneless (sirloin tip roast, pork knuckle roast). At 3 to 4 pounds, a lean and compact roast when netted or tied.

MY FAVORITE PORK ROASTS

I love the rib section of the center-cut loin, which offers more fat and flavor than the adjoining T-bone loin section. I usually buy at least 3 bones, and up to 8 bones, for roasting.

When I'm serving a larger group I buy a whole or half fresh ham (leg of pork) with the skin on. Fresh ham is an inexpensive cut with little waste. It has a great robust flavor — and then there are all those lovely cracklings to munch on.

Sometimes I crave the old-fashioned flavor of well-done pork. Those are the times when I slow-roast a whole bone-in Boston butt. It has ample fat, so it can be cooked to very well-done and still provide juicy and succulent meat. I love the budget price and the added plus of filling my house with great porky aromas.

Cooking Pork Tenderloin on the Grill

Use direct heat for unstuffed tenderloins. See page 11 for more on grilling.

IF USING A CHARCOAL GRILL

- Layer the coals so that you have three degrees of heat: medium-high, medium, and no fire at all.
- To determine the heat intensity of each area of the grill, hold your hand about 2 inches above the grate. If you can keep your hand there for a count of 2 to 3, you have medium-high heat; a count of 4 to 6 is medium heat.
- Put the meat directly above the hottest part of the fire. If flare-ups occur, move the meat to a cooler part of the grill and cover the grill until the flames die down. Cook the meat for about 1½ minutes on each side. Then move the meat to the area with medium heat, cover the grill, and cook until the meat is firm to the touch and registers an internal temperature of 135°F to 140°F on an instant-read thermometer, 2 to 3 minutes more per side. Cover loosely with aluminum foil and let rest for 5 to 10 minutes before serving.

IF USING A GAS GRILL

- Cook the meat over medium-high heat for 1½ minutes per side to sear. If flare-ups occur, lower the flame and cover the grill until the flames die down. Once the meat is seared, lower the fire to medium heat, cover the grill, and cook until the meat is firm to the touch and registers an internal temperature of 135°F to 140°F on an instant-read thermometer, 2 to 3 minutes more per side. Cover loosely with aluminum foil and let rest for 5 to 10 minutes before serving.

Use indirect heat for stuffed tenderloins or as an option for unstuffed double tenderloin roasts. See page 12 for more on grill-roasting.

IF USING A CHARCOAL GRILL

- Build the fire. Once the coals are burning, mound them into banks on either side of the barbecue grate with a drip pan (a small roasting pan or a disposable aluminum pan) in between. You can sprinkle 2 cups soaked wood chips (oak, hickory) over the coals at this time, dividing them equally between the two mounds.
- Sear the tenderloins directly over the hot coals, 1½ to 2 minutes per side. If flare-ups occur, move the meat to a cooler part of the grill. Move the tenderloins to the center of the grill, over the drip pan. Cover the grill and cook the meat until the internal temperature reaches 135°F to 140°F on an instant-read thermometer, 10 to 15 minutes. Turn

the meat from time to time and refresh the wood chips (if using) as needed. Remove the meat from the grill, cover loosely with aluminum foil, and let rest for 5 to 10 minutes.

IF USING A GAS GRILL

- Preheat all burners of the grill, then shut off half the grill, for a 2-burner grill, or the middle section, for a 3-burner grill. If your grill has a smoke box, you can add soaked wood chips for a smoky flavor.
- Sear the meat on all sides over the flame, 1½ to 2 minutes total; if flare-ups occur, move the meat off the flame and cover the grill. After the meat is seared, move it to the turned-off area of the grill, cover, and cook until the internal temperature reaches 135°F to 140°F on an instant-read thermometer, 10 to 15 minutes. Turn the meat from time to time. Remove the meat from the grill, cover loosely with aluminum foil, and let rest for 5 to 10 minutes.

PORK TENDERLOIN STUFFED WITH PORCINI MUSHROOMS WITH TOMATO SALSA VERDE

Fit for Company, Heirloom Pork

Serves 6

Stuffing this lean cut of pork with mushrooms adds elegance as well as flavor and juiciness. Look for an heirloom breed, such as Berkshire, Duroc, Tamworth, or Gloucestershire Old Spot, or pampered pork from your local farmers' market. These tenderloins are even better cooked indirectly on a grill (grill-roasting). Follow the directions for grill-roasting tenderloins on page 322.

Porcini Stuffing

- 1 pound fresh porcini mushrooms, cut into ¼-inch-thick slices
- 4 garlic cloves, thinly sliced
- 1 teaspoon chopped fresh sage
- 1 teaspoon chopped fresh thyme
- 2 tablespoons extra-virgin olive oil
- Salt and freshly ground black pepper

- 2 1- to 1¼-pound pork tenderloins
- 1 teaspoon chopped fresh thyme
- 1 teaspoon chopped fresh sage
- 1 teaspoon salt
- 2 teaspoons freshly ground black pepper
- 1 tablespoon extra-virgin olive oil
- Tomato Salsa Verde (recipe follows)

1 Preheat the oven to 400°F.

2 **Stuffing:** In a bowl, toss the mushrooms with the garlic, sage, thyme, oil, and a sprinkling of salt and pepper. Spread the mushroom mixture and all the oil in a roasting pan and roast for 5 minutes. Stir and roast for 5 minutes more, or until the mushrooms are soft and fragrant. Set aside to cool. Increase the oven temperature to 450°F.

3 To butterfly the tenderloins, make a deep lengthwise cut down the center of one, being careful not to cut all the way through. Open up the meat like a book and place it between 2 pieces of plastic wrap. Pound the tenderloin with a mallet until it is about ¼ inch thick. Repeat with the other tenderloin. Spread a layer of mushrooms over each tenderloin, leaving at least a 1-inch border all around. With a long side toward you, roll up the meat to enclose the filling. Tie the tenderloins at 2-inch intervals with butcher's twine.

4   Combine the thyme, sage, salt, and pepper in a small bowl. Rub the mixture all over the tenderloins.

5   Heat the oil in a large heavy ovenproof skillet over medium-high heat. Sear the tenderloins on all sides, 3 to 4 minutes total. Transfer to the oven and roast for 15 minutes. Check the internal temperature with an instant-read thermometer: When it reaches 135° to 140°F, the meat is done. If not done, continue roasting, checking the temperature every 5 minutes. Transfer the meat to a platter and tent loosely with aluminum foil. Let rest for 5 to 10 minutes.

6   Remove the strings and carve the meat into 1-inch-thick slices. Serve with Tomato Salsa Verde.

Alternative Cuts: Pork cutlets from the leg or boneless sirloin, cut or pounded to ¼ inch thick, or 1-inch-thick boneless pork chops, pounded to a thickness of ¼ inch. Stuff with the mushrooms, form into packets, and tie with string.

Cook's Notes
- Instead of fresh porcini, you can substitute an equal amount of cremini mushrooms, portobellos, or shiitakes. If you are using shiitakes, be sure to remove and discard the tough stems.
- Instead of butterflying the tenderloins, you can sandwich the mushrooms between the 2 tenderloins, matching the tail of one opposite the thicker head of the other, then tie them together to make a double tenderloin roast. Tie the roast with several loops of butcher's twine. Halve the porcini stuffing recipe for this method.

TOMATO SALSA VERDE

Makes 3 cups

3 anchovy fillets, rinsed and chopped	½ cup good extra-virgin olive oil
⅓ cup packed chopped fresh basil	2 tablespoons balsamic vinegar
⅔ cup packed chopped fresh flat-leaf parsley	2 cups seeded and diced vine-ripe tomatoes
½ cup packed chopped celery leaves	(preferably heirloom varieties)
1 garlic clove, peeled	Salt and freshly ground black pepper

Put the anchovies, basil, parsley, celery leaves, and garlic in a food processor. Add the oil and vinegar and pulse until blended. Transfer to a bowl and stir in the tomatoes. Season to taste with salt and pepper.

PROSCIUTTO-WRAPPED PORK TENDERLOIN

Fit for Company, Great Leftovers
Serves 4 to 6

As one of the entrées at her restaurant, Boulevard, my wife serves mixed plates of heirloom porky delights. Her current favorite is a chunk of slowly braised pork cheek, a dry-rubbed and roasted pork rib, and a piece of ever-so-juicy tenderloin wrapped in prosciutto di Parma. The prosciutto, even though thinly sliced, lends a surprisingly robust flavor that permeates the meat and imbues the outer layer with a slightly pink tinge. You'll need to wrap the tenderloin a day ahead and refrigerate it overnight.

1 teaspoon chopped fresh thyme or rosemary	6–8 thin slices prosciutto or other cured ham (see Cook's Notes)
1 teaspoon chopped fresh sage	
2 teaspoons freshly ground black pepper	1 tablespoon extra-virgin olive oil
2 1- to 1¼-pound pork tenderloins	

1 Combine the thyme, sage, and pepper in a small bowl. Rub the mixture all over the tenderloins. Wrap each tenderloin with the prosciutto in a spiral pattern. It's okay if there is some overlap or if some areas of the tenderloin remain exposed. Tie each tenderloin at 2-inch intervals with butcher's twine, then wrap in plastic wrap and refrigerate overnight.

2 The next day, allow the meat to rest at room temperature for 1 hour.

3 Preheat the oven to 350°F.

4 Heat the oil in a large nonstick skillet over medium heat. Add the tenderloins and cook, turning, until lightly colored on all sides, about 4 minutes total. Place in a roasting pan and roast for 10 to 15 minutes, or until the internal temperature registers 135°F to 140°F on an instant-read thermometer. Remove the tenderloins to a platter and let rest, tented with aluminum foil, for 10 minutes.

5 Remove the twine, slice the pork ½ inch thick, and serve at once.

Alternative Cuts: Boneless pork loin, sirloin roast, or top round (inside); or boneless sirloin tip (knuckle) roast.

Cook's Notes

- Buy the best prosciutto you can find, such as Italian prosciutto from Parma or San Daniele. Some domestic brands can be quite salty and harsh, so taste a little sample before you buy them. However, brands such as La Quercia from Iowa (see Sources), are as good as the very best Italian.

- You can wrap the tenderloins in thin slices of pancetta, coppa, or even bacon instead of the prosciutto. Try serrano ham from Spain or some of the salty American country hams that are marketed as American prosciutto, such as Newsom's country ham. I also like Surryano from Wallace Edwards & Sons, in Surry, Virginia (see Sources), an air-dried ham in the Spanish style. For a smoky flavor, use Italian speck or German Westphalian ham.

- You can turn the roast into a complete meal by making a pan sauce and then serving slices of the meat over creamy polenta. To make a pan sauce, deglaze the roasting pan with ½ cup marsala or Madeira. Add 1 cup diced ripe tomatoes, ½ pound sliced mushrooms, 2 sliced garlic cloves, and 3 or 4 fresh sage leaves. Boil until the mushrooms are cooked and the liquid just becomes syrupy. Ladle some of the sauce over the polenta and top with the sliced pork tenderloin.

Leftovers

- Slice cold leftover tenderloin ¼ inch thick and lay on a split Italian roll. Add a little fontina or provolone cheese, some shredded lettuce, sliced onions, sliced tomatoes, and peperoncini, then drizzle with a little extra-virgin olive oil and vinegar.

- Fill a split square of focaccia with leftover sliced tenderloin and fontina cheese and heat in a panini press or grill pan.

SPANISH-STYLE ROASTED RACK OF PORK WITH PAN-ROASTED ROMESCO SAUCE

Fit for Company, Heirloom Pork

Serves 6

Normally romesco sauce is served at room temperature. In this recipe, I roast the peppers, garlic, and tomato while the pork cooks and then combine them with the pan juices to make a warm sauce. I prefer an heirloom breed of pork. If you use supermarket pork, I recommend flavor-brining the meat first in a Spanish-inspired flavor brine (see Cook's Notes). If you are brining the meat, you'll need to begin the recipe 2 days in advance. Piquillo peppers are a supercharged Spanish pimiento. Even in Spain, they are seldom used fresh but are sold roasted, in cans or jars. If you can't find them, substitute canned whole pimientos or fire-roasted red bell peppers (see page 284).

Spanish Spice Paste

- 1 tablespoon salt
- 2 teaspoons freshly ground black pepper
- 1 tablespoon chopped fresh marjoram
- 1 tablespoon Spanish paprika (*pimentón de la Vera*; see Sources)
- 2 teaspoons minced garlic
- 2 tablespoons olive oil

- 1 6- to 8-bone center-cut pork loin rib roast (rack of pork; 4–5 pounds), chine bone removed
- 6 garlic cloves, sliced
- 4 whole piquillo peppers or pimientos
- 1 Roma tomato, peeled, halved, and seeded
- ¼ cup olive oil
- 1 cup Spanish dry sherry
- ½ cup roasted almonds (I use Spanish Marcona; see Cook's Notes)
- ¼ cup fresh bread crumbs
  Salt and freshly ground black pepper

1 **Paste:** Combine all the ingredients in a small bowl to make a paste. Rub all over the pork roast. Let the roast stand at room temperature for 2 hours.

2 Preheat the oven to 425°F.

3 Lay the roast bone side down in a roasting pan and roast for 15 minutes. Lower the oven temperature to 325°F. Scatter the sliced garlic over the bottom of a baking dish,

lay the peppers and tomato on top, pour over the oil, and roast along with the pork for 30 minutes. Remove the dish with the peppers and tomato and let cool.

4   Check the internal temperature of the roast with an instant-read thermometer. If it registers 135°F to 140°F, it's done. If not done, continue to roast, checking the temperature every 15 minutes. Transfer the roast to a cutting board, cover loosely with aluminum foil, and let rest for 15 to 20 minutes while you finish the sauce.

5   Pour off any fat from the roasting pan and pour in the sherry. Place over medium heat and scrape up any browned bits from the bottom of the pan. Pour all the liquid into a small saucepan and boil until reduced to about ¼ cup. Set aside.

6   Finely chop the almonds in a food processor. Add the roasted pepper and tomato mixture, with its oil, and the bread crumbs. Pulse a few times, then add the reduced sherry and process to form a smooth paste. Season to taste with salt and pepper.

7   To serve, cut the roast into individual chops. Serve the warm sauce on the side.

Alternative Cuts: Boneless pork loin, pork inside roast (top round), pork sirloin roast, pork knuckle roast, or Boston butt (increase the roasting time).

Cook's Notes

- To flavor-brine the pork, combine 7 cups water with ½ cup salt, ⅓ cup firmly packed light brown sugar, ¼ cup sherry vinegar, ¼ cup sweet sherry, ¼ teaspoon saffron threads, and 1 tablespoon Spanish paprika (*pimentón de la Vera*; see Sources). Stir until the salt and sugar are dissolved, and add 2 cups of ice cubes. Place the pork in a bowl or plastic storage tub. Cover with the flavor brine and refrigerate for 48 hours. Remove from the flavor brine, pat dry, and proceed with the recipe, omitting the salt from the rub.

- Roasted and salted Marcona almonds from Spain are sold at specialty food shops and online (see Sources). If you can't find them, use Blue Diamond roasted almonds.

PANCETTA-HERB-FLAVORED PORK LOIN WITH RHUBARB SAUCE

Fit for Company, Great Leftovers

Serves 6

The tart, fruity flavor of rhubarb is a superb match with roast pork. A pancetta and herb mixture gives this roast a delicate cured-pork taste.

1 3-pound boneless pork loin roast
   Double recipe Turkish Flavor Brine (page 252; see Cook's Notes)

Pancetta-Herb Paste

¼ pound pancetta, diced
2 teaspoons chopped fresh rosemary
2 teaspoons chopped fresh sage
2 garlic cloves, peeled
2 teaspoons freshly ground black pepper

Rhubarb Sauce

2 cups homemade pork stock (see page 168) or canned low-sodium chicken broth
1 cup pomegranate juice
2 cups sliced rhubarb
2 teaspoons dark brown sugar
¼ cup honey, plus more to taste
   Fresh lemon juice (optional)
2 teaspoons cornstarch (optional), mixed with 1 tablespoon cold water

1 Place the roast in a plastic storage container and pour over the flavor brine, making sure the pork is fully submerged. Refrigerate overnight, or for up to 24 hours.

2 **The next day, make the paste:** Place all the ingredients in a food processor and pulse several times to create a paste.

3 Remove the roast from the flavor brine and pat dry. Place fat side up on a work surface and cut 15 to 20 slits in the pork. Fill each slit with some of the paste and rub the remaining paste over the surface of the roast. Let the roast stand at room temperature for 2 hours.

4 Preheat the oven to 350°F.

5 Place the roast on a rack set in a roasting pan and roast for 1 hour and 15 minutes, until the internal temperature reaches 135°F to 140°F on an instant-read thermometer. If not done, continue to roast, checking the temperature every 15 minutes.

6 **Meanwhile, make the sauce:** Combine the stock, pomegranate juice, rhubarb, brown sugar, and honey in a small saucepan and bring to a boil. Reduce the heat to a simmer

and cook for 10 minutes, or until the rhubarb is tender. Taste and add more honey and/or some lemon juice. Set aside.

7   Remove the roast from the oven when done, transfer to a cutting board, and cover loosely with aluminum foil. Let rest for 15 minutes while you finish the sauce.

8   Remove the roasting rack from the pan and skim off any fat from the pan juices. Set the pan over medium heat and add the rhubarb sauce, scraping up any browned bits from the bottom of the pan. Pour the sauce back into its saucepan. Bring to a boil, reduce the heat to a simmer, and cook for 5 minutes. Season to taste with salt, pepper, honey, and/or lemon juice. For a slightly thicker sauce, whisk the cornstarch mixture into the sauce and bring to a boil. Cook for 10 to 15 seconds, or until the sauce is just thickened and lightly coats the back of a spoon.

9   Slice the roast, spoon over the sauce, and serve.

Alternative Cuts: Bone-in pork loin center-cut roast, any boneless roast cut from the leg, or boneless sirloin roast.

Cook's Notes

- If using heirloom or well-marbled pork, omit the flavor-brining step.

- If you don't have pancetta, use bacon or replace the pancetta with 4 tablespoons olive oil.

- Try this recipe with other semitart fruits, such as tart cherries, fresh or dried apricots, sour plums, or quinces.

DOUBLE RACK OF PORK, HONOR-GUARD STYLE, WITH MOREL PAN SAUCE

Fit for Company, Fit for a Crowd
Serves 12, with leftovers

Crown roast of pork was once considered the elegant presentation of choice for a proud Christmas table. But today's pork is leaner, and with a crown roast, which is made by cutting between each rib chop and forming the chops into a circle, the meat is easily overcooked before the bone side is done. Shame, shame, shame. For a spectacular but less-risky preparation, have the butcher french the bones of two 7-bone rib racks. Then face them back to back, bones crisscrossed like a military salute of a "guard of honor."

The honor guard presentation lends itself to a savory stuffing, such as Chestnut, Bacon, and Corn Bread Stuffing (page 338). Bake the stuffing separately, then spoon it into the tunnel created by the two loins. For my family's Christmas dinner, I serve this dish with braised escarole and roasted potatoes.

Garlic, Shallot, and Herb Paste

- 3 garlic cloves, peeled
- ¼ cup coarsely chopped shallots
- 2 tablespoons chopped fresh sage
- 2 tablespoons chopped fresh rosemary
- 2 tablespoons salt
- 1 tablespoon freshly ground black pepper
- 3 tablespoons olive oil

- 2 7-bone center-cut pork loin rib roasts (rack of pork), chine bones removed, bones frenched, and fat trimmed to ¼ inch
- Morel Pan Sauce (recipe follows)

1   **Paste:** With the motor running, drop the garlic and shallots through the feed tube of a food processor and chop. Scrape down the sides of the bowl with a rubber spatula. Add the remaining ingredients and pulse several times to form a paste.

2   Lay each roast, bone side down, on a work surface and, using a sharp paring knife, cut 6 to 8 diagonal slices through the fat only (each cut about ¼ inch deep and 3 inches long). Rub the paste into the slits and over the fat, sides, and ends of the roast. Lay the roasts back to back in a roasting pan with the bones crisscrossing and pointing upward. Let rest at room temperature for 2 hours.

3   Preheat the oven to 350°F, with a rack in the lower third of the oven.

4   Place the roast in the oven, insert a continuous-read digital thermometer into the meat so that the tip is positioned dead center, and set it for 135°F. The roast should take 1¼

to 1½ hours to reach this temperature. If you are not using a continuous-read thermometer, begin checking the internal temperature of the roast with an instant-read thermometer after 1 hour. If not yet done, continue to roast, monitoring the temperature every 15 minutes. When done, remove the pork and tent loosely with aluminum foil. Let rest for at least 15 minutes, or up to 25 minutes. The meat will reach a final temperature of 140°F to 150°F (providing faintly pink meat). Make the sauce.

5   To carve the roast, you have two options: You can cut between the rib bones so that each guest gets a thick chop, or you can remove the bones by slicing between the bones and meat, cut the meat into ¼- to ½-inch-thick slices, and serve the bones separately (this will stretch the roast and accommodate variations in individual appetites). Serve with the Morel Pan Sauce on the side.

Alternative Cuts: None for the "honor guard" presentation, but you can use a boneless loin or T-bone loin roast for a less-fancy effect. Also good is the inside roast (top round) from the leg. If you use loin or leg, you may want to flavor-brine it first.

Cook's Notes

- Because today's commercial pork is so lean, I often recommend flavor-brining to improve the meat's juiciness and texture. However, if you cook the pork to no more than a final temperature of 145°F after resting (remove it from the oven at 135°F), the meat should be tender and juicy without flavor-brining. If your family insists on more well-done pork or you don't trust your ability to get the pork out of the oven quickly enough, you should flavor-brine the pork; don't cook it to more than 150°F, for a final internal temperature of 160°F after resting. (For those of you who still think pork should be cooked to 180°F, not even flavor-brining will help.) See page 249 for information on flavor-brining.

- If you are cooking this recipe for a special occasion, splurge on a rib-end center-cut loin roast from your local farmers' market or from an heirloom breed, such as Berkshire.

- For a less-gussied-up version, roast a single 7-bone rib end loin roast and cut the paste recipe in half. You can serve it as is or with a modified pan sauce, substituting less-expensive dried porcini for morels. For a sauce even kinder on the pocketbook, instead of dried mushrooms, use ½ pound sliced white or cremini mushrooms cooked with the butter and shallots until soft.

MOREL PAN SAUCE
Makes 1½ to 2 cups

2 ounces dried morel mushrooms
2 cups boiling water
1 tablespoon butter
2 tablespoons finely chopped shallots
2 tablespoons brandy

2 cups homemade pork stock (see page 168)
    or canned low-sodium chicken broth
1 cup heavy cream or crème fraîche
1 cup medium-dry sherry, such as Dry Sack
    Salt and freshly ground black pepper

1 Place the morels in a small bowl and pour over the boiling water. Soak for at least 45 minutes, or up to several hours, until soft. Remove the mushrooms from the liquid with a slotted spoon. Strain the soaking liquid, leaving behind any grit in the bottom of the bowl. Set aside.

2 Heat the butter in a medium saucepan over medium heat. Add the shallots and cook, stirring, for 2 minutes, or until they begin to color. Remove from the heat and add the brandy. Return to the burner and carefully tilt the pan to ignite or use a long match. Shake the pan until the brandy has almost evaporated. Whisk in the stock and cream. Add the mushroom soaking liquid and the mushrooms. Bring to a boil, reduce the heat to a simmer, and cook until the sauce lightly coats the back of a spoon, 10 to 15 minutes. Set aside. (*You can make the sauce to this point several hours ahead.*)

3 Pour off any fat from the roasting pan, leaving any meat juices behind. Place the pan over medium heat and pour in the sherry, scraping up any browned bits from the bottom of the pan. Bring to a boil and boil for 30 seconds, then pour through a strainer into the mushroom sauce. Bring the sauce back to a boil and cook, whisking, until it reduces to the consistency of heavy cream. Season to taste with salt and pepper and serve.

CHESTNUT, BACON, AND CORN BREAD STUFFING

Makes about 12 cups

---

3 cups fresh chestnuts (about 1 pound)

3 cups homemade chicken or turkey stock or canned low-sodium chicken broth, or more if needed

½ pound thick-sliced bacon, cut crosswise into ½-inch-wide strips

3 cups chopped onions

2 cups chopped celery

1 cup chopped dried apples

1 tablespoon chopped fresh thyme

2 teaspoons chopped fresh sage

8 cups store-bought dried corn bread stuffing mix or 8 cups coarse crumbs unsweetened homemade corn bread, dried in the oven

Salt and freshly ground black pepper

2–3 tablespoons butter

1 Preheat the oven to 450°F.

2 Cut a deep cross in the flat side of each chestnut. Spread the chestnuts on a baking sheet and roast until the shells begin to open, about 15 minutes. Remove from the oven and let cool just until cool enough to handle. Use a sharp paring knife to remove the shells and as much inner skin as possible (the remaining inner skin should rub off easily after the chestnuts are boiled).

3 Bring the stock and chestnuts to a boil in a medium saucepan. Reduce the heat to a simmer, cover, and cook until the chestnuts are tender, about 20 minutes. Remove the chestnuts with a slotted spoon and remove any remaining skin. Coarsely chop the chestnuts and set aside. Strain the stock and reserve.

4 Fry the bacon in a large heavy skillet over medium heat, stirring, until lightly crisped. Remove with a slotted spoon, leaving the fat behind in the pan. Add the onions and celery, cover, and cook until soft, stirring from time to time, about 5 minutes. Add the dried apples, thyme, sage, and 1 cup of the reserved stock and cook for 1 to 2 minutes more. Remove from the heat.

5 Place the corn bread, bacon, and chestnuts in a large bowl, add the onion mixture and liquid, and stir until the stuffing is moist but not wet. It should easily mound when pressed into a large spoon. Add more stock if the stuffing is too dry. Season to taste with salt and pepper.

6 Preheat the oven to 350°F. Butter a 3- to 4-quart casserole.

7 Place the stuffing in the casserole and dot the surface with the remaining butter. Cover the casserole and bake for 20 minutes. Uncover and continue baking until the top browns lightly, 20 to 25 minutes. Spoon as much stuffing as you can into the tunnel created by the pork loins and serve the rest in a serving bowl.

MELT-IN-YOUR-MOUTH PORK SHOULDER

Comfort Food, Cheap Eats, Rewarms Well, Heirloom Pork
Serves 6 to 8

This is an Italian-flavored version of pulled pork, and the slower you cook it, the more succulent and juicy the outcome. I prefer to cook it in a low (250°F) oven, but if your oven cannot reliably maintain that temperature, cook it at 300°F for 3 to 4 hours. The recipe, which has peasant roots, is sublime when made with pasture-raised heirloom pork.

Slow-Roast Herb Mix

- 2 tablespoons chopped fresh sage
- 2 tablespoons chopped fresh rosemary
- 2 tablespoons chopped garlic
- 1 teaspoon ground fennel seeds
- 1 tablespoon salt
- 2 teaspoons freshly ground black pepper

- 1 5- to 6-pound boneless Boston butt (pork shoulder butt), preferably from Berkshire, Duroc, Tamworth, or other heirloom breed
- 1 tablespoon olive oil

Green Olive Relish

- 2 anchovy fillets
- 1 small garlic clove, peeled
- ½ cup chopped fresh flat-leaf parsley
- ½ cup pitted green olives, such as picholine
- ¼ cup leafy celery tops
- 2 teaspoons finely grated lemon zest
- 1 teaspoon chopped fresh rosemary
- 1 teaspoon chopped fresh sage
- 2 teaspoons red wine vinegar
- 1 tablespoon fresh lemon juice
- ⅓ cup good extra-virgin olive oil
- Salt and freshly ground black pepper

1. Preheat the oven to 450°F, with a rack in the lower third of the oven.

2. **Herb mix:** Combine all the ingredients in a small bowl. Lay the roast fat side up on a work surface. Brush the oil all over the top and sides of the roast and rub the herb mix over the top and sides. If the roast is not tied, tie it with 4 or 5 loops of butcher's twine.

3. Place the roast fat side up on a rack in a roasting pan. Roast for 20 minutes. Reduce the heat to 250°F and continue to roast for 4 hours more. Check the roast. It is done when a fork can be inserted into the meat with little or no resistance and the meat is just shy of falling apart (the internal temperature will register 185°F to 190°F on an instant-read thermometer). If not done, continue roasting, checking the temperature

every 30 minutes or so; this may take 6 to 8 hours total. Remove from the oven, cover loosely with aluminum foil, and let rest for 15 to 20 minutes.

4   **Meanwhile, make the relish:** With the motor running, drop the anchovies and garlic through the feed tube of a food processor. Stop and scrape down the sides of the bowl and add the remaining ingredients except the oil, salt, and pepper. Pulse to chop everything quite fine. With the motor running, pour in the oil, then scrape into a small serving bowl and season to taste with salt and pepper.

5   Remove the twine from the roast. Cut the pork into chunks or pull into shreds and serve with the Green Olive Relish on the side.

Alternative Cuts: Bone-in Boston butt, bone-in picnic shoulder, or fresh pork belly.

Leftovers

- Shred leftover meat and warm briefly in a microwave. Toast French rolls. Combine the meat with some Green Olive Relish and a little mayonnaise and pile onto the rolls.

- Combine 2 cups shredded or diced meat with 1 to 2 cups Gary's Heirloom Tomato Sauce (page 316). Heat for 5 to 10 minutes, then toss with cooked fresh linguine or tagliatelle. Serve with freshly grated Parmigiano-Reggiano.

- Combine 1 cup shredded meat with 4 beaten eggs. Scramble, leaving the eggs moist. Sprinkle with shredded fontina cheese and serve on thick-cut toasted Italian or French bread, garnished with Green Olive Relish.

- Use as a filling for cannelloni or ravioli (see Veal Shank Ravioli with Brown Butter and Sage, page 588), mixed with a little ricotta and/or cooked spinach.

- Use as a filling for little half-moon-shape pastries (use the dough for Jamaican Beef Patties, page 150).

- Use as a filling for pierogi (page 305).

DRY-SALTED FRESH LEG OF PORK

Fit for Company, Fit for a Crowd, Family Meal, Great Leftovers
Serves 8 to 12

Not far from Des Moines, some of the best prosciutto produced anywhere on earth (including Italy) is made by artisans with very strict standards. The brand is La Quercia, meaning "the oak," in Italian, and the artisans are Herb and Kathy Eckhouse. One of the requirements the Eckhouses insist on for the pork they buy is that the pigs live an outdoor life, with room to run and root. When they can, they use heirloom breeds such as Berkshire and Tamworth. Much of the meat comes from pigs raised with organic methods. The result is prosciutto that is faintly sweet, deliciously porky, and silky in texture.

Herb and Kathy's favorite roast is leg of pork (fresh ham), which Kathy makes extra juicy by rubbing it with a generous amount of salt and fresh sage. This process, ironically, is adapted from the Jewish practice of "koshering" meat. Kathy's recipe is for a half ham, and she recommends using 1 teaspoon kosher salt per pound of meat or 2 to 3 tablespoons for a 6- to 9-pound half ham. For a 12- to 18-pound whole ham, use 4 to 6 tablespoons. While this roast is a lengthy endeavor, taking 5 days to prepare, most of the prep is hands off, and the results are well worth the wait. The skin comes out crispy and delicious.

½ bone-in leg of pork (fresh ham), shank or rump end, skin on (6–9 pounds)

2–3 tablespoons salt

2½ tablespoons chopped fresh sage

2 tablespoons freshly ground black pepper

2 tablespoons minced garlic

1 Wash the ham and pat it dry. Scrape the skin all over, using a fish scaler or stiff wire brush. Lay the ham on a work surface with the thickest part of the fat up and cut a 1-inch crosshatch pattern into the skin, going about ½ inch into the fat.

2 Combine the salt, 1½ tablespoons of the sage, and 1½ tablespoons of the pepper in a small bowl and sprinkle over all sides of the ham, working it into the gashes of the crosshatch pattern. Place the ham in a 2-gallon zipper-lock bag, press out as much air as possible, seal, and refrigerate overnight.

3 The next day, redistribute the salt by opening the bag and massaging the salt into the meat. Squeeze out as much air as possible from the bag, reseal it, and refrigerate overnight. Repeat the salt redistribution and massaging every day for a total of 4 days.

4 About 16 hours before roasting, remove the ham from the bag. Wipe the ham with paper towels until there is no visible salt and the meat is moist but not wet. Place in

a roasting pan with the crosshatch side up and refrigerate, uncovered, for at least 8 hours, or up to 12 hours. This drying helps to make the skin bubble and become crisp.

5   About 4 hours before roasting, remove the roast from the refrigerator and let warm at room temperature.

6   Preheat the oven to 450°F.

7   When ready to roast, sprinkle the meat with the remaining 1 tablespoon sage, the remaining ½ tablespoon pepper, and the garlic and work the herbs and garlic into the slashes created by the scoring. Roast the ham for 20 minutes. Reduce the heat to 325°F, roast for 2½ hours more, and begin checking the internal temperature every 15 minutes with an instant-read thermometer. Remove the roast at 135°F to 140°F. Let rest for 30 to 45 minutes, then carve and serve.

Alternative Cuts: Boston butt (reduce the salting to 2 days and roast to an internal temperature of 150°F to 160°F) or whole skin-on leg of pork.

Cook's Note
- The skin should be bubbly and crispy. If it is not, at the end of the cooking, turn up the oven to 400°F and roast for 10 minutes more.

Ham

Technically a ham is the meat of the thigh of a hog, but that says nothing about whether that thigh meat is raw, salted, or cured in salt brine — and a ham can be any of these. In this chapter, I focus on ham that is cured in salt brine, then smoked and cooked.

These brine-cured hams are referred to as **city hams**. They're different from country hams, which are rubbed with a mixture of salt and sugar (and sometimes nitrates or nitrites; see page 347) and aged after smoking.

Back in the day, fine city hams were made by time-honored methods that involved immersing the pork thighs in a solution of salt, sugar, and sodium nitrites. Five or six weeks later, the thighs were smoked for several days, then partially cooked. The hams were labeled "ham, partially cooked" and required baking before eating. Only a few mail-order sources exist for this sort of ham today (see Sources).

Most of the hams you find in supermarkets now are fully cooked, and they've been made much more quickly. The meat is injected with a curing solution of water, salt, sometimes sugar, phosphates, sodium lactate, sodium diacetate, and nitrites. Injecting the cure immediately disperses it throughout the ham, causing the muscle tissue to act like a sponge and swell and distort. Sodium lactate and sodium diacetate prevent the growth of disease-causing bacteria, such as listeria. Phosphates ensure that the water pumped into the muscle stays there after processing, smoking, and cooking. It's this extra water that gives this type of ham its soft, spongy, and rubbery texture.

For all the recipes in this book, I assume a ham quality of at least "ham with natural juices" or, better still, simply labeled "ham" (see page 345).

Hams and hams with natural juices are sold whole and as halves. Whole hams are the more flavorful and least wasteful cut. They weigh from 12 to 20 pounds and will serve 20 to 25 people, with leftovers. The **shank half** is from the lower part of the leg and is relatively easy to carve. A 6- to 10-pound shank half serves 10 to 12 people. The **butt half** (also called the rump half) is from the upper part of the leg; it includes part of the hip bone (the aitchbone), which makes carving more difficult, but the butt end has more tender and flavorful meat. A 6- to 10-pound butt half serves 12 people.

Some companies offer a **partially boned whole ham**, which may also be called a club ham (see Sources). These hams have the aitchbone (hip) removed and are very easy to carve. And you may also find butt halves that are partially boned. Expect to pay more for these.

Partially boned hams are often sold sliced — what are called **spiral-cut hams**. I don't like them, because they come with a commercial-tasting glaze and tend to dry out when you warm them in the oven.

BEWARE THE WATER — CHOOSING A HAM

The more water remaining in a finished ham, the spongier the texture and the lower the quality and the price. Here are the USDA definitions, from the highest quality to the lowest. Unless you have a very tight budget, I recommend buying "ham" or "ham with natural juices" (the most common type).

Ham: This contains the highest percentage of protein — 20.5 percent — and the least amount of added water — none (the rest of the weight is fat and the natural juices in the meat tissue). It's worth searching out because it doesn't have the soft, spongy texture of a lesser-quality ham.

Ham with Natural Juices: Once smoked and cooked, this ham must contain at least 18.5 percent protein by weight. It will contain less than 10 percent added water — the "natural juices." All bone-in varieties will have a natural leg shape. Boneless varieties with a natural leg shape are suitable for baking; the reshaped, pressed, or cylindrical varieties should be used without cooking in sandwiches or salads.

Ham, Water Added: This ham must contain at least 17 percent protein; the percentage of water added is 10 percent and is not stated on the label. That means the ham weighs 10 percent more than its raw weight, and you pay for that water at ham prices.

Ham and Water Product: This is the cheapest of all supermarket hams, and it contains as much water as the manufacturer can shamelessly pump into it — up to 50 percent. The percentage of excess water compared with the raw weight must be stated on the label.

Water and Ham Product: This ham-like product contains more than 50 percent water and is sold to prisons, the military, and cheap mass feeders. I hope your paths never cross with these bags of salty water.

BONE-IN VERSUS BONELESS HAMS

I prefer bone-in hams for baking. To me, meat cooked on the bone always tastes better, but in the case of ham, there are more reasons than taste. When the bone is removed, manufacturers have to find a way to re-form a solid chunk of meat so that it doesn't fall apart when sliced. To do this, they usually process the boned-out ham in a machine called a vacuum tumbler. The result? A boneless ham has a slightly spongier texture than bone in. Not to mention the fact that leftover ham bones add great flavor to soups, greens, and bean dishes and can be used to make Ham Stock (page 363).

Hams at a Glance

From the Leg

Whole smoked ham, bone in. This ham can weigh between 14 and 20 pounds and is ideal for feeding 16 to 25 people.

Rump half, smoked ham, bone in (ham butt half, club ham). Look for hams with the aitchbone (hip bone) removed, which makes for much easier carving.

Shank half, smoked ham, bone in (ham shank half, half ham shank end). A little more waste than a rump half that does not have the aitchbone removed. Less expensive than the rump half.

Smoked ham, boneless. Comes in various sizes from whole and halves to smaller re-formed pieces. I prefer boneless versions that have the natural shape of the leg.

Country ham, bone in or boneless. Many varieties, depending on the producer. Drier and saltier than smoked "city" ham. Some companies also sell fully cooked versions (see Sources).

From the Shoulder

Whole shoulder picnic (picnic ham, smoked picnic, smoked callie). Much cheaper than a pork leg ham. This has more waste, fat, and sinew and can fall apart when sliced. Great for braising or for flavoring soups and bean dishes.

Smoked pork shoulder roll (smoked shoulder butt, cottage butt, cottage ham, daisy ham). Made from the Boston butt. This is boned, netted, and smoked. At 3 to 6 pounds, it is a nice alternative to traditional ham. Has ample fat for moist-heat cooking.

THE GREAT HAMS OF EUROPE

Prosciutto di Parma (Parma Ham). *Prosciutto* is the Italian word for "ham." It is cured by rubbing with salt only, then it's air dried and aged for at least ten months and sometimes as long as two years. Only prosciutto produced in Parma can be called prosciutto di Parma, but many other areas of Italy make prosciutto (an excellent prosciutto that comes from Friuli is labeled San Daniele). Prosciutto is usually thinly sliced and eaten uncooked. Cooked prosciutto, called prosciutto cotto, is sold sliced in delis.

Serrano Ham. Like prosciutto, this Spanish ham is cured by rubbing with salt (though sometimes with nitrites as well), then air-dried and aged. The best serrano hams are aged for two years or more. They are usually served thinly sliced and eaten raw. Because serrano is aged at higher temperatures than prosciutto, it has a different taste, with the deep flavors associated with well-aged cheeses. Until quite recently, it was not available in the United States; it is sold in better delis or markets.

Ibérico Ham. Made just like serrano ham, these hams are made from the meat of the semi-wild indigenous Ibérico pig, which is often fattened on acorns (called *bellota*), resulting in fattier hams. Acorn-fed Ibérico ham from Spain is now available in the United States, but this rare and unctuous treat sells at about $200 per pound. It is always served sliced and raw.

Bayonne Ham. This salted and dry-cured ham comes from the Southwest of France. True Bayonne ham is made under strict regulations, beginning with how specific breeds of pigs are raised. During the aging process — at least seven months, but usually nine or ten — the ham is rubbed with a ground red pepper called *piment d'Espelette*, which gives the ham a slightly tangy flavor. Once fully aged and ready for market, true Bayonne ham is marked with a cross topped with the name "Bayonne." It is not currently sold in the United States, but it is available in Canada.

Westphalian Ham. This partially cooked German ham is cured with juniper and then heavily smoked, sometimes with juniper. It is usually eaten thinly sliced, with no further cooking. Some good brands are made in the United States (see Sources).

Jambon de Paris. This mild cooked ham is brine-cured and poached. Most often, it's not smoked. Jambon de Paris is usually sliced and eaten in sandwiches, the most famous being the melted ham and cheese called croque monsieur. Unlike deli boiled ham, jambon de Paris is not pumped with water and thus has a firm, not spongy, texture. It is available in the United States, or see the recipe on page 444 to make a similar-style ham.

Speck. Similar to Westphalian ham, this Italian dry-cured ham is flattened and smoked. It is less smoky than Westpahalian ham, and its taste and texture are similar to that of a lightly smoked prosciutto. Excellent speck is made in Iowa by La Quercia (see Sources).

York Ham. This English brine-cured or dry-cured ham is mild, not too salty, and similar in taste and texture to jambon de Paris. York ham can be baked with a sweet glaze. Cold and sliced, it makes a great sandwich. York ham is not available in the United States, but to make a similar ham on your own, see page 444.

Uncured "Nitrite-Free" and "All-Natural" Hams

Nitrates (NO_3) and nitrites (NO_2) have been used in curing hams for centuries. They not only give cured meat its characteristic red color but they help preserve the meat and inhibit the growth of certain bacteria, including the botulinum toxin.

Hams labeled "uncured" still contain nitrites, but the nitrites come from a vegetable source, such as celery juice, that is high in the compound. Manufacturers add special fermentation bacteria to the curing mixture, which will convert the nitrate in the juice to nitrite. Even though the ingredients list celery juice, the label will often say "no nitrites or nitrates added." This is because the USDA does not require manufacturers to declare nitrites unless they are used as an added chemical. Trust me: There is plenty of nitrite in "uncured" products.

These hams do not keep as well as hams that get their nitrites from an inorganic source, but some excellent-tasting "uncured" hams are available (see Sources).

Since the USDA defines "all natural" as "minimally processed," ham, which is by definition processed, cannot be called all natural. Meat companies that make the all-natural claim usually mean that the ham comes from an animal not treated with antibiotics or growth stimulants, but just saying "all natural" without such qualifiers means very little indeed.

"HAMS" THAT DON'T COME FROM THE HIND LEG

Picnic Hams. Made from the picnic shoulder (which is from the front leg), these hams are inexpensive but have more fat and usually more water than hind-leg hams. They are ideal to use in soups, bean dishes, and peasant-style dishes like braised cabbage and kraut. I don't recommend picnic ham for slicing because it is composed of several muscle groups that separate and fall apart.

Cottage Ham (Smoked Boston Butt). This smoked upper part of the pork shoulder (also called a daisy ham) may come boned and rolled. Like the picnic ham, it's great for braising and using in casseroles. Cottage ham can be sliced thin and fried like bacon. See page 442 for a recipe.

STORING HAM

- Refrigerate unbaked ham in its original vacuum packaging for up to 10 days.
- Once baked, ham can be refrigerated, tightly covered, for up to 5 days.
- Sliced ham is best used within 2 days. If it's vacuum-packed, it will keep for 1 week.
- Unsliced dry, cured, and aged country ham, such as Smithfield hams and hams like prosciutto and serrano, can be kept in a cool, dry, dark place almost indefinitely.

- Ham can be frozen for up to 2 months, but the salt used in the curing process increases the deterioration of quality and flavor. Due to its high water content, canned ham is especially vulnerable. Leave the ham in its original vacuum packaging. Pack leftover ham in a freezer-weight zipper-lock bag.
- Rainbow iridescence on sliced ham is due to light refraction on the film caused by the injected phosphates; it doesn't mean the ham is spoiled.

BAKED HAM WITH GLAZE AND SAUCE

Fit for Company, Fit for a Crowd, Great Leftovers

Half ham serves 10 to 12; whole ham serves 20 to 25

Nowadays, supermarket hams are sold fully cooked. Baking a ham serves to warm it through, remove some of the excess moisture and concentrate flavor, improve texture, and add flavor via a glaze or sauce.

½ bone-in (6–10 pounds) or boneless ham (5–9 pounds), or 1 whole bone-in (12–20 pounds) or boneless ham (10–18 pounds)

1 recipe Glaze/Sauce (pages 351–54) for ½ ham, or a double recipe for a whole ham

1 Preheat the oven to 325°F, with a rack in the lower third of the oven.

2 Trim away any skin from the ham and trim the external fat to a thickness of about ¼ inch. Place the ham fat side up on a work surface and score the fat to a depth of about ¼ inch in a 2-inch diamond pattern over the top surface.

3 Place the ham in a roasting pan. Insert a cable-type digital continuous-read thermometer, if you have one, in the center of the ham and set it for 115°F. Add enough of the liquid called for in the glaze/sauce recipe of your choice so that there is at least ¼ inch covering the bottom of the pan, and place in the oven. If you don't have a continuous-read thermometer, use 10 minutes per pound as a rough estimate of the minimum time at which to begin checking the internal temperature of the ham with an instant-read thermometer. As the ham bakes, continue to add water so that the bottom of the pan is always covered to a depth of at least ¼ inch.

4 When the internal temperature of the ham reaches 115°F, it is time to apply the glaze. Remove the ham from the oven and increase the heat to 425°F. Add more water to the pan, making sure there is now about ½ inch covering the bottom. Smear some of the glaze generously over the top surface of the ham, using a large spoon or pastry brush. Return the ham to the oven for 10 to 15 minutes, or until the glaze bubbles and begins to darken and the internal temperature reaches 130°F.

5 Remove the ham from the oven, transfer to a carving board or large platter, and let rest, loosely covered with aluminum foil, for 20 to 40 minutes. While the ham rests, the internal temperature will reach 140°F to 145°F.

6 Meanwhile, pour the pan juices into a heavy 2-quart saucepan and spoon off all of the grease. Whisk in the remaining glaze/sauce ingredients except for the cornstarch and

bring to a boil. Taste the sauce to determine if the flavors have concentrated to your liking. If not, continue to boil to concentrate the flavors. You may serve the sauce as is or, if you prefer the sauce thicker, stir in the cornstarch mixture in the recipe and whisk for about 30 seconds to lightly thicken the sauce to the consistency of maple syrup. Set aside and keep warm.

7 Carve the ham and arrange the slices on a platter. Pour the sauce into a small serving bowl or gravy boat and serve with the ham.

Leftovers

- Use leftovers for ham sandwiches or make any of the leftover ham recipes (pages 358–65). Keep the bone for Ham Stock (page 363) or soup (page 362).

Glazes and Sauces for Baked Ham

I like to do more than just flavor the outside of a ham with glaze. For extra flavor and juiciness, I use the glaze ingredients and pan juices to make a sauce to serve with the ham slices.

Soft drinks, such as root beer, Dr Pepper, ginger ale, and Coke, and fruit juices, such as orange and apple, go really well with ham and provide a great base for glazes and sauces.

ROOT BEER AND MUSTARD GLAZE/SAUCE

Makes enough for a half ham

3 cups root beer (don't use diet)

⅓ cup yellow mustard (I use French's)

¼ cup firmly packed dark brown sugar

¼ cup malt vinegar or cider vinegar

1 tablespoon cornstarch, mixed with ¼ cup cold water (optional)

1 Pour 2 cups of the root beer and enough water into the roasting pan to cover the bottom to a depth of at least ¼ inch as directed in step 3 of Baked Ham with Glaze and Sauce (page 349). Add more water to the roasting pan as needed to maintain a ¼-inch depth during the baking process.

2 Make the glaze while the ham is baking: Combine the remaining 1 cup root beer with the mustard, brown sugar, and vinegar in a small nonreactive saucepan. Bring to a boil and cook, stirring, until the glaze thickens to the consistency of molasses. Set aside.

3 Smear some of the glaze over the ham as directed in step 4 of Baked Ham. (If the glaze becomes too thick while sitting, rewarm gently and stir in a few spoonfuls of water.) Save the extra glaze to make the sauce.

4 To make the sauce, add the remaining glaze to the degreased pan juices as directed in step 6 of Baked Ham and bring to a boil. Thicken with the cornstarch mixture (if using) as directed.

DR PEPPER GLAZE/SAUCE

Makes enough for a half ham

3 cups Dr Pepper (don't use diet), or more as needed

½ cup pitted prunes

⅓ cup Dijon mustard

⅓ cup firmly packed dark brown sugar

2 tablespoons cider vinegar

1 tablespoon cornstarch, mixed with ¼ cup cold water (optional)

1 Pour 2 cups of the Dr Pepper and enough water into the roasting pan to cover the bottom to a depth of at least ¼ inch as directed in step 3 of Baked Ham with Glaze and Sauce (page 349). Add more water to the roasting pan as needed to maintain a ¼-inch depth during the baking process.

2 Make the glaze while the ham is baking: Combine the remaining 1 cup Dr Pepper with the prunes in a small nonreactive saucepan. Bring to a boil, reduce the heat to a simmer, and cook until the prunes are soft, adding more Dr Pepper if necessary so that the prunes remain covered, about 10 minutes. Remove the prunes with a slotted spoon and set aside. Whisk in the mustard, brown sugar, and vinegar, bring to a boil, and cook, stirring, until the glaze thickens to the consistency of molasses. Set aside.

3 Smear some of the glaze over the ham as directed in step 4 of Baked Ham. (If the glaze becomes too thick while sitting, rewarm gently and stir in a few spoonfuls of water.) Save the extra glaze to make the sauce.

4 To make the sauce, add the remaining glaze to the degreased pan juices as directed in step 6 of Baked Ham and bring to a boil. Thicken with the cornstarch mixture (if using) as directed. Add the reserved prunes just before serving and cook until they are heated through.

ORANGE JUICE AND MARMALADE GLAZE/SAUCE

Makes enough for a half ham

I like tangerine marmalade for this recipe, but you can also use orange, lemon, or any citrus marmalade. I have even used apricot preserves.

3 cups orange juice

1 cup marmalade, such as tangerine, or apricot preserves

½ teaspoon ground ginger

¼ teaspoon ground cloves

½ cup firmly packed light brown sugar

¼ cup fresh lemon juice, or more to taste

1 tablespoon cornstarch, mixed with ¼ cup cold water (optional)

1 Pour 2 cups of the orange juice and enough water into the roasting pan to cover the bottom to a depth of at least ¼ inch as directed in step 3 of Baked Ham with Glaze and Sauce (page 349). Add more water to the roasting pan as needed to maintain a ¼-inch depth during the baking process.

2 Make the glaze while the ham is baking: Combine ½ cup of the marmalade with the ginger, cloves, and brown sugar in a small nonreactive saucepan. Bring to a boil and cook, stirring, until the glaze thickens to the consistency of molasses. Keep warm.

3 Smear some of the glaze over the ham as directed in step 4 of Baked Ham. Save the extra glaze to make the sauce.

4 To make the sauce, add the remaining glaze, the remaining 1 cup orange juice, and the remaining ½ cup marmalade to the degreased pan juices as directed in step 6 of Baked Ham. Stir in the lemon juice, bring to a boil, and boil to concentrate the flavors to suit your taste. Add more lemon juice if desired. Thicken with the cornstarch mixture (if using) as directed.

APPLE CIDER, BOURBON, MOLASSES, AND PECAN GLAZE/SAUCE

Makes enough for a half ham

3 cups apple cider or apple juice

½ cup pecans

1 cup firmly packed dark brown sugar

2 tablespoons unsulfured molasses

1½ tablespoons dry mustard powder (I use Colman's)

¼ cup bourbon

1 Pour 2 cups of the apple cider and enough water into the roasting pan to cover the bottom to a depth of at least ¼ inch as indicated in step 3 of Baked Ham with Glaze and Sauce (page 349). Add more water to the roasting pan as needed to maintain a ¼-inch depth during the baking process.

2 Make the glaze while the ham is baking: Heat a 10-inch skillet over medium heat. Add the pecans in a single layer and toast, shaking the pan frequently, until the pecans begin to color and give off a lovely nutty aroma, about 5 minutes. Transfer the nuts to a bowl and let cool. Add the nuts to a food processor and pulse to coarsely chop; don't overchop. Scrape the nuts into a small bowl and stir in the brown sugar, 1 tablespoon of the molasses, the mustard, and 2 tablespoons of the bourbon. Set aside.

3 Smear some of the glaze over the ham as directed in step 4 of Baked Ham. Save the extra glaze to make the sauce.

4 To make the sauce, add the remaining 1 cup apple cider and the remaining 2 tablespoons bourbon to a small saucepan, bring to a boil, and cook to reduce by half, about 10 minutes. Pour the degreased pan juices into the saucepan and stir in the remaining 1 tablespoon molasses along with any remaining glaze as directed in step 6 of Baked Ham. Bring to a boil and boil to concentrate the flavors to suit your taste. Thicken with the cornstarch mixture (if using) as directed.

Country Ham

Most country hams are made by small producers who use methods that were perfected two hundred to three hundred years ago. The hams tasted good then, and they taste good now. In the old days in America, country hams were made wherever pigs were raised, but today most are produced in Virginia (the most common being Smithfield), Tennessee, the Carolinas, Georgia, Mississippi, Kentucky, Missouri, and Texas (for my favorite ham producers, see Sources).

Unlike city hams, country hams are made without water. Each leg is rubbed with a mixture of salt and sugar (some producers add nitrites or nitrates, spices, pepper, and other flavorings) and cured for one to three months. The hams may (or may not) be smoked over hickory, oak, or other aromatic woods. Then they are aged for several months to three years. Each producer creates unique flavor nuances in the ham. It all depends on the breed of pig, its diet, the cure, the temperature and wood used for smoking, aging times, and humidity.

While all country hams are saltier than city hams, the salt level will vary from one producer to the next. How long a ham has been aged will also affect saltiness and flavor. My recipe for cooking country ham is designed to extract as much salt as possible, but if you are not familiar with country ham, you may still find it salty.

Most likely your ham will have some greenish mold on the outside. This is normal and harmless, but you do have to scrub it off. You also need to soak the ham for 48 hours, then parboil it three times before you can begin to cook it. Yes, this is a commitment, but it is well worth it. Country ham is not for the timid (maybe that's why I like it). Real ham lovers think nothing beats the flavor of a well-aged country ham, which intensifies in the mouth, somewhat like two-year-old Parmigiano-Reggiano.

Many producers now sell fully cooked versions of their country hams in various sizes. This means they did all the scrubbing, soaking, parboiling, and poaching at their plant, and all you have to do is slice it thin and eat it, or bake it — with a glaze, if you like — to get it warm. This is an ideal way for a novice to get acquainted with the joys of country ham.

Other producers, aware of the popularity of dry-cured European hams like serrano and prosciutto — which are eaten raw — now sell less salty country hams, which they call prosciutto or American prosciutto. My recipes assume you will be using the traditional, saltier country ham.

COUNTRY HAM WITH MAPLE, TEA, AND CARDAMOM GLAZE AND SAUCE

Fit for Company, Fit for a Crowd, Great Leftovers
Serves 16 to 20

Unless you live in the South, you may not find country hams at your supermarket. Most of the smokehouses that make them, however, sell them over the Internet (see Sources). Country hams vary considerably in their level of saltiness, smokiness, length of aging, and quality, so you may want to try a few to see which ones suit your taste.

The best way to enjoy the ham is very thinly sliced and served on warm biscuits with a drizzle of the sauce and a side of sweet potatoes.

1 12- to 16-pound bone-in country ham (see Cook's Notes)	1 cup real maple syrup
3 cups brewed black tea	½ teaspoon ground cardamom
2 cups apple cider or apple juice	½ cup firmly packed light brown sugar
¼ cup bourbon (optional)	¼ cup cider vinegar

1 Wash the ham under cold water, scrubbing the skin with a stiff brush to remove any black pepper coating or mold. Put the ham in a very large pot or tub or a clean sink, big enough so that the ham can be completely submerged in cold water. Soak the ham for 48 hours, changing the water six to eight times to extract as much of the salt as possible. Drain and scrub the ham again to remove any remaining pepper or mold. Rinse the ham thoroughly.

2 Put the ham in a very large pot and cover it completely with cold water. Bring to a boil, then drain and discard the water. Refill the pot with water to cover the ham, bring to a boil, and discard the water two more times. Finally, cover the ham again with cold water, bring to a boil, and reduce the heat to barely a simmer. Take care not to let the water actually boil; it should read about 180°F on an instant-read thermometer. Poach the ham, uncovered, for 4 hours at a slow simmer.

3 Slice off a bit of ham and taste it. It should be firm but tender and palatable, and it will probably still be quite salty. You may need to cook it for 1 to 2 hours more, depending on its salt level and how long it was aged. Taste it from time to time to judge its progress, until it is cooked to your liking. (*At this point, you can let the ham cool in its poaching liquid, then remove it, wrap it tightly in aluminum foil, and refrigerate it to bake and glaze the next day. Discard the liquid.*)

4   Preheat the oven to 350°F.

5   Drain the ham and discard the liquid. Carefully remove all the skin and any dark or discolored meat. Trim the fat, leaving a ⅛- to ¼-inch-thick layer, and score a criss-cross grid in the top of the fat, if you like. Place the ham fat side up in a roasting pan. Pour in 2 cups of the tea and enough water so that there is ¼ inch of liquid in the bottom of the pan. Bake for 30 minutes. (Or, if you have refrigerated the boiled ham, bake it for 2 hours, or until it reaches an internal temperature of 115°F.) Add water to the pan to maintain a ¼-inch depth during the baking process.

6   While the ham is baking, make the glaze: Combine the remaining 1 cup tea, the apple cider, bourbon (if using), maple syrup, cardamom, brown sugar, and vinegar in a small saucepan. Bring to a boil and cook until the glaze becomes syrupy. Set aside.

7   Increase the oven temperature to 425°F. Generously brush some of the glaze over the ham. Roast for 10 minutes, brush with the glaze again, and roast for 5 minutes more, or until the surface is glazed and bubbly. Reserve the remaining glaze to make the sauce. Place the ham on a cutting board or platter and let it rest, covered loosely with aluminum foil, for 20 to 45 minutes.

8   Taste the liquid in the pan and if it is not too salty, add 1 cup to the remaining glaze. If it is salty, add 1 cup water instead. Bring to a boil, and reduce until the sauce becomes syrupy.

9   Cut the ham into thin slices. Serve warm or at room temperature with the sauce on the side.

Cook's Notes

- If you are using a fully precooked country ham, start with step 4. There is no need to trim the ham, because that has already been done. Roast for about 10 minutes per pound, then check the internal temperature. When it reaches 115°F, begin to apply the glaze as directed.

- You may use any of the other glaze/sauce recipes on pages 351–54.

- Instead of glazing the ham, you can sprinkle it with a generous amount of confectioners' sugar, which will melt into a blanket of sweetness as you heat the ham for 10 minutes at 425°F. However, you will not have a sauce.

Leftovers

- Leftover ham can be served cold or rewarmed and stuffed into warm biscuits.

- Thick slices of cooked country ham can be fried and served with steamed greens.

- You can use country ham in the leftover ham recipes (pages 358–65).

HAM LEFTOVERS
HAM IN PORT AND RAISIN SAUCE

In a Hurry, Family Meal

Serves 4

This sauce is great made with leftover baked ham or with a ham steak or smoked pork chops. The sweet-and-sour sauce is also well suited to the saltiness of leftover country ham.

1 tablespoon butter	2 teaspoons Dijon mustard
1½ pounds leftover ham slices, one 1½-pound ham steak, or 4 smoked pork chops	1 cup canned low-sodium chicken broth
½ cup finely chopped onion	2 cups raisins
Salt and freshly ground black pepper	1 cup port
	2–3 tablespoons balsamic vinegar

1 Melt the butter in a 12-inch nonstick skillet over medium-high heat. Add the sliced ham in batches and fry for 1 minute, or until the slices begin to color. Turn and fry for 1 minute more, then transfer to a platter. Or, if using ham steak or smoked pork chops, sauté the meat in the butter for 3 minutes instead of 1 minute per side. Transfer to a platter.

2 Add the onion to the pan and season with a pinch each of salt and pepper. Reduce the heat to medium, cover, and cook, stirring occasionally, until the onion softens and begins to color, 5 to 7 minutes. Stir in the mustard, then the broth and raisins. Bring to a boil and cook, stirring, until the mustard is completely dissolved. Stir in the port and 2 tablespoons vinegar or to taste and continue to boil until the sauce is just syrupy.

3 Reduce the heat to a simmer, add the ham, cover, and cook for a minute or so more to rewarm the meat thoroughly. Transfer the ham to a serving platter and spoon the sauce and raisins over the ham.

BOURBON, STOUT, AND SWEET POTATO WAFFLES WITH HAM AND MAPLE SAUCE

Comfort Food, Family Meal

Serves 4

Perfect for an autumn breakfast or brunch, this dish is excellent made with country ham or regular ham and a great use of holiday-meal leftovers. You can use leftover sweet potatoes for the waffles as long as they don't have too many extra ingredients in them (no marshmallows, please). Otherwise boil, bake, or microwave a sweet potato (these are often mistakenly called yams in supermarkets) and mash it fresh. Just be sure it cools before you stir it into the batter.

Waffles
- 1½ cups all-purpose flour
- 1 tablespoon baking powder
- ½ teaspoon salt
- Pinch each freshly grated nutmeg, ground cardamom, and ground ginger
- 3 large eggs, separated
- ½ cup whole milk
- ½ cup Guinness or other stout or dark beer
- 2 tablespoons bourbon
- 1 cup cooked and mashed sweet potatoes
- 2 tablespoons butter, melted

Ham and Maple Sauce
- 2 tablespoons butter
- 2 cups ½-inch-diced leftover ham
- ⅓ cup chopped onion
- 1 cup heavy cream
- 1 cup leftover sauce from Baked Ham (page 349), Ham Stock (page 363), or home-made pork stock (see page 168)
- ¼ cup real maple syrup
- 2 tablespoons Dijon mustard
- Salt and freshly ground black pepper

Chopped fresh chives

1 **Waffles:** Stir together the flour, baking powder, salt, and spices in a large bowl. In another bowl, stir together the egg yolks, milk, stout, bourbon, sweet potatoes, and butter. Pour the wet mixture into the dry mixture, stirring until just combined.

2 Using a standing mixer or a hand mixer, beat the egg whites to stiff peaks. Gently fold them into the batter (it's okay if a few streaks of egg white remain).

3 **Sauce:** Melt the butter in a large nonstick skillet over medium-high heat. Add the ham and cook, stirring, until it begins to brown, 1 to 2 minutes. Stir in the onion and

cook until soft, about 5 minutes. Stir in the cream, leftover sauce, maple syrup, and mustard. Simmer until the sauce is slightly thickened, 5 to 8 minutes. Season to taste with salt and pepper. Keep warm.

4   Meanwhile, bake the waffles as directed by the waffle iron manufacturer.

5   Top the waffles with the ham sauce, garnish with the chives, and serve.

Alternative Cuts: Chopped ham steak; diced smoked pork chops or smoked pork loin (Canadian bacon); or slab bacon, cut into small chunks (pour off the grease before adding the cream). Cooking times may vary.

Cook's Notes

- If you don't have any stout or other dark beer, use light beer or even water.
- Maple syrup can be pricey, but the lower-grade, and often lower-priced, maple syrups are fuller in flavor. Feel free to go for the budget-friendly Grade B maple syrup for this recipe; its deeper flavor is a perfect match for the smoky ham.

GREENS, FRESH PEAS, AND HAM SOUP

In a Hurry, Cheap Eats, Meat as a Condiment, Fit for a Crowd, Family Meal

Serves 8

This light but satisfying soup captures the essence of spring, when sweet green peas first make their appearance. Unfortunately, unless they are used within a day or so after picking, the peas change from sweet to starchy. If you can't get really fresh peas, the solution is to use frozen, which are processed before they have turned starchy. That way, you can make this soup at any time of year.

1 tablespoon olive oil

1½ cups coarsely chopped onions

2 garlic cloves, minced
Salt and freshly ground black pepper

6 cups Ham Stock (recipe follows), homemade pork stock (see page 168), or canned low-sodium chicken broth

1 pound Yukon Gold potatoes, peeled and cut into ½-inch cubes

½ pound greens, such as kale, Swiss chard, mustard greens, or collard greens, ribs discarded, leaves coarsely chopped

1 fresh rosemary sprig

2 bay leaves

2 cups diced canned tomatoes (I use San Marzano)

1 pound leftover ham, cut into ½-inch cubes (about 2½ cups)

1 cup cooked white beans, such as Great Northern or zolfini

2 cups fresh or frozen peas

2 tablespoons fresh lemon juice, or more to taste

3 tablespoons finely chopped fresh flat-leaf parsley

Garnish

8 poached large eggs (optional)
Good extra-virgin olive oil
Freshly grated Parmigiano-Reggiano

1 Heat the oil in a large saucepan or soup pot over medium-high heat. Add the onions, garlic, and a sprinkle of salt and pepper and cook, stirring frequently, until the onions are translucent and beginning to brown, about 10 minutes. Add the stock, potatoes, and greens. Bring to a boil, reduce the heat to a simmer, and cook until the potatoes are just tender, about 15 minutes.

2 Tie the rosemary and bay leaves in a bundle with butcher's twine and add to the soup, along with the tomatoes, ham, and beans. Cook at a low simmer for 15 minutes.

3   Add the peas and cook for 5 minutes more. Discard the herb bundle. Add the lemon juice and season to taste with salt and pepper. Taste for seasonings and add more lemon juice, salt, and/or pepper. Stir in the parsley. Ladle the soup into heated soup bowls. Add a poached egg to each bowl (if using), drizzle with olive oil, and sprinkle with cheese.

Alternative Cuts: Diced smoked pork chops, meat from cooked ham hocks, or diced Canadian bacon.

Cook's Note
- Adding the poached eggs makes this a substantial lunch.

HAM STOCK

Makes about 2 quarts

This stock provides a hearty underpinning for soup.

1 meaty ham bone or 2–3 ham hocks (about 2 pounds total)	2 celery stalks, each broken into 3 or 4 pieces
1 onion, not peeled, studded with 2 cloves	1 fresh thyme sprig
3 garlic cloves, not peeled	3 bay leaves
1 carrot, peeled and cut into 3 pieces	1 teaspoon black peppercorns

1   Throw the ham bone or hocks into a soup pot and add everything else. Cover with cold water. Bring to a boil, then reduce the heat to a simmer, cover, and cook for 2½ to 3 hours, or until the broth has a nice hammy flavor or the ham hocks are tender. Strain and reserve any bits of ham or ham hock meat.

2   Refrigerate the meat and stock separately and remove any congealed fat before using.

GAMMY BROWN'S DEVILED HAM

Fit for a Crowd, Fit for Company

Makes 3 cups (enough for 12 as an hors d'oeuvre or 6 sandwiches)

This recipe was passed down from my wife's grandmother Gammy Brown to my wife's mother, Audrey, and eventually to Nancy. Neither of them ever measured anything or wrote down recipes. No two deviled hams were alike, but damned if they weren't all good.

Gammy Brown came from New Hampshire, where cob-smoked hams were enjoyed during the holidays. There were always plenty of leftovers, which were needed to feed the family members still hanging around a day or two after the feast. Deviled ham was a popular solution.

Spread it on sandwiches, or serve it as a snack or hors d'oeuvre on rye toasts, crackers, or crostini, or piped (or spooned) into celery stalks. Gammy Brown would never have used shallots or olive oil, but this is Nancy's interpretation. Feel free to change it to suit your family's tastes.

1 tablespoon olive oil

¼ cup chopped shallots

2½ cups ½-inch-diced leftover ham

½ cup finely chopped celery, including leafy tops

¼ cup chopped fresh flat-leaf parsley

1 tablespoon prepared horseradish, or more to taste

2 tablespoons Dijon mustard, or more to taste

⅓ cup mayonnaise, or more if needed

¼ cup finely chopped dill pickles, sweet pickles, or cornichons (optional)

Freshly ground black pepper

1 Heat the oil in a small skillet over medium heat. Add the shallots and cook until soft, about 3 minutes. Transfer to a medium bowl.

2 Put the ham into a food processor and pulse until coarsely chopped. Transfer to the bowl with the shallots. Add the celery, parsley, horseradish, mustard, mayonnaise, pickles (if using), and pepper to taste and stir to combine. Taste for seasonings. Add more horseradish, mustard, and/or pepper to taste and add more mayonnaise if the mixture seems too dry.

3 Pack the deviled ham into an attractive crock or serving bowl and serve at room temperature. (*Or cover and refrigerate for up to 1 week. Let sit at room temperature for 30 minutes before serving.*)

Pork Stews, Pot Roasts, and Other Braises

In order to yield moist, tender meat, pork cooked by moist-heat methods must have ample fat and some connective tissue. Ideal cuts for moist-heat cooking come from the shoulder (Boston butt and picnic shoulder), the blade end of the loin, and the belly; the ribs, shanks, neck, and trotters also work well.

For stews, I like Boston butt, picnic shoulder, country-style ribs, neck bones, spareribs, cheeks, shanks, and ham hocks. For pot roasts, I recommend Boston butt and the blade end of the loin.

Picnic ham and sausages also have ample fat. Take care, though, not to cook sausages too long in liquid; long cooking will leach out all of their flavor.

Tails, head, ears, and trotters are used in traditional peasant-style stews, such as Feijoada from Brazil (page 193). These cuts may be humble, but they're packed with flavor and texture.

Cuts from the center-cut loin, sirloin, tenderloin, and leg are too lean for braising.

Pork Braising Cuts at a Glance

From the Shoulder

Blade Boston butt roast, bone in (fresh pork butt, Boston shoulder, Boston butt, pork butt roast, Boston-style butt, pork shoulder butt). By far the most versatile cut for moist-heat cooking. Can be pot-roasted, stewed, or barbecued. Sold whole, halved, and cut into shapes. See country-style ribs, below. Inexpensive.

Blade Boston roast, boneless (boneless Boston Butt, boneless pork shoulder roast, rolled butt roast, butt roast, Boston roast). See bone-in blade Boston roast, above. Sold as whole, half, or in pieces. Should be tied or netted.

Country-style ribs, bone in or boneless (country ribs, blade-end country spareribs). Thick 4- to 6-inch-long strips cut from the Boston butt. Can be braised as is or cut up for stews.

Blade steaks, bone in or boneless (7-rib cut, pork steak). Can be braised as is or cut up for stews.

Arm picnic, usually bone in but sometimes boneless (fresh picnic, picnic shoulder, picnic). Sold whole or half, often with skin on, which adds body to a sauce. Can be pot-roasted, barbecued, or cut up for stew. Cheap, but has more waste than blade Boston butt roast. Also sold in a smaller piece as a pork shoulder arm roast.

Neck bones. Great for soups and stews, to add body and flavor. Sometimes sold smoked. Not much meat but very cheap.

Hocks (pork shanks, pork hocks). Sold whole or cut into thick rounds. Great for stews or other braised dishes. The skin and bones add rich flavor and body to sauces.

Smoked pork hock (ham hock, smoked ham hock, smoked pork shank). Sold skin on or without skin. Adds great flavor to bean dishes, soups, and sauerkraut.

Whole shoulder picnic (picnic ham, smoked picnic, smoked callie). Much cheaper than a pork leg ham. This has more waste, fat, and sinew and can fall apart when sliced. Great for braising or for flavoring soups and bean dishes.

Smoked pork shoulder roll (smoked shoulder butt, cottage butt, cottage ham, daisy ham). Made from the Boston butt. This is boned, netted, and smoked. At 3 to 6 pounds, it is a nice alternative to traditional ham. Has ample fat for moist-heat cooking.

From the Loin

Blade roast, bone in (blade-end pork loin roast, pork blade roast). Similar to the blade Boston butt roast but leaner and smaller. Can be pot-roasted, cut up for stew, or cut into blade chops or thick strips.

Blade chop, bone in or boneless (pork chop end cut, blade steak). The bone in are often cut into 2 pieces and sold as country-style ribs. These have ample fat for braising.

Country-style ribs, bone-in or boneless (country ribs). Made by butterflying boneless loin blade chops. Ideal for stews and braises.

From the Belly

Pork belly, boneless (fresh pork side meat, fresh belly, streak of lean, chunk side of pork, fresh bacon). Sold whole or in chunks of varying sizes. Can be braised until tender, then roasted or cut into pieces and fried.

Spareribs (fresh spareribs). Cut into separate ribs or pieces, ideal for rustic peasant dishes, bean dishes, and Asian dishes.

CUBAN-STYLE PORK AND RICE

Meat as a Condiment, Comfort Food, Cheap Eats, Rewarms Well

Serves 6

Ideal if you are pressed for time, this braise, a quick, spicy take on Spanish paella, uses the lean meat from the loin, which would dry out if cooked for longer. Marinate the pork ahead if you can. Leftovers can easily be rewarmed in a microwave.

Cuban Spice Paste

- ¼ cup Spanish paprika (*pimentón de la Vera*; see Sources) or sweet Hungarian paprika
- 2 teaspoons minced garlic
- ¼ cup fresh lime juice
- 2 tablespoons rum (optional)
- 1½ teaspoons salt
- 1 teaspoon freshly ground black pepper
- 2 teaspoons chopped fresh oregano
- ½ teaspoon ground cumin
- 2 tablespoons olive oil

- 1½ pounds boneless pork loin chops (1 inch thick), cut into 1-inch cubes
- 1 tablespoon olive oil

- 2 cups chopped onions
- 2 tablespoons chopped garlic
- 2 cups Arborio rice
- 3 cups canned low-sodium chicken broth
- 1 cup drained canned diced tomatoes
- ¼ teaspoon saffron threads
- 2 tablespoons capers, rinsed
- ½ cup fire-roasted red bell peppers (see page 284) or jarred piquillo peppers, cut into strips
- 16 large shrimp in their shells (optional)
- 2 cups (1 package) frozen artichoke hearts, thawed, or 2 cups cooked fresh green beans, or frozen, thawed
- Salt and freshly ground black pepper

1 **Spice paste:** Combine all the ingredients in a medium bowl and mix to make a homogenous paste. Add the pork and toss to coat well. (*For the best flavor, refrigerate the pork, covered, for up to 16 hours.*)

2 Preheat the oven to 350°F.

3 Heat the oil in a large nonstick ovenproof skillet over medium-high heat. Remove the pork from the spice paste and pat dry, reserving the spice paste in the bowl. Add the pork to the pan and cook, turning occasionally, for 5 minutes, or until browned on all sides. Remove the pork and set aside. Reduce the heat to medium, add the onions and garlic, and cook, scraping up any browned bits from the bottom of the pan, for 5 minutes, or until soft. Add the rice, stirring until well coated with the onion mixture.

Stir in the broth, tomatoes, saffron, and the reserved spice paste. Bring to a boil, reduce the heat to a simmer, and cook for 15 minutes.

4   Stir in the capers, cover, and transfer to the oven. Bake for 10 minutes. Stir in the pork, then scatter the the peppers, shrimp (if using), and artichoke hearts over the rice. Cover and bake for 10 minutes more, or until the rice is tender, the liquid has been absorbed, and the shrimp (if using) are opaque and pink.

5   To serve, stir the rice to incorporate all the ingredients and season to taste with salt and pepper.

Alternative Cuts: Cubes cut from the leg, sirloin, or tenderloin.

Cook's Note

- For a more flavorful and longer-cooking version of pork and rice, use cubed Boston butt or cubed boneless country-style ribs. Don't remove the pork from the skillet once it is browned; simply proceed with the recipe. Add an extra 10 minutes to the baking time before adding the peppers.

Leftovers

- Combine 2 to 3 cups leftovers with 6 beaten eggs to make a Spanish *tortilla* ("flat omelet"). Garnish with shredded Manchego cheese.

- For a great cold dish, toss some of the leftover rice mixture with cooked vegetables, such as carrots, green beans, asparagus, peas, cauliflower, or broccoli, and dress with a vinaigrette made with fresh lime juice.

PORK STEW WITH FENNEL AND BUTTERNUT SQUASH

Cheap Eats, Two-for-One, Family Meal, Rewarms Well, Freezes Well, Heirloom Pork

Serves 4, with leftovers

Nothing suggests that colder days are ahead more than the appearance of winter squash. There are many varieties, but I keep coming back to butternut squash as my favorite. Readily available, it keeps well for months, has a deep, sweet flavor, and holds its shape well when stewed. Combined with pork, fresh fennel, and tomato, it produces a stew that is much greater than the sum of its parts. I like to cut the pork into big chunks; they hold their shape and are much more appealing than little cubes.

Aromatic Spice Rub

- 2 teaspoons salt
- 1 teaspoon freshly ground black pepper
- ½ teaspoon cayenne pepper
- ¼ teaspoon ground ginger
- 1 teaspoon dried rubbed sage
- ¼ teaspoon freshly grated nutmeg
- 1 teaspoon fennel pollen (see Sources) or ground fennel seeds

- 3 pounds boneless Boston butt, trimmed of external fat and cut into 3-inch chunks

- ¼ pound pancetta, diced into ¼-inch cubes
- 2 cups chopped onions
- 2 tablespoons chopped garlic
- 2 cups homemade pork stock (see page 168) or canned low-sodium chicken broth
- 1 cup dry red wine
- 2 cups peeled, seeded, and diced tomatoes (fresh or canned)
- 2 large fennel bulbs, fronds chopped, stalks discarded, bulbs cut into 1-inch chunks
- 3 cups 1½-inch cubes peeled butternut squash
- Salt and freshly ground black pepper

1. **Rub:** Combine all the ingredients in a small bowl. Rub all over the pork chunks. Set aside for 1 hour, or cover and refrigerate overnight.

2. Preheat the oven to 350°F.

3. Heat a large Dutch oven over medium heat. Add the pancetta and cook until it is browned and the fat has rendered, about 5 minutes. Remove the pancetta with a slotted spoon and set aside, leaving about 3 tablespoons fat in the pot. Increase the heat to medium-high, add the pork, and brown on all sides, 7 to 10 minutes. Remove the pork with a slotted spoon and set aside. Pour off all but 2 tablespoons of the fat.

4   Add the onions and garlic and cook, stirring, until soft, about 5 minutes. Add the stock, red wine, and tomatoes and bring to a boil, scraping up any browned bits from the bottom of the pot. Add the pancetta and pork.

5   Cover and bake for 1 hour.

6   Remove the pot from the oven and add the fennel fronds and bulbs and squash. Bake, covered, for 30 minutes more, or until the meat and vegetables are quite tender. Remove from the oven and, with a slotted spoon, remove the meat and vegetables to a warm platter or serving bowl. Degrease the surface of the sauce, and if the sauce is thin, bring to a boil and reduce it until it begins to thicken and become syrupy. Season to taste with salt and pepper. Add the meat and vegetables and heat through, then return to the platter and serve at once.

Alternative Cuts: Boneless country-style ribs, blade steaks, shoulder steaks, pork cheeks, or neck bones. Or shanks, cut into 2-inch-thick rounds. Cheeks, neck bones, and shanks will require longer cooking times.

Cook's Note
- For a deeper, more intense porky flavor, try this stew with meat from heirloom breeds, such as Berkshire, Tamworth, or Duroc. Using the homemade pork stock will also provide more flavor.

Leftovers
- Serve leftover stew over large pasta shapes such as farfalle, rotini, or rigatoni, and make sure to provide Parmigiano-Reggiano to sprinkle over the top.
- If you have lots of stew left over, make a delicious pie by covering the stew with your favorite corn bread recipe or the one from Pot-Roasted Veal on a Cloud (page 573). You can also make a great topping with biscuits.

CARCAMUSAS (SPANISH-STYLE PORK STEW WITH CHORIZO AND PAPRIKA)

Rewarms Well, Great Leftovers
Serves 4 to 6

As a guest of the Trade Commission of Spain, I went with a group to the ancient walled city of Toledo in Castilla–La Mancha to learn about the foods of the region. Shortly after arriving, we settled in at a small bar-restaurant called Cámara de Toledo, located off the main square, for some tapas. First to arrive were plates of hand-cut local serrano ham, thinly sliced rounds of air-dried chorizo, and Manchego cheese. Then came cubes of crispy fried potatoes and *carcamusas,* a stewy concoction of chorizo and diced tender pork. It took only a single bite for me to realize I had to have the recipe for this specialty. When I asked the host for the recipe, I got a vague list of ingredients with no measurements or instructions. Through trial and error, I came up with something pretty close to what I remember. I recommend serving *carcamusas* with diced potatoes (Yukon Gold potatoes are best), cooked in olive oil until golden and crisp.

The stew is best made ahead so the assertive flavors of the chorizo and ham can mellow and penetrate the pork.

1 tablespoon extra-virgin olive oil

½ pound Spanish-style chorizo (see Cook's Note) or linguica, diced

3 cups thinly sliced onions

2 tablespoons finely chopped garlic

2 tablespoons Spanish paprika (*pimentón de la Vera*; see Sources)

2 pounds boneless country-style ribs, cut into 1-inch chunks

Salt and freshly ground black pepper

3 cups dry white wine

2 cups canned low-sodium chicken broth, or more if needed

2 generous pinches saffron threads (I use Spanish)

2 teaspoons chopped fresh marjoram or oregano

¼ cup chopped fresh flat-leaf parsley

2 cups peeled, seeded, and diced vine-ripened tomatoes, canned diced tomatoes (I use Muir Glen), or Gary's Heirloom Tomato Sauce (page 316)

1 12-ounce package frozen peas

1   Heat the oil in a large pot or Dutch oven over medium heat and add the chorizo. Cook until the edges begin to color, stirring from time to time, about 5 minutes. Add the onions and garlic, cover, and cook, stirring occasionally, until the onions are quite

soft, about 10 minutes. Sprinkle over the paprika, stir to coat, and cook for 1 minute. Add the ribs and a sprinkle each of salt and pepper, stir well, and cook, stirring, for 5 minutes. Add the white wine and increase the heat to high. Boil to reduce the wine to about 1 cup, about 10 minutes.

2 Meanwhile, bring the chicken broth and saffron to a boil in a saucepan. Remove from the heat.

3 When the wine has reduced, add the warm broth, marjoram, parsley, and tomatoes. Simmer, uncovered, for 45 to 65 minutes, or until the pork is tender and the sauce is just beginning to thicken. If it's too thick, add more broth. *(At this point you can cool and refrigerate overnight.)*

4 Degrease the surface. If it's been refrigerated, rewarm the stew over low heat. Add the peas and cook for about 5 minutes. Season to taste with salt and pepper, and serve.

Alternative Cuts: Boneless Boston butt, bone-in blade steak, blade pork chops, or back ribs (cooked on the bone).

Cook's Note

- Do not use Mexican chorizo. Look for Spanish chorizo that is not fully dried but somewhat soft when squeezed, called *semicurado* (see Sources). To make your own, see page 414.

Leftovers

- Serve leftovers over wide noodles like pappardelle or over linguine and garnish with grated aged Manchego cheese.

- *Carcamusas* is also great served over bulgur, brown rice, or couscous.

- For a great casserole, combine 2 to 3 cups leftover *carcamusas* with 3 to 4 cups cooked bulgur, brown rice, or couscous in a baking dish. Dot the top with butter and bake in a 350°F oven for 20 minutes, until heated through.

PORK STEW WITH HARD CIDER, BABY ONIONS, AND POTATOES

Family Meal, Great Leftovers, Rewarms Well

Serves 6

I often look for alcoholic beverages other than wine and beer to add flavor and depth to stews. For pork stews, hard cider fits this role perfectly. It's not too sweet, yet its subtle apple flavors marry perfectly with pork and ingredients such as onions and potatoes. In the last few years, several artisanal producers have responded to the demand for hard ciders. Check out your local specialty liquor store to see what is available in your area, and buy extra to serve with the stew. I like Two Rivers Cider from Sacramento, California.

¼ pound bacon (I use applewood-smoked; see Sources), cut crosswise into ¼-inch-wide strips	1½ cups hard cider, still or sparkling
3 pounds boneless Boston butt or boneless country-style ribs, trimmed of excess fat and cut into 2-inch cubes	2 cups homemade pork stock (see page 168) or canned low-sodium chicken broth
	30 small boiling onions, trimmed and peeled
Salt and freshly ground black pepper	1½ pounds small red potatoes (about 2 inches in diameter), scrubbed and cut in half
½ cup chopped shallots	2 semitart apples (Granny Smith, Pippin, or Jonathan), peeled, cored, and cut into 1-inch dice
½ cup finely chopped peeled parsnips	
2 teaspoons chopped fresh sage	1 tablespoon coarse-grain mustard
½ cup Calvados (optional)	

1   Heat a large Dutch oven over medium heat. Add the bacon and fry until lightly browned. Remove with a slotted spoon and set aside, leaving about 3 tablespoons of fat in the pot.

2   Season the pork with salt and pepper and place in the pot. Increase the heat to medium-high and brown the pork on all sides, 5 to 7 minutes. Remove with a slotted spoon and set aside.

3   Reduce the heat to medium, add the shallots and parsnips, and cook, covered, for 5 minutes, stirring from time to time. Stir in the sage and cook for 1 minute more. Add the Calvados (if using) and reduce until almost evaporated, 5 minutes. Add the cider, stock, and reserved bacon and pork and scrape up any browned bits from the bottom of the pot. Bring to a boil, reduce the heat to a simmer, cover, and cook for 40 minutes.

4 Add the onions and potatoes and cook for 10 minutes more. Add the apples and cook for an additional 10 minutes, or until the potatoes and pork are fork-tender. Strain the solids from the liquid and reserve.

5 Return the liquid to the pot and skim off the fat from the surface. Whisk in the mustard, bring to a boil, and cook until just thickened and syrupy, 10 minutes. Return the solids to the pot and heat for 1 minute. Season to taste with salt and pepper and serve in shallow soup bowls.

Alternative Cuts: Shanks, cut into 2-inch rounds (cook for 1½ hours before adding the potatoes) or cheeks (cook for 1½ to 2 hours before adding the potatoes).

Cook's Notes

- Instead of Calvados, you can use brandy.

- For a great variation, substitute yellow or orange sweet potatoes for the red potatoes. Cut them into 2-inch chunks.

Leftovers

- Turn leftovers into a deep-dish pie. You'll need about 4 cups. Pour into a deep-dish pie plate or a casserole dish and top with your favorite flaky biscuit recipe, or use the crust from Irish Beef-Cheek Pie with Stout (page 222).

WINE AND VINEGAR–BRAISED PICNIC SHOULDER

Cheap Eats, Rewarms Well, Great Leftovers
Serves 6, *with leftovers*

Picnic shoulder, which is the leg portion of the front shoulder, is one of the only cuts customarily sold with the skin still on. When slowly braised, the skin gives the resulting sauce great body. While the picnic shoulder has lots of bone and gristle, the meat is usually well marbled and becomes soft and tender during braising. Leftovers provide lots of opportunities for tasty fillings for stuffed pasta, such as ravioli.

Sage and Thyme Rub

- 1 tablespoon chopped fresh sage
- 1 tablespoon chopped fresh thyme
- 2 garlic cloves, peeled
- 1 teaspoon salt
- 1 teaspoon freshly ground black pepper
- 1 tablespoon olive oil

- 1 3½- to 4-pound bone-in picnic shoulder (with skin), tied with 3 or 4 loops of butcher's twine
- 1 tablespoon olive oil
- ¼ pound pancetta or dried coppa, chopped
- 2 cups thinly sliced onions
- ½ cup finely chopped peeled carrots

- ½ cup thinly sliced shallots
- 1 cup finely chopped celery
- 2 tablespoons minced garlic
- 1 teaspoon chopped fresh thyme
- 2 bay leaves
- ½ teaspoon ground ginger
- Salt and freshly ground black pepper
- ½ cup grappa, Calvados, or brandy (optional)
- ½ cup cider vinegar or white vinegar
- 2 cups dry white wine
- 2 cups homemade pork stock (see page 168) or canned low-sodium chicken broth
- 12 cipollini onions or 24 boiling onions, trimmed and peeled
- Sugar

1. **Rub:** Combine the sage, thyme, garlic, and salt in a mortar, and with the pestle, pound and mash to form a paste. Stir in the pepper and olive oil. Score the skin of the pork to form a 1-inch crosshatch pattern about ¼ inch deep. Make slits all over the rest of the pork and press the rub into the slits and crosshatches. Smear any extra rub over the surface of the pork. Set aside for 1 hour, or cover and refrigerate overnight.

2. Preheat the oven to 325°F.

3. Heat the oil in a large Dutch oven over medium heat. Add the pancetta and cook, stirring, until it browns and begins to crisp, about 5 minutes. Remove with a slotted spoon

and set aside. Turn up the heat to medium-high, add the pork, and brown on all sides, about 10 minutes. Remove and set aside.

4. Pour off all but 2 tablespoons of fat from the pot and reduce the heat to medium. Add the sliced onions, carrots, shallots, and celery, cover, and cook, stirring from time to time, until the vegetables are soft, about 10 minutes. Add the garlic, thyme, bay leaves, ginger, and a pinch each of salt and pepper and cook for 1 minute more. Add the grappa (if using) and bring to a boil, scraping up any browned bits from the bottom of the pot. Boil until the liquor has almost evaporated, 3 to 5 minutes. Add the vinegar, bring to a boil, and continue to boil until reduced by half, 3 to 5 minutes. Add the white wine and stock and bring to a boil again.

5. Return the pancetta and pork, fat side up, to the pot. Cover, place the pot in the oven, and braise for 2½ to 3 hours, turning the roast every hour, until the pork is very tender. Taste it to tell. (*At this point, you can cool the roast in the liquid and refrigerate for up to 3 days.*)

6. Transfer the roast to a platter and cover loosely with aluminum foil. Skim any fat from the surface of the sauce. Discard the bay leaves. Add the cipollini onions, cover, and cook over medium heat for 10 minutes, or until tender. If the sauce is thin, remove the solids and reduce until it just turns syrupy. Season to taste with salt, pepper, and sugar; the sauce should have a mild sweet-and-sour taste. Remove the twine from the roast and discard. Slice the pork, arrange on a platter, and ladle some sauce and onions over the top. Serve the extra sauce on the side.

Alternative Cuts: Boston butt, blade-end pork loin roast (decrease the cooking time), or whole pork shank.

Leftovers
- Finely dice or shred the pork and rewarm in the sauce. Serve over penne.
- Use the leftover meat instead of veal to fill Veal Shank Ravioli with Brown Butter and Sage (page 588).

BEER AND TEQUILA CARNITAS TACOS

Cheap Eats, Comfort Food, Fit for a Crowd, Great Leftovers

Serves 8 (about 24 tacos)

Agustin Martinez, who is married to my wife's partner, Kathy King, hails from Mexico City. He's a sophisticated kind of guy and an accomplished chef who likes carnitas that have a little more flair and sophistication than just deep-fried chunks of seasoned pork. This recipe comes from his grandmother, an independent woman who did things her own way. According to Agustin, few in the family ever disagreed with her, because she kept a loaded shotgun behind the stove. With a little coaxing, I was able to get him to share his recipe, which incorporates beer and aged tequila (*reposado*) to give it a very special flavor. Serve the carnitas with warm tortillas and all the fixings for your guests to make their own soft tacos.

4–5 pounds boneless Boston butt (pork shoulder butt)

2 tablespoons finely chopped garlic

2 cups chopped white onions

4 poblano chiles, stemmed, seeded, and cut into ¼-inch dice

Salt and freshly ground black pepper

3 cups peeled, seeded, and chopped tomatoes, fresh or canned

1 cup tequila *reposado*

2 12-ounce bottles dark Mexican beer, such as Negra Modelo

24 corn tortillas, warmed

Garnishes

Finely chopped white onion

Chopped fresh cilantro

Pico de Gallo (page 259)

Salsa Verde (page 260)

1. Trim enough fat from the meat to give you about ⅓ cup of finely diced fat. Cut the pork into 1½-inch cubes. Set aside.

2. Heat a large Dutch oven over medium-low heat and add the fat. Cook until the fat is rendered and there are little crisp pieces left, about 10 minutes. Increase the heat to medium. Add the garlic, onions, chiles, and a good sprinkling of salt and pepper. Cook, stirring, until the onions are soft and translucent, about 10 minutes. Add the pork and cook, stirring from time to time, for 30 minutes, or until any liquid has evaporated and the pork has browned.

3. Stir in the tomatoes and cook for 10 minutes more. Add the tequila and cook until the liquid has evaporated, about 5 minutes. Add the beer, increase the heat, and bring to a

gentle boil. Cook until all the liquid has evaporated, about 15 minutes. Taste the meat to see if it is tender. If not, add ½ cup water and cook until the meat is tender and all the liquid has evaporated, about 5 more minutes. Repeat if necessary. Season to taste with salt and pepper. Scrape the carnitas and any browned bits from the bottom of the pot onto a serving platter and let guests assemble their own tacos with the tortillas and garnishes.

Alternative Cuts: Picnic shoulder, trimmed of excess fat and gristle; blade-end pork loin roast; boneless country-style ribs cut from the shoulder.

Cook's Note
- To rewarm carnitas, gently fry in a little oil in a nonstick pan or microwave in a covered container.

Leftovers
- Use leftover carnitas to make burritos, sandwiches, or quesadillas.

CHILE-BRAISED PORK BELLY

Comfort Food, Rewarms Well, Great Leftovers

Serves 6 to 8

Pork belly has become the rage on restaurant menus all across the land. Our neighbors south of the border enjoy pork and particularly love chile-spiked meats that are slow-cooked and eaten wrapped in tortillas with plenty of rice, beans, and salsas. This tradition inspired my recipe.

Ancho Chile Spice Rub

- 2 dried ancho chiles, torn into pieces, seeds and stems discarded
- 1 cup boiling water, or more if needed
- 2 teaspoons cumin seeds
- 2 teaspoons fennel seeds
- 1 teaspoon coriander seeds
- 1 tablespoon chopped fresh marjoram or oregano (I use Mexican)
- 1 teaspoon cayenne pepper
- Salt and freshly ground black pepper

- 1 2- to 3-pound piece fresh pork belly, skinned
- 2 cups chopped onions
- 2 tablespoons chopped garlic
- 1 cup thinly sliced scallions
- ½ cup finely chopped cilantro stems
- 1 cup fresh orange juice
- ½ cup dry white wine
- ¼ cup fresh lime juice
- 1½–2 dozen corn tortillas, warmed
- Cooked long-grain rice
- Cooked pinto beans
- Salsas, homemade (pages 259–60) or store-bought

1   **Rub:** Add the chile pieces to a small skillet and stir over medium heat until they start to crisp and become fragrant, 30 seconds to 1 minute. Transfer to a small bowl and cover with the boiling water. Soak until soft, about 30 minutes. Drain, reserving the soaking liquid and the chiles separately.

2   Add the cumin, fennel, and coriander seeds to the same skillet and toast over medium heat, shaking the pan, until the spices begin to color and become fragrant, 2 to 3 minutes. Immediately transfer to a spice grinder or a mortar with a pestle and grind into a powder. Place the softened chiles, ground spices, marjoram, cayenne, ¼ cup of the chile soaking liquid, 2 teaspoons salt, and 1 teaspoon black pepper in a blender and blend to a smooth paste. Remove 2 tablespoons and set aside.

3   Place the pork belly fat side up on a work surface and cut a crosshatch pattern about ¼ inch deep into the fat. Rub the spice rub all over the meat, wrap, and refrigerate for at least 6 hours, or, preferably, overnight.

4 Preheat the oven to 250°F.

5 Unwrap the belly, but don't rub off the spices. Heat a large heavy ovenproof skillet over medium-low heat. Add the belly, fat side down, and slowly brown, taking care not to burn the spices but to get them nice and brown, 5 to 10 minutes. Flip over the belly and brown the other side, 5 to 10 minutes more. Transfer to a platter and pour off all but 2 tablespoons of the fat from the pan.

6 Increase the heat to medium, add the onions, cover, and cook until soft, stirring from time to time, about 10 minutes. Add the garlic and scallions and cook, stirring, for 1 minute more. Add the reserved 2 tablespoons spice paste and ½ cup of the reserved chile soaking liquid and stir, scraping up any browned bits from the bottom of the pan. Add the cilantro stems, orange juice, white wine, and lime juice and bring to a boil.

7 Return the belly to the skillet, fat side up, and place in the oven. Bake, uncovered, for 1 hour, basting the belly once or twice with the liquid. Make sure the liquid does not boil; if it does, reduce the temperature to 225°F. Turn over the belly and bake for 1 hour more, basting every 30 minutes. Add more wine or water if the liquid evaporates. Flip again so that the fat side is up and continue to cook until the belly is quite tender. It may take 3 to 4 hours total. Transfer the belly to a warm platter and loosely tent with aluminum foil.

8 Skim the fat from the liquid and boil on the stove top to reduce the sauce until just syrupy, about 5 minutes. Cut the belly into ½-inch-thick slices, then slice again into ½-inch-wide fingers, and return to the platter. Ladle the sauce over the slices and serve with the tortillas, rice, beans, and salsas.

Alternative Cuts: Smoked slab bacon, roasted for 1½ to 2 hours, or until fork-tender, and served using the glazed method (see Cook's Notes).

Cook's Notes

• You can also serve the belly glazed with the sauce. Once the sauce has reduced, heat the oven to 400°F. Line a baking sheet with aluminum foil and set the belly on it, fat side up. Spoon over some of the sauce and roast for 10 to 15 minutes, or until the meat is sizzling, nicely browned, and shiny. Cut the glazed belly into ¼-inch-thick slices or into the ½-inch-wide fingers. You can also refrigerate the belly and sauce and then glaze a day or two later, when ready to serve.

• Another great way to serve cooked belly is to cut it into ½-x-2-inch pieces, skewer, and grill, brushing it with the sauce.

STINCO (BRAISED AND ROASTED PORK SHANKS)

Cheap Eats, Fit for Company, Great Leftovers, Rewarms Well

Serves 4 to 6

No, *stinco* is not the aroma of this classic Italian pot roast. It's the Italian word for "shank." I prefer to use the larger and meatier shanks cut from the hind legs. Each will weigh 2 to 2½ pounds and will feed two or three people. If you can't find them, use the smaller shanks from the front legs. Serve the *stinco* with mashed potatoes. You might plan on making extra *stinco*, because there are some very delicious ways to serve leftovers.

1 ounce dried porcini mushrooms

1½ cups boiling water

2 large or 4 small pork shanks (4 to 5 pounds total), trimmed of any skin or hair

Salt and freshly ground black pepper

3 tablespoons olive oil

2 ounces prosciutto or dried coppa, chopped

2 cups chopped onions

1 cup finely chopped peeled carrots

½ cup chopped celery

1 cup chopped leeks (white and pale green parts)

2 tablespoons chopped garlic

1 cup dry white wine

1 cup homemade pork stock (see page 168) or canned low-sodium chicken broth, plus more if needed

1 tablespoon chopped fresh sage

2 teaspoons chopped fresh rosemary

1 Place the mushrooms in a small bowl and cover with the boiling water. Soak for at least 45 minutes, or up to several hours. Remove the mushrooms from the liquid with a slotted spoon. Chop and set aside. Strain the soaking liquid, leaving behind any grit in the bottom of the bowl, and set aside.

2 Preheat the oven to 325°F.

3 Tie each shank with 3 loops of butcher's twine. Generously season the shanks with salt and pepper. Heat 2 tablespoons of the oil in a large Dutch oven over medium-high heat. Add the shanks (you may have to brown them in batches) and sear until nicely browned on all sides, about 10 minutes. Set aside the shanks and pour off all but 2 tablespoons of the fat.

4 Reduce the heat to medium and add the prosciutto, onions, carrots, celery, and leeks. Cover and cook until soft, stirring occasionally, about 10 minutes. Scrape up any browned bits from the bottom of the pot. Add the garlic, reserved mushrooms, and

white wine and bring to a boil, scraping up any remaining browned bits from the bottom. Add the reserved mushroom liquid, the stock, 1 teaspoon of the sage, 1 teaspoon of the rosemary, and the shanks. Bring to a boil.

5 Cover and bake for 30 minutes, then turn the shanks, re-cover the pot, and bake for another 30 minutes. Remove the lid and, after another 30 minutes, begin checking the shanks, adding more stock or water if the liquid evaporates. The shanks are done when the meat is almost falling off the bone and is quite tender.

6 Transfer the pot to the top of the stove and transfer the shanks to a shallow roasting pan. Increase the oven temperature to 425°F. Brush the shanks with the remaining 1 tablespoon olive oil and sprinkle with some pepper and the remaining 2 teaspoons sage and 1 teaspoon rosemary. Roast the shanks in the oven for 15 to 20 minutes, or until slightly browned.

7 Meanwhile, degrease the braising liquid in the pot and, if necessary, boil it down until it just turns syrupy. Season to taste with salt and pepper. To serve, remove and discard the twine, cut chunks of meat from the shanks, transfer to plates, and ladle on some of the sauce. Pass the extra sauce at the table.

Alternative Cuts: Large, meaty veal shanks or lamb shanks.

Cook's Note
- This is a great recipe if you can find shanks from heirloom pork, which have ample marbling and great flavor. This underappreciated cut will have a friendly price.

Leftovers
- Leftover *stinco* makes a great sauce for pasta. Combine 2 cups chopped meat with 1 cup leftover sauce, 1 cup cooked white beans (I use cannellini beans), and 1 cup diced tomatoes and simmer for 20 minutes. Serve with 1 pound cooked penne, with a drizzle of extra-virgin olive oil, and lots of grated pecorino cheese.

- You can also use leftover shank meat as a filling for ravioli (see Veal Shank Ravioli with Brown Butter and Sage, page 588).

- Use the leftover bones and any sauce as a base for a pot of cabbage, bean, or lentil soup.

- If you have some of Gary's Heirloom Tomato Sauce (page 316) in your freezer, combine it with some shredded stinco meat and a little leftover braising sauce and serve over the fresh or dried pasta of your choice.

THAI BRAISED AND GLAZED PORK NECK

Cheap Eats, Rewarms Well

Serves 4

Several years back, my wife, Nancy, and a few other American chefs did a promotional cooking exhibition for a luxury hotel in Bangkok. They were rewarded for their efforts with a stay at a resort in the mountainous area of Chiang Mai. While in that area, they visited a private home where they were served chunks of pork neck with sweetly glazed meat. My wife asked for the recipe, but she could ascertain only that the bones were first braised until the meat was tender, then slowly grilled and basted with a spicy sweet sauce. I did lots of research and, through trial and error, eventually came up with something that Nancy said was close to what she remembered.

If you can't find pork neck bones with a fair amount of meat attached, use bone-in country-style ribs instead. Serve the stew over jasmine rice with lots of chopped fresh cilantro.

Braise

- 3 cups water
- 2 lemongrass stalks, cut into 2-inch-long pieces
- 8 garlic cloves, peeled
- 3 ⅛-inch-thick slices fresh ginger
- 8 scallions, cut into 3-inch lengths
- 1 onion, coarsely chopped
- ¼ cup soy sauce
- 3 tablespoons Asian fish sauce
- 1 tablespoon dark brown sugar
- 1 tablespoon Thai red curry paste
- Stems from 1 bunch fresh cilantro (reserve the leaves for garnish)
- 2 tablespoons rice vinegar
- 5 pounds pork neck bones or 3 pounds bone-in country-style ribs

Thai Red Curry Glaze

- 5 tablespoons ketchup
- 1 tablespoon Thai red curry paste
- 2 tablespoons honey
- 2 tablespoons dark brown sugar
- 1 tablespoon Sriracha sauce, or more to taste
- 2 tablespoons fresh lime juice, or more to taste
- 1 tablespoon Asian fish sauce

Garnish

- Chopped fresh cilantro leaves
- Lime wedges

1 **Braise:** Place all the ingredients for the braise in a large Dutch oven. Bring to a boil, then reduce to a simmer. Add the pork and cook for 1 hour 15 minutes, or until tender (neck bones may take longer than ribs). Remove the meat and set aside. Strain the liquid and discard the solids. Reserve ¼ cup of the braising liquid for the glaze (save the rest to use in a pork curry or other dish). (*At this point, you can refrigerate the meat and ¼ cup of the liquid separately, covered, for up to 1 day.*)

2   Set up a charcoal or gas grill for indirect heat (see page 11 for more on grilling).

3   **Glaze:** Whisk together the ketchup, curry paste, honey, brown sugar, and the reserved ¼ cup braising liquid in a small bowl until smooth. Whisk in the Sriracha, lime juice, and fish sauce. Taste and add more Sriracha and/or lime juice as needed.

4   Brush the meat on one side with the glaze. Grill over medium-high heat, basting and turning the meat until well glazed but not heavily charred (a little black edge is okay), 2 to 3 minutes per side. Move to an area with no fire if the meat begins to burn. When the meat is nicely glazed all over, transfer to a platter, sprinkle with cilantro, and serve with lime wedges on the side.

Alternative Cuts: Pork shanks, blade-end chops, or spareribs.

Cook's Notes
- For a nice variation, add 1 cup unsweetened coconut milk to the braising liquid during the last 2 minutes of cooking.

- You can also turn the braising liquid into a delicious soup. Add 1 cup quartered mushrooms, 2 cups sliced bok choy, 2 cups diced leftover meat, and 1 cup unsweetened coconut milk. Cook for 5 to 10 minutes, then ladle into bowls filled with hot cooked rice noodles.

HAM HOCKS WITH LEEKS AND WHITE BEANS

Cheap Eats, Fit for Company, Rewarms Well

Serves 6

The traditional way to serve this rib-sticking winter feast is to provide each diner with a large ham hock nestled in a bed of white beans, but a leaner approach is to fully cook the ham hocks a day ahead, refrigerate them overnight, spoon off the congealed surface fat, and separate the meat from the skin, fat, and bones. Then the stock from the ham hocks, plus the bones and any skin, is used to cook the beans, and the meat is added near the end. Instead of collards, you can try other varieties of winter greens, such as kale, Swiss chard, turnip greens, or mustard greens, or a mixture of any of these.

Great Northern and navy beans are the easiest to find, but Italian cannellini beans and small white beans are particularly nice. Each bean may vary somewhat in cooking time, so taste them before serving (check out Rancho Gordo and Phipps Country Store for heirloom varieties of beans; see Sources).

Ham Hocks

- 4–6 meaty smoked ham hocks (about 4 pounds total)
- 1 medium onion, spiked with 3 cloves
- 3 garlic cloves, not peeled
- 1 carrot, cut into chunks
- 2 celery stalks, cut into chunks
  Dark green tops from 3 medium leeks (from below)
- 4 bay leaves
- 1 fresh thyme sprig or ½ teaspoon dried
- 3 fresh sage leaves or ½ teaspoon dried
- 1 teaspoon black peppercorns

White Beans

- 1½ cups dried white beans (see headnote), picked over and rinsed
- 5 cups ham hock stock (from above), or more as needed

- 2 teaspoons chopped fresh thyme or 1 teaspoon dried
- 1 teaspoon crushed fennel seeds
- 1 teaspoon chopped fresh marjoram or ½ teaspoon dried
- 6 sun-dried tomatoes (not oil-packed), chopped
- 2 tablespoons bacon fat or olive oil
- 3 leeks, white and pale green parts, chopped
- 1 medium onion, chopped
- 2 carrots, peeled and chopped
- 1 celery stalk, chopped
- 2 teaspoons minced garlic
- 3 cups chopped stemmed collard greens or other leafy greens (see headnote)
  Salt and freshly ground black pepper

- 2 tablespoons chopped fresh flat-leaf parsley
- 2 tablespoons chopped fresh basil
- 2 tablespoons finely chopped scallions
  Tabasco or other hot sauce

1. **Ham hocks:** Throw the ham hocks into a large pot and cover with at least 2½ quarts water. Add the remaining ingredients and simmer, uncovered, over medium-low heat for 2½ to 3 hours, or until the meat is quite tender. Remove the hocks, strain the stock, and discard the vegetables and herbs. Refrigerate the hocks and stock separately in airtight containers overnight.

2. **Meanwhile, for the beans:** Soak the beans overnight in cold water to cover by 2 inches.

3. Remove and discard the fat from each ham hock. Pull the meat off the bone in relatively large pieces and set aside. Save the bones and any skin for cooking the beans. Remove the congealed fat from the stock.

4. Drain and rinse the beans. Drop them into a 4-quart pot or Dutch oven and cover with the 5 cups ham hock stock. Add the thyme, fennel seeds, marjoram, sun-dried tomatoes, and the reserved bones and skin. Bring to a boil, reduce the heat to a simmer, and cook for 1¼ hours, adding more stock or water if the beans become dry. Check the beans to see if they are tender. If not, continue to cook, adding more stock or water as necessary. When the beans are done, drain the beans and reserve the liquid. Discard the bones and skin. Place the beans back in the pot.

5. Heat the bacon fat in a large skillet over medium heat. Add the leeks, onion, carrots, celery, garlic, collards, and a pinch each of salt and pepper. Cover and cook until the vegetables are soft and the greens have wilted, about 10 minutes, stirring from time to time. Stir the vegetables into the beans. Add the reserved ham hock meat and 2 cups of the reserved bean-cooking liquid. Simmer for 10 minutes, adding more reserved liquid if the beans become too dry. Season to taste with salt and pepper.

6. To serve, spoon the beans into shallow bowls. Sprinkle with the parsley, basil, and scallions. Let guests add Tabasco to suit their tastes.

Alternative Cuts: Ham, smoked pork chops, or smoked sausages, such as andouille. Ham and pork chops should be cooked in the beans; add sausages to the beans with the vegetables to cook for 10 minutes. Use canned low-sodium chicken broth instead of the ham hock stock.

Cook's Note
- You can also serve the beans over steamed rice, Louisiana style.

Pork Ribs

I love to gnaw on bones, so ribs are my favorite pork-eating experience. Yes, ribs are fatty, but it's that fat that allows for long, slow cooking with juicy, succulent results.

While ribs are a popular summertime barbecue item, they are a great cut to consider throughout the year. During the winter months, they are often sold at bargain prices. Slabs of spareribs or back ribs can be marinated or rubbed with spices and then roasted. They can also be used in stews and other braises and are good in bean dishes and rice dishes. Country-style ribs, especially the boneless variety, are ideal for stews and kebabs.

Choosing Ribs

Spareribs

- Spareribs contain the most fat and are the least likely to dry out.
- The bigger the slab, the better (thicker, meatier ribs).
- Seek out slabs from the heirloom Duroc breed (see Sources), which have just the right ratio of fat to lean and make for great eating.
- Figure on 3 to 4 servings for a 3-pound-plus slab from any breed.
- Avoid frozen ribs, which may be left over from the summer season and could be freezer-burned.

St. Louis–Style Ribs

- St. Louis–style ribs are essentially spareribs with the breastbone (sternum) removed, creating a uniform rectangular shape.
- They are less fatty than spareribs, but meatier and more succulent than back ribs.
- Look for 2- to 2½-pound slabs and figure on 2 to 3 servings per slab.

Back Ribs

- Often called "baby" back ribs, these ribs are nothing more than the bones from rib pork chops. Because they usually have so little meat attached, they are by far the most expensive cut of pork.
- Because they are lean, they will dry out if overcooked.
- Select slabs with the most amount of meat on the bone, weighing 1½ to 2 pounds per slab. Figure on 1½ to 2 servings per slab.

Country-Style Ribs

- Occasionally labeled "country ribs," these are typically made by cutting blade-end pork chops in half between the blade bone and the under blade meat or by butterflying them.
- These contain the highest ratio of meat to bone and have less fat than spareribs. They come boneless as well.
- Country-style ribs are excellent for stews, kebabs, soups, and bean dishes, but not for barbecuing.

Pork Shoulder Country-Style Ribs

- These are pieces of Boston butt cut into 1- to 2-inch-thick boneless or bone-in strips.
- These can be used interchangeably with country-style ribs in my recipes.

Pork Ribs at a Glance

From the Belly

Spareribs (fresh spareribs). Look for large, thick slabs weighing 3 pounds or more. Ample fat and meat; will stay juicy and succulent after long, slow roasting.

Spareribs, St. Louis style (St. Louis-style ribs, pork spareribs breastbone off). Made by trimming the fatty breastbone away and trimming the ends and edges to produce a rectangular shape. Look for slabs weighing 2 pounds or more. I prefer St. Louis ribs to the much more expensive back loin ribs.

From the Loin

Loin back ribs (baby back ribs, back ribs, country back ribs). Cut from the rib section of the pork loin. These pork chop bones often have little meat attached, so look for thicker, larger slabs weighing at least 1½ pounds. They cook more quickly than other cuts, but can dry out. Expensive.

Country-style ribs, bone-in or boneless (country ribs). Made by cutting blade-end pork chops in half or butterflying them. These are ideal for grilling, but can dry out if cooked long and slow or barbecued. Very meaty and a good bargain. See also pork shoulder country-style ribs, below.

From the Shoulder

Country-style ribs, bone in or boneless (pork shoulder country-style ribs, country ribs, blade-end country spareribs). Cut from the Boston butt. Reasonably priced and can be grilled; not good for long, slow roasting or real barbecuing.

Roasting the Perfect Slab of Ribs

IF USING THE OVEN

- Preheat the oven to 350°F.
- If the ribs have been marinated, remove them from the marinade and shake off any excess (save the marinade if instructed in the recipe). For dry rub–coated ribs, leave the coating alone.
- Place a rack on a baking sheet. Set the ribs flat on the rack, fat side up.
- Roast until the meat begins to pull away from the bone. Back ribs will take 45 minutes to 1 hour; St. Louis–style ribs will take 1½ to 2 hours; spareribs will take 2 to 2½ hours.
- If there is a glazing step, cook under the broiler; watch carefully so it does not burn.
- Remove from the oven, cover loosely with aluminum foil, and let rest for 15 minutes before cutting and serving.

IF USING A GAS GRILL

- Preheat all burners of the grill, then shut off half the grill for a 2-burner grill or the middle section for a 3-burner grill (see page 11 for more on grilling).
- If the ribs have been marinated, remove them from the marinade and shake off any excess (save the marinade if instructed in the recipe). For dry rub–coated ribs, leave the coating alone.
- Place the ribs fat side up over the side of the grill with no heat; make sure there is no fire under the ribs. You may have to use a rib rack (a vertical rack designed especially for cooking several rib racks at a time).
- Close the lid and adjust the heat to maintain a consistent temperature of 300°F to 350°F.
- Grill-roast until the meat begins to pull away from the bone. Back ribs will take 45 minutes to 1 hour; St. Louis–style ribs will take 1½ to 2 hours; spareribs will take 2 to 2½ hours.
- If there is a glazing step, cook over direct heat as instructed in the recipe.
- Remove from the grill, cover loosely with aluminum foil, and let rest for 15 minutes before cutting and serving.

IF USING A CHARCOAL GRILL

- Set up a charcoal grill with coals in one half of the grill, leaving the other half without coals (see page 11 for more on grilling). Follow the directions above for using a gas grill. You will need to replenish the charcoal from time to time.

GRILL-ROASTED CHERRY-GLAZED ST. LOUIS RIBS

Comfort Food, Family Meal

Serves 6

The secret to great ribs is slow and steady cooking. I prefer the meatier and somewhat fatty spareribs to the ever-popular back ribs. Buy St. Louis–style spareribs, for which the gristly and fatty brisket portion (the sternum) is cut away, leaving a nice rectangular-shape rack. For flavor, these ribs are marinated in a pomegranate and soy marinade. So they don't burn, they are cooked over indirect heat. After they have cooked to perfection, they are brushed with a cherry glaze and finished briefly over direct heat. You can also cook them in the oven (see Cook's Notes).

Pomegranate Marinade

- 2 cups pomegranate, cherry, or cranberry juice
- ⅓ cup soy sauce
- ½ cup finely chopped red onion
- 2 teaspoons minced garlic
- 1 teaspoon ground ginger
- 1 teaspoon freshly ground black pepper
- ½ teaspoon freshly grated nutmeg
- ¼ teaspoon ground cinnamon

- 2 slabs St. Louis–style spareribs (4–5 pounds total)

Cherry Glaze

- ½ cup cherry jam (I use one made with tart cherries)
- 2 tablespoons Dijon mustard
- 1 tablespoon light brown sugar

1 **Marinade:** Put all the ingredients in a medium bowl and whisk to combine. Place the ribs in a large zipper-lock bag (you may have to fold them in half) and pour in the marinade. Seal the bag and turn over several times to coat the ribs. Place the ribs in a large rectangular pan (in case the bag leaks) and refrigerate for 16 to 24 hours, turning the bag from time to time to redistribute the marinade. The next day, remove the ribs from the marinade. Reserve ½ cup of the marinade for the glaze and discard the rest.

2 To grill-roast the ribs, build a fire on one side of a charcoal grill, or, if using a gas grill, preheat all the burners of the grill, then turn off one burner. (See page 394 for more on grill-roasting ribs.) Place the ribs so there is no fire under the meat. Cover the grill and try to maintain a temperature of 300°F to 350°F. The ribs are done when the meat

begins to pull away from the bone, 1½ to 2 hours, depending on the temperature of the grill.

3   **Meanwhile, make the glaze:** Bring the reserved ½ cup marinade to a boil in a small saucepan. Stir in the jam, mustard, and brown sugar and boil for 1 minute, or until the glaze has the viscosity of light syrup.

4   Brush some of the glaze over the rib slabs, place them directly over a medium-hot fire, and grill for 2 to 3 minutes, or until the glaze is bubbly and just beginning to brown. (You may have to do this in batches or rebuild a fire to cover the rest of the grill.) Turn, brush the other side with glaze, and grill for 2 to 3 minutes more, or until the glaze is bubbly and beginning to color. Remove from the grill, cover loosely with aluminum foil, and let rest for 15 minutes.

5   Slice between the ribs to separate them and serve.

Alternative Cuts: Regular spareribs, which will take longer; or bone-in country-style ribs and back ribs, which will take less time.

Cook's Notes
- Depending on the size of your grill, you may need to use a vertical rib rack (see page 394).

- This recipe lends itself to many flavor variations. For grape, substitute grape juice in the marinade and grape jam in the glaze. For apricot, use apricot nectar or orange juice in the marinade and apricot jam in the glaze. For orange, use orange juice in the marinade and orange marmalade in the glaze. For berry, use berry-flavored liqueur in the marinade and berry jam in the glaze.

- You can also roast these ribs for 1½ to 2 hours in a 350°F oven, or until the meat begins to pull away from the bones and is tender to the tooth. Brush the ribs with the glaze and broil for 2 to 3 minutes per side.

GRILLED BACK RIBS IN SMOKY CHILE MARINADE

Fit for Company, Fit for a Crowd

Serves 6 as a main course, or 10 as an hors d'oeuvre

Pork ribs work well in this spicy recipe, but you can also use boneless pork loin chops. Reserve some of the unused marinade to make a dipping sauce for additional flavor. The marinade is also ideal for skirt steak or flank steak for fajitas, but be sure to marinate the beef overnight. It's great with pork kebabs or pork tenderloins, too. If you use back ribs, the recipe makes a great hors d'oeuvre for parties; don't forget to provide a bowl for bones.

Smoky Chile Marinade
- 1 habanero or other hot chile, stemmed, seeded, and chopped
- 2 teaspoons finely grated lime or lemon zest
- 2 scallions, finely chopped
- 1 cup fresh orange juice
- ¼ cup fresh lime juice
- ¼ cup soy sauce
- 1 teaspoon dried oregano (I use Mexican)
- 1 tablespoon New Mexico or ancho chile powder
- 1 teaspoon ground cumin
- ½ teaspoon ground coriander

- 2 teaspoons sugar
- 2 teaspoons minced garlic
- 1 tablespoon chopped chipotle chile in adobo (I use Herdez brand)
- ⅓ cup vegetable oil
- 2 teaspoons salt
- 1 teaspoon freshly ground black pepper

- 3 slabs back ribs (about 5 pounds total) or 2 slabs St. Louis–style spareribs (about 5 pounds total)
- 1 cup fresh orange juice

1. **Marinade:** Combine all the ingredients in a small bowl. Set aside ½ cup. Put the ribs in a large zipper-lock bag (you may have to fold them in half), pour over the remaining marinade, and seal the bag. Place in a large rectangular pan to catch leaks and marinate at room temperature for 2 hours, or up to 24 hours in the refrigerator, turning the bag from time to time to redistribute the marinade.

2. Set up a charcoal or gas grill as directed on page 394. Remove the ribs from the marinade, shaking off the excess, and discard the marinade.

3 Follow the directions for grill-roasting in step 2 of Grill-Roasted St. Louis Ribs (see page 395). When the ribs are done, remove from the grill, cover with aluminum foil, and let rest for 15 minutes.

4 Meanwhile, bring the reserved ½ cup marinade and the orange juice to a boil, reduce the heat, and simmer for 3 minutes. Set the sauce aside.

5 Transfer the ribs to a warm platter, cut into individual ribs, and serve with the dipping sauce.

Alternative Cuts: Regular spareribs, bone-in country-style ribs, or rib or blade-end pork chops.

Cook's Notes

- For a less spicy version, eliminate the habanero chile or replace it with finely chopped jalapeño chile.
- You can also roast the ribs indoors in the oven (see Cook's Notes, page 396).

BAKED SPARERIBS WITH LEMON CONFIT RUB

Fit for Company, Fit for a Crowd

Serves 6 as a main course, or 10 as an hors d'oeuvre

A staple in Mediterranean cooking, Moroccan preserved lemons have a distinctive sweet-salty-tart flavor. They're quite expensive in specialty markets, and some advance thought is required to make them at home. As a substitute, my wife, Nancy, came up with a clever and thrifty way to microwave the lemons. While they taste different from true pickled lemons, they are quick and a reasonable facsimile. The rub that I use here is equally good on lamb and chicken. If you use back ribs, these make a great hors d'oeuvre, especially for stand-up parties.

Lemon Confit Rub

- 4 lemons (see Cook's Notes)
- 8 garlic cloves, peeled
- 3 tablespoons fresh rosemary leaves
- 3 tablespoons fresh thyme leaves
- 2 tablespoons crushed fennel seeds
- 2 tablespoons salt
- 1 tablespoon freshly ground black pepper
- 2 teaspoons light brown sugar
- ¼ cup olive oil

- 2 2½-pound slabs St. Louis–style spareribs (about 5 pounds total), 2 slabs regular spareribs (about 6 pounds total), or 3 slabs back ribs (about 4½ pounds total)

1 **Rub:** Cut 4 or 5 deep lengthwise slashes — equally spaced — into each lemon. Put the lemons and garlic cloves in a microwavable container, cover, and cook on high for 2 minutes, or until the skins are quite soft and juice has exuded from the lemons. If the lemons are not quite soft, continue to microwave, checking every 30 seconds. Pour the lemon juice into a measuring cup and set aside. When the lemons are cool enough to handle, cut through the slashes into sections and, using a spoon, scrape away the pulp and white pith from the lemon rind; discard the pulp and pith. (The pith is bitter, so scrape away as much as possible.) Put ⅓ cup of the reserved lemon juice in a blender with the lemon rinds, garlic, rosemary, thyme, fennel seeds, salt, pepper, brown sugar, and oil. Puree, scraping down the sides of the blender once or twice, until the mixture forms a thick paste.

2 Generously smear some of the paste on both sides of each slab of ribs; reserve the remainder. Put the ribs on a baking sheet, cover with plastic wrap, and refrigerate for 16 hours to 24 hours.

3 Preheat the oven to 350°F.

4 Arrange the ribs, fat side down, on a rack over a baking sheet or a roasting pan (you may need two pans). Bake for 20 minutes. Turn over the ribs and baste with the reserved paste. Bake for 20 minutes more, turn, and baste again. Bake for 20 minutes more, turn, baste, and continue to cook until the ribs are done, 1¼ to 2½ hours total (back ribs will take the least amount of time, regular spareribs the most). If you have two pans on separate oven racks, reverse the positions of the pans halfway through. The ribs are done when the meat begins to pull away from the bones. Remove from the oven, cover loosely with aluminum foil, and set aside for 15 minutes.

5 Cut into individual ribs and serve.

Alternative Cuts: Country-style pork ribs, thick-cut blade pork chops, breast of lamb, or beef back ribs.

Cook's Notes
- If you can find them, use Meyer lemons.
- If you have preserved lemons in your pantry, you can substitute them for the lemon confit in this recipe. Use 2 preserved lemons and reduce the salt to 1 tablespoon. Squeeze enough fresh lemon juice to equal ⅓ cup.
- If you'd like to make authentic preserved lemons, see page 499.
- You can also grill-roast these ribs following the directions on page 394.
- You can also use this versatile rub for pork kebabs, chops, and leg or loin roasts. (For roasts, cut deep slashes into the fat and meat and stuff the paste into the slashes.)

Sausages, Pâtés, Potted Meats, & Cured Meats

Sausages, Pâtés, Potted Meats, and Cured Meats

RECIPES

From Necessity to Art

The act of preserving meat has historically centered around the pig. In France, turning pork into such long-lasting treats as hams, pâtés, rillettes, and sausages is called *charcuterie*; in Italy, it is the art of *salumi*; and in Germany, *delicatessen*. While specialists practice the art of preserving at butcher shops, it began on the farm, when pigs were slaughtered and the meat had to be preserved for the family.

On the farm, the jobs of slaughtering the pig and making the ham, sausages, and other preserved meats were assigned to the men. These men weren't skilled cooks, so the recipes needed to be simple and very straightforward. Most of these early recipes are based on salt, a few spices, and the right environment for curing and aging. Salt is the key ingredient needed to preserve meat. It pulls moisture from the meat and creates an environment that is unfriendly to bacteria.

The sausages and preserved meats you make on your own will be much better than anything you can buy, and the recipes are very simple. Don't worry: You won't need any special equipment. A food processor is fine for making sausage mixtures, and you can use a kettle-style barbecue as a smoker.

Now, let's get started.

Sausages

If you can operate the pulse switch on your food processor or install the meat grinder attachment for your stand mixer, you have all the skill it takes to make sausages at home. It's that easy. You don't even need to stuff the sausage into a casing.

Pretty much every country and every cuisine has found tasty ways to use bits of meat and fat and an array of seasonings and flavorings to come up with an endless variety of sausages. Each recipe in this section is based on a cuisine—American, Spanish, French, Thai, Mexican, and Italian—that is well represented in the book. All these sausages can certainly be enjoyed on their own, but they can also be used to flavor many other dishes. A good example is Spanish chorizo, which you'll find in many of the book's recipes for stews, rice dishes, soups, and appetizers.

When you make sausages at home, you have complete control over the quality and type of meat, the amount of fat, and the array of ingredients you use to flavor your sausages. Once you've tried the recipes here, why not experiment? For example, try using honey instead of maple syrup in the Maple and Sage Pork Sausage Patties and adding some diced dried apple or apricot. Making sausages is one of the most satisfying activities of meat cookery. Once you start making your own, you may never purchase store-bought sausages again.

MAKING SAUSAGE LINKS

Equipment: You need either a sausage horn attachment for a meat grinder or stand mixer or a disposable pastry bag fitted with a plain tip.

Casings: For 4 pounds of sausage you need about 8 feet of medium hog casings (available from specialty butchers or by mail-order; see Cook's Notes). Soak the casings in a large bowl of warm water for at least 30 minutes. Then put one end of each casing over the end of a faucet and flush the inside of the casing with warm water. Rinse out the bowl and cover the casings with fresh warm water.

- **If you're using a grinder:** Remove the plate and knife and fit it with the sausage horn. Pull almost the entire length of a casing over the tip of the horn, gathering it up and leaving a little bit dangling. Tie a knot in the dangling end. Fill the bowl of the grinder with the chilled sausage meat and crank the meat through the grinder to fill the casing. Use a skewer, pin, or needle to prick any air bubbles that form as the casing fills. The casing should be full, but not tightly packed, or it will burst when you form the links. When the casing is filled, remove it from the horn.

- **If you're using a pastry bag:** Pull as much of a casing over the end of the tip as will fit (if necessary, cut the casings into shorter lengths), gathering it up and leaving a little bit dangling. Tie a knot in the dangling end. Fill the pastry bag with the chilled sausage meat. Squeeze the bag with one hand to push the meat into the casing while you use your other hand to hold the casing on the metal tip, filling the casing as described above. As the casing is filled, remove it from the pastry bag.

- **To form the links:** Begin at the knotted end and pinch the casing between your fingers 5 inches from the end (you may vary the length if you wish). Move down the casing another 5 inches — that is, 10 inches from the first knot — and pinch again. Twist the second 5-inch section with your fingers to make a link. Proceed down the casing, repeating this process and twisting every other pinch to make links. When you reach the end, tie another knot. To separate the chain into links, use a sharp knife to cut through the twisted casings to make individual sausages. Refrigerate right away and use within 2 days. You can pack the sausages in zipper-lock bags and freeze for up to 3 months.

Cook's Notes

- Casings aren't hard to find. Search the Internet or your local yellow pages under "Sausages, Supplies" or "Butcher's Supplies," and you're likely to locate them, especially if you live in a city with ethnic neighborhoods. If your local butcher makes his or her own sausages, ask for some casings, along with the pork and fat for making sausages. Or see Sources.

- Casings come packed in salt, so they will last forever in the back of your refrigerator.

MAPLE AND SAGE PORK SAUSAGE PATTIES

Family Meal, Freezes Well

Makes 3½ pounds; serves 4 to 6 with 2 pounds left over to freeze

It's hard to beat the aroma of homemade pork sausage frying on the stove, urging all to come and eat a great breakfast. Making the patties couldn't be easier, and the only equipment needed is a sharp knife and your trusty food processor. In less than 30 minutes, you'll have homemade sausage that will taste better than almost any store-bought version you can find. Besides breakfasts, you can use your sausages for turkey stuffing or for a quick sandwich for lunch. It's also excellent in Cassoulet (page 312).

I like the hint of sweetness provided by maple sugar. If you can't find maple in sugar form, use real maple syrup. If you can get Grade B maple syrup, which is darker and more intensely flavored, all the better. Do seek out the real thing, though. The surprising fact about real versus imitation maple flavoring is that the genuine article has a much more subtle flavor that isn't overly sweet. Fenugreek brings out the flavors of the maple, but if you can't find it, leave it out or substitute ⅛ teaspoon ground cinnamon.

2¼ pounds boneless Boston butt (pork shoulder butt), cut into 1-inch cubes	½ teaspoon pure vanilla extract
¾ pound pork fatback (see Cook's Notes), cut into ½-inch cubes	½ teaspoon ground fenugreek (see Sources) or ⅛ teaspoon ground cinnamon
1 tablespoon plus 1 teaspoon maple sugar (see Sources) or ¼ cup real maple syrup (I use Grade B)	¼ teaspoon freshly grated nutmeg
	¼ cup cold water (if using maple syrup, reduce the water to 2 tablespoons)
2 teaspoons finely chopped fresh sage or ¾ teaspoon rubbed	Salt and freshly ground black pepper

1 Place half the cubed pork and half the fat in a food processor. Process with short pulses until the mixture has a coarse texture, with each particle about ⅜ inch in diameter. Scrape into a large bowl and repeat with the remaining meat and fat.

2 Add all the remaining ingredients to the meat mixture plus 1 tablespoon salt and 2 teaspoons pepper. Using clean hands, knead and squeeze the meat until everything is well blended. Cook a small patty in a small skillet until done and taste for salt, pepper, and other seasonings; adjust as necessary. *(If you have time, wrap the sausage meat in*

plastic wrap and refrigerate for up to 2 days so the flavors develop, or refrigerate what you will use in 2 days and freeze the rest in 2 or 3 small zipper-lock bags; it will keep for 3 months.)

3. When you are ready to cook the sausage, form 1½ pounds of the mixture into 8 to 12 oval patties, about ½ inch thick. Heat a large heavy skillet over medium-high heat and add the patties, without crowding. You may need to cook them in 2 batches. Fry for 5 to 6 minutes, or until nicely browned. Flip and fry for 5 minutes more, or until the centers are faintly pink or gray. Drain the patties on paper towels. You can keep them warm in a low (200°F) oven. Arrange on a serving platter and serve.

Alternative Cuts: Boneless country-style ribs, boneless country-style ribs cut from the shoulder, or boneless blade-end pork loin.

Cook's Notes

- Fatback is not easily found in most supermarkets or butcher shops. Ask for fat trimmings from the shoulder or loin, or trim fat from your own pork roasts and bag and freeze it until you have enough to make a batch of sausage.

- When freezing the uncooked sausage, portion it into amounts big enough for breakfast.

- Dried fruits and berries, such as dried cranberries, dried tart cherries, dried blueberries, dried apples, chopped dried apricots, chopped pitted prunes, raisins, and dried currants go well with this sausage mixture. Add ½ cup or more to suit your taste.

HYGIENE AND SAFETY WHEN MAKING SAUSAGES

- Wash your hands frequently with soap and very hot water.
- Keep the meat cold at all times. Refrigerate the meat before and between all steps.
- Never leave meat unrefrigerated in the grinder or pastry bag for more than 10 minutes.
- Never taste raw sausage meat. Fry up a small patty, taste it, and adjust the seasonings.
- Wash all your utensils and equipment as soon as you've used them, even if you're just taking a short break.
- If you don't intend to use all the sausage in the next 2 or 3 days, freeze it immediately. Don't wait for 2 or 3 days to pass and then freeze it.
- Clean everything. Chill everything. When in doubt, throw it out!

SWEET ITALIAN SAUSAGE

Family Meal, Freezes Well, Heirloom Pork

Makes about 3½ pounds

When I think Italian sausage, this is the recipe that comes to mind: pork flavored with fennel and a kiss of garlic. It's simple but so delicious, whether grilled and stuffed into a roll with onions and bell peppers, used to stuff roasts or poultry, or slapped on a pizza. It's not too shabby as a breakfast link either. The key to making this sausage rise from the ordinary to the sublime lies in the quality of pork you use and the freshness of the spices. Go the extra mile and seek out pork from one of the great heirloom breeds.

For sausage safety, see page 409.

3 pounds boneless Boston butt (preferably from an heirloom breed), cut into 1-inch pieces

½ pound pork fatback (see Cook's Notes, page 409), cut into ½-inch pieces

Salt and freshly ground black pepper

2 teaspoons fennel pollen (see Sources) or ground fennel seeds

1 tablespoon fennel seeds

1 tablespoon minced garlic

¼ cup dry white wine

1 tablespoon chopped fresh basil (optional)

Medium hog casings

1. Using a meat grinder fitted with a ⅜-inch plate, coarsely grind the pork and fatback into a large bowl or coarsely chop in batches in a food processor as directed in step 1 of Maple and Sage Pork Sausage Patties (page 408). Add 4 teaspoons salt, 2½ teaspoons pepper and the remaining ingredients (except the casings). Using clean hands, knead and squeeze the mixture to blend thoroughly. Cook a small patty in a small skillet and taste for salt, pepper, and other seasonings; adjust as necessary.

2. Stuff the sausage meat into casings and twist into 5-inch links (see page 407). Refrigerate and use within 2 days or freeze in 4-link zipper-lock packages for up to 3 months.

Alternative Cuts: Boneless country-style ribs cut from the pork shoulder butt or boneless blade-end pork loin roast.

Cook's Note
- To turn sweet Italian sausage into hot, add 1 teaspoon cayenne pepper, 2 teaspoons crushed red pepper flakes, and 2 tablespoons hot Hungarian paprika.

THAI PORK SAUSAGE

Freezes Well

Makes about 4 pounds

With a little of this sausage in your freezer, you can produce a Thai-flavored dish in no time flat. Stir-fry it with vegetables and a bit of coconut milk and serve over rice, or use in fried rice. Or stir-fry, then add chicken stock, rice noodles, diced zucchini, and mushrooms for a quick soup. The sausage is ideal in steamed or fried dumplings as well. Cilantro roots and stems have a more intense flavor than the leaves. For sausage safety, see page 409.

3 pounds boneless Boston butt (pork shoulder butt), cut into 1-inch pieces	3 tablespoons chopped fresh Thai basil or ordinary basil
½ pound pork fatback (see Cook's Notes, page 409), cut into ½-inch pieces	3 tablespoons chopped fresh mint
Salt and freshly ground black pepper	1½ tablespoons finely chopped garlic
1 tablespoon Thai green curry paste	1½ tablespoons minced fresh ginger
1 bunch fresh cilantro, leaves coarsely chopped, stems and roots finely chopped (about 2 packed cups)	¼ cup Asian fish sauce
	1 teaspoon crushed red pepper flakes
	1 teaspoon cayenne pepper
	Medium hog casings (optional)

1. Using a meat grinder fitted with a ⅜-inch plate, coarsely grind the meat and fat into a large bowl or chop coarsely in batches in a food processor as directed in step 1 of Maple and Sage Pork Sausage Patties (page 408).

2. Add 2 teaspoons salt, 1 tablespoon pepper, and the remaining ingredients (except the casings) and, using clean hands, knead and squeeze the mixture to blend thoroughly. Cook a small patty in a small skillet and taste for salt, pepper, and other seasonings, especially the green curry paste; adjust as necessary.

3. Divide the sausage into 8 portions of about ½ pound each. Or stuff into casings and tie into 5-inch links (see page 407). Refrigerate for no more than 1 day, or freeze for up to 3 months.

Alternative Cuts: Boneless country-style ribs, boneless country-style ribs cut from the pork shoulder butt, or boneless blade-end pork loin.

Cook's Note
- You can replace ½ pound of the pork with finely chopped shrimp.

KALE AND GARLIC SAUSAGE

Comfort Food, Great Leftovers, Freezes Well

Makes about 4 pounds

The area around Lyon, France, is renowned for various styles of *cervelas,* or Lyonnaise sausages. They usually contain lots of garlic and are briefly hung to concentrate their flavors, then poached. Some even contain luxury ingredients like black truffles, morels, or pistachios. Often they are eaten with boiled potatoes or warm potato salad. They are great in soups, with lentils or beans, or in Cassoulet (page 312). My version, which contains kale and garlic, was inspired by a recipe from Chez Panisse in Berkeley, California, a restaurant I've enjoyed for more than forty years.

For sausage safety, see page 409.

2 tablespoons olive oil	Salt and freshly ground black pepper
½ cup finely chopped onion	½ pound ham, cut into ¼-inch dice
⅓ cup finely chopped shallots	1½ tablespoons Spanish paprika (*pimentón de la Vera*; see Sources) or sweet Hungarian paprika
12 large garlic cloves, peeled	
1½ pounds green kale or lacinato kale (also called cavolo nero or dinosaur kale), stems removed	1 teaspoon crushed red pepper flakes
	½ teaspoon ground coriander
½ cup dry white wine	¼ teaspoon freshly grated nutmeg
½ cup water	1 tablespoon chopped fresh basil
2 pounds boneless Boston butt (pork shoulder butt), cut into 1-inch pieces	2 teaspoons chopped fresh thyme
	2 teaspoons chopped fresh sage
¼ pound pork fatback (see Cook's Notes, page 409), cut into ½-inch pieces	2 tablespoons cognac (optional)
	Medium hog casings
2 ounces pancetta or bacon	

1. Heat the oil in a large skillet over medium-high heat. Add the onion, shallots, and garlic. Cover and cook until soft, stirring occasionally, about 5 minutes. Add the kale, white wine, and water. Reduce the heat to medium and cook until the kale is wilted and soft, about 15 minutes. Drain the kale mixture, squeezing out as much moisture as you can; save ¼ cup of the liquid. Transfer to a bowl and cool in the refrigerator for 30 minutes.

2. Using a meat grinder fitted with a ⅜-inch plate, coarsely grind the pork butt and the cooled kale mixture into a large bowl or coarsely chop in batches in a food processor as directed in step 1 of Maple and Sage Pork Sausage Patties (page 408). Change to an

⅛-inch plate and grind the fatback and pancetta into the bowl with the pork butt or chop in the food processor into about ⅛-inch pieces. Add 2½ teaspoons salt, 2 teaspoons pepper, and the remaining ingredients (except the casings) and the reserved kale cooking liquid to the bowl with the ground meats. Using clean hands, knead and squeeze the mixture to blend thoroughly. Cook a small patty in a small skillet and taste for seasonings; adjust as necessary.

3   Stuff the mixture into the hog casings and tie into 8-inch links (see page 407). Place the sausages in a single layer on a baking sheet and refrigerate, uncovered, overnight so that the flavors develop. (*The sausages can be refrigerated for up to 2 days or frozen for up to 3 months.*)

4   Bring a large pot of salted water to a boil. Add the sausages and, when the water returns to a boil, turn off the heat. Let them sit in the water for 15 minutes, then drain. To serve, grill or panfry the sausages.

Alternative Cuts: Boneless country-style ribs, boneless country-style ribs from pork shoulder butt, or boneless blade-end pork loin.

Cook's Notes

- Another great way to serve these sausages is to cut them into ½-inch-thick slices and gently brown them in butter. Serve for breakfast or add to a pot of cooked lentils or white beans.

- For an elegant variation, add 1 cup roasted pistachios to the meat mixture.

- You can also add ½ cup soaked dried morel mushrooms, coarsely chopped.

SEMIDRIED (SEMICURADO) SPANISH CHORIZO

Great Leftovers, Freezes Well
Makes about 3 pounds

There are many types of Spanish chorizo, from hard, cured, air-dried sausages meant to be eaten as is to much softer and only partially dried (*semicurado*) versions, like the one here, that are used to add flavor to many dishes such as paella, bean dishes, and stews. Making semidried chorizo is simple, and the sausages can be frozen in small batches to be used whenever you have a hankering for Spanish-inspired recipes calling for *semicurado* chorizo. Do not use Mexican chorizo as a substitute for Spanish chorizo and vice versa.

If you wish to dry these links for longer than 3 days or smoke them, you must add the Insta Cure for safety. For more on sausage safety, see page 409.

3 pounds boneless Boston butt (pork shoulder butt), cut into 1-inch pieces

½ pound pork fatback (see Cook's Notes, page 409), cut into ½-inch pieces

½ teaspoon Insta Cure No. 1 (see page 415 and Sources; optional)

¼ cup cold water (if using Insta Cure No. 1)
Salt and freshly ground black pepper

¼ cup sweet Hungarian paprika or California chile powder

2 tablespoons Spanish paprika (*pimentón de la Vera*; see Sources)

1 tablespoon minced garlic

2 teaspoons sugar
Pinch of ground cinnamon
Medium hog casings

1 Using a meat grinder fitted with a ⅜-inch plate, coarsely grind the pork into a large bowl or coarsely chop in batches in a food processor in batches as directed in step 1 of Maple and Sage Pork Sausage Patties (page 408). Change to an ⅛-inch plate and grind the fatback through or chop in the food processor into about ⅛-inch pieces.

2 If using the Insta Cure No. 1 (see Cook's Note), stir it into the cold water and pour over the pork mixture. Add 4 teaspoons salt, 2 teaspoons pepper, and the remaining ingredients (except the casings; see Cook's Note). Using clean hands, knead and squeeze the mixture to blend thoroughly. Cook a small patty in a small skillet and taste for salt, pepper, and other seasonings; adjust as necessary.

3 Stuff the mixture into casings and twist into 6-inch links (see page 407).

4 To partially dry the sausage, hang them over a stick at room temperature for 30 minutes, then place the links directly on a refrigerator shelf, so that air can circulate all

around them. (If your refrigerator has glass shelves, suspend the links from a shelf.) Hang for 3 days or up to 8 days before using. After the drying period, the sausages can be refrigerated for up to a week or frozen, in small batches, for up to 3 months.

Alternative Cuts: Boneless country-style ribs, boneless country-style ribs from pork shoulder butt, or boneless blade-end pork loin.

Cook's Note
- You can also smoke these links for 2 to 3 hours, depending on how smoky you want them. See page 439 for cold-smoking instructions.

USING CHORIZO
- Braise chunks in sherry
- Use in rice dishes such as paella
- Mix with beans or chickpeas in classic dishes such as Feijoada (page 193)
- Stuff slices into dates or prunes, wrap in serrano ham, skewer, and grill
- Skewer with shrimp and vegetables and grill
- Use to flavor slow-cooked greens such as kale, collards, or cabbage
- Use as a filling for turnovers and other pies
- Stew slowly with potatoes
- Add to soups, especially bean or winter vegetable soups
- Braise with clams or other seafood
- Use as a filling for seafood such as squid
- Panfry with chicken livers and sweet bell peppers
- Add to braised chicken dishes
- Use in Spanish boiled dinners (see Cocido, page 209)
- Add to stuffings for fish or poultry
- Add to egg dishes

INSTA CURE NO. 1

Some of the recipes in this section call for Insta Cure No. 1. This preservative must be used in recipes where the meat is aged or smoked above refrigerator temperatures, which are ideal breeding grounds for bacterial growth, like the botulinum toxin. For safety reasons, do not leave Insta Cure out of any recipe that calls for it. However, some recipes, such as pâtés or brined meats like corned beef, call for Insta Cure as an option, to preserve the meat's pink color; if you wish, you may leave it out of these recipes.

A mixture of 1 part sodium nitrite to 15 parts table salt, Insta Cure is colored pink so that it won't be mistaken for regular salt. Because only minuscule amounts of the nitrite are used for the curing process — quantities too small to be measured with normal scales or measuring cups and spoons — it is mixed with salt to bulk it up.

To obtain Insta Cure No. 1, see Sources.

BASIC MEXICAN-STYLE CHORIZO

Comfort Food, Great Leftovers, Freezes Well

Makes about 4 pounds

In Mexican cooking, chorizo is most often used to flavor dishes such as chilis and other stews, enchiladas, tacos, and egg dishes. There is no need to stuff the mixture into casings; simply package the mixture in ½-pound or 1-pound quantities and store in the freezer until you need it.

This is a basic recipe, but I have made some suggestions for embellishments, as well as substitutions; see Cook's Notes. For sausage safety, see page 409.

2 dried ancho, New Mexico, California, or guajillo chiles, or a combination	Salt and freshly ground black pepper
2 teaspoons cumin seeds	1 teaspoon dried oregano (I use Mexican)
½ teaspoon coriander seeds	1 teaspoon cayenne pepper, or more to taste
3 pounds boneless Boston butt (pork shoulder butt), cut into 1-inch pieces	⅛ teaspoon ground cinnamon
	1 tablespoon minced garlic
½ pound pork fatback (see Cook's Notes, page 409), cut into ½-inch pieces	1 tablespoon agave syrup (see Cook's Notes) or 1 teaspoon sugar
	3 tablespoons white vinegar, or more to taste

1 Tear the chiles into large pieces and discard the seeds and stems. Toast in a small dry skillet over medium heat, stirring, for 1 or 2 minutes, or until the chiles start to darken and become aromatic. Take care not to burn them. Transfer to a small bowl, pour over boiling water to cover, and soak for at least 30 minutes, or until the chiles have softened.

2 Add the chiles to a blender with a few tablespoons of the soaking liquid and puree. Set aside.

3 Add the cumin and coriander seeds to the skillet and toast over medium heat, shaking the pan, until the seeds become aromatic and just begin to smoke, 2 to 3 minutes. Transfer to a mortar with a pestle or a spice grinder and grind to a powder. Set aside.

4 Using a meat grinder fitted with a ¼-inch plate, coarsely grind the pork and fatback into a large bowl or coarsely chop in batches in a food processor as directed in step 1 of Maple and Sage Pork Sausage Patties (page 408). Add the reserved chile puree, toasted spices, 4 teaspoons salt, 1½ teaspoons pepper, and the remaining ingredients and, using clean hands, knead and squeeze the mixture to blend thoroughly. Cook a small patty in a small skillet and taste for salt, pepper, cayenne, and vinegar; adjust

as necessary. Refrigerate what you need immediately and freeze the rest in ½- to 1-pound amounts in zipper-lock freezer bags. The chorizo can be refrigerated for up to 2 days or frozen for up to 3 months.

Alternative Cuts: Boneless country-style ribs, boneless country-style ribs from pork shoulder butt, or boneless blade-end pork loin.

Cook's Notes

- Agave syrup is made from the agave cactus and has a nice fruity flavor. It is sold at Whole Foods and health-food stores, as well as many supermarkets.

- Add as many of the embellishments as you desire to suit your tastes:

    1 cup or more chopped fresh cilantro

    1 teaspoon or more grated unsweetened dark chocolate

    ¼ cup tequila or beer, preferably Mexican

    ½ cup fire-roasted and chopped mild chiles, such as poblano or bell pepper (see page 284)

    2 teaspoons finely grated lime zest

    ½ cup finely chopped and cooked onion

- Or make any of these substitutions:

    Replace the cayenne pepper with 1 seeded and finely chopped hot chile, such as jalapeño or serrano

    Replace the dried chiles and the cayenne with ½ teaspoon seeded and finely chopped habanero chile (warning: this will make a very hot sausage)

    Replace the vinegar with ¼ cup fresh lime juice

    Replace the dried oregano with 1 tablespoon chopped fresh oregano

    Replace the agave syrup or sugar with 1 tablespoon finely chopped raisins or pureed pitted prunes

Pâtés and Mousses

Many of us think of **pâté** as a rich, creamy spread made of liver. But technically, it's a blend of various ground meats, including liver, that is cooked in a crust (also called *pâté en croûte*). A **terrine** refers to a ground meat mixture cooked in a mold or loaf pan. A **mousse** is a smoother blend, usually of liver and fat, that is formed in a mold. Often a mousse is made by pureeing warm cooked livers with fat to produce a homogeneous blend, but it can also be made by combining raw liver and fat, then baking the mixture in a mold.

Nowadays we use the word "pâté" to cover all three types of ground meat mixtures. They're usually eaten cold and make an ideal first course or hors d'oeuvre for both informal and formal gatherings.

Making pâté takes no more skill than making meat loaf, and I have chosen recipes that are good and basic and that leave you plenty of room to express your own creativity. You can add or substitute other ingredients, such as pistachios, hand-diced meats (ham, smoked sausage, smoked tongue, duck breast, game), wild mushrooms, or truffles. Remember that a good pâté is about texture and richness. In order to attain the right consistency, pâtés — especially liver mousses — must contain ample fat. Don't reduce the fat in my recipes; the results will be dry and grainy.

TECHNIQUES FOR MAKING PÂTÉS

Recipes for terrines often call for lining the pan with strips of fat or caul fat, perhaps to make the mixture more moist. This is unnecessary, and I recommend cooking the pâté mixture just as you would a meat loaf, in an unlined pan. But if you do want to line the pan, use strips of bacon or pancetta, which will give the pâté a nice appearance.

I sometimes weight a cooked pâté, which compresses it so that you get firm, intact slices, but my recipes include ingredients that provide ample natural gelatin to bind the mixture and produce firm slices.

For moist results, pâtés — especially liver mousses — need to cook slowly to prevent the ingredients from separating. Placing the pâté mold in a water bath slows down the cooking and is an important part of the process.

ITALIAN COUNTRY TERRINE

Fit for Company, Fit for a Crowd, Keeps Well
Serves 10 to 12

Franco Dunn, the founding chef of the former Santi Restaurant in Santa Rosa, in California's Sonoma County wine-growing region, is known for his authentic rustic Italian fare. Franco is justifiably proud of his Italian *salumi*, especially this peasant-style terrine, which is an Italian cousin to the rustic French *pâté de campagne*. This one was inspired by a similar dish he ate in Umbria, where it was made with wild boar instead of pork, which is a great substitution.

1 tablespoon bacon fat or olive oil	2 tablespoons salt
1 cup chopped onions	2 teaspoons freshly ground black pepper
1 10-ounce bag cleaned spinach	1½ teaspoons fennel pollen (see Sources)
1 pound boneless Boston butt (pork shoulder butt), cut into 1-inch cubes	or ground fennel seeds
½ pound pork fatback (see Cook's Notes, page 409), cut into ½-inch cubes	¼ teaspoon ground allspice
	¼ teaspoon freshly grated nutmeg
1 pound pork liver or chicken or duck livers, cut into ½-inch cubes	2 garlic cloves, minced
	2 tablespoons grappa or brandy
¼ pound pork skin, boiled and cut into 1-inch cubes, or 2 packets (4½ teaspoons) unflavored gelatin, dissolved in ¼ cup warm water (see Cook's Notes)	2 teaspoons finely grated lemon zest
	2 teaspoons chopped fresh thyme
	2 teaspoons sugar
	1 large egg, lightly beaten
	2 fresh thyme sprigs

1   Heat the fat in a medium skillet over medium heat. Add the onions, cover, and cook, stirring occasionally, until quite soft, about 10 minutes. Transfer the onions to a bowl and refrigerate for at least 30 minutes.

2   Bring a large pot of water to a boil. Cook the spinach until just wilted, about 1 minute, then drain in a colander. Rinse under cold running water and squeeze dry. Chop roughly and cool in the refrigerator for at least 30 minutes. (*The onions and spinach can be covered and refrigerated overnight.*)

3   Using a meat grinder fitted with a ⅜-inch plate, grind the pork into a large bowl (if you have one, use the bowl for a standing electric mixer, because you'll be using a mixer to combine the pâté ingredients) or coarsely chop in a food processor into about ⅜-inch pieces (see Cook's Notes). Change to an ⅛-inch plate. In another bowl, stir together the fatback, ½ pound of the liver, the pork skin or gelatin, and cooked onions and spinach

and grind the mixture into the bowl with the pork butt or chop in the food processor into about ⅛-inch pieces. Add the remaining diced liver and all the remaining ingredients except the thyme sprigs and mix on medium speed with an electric stand or hand mixer until well combined, 2 to 3 minutes. Or, beat well by hand with a sturdy wooden spoon.

4   Preheat the oven to 300°F, with a rack in the middle of the oven.

5   Put on some water to boil. Meanwhile, lay the thyme sprigs in the bottom of a 9-x-5-inch (7-cup) loaf pan or terrine. Scrape the meat mixture into the pan. Cover tightly with aluminum foil and put the pan in a roasting pan or baking dish. Place in the oven and add enough boiling water to the roasting pan to come two thirds of the way up the sides of the loaf pan. Bake for 1¾ to 2 hours, or until the internal temperature registers 155°F to 160°F on an instant-read thermometer. Remove from the oven and let cool for 2 hours, then cover with plastic wrap and refrigerate overnight. (*The terrine can be refrigerated for up to 1 week.*)

6   To serve, unmold the terrine onto a cutting board. Remove the thyme sprigs and discard. Cut the terrine into ½-inch-thick slices. Allow to warm at room temperature for 10 to 15 minutes before serving.

Cook's Notes

- Pork liver can be rather strong and is not to everyone's taste (although some of the strong taste will be removed if you soak the pork liver as instructed in step 1 of Pork Liver Mousse, page 424). If you prefer a milder taste, use chicken or duck livers, or a mixture.

- Boiled pork skin provides the gelatin that makes the slices firm so that they don't fall apart. You can get pork skin from farmers' markets or special-order it from your butcher. It also contributes an earthy taste. To prepare the skin, simmer in water to cover for at least 2 hours, or until very soft. Drain. (*The skin can be stored in a covered container in the refrigerator for up to 4 days or in the freezer for up to 3 months.*) You can also use the rind trimmed from slab bacon.

- If you're using gelatin, dissolve it by sprinkling it over ¼ cup warm water in a small bowl. Let sit for about 5 minutes.

- If you chop the ingredients in a food processor, it's better to err on the side of too coarse than to turn the meat into a puree.

- Sometimes I weight my pâtés and terrines so that they have a firmer texture. To do this, cut a piece of cardboard to just fit on top of the pâté inside the pan. Wrap the cardboard in aluminum foil and set a few heavy cans on top, or find a brick that will fit inside the mold (wrap it in aluminum foil first).

SMOOTH LAMB LIVER PÂTÉ WITH VIN SANTO

Fit for Company, Fit for a Crowd, Cheap Eats

Serves 8 to 10

Vin Santo is a sweet dessert wine from Tuscany. If you can't find it, use any sweet white wine, such as Muscat, Riesling, or Sauternes, or sweet sherry. This recipe came from chef Cathy Whims, owner of Nostrana in Portland, Oregon. The pâté is creamy textured, with sweet notes from the honey, currants, and Vin Santo. If you can't find lamb's liver, use beef or pork liver, chicken livers, or a combination.

1¾ pounds pork fatback (see Cook's Notes, page 409), cut into 1-inch cubes	1½ pounds lamb's liver, cut into 1-inch cubes
⅓ cup Vin Santo or other sweet dessert wine (see headnote)	5 large egg yolks, lightly beaten, at room temperature
1 cup homemade pork stock (see page 168) or canned low-sodium chicken broth	5 teaspoons salt
1½ cups heavy cream	2 teaspoons freshly ground black pepper
1 cup chopped fresh flat-leaf parsley	½ teaspoon ground coriander
⅔ cup dried currants	¼ teaspoon ground ginger
2 tablespoons honey	¼ teaspoon freshly grated nutmeg
	⅛ teaspoon ground cloves

1   Bring a large pot of water to a boil. Boil the fatback for 5 minutes. Drain and cool in the refrigerator for about 30 minutes, or until it reaches 60°F to 65°F.

2   Meanwhile, combine the wine, stock, heavy cream, parsley, currants, and honey in a medium saucepan and bring to a simmer. Remove from the heat and cool in the refrigerator for about 30 minutes, or until the mixture reaches 60°F to 65°F.

3   Preheat the oven to 300°F. Line a 2-quart terrine mold with plastic wrap. Put on some water to boil.

4   In a large bowl, combine the liver, fatback, wine mixture, egg yolks, salt, and the remaining spices. Place half of the mixture in a blender and blend at medium speed until very smooth. Transfer to a bowl. Repeat with the second half of the mixture, and combine both batches. (For a supersmooth pâté, strain through a fine-mesh strainer.) Pour the mixture into the terrine mold. Place an oiled piece of parchment paper over the top, then wrap the entire mold tightly with aluminum foil.

5 Set the mold in a deep roasting pan and pour boiling water into the roasting pan to reach the level of the mixture in the mold. Bake for 30 minutes. Reduce the oven temperature to 225°F and bake for 2 hours more, or until the internal temperature of the pâté reaches 150°F on an instant-read thermometer. Cool to room temperature, then refrigerate overnight before serving.

Alternative Cuts: Pork liver (soak overnight in buttermilk; see step 1 of Pork Liver Mousse, page 424), calf's liver, beef liver, or chicken or duck livers, or, better still, a combination of any of these.

Cook's Notes
- Use liver from grass-fed lambs, if you can.
- In order to get a homogenous mixture of fat and liver, it is critical that the ingredients be cooled to 60°F to 65°F. If they are too warm, the fat will melt and separate; if too cool, the fat will remain in little granules.

PORK LIVER MOUSSE

Fit for Company, Fit for a Crowd
Serves 8 to 12

This mousse, which is made with cooked liver and lots of onions and shallots, is fairly easy to prepare, but unlike most pâtés, it does not keep longer than 3 or 4 days in the refrigerator. I like the sweet undertones provided by the apples, but you can omit them. Because pork liver is stronger tasting than other liver, I soak it in buttermilk to leach out some of its stronger flavors. Feel free to replace a portion of it with chicken, duck, calf's, or beef liver if you prefer. Just make sure that whatever kind of liver you use is impeccably fresh. Avoid frozen liver, which becomes watery and would give the mousse a grainy texture.

2	cups buttermilk	1½	cups chopped onions
2	teaspoons sugar	½	cup chopped shallots
1½	pounds pork liver, or ¾ pound pork liver plus ¾ pound chicken or duck livers or calf's or beef liver	6	garlic cloves, chopped
		2	tablespoons brandy
		2	tablespoons sweet sherry or Madeira
1	pound (4 sticks) butter	1	small Granny Smith apple, peeled, cored, and diced (optional)
	Salt and freshly ground black pepper		
⅛	teaspoon *each* ground allspice, nutmeg, ginger, coriander, and cloves, combined, or more to taste	3	pitted prunes, soaked in hot water for 10 minutes and drained (optional)
			Crostini, toast, or crackers

1 Put the buttermilk in a large bowl and stir in the sugar. Add the pork liver and stir to combine. Cover and refrigerate for at least 2 hours, or up to 24 hours.

2 Drain the pork liver in a colander and wash well under cold running water until all the milky coating is gone. Pat dry with paper towels. Cut away any large blood vessels or connective tissue from the pork liver and calf's or beef liver (if using) and cut into 2-inch pieces. If using poultry livers, leave them whole.

3 Heat 4 tablespoons of the butter in a large skillet over medium-high heat. When it begins to sizzle, add half of the liver and sprinkle with 1 teaspoon salt, ½ teaspoon pepper, and half of the spice mixture. Shaking the pan and stirring, cook the liver until lightly browned and firm but still slightly pink on the inside. Transfer the liver and pan juices to a large bowl. Repeat with an additional 2 tablespoons of the butter, the remaining liver, another 1 teaspoon salt, ½ teaspoon pepper, and the remaining

spices. Set 3 sticks of butter to soften on top of the warm liver while you cook the vegetables.

4 Reduce the heat to medium and add the remaining 2 tablespoons butter to the skillet. Add the onions, shallots, and garlic and sprinkle with 2 teaspoons salt and 1 teaspoon pepper. Reduce the heat to medium-low, cover, and cook for 5 minutes. Stir in the brandy and sherry and scrape up any browned bits from the bottom of the pan. Cover and cook until the vegetables are quite soft, 10 to 15 minutes. Add the apple and/or prunes (if using), and cook for 5 minutes more, or until the fruit is soft. Scrape the mixture and any juices into the bowl with the liver and butter. Stir the mixture and allow to cool at room temperature for 30 minutes.

5 Puree the mixture in 2 or 3 batches in a food processor until smooth and transfer to a large bowl. Season to taste with salt, pepper, and spices. Stir until well mixed. Scrape the mousse into a serving bowl or 9-x-5-inch (8-cup) loaf pan, smooth the top, and cover with plastic wrap. Refrigerate for at least 24 hours, or until firm.

6 Allow it to sit at room temperature for 30 minutes. If the mousse is in a loaf pan, dip the pan into a large container of hot water for 10 to 20 seconds, then turn it out onto a platter. Or, serve directly from the serving bowl. Serve with crostini, toast, or crackers.

Alternative Cuts: Lamb's liver, alone or in combination with the pork.

Cook's Notes

- For a more intensely porky flavor, replace some of the butter with an equal amount of homemade lard (see page 434).

- For an Asian flavor, use ½ teaspoon Chinese five-spice powder instead of the spices called for in the recipe.

- After the liver mixture is processed, it will still have a slightly grainy texture. If you prefer a supersmooth mousse, strain the mixture through a fine-mesh sieve before putting it into the mold.

TONGUE MOUSSE

Fit for Company, Fit for a Crowd, Great Leftovers
Serves 10

Every time I serve this amazingly simple spread, it draws oohs and aahs. It's my go-to offering for numerous couch-potato gatherings: Super Bowl, March Madness, and the World Series. The delicate salty meat flavor of the tongue combines perfectly with the tangy sour cream and cream cheese. The mousse can be made up to 3 days ahead, leaving you free to join the gang in front of the TV. The mousse is best made with smoked or pickled beef or veal tongue, which you can prepare yourself (see page 448 for a recipe) or buy slices of smoked tongue loaf or sliced pickled tongue from a deli.

1¼ pounds cold cooked, smoked, or pickled tongue (see headnote), cut into ½-inch dice (about 3 cups)

Salt and freshly ground black pepper

1 cup sour cream

1 8-ounce block Philadelphia cream cheese (use the original, which contains guar gum), at room temperature

1 tablespoon smooth or coarse-grain Dijon mustard

½ cup chopped fresh flat-leaf parsley

¼ cup finely chopped shallots or fresh chives

2 tablespoons dry sherry, plus more if needed

Crackers or toasted rye or pumpernickel bread for serving

Place the tongue in a food processor and pulse several times to finely chop. Add a sprinkling of salt, 2 teaspoons pepper, and the remaining ingredients, except the crackers. Pulse several times to produce a homogeneous mixture. Taste and add sherry and/or salt and pepper if needed. Scrape into a serving bowl just large enough to hold the mousse. Cover with plastic wrap and refrigerate for at least 2 hours, or until firm (overnight is best). (*The mousse keeps refrigerated for 3 to 5 days.*) Serve from the bowl with the crackers or toast.

Alternative Cuts: Pastrami, corned beef, or smoked ham.

Cook's Notes

- The addition of gelatin turns this mousse into a sliceable terrine. Dissolve 2 packets (4½ teaspoons) unflavored gelatin by sprinkling it over ¼ cup warm water in a small bowl. Let sit for about 5 minutes, and add the gelatin mixture when you add the sherry. Place the mixture in a loaf pan lined with plastic wrap and chill until firm, or overnight. Unmold and slice to serve as a first course.

- You can use this mousse as a filling for tea sandwiches or canapés, garnished with thin slices of dill pickles or cornichons.

HAM AND GOAT CHEESE TERRINE

Fit for Company, Great Leftovers
Serves 6 to 8

The success of this incredibly simple terrine depends on the quality of the ham that you use. Leftover baked ham works well; cut your slices as thin as you can. If you purchase ham from a deli, ask for the best smoked ham, sliced about 1/16 inch thick (see Sources for my favorite producers). Serve on a salad of curly endive or frisée, dressed with a mustardy vinaigrette. Accompany the terrine with cornichons and pickled pearl onions and thin slices of good peasant bread (I'm partial to German-style rye breads).

8 ounces fresh goat cheese (a mild, soft one, such as Laura Chenel or Montrachet), at room temperature

1 8-ounce block Philadelphia cream cheese (use the original, which contains guar gum), at room temperature

¼ cup sour cream or crème fraîche

¼ cup chopped fresh chervil or flat-leaf parsley

¼ cup chopped fresh chives or scallion greens

2 tablespoons finely chopped shallot

2 tablespoons port, Madeira, or sweet sherry

2 packets (4½ teaspoons) unflavored gelatin, dissolved in ¼ cup warm water

Salt and freshly ground black pepper

8–12 1/16-inch-thick slices good smoked ham or 1/8-inch-thick slices leftover baked ham (about 1 to 1½ pounds)

1. Place the cheeses, sour cream, herbs, shallot, and port in a food processor and scrape the gelatin mixture over. Pulse several times, until well combined. Season to taste with salt and pepper. The cheese mixture will pick up salt from the ham, so it's best to undersalt; you may find you don't need any at all.

2. Line an 8½-x-4½-inch (6-cup) loaf pan with plastic wrap so that it overhangs the sides. Cover the bottom of the pan with a layer of ham (if a single ham slice doesn't cover the pan, use several pieces fitted together). Using a rubber spatula or offset spatula, cover the ham with a thin layer (¼ to ½ inch) of the cheese mixture, then cover with another layer of ham. Repeat the layering until all the ham and cheese are used. Cover the top with the overhanging plastic wrap (if necessary, use additional wrap so that it is sealed). Refrigerate the terrine overnight to firm and let the flavors meld. (*Refrigerated, the terrine will keep for 3 to 4 days.*)

3. To unmold, gently pull on the plastic wrap to loosen the terrine. If it sticks, immerse the mold in a pan of very hot water for 10 to 15 seconds to melt some of the gelatin. Invert the mold over a platter and unmold. Remove and discard the plastic wrap. To serve, use a serrated or electric knife to cut the terrine into ½-inch-thick slices.

Alternative Cuts: To vary the flavor of the terrine, use other types of ham, such as prosciutto, serrano, or Westphalian ham.

Cook's Note

- You can also make this mixture into pinwheels, which are ideal for a passed hors d'oeuvre. You won't need the gelatin; you will need uniform ¹⁄₁₆-inch-thick ham slices purchased from a deli. Using a rubber spatula or offset spatula, spread a thin layer of the filling on a ham slice, leaving a ¼-inch border all around. Roll up the ham into a cylinder and tightly wrap in plastic wrap. Repeat with the remaining ham slices and the filling mixture until all the filling is used. Refrigerate the rolls for at least 1 hour, or up to overnight. Just before serving, remove the plastic wrap and cut each roll into ¾- to 1-inch-thick rounds. You can skewer each round with a toothpick or just lay them cut side down on a platter and let your guests grab them with their fingers.

Confit and Rillettes

Confit is an ancient French method for preserving meat, mainly pork or fatty fowl, by cooking it slowly in fat. Typically, fattier cuts of pork, such as Boston butt, are well salted for a few days (as with salt-preserved meat), then the meat is covered completely in fat and cooked slowly until very tender. The meat is removed and placed in a crock or similar container, and the fat is strained and poured over the meat, covering it completely. Between the salt-curing and the fat keeping it from direct contact with air, the meat could be stored in a cool place for as long as a year.

With refrigeration, making a confit is less about preservation than about the great flavor that the seasoned and aged meat gains from the technique. Confit pork or fowl contributes great flavor to such classics as cassoulet, and it is delicious panfried and served over dressed bitter salad greens.

Rillettes, also called potted meats, are a close cousin to confit. Fatty cuts of pork shoulder and/or pork belly are slowly cooked to render out the fat. Once the juices evaporate and the meat begins to fall apart, the meat is shredded and blended with the fat to produce a spreadable paste, which is packed into a mold (a small deep bowl works well). Rillettes are best after aging for 2 to 3 days in the refrigerator.

PORK CONFIT

**Fit for Company, Cheap Eats, Comfort Food,
Great Leftovers, Keeps Well**

Makes about 3 pounds

This is a much less salty version of the classic confit from southwestern France, which is usually made with fatted duck or goose. I've adapted a recipe that my wife, Nancy, uses at her restaurant, Boulevard, in San Francisco. Slow-poaching fatty cuts of pork in fat gives the meat an intense taste without drying it out. The unique flavors are mellowed and improved as the pork ages. Packed in the fat in which it was cooked, the pork will keep for 2 months in the refrigerator, ready for an impromptu family dinner or an important occasion. You can use pork confit in Cassoulet (page 312) or fry up chunks to crisp the outside and serve warm in a salad of radicchio (page 432). For a great sandwich filling, gently warm it, then pour off the fat, chop the meat with cornichons and shallots, and combine with mayonnaise and a bit of coarse-grain Dijon mustard.

Herbes de Provence Rub

- 2 teaspoons herbes de Provence
- 2 tablespoons salt
- 2 teaspoons freshly ground black pepper
- ½ teaspoon ground coriander
- ¼ teaspoon ground allspice
- 6 bay leaves, crushed
- 2 fresh sage leaves, chopped
- 1 teaspoon chopped fresh thyme

- 4 pounds boneless Boston butt (pork shoulder butt), cut into 3-inch chunks (don't trim too much fat from the meat)
- 2 onions, sliced
- 8 garlic cloves, peeled
- 6 fresh thyme sprigs
- 1 fresh rosemary sprig
- About 4 cups melted lard (see page 434) and/or olive oil

1 **Rub:** Combine all the ingredients in a small bowl. Rub generously over the pork chunks. Put the pork in a large zipper-lock bag and refrigerate for 24 to 30 hours, shaking and turning the bag from time to time to redistribute the rub.

2 Preheat the oven to 225°F.

3 Put the onions, garlic, thyme, and rosemary in a Dutch oven. Pat the pork dry with paper towels (don't scrape off the spice rub) and lay it on top of the onions. Pour on the melted lard and/or olive oil to cover the meat. Bake for 4 to 5 hours, or until the meat is quite tender, turning the meat in the fat occasionally. The meat should be completely covered with fat at all times; add more lard or olive oil if necessary.

4   Using a slotted spoon, remove the pork from the fat and pack it snugly into a storage container. Strain the fat and juices into a glass measuring cup (discarding the onions, garlic, thyme, and rosemary) and let the juices settle to the bottom, about 5 minutes. Pour enough of the fat over the pork so that it's completely covered by ½ inch and seal the container. Refrigerate for at least 2 weeks and up to 2 months before serving, making sure the pork is always completely immersed in fat. Pour the juices into another container and refrigerate or freeze for another use (see Cook's Notes).

5   To serve the pork, remove the chunks of meat from the fat and scrape off any fat clinging to them. Heat the pork in a nonstick skillet over medium-high heat until crisped (see Panfried Pork Confit and Radicchio Salad, page 432).

Alternative Cuts: Pork cheeks; boneless country-style ribs; pork belly; or picnic shoulder, trimmed of skin and gristle.

Cook's Notes
- If you don't have herbes de Provence, use a mixture of equal parts dried marjoram, sage, thyme, rosemary, savory, fennel seeds, and basil — and, if you want to be truly traditional, dried lavender.

- The juices from the pork confit can be refrigerated for 3 to 4 days or frozen for several months and used in vinaigrettes or other dishes such as Cassoulet (page 312) and stews to lend an intense porky flavor.

PANFRIED PORK CONFIT AND RADICCHIO SALAD

Serves 4

¼	cup juices from Pork Confit (see page 431)		Salt and freshly ground black pepper
½	cup dry red wine	1	tablespoon fat from Pork Confit (page 430)
2	tablespoons red wine vinegar	1	cup coarsely shredded or chopped Pork Confit
2	shallots, sliced into rings		(page 430)
2	garlic cloves, thinly sliced	2	small heads radicchio, very thinly sliced
¼	cup olive oil	½	cup toasted sliced almonds

1   Combine the confit juices, red wine, vinegar, shallots, and garlic in a small pan. Boil to reduce the liquid to ¼ cup, 3 to 5 minutes. Let cool, then whisk in the oil. Season to taste with salt and pepper. Set aside.

2   Heat the confit fat in a medium skillet over medium-high heat. Add the confit and fry until the edges of the meat begin to brown and crisp, 2 to 3 minutes.

3   Combine the confit with the radicchio and almonds in a bowl and toss with the dressing. Divide among four salad plates and serve.

STAR ANISE-FLAVORED PORK RILLETTES

Comfort Food, Great Leftovers, Keeps Well

Serves 6 to 8

For rillettes, the French version of potted pork, fattier cuts are cooked long and slow until the meat is easily shredded, and then the meat and fat are combined and stored in a crock or mold with the top surface covered in more fat. For optimum flavor, allow the rillettes to mellow and mature for 2 to 3 days in the refrigerator before serving. I like the sweet flavor of star anise with pork. If you prefer, you can leave it out or replace it with ½ teaspoon crushed fennel seeds.

1 pound boneless Boston butt (pork shoulder butt) or boneless country-style ribs, cut into 1-inch pieces	1 teaspoon chopped fresh thyme
	1 whole star anise
	1 whole allspice berry
1½ pounds skinless pork belly, cut into ½-inch pieces, or 1 pound trimmed fat from Boston butt	¼ cup chopped shallots
	1 tablespoon chopped garlic
	½ cup dry white wine or beer
Salt and freshly ground black pepper	1 cup water
2 bay leaves	Toasted baguette slices

1 Place the meat and fat in a heavy saucepan or heatproof casserole. Stir in 2 teaspoons salt, 1 teaspoon pepper, and the remaining ingredients (except the baguette slices) and bring to a boil. Reduce the heat to a simmer and cook for 3 to 4 hours, until the meat is very tender and the water has evaporated, leaving only fat in the pan. Stir the rillettes occasionally to make sure the meat does not stick to the bottom of the pan.

2 Remove from the heat and discard the bay leaves, star anise, and allspice. Cool for 10 minutes, then shred the meat with a fork. Stir the shredded meat and fat together until well combined. Season to taste with salt and pepper. Scrape the rillettes into a 4-cup bowl, soufflé dish, or terrine. Cover with plastic wrap and refrigerate for at least 12 hours, or, ideally, 2 to 3 days before serving. (*Rillettes will keep for up to 2 weeks in the refrigerator.*)

3 Serve with toasted rounds of baguette.

SHANNON HAYES'S LARD

Cheap Eats, Keeps Well, Freezes Well
Makes 5 to 8 quarts

This technique for rendering pork fat into lard comes from Shannon Hayes, who has a Ph.D. in sustainable agriculture and works on her family's farm, which pasture-raises pigs, sheep, and cattle. The recipe produces pure lard with a mild taste, and the addition of the small amount of baking soda makes it pure white. Although the rendering is time-consuming (4 to 6 hours), it's not at all labor-intensive.

Pork fat can be acquired at little to no cost from a butcher or local farmer. This recipe is a must-have if you raise pigs and will give you a year's supply of lard.

5 pounds pork fat (see Cook's Notes)	¼ teaspoon baking soda

1 Have ready a large kettle or Dutch oven with a lid or splatter screen and several airtight containers, such as canning jars, for storing the finished lard.

2 Remove any skin from the fat and discard. Cut the pork fat into strips or chunks, none more than ½ inch wide, and toss them into the kettle. To avoid boilover, do not fill the kettle more than halfway. Sprinkle the fat with the baking soda, cover, and begin cooking at the lowest heat your stove top or oven can achieve. New stoves often come equipped with a "simmer" burner that, at its lowest setting, will provide ample heat for even a large kettle of fat. Alternatively, put the kettle in the oven at its lowest temperature setting. Stir the fat occasionally (a few times per hour) and check the temperature: It should not go above 250°F.

3 After the first hour, replace the lid with a splatter screen or move it so that it is slightly askew to allow as much water as possible to evaporate without creating a mess in your kitchen. As the fat cooks, it will occasionally pop and splatter, so avoid putting your face directly over the kettle for inspection.

4 After 4 to 6 hours, the liquid will turn clear and the cracklings (bits of meat remaining after the fat has melted) will float up to the top. When the cracklings are brown, shriveled, and have little bubbles on them, remove the kettle from the heat — be sure to stop the rendering process before the cracklings sink back down to the bottom and burn. Skim the cracklings off the top and allow them to drain on paper towels or brown paper bags — they're a delicious reward for all the work you've done. (See Cook's Notes for what to do with them.)

5 Use a ladle to spoon the lard into a large metal bowl, leaving any water at the bottom of the kettle. Discard the water. The lard will be extremely hot. Once it has cooled enough so that you can handle the bowl, strain the lard through a cheesecloth-lined colander into another large bowl. Divide the strained lard among the airtight containers and refrigerate quickly. The lard can be refrigerated for up to 6 months or frozen for up to a year.

Cook's Notes

- If you have a portable burner, you may want to make the lard outside.

- One way to speed up the rendering process is to grind the fat with a meat grinder. These smaller particles will render much more quickly.

- Use the cracklings in corn bread or biscuits or gently reheat and serve as a garnish for salads.

- I use fatback that I purchase from my local farmers' market. You can also use fat trimmings from pork shoulder or loin, but make sure they are mostly fat with no meat. (Freeze the trimmings until you have enough to make a batch of lard.)

LARD: THE SURPRISING FACTS

Why on earth would you want to make your own lard?

If you love flaky piecrusts and biscuits and moist corn bread, you should consider keeping a jar of lard in your fridge. It's also great for deep-frying, producing crispy fries, cutlets, and fried chicken.

Until recently, fear had driven lard out of most kitchens, despite the fact that it was the preferred fat in American cooking before World War II. Now it turns out that besides its stellar culinary attributes, lard has a lot going for it. It actually contains less saturated fat (which can increase risk of cardiovascular disease) than butter: 40 percent as compared with butter's 60 per-

cent. It is much higher in monounsaturated fats (said to decrease the risk of heart disease) than butter and contains three times more beneficial polyunsaturated fats. Lard also helps our skeletons absorb calcium, protects our liver from toxins, and bolsters our immune system. In addition, it's a good source of vitamin D.

Homemade lard contains none of the unhealthy trans fats that are produced when fats are hydrogenated to make them solid at room temperature. For that reason, don't even consider purchasing store-bought lard sold on supermarket shelves in block form — it's loaded with nasty trans fats.

Once you begin cooking with your own lard, I think you'll find homemade to be a necessity.

Cured and Smoked Meat

Using salt to preserve meat, called curing, may predate recorded history. The process, in which the water in the meat is replaced with salt through osmosis, retards spoilage caused by bacteria and other microorganisms. Depending on how much water is removed, the meat may be preserved almost indefinitely. With the advent of refrigeration, the primary reason for curing became not preserving but the taste that we've developed for such delicacies as bacon, ham, corned beef, and pastrami.

There are two common ways of curing meat. **Dry-curing** involves coating the meat with salt. **Wet-curing** (also called brining, corning, or pickling) uses a solution of salt and water. Often ingredients such as sugar, sodium nitrite (which gives cured meat its reddish-pink hue and prevents the growth of bacteria), spices, and other flavorings are added to both wet and dry cures.

Any kind of meat and any cut can be cured, but pork is the most common choice for curing because its fatty richness goes well with salt and because it won't become hard and dry, as beef does. Centuries of tradition have led to such classic cured delacacies as bacon, ham, ham hocks, pork loin, French *petit salé* ("brined pork"), corned beef, and pastrami. Once cured, the meat can be smoked, adding another layer of flavor to complement the salty tang.

BASIC WET BRINE

Makes 5 quarts

This is a basic brine that I use for bacon, corned beef, pickled tongue, ham, smoked pork loin, and *petit salé* pork. The method for brining is the same in each case. The only variations in the individual recipes are the addition of spices, herbs, or other flavorings and the time spent in the brine.

1 gallon cold water

1 pound (3 cups) kosher salt (I use Diamond Crystal; see page 20)

1 cup (½ pound) firmly packed light brown sugar

3 tablespoons Insta Cure No. 1 (optional if meat is not to be smoked; see page 415 and Sources)

Pour the water into a nonreactive container, such as a plastic storage tub or stainless steel bowl, large enough to hold the brine and the meat you wish to cure. Add the salt, brown sugar, and Insta Cure (if using) and stir until completely dissolved. Add the meat to the brine and weight it down with a plate so that it is completely submerged. Refrigerate for the time recommended in the individual recipe.

Cook's Notes

- If you prefer a sweeter flavor in your cured meats, increase the brown sugar by ¼-cup (2-ounce) increments each time you cure something to determine what sweetness level you prefer. If the basic cure is too sweet, then reduce the sugar by ¼-cup increments. You can replace some or all of the light brown sugar with other sweeteners, such as dark brown sugar, molasses, maple syrup, agave syrup (see Cook's Notes, page 417), treacle (see Sources), white sugar, turbinado sugar, honey, or malt syrup. Be sure to take notes each time you cure something so that you can adjust the sweetness and salt levels and curing times to your taste.

- You can also replace some of the water with other liquids, such as beer, sweet or hard cider, red or white wine (take care, because wine is acidic), rum, bourbon, scotch, brandy, Drambuie, or Irish whiskey; consult the individual recipes for specifics.

- If the brining container won't fit in your refrigerator, you can use a cooler. Add several gel ice packs sealed in zipper-lock bags and replace them as necessary to maintain a temperature no higher than 40°F.

HOME-CURED BACON

Comfort Food, Great Leftovers, Keeps Well, Freezes Well

Makes 5 to 8 pounds

Making your own bacon couldn't be easier, and you will be very happy when you eat the results. Keep it in the freezer to add flavor to soups, stews, and pot roasts.

1 6- to 10-pound skinless pork belly
Basic Wet Brine (page 437) made with Insta Cure No. 1

3 tablespoons coarsely ground black pepper, (optional)

1 Cut the belly crosswise into 3 or 4 equal-sized pieces. Lay the pieces in a rectangular storage tub large enough to hold them and the brine. Pour the brine over the meat. If the pieces are not completely submerged, weight them down with a plate. Cover and refrigerate for 2 days for smaller bellies (6 to 7 pounds) and 3 days for bellies more than 7 pounds. After 1 day, remove the belly pieces, stir the brine, and resubmerge the meat, changing the order of the pieces in the brine.

2 Remove the belly pieces from the brine. Wash under cold water and pat dry with paper towels. If you desire, sprinkle the belly pieces evenly with the pepper. Smoke the bellies (see Cold-Smoking, page 439). Cool to room temperature. Use a long, sharp knife to cut into ⅛-inch thick slices, then wrap in plastic wrap and refrigerate. (*Refrigerate for up to 1 week or freeze for up to 2 months.*)

3 Cook in a skillet over medium heat until nicely browned but not overly crisp and brittle, about 5 minutes per side. Drain on paper towels.

Cook's Notes

- For molasses-flavored bacon, replace ¼ cup of the brown sugar in the brine with ½ cup unsulfured molasses.

- For tropical-flavored bacon, replace 1 cup of the water in the brine with 1 cup dark rum and replace ¼ cup of the brown sugar with ½ cup unsulfured molasses.

- For scotch-and-Drambuie-flavored bacon, replace 2 cups of the water in the brine with 1 cup scotch and 1 cup Drambuie and replace ½ cup of the brown sugar with 1 cup honey.

- For maple-flavored bacon, replace ¼ cup of the brown sugar in the brine with ½ cup real maple syrup (I use Grade B) or replace all the brown sugar with maple sugar. Add 1 tablespoon pure vanilla extract to the brine.

- For honey-flavored bacon, replace ¼ cup of the brown sugar in the brine with ½ cup honey.

- For treacle–flavored bacon, replace ¼ cup of the brown sugar in the brine with ½ cup dark treacle (see Sources).

- For malt-flavored bacon, replace ¼ cup of the brown sugar in the brine with ½ cup malt syrup (see Sources).

- For Kentucky-inspired bacon, replace 1 cup of the water in the brine with 1 cup bourbon and use dark brown sugar instead of light brown sugar.

COLD-SMOKING

In contrast to hot-smoking, which cooks the meat while adding smoke and is usually done at temperatures between 175°F and 250°F, cold-smoking does not cook the food, and it is conducted at temperatures of 70°F to 110°F. You'll need a kettle-style grill.

1 Open the vents in the bottom of the grill and the lid. Remove the lid and the top rack from the grill, and center a disposable aluminum roasting pan on the lower rack. Add 6 cups hardwood sawdust to the pan.

2 Light 5 charcoal briquettes in a chimney starter. When the briquettes are glowing and completely covered with gray ash, transfer them with tongs to the sawdust, spacing them evenly.

3 When the sawdust begins to smolder, replace the top rack and arrange the pieces of meat on the rack at least 1 inch apart to allow the smoke to circulate. Cover the grill, and insert an instant-read thermometer into a vent hole in the lid to monitor the temperature. Maintain a temperature inside the grill of 70°F to 110°F. If the temperature rises above 120°F, remove 1 or more briquettes or uncover the grill slightly until the temperature falls. If the sawdust stops burning, light more briquettes in the charcoal chimney starter and reignite the sawdust. Every 1½ hours, add 1 cup sawdust to the pan and stir with tongs to ignite it. Smoke the meat for 4 to 6 hours, depending on how smoky you want it. Cool the meat completely, then wrap it in plastic wrap and refrigerate it until ready to use.

Cook's Note
- Try various types of hardwood sawdust, such as hickory, cherry, alder, oak, or apple and other fruitwood. You can also experiment with a mixture of different woods (see Sources for hardwood sawdust for smokers).

THE PERFECT BLT

In a Hurry, Comfort Food

Serves 2

Certain sandwiches may be simple, but they stand out if every component is of the best quality. This BLT should be made with lightly toasted white or egg bread that is impeccably fresh. The tomato must be vine-ripened at the height of the season, sweet and bursting with juices. And, most important, the bacon must be lean, smoky, and succulent. After these ingredients have been procured, slather on some homemade mayonnaise and add some tender Boston or Bibb lettuce or crisp iceberg. Oh, and don't forget the napkins.

6 thick slices good bacon, homemade (page 438) or artisanal (see Sources)

4 slices good white or egg bread (I use home-made), lightly toasted

Mayonnaise (I use homemade)

2 Boston, Bibb, or iceberg lettuce leaves

2–4 ¼-inch-thick slices large vine-ripened tomato

Salt and freshly ground black pepper

1 Cook the bacon in a medium skillet over medium heat until nicely browned but not overly crisp and brittle, about 5 minutes per side. Drain on paper towels.

2 To assemble the sandwiches, spread each slice of toasted bread generously with mayonnaise. For each sandwich, put the lettuce on one piece of toast, then put 1 or 2 tomato slices on the lettuce, and sprinkle with salt and pepper to taste. Lay 3 pieces of bacon over the tomatoes and cover with the other slice of toast. Cut in half and serve.

Alternative Cuts: Slices of fried ham, smoked pork loin, or smoked Boston butt.

Cook's Note

- Bacon should be cooked until it just begins to brown and is still soft enough to bend without shattering; you want to taste the subtleties and nuances rather than burned fat.

SMOKED PORK LOIN (CANADIAN BACON)

Comfort Food, Great Leftovers, Keeps Well, Freezes Well
Makes 3 to 5 pounds

Most store-bought Canadian bacon is flabby, spongy, and pricey. This recipe produces bacon that is delicately smoked and porky, with a firm texture. See Cook's Notes for other flavoring suggestions for the brine.

2 2- to 3-pound pieces boneless pork loin, preferably cut from the rib or blade section of the center-cut loin (2–3 inches thick)
Basic Wet Brine (page 437) made with Insta Cure No. 1

1 tablespoon coarsely ground black pepper (optional)

1. Follow the directions in step 1 of Home-Cured Bacon (page 438), curing the loin for 2 days (if the loin is more than 3 inches thick, increase the curing time to 3 days).

2. Remove the loin from the brine. Rinse, and pat dry. Sprinkle evenly with the pepper (if using). Smoke (see Cold-Smoking, page 439). Cool to room temperature, then wrap in plastic wrap and refrigerate. (*Refrigerate for up to 1 week or freeze for up to 2 months.*)

3. Cut into ⅛-inch-thick slices and lightly panfry or roast whole to an internal temperature of 135°F to 140°F. Eat hot or refrigerate for cold sandwiches.

Cook's Notes

- Panfried slices are great for breakfast, but should never be cooked to the point of becoming crisp, or they will be inedible.

- Cut into ¾-inch chops, Canadian bacon can be used in any recipe calling for smoked pork chops.

- Vary the brine as suggested in the Cook's Notes following the bacon recipe (page 438).

- To make the traditional cornmeal-coated Canadian bacon known as peameal bacon, roll the cured and still-damp loin in fine cornmeal. Hang and air-dry for 1 hour, then smoke.

- Use this curing recipe to make smoked pork chops using a 6- to 8-rib bone-in center-cut loin rib section. Cure for 4 days and cold-smoke as directed on page 439. Cut between the ribs into chops and panfry or grill; or roast the whole piece to an internal temperature of 130°F to 140°F on an instant-read thermometer.

SMOKED BOSTON BUTT
(COTTAGE HAM/BACON)

Comfort Food, Great Leftovers, Keeps Well, Freezes Well
Makes 3 to 5 pounds

A boneless Boston butt can be cured and smoked, then slow-roasted. From there, you can serve it as is or chill it, slice it across the grain into ⅛-inch-thick slices, and panfry as a very meaty bacon.

1 4- to 6-pound whole boneless Boston butt (pork shoulder butt)	2 tablespoons coarsely ground black pepper (optional)
Basic Wet Brine (page 437) made with Insta Cure No. 1	

1 Lay the meat fat side up on a cutting board. With your knife held parallel to the work surface, cut the meat into 2 pieces, each 1½ to 2½ inches thick. Follow the directions in step 1 of Home-Cured Bacon (page 438), curing the meat for 2 days.

2 Remove the pork from the brine, rinse, and pat dry. Sprinkle evenly with the pepper (if using). Smoke (see Cold-Smoking, page 439). Cool to room temperature, then wrap in plastic wrap and refrigerate. (*Refrigerate for up to 1 week or freeze for up to 2 months.*)

3 To roast the smoked butt, preheat the oven to 225°F.

4 Put the meat in a roasting pan and roast for 2 to 2½ hours, or until the internal temperature reaches 150°F on an instant-read thermometer.

Alternative Cuts: Boneless blade-end pork loin roast, left whole, cured in the brine for 2 days.

Cook's Notes
- Vary the brine as suggested in the Cook's Notes following the bacon recipe (page 438). I particularly like this with treacle or malt syrup added to the brine.
- To use in place of bacon, refrigerate for up to 5 days, then slice into ⅛-inch-thick slices across the grain and fry for 2 to 3 minutes per side (don't try to fry until crisp, or it will become tough and dry).

DICK VENNERBECK'S OVERNIGHT "HAM"

Comfort Food, Great Leftovers
Makes 1¾ to 5 pounds

This isn't really a ham, but a smoked pork tenderloin with a great hamlike flavor that spends only 16 to 24 hours in the cure. It's a perfect recipe for beginners. Dick Vennerbeck is one of my buddies who loves making sausage.

2–4 1- to 1½-pound pork tenderloins

½ recipe Basic Wet Brine (page 437) made with Insta Cure No. 1

1 Follow the directions in step 1 for Home-Cured Bacon (page 438), curing the tenderloins for 16 to 24 hours.

2 Remove the tenderloins from the brine, rinse, and pat dry. Smoke (see Cold-Smoking, page 439). Cool to room temperature, then wrap in plastic and refrigerate. (*Refrigerate for up to 1 week or freeze for up to 2 months.*)

3 To roast the tenderloins, preheat the oven to 225°F.

4 Put the tenderloins on a baking sheet and roast for 30 to 45 minutes, or until the internal temperature reaches 140°F to 145°F on an instant-read thermometer. Eat as is or wrap and chill, then slice and use cold in sandwiches.

Cook's Note
- Vary the brine as suggested in the Cook's Notes following the bacon recipe (page 438). I particularly like using honey or maple syrup in the cure for this.

HOME-CURED HAM

Fit for Company, Fit for a Crowd, Comfort Food, Great Leftovers

Makes 1 ham

Curing a whole bone-in ham by immersing the leg in brine is not feasible at home because it would take roughly 40 days for the cure to penetrate to the bone, long enough for the leg to spoil. To reduce the distance the brine has to penetrate, this recipe uses boneless roasts.

The amount of time the meat will spend in the cure depends entirely on how thick the piece of meat is. If your roast comes rolled and tied or netted, you must remove the string or net so that the thickness is lessened. The curing times I provide are approximate, and you may have to experiment, keeping good notes on the diameter of the roast, any variations you made in the brine recipe (see Cook's Notes), and how salty the meat is.

1 3- to 5-pound fresh ham inside roast (top roast), 4- to 6-pound fresh ham outside roast (bottom roast), 3- to 4-pound fresh ham knuckle roast (sirloin tip), 2- to 3-pound boneless sirloin, or a boneless whole or half pork leg (fresh ham)

Basic Wet Brine (page 437) made with Insta Cure No. 1

1. Brine the ham, following the directions in step 1 of Home-Cured Bacon (page 438). Make sure the meat is submerged at all times. For inside roast, knuckle roast, and sirloin roast, 3 to 4 inches thick, cure for 3 to 4 days. For outside roast and boneless leg, whole or half, at least 4 inches thick, cure for 3 days, then remove the meat, stir the brine, replace the meat, and cure for 2 days more.

2. Once the meat is cured, roll it and tie to form a uniform roast before smoking. Follow the directions on page 439 for cold-smoking. Cool to room temperature, then wrap in plastic wrap and refrigerate. *(Refrigerate for up to 1 week or freeze for up to 2 months).*

3. To serve, roast the ham in a 325°F oven until it reaches an internal temperature of 140°F to 145°F on an instant-read thermometer. If you wish to glaze the ham, see Baked Ham with Glaze and Sauce (page 349). Roasting times are approximate and will vary depending on the size of the ham.

APPROXIMATE ROASTING TIMES TO REACH 140°F TO 145°F

CUT	ROASTING TIME
Knuckle or sirloin	1 to 1¼ hours
Inside roast	1½ to 2 hours
Outside roast	2 to 2½ hours
Boneless half leg	2½ to 3 hours
Boneless whole leg	3 to 4 hours

Cook's Notes

- Vary the brine as suggested in the Cook's Notes following Home-Cured Bacon (page 438). I am partial to the honey, maple, and tropical variations for brining ham.

- For a ham similar to the French jambon de Paris (see page 347), instead of roasting, poach it in a broth made with water, wine, or beer, thyme sprigs, sage sprigs, bay leaves, onions, celery, carrots, and pickling spices (see below) for 1½ to 3 hours.

PICKLING SPICES

Makes ½ cup

1 tablespoon black peppercorns, crushed

2 tablespoons coriander seeds, cracked

2 teaspoons dill seeds

2 teaspoons caraway seeds

1 teaspoon celery seeds

1 tablespoon whole allspice berries

1 teaspoon whole cloves

8 bay leaves, broken into pieces

1 tablespoon mustard seeds

2 teaspoons crushed red pepper flakes

2 2- to 3-inch cinnamon sticks, broken into pieces

Combine all the spices in a small bowl until well mixed. Store in a tightly sealed container. *(The pickling spice mix keeps for 2 to 3 months at room temperature.)*

HOME-CURED CORNED BEEF AND PASTRAMI

Comfort Food, Great Leftovers, Keeps Well

2 whole briskets make 6–9 pounds; 2 flat-cut or 3 point-cut briskets make 4½–6 pounds

To turn corned beef into pastrami, simply coat the cured meat with cracked black pepper and coriander and smoke it. I like corned beef and pastrami with some fat, so I prefer to use the whole brisket, which contains the fatty "point" and the leaner "flat," or first cut (see page 161). If you prefer leaner corned beef and pastrami, use only the flat cut; if you prefer fattier versions, use only the point cut.

Using Insta Cure No. 1 is optional for corned beef but not for pastrami, which needs the cure for safe smoking. If you leave it out of the corned beef, the meat will be gray, not pink, but the flavor will not be affected.

2 whole briskets (8–12 pounds), or 2 flat-cut briskets (6–8 pounds), or 3 point-cut briskets (6–8 pounds), fat trimmed to ¼ inch
Basic Wet Brine (page 437), substituting two 12-ounce bottles lager beer for 3 cups of the water and made with Insta Cure No. 1 if making pastrami (optional for corned beef)

½ cup pickling spices, homemade (page 445) or store-bought
8 garlic cloves, crushed (optional)
½ cup cracked black peppercorns for pastrami
½ cup cracked coriander seeds for pastrami

1 Submerge the briskets in the brine in a large plastic storage tub. Add the pickling spices and garlic (if using), and weight the meat with a plate. Cover and refrigerate for 3 days, then remove the beef and rinse. Stir the brine, return the beef to the brine, and refrigerate for 2 days more. Remove the brisket from the brine, rinse, and pat dry. (*At this point, the brisket can be covered and refrigerated for up to 2 days.*)

2 If making pastrami, mix together the peppercorns and coriander seeds and spread in a shallow baking pan. Press the meat into the peppercorn mixture on all sides. Cold-smoke as directed on page 439.

3 Steam the corned beef or pastrami in a closed pot until tender, 3 to 4 hours. Or see pages 179–184 for recipes using corned beef. (*Refrigerate for up to 1 week or freeze for up to 2 months.*)

PETIT SALÉ PORK (BRINED PORK)

Comfort Food, Great Leftovers
Makes 3½ to 7 pounds

This is the French answer to corned beef, a tradition in which tougher and/or fattier cuts of pork were cured in an aromatic brine by the local butcher. Patrons could purchase their favorite pieces to cook in the French version of a "boiled dinner." *Petit salé* pork has a different flavor from that of corned beef, but it can be substituted (see Cook's Notes).

My preferred cuts for *petit salé* pork are picnic shoulder, Boston butt, and, especially, pork belly with the spareribs attached. Whole skinned boneless pork belly without the ribs is also good, as is blade-end pork loin. When making *petit salé* pork, try an assortment of various cuts.

If using a picnic shoulder, cut into 2 smaller pieces so that they can be cured in less time. If using a Boston butt, split the butt into 2 pieces, cutting parallel to the fat cap. If using pork belly, cut into 2- to 3-pound pieces.

4–8 pounds various pork cuts (see headnote)	6 bay leaves
Basic Wet Brine (page 437)	1 tablespoon pickling spices, homemade (page 445) or store-bought
1 cup dry white wine	12 whole allspice berries
2 tablespoons crushed juniper berries	4 whole cloves
6 fresh thyme sprigs	6 garlic cloves, crushed
4 shallots, thinly sliced	

1   Put the meat in a large plastic storage container or large zipper-lock bag and add the brine and all the remaining ingredients. Weight with a plate and cure in the refrigerator for 4 days. (This is a rough estimate; keep notes and make adjustments to the curing time the next time you prepare the recipe.)

2   Remove the pork from the brine, rinse, and pat dry. Poach in water until tender, 1½ to 3 hours, depending on the cut. (*Refrigerate for up to 1 week or freeze for up to 2 months.*)

Cook's Note

- To substitute *petit salé* pork in the Irish Corned Beef and Vegetables (page 179), replace the Guinness with 2 cups dry white wine. Add 2 chopped leeks and 4 peeled turnips and replace the green cabbage with savoy cabbage.

PICKLED BEEF TONGUE

Comfort Food, Great Leftovers

1 tongue makes 2½ pounds; 2 tongues make 4 to 5 pounds

Once you've eaten a warm pickled tongue sandwich slathered with mustard and/or coleslaw, I think you'll want to indulge on a regular basis. But unless you live in a town that has an old-fashioned Jewish deli, pickled tongue is hard to come by. Making your own is the way to go. And even if you do have a deli near you, I'm willing to bet that this version will taste oh-so-much better than the one you can buy. Beef tongue should be well washed before pickling. A beef tongue can be pickled using the recipe for Corned Beef (page 446) or the one below.

½ recipe Basic Wet Brine (page 437), made with Insta Cure No. 1 (if cold-smoking, otherwise optional)

¼–½ cup pickling spices, homemade (page 445) or store-bought

1–2 2- to 3-pound beef tongues, well washed and scrubbed

1   Combine the brine and pickling spices in a plastic storage container, and submerge the tongues in it. Cure in the refrigerator for 6 days; after 3 days, remove the tongues, stir the brine, and return the tongues to the brine.

2   Remove the tongues from the brine, rinse well, and pat dry. Wrap in plastic wrap and store in the refrigerator until ready to cook. (*Pickled tongue will keep for 2 to 3 days.*)

3   To cook the pickled tongue, place in a large pot, cover with water, and bring to a boil. If you wish, add ¼ cup pickling spices. Reduce the heat to maintain a simmer, cover, and cook for 3 to 4 hours, until the tongue is fork-tender. When the tongue is cool enough to handle, peel off the skin. Slice the meat thinly, crosswise, and serve warm, or chill overnight and use cold in sandwiches or salads. You can gently warm sliced tongue in a little water in a covered pan or in the microwave and use for warm tongue sandwiches.

Cook's Note
- You may also dry the tongues well and smoke them, following the directions on page 439.

Lamb & Goat

Lamb and Goat

R E C I P E S

GROUND LAMB AND GOAT

LAMB AND GOAT STEWS, POT ROASTS, AND OTHER BRAISES

In Praise of Lamb

In Pakistan and India and in the countries that border the Mediterranean, lamb is the meat of choice. It is also popular in the British Isles, particularly Scotland and Ireland. That's not the case in the United States. On a per capita basis, Americans consume less than one pound of lamb per year. That means that most of us eat none whatsoever. In fact, as I travel, I talk with cooks from the Midwest and the South who complain that they can't even *find* lamb in their supermarkets.

That's a shame. Lamb is a versatile and delicious culinary treasure. Its ever-so-slightly gamy flavors marry deliciously with chiles, garlic, rosemary, and strong spices, such as curry blends. It's one of the few meats that can be cooked with sweet ingredients, such as honey, dried fruits, and pomegranate, without sacrificing its own unique flavor. Roasting in the oven, slathered with herbs and olives or coated with chopped nuts, lamb will fill the kitchen with luscious aromas. Savvy cooks have discovered that a boneless leg of lamb is an ideal cut for grilling and perfect for a group when you need various degrees of doneness.

Because I am a lover of lamb in all forms and shapes, I ask people I meet on my travels why they don't like it. Often the answer is based on the misconceived notion that it tastes like mutton (mutton comes from mature sheep, one year old or older), which has a strong smell and a powerful flavor. This idea makes little sense, because old lamb has not been available in our markets for perhaps fifty years. I hope these recipes will help you discover just how delicious lamb is.

Goat: A Growing Supply

Two of the best meat dishes I've eaten in recent memory featured goat. One was a baby goat shoulder slowly spit-roasted over a hardwood fire in the hills of Piemonte, in northern Italy. The shoulder was tender, succulent, and simple, basted only with olive oil that had been infused with wild herbs. I ate the other dish much closer to home, at my local Pakistani curry house: bony chunks of goat neck stewed long and slow in a curry sauce packed with chiles, onions, and chunks of garlic. Soft and tender bits of meat clung to the bones, waiting to be sucked off. A mess to eat, but, oh, what a joy!

What has kept this delicious meat out of the American dining mainstream? Well, part of the reason has been lack of supply. Until recently, we didn't raise much goat in America. In the past few years, however, farmers have begun raising meat goats, in particular, the superior breed known as the South African Boer. Because it is relatively easy to graze Boer goats in many parts of the country, the meat is becoming increasingly available.

These animals, often sold under the French name *chevon,* are slaughtered young, when they are six to nine months old and weigh around sixty pounds. Some farmers sell even younger milk-fed goats at one to two months and about twenty-five pounds. You might find these sold as *cabrito,* from the Spanish word meaning "kid." Young goat meat is lean, relatively tender, and has an excellent, very slightly gamy flavor, like lamb, but more mild.

The best place to find goat is at markets serving Middle Eastern, Caribbean, Pakistani, or Mexican communities. There are websites that offer young goat (see Sources) as well.

Farmers' markets are another good source. Some vendors may primarily raise dairy goats, selling unwanted young males or older females that are no longer producing sufficient milk, while others may raise different breeds of meat goats. The tenderness and flavor of the meat will vary accordingly. To learn more, ask the farmer if he or she is selling actual meat goats and at what age or size they were slaughtered. The meat from older goats will be tougher, but is great for moist-heat cooking in stews and pot roasts. Young dairy males may produce cuts tender enough for dry-heat cooking, or they may be a bit chewy. If you're lucky enough to have a supplier who sells meat from a variety of meat goats, make sure the goats are young.

Because lamb and goat have a similar anatomy and taste, they can be substituted for each other in any of the recipes in this chapter. Young goat is very lean, so take care not to overcook it in recipes calling for dry heat, such as grilling and roasting.

What Is Lamb?

Lamb is meat that comes from sheep less than one year old. Most lambs are marketed at six to eight months of age and produce sixty to seventy pounds of meat. Baby lambs are slaughtered at six to eight weeks, when the whole carcass weighs twenty-five pounds or less. Some small producers offer these whole or split — through specialty butchers, at farmers' markets, or on the Web — but most are sold to restaurants.

According to the USDA, any lamb slaughtered between March and October can be called "spring lamb." (Now that's eternal spring!) The truth is that today's lambs are raised with superior methods of animal husbandry, and this isn't really seasonal meat. Old habits die hard, however, and for many people, lamb is still considered a meat to enjoy in the spring. There may be some logic to this if the lamb is raised and finished on grass. In a number of lamb-producing states, spring is the time when grass is at its peak. Green and lush pasturage allows the animals to fatten and the meat to marble.

MY IDEAL LAMB

The best lamb I've ever had came from Coffelt Farm, a producer on Orcas Island in the San Juan Islands off the coast of Washington State, which sells grass-fed lamb directly to consumers. I visited in the fall, when the sheep were grazing on lush green pastures situated between stands of Douglas firs. I bought a leg, chops, and neck. The neck, which I stewed, had a particularly wonderful flavor. The lamb was not heavily marbled, but it was succulent, moist, and juicy, and the fat was delicious.

Grass-Fed and Grain-Finished Lamb

Lamb from New Zealand is raised on grass, from weaning to slaughter. Most lamb imported from Australia is raised and finished on grass, but some of that country's producers finish their lamb on grain to appeal to the American market.

The story of American lamb is more complicated. Ranchers in areas where the grass is rich for a long growing season can produce lambs that are finished exclusively on grass. Ranchers in regions where grass doesn't provide adequate nutrition for the entire growing season supplement the animals' diet with grain — in the pasture or other locations on the farm. Still other ranchers finish their lambs at a feedlot, where the lambs may be given hormones and antibiotics. In general, lambs produced east of the Mississippi are grass-fed, because there are high-quality grasses suitable for finishing. Most lambs raised in the West, where the grass dies out in summer months, are finished on grain and alfalfa. In most cases, how the lamb is finished — whether on grass or grain — is not noted on the label, but some farms are now realizing that consumers may prefer lamb fed only on grass and may indicate that.

Large brands, such as Superior Farms in California (see Sources), contract with many small ranchers throughout the country, and they don't specify which of the lamb they sell is grass-fed and which is grain-finished. However, Superior does offer a separate brand that is raised without hormones or antibiotics, which they call Pure Lamb. Other lamb ranchers may use different terms for lamb raised the same way; look for a label that states that antibiotics and hormones are not used.

While some producers market their lamb as grass-fed, small operations that raise their lamb on grass may not bother to make that claim. Because it is relatively easy to raise lamb in just about every area of the country, you may be able to find some of this lamb at your local farmers' market. Ask the farmer to tell you how he or she raises the animals.

There is also lamb that carries the USDA Certified Organic label. As with beef, this does not mean the lamb hasn't been finished on grain, though the grain (if any) must be organic. Check out www.eatwild.com for more details and to find lamb producers near you.

TERMS AT A GLANCE

Grass-Fed Lamb
- Rarely given antibiotics or hormones
- Fed only grass and forage
- Can be kept in corrals during non-grazing season but usually are not
- Some larger producers indicate grass-fed, but usually the term is not noted on labels or in marketing materials

USDA Certified Organic Lamb
- Cannot be given antibiotics, hormones, or animal by-products
- Must be kept in organic pasture during grazing season
- Can be kept in corrals in non-grazing season, but must have access to pasture
- Can be finished on organic grain and/or grass in pasture or in corrals
- Claim must be verified by approved third-party auditors

Natural Lamb with a label stating "raised without antibiotics or hormones and fed a vegetarian diet"
- Cannot be given antibiotics, hormones, or animal by-products
- Can be finished on grain or grass in pasture or in corrals
- Some producers may follow other practices, such as humanely raising their animals or raising them solely in pasture

Natural Lamb with no other claims
- Essentially a term for commodity lamb
- May be given antibiotics and hormones, and the diet may not be 100-percent vegetarian
- Can be given grain in corrals

Naturally Raised Lamb
- Same as natural lamb with a label stating "raised without antibiotics or hormones and fed a vegetarian diet"
- Term has not yet been approved for use by specific meat companies

Commodity Lamb
- May or may not be finished on grass or grain without any notation on the label
- May be given antibiotics and hormones, and the diet may not be 100-percent vegetarian

HEIRLOOM LAMB BREEDS

With the growing interest in heirloom breeds of livestock, farms around the country are raising heirloom varieties of lamb. Much of this fine meat finds its way into local farmers' markets or is sold directly to consumers. One well-known national supplier, www.heritagefoodsusa.com, features lamb from Romney, Katahdin, St. Croix, and Targhee sheep — all rare breeds known to produce great lamb. Many farms that raise heirloom breeds do so without antibiotics or hormones, and they may feed their lambs solely on grass. Because small producers often don't go through the expense of USDA labeling, ask your farmer for details.

Raising Goats

The goat meat industry is growing, but it's still very small. Thankfully, the farmers who raise goats have resisted the temptation to industrialize their practices.

Goats are kept in pasture and allowed to eat their favorite things, including brush, twigs, and leaves. They may be given antibiotics for a short period of time to prevent and treat diseases, but they are not given hormones, and they are not kept in feedlots. As its popularity increases (and I believe it will), young goat meat from meat breeds will be more widely available. When it comes to your market, ask the purveyor to give you details on how the goats are raised.

How to Buy Lamb and Goat

Lamb

A significant percentage of lamb in the U.S. market is imported from New Zealand and Australia. New Zealand and Australian sheep are smaller than those raised in the United States, so the cuts are small but consistent in size. American lamb varies a lot in terms of carcass size, based on how old the animals are, what they are fed, and what breed they come from. This leads to considerable variation in the size of cuts; legs of lamb, for example, can range from five to ten pounds.

The size of the cut isn't an indication of tenderness. In general, most lamb cuts are relatively tender, because they come from young animals, and they can be cooked by dry heat. Shank and neck, however, have lots of connective tissue and must be braised.

- Lamb meat should be fine grained and light red in color. Dark purplish meat has come from an old sheep.
- The meat should be moist but never sticky.
- If you like a richer flavor, look for more marbling (but leanness does not necessarily mean lack of flavor or tenderness).
- The fat should be white, with no blemishes or brown edges, and it should have been well trimmed.
- The bones should be red, moist, and porous. A dry, white bone indicates an old sheep.
- There should be a faint lamby smell, but no strong odors.

Goat

Unless you prefer mature goat meat (which will be stronger in flavor and is best cooked with moist heat), buy young goat (*chevon* or *cabrito*). Young goat chops and roasts will be smaller than equivalent lamb cuts, but the other criteria for buying lamb apply to goat.

The details on color of the meat, fat, and bone are much the same as for lamb. Again, there should be no off aromas and only a faint smell of goat.

Lamb and Goat Grades

Lamb. The USDA provides grading for lamb as it does for beef. Because grading is voluntary and costs the producer extra money, many small ranchers may choose not to have their lamb graded (it still must be slaughtered and processed under government inspection for wholesomeness). So ungraded lamb can be as delicious as graded lamb.

The grading system is based on overall marbling. The highest grade is Prime, followed by Choice and Good (lower grades are not sold at retail). About 80 percent of American lamb is graded Prime or Choice, but Prime grade makes up just a small percentage, and most of it is snapped up by high-end restaurants. The lamb you'll find in supermarkets is mostly graded Choice or Good. Because lamb is harvested at a young age, the meat doesn't need to be highly marbled to be juicy and tender. However, the really tender cuts, such as loin and sirloin, will dry out if cooked to well-done, so pay attention. If you like well-done lamb, buy shoulder chops and braise them.

Goat. Goat is not graded, but it must be slaughtered and processed under government inspection.

Primal Cuts of Lamb and Goat

Once you decide what type of dish you're going to make, you need to choose a cut that matches your cooking method. Both lamb and goat are divided into five primals.

- The most tender and most expensive cuts come from the back (the **rib** and **loin** primals).
- The best large roasts come from the **leg** primal.
- Cuts from the **shoulder** primal and the **foreleg** and **breast** primals are best cooked with moist heat (though they can be roasted). Shanks (cut from the foreleg primal) and neck (from the shoulder primal) are ideal for long, slow braises and stews.

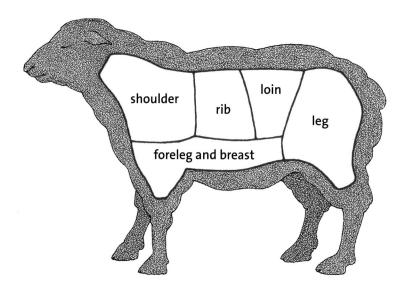

STORING LAMB AND GOAT

Lamb and goat will keep for 2 to 4 days in the refrigerator and for 4 to 6 months in the freezer.

Follow the guidelines on page 6 for storing raw and cooked meat and for thawing meat.

Cooking and Serving Lamb and Goat

In general, you can cook all goat cuts as you would lamb, but keep in mind that young goat is leaner than lamb, so take care not to dry out chops and roasts by overcooking.

- Lamb and goat are ideal meats for grilling, and the gnarly cuts make great one-pot dishes.
- Lamb and goat meat are covered in a papery membrane called "fell." Don't remove it from large roasts such as leg, shoulder, and breast, because it helps hold the meat in place. If the butcher hasn't trimmed it from small cuts such as chops and racks of lamb, you should; it can cause chops to curl during high-heat cooking.
- Lamb and, especially, goat are tender, lean meats, so it's best not to overcook them (except when cooking with moist heat). Lamb remains juicy cooked up to medium, but it will begin to dry out if cooked beyond 140°F. Goat, especially chops, should be cooked to medium-rare.
- Serve lamb hot, on a heated platter or heated dinner plates. Lamb fat tends to congeal quickly at room temperature, becoming unpleasantly waxy. If you must serve lamb at room temperature or less than hot (as on a buffet), choose cuts with little fat or trim away external fat.

Lamb and Goat Doneness

The following charts are based on what I believe will give the best cooking results. The temperatures are lower than what the USDA recommends. When cooking for those who are immunologically compromised or pregnant, you should err on the side of caution.

With moist-heat cooking (braising and stewing), meat is usually cooked to temperatures of 160°F to 190°F or more; it relies on the collagen turning into gelatin, as well as the ample fat in the meat, to produce tender and juicy results. Here the best way to determine doneness is to see how easily a fork can penetrate the meat — or to taste it.

Use the following temperatures for lamb and goat cooked by dry-heat methods, such as roasting, grilling, and frying. Because carry-over heat will vary depending on the size of the piece of meat and the intensity of the heat source, consult the individual recipes to determine exactly what internal temperature the meat should be when it is removed from the heat source and what the resting time should be.

Very Rare. The center of the meat will be soft and the color of raw meat (purple-red for lamb and goat). The rest of the meat will be bright pink and quite juicy.

MEAT	REMOVE FROM HEAT	IDEAL TEMPERATURE (AFTER RESTING)	USDA RECOMMENDS
Lamb and goat chops	110°F to 115°F	115°F to 120°F	Does not recommend
Lamb and goat roasts	105°F to 110°F	115°F to 125°F	Does not recommend

Rare. The meat will be fairly soft and bright pink to red in the center, not purple-red as in very rare, though some purple-red areas may remain near the bones and in the very center of large roasts. The meat will be very juicy.

MEAT	REMOVE FROM HEAT	IDEAL TEMPERATURE (AFTER RESTING)	USDA RECOMMENDS
Lamb and goat chops	120°F to 125°F	125°F to 130°F	Does not recommend
Lamb and goat roasts	110°F to 115°F	125°F to 130°F	Does not recommend

Medium-Rare. Lamb and goat can be reliably cooked to this popular degree of doneness. The meat will be quite pink in the center with no bloodred areas and will have begun to turn grayish around the edges. It is firmer than rare but still quite juicy. Restaurants often describe lamb cooked to this temperature as rare.

MEAT	REMOVE FROM HEAT	IDEAL TEMPERATURE (AFTER RESTING)	USDA RECOMMENDS
Lamb and goat chops	125°F to 130°F	130°F to 135°F	145°F
Lamb and goat roasts	120°F to 125°F	130°F to 135°F	145°F

Medium. This doneness is fine for marbled cuts such as rack of lamb. The meat will be pink in the center and gray at the periphery, the texture quite firm, and the grain compact.

MEAT	REMOVE FROM HEAT	IDEAL TEMPERATURE (AFTER RESTING)	USDA RECOMMENDS
Lamb and goat chops	130°F to 135°F	140°F to 145°F	N/A*
Lamb and goat roasts	125°F to 130°F	140°F to 145°F	N/A*

Medium-Well. The meat will usually be uniformly gray, with a pinkish tint near the bone. Lean lamb or goat should be cooked by low heat to this range, but it may still be dry. Fatty cuts, such as lamb and goat shoulder, will still be juicy.

MEAT	REMOVE FROM HEAT	IDEAL TEMPERATURE (AFTER RESTING)	USDA RECOMMENDS
Lamb and goat chops	140°F to 145°F	150°F to 155°F	N/A*
Lamb and goat roasts	140°F to 145°F	150°F to 155°F	N/A*

Well-Done. Meat is overcooked at this stage unless it is fatty and naturally juicy, such as the shoulder.

MEAT	REMOVE FROM HEAT	IDEAL TEMPERATURE (AFTER RESTING)	USDA RECOMMENDS
Lamb and goat roasts	150°F to 155°F	160°F to 165°F	N/A*

* The USDA does not provide temperatures for this degree of doneness.

Lamb and Goat Chops

Lamb and goat chops are perfect for grilling, panfrying, and broiling, and they take well to marinades, rubs, and spice pastes. Because lamb and young goat are so tender, all areas except the shank, neck, and breast can be sliced into chops.

Look for rib and loin chops 1 to 2 inches thick (if the 2-inch chops include two rib bones, they are often called double chops). My favorite are 2-inch-thick chops cut from the rib or rack. They have the most marbling and — depending on how they're trimmed — some pockets of delicious fat as well, but they are expensive. Leaner but very tasty are the T-bone loin chops. I buy them 2 to 2½ inches thick, and I love grilling them over direct heat, then moving them to an area of the grill without heat to finish cooking indirectly. Medium-rare is the perfect level of doneness for my taste.

For chops from the shoulder or leg, which are sometimes called steaks or cutlets and have a larger diameter, ¾-inch-thick is fine. Shoulder chops can contain some tender meat near the rib and tougher meat around the blade or round bone. They can be grilled or cooked by dry heat, but you'll get better results when you use moist heat. Using a Jaccard (see page 49) or pounding these chops can improve their tenderness.

In general, don't buy thin chops. It's very difficult to get a nice sear on thin chops without overcooking them.

Lamb and Goat Chops and Cutlets at a Glance

From the Rib and Loin

Lamb rib chop, bone in (rack of lamb chop, rib chop). Cut from ribs 5 to 12. The four chops closest to the rear will have fewer pockets of fat than the four chops closest to the shoulder. Should be 1 to 2½ inches thick.

Goat rib chop, bone in. When cut from a small goat (*cabrito*), these chops will be tender and succulent. Should be 1 to 2 inches thick. Use in any recipe calling for lamb chops.

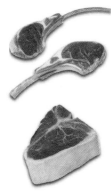

Frenched lamb or goat rib chop, bone in (frenched chop, rib kebab). May still contain some of the fatty tail and some of the flap meat at the shoulder end or may be trimmed. This is my favorite chop. I like it 2 inches thick.

Lamb loin chop, bone in (T-bone loin chop). Lean and very tender. Look for chops that have a bit of both loin and tenderloin muscle. Should be 1½ to 2½ inches thick.

Goat loin chop, bone in (T-bone loin chop). Should be 2 inches thick. Very lean and should not be overcooked. Use in any recipe calling for lamb chops.

Lamb or goat double loin chop, bone in (English chop, saddle chop). Cut from both sides of the backbone. Should be 1 to 2½ inches thick. Ideal for grilling and special occasions. May have to be special-ordered.

From the Leg

Lamb or goat sirloin chop, bone in or boneless (lamb sirloin steak). Sometimes sold with a small piece of hip bone, but often sold boneless, these are tender and well priced. Great marinated and grilled. Should be ¾ to 1½ inches thick. Thick chops can be cut into kebabs.

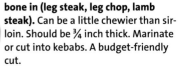

Center-slice lamb or goat leg steak, bone in (leg steak, leg chop, lamb steak). Can be a little chewier than sirloin. Should be ¾ inch thick. Marinate or cut into kebabs. A budget-friendly cut.

Lamb or goat leg cutlet, boneless. These slices are cut across any of the muscles that make up the leg, including the sirloin tip, outside, inside, and sirloin; usually not identified. Ideal pounded and breaded for lamb milanese or lamb scaloppine, but, like any chop, can be grilled or pan-broiled. For grilling, I prefer cutlets at least ¾ inch thick; for pounding and breading, ½ to ¾ inch thick is fine.

From the Shoulder

Lamb blade chop, bone in (shoulder chop, blade shoulder chop, blade cut chop). Contains some very tender meat next to the rib bone and some chewier meat around the blade bone. If you plan to grill or cook by dry heat, look for chops with the smallest amount of blade bone and the largest amount of rib eye meat. For moist-heat cooking, any chop will do. Should be ¾ to 1 inch thick. A budget-friendly cut.

Goat blade chop, bone in. When cut from young goats (*cabrito*), suitable for dry-heat cooking. Should be ¾ to 1½ inches thick. Braise chops from somewhat older goats (*chevon*). Great in curries and tagines.

Lamb or goat arm chop, bone in (round-bone chop, arm cut chop). Ideal for moist-heat cooking. Tender enough for dry-heat cooking. Should be ¾ to 1 inch thick. A budget-friendly cut.

GRILLED LAMB CHOPS

In a Hurry, Fit for Company

Serves 4

Rib and loin (T-bone) lamb chops are expensive, tender cuts that don't need to be marinated. They taste great with nothing more than an ample sprinkling of salt and pepper and maybe a little chopped fresh herb. Another choice is to finish the chops with a pat of flavored butter (see pages 58–59) or flavor with a spice paste (see pages 464–66).

Sirloin and leg chops are less expensive than rib and loin chops and only slightly less tender, but they are also less flavorful and can be improved with a marinade. Shoulder lamb chops are the cheapest and have great flavor but can be chewy. If you substitute shoulder chops, cook them to at least medium-rare or medium (see Cook's Notes).

8 1- to 1¼-inch-thick rib or T-bone loin lamb or goat chops (2–3 pounds total)
Salt and freshly ground pepper

2 tablespoons freshly chopped rosemary, thyme, or oregano (optional)

1 Season the chops with salt and pepper to taste, and coat with the herbs (if using).

2 Set up a charcoal or gas grill for medium-high heat (see page 11 for more on grilling).

3 Grill the chops, covered, for 3 to 5 minutes per side, or until the internal temperature reaches 125°F to 130°F on an instant-read thermometer, for medium-rare. Set the chops aside on a warm platter, cover loosely with aluminum foil, and let rest for 5 minutes before serving.

Alternative Cuts: Lamb sirloin chops, leg chops, or shoulder chops (see Cook's Notes).

Cook's Notes

- If using sirloin, leg, or shoulder chops, marinate the chops in the marinade of your choice. Good choices include Persian Pomegranate Marinate (page 465), Basic Olive Oil and Fresh Herb Marinade (page 64), Mustardy Marinade (page 65), or Herb Marinade (page 90).

- Instead of grilling, you can broil the chops for 4 to 5 minutes per side.

- Sirloin and leg chops can be grilled as in step 3, above. If using shoulder chops, set up the grill for indirect grilling. Sear the chops for 2 to 3 minutes per side, then move them to an area of the grill with no fire, cover, and cook for 7 to 10 minutes more, or until 130°F to 135°F for medium-rare to medium.

Marinades and Pastes for Lamb Chops

Each recipe makes enough for 6 to 8 chops.

MOROCCAN MINT AND LEMON PASTE WITH TAHINI SAUCE

Mint and Lemon Paste

- 2 small garlic cloves, peeled
- ½ cup fresh cilantro leaves, plus more for garnish
- 2 tablespoons chopped fresh mint
- ⅓ cup fresh lemon juice
- 2 tablespoons olive oil
- 1 teaspoon salt
- 1 teaspoon freshly ground black pepper
- ½ teaspoon cayenne pepper
- 2 teaspoons sweet Hungarian paprika
- 1 teaspoon ground cumin
- 1 teaspoon turmeric
- 1 teaspoon ground fennel seeds
- Pinch of ground cinnamon

Tahini Sauce

- 2 tablespoons tahini (sesame paste)
- 3 tablespoons fresh lemon juice
- 3 tablespoons extra-virgin olive oil
- 1 tablespoon water, or more if needed
- Salt

1 **Paste:** With the motor running, drop the garlic through the feed tube of a food processor and process until chopped. Scrape down the sides of the bowl and add the cilantro and mint. Pulse until the leaves are chopped. Scrape down the sides of the bowl, then add the remaining ingredients and process to form a thick paste. Rub the mixture all over the chops and place them on a plate. Cover with plastic wrap and refrigerate for at least 2 hours or up to 16 hours for rib and loin chops and up to 36 hours for sirloin, leg, or shoulder chops. Turn the chops from time to time.

2 Shake the excess paste off the chops and discard. Follow the directions in Grilled Lamb Chops (page 463) to cook the chops.

3 **Sauce:** While the chops are resting, make the tahini sauce. Combine the tahini, lemon juice, and oil in the (clean) food processor and process until smooth. Add the water, then add more water 1 tablespoon at a time if necessary, until the sauce is thin enough to drizzle. Season to taste with salt.

4 Arrange the chops on a platter and drizzle the tahini sauce over them. Garnish with cilantro and serve.

PERSIAN POMEGRANATE MARINADE

Pomegranate syrup and molasses can be found in Middle Eastern and gourmet markets, and health-food stores. This marinade is ideal for lamb sirloin and leg chops, and goat chops.

½ cup pomegranate syrup or molasses

¼ cup pomegranate juice

½ teaspoon ground ginger

½ teaspoon ground cumin

Pinch of ground allspice

2 teaspoons minced garlic

2 teaspoons chopped fresh rosemary

2 teaspoons chopped fresh marjoram

1 teaspoon salt

½ teaspoon freshly ground black pepper

2 tablespoons olive oil

Pomegranate seeds

Chopped fresh basil

1 Whisk the ingredients, except the pomegranate seeds and basil, together in a small bowl. Place lamb chops in a large zipper-lock bag, pour in the marinade, seal, and place the bag in a bowl to catch any leaks. Refrigerate overnight, turning and shaking the bag from time to time to redistribute the marinade.

2 Remove the chops from the marinade, shake off the excess, and discard the marinade. Follow the directions in Grilled Lamb Chops (page 463) to cook the chops. Garnish with pomegranate seeds and chopped basil (if using), and serve.

TURKISH SPICE PASTE

⅛ teaspoon ground cinnamon

¼ teaspoon ground allspice

¼ teaspoon ground fennel seeds

Pinch of ground cloves

½ teaspoon ground cumin

½ teaspoon ground coriander

½ teaspoon ground mustard seeds

½ teaspoon cayenne pepper

1 tablespoon sweet Hungarian paprika

1 teaspoon dried mint

1 teaspoon dried oregano

1 teaspoon salt

½ teaspoon freshly ground black pepper

1 teaspoon minced garlic

2 teaspoons tomato paste

2 teaspoons fresh lemon juice

1 tablespoon olive oil

1 Combine all the ingredients in a medium bowl. Add lamb chops and turn to coat completely. Cover with plastic wrap, and refrigerate overnight. Turn the chops from time to time.

2 Follow the directions in Grilled Lamb Chops (page 463) to cook and serve.

SPICY THAI PEANUT PASTE AND SAUCE

2 garlic cloves, peeled

⅓ cup fresh cilantro leaves

⅓ cup unsalted natural crunchy peanut butter

1 tablespoon Thai green curry paste

1 tablespoon fresh lime juice

2 tablespoons ketchup

1 tablespoon Asian fish sauce

1 tablespoon soy sauce

1 teaspoon sugar

2 tablespoons peanut oil

1 With the motor running, drop the garlic through the feed tube of a food processor and process until chopped. Scrape down the sides of the bowl. Add the cilantro and pulse until chopped. Add the remaining ingredients and pulse to form a soft paste. Smear some of the paste over both sides of each lamb chop and place on a plate. Cover with plastic wrap and refrigerate for 2 hours, or up to 6 hours. Reserve the rest of the paste.

2 Follow the directions in Grilled Lamb Chops (page 463) to cook the chops.

3 Meanwhile, gently heat the reserved peanut paste in a small saucepan, stirring in enough water to make a thick but pourable sauce. Spoon the sauce over the lamb chops and serve.

PROVENÇAL ANCHOVY AND HERB PASTE

1 anchovy fillet, minced

2 teaspoons finely chopped capers

2 garlic cloves, minced

1 tablespoon chopped fresh basil

1 tablespoon chopped fresh thyme

2 teaspoons Dijon mustard

½ teaspoon freshly ground black pepper

1 teaspoon salt

2 tablespoons extra-virgin olive oil

1 Combine all the ingredients except the oil in a small bowl. Whisk in the oil to make a paste. Smear the paste all over the lamb chops and place on a plate. Cover with plastic wrap and refrigerate for at least 2 hours, or up to overnight, turning the chops from time to time.

2 Follow the directions in Grilled Lamb Chops (page 463) to cook and serve.

SAUTÉED LAMB CHOPS WITH TOMATO-EGGPLANT VINAIGRETTE

In a Hurry, Family Meal

Serves 4

In northern Sonoma County, where I live, we grow many varieties of heirloom tomatoes, which reach their peak in late summer and early fall. Some years, when the weather is particularly mild, we have locally grown heirlooms into November. This recipe uses tomatoes and another late-summer vegetable, eggplant, in a light and fresh vinaigrette to serve over sautéed lamb chops.

1 large eggplant, cut into 1-inch dice
¼ cup plus 1 tablespoon olive oil, or more if needed
   Salt and freshly ground black pepper
8 1½-inch-thick rib or T-bone lamb loin chops (about 2 pounds total)
2 teaspoons chopped fresh thyme

Tomato-Eggplant Vinaigrette
¼ cup dry white wine or dry sherry
2 tablespoons good red wine vinegar (I use Banyuls), or more to taste
2 teaspoons Dijon mustard
¼ cup extra-virgin olive oil
1 cup diced (1-inch) vine-ripe tomatoes (I use an heirloom variety)
   Salt and freshly ground black pepper

1 tablespoon shredded fresh basil leaves
2 teaspoons shredded fresh mint leaves

1   Preheat the oven to 375°F.

2   Toss the eggplant with ¼ cup of the oil and salt and pepper to taste in a large bowl until well coated. Spread the eggplant and any oil remaining in the bowl on a large baking sheet and roast for 10 minutes. Stir and, if the eggplant is dry, brush with more olive oil. Roast for 5 to 10 minutes more, or until the cubes are very soft. Set aside.

3   Season the chops to taste with salt and pepper and sprinkle with the thyme. Heat a large skillet over medium-high heat and add the remaining 1 tablespoon oil. Sear the chops for 2 to 3 minutes per side, in batches if necessary, until medium-rare. The internal temperature should be 125°F to 130°F on an instant-read thermometer. Remove and set aside on a warm platter, covered loosely with aluminum foil, to rest while you make the vinaigrette.

4 **Vinaigrette:** Pour off the fat from the skillet. Pour the white wine into the pan and whisk to loosen any browned bits from the bottom. Boil to reduce by half, 2 to 3 minutes. Stir in the vinegar and cook for 30 seconds. Remove from the heat and whisk in the mustard, then gradually whisk in the oil to form a homogenous vinaigrette. Stir in the reserved eggplant and the tomatoes. Season to taste with salt, pepper, and/or vinegar.

5 To serve, spoon the vinaigrette over the chops and sprinkle with the basil and mint.

Alternative Cuts: Lamb sirloin or shoulder chops (cook for 5 to 10 minutes longer, or until medium) or goat chops.

Cook's Note
- Instead of fresh tomatoes, you can use 1 cup frozen Oven-Roasted Tomatoes (see below) that you made during the summer.

OVEN-ROASTED TOMATOES

Makes about 3 cups

Once roasted, the tomatoes can be packed into ½-pint freezer containers and frozen to be used throughout the year for a simple and delicious tomato sauce.

2 pounds plum tomatoes, cored, peeled, and halved lengthwise	2 tablespoons chopped fresh herbs, such as basil, oregano, or thyme, or 2 teaspoons dried herbs (use one herb or a combination)
2 tablespoons olive oil	Salt and freshly ground black pepper
2 tablespoons finely chopped garlic	

1 Preheat the oven to 250°F.

2 Arrange the tomatoes, cut sides up, on a baking sheet or in a roasting pan. Drizzle with the oil and sprinkle with the garlic, herbs, and salt and pepper to taste. Roast until the juices given off by the tomatoes have begun to thicken, 1 to 2 hours. Using a spatula, scrape the tomatoes and all the juices into nonreactive containers. (*Use at once, or cool, cover, and refrigerate for up to 1 week or freeze for up to 1 year.*)

Cook's Note
- You can use any variety of tomato. Juicier tomatoes will need to roast longer. Cut large tomatoes into ½-inch-thick slices before roasting.

MUSHROOM-STUFFED LAMB T-BONE LOIN CHOPS

Fit for Company, In a Hurry, Wood-Fired Oven

Serves 4

By partially separating the meat from the T-shaped bone, you can create a space to insert a few tablespoons of a richly flavored stuffing that elevates these chops from great to sublime. Best of all, this method couldn't be easier. Besides the mushroom and cheese stuffing here, you can use other combinations. My wife, Nancy, who gave me the idea, makes a great stuffing of chopped cooked broccoli rabe and mascarpone or cream cheese (see Cook's Notes for other ideas).

Mushroom and Cheese Stuffing

- 2 tablespoons butter
- ½ pound cremini mushrooms, thickly sliced
  Salt and freshly ground black pepper
- 1 tablespoon chopped garlic
- ½ cup soft bread crumbs made from day-old bread
- ¼ cup grated Comté or Gruyère cheese
- ¼ cup freshly grated Parmigiano-Reggiano
- 2 teaspoons chopped fresh thyme
- 2 teaspoons chopped fresh rosemary
- 3 tablespoons chopped fresh flat-leaf parsley

- 2 tablespoons homemade beef stock (see page 168) or canned low-sodium chicken broth, or more if needed

- 8 2-inch-thick lamb T-bone loin chops (if possible, have the butcher leave the tail flaps on the chops)
- 1 teaspoon chopped fresh thyme
- 1 teaspoon chopped fresh rosemary
  Salt and freshly ground black pepper
- 2 tablespoons olive oil

1 **Stuffing:** Heat the butter in a large nonstick skillet over medium heat. Add the mushrooms, sprinkle generously with salt and pepper, and cook, stirring, for 3 minutes. Stir in the garlic and cook until the mushrooms are soft, about 5 minutes. Transfer the mushrooms and any liquid to a food processor and pulse several times to coarsely chop. Add the bread crumbs, cheeses, thyme, rosemary, and parsley. Pulse several more times to combine. Transfer to a large bowl and stir in the stock 1 tablespoon at a time. The stuffing should be moist but not wet. Add more stock if needed. Season to taste with salt and pepper. To firm up the stuffing, cover and refrigerate for at least 30 minutes, or overnight.

2 Preheat the oven to 350°F.

3   Stand the chops on the flat part of the T (like an upside-down capital T) and, using a sharp boning knife, cut between the meat and the T-bone to separate the meat from both sides of the bone, leaving the meat attached at the base of the bone. Firmly press about 2 tablespoons stuffing onto each side of the T-bone and then re-form the chop. If the tail is attached, put a little stuffing between the tail and the body of the chop. Secure each chop by wrapping butcher's twine twice around the perimeter. Sprinkle the chops all over with the thyme, rosemary, and salt and pepper to taste.

4   Heat the oil in a large ovenproof skillet over medium-high heat. Add the chops to the pan and brown for 2 to 3 minutes. Flip and brown the other side for 2 to 3 minutes more. You may have to do this in batches.

5   Remove the chops, pour off the fat, and then stand the chops up in the pan — use the flat part of the T-bone to stabilize them, keeping the meat from contacting the pan. Roast for 10 minutes, or until the internal temperature reaches 125°F on an instant-read thermometer, for medium-rare. Transfer the chops to a platter, cover loosely with aluminum foil, and let rest for 5 to 7 minutes. Remove the twine before serving.

Alternative Cuts: Lamb rib chops (at least 1½ inches thick) into which you can cut a pocket; the stuffing will not cook for long, so use precooked ingredients, as in the bulgur, mint, and feta stuffing (see below).

Cook's Notes
- To roast the chops in a wood-fired oven, omit the browning step. Arrange the chops vertically, resting on the flat side of the T-bone, in an ovenproof skillet and roast for about 15 minutes, or until they reach an internal temperature of 120°F on an instant-read thermometer, for medium-rare. Let rest for 5 minutes.

- Here are some other ideas for stuffing:

    Soft bread crumbs, fresh goat cheese, cooked spinach, and fresh chives

    Soft bread crumbs, chopped picholine olives, and chopped fresh basil

    Soft bread crumbs, finely chopped prosciutto or smoked ham, and fontina cheese

    Soft bread crumbs, porcini mushrooms, Parmigiano-Reggiano, and fresh thyme leaves

    Soft bread crumbs, chopped pitted prunes, and chopped sautéed fennel

    Cooked rice, dried cherries, and chopped fresh rosemary

    Cooked bulgur, chopped fresh mint, and feta cheese

TANDOORI LAMB SHOULDER CHOPS

Cheap Eats, Fit for Company

Serves 4

Lamb shoulder chops are usually a good bargain. An acid-based marinade helps to tenderize them. For the best flavor and tenderness, cook them to medium, which means they will be pink to faintly pink on the inside. Adjust the heat on your grill so it is not blazing hot: Medium to medium-high is best. For even cooking and so that the marinade penetrates to the center, buy chops that are ½ to ¾ inch thick.

Tandoori Marinade

1 cup plain whole-milk Greek yogurt
1 tablespoon finely grated lemon zest
¼ cup fresh lemon juice
1 tablespoon minced garlic
1 tablespoon minced fresh ginger
½ teaspoon ground cardamom
1 tablespoon sweet Hungarian paprika or California chile powder
1 teaspoon ground fennel seeds
Pinch of ground cloves

1 teaspoon ground cumin
1½ teaspoons ground coriander
1 teaspoon turmeric
¼ cup finely chopped fresh cilantro
¼ teaspoon ground fenugreek (see Sources)
½ teaspoon cayenne pepper
2 teaspoons salt

6–8 ½–¾-inch-thick lamb shoulder chops (about 3 pounds total)
Lemon wedges

1. **Marinade:** Combine all the ingredients in a small bowl, stirring until well blended. Coat the lamb chops with the marinade and place on a plate. Cover with plastic wrap and refrigerate overnight.

2. Set up a charcoal or gas grill for medium to medium-high heat (see page 11 for more on grilling). Lightly oil the grill.

3. Remove the lamb chops from the marinade, leaving some of the marinade on the chops. Grill the chops for 4 minutes per side. Cut into one chop to see if it is medium pink. If not, grill for 2 to 3 minutes more. Transfer to a warm platter and let the chops rest, loosely covered with aluminum foil, for 5 minutes before serving with lemon wedges.

Alternative Cuts: Pork leg or sirloin chops or goat chops.

SAUTÉED GOAT T-BONE LOIN CHOPS WITH PECORINO AND TOASTED ALMONDS

In a Hurry, Fit for Company
Serves 4

The crispy texture of the toasted flavored bread crumbs makes a delicious topping for steaks or chops, whether lamb, goat, pork, beef, or veal. The crumbs can also be sprinkled over slices of roasted meat. If the flavor of pecorino cheese is too strong for you, substitute Parmigiano-Reggiano. You can make the crumbs up to several hours ahead.

8 1¼–1½-inch-thick goat T-bone loin chops
    (4–6 ounces each)
   Salt and freshly ground black pepper
4 teaspoons chopped fresh sage
2 teaspoons chopped fresh mint
3 tablespoons olive oil
¼ cup finely chopped shallots
1 tablespoon chopped garlic
1 cup dry white wine
½ cup homemade beef stock (see page 168)
    or canned low-sodium chicken broth

Pecorino and Toasted Almond Bread Crumbs

¼ cup olive oil
1 anchovy fillet, minced
2 teaspoons finely chopped garlic
1 tablespoon chopped fresh sage
1 cup soft bread crumbs made
    from day-old sourdough or other
    coarse-textured bread
¼ cup freshly grated pecorino cheese
¼ cup chopped toasted almonds

Garnish

1 tablespoon shredded fresh mint leaves

1   Season the chops to taste with salt and pepper and sprinkle with the sage and mint. Let rest at room temperature for 30 minutes to 1 hour to allow the seasoning to penetrate the meat, or wrap the chops in plastic wrap and refrigerate overnight.

2   Heat the oil in a large skillet over medium-high heat. Add the chops and sear for 3 to 4 minutes per side; you may have to do this in batches. Remove the chops to a platter. Reduce the heat to medium, add the shallots and garlic, and cook for 1 minute. Add the white wine and bring to a boil, scraping up any browned bits from the bottom of the pan. Boil for 2 to 3 minutes, then add the stock and chops. Reduce the heat to medium and cook for 5 minutes, or until an instant-read thermometer reads 125°F to 130°F for

medium-rare. Set the chops aside, covered loosely with aluminum foil, to rest while you make the bread crumbs.

3   **Bread crumbs:** Heat the oil in a medium nonstick skillet over medium heat. Add the anchovy and garlic and cook, stirring, for 1 minute, making sure the garlic does not brown. Stir in the sage and cook for 1 minute more. Stir in the bread crumbs and cheese and cook, stirring, for 3 to 4 minutes more, or until the crumbs are nicely golden. Stir in the almonds. Set aside.

4   To serve, arrange the chops on a platter and drizzle over the pan juices. Scatter the bread crumbs over the top and sprinkle on the mint.

Alternative Cuts: Lamb or veal rib or loin chops; pork rib or loin chops; goat rib chops; or lamb or goat shoulder chops (cook, covered, for 15 minutes in the stock).

Lamb and Goat Roasts

If bold and meaty leg of lamb is king, the dainty and elegant rack of lamb is queen. You can even form it into a circle and give her a crown. These are my two favorite roasts.

The **leg** is a versatile cut. When whole, it's large enough to feed 8 to 10 people; sold as a half, it's perfect for a family meal. If the bone is removed, you have an uneven slab of meat that can be marinated and grilled to rare, medium, or even medium-well to suit the tastes of a mixed crowd. **Leg of goat** can be used in any recipe for leg of lamb with equally delicious results.

Rack of lamb is expensive, but its small size makes it perfect for a romantic meal for two. For easy slicing and great presentation, buy the rack with the chine bone removed. The flap meat should also be removed, the external fat trimmed to about ¼ inch, and the bones frenched. A **lamb crown roast**, consisting of two 8-bone racks tied into a round, is an extravagant cut to serve at a special dinner party. **Goat rack** is equally elegant, but it's leaner than lamb, so don't cook it beyond medium-rare.

Other Cuts for Roasting

Lamb shoulder is kind on the budget. It does contain chewier meat than the leg and a few pockets of fat and gristle, but when cooked long and slow, it produces succulent well-done meat.

A **lamb sirloin roast** may weigh only 1 to 3 pounds, but it's lean and tender, and it roasts quickly for evenings when your time is limited.

Legs are sometimes boned and divided into small roasts made up of individual leg muscles. If you can find them at 1 to 3 pounds, they, too, make quick, tender little roasts.

A **boneless loin** will weigh 1 to 2 pounds. It roasts quickly and can easily be sliced to feed 3 or 4 people. It isn't cheap, and you'll find it only at fancy markets, but it sure tastes good.

A double loin left on the bone and tied is called a **saddle of lamb**. It makes an impressive presentation, but it's a little difficult to carve.

Lamb and Goat Roasts at a Glance

From the Shoulder

Lamb whole square-cut shoulder, bone in (shoulder roast, shoulder blade roast). Ideal for long, slow roasting. Difficult to carve because of the bones. Sometimes butchers saw the shoulder through the bone into choplike pieces and tie them together. Other times lamb shoulder is cut into a blade roast and an arm roast. Shoulder is well priced and my favorite cut for roasting and braising.

Goat shoulder, bone in. My favorite. Roast it long and slow.

Lamb or goat shoulder roast, boneless (rolled shoulder roast, Saratoga roast). Sold whole or in smaller pieces. Easy to carve but may have pockets of fat and some gristle. Best when roasted medium to medium-well, but can even be cooked to well-done. Can be unrolled, stuffed, and re-tied.

Lamb or goat cushion roast, shoulder, boneless (shoulder clod roast, boneless outside arm roast, boneless shoulder roast). This nifty little roast includes the whole arm and foreshank. If you have a good butcher, ask him or her to separate the foreleg from the shoulder blade and remove the upper arm bone; this leaves a great pocket for stuffing. This is my favorite for stuffing and roasting.

From the Rib and Loin

Lamb rib roast, bone in (rack of lamb, lamb rack, rib rack). Easy and quick to roast. Have the butcher remove the chine bone so you can slice between the ribs. Lots of fat, especially on the large end. Has 7 to 8 ribs and will feed 3 to 4 people. Expensive.

Goat rib roast. Smaller than a lamb rack, but treat it the same way. Figure 2 portions from an 8-bone rack.

Frenched lamb or goat rib roast (rack of lamb, lamb rack). More elegant in presentation than the rib roast, but still plenty of fat over the rib bones.

Frenched lamb or goat rib roast, cap off. Trimmed down to a single rib eye and cut with the rib fat removed. Ideal for small, fancy parties. Very expensive. An 8-rib rack will feed 2 to 3 people.

Lamb or goat crown roast, bone in. Contains 16 ribs, ideal for an elegant meal to serve 6 to 8. Requires a special-order.

Lamb or goat loin roast, bone in (saddle roast, full trim loin roast). Have the butcher cut between each chop for easy carving. An elegant roast for small gatherings; will feed 3 to 4 people.

Lamb or goat double-roast loin, boneless (double saddle roast, double loin roast). Weighs 2 to 3 pounds. Easy to unroll, stuff, and re-tie (some fine butcher shops sell this already stuffed) and easy to carve. Very expensive. Will feed 4 to 6 people.

From the Leg

Lamb or goat sirloin leg, boneless (lamb chump, lamb sirloin roast). A relatively inexpensive, tender roast for 2 to 4 people. Weighs 1 to 2 pounds. Best cooked medium-rare because it's lean.

Lamb whole leg, bone in (whole leg of lamb, sirloin-on full-trimmed leg roast). The whole leg includes the sirloin area, which is part of the hip. Make sure the aitchbone is removed, so you can carve the leg easily. Whole legs can weigh 6 to 9 pounds with the aitchbone removed. Will feed 8 or more people.

Goat leg. Smaller than a lamb leg; it will weigh only about 4 pounds. Treat as you would leg of lamb. Cook rare to medium.

Lamb or goat sirloin-off leg, bone in (short-leg roast). The sirloin area is removed, leaving a smaller leg that is easier to carve. Many stores now sell this as "whole leg of lamb," because it is much more consumer friendly. These legs weigh 5 to 8 pounds and should feed 6 to 8 people.

Lamb or goat leg, boneless (boneless leg roast, boned and tied leg of lamb). Easy to carve and easy to roast. Can be cooked rare to medium, depending on your preference.

Butterflied lamb or goat leg roast. Unrolled, it's ideal for grilling and grill-roasting. Takes well to many different marinades.

Lamb or goat sirloin half leg, bone in or boneless (leg of lamb butt half). Ideal for 4 to 6 people. Easy to carve when aitchbone is removed. More tender than the shank.

Lamb or goat shank half leg, bone in. Less tender than the sirloin, but a good roast for smaller groups.

Lamb American-style leg roast. Some of the shank and sirloin portions are removed from the whole leg, leaving a 3- to 4-pound roast that's easy to carve. May be more expensive than shank or sirloin half legs.

ROAST LEG OF LAMB WITH ROSEMARY-SCENTED POTATOES

Family Meal, Fit for Company, Fit for a Crowd, Great Leftovers

Serves 8, with leftovers

Sometimes it's hard to beat the classics. Such is the case with this recipe, which relies on traditional Mediterranean ingredients for its flavor: lemon, rosemary, and olive oil. Because the potatoes are roasted right in the pan alongside the lamb, they not only turn brown, but also pick up the flavors of the lamb herb paste. The paste is best applied to the roast a day ahead, but if time does not allow, rub it on anytime before roasting. This is a perfect roast for Easter dinner.

Lemon-Rosemary Paste

- 4 garlic cloves, peeled
- 4 teaspoons salt
- 2 tablespoons finely grated lemon zest
- ¼ cup fresh rosemary leaves
- 2 teaspoons freshly ground black pepper
- 2 tablespoons fresh lemon juice
- ¼ cup olive oil

- 1 6- to 8-pound whole bone-in leg of lamb, fat trimmed
- 8 medium Yukon Gold potatoes (about 3½ pounds total), peeled and halved lengthwise
- 1 cup olive oil
- 3 tablespoons finely chopped fresh rosemary
  Salt and freshly ground black pepper

1. **Paste:** Pound the garlic with the salt in a mortar with a pestle, or pulse in a small food processor until it forms a paste. Add the lemon zest and rosemary and pound or pulse to bruise the rosemary, about 1 minute. Stir in the pepper, lemon juice, and oil to make a soft, spreadable paste.

2. Place the lamb fat side up on your work surface and cut shallow diagonal gashes across the fat, about ½ inch apart. Coat the top of the lamb with the rub, working some into the gashes. If any rub remains, rub some onto the ends and the underside of the lamb. Wrap the lamb in plastic wrap and refrigerate, preferably overnight, or for up to 24 hours. (If time does not allow, try to apply the lemon-rosemary rub at least 2 hours before roasting and let it marinate at room temperature.)

3. The next day, remove the lamb from the refrigerator, unwrap, and let it sit at room temperature for 2 hours.

4. Preheat the oven to 425°F, with a rack in the middle.

5   Place the lamb fat side up in a roasting pan, preferably nonstick. Roast for 15 minutes.

6   Meanwhile, place the potatoes in a large bowl and toss with the oil, rosemary, and salt and pepper to taste.

7   Remove the lamb from the oven and reduce the heat to 350°F. Lay the potatoes cut side down around the lamb and return the pan to the oven. Roast for 40 minutes. Using a small metal spatula, turn over the potatoes, taking care that the crisp brown bottoms do not remain stuck to the pan. Brush the potatoes with the pan juices. Roast for 15 minutes more, or until the internal temperature of the lamb registers 120°F to 125°F on an instant-read thermometer, for medium-rare, and the cut sides of the potatoes are browned and crisp. Transfer the potatoes to a warm platter and let the lamb rest, loosely covered with aluminum foil, for 20 minutes before carving. (If the potatoes have not adequately browned and crisped but the lamb is done, transfer the lamb to a platter, increase the oven temperature to 400°F, and continue to roast the potatoes while the lamb is resting.) If the potatoes cool down, reheat in the oven for 10 minutes before serving.

8   To serve, slice the lamb and arrange on the platter with the potatoes.

Alternative Cuts: Boned, rolled, and tied whole leg of lamb; rack of lamb (reduce the rosemary rub by one quarter and the roasting time to 25 to 30 minutes; leave out the potatoes, or begin them in a separate pan 30 minutes before roasting the lamb); or lamb shoulder roast (add 30 to 45 minutes more to the cooking time and roast to an internal temperature of 145°F to 150°F; make sure to remove the potatoes when they are done). A goat leg of the same weight.

Cook's Note
- This lamb goes well with an earthy, full-flavored wine, such as Châteauneuf-du-Pape, Côte-Rôtie, Gigondas, or California Syrah.

Leftovers
- See Two Lamb Sandwiches, page 482.

Two Lamb Sandwiches

ROAST LAMB SANDWICH WITH FENNEL SLAW

This is also good on a kaiser roll or sliced and toasted sourdough bread.

Combine 1 cup thinly shaved fennel with ¼ cup chopped fresh flat-leaf parsley, 2 tablespoons finely chopped shallots, 1 tablespoon chopped capers, 1 finely chopped anchovy fillet, 2 tablespoons mayonnaise, 1 tablespoon Dijon mustard, 1 tablespoon fresh lemon juice, and 1 tablespoon extra-virgin olive oil.

Spread mayonnaise and Dijon mustard on both sides of a split 6-inch piece of baguette. Pile with sliced roast lamb, then add a thick layer of fennel slaw, close the sandwich, and serve.

ROAST LAMB SANDWICH WITH JEFF'S ROASTED RED PEPPER MAYONNAISE

Combine ½ cup finely chopped fire-roasted red bell peppers (see page 284) with 1 teaspoon minced garlic, ¼ cup finely chopped toasted almonds, 2 teaspoons sherry vinegar, 2 tablespoons olive oil, 2 tablespoons mayonnaise, and 2 tablespoons Harissa (page 530) or bottled Sriracha sauce, if you like things spicy.

Smear the mayonnaise on both sides of a split ciabatta roll or sliced and toasted sourdough bread. Top with thin slices of roast lamb and arugula, watercress, or radicchio leaves. Or, for a great rolled sandwich, smear the red pepper mayonnaise on warmed naan or lavash; cover with thinly sliced roast lamb and arugula, watercress, or radicchio, roll up, and cut into 4-inch lengths.

THYME AND FENNEL–RUBBED ROAST RACK OF LAMB

In a Hurry, Fit for Company

Serves 2 to 4

Rack of lamb is elegant and expensive, but it is one of the simplest roasts to prepare. For the best presentation, have the butcher trim it to a single eye of meat and french the bones. Because rack of lamb is so delicate, I keep the added flavors to a minimum. Fennel pollen has a subtler flavor than fennel seeds.

1 large 7- to 8-bone rack of lamb (1½–1¾ pounds) or 2 small 7-bone racks of lamb (about 1½ pounds total), trimmed and frenched

Salt and freshly ground black pepper

2 garlic cloves, finely chopped

2 tablespoons finely chopped fresh thyme

1 teaspoon fennel pollen (see Sources) or ground fennel seeds

1 tablespoon olive oil

1   Let the lamb rest at room temperature for 1 hour.

2   Preheat the oven to 450°F.

3   Sprinkle the lamb generously all over with salt and pepper. Heat a heavy 10-inch skillet over high heat. Place the rack in the pan, fat side down, and sear for 1 to 2 minutes. If cooking 2 racks, do this in batches. Using tongs, hold the rack upright, with the bones vertical, and sear for another 1 to 2 minutes. Flip to the backbone side and sear for 1 to 2 minutes more. Remove from the heat.

4   Combine the garlic, thyme, fennel, and oil in a small food processor and process to make a paste. Smear the paste over the fat side and ends of the roast(s). Place the rack(s) bone side down in a roasting pan. Cover the exposed part of the bones with aluminum foil.

5   Roast for 12 minutes for smaller racks and 15 minutes for a larger rack. With an instant-read thermometer, check the internal temperature; it should be 110°F to 115°F for rare or 120°F to 125°F for medium-rare. If not yet done, roast for 5 minutes more and check again; continue to check every 5 minutes. Place the rack(s) on a cutting board, cover loosely with aluminum foil, and let rest for 7 to 10 minutes. Carve the roasts between the bones and serve.

Alternative Cuts: Saddle roast; bone-in lamb loin roast or lamb sirloin roast (sirloin will take about 20 minutes longer); or rack of goat.

PROVENÇAL BUTTERFLIED LEG OF LAMB WITH OLIVE CRUST

Fit for Company, Great Leftovers, Wood-Fired Oven

Serves 6 to 8, with leftovers

The Provence region of France produces some of the finest olives in the Mediterranean. Often ground and blended with olive oil to make a paste called tapenade, they are also an important ingredient in Provençal stews and other braises. You can purchase tapenade in small jars in the specialty food area of most supermarkets. Do not use the mild-flavored canned black olives from California; do make sure to use extra-virgin olive oil.

To oven-roast the lamb, see Cook's Notes.

Olive Paste

- ¼ cup French black olive tapenade or ½ cup Nyons or kalamata olives, pitted
- 2 garlic cloves, peeled
- 1 tablespoon finely grated lemon zest
- 1 tablespoon chopped fresh savory
- 1 tablespoon chopped fresh thyme

- 1 teaspoon freshly ground black pepper
- 1 tablespoon red wine vinegar
- 1 tablespoon extra-virgin olive oil, or more if needed

- 1 4- to 5-pound boneless leg of lamb

1. **Paste:** If starting with pitted olives, place them in a food processor and pulse several times to chop, then add the remaining paste ingredients. Otherwise, combine the tapenade with the remaining paste ingredients in the processor and pulse to form a soft paste. If too dry, add olive oil as needed.

2. If your lamb is tied or netted, untie or remove the netting and lay the lamb flat, fat side up. Trim most of the external fat, then place the lamb in a baking dish or shallow bowl and generously rub the paste all over it. Cover with plastic wrap and marinate for 2 hours at room temperature, or for up to 24 hours in the refrigerator.

3. Before grilling, remove the lamb from the refrigerator and let sit at room temperature for 2 hours.

4. Set up a charcoal or gas grill for indirect heat (see page 11 for more on grilling).

5. Place the lamb, fat side down, directly over a medium-hot fire (do not remove the olive paste) and sear for 5 to 7 minutes, or until it begins to color and brown. Turn and repeat on the boned side of the lamb. Transfer to the area of the grill without a fire,

fat side up, cover the grill, and continue to grill for 40 minutes, or until the internal temperature reaches 125°F on an instant-read thermometer inserted in the thickest part of the roast. This area will yield medium-rare meat, while thinner areas will be more well-done (if you like rare lamb, remove it when it has an internal temperature of 110°F to 115°F). Let the lamb rest on a platter, loosely tented with aluminum foil, for 15 to 20 minutes before carving.

6   Slice lamb into ¼-inch-thick slices and serve.

Alternative Cuts: Bone-in leg (cook over indirect heat only for 50 to 70 minutes, or until done); rack of lamb (reduce cooking over direct heat to 2 to 3 minutes per side and over indirect heat, 20 to 25 minutes); boneless or bone-in goat leg.

Cook's Notes

- This is an ideal roast for your wood-fired oven. Don't sear the lamb. Place it in a heavy roasting pan, fat side up. Insert a cable-type digital continuous-read thermometer in the lamb. Pop the pan into your oven when the oven temperature reaches about 450°F, and roast until the internal temperature of the lamb reaches 120°F. Let rest for 20 minutes, loosely tented with aluminum foil; the temperature will rise to around 135°F.

- To roast the lamb in an ordinary oven, preheat it to 450°F. Place the lamb in a heavy roasting pan and roast for 15 minutes. Reduce the heat to 350°F and continue to roast until the internal temperature reaches 125°F, about 40 minutes. Let rest for 15 to 20 minutes, loosely tented with aluminum foil, before carving.

Leftovers

- Use for lamb sandwiches; see page 482.
- Thinly slice the lamb and serve over salad greens with a lemony vinaigrette.

PORCINI AND ARTICHOKE–STUFFED LEG OF LAMB

Fit for Company, Fit for a Crowd, Great Leftovers

Serves 8

Stuffing a roast elevates it to something so special that it can become the centerpiece of a meal for important guests. All you need to do is untie and unroll this roast, spoon on the Italian-inspired stuffing, roll it back up, and re-tie it.

Porcini and Artichoke Stuffing

- 1 ounce dried porcini mushrooms
- 1 cup boiling water
- 1 tablespoon olive oil
- 3 tablespoons chopped shallots
- 1 tablespoon finely chopped garlic
- 1 cup coarsely chopped artichoke hearts (freshly cooked or thawed frozen)
- 1 cup soft bread crumbs made from day-old sourdough or other coarse-textured bread
- ½ cup freshly grated Parmigiano-Reggiano
- 1 teaspoon chopped fresh tarragon
- 1 large egg, beaten
  Salt and freshly ground black pepper

- 1 4- to 5-pound boneless leg of lamb
- 3 tablespoons chopped fresh oregano
- 2 teaspoons salt
- 2 teaspoons freshly ground black pepper
- 3 tablespoons olive oil

1. **Stuffing:** Place the porcini in a small bowl and pour the water over to cover. Soak for at least 45 minutes, or up to several hours, until soft.

2. Remove the porcini from the liquid with a slotted spoon, finely chop, and set aside. Strain the soaking liquid, leaving behind any grit in the bottom of the bowl, and save to make a pan sauce (see Cook's Notes) or to use in another recipe.

3. Heat the oil in a small skillet over medium heat. Add the shallots and garlic and cook until soft, about 3 minutes. Add the artichokes and cook, stirring, for 2 minutes more.

4. Combine the artichoke mixture, the reserved mushrooms, the bread crumbs, cheese, tarragon, and egg in a medium bowl and mix until well combined. Season to taste with salt and pepper. Let cool until firm, about 30 minutes.

5. Meanwhile, open out the lamb, fat side down, on a work surface and allow to rest at room temperature for 1 hour.

6. Preheat the oven to 350°F.

7   Spread the stuffing over the lamb, pressing it into the gashes and other areas left by the removal of the bones. Re-form the lamb into a cylindrical shape and tie it in 4 to 6 places with butcher's twine.

8   Combine the oregano, salt, pepper, and oil in a small bowl and brush all over the lamb. Place the lamb fat side up on a rack in a roasting pan. Roast for 1 hour, or until the internal temperature of the thickest part is 120°F to 125°F on an instant-read thermometer; the lamb will be mostly medium-rare except for the more cooked ends. Let rest, loosely covered with aluminum foil, for 15 to 20 minutes.

9   Remove the twine, slice the meat into ½-inch-thick slices, and serve.

Alternative Cuts: Boneless lamb shoulder roast (cook until medium-well) or boneless goat leg.

Cook's Notes
- This roast is also delicious cooked on the grill over indirect heat.
- You can easily turn the roasting juices into a simple pan sauce. Skim off the fat from the roasting pan, leaving the juices behind. Add 1 cup dry white wine or dry vermouth and scrape up any browned bits from the bottom of the pan. Pour into a saucepan and boil to reduce by half. Add the reserved mushroom soaking liquid and boil until the sauce just turns syrupy. Stir in ½ cup chopped artichoke hearts and 1 teaspoon chopped fresh oregano. Season to taste with salt and pepper and serve with the lamb.

Leftovers
- Thinly sliced, this roast makes great sandwiches; see page 482.

SLOW-ROASTED LAMB SHOULDER WITH ROSEMARY-PANCETTA PASTE

Cheap Eats, Family Meal, Great Leftovers

Serves 6

Cuts of lamb, such as the shoulder and breast, that have rich, deep flavor and ample fat are delicious when well-done. You can serve the lamb with a pan sauce, if you like (see Cook's Notes). I like to accompany this dish with cannellini or flageolet beans cooked with sage and garlic.

Rosemary-Pancetta Paste

- 8 garlic cloves, peeled
- ¼ pound pancetta, diced
- 3 tablespoons chopped fresh rosemary
- 2 teaspoons freshly ground black pepper

- 1 3- to 4-pound boned and rolled lamb shoulder roast

  White Beans with Sage (page 490)

1 **Paste:** With the motor running, drop the garlic through the feed tube of a food processor and pulse until chopped. Stop and scrape down the sides of the bowl. Add the pancetta, rosemary, and pepper and pulse several times to form a paste.

2 Trim the lamb of excess fat. Make ½-inch-deep gashes 1 to 2 inches long at an angle all over the surface of the meat, taking care not to cut any of the strings. Fill each gash with some of the rosemary-pancetta paste. Smear the remaining paste over the surface of the roast. *(The meat can be wrapped in plastic wrap and refrigerated overnight. Let the roast sit for 1 hour at room temperature before cooking.)*

3 Preheat the oven to 275°F.

4 Place the roast fat side up in a roasting pan and roast for 3 hours, until the meat registers 160°F on an instant-read thermometer. If not done, continue to roast, checking every 30 minutes. Let rest, loosely covered with aluminum foil, for 20 minutes before carving.

5 Slice the meat into thick slices. Spoon the beans into a large shallow serving bowl and top with the lamb. Drizzle any juices (or the pan sauce; see Cook's Notes) over the top, and serve.

Alternative Cuts: Breast of lamb (you will need about 6 pounds), bone-in lamb shoulder, or boneless or bone-in goat shoulder.

Cook's Notes

- If you don't have time to make the beans from scratch (see below), use canned beans. Cook 1 cup chopped onions, 1 tablespoon chopped garlic, and some chopped fresh sage in olive oil until soft. Add the canned beans and some water or stock and simmer for 20 minutes. Season to taste with salt and pepper.

- You can serve the lamb as is or make a simple pan sauce: Skim off the fat from the roasting pan and deglaze the pan juices with ½ cup dry white wine, 1 cup home-made or canned low-sodium chicken broth, and ½ chopped fresh or canned tomato. Cook the sauce until it just turns syrupy.

WHITE BEANS WITH SAGE

1 pound (2½ cups) dried white beans, such as cannellini or flageolet, picked over and rinsed	12 fresh sage leaves
	2 bay leaves
	Salt and freshly ground black pepper
4 garlic cloves, sliced	2 tablespoons extra-virgin olive oil

1 Bring 3 quarts water to a boil in a casserole or large saucepan. Add the beans, bring to a boil, and boil for 3 minutes. Remove from the heat and let the beans soak for 1 hour. Drain, discard the liquid, and return the beans to the pot.

2 Add another 3 quarts water to the beans. Bring to a boil, add the garlic, sage, bay leaves, and 1 teaspoon pepper. Reduce the heat, and simmer until the beans are just tender and not falling apart (begin sampling them after 20 minutes of cooking). Drain and reserve the liquid. Discard the bay leaves and put the beans back in the pot. Stir in enough cooking liquid to keep them moist. Stir in 1 teaspoon salt and the olive oil, cover, and set aside. Gently rewarm before serving, and season to taste with more salt and pepper.

CROWN ROAST OF LAMB

Fit for Company, Fit for a Crowd

Serves 10

A crown roast of lamb makes for a truly regal presentation. Plan on 2 to 3 chops per person. Two crown roasts, which consist of 14 to 16 chops each, should be adequate for 10, unless you have big eaters, in which case you'll need three. You could also get two crown roasts and a 7-bone rack of lamb for second helpings. You'll need to order the crown roasts ahead of time from the butcher. Because more of the meat is exposed to the oven heat than in a normal rack of lamb, expect cooking times to be a little less. If you wish, fill the crown with Bulgur Mint Stuffing (see Cook's Note) before serving.

2 crown roasts of lamb (14–16 chops each)	3 tablespoons minced garlic
Olive oil for brushing	1 tablespoon salt
¼ cup chopped fresh rosemary	2 teaspoons freshly ground black pepper
2 tablespoons chopped fresh oregano	

1. Put the roasts bone side up in two shallow roasting pans. Brush the meat with the oil, making sure to cover the exposed cracks between the chops. Combine the remaining ingredients in a small bowl and rub the mixture all over the meat and fat. Let the lamb rest at room temperature for 1 to 2 hours.

2. Preheat the oven to 450°F.

3. Cover the bones tightly with aluminum foil to protect them from burning. Roast the lamb for 15 to 20 minutes. Check the internal temperature by inserting an instant-read thermometer into several chops, without touching the bones. For rare meat, remove at 110°F to 115°F; for medium-rare, 120°F to 125°F; and for medium, 130°F to 135°F. If the roast is not done to your liking, continue roasting, checking every 5 minutes. Let the roast rest, loosely covered with aluminum foil, for 10 to 15 minutes before carving, then slice the meat into chops between the ribs and serve.

Cook's Note

- For a dramatic presentation, fill the centers of the crowns with roasted root vegetables, Bulgur Mint Stuffing (recipe follows), or your favorite stuffing, cooked separately. Do not stuff a crown roast of lamb before cooking; the stuffing takes too long to cook, resulting in overcooked lamb.

BULGUR MINT STUFFING

Serves 10

5 tablespoons butter

2 cups finely chopped onions

½ cup finely chopped peeled carrots

¼ cup finely chopped shallots

2 cups bulgur

1 cup dried currants

¼ teaspoon ground allspice

⅛ teaspoon ground cinnamon

4 cups homemade lamb stock (see page 168) or canned low-sodium chicken broth

Salt and freshly ground black pepper

2 tablespoons chopped fresh mint

½ cup toasted pine nuts (optional; see page 273)

1 Heat 3 tablespoons of the butter in a large heavy saucepan over medium heat. Add the onions, carrots, and shallots, cover, and cook, stirring from time to time, for 10 minutes, or until soft and beginning to color.

2 Stir in the bulgur until well coated. Stir in the currants, allspice, cinnamon, stock, ½ teaspoon salt, and ½ teaspoon pepper. Bring to a boil, cover, and reduce to a simmer. Cook for 15 to 20 minutes, or until the bulgur is tender.

3 Stir in the remaining 2 tablespoons butter, the mint, and pine nuts (if using). Season to taste with salt and pepper. Mound half the stuffing in the center of each crown roast.

GRILL-ROASTED GOAT SHOULDER

Fit for Company, Family Meal

Serves 6

Since goats tend to be lean, the shoulder is one of the few cuts (the breast is the other) that has enough fat to withstand long, slow roasting, yielding well-done and succulent meat. Goat holds up well to strong flavors. In this recipe, adapted from *Corsican Cuisine: Flavors of the Perfumed Isle* by Arthur L. Meyer, it is smeared with anchovies and herbs and basted with an herb-infused olive oil. If you can get a baby goat (*cabrito* or kid), which weighs 30 pounds or less, by all means use this recipe and roast the whole kid on a spit or in a large oven.

Anchovy-Herb Paste

- 4 anchovy fillets
- 6 garlic cloves, peeled
- 2 tablespoons finely grated lemon zest
- 1 tablespoon chopped fresh marjoram or oregano
- 2 teaspoons chopped fresh mint
- 2 teaspoons freshly ground black pepper
- ¼ cup olive oil

- 1 4- to 6-pound whole bone-in goat shoulder
- 2 cups dry white wine, or more as needed

Mint-Herb Basting Oil

- 2 tablespoons chopped fresh mint
- 1 tablespoon chopped fresh rosemary
- 1 tablespoon chopped fresh marjoram or oregano
- ⅓ cup extra-virgin olive oil
- 3 tablespoons red wine vinegar

1   **Paste:** With the motor running, drop the anchovies and garlic through the feed tube of a food processor. Scrape down the sides of the bowl and add the remaining ingredients. Pulse several times to form a paste.

2   Place the shoulder fat side up on a cutting board and cut several ½-inch-deep gashes into the fat and the meat below. Work some of the paste into the gashes and rub the rest over the shoulder. (*You can wrap the shoulder in plastic wrap and marinate overnight in the refrigerator.*)

3   Set up a charcoal or gas grill for indirect grilling (see page 12). Adjust the heat to as close as you can get to 275°F.

4   Place the shoulder in a roasting pan. Pour in the white wine and enough water to reach a depth of 1 inch. Place the pan on the grill where there is no fire, cover the grill, and roast for 1 hour.

5   **Meanwhile, make the basting oil:** Combine all the ingredients in a small bowl. Set aside.

6   After 1 hour of roasting, brush the basting oil all over the goat. Continue to baste every 45 minutes, and make sure there is at least ½ inch of liquid in the pan, adding more wine or water as needed. After 2½ hours, check the meat. It should be quite tender and almost coming off the bone. If the meat is not done, continue to roast, checking every 30 minutes.

7   When the meat is done, transfer it to a platter and loosely tent with aluminum foil to keep warm. Pour the liquid from the pan into a saucepan and degrease the surface. Taste the sauce; it should have a rich flavor. If it does not, boil for a few minutes to concentrate the flavor. Do not attempt to reduce the sauce, because it may become too salty.

8   Cut the shoulder into chunks. Pour some sauce over and pass the rest at the table.

Alternative Cuts: Boneless goat shoulder, breast of goat, bone-in or boneless lamb shoulder, or breast of lamb.

Cook's Note
- You can roast the goat shoulder in a 275°F oven for 3 to 4 hours.

Lamb and Goat Kebabs

First made from lamb, kebabs originated in Persia and soon spread throughout the Middle East, where lamb and goat remain the meats of choice for these succulent cubes. They are my first choice too.

Lamb skewers can easily be embellished with a host of garnishes and accompaniments, from simple aromatic herbs to the classic accompaniment of sweet onion and bell peppers to chunks of fruit, such as dried apricots. Vegetables to skewer along with the meat include eggplants, mushrooms, summer and winter squashes, and even cucumbers. The list can also include leafy vegetables, such as chicory, radicchio, cabbage, and bok choy—in fact, just about any vegetable that will stay put on the skewer.

When it comes to choosing a marinade, in addition to the recipes in this chapter, check out the marinades suggested for beef (see page 129) or pork kebabs (see page 291).

LAMB AND GOAT CUTS FOR KEBABS

I recommend cutting the meat into 1½- to 2-inch chunks—large enough so that you can brown the exterior nicely and not overcook the meat. Try to keep your cubes uniform so that they all cook evenly.

Meat from the loin and rib is too expensive to use for kebabs, and this ultra-tender meat can easily be overmarinated, which will turn it mushy.

- Ideal cuts are sirloin and boneless leg.
- If you are on a budget and have plenty of time on your hands, you can use boneless shoulder, but you will need to carefully trim away any unwanted fat and gristle.

MOROCCAN-STYLE LAMB KEBABS

Family Meal

Serves 6

I'm drawn to Moroccan food because of its copious use of spices and fruits. Fresh lemon juice flavors marinades, condiments, and stews, and lemons are also preserved, to be used throughout the year, when fresh ones are out of season. Preserving lemons in salt and lemon juice mellows the bitterness, while balancing their aromatic notes. Preserved lemons go particularly well with lamb. You can purchase them (see Sources), but they are easy to make yourself (see page 499).

Serve these kebabs over basmati rice or couscous with lots of Yogurt-Lemon Sauce drizzled over.

Lemon Marinade

- 4 wedges Preserved Lemons (recipe follows)
- ¼ cup fresh lemon juice
- 6 garlic cloves, peeled
- 1 ⅛-inch-thick slice fresh ginger
- 1 teaspoon dried marjoram
- 1 teaspoon ground coriander
- 1 teaspoon ground cumin
- 1 teaspoon salt
- 1 teaspoon freshly ground black pepper
- ½ teaspoon turmeric
- 3 tablespoons olive oil

- 2½ pounds boneless leg of lamb or lamb sirloin steak, trimmed of excess fat and cut into 2-inch chunks
- 1 sweet onion (such as Walla Walla) or red onion, cut into 1-inch pieces

- 1 red bell pepper, cored, seeded, and cut into 1-inch squares
- 1 yellow bell pepper, cored, seeded, and cut into 1-inch squares

Yogurt-Lemon Sauce

- 2 tablespoons reserved lemon marinade paste
- 1 seedless cucumber, cut into ½-inch dice
- ½ cup chopped fresh cilantro
- 2 cups plain whole-milk Greek yogurt
  Salt

  Cooked basmati rice or couscous (optional)

- 4 12-inch metal skewers

1   **Marinade:** Put all the ingredients in a blender and puree to make a coarse paste. Set aside 2 tablespoons for the yogurt sauce. Put the lamb in a large zipper-lock bag and scrape in the remaining marinade. Seal the bag and massage it to coat all the lamb. Marinate for 2 hours at room temperature, or as long as overnight in the refrigerator, turning from time to time to redistribute the marinade.

2   Set up a charcoal or gas grill for medium-high heat (see page 11 for more on grilling). Oil the grill grate.

3   Remove the lamb from the marinade and place in a bowl. Put the onion and peppers in the bag and massage them to coat with the marinade (it's okay if the onion pieces break apart). Transfer to another bowl and discard the marinade. Thread the lamb and vegetables onto the skewers, threading a piece of onion and pepper between each chunk of lamb. If there are extra peppers or onion, thread them onto separate skewers, if you like.

4   Grill the skewers, turning every 3 to 4 minutes, for about 10 minutes for medium-rare. Cut into a few pieces of lamb to be sure they are done.

5   **Meanwhile, make the sauce:** Combine the reserved 2 tablespoons marinade with the cucumber, cilantro, and yogurt in a bowl. Season with salt to taste. Mix well. (Don't make the sauce more than an hour before serving, or it will be become watery.)

6   Remove the lamb and vegetables from the skewers and serve them in a mound, heaped over basmati rice or couscous (if using). Drizzle some of the sauce over the kebabs and pass the rest at the table.

Alternative Cuts: Boneless lamb shoulder, but take care to trim away any sinew and excess fat. Goat leg meat. This is also a great marinade for rib or loin lamb chops.

Cook's Note

- During the summer, complete the meal with slices of grilled summer squash, such as yellow crookneck, zucchini, or pattypan. When the squash is done, brush it with a bit of the Yogurt-Lemon Sauce.

PRESERVED LEMONS

Makes 4 cups

This Moroccan delicacy is easy to make and adds an intense lemony flavor to tagines and marinades. Allow about a week at room temperature for the salt and lemon juice to pickle and preserve the lemons.

8 lemons	1½–2 cups fresh lemon juice
1 cup kosher salt (I use Diamond Crystal)	Olive oil

1 Wash the lemons well, using plenty of hot water to get rid of any wax. Dry them well. Cut each lemon lengthwise into 8 wedges. Remove any visible seeds. Put the wedges in a bowl and toss with the salt.

2 Pack the lemons into a 1-quart jar with a glass or plastic lid (metal will rust), scraping any salt and juice from the bowl into the jar. Cover the lemons with lemon juice, leaving about ½ inch of space at the top. Put the lid on loosely and let the jar sit at cool room temperature for 1 week to pickle. Tighten the lid and shake the jar from time to time to redistribute the salt and juices, then loosen the lid again.

3 After a week at room temperature, add enough olive oil to fill the air space at the top. Cover tightly and refrigerate. (*The preserved lemons will keep well in the refrigerator for up to 6 months.*)

SPICY AND SMOKY MEXICAN GOAT KEBABS

Family Meal

Serves 4

I like to serve these kebabs in the fall when butternut squash is just coming to market. If you want a summertime dish, use yellow or green pattypan squash or zucchini or summer squash cut into 1-inch chunks and don't precook it in boiling water. Another great choice is corn on the cob: Set aside some marinade to brush over the ears, and grill the corn along with the kebabs.

You can use any variety of hot fresh chiles you can find instead of poblanos. Serve the kebabs with warm tortillas, rice, black beans, and some salsa (see Cook's Notes) on the side.

2½ pounds boneless goat leg or sirloin, cut into 1½-inch cubes	2 cups 1-inch cubes peeled butternut squash or various summer squashes (see headnote)
Smoky Chile Marinade (page 398)	16 scallions, root ends trimmed
1 red onion, cut into 1-inch squares	2 tablespoons vegetable oil
16 medium radishes, trimmed	Salt and freshly ground black pepper
2 poblano chiles (see headnote), cored, seeded, and cut into 1-inch squares	4 12-inch metal skewers

1   Place the goat in a large zipper-lock bag. Reserve ½ cup of the marinade. Pour the rest over the goat, seal the bag, and shake and turn the bag to coat all the pieces with marinade. Marinate at room temperature for 2 hours, or overnight in the refrigerator.

2   Set up a charcoal or gas grill for medium-high heat (see page 11 for more on grilling).

3   Remove the goat from the marinade. Thread the goat onto the skewers, alternating with the onion, radishes, and chile. Set aside.

4   Bring a large pot of water to a boil. Add the butternut squash and boil until tender but still firm, about 10 minutes. Drain in a colander and cool under cold running water. (Omit this step if using summer squash.) Thread the squash onto the remaining skewers. Brush with some of the reserved marinade.

5   Place the skewers on the grill. Cook, turning the skewers every 2 to 3 minutes, basting each time with the reserved marinade. The goat skewers are done when the meat is

firm to the touch and the edges have begun to brown (cut into a piece to make sure that it is just reddish pink inside) and the vegetables have begun to color and soften, 10 to 12 minutes. The squash is done when nicely colored and tender. Stack the skewers on a warm platter, cover with aluminum foil, and set aside.

6   Brush the scallions with some of the oil and sprinkle with salt and pepper to taste. Grill until they begin to brown and soften, turning and brushing with oil frequently, about 5 minutes, depending on how hot the fire is. When done, brush with some of the reserved marinade.

7   Remove the meat and vegetables from the skewers and mound on the platter. Garnish the edges of the platter with the scallions and serve.

Alternative Cuts: Boneless lamb leg or sirloin; or boneless lamb or goat shoulder, well trimmed of sinew and fat.

Cook's Notes

- The marinade is also good for goat or lamb chops.

- Serve the kebabs with salsa — I particularly like Pico de Gallo (page 259) with the addition of some diced peaches, plums, or apricots — and warm tortillas, and let guests fill them with the meat and vegetables.

Ground Lamb and Goat

Ground lamb and goat are particularly popular in countries such as Greece, Turkey, India, Pakistan, and Iraq, where these animals are the main source of red meat. If you buy the meat already ground, make sure that it isn't too fatty (some stores use the fatty breast meat for their ground lamb). Ground goat can be difficult to find. The best source is a Middle Eastern market — or grind your own.

The best cuts for grinding are boneless sirloin, leg, or shoulder. Cut the meat into ½-inch cubes and chop in a food processor. Aim for 15 to 20 percent fat.

Lamb and goat can be used interchangeably in the following recipes.

GRINDING MEAT AT HOME

Plan to grind meat the day that you purchase it so that it's at maximum freshness. If you want to be extra cautious, follow the advice of the food science writer Harold McGee. To kill surface bacteria, he brings a pot of water to a boil and blanches the large chunk of meat for 30 to 60 seconds. He immediately transfers the meat to an ice bath, then drains it and pats it dry. Otherwise, simply use freshly purchased meat directly from the refrigerator.

- To keep the fat firm and the meat cold during chopping, place the clean food processor bowl and the blade in the freezer for 30 minutes before you begin.
- Cut the meat into ¾-inch cubes. If you are not grinding the meat immediately, refrigerate it.
- Place no more than ¾ pound meat at a time in the food processor. Use the pulse switch in 2-second bursts to produce ⅛- to ¼-inch pieces of meat. Don't overprocess, or you'll end up with meat slurry.
- You can also use a meat grinder fitted with the ¼-inch plate.
- Use the ground meat immediately, or wrap it and freeze (see page 7) for up to 2 months.

LEBANESE-STYLE LAMB AND BULGUR BURGERS

In a Hurry, Family Meal

Serves 4

This simple little burger is a great way to appreciate the joys of Lebanese cooking. Heavy on spices but light on the waistline, it's sure to become a family favorite. Instead of forming into patties to be stuffed into warm pita bread, you can also roll the meat mixture into meatballs and serve with the yogurt sauce on the side as a great party hors d'oeuvre.

Burgers

- 1½ cups finely chopped onions
- 2 tablespoons chopped garlic
- 2 teaspoons coriander seeds
- 2 teaspoons cumin seeds
- 1 pound lean ground lamb (80%–85% lean)
- ¾ cup cooked bulgur
- ½ teaspoon cayenne pepper
- ¼ teaspoon ground allspice
  - Pinch of ground cinnamon
- ¼ cup chopped fresh flat-leaf parsley
- 1 large egg, lightly beaten
- 1½ teaspoons salt
- 1 teaspoon freshly ground black pepper

Yogurt Sauce

- ½ cup plain whole-milk Greek yogurt
- 2 tablespoons chopped fresh mint
- 2 tablespoons chopped fresh flat-leaf parsley

- 1 teaspoon finely grated lemon zest
- 1 tablespoon fresh lemon juice
- 1 teaspoon sugar
- 1 tablespoon chopped fresh oregano
- ¼ cup finely chopped scallion greens
- ½ teaspoon salt
- ½ teaspoon freshly ground black pepper
  - Reserved spice mixture (from Burgers)

Garnish

- ½ cup finely chopped red onion
- 1 cup chopped fresh flat-leaf parsley
- 1 cup diced tomatoes
- 2 tablespoons olive oil
  - Pinch of salt

- 4 pita breads (I use whole wheat)
- 1 tablespoon olive oil

1 Preheat the oven to 350°F.

2 **Burgers:** Bring a pot of lightly salted water to a boil. Blanch the onions and garlic in the boiling water for 2 minutes. Drain and cool in the refrigerator.

3 Toast the coriander seeds and cumin seeds in a small dry skillet over medium heat until they begin to pop and are fragrant and lightly browned. Transfer to a small bowl

to cool, then crush in a mortar with a pestle or a spice grinder. Divide the spices in half and reserve one half for the yogurt sauce.

4. Combine the lamb, bulgur, blanched onions and garlic, half of the toasted spices, and the remaining burger ingredients in a medium bowl. Knead, and squeeze the mixture with your hands until well blended. Form into 12 equal-sized balls, then form each ball into an oval patty about ½ inch thick. Set aside.

5. **Sauce:** Combine all the ingredients in a small bowl until well blended. Refrigerate until ready to serve.

6. **Garnish:** Combine the ingredients in a small bowl and set aside.

7. Wrap the pitas in aluminum foil and warm in the oven for 10 minutes.

8. Meanwhile, heat the oil in a large nonstick skillet over medium-high heat. Add the burgers, in 2 batches if necessary, and cook for 5 minutes per side for medium-rare.

9. Cut a 1-inch slice off each pita and gently open the pockets. Fill each pocket with 3 patties and spoon over some yogurt sauce. Add some of the tomato-onion garnish, followed by a bit more yogurt sauce, and serve.

Alternative Cuts: Ground goat or a mixture of ground lamb and goat and lean ground beef (85% lean) or bison.

Cook's Notes
- You can cook the bulgur and blanch the onions and garlic a day ahead and refrigerate.
- You can also grill the burgers.

SICILIAN LAMB MEATBALLS BRAISED WITH EGGPLANT, BELL PEPPER, AND TOMATOES

Family Meal, Great Leftovers, Rewarms Well

Serves 4

Fall is a great time to enjoy eggplants and bell peppers, whose season begins in late summer and extends well into September. Heirloom varieties of tomatoes are still abundant during this time, too. Put these three ingredients together with lamb, and you have a great marriage. You can serve this over polenta or a shaped pasta, such as penne, ziti, or rigatoni. Don't forget a generous sprinkling of pecorino cheese.

Meatballs

- ½ cup fresh bread crumbs
- ¼ cup water
- 1¼ pounds ground lamb (85% lean)
- 1 teaspoon salt
- ½ teaspoon freshly ground black pepper
- 1 large egg, lightly beaten
- ½ cup freshly grated pecorino cheese
- 1 tablespoon freshly grated nutmeg
- ⅛ teaspoon ground cinnamon
- 1 tablespoon chopped fresh marjoram

Eggplant, Bell Pepper, and Tomato Sauce

- 1 medium eggplant, cut into 1-inch chunks
- 6 tablespoons extra-virgin olive oil, plus more if needed
  Salt and freshly ground black pepper
- 1 red bell pepper, cored, seeded, and cut into ½-inch-wide strips
- 1 cup finely chopped onions
- 1 cup dry white wine
- 1 tablespoon minced garlic
- 2 cups peeled, halved, seeded, and chopped vine-ripened tomatoes (I use an heirloom variety)
- 2 teaspoons chopped fresh marjoram
  Freshly grated pecorino cheese

1   Preheat the oven to 400°F.

2   **Meatballs:** Soak the bread crumbs in the water and squeeze out the excess. Combine the bread crumbs with the remaining meatball ingredients in a large bowl. Using clean hands, knead and squeeze the mixture until well combined. Form into ten to twelve 2-inch meatballs. Set aside.

3   **Sauce:** Toss the eggplant with 5 tablespoons of the oil in a medium bowl and sprinkle with salt and pepper to taste. Spread the eggplant in a single layer on a baking sheet and bake for 7 minutes. Turn with a spatula and bake for 5 minutes more, or until very soft. If dry, brush with more oil. Set aside.

4   Heat the remaining 1 tablespoon oil in a large deep skillet over medium-high heat. Add the meatballs and brown on all sides, about 5 minutes. Remove and set aside.

5   Add the bell pepper strips to the pan and cook, stirring, until soft, about 5 minutes. Remove and set aside. Reduce the heat to medium, add the onions, cover, and cook, stirring from time to time, until soft, about 5 minutes. Add the white wine and garlic and cook until the wine has almost evaporated, scraping up any browned bits from the bottom of the pan. Add the meatballs, bell pepper, eggplant, tomatoes, and marjoram and bring to a simmer. Cover and simmer for 10 to 15 minutes, then uncover and boil to reduce if the sauce is too thin. Degrease the sauce and season to taste with salt and pepper.

6   Spoon the meatballs onto a serving platter. Spoon the vegetable mixture and sauce over the top, sprinkle with pecorino, and serve.

Alternative Cuts: A mixture of ½ pound lamb and ¾ pound hot or sweet Italian sausage, ground goat, beef, bison, or pork, or a mixture of any or all.

Cook's Note
- You can also make 1-inch meatballs and serve as an hors d'oeuvre; omit the sauce.

Leftovers
- Use as a filling for a meatball sub.
- Layer with rigatoni or penne, ricotta, and grated pecorino cheese in a casserole and bake at 350°F until hot.

LONI'S PASTITSIO (THE ULTIMATE GREEK MAC AND CHEESE)

Cheap Eats, Fit for a Crowd, Family Meal, Great Leftovers, Rewarms Well

Serves 6, with leftovers

I first encountered pastitsio many years ago at a Greek festival put on by a local Greek Orthodox church. The wonderful aromas drew me immediately to the stall where huge squares of baked pasta were being cut from a large hotel pan. One bite, and I knew I was eating the "ultimate" mac and cheese. The recipe comes from my mentor and good friend Loni Kuhn. Loni ran a cooking school in her San Francisco home for more than twenty years, and she generously supplied me with many of her best recipes. Loni passed away in 1997, but her enthusiasm and love of good, simple food lives on in her recipes.

¼ cup olive oil	1 pound elbow macaroni
1½ cups finely chopped onions	8 tablespoons (1 stick) butter
3–4 garlic cloves, minced	½ cup all-purpose flour
2 pounds lean ground lamb (85% lean)	4 cups whole milk
2 cups tomato puree	Pinch of freshly grated nutmeg
1 tablespoon dried oregano (I use Greek)	2 cups freshly grated kefalotiri or pecorino cheese
1 4-inch cinnamon stick	5 large eggs
2 bay leaves	1 cup panko or homemade dried bread crumbs
¼ teaspoon freshly grated nutmeg	
Salt and freshy ground black pepper	

1   Heat the oil in a large skillet over medium heat. Add the onions and cook until soft, about 5 minutes. Add the garlic and lamb, breaking up any lumps with a heavy spoon. Stir in the tomato puree, oregano, cinnamon, bay leaves, nutmeg, 1 teaspoon salt, and pepper to taste. Cover and simmer over medium heat for about 2 minutes. Uncover and cook until most of the liquid has evaporated, 10 to 15 minutes. Remove from the heat and discard the cinnamon stick and bay leaves.

2   Meanwhile, bring a large pot of salted water to a boil. Add the macaroni and cook until slightly less than al dente. Drain in a colander. Rinse well with cold water, then drain again and set aside.

3   Preheat the oven to 350°F.

4   Melt the butter in a large skillet over medium heat. Add the flour and stir constantly until the mixture bubbles, 2 to 3 minutes. Rapidly stir in the milk and nutmeg and cook until the sauce comes to a simmer and is thick and smooth. Stir in 1 cup of the cheese until well blended. Remove from the heat and set the sauce aside to cool slightly.

5   Break the eggs into a bowl, whisk well, and stir in a couple of spoonfuls of the warm sauce to temper them. Rapidly beat the egg mixture into the rest of the sauce. Season to taste with salt and pepper.

6   To assemble the pastitsio, place half of the macaroni in a buttered 9-x-13-inch baking pan and sprinkle with ½ cup of the cheese. Top with the meat sauce. Top the meat sauce with the remaining macaroni, then the remaining ½ cup cheese. Spoon the cheese sauce over the whole pan, then sprinkle on the bread crumbs. (*The pastitsio can be assembled a day ahead, refrigerated, then baked when you are ready; add 20 minutes to the cooking time.*)

7   Bake for 45 minutes, or until the top is lightly browned. Remove from the oven and let rest for about 20 minutes. Cut into 3-x-4-inch rectangles (9 rectangles total) and serve.

Alternative Cuts: A mixture of ground beef and lamb or ground goat or a mixture of ground goat and ground lamb.

Leftovers
- You can rewarm leftovers by wrapping squares in aluminum foil and heating for 20 minutes in a 375°F oven.

Lamb and Goat Stews, Pot Roasts, and Other Braises

As you do with beef, avoid buying lamb stew meat already cubed. You won't know what cut it's from, and the pieces are usually too small.

The **neck**, which is one of the cheapest cuts, makes the best lamb or goat stew. It's got enough collagen to give wonderful body to the sauce, and the meat cooks up tender and silky. However, there are lots of bones to deal with. For boneless stews, buy a chunk of boneless lamb or goat shoulder, which is also kind to the wallet. Cut it into 2- to 3-inch chunks (they will shrink as they cook) and trim away excess fat and large chunks of gristle. If you don't mind fattier cuts, you can use **lamb breast** for stew; it's downright cheap. It can be hard to find, but it is worth looking for. If you cut cubes from bone-in shoulder or breast, throw the bones into the stew for added flavor. I like to stew **lamb shanks** cut into 2-inch sections (called osso buco), because they offer the added treat of the wonderful bone marrow to feast on.

I find that **leg meat** can dry out and/or fall apart when it's stewed. If you must use leg meat, choose the shank half; it has a little more collagen.

For pot-roasting, a boneless **lamb shoulder** is hard to beat. Some stores separate the shoulder into the smaller **blade portion** and **arm portion** for feeding smaller groups. If you can find the outside arm (also called a lamb shoulder cushion roast), ask the butcher to remove the upper arm bone. That leaves a great pocket for stuffing, and I think it makes the best braised stuffed lamb roast.

Whole lamb shanks are great to braise, and the meat cooks up soft and tender. The disadvantage is that they've become so popular that their price has gone up.

Lamb breast can be braised whole as a pot roast, or you can cut a pocket into it and fill it with a delicious stuffing, turning a humble cut into a crowd-pleaser. If you don't have a friendly butcher to cut the pocket, see the recipe for stuffed veal breast on page 580. It's delicious, but on the fatty side.

Goat neck, shoulder, and shank can be used in any braising recipe that calls for lamb.

Lamb and Goat Braising Cuts at a Glance

From the Shoulder

Lamb neck slices, bone in. Bony, yes, but delicious, particularly with Indian or Middle Eastern spices.

Goat neck. Like lamb, ideal for stews, especially curries.

Square-cut lamb shoulder, bone in (shoulder roast). Pot-roast whole, stuff, or cut into chunks for stew. Will feed 6 to 8. You can also buy smaller pieces.

Lamb shoulder roast, boneless (rolled shoulder roast, Saratoga roast). Pot-roast whole, stuff, or cut into chunks for stew.

Goat shoulder roast, bone in or boneless. Makes a great pot roast. Can also be cut up for stews. Good for grill-roasting.

From the Shoulder

Lamb blade chop, bone in (shoulder chop, blade shoulder chop, blade cut chop). Contains some very tender meat next to the rib bone and some chewier meat around the blade bone. If you plan to grill or cook by dry heat, look for chops with the smallest amount of blade bone and the largest amount of rib eye meat. For moist-heat cooking, any chop will do. Should be ¾ to 1 inch thick. A budget-friendly cut.

Goat blade chop, bone in. When cut from young goats (*cabrito*), suitable for dry-heat cooking. Should be ¾ to 1½ inches thick. Braise chops from somewhat older goats (*chevon*). Great in curries and tagines.

Lamb or goat arm chop, bone in (round-bone chop, arm cut chop). Ideal for moist-heat cooking. Tender enough for dry-heat cooking. Should be ¾ to 1 inch thick. A budget-friendly cut.

From the Breast

Whole lamb or goat breast, bone in. Cook whole or cut between ribs for stews and pot roast. Can also be stuffed.

Lamb or goat breast, boneless. Cut a pocket, stuff, and pot-roast, or cut into stew meat.

Lamb or goat spareribs. The breast-bone has been removed, leaving only a slab of ribs. Grill or braise. Can also be stuffed.

Rolled lamb or goat breast (pinwheels, breast pot roast). An inexpensive, rich, and delicious pot roast. A bit fatty, but oh so good.

From the Foreleg and Hind Shank

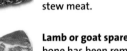

Lamb shanks (osso buco). Sold whole or crosscut. A great braise. Figure 1 shank per person. Usually sold from the foreshank, but hind shanks cut from the hind leg will be larger and more meaty.

Goat shanks. Great for strongly spiced dishes, such as chili, curries, and tagines.

WEST INDIAN GOAT CURRY

Family Meal, Rewarms Well

Serves 6

For several years, each July I visited the island of Anguilla to participate in a food and wine event. Anguilla, which is in the British West Indies, is a small, mostly barren island with little fresh water and minimal agriculture, but there are enough bushes and scrawny trees to support the wandering goats that populate the island. Occasionally some of the goats make it into one of the few island specialties, goat soup. Goat soup is actually more of a soupy curry than a soup. Many of the Caribbean islands have their own versions of goat curry that have been influenced by the strong migration of East Indians who now populate these islands.

Goat curry is served over rice and is usually accompanied by fried plantains and a bottle of very spicy homemade hot sauce.

Caribbean Curry Paste

- 1 large bunch fresh cilantro (about ½ pound), stems and leaves separated, leaves reserved for the curry
- ½ cup chopped onion
- 1 or more serrano chiles or other spicy green chiles, stemmed and seeded
- 1 2-inch piece peeled fresh ginger
- 2 teaspoons chopped fresh thyme
- 2 tablespoons Bruce's Curry Powder (page 526)
- ½ teaspoon ground allspice
- ⅛ teaspoon ground cloves
- 2 teaspoons ground cumin
- 2 teaspoons turmeric
- 2 tablespoons fresh lime juice
- 2 teaspoons ground annatto seeds (achiote; see Sources) or sweet Hungarian paprika

- 2 teaspoons salt
- 1 14-ounce can unsweetened coconut milk, stirred well

- 3 pounds boneless goat shoulder, cut into 1½-inch cubes
- 2 tablespoons peanut oil
- 2 cups chopped onions
- 1 tablespoon chopped garlic
- 1 14.5-ounce can diced tomatoes (I use Muir Glen fire-roasted)
- 2 teaspoons dark brown sugar, plus more to taste
- Salt
- Fresh lime juice
- Fresh cilantro leaves (from above)
- Cooked rice

1   **Paste:** Coarsely chop the cilantro stems and add to a blender, along with the remaining ingredients except for the coconut milk. Pour in about ¼ cup of the coconut milk and blend to form a soft paste. If it is dry, add more coconut milk; set aside the rest of the coconut milk.

2 Place the meat in a bowl and pour over the paste. Massage the paste into the meat until all the pieces of meat are well coated. Cover with plastic wrap and marinate at room temperature for 1 hour, or overnight in the refrigerator.

3 Heat the oil in a large pot or Dutch oven over medium-high heat. Add the onions and cook until soft, stirring frequently, about 5 minutes. Add the garlic and cook for 1 minute more, until softened. Scrape in the meat and all the paste. Reduce the heat to medium and cook for 5 minutes more. Stir in the tomatoes, brown sugar, and the remaining coconut milk. Bring to a boil, reduce to a simmer, cover, and cook for 1 hour. Test a piece of meat to see if it is tender. If not, cook until it is, checking every 20 minutes or so.

4 Degrease the surface of the curry. If the sauce is thin, boil to reduce the liquid and concentrate the flavors, but leave it soupy. Coarsely chop the cilantro leaves and stir half of them into the curry. Taste and add more salt, brown sugar, and/or lime juice. Serve the curry in shallow bowls over rice, garnished with the remaining cilantro leaves.

Alternative Cuts: Boneless beef chuck or lamb shoulder. Goat or lamb shanks or neck (increase the cooking time to 3 hours, or until the meat is falling off the bone). Or, if you want to be authentic, use goat ribs and let guests pick through the bones as they eat.

Cook's Notes
- During the last 20 minutes of cooking, you can add 2 cups diced (1-inch) sweet potatoes to the curry.
- This curry is nice served with Green Papaya Salad (page 271).

MEXICAN BRAISED GOAT WITH CHILES (BIRRIA DE CHIVO)

Family Meal, Fit for a Crowd, Great Leftovers, Two-for-One, Rewarms Well

Serves 8

On my frequent visits to the Mexican neighborhood of Santa Rosa, California, I often enjoy steaming bowls of various stews. One of my favorites is *birria,* a rich soupy stew made with lamb or goat. I prefer the goat version (*birria de chivo*), which is very flavorful and made with tougher bony cuts, such as ribs, shank, or neck. The meat is cooked long and slow until it almost falls off the bones, so I simply tease it off, suck on the bones, and dive into any bits of meat left behind. If you prefer, you can make your *birria* with boneless meat from the leg or shoulder.

Chile Marinade/Sauce

- 8 assorted dried chiles, such as guajillo, ancho, New Mexico, California, and/or mulato
- 1 or more jalapeño chiles, stemmed, seeded, and coarsely chopped
- 1 large onion, coarsely chopped
- 8 garlic cloves, peeled
- 1 bunch fresh cilantro, stems and leaves separated, leaves reserved for garnish
- 1 12-ounce bottle Mexican beer
- 2 teaspoons dried oregano (I use Mexican)
- 2 teaspoons cumin seeds
- ¼ teaspoon ground cinnamon
- ⅛ teaspoon ground cloves
- 1 teaspoon dried thyme
- 2 teaspoons salt
- 2 tablespoons white vinegar, or more to taste

- 8 pounds bony goat pieces, such as ribs, neck, shank, and/or shoulder, or 4 pounds boneless goat shoulder
- 2 bay leaves
  Freshly ground black pepper
  Warm corn tortillas

Garnishes

  Lime wedges
  Chopped red onion
  Salsa Verde (page 260)
  Finely shredded cabbage
  Fresh cilantro leaves (from above)

1 **Marinade:** Heat a large dry skillet over medium heat and add the dried chiles. Toast them, turning, until fragrant; take care not to burn them. Remove from the heat. When they are cool enough to handle, tear up the chiles and discard the seeds and stems. Place the chiles in a bowl and pour over enough boiling water to cover. Soak for 30 minutes, or until they are soft.

2   Drain the chiles, reserving the soaking liquid. Place the chiles in a blender with the remaining sauce ingredients and blend until a homogenous sauce forms. Place the meat in a large bowl, pour the sauce over, and mix well. Marinate for 2 hours at room temperature, or cover with plastic wrap and refrigerate overnight.

3   Preheat the oven to 325°F.

4   Place the meat and sauce in a large Dutch oven. Add the bay leaves, cover, and bake for 2½ to 3 hours, or until the meat is tender and falling off the bone. Check the stew from time to time and add some of the reserved chile soaking liquid or water if the meat is not covered with liquid. Discard the bay leaves and degrease the sauce. (*The stew can be cooled and refrigerated overnight. Remove the congealed fat and rewarm.*)

5   The sauce should be soupy but intensely flavored. If not, remove the meat and boil to reduce the sauce to suit your taste, then return the meat to the pot. Season to taste with salt, pepper, and/or vinegar.

6   Ladle into large soup bowls and serve with the tortillas and garnishes.

Alternative Cuts: Bony lamb, such as neck, shoulder, shank, or breast, or boneless lamb shoulder.

Cook's Note
- If you want to be a gracious host, remove the meat from the bones and return it to the stew before serving.

Leftovers
- Turn leftovers into soup by adding any combination of chunks of carrot, rutabaga, turnip, summer or winter squash, chayote, corn on the cob, and/or cabbage and dilute with pork or chicken stock.

THAI GOAT AND NOODLE SOUP (KHAO SOI)

Family Meal, Rewarms Well
Serves 6

Dana Younkin, the chef de cuisine of Boulevard, my wife's restaurant, oversees the cooking line and provides ideas to keep the menu exciting. I asked her to give me a recipe for the kind of food she likes to eat at home when she doesn't have to impress a roomful of paying guests. She chose *khao soi,* a simple noodle soup from Thailand, where her parents have roots.

Khao soi is a popular dish eaten at home or at simple stalls on the street. It is made with goat or lamb, or beef, chicken, or pork. Fresh kaffir lime leaves have a wonderful aromatic flavor. If you can't find them, substitute grated lime zest.

3 pounds boneless goat shoulder, cut into
    2-inch chunks

Khao Soi Marinade
1 tablespoon Thai red curry paste
1 tablespoon Asian fish sauce
2 garlic cloves, finely chopped
1 1-inch piece fresh ginger, peeled and minced
    Juice of 1 lime

Soup
1 14-ounce can unsweetened coconut milk
    (do not shake the can before opening)
2 tablespoons Thai red curry paste, or more
    to taste
2 tablespoons turmeric
1 white onion, chopped
3 garlic cloves, finely chopped
1 lemongrass stalk, tough outer leaves dis-
    carded, tender inner leaves chopped
1 2-inch piece fresh ginger, peeled and minced

4 kaffir lime leaves (see Sources) or 2 teaspoons
    finely grated lime zest
3 tablespoons Asian fish sauce, or more to taste
3 tablespoons *kecap manis* (sweet soy sauce),
    or 3 tablespoons soy sauce plus 2 teaspoons
    unsulfured molasses, or more to taste
¼ cup firmly packed dark brown sugar
¼ cup fresh lime juice, or more to taste
8 cups homemade chicken stock, canned
    low-sodium chicken broth, or water

1 pound fresh Chinese egg noodles (available
    in most Asian grocery stores) or dried
    linguine

Garnish
2 cups bean sprouts
½ cup chopped fresh cilantro
½ cup thinly sliced cucumber
½ cup thinly sliced scallions

1 **Marinade:** Place the meat in a bowl. Combine the marinade ingredients and rub all over the meat. Cover with plastic wrap and marinate for at least 2 hours at room temperature, or overnight in the refrigerator.

2   **Soup:** Remove the "cream" on top of the coconut milk and add it to a large pot. Reserve the remaining liquid. Heat the cream over medium heat until it is fragrant and separating. Add the red curry paste and turmeric and cook for 2 to 3 minutes. Add the onion, garlic, lemongrass, and ginger and cook for 5 minutes, or until soft.

3   Add the remaining soup ingredients and the reserved coconut milk and bring to a simmer. Add the goat meat and its marinade. Cover and simmer for 30 minutes. Taste and add more red curry paste if you want the soup spicy. Cover and continue to simmer for a total of 1½ to 2 hours, or until the meat is tender. Adjust the seasonings, adding more *kecap manis*, fish sauce, and/or lime juice to taste. Remove the lime leaves.

4   Meanwhile, bring a pot of water to a boil. Cook the noodles until tender and drain.

5   Divide the noodles among six large shallow bowls. Ladle the meat and soup over the noodles and serve with the garnishes.

Alternative Cuts: Goat ribs; boneless beef short ribs or chuck; Boston butt or country-style pork ribs (reduce the cooking time by 30 minutes); or boneless lamb shoulder or shoulder chops.

Leftovers
- This soup rewarms very well. Gently reheat and serve over freshly cooked noodles.

TURKISH POMEGRANATE-GLAZED LAMB SHOULDER CHOPS AND CARROTS

Cheap Eats, Rewarms Well

Serves 6

I've never been to Turkey, but I love Turkish food, especially the way aromatic spices and sweet-tart pomegranate syrup are used to flavor stews like this one. Here the braising liquid is reduced until it becomes thick and sticky and deliciously coats the meat and carrots. For best results, buy carrots that are ½ to ¾ inch thick and 6 to 7 inches long. Serve this dish with bulgur or a rice pilaf.

6 lamb blade shoulder chops (about ½ pound each)

Turkish Spice Rub

1 teaspoon Aleppo pepper (see Sources), crushed red pepper flakes, or cayenne pepper

1 teaspoon salt

1 teaspoon ground cumin

¾ teaspoon freshly ground black pepper

½ teaspoon ground cardamom

¼ teaspoon freshly grated nutmeg

2 tablespoons olive oil

1 tablespoon butter

2 tablespoons grated fresh ginger

½ cup finely chopped shallots

1 cup finely chopped onions

1 cup homemade lamb stock (see page 168) or canned low-sodium chicken broth

1 cup pomegranate molasses or syrup (see Sources)

2 pounds medium carrots of various colors, peeled and halved lengthwise

½ pound parsnips, peeled and halved lengthwise

Salt and freshly ground black pepper

Garnish

½ cup fresh pomegranate seeds (see Cook's Notes)

¼ cup toasted pine nuts (see page 273)

2 tablespoons shredded fresh basil leaves (see Cook's Notes)

2 tablespoons shredded fresh mint leaves (see Cook's Notes)

1 Cut each chop into 2 pieces by cutting between the flat side of the blade bone and the meat.

2 **Rub:** Combine all the rub ingredients in a small bowl. Sprinkle the rub over the chops. Let sit for at least 30 minutes at room temperature, or wrap in plastic wrap and refrigerate overnight.

3. Heat the oil and butter in a large deep skillet or Dutch oven over medium-high heat. Add the chops (you may need to do this in batches) and brown for 2 to 3 minutes per side. Set the chops aside. Add the ginger, shallots, and onions to the pan, reduce the heat to medium, and cook until soft, about 5 minutes. Add the stock and bring to a boil, scraping up the browned bits from the bottom of the pan. Add the pomegranate molasses and the chops. Reduce the heat to a simmer, cover, and cook for 40 minutes, until the chops are tender. If not yet tender, continue cooking, checking every 15 minutes. Remove the chops and set aside. Degrease the liquid.

4. Add the carrots and parsips to the pan, cover, and cook for 10 minutes, or until tender. Remove the carrots and parsnips and set aside. Bring the liquid to a boil and reduce until it thickens and becomes very syrupy, 5 to 10 minutes. Return the carrots and parsnips to the pan and reheat over very low heat, turning frequently. When the sauce forms a glaze, add the chops and turn them until they are reheated and coated in the glaze. Season to taste with salt and pepper.

5. Place the chops on a platter and arrange the vegetables over them. Spoon over any remaining glaze, scatter on the pomegranate seeds and pine nuts, sprinkle over the basil and mint, and serve.

Alternative Cuts: Goat or pork blade chops.

Cook's Notes

- Instead of the spices called for in the rub, you can substitute 1 tablespoon Baharat (page 536).

- To remove the seeds from a pomegranate, cut the pomegranate in half through the stem and flower ends. Hold each half cut side down over a bowl and give it a good smack with a large wooden spoon. The seeds will drop out. Remove and discard any pieces of white membrane.

- To shred basil and mint leaves (a technique known as *chiffonade*), stack 2 or 3 leaves and roll them lengthwise into a tight cylinder. Thinly slice into ⅛-inch-wide slices. Unroll, and you will have nice, even-looking shreds.

FLORENTINE LAMB POT ROAST WITH BLACK OLIVES

Family Meal, Great Leftovers, Rewarms Well

Serves 6 to 8

While steak Florentine cooked over wood is justifiably famous, fine braised dishes are also typical of Tuscan cuisine. After we tried this dish at a friend's home in Tuscany, Cathy Whims, the chef at Nostrana in Portland, Oregon, and the Italian food expert Faith Willinger talked our host into sharing her recipe. Cathy fine-tuned it a bit and shared her version with me. Like so many great Italian recipes, this relies on only a few good ingredients to produce a delicious result. Cathy likes to use Italian olives, such as brine-cured Gaeta olives or mild, herby, and aromatic taggiascas. If you can find them, use them, but she has also had good results with niçoise olives and the easy-to-find Greek kalamata olives.

1 3- to 4-pound boned and tied lamb shoulder roast, trimmed of excess fat	1 cup dry white wine
Salt and freshly ground black pepper	1 28-ounce can whole tomatoes (I use San Marzano), drained and chopped
¼ cup extra-virgin olive oil (I use Tuscan)	1¼ cups pitted Gaeta, taggiasca, niçoise, or kalamata olives (see Cook's Notes)
5 garlic cloves, minced	
1 tablespoon minced fresh rosemary	

1 Season the lamb all over with salt and pepper. Heat the oil in a Dutch oven over medium-high heat. Add the lamb and brown on all sides, about 10 minutes. Transfer to a plate.

2 Reduce the heat to medium, add the garlic and rosemary, and cook, stirring, until the garlic is pale gold, about 2 minutes. Add the white wine, scrape up any browned bits from the bottom of the pot, and boil until the wine has almost evaporated, about 5 minutes.

3 Add the tomatoes and olives and return the lamb to the pot, fat side up. Cover and cook over low heat for 1½ to 2 hours, or until the meat is tender. Remove the lamb from the sauce and cover with aluminum foil. Degrease the sauce and, if it is too thin, boil to reduce it and concentrate the flavors. Season to taste with more salt and pepper.

4 Remove the twine from the lamb and discard. Slice the meat and spoon over some sauce. Serve, passing the remaining sauce at the table.

Alternative Cuts: Bone-in lamb shoulder; shoulder lamb chops; boneless leg of lamb, whole or cut into 2-inch chunks; or bone-in goat shoulder, whole or cut into chops.

Cook's Notes

- Gaeta olives come from the village of Gaeta in central Italy and are sold salt-cured or wet-brined; use the brined variety. They have a pleasant taste and a mild, salty flavor. Taggiasca olives are also mild and are cured in brine with herbs, such as bay, rosemary, and thyme.

- Serve the meat over creamy polenta.

- To cook this as a stew, cut the meat into 2-inch chunks, season with salt and pepper, toss in all-purpose flour to coat, and proceed with the recipe. You may have to brown the meat in batches.

Leftovers

- Serve leftovers cut into pieces, along with the sauce, over pasta. Or use the braising liquid as a sauce for pasta and serve with grated pecorino cheese.

PAKISTANI FEAST-DAY LAMB WITH LIME AND FRESH CILANTRO

Fit for Company, Fit for a Crowd, Two-for-One, Rewarms Well, Great Leftovers

Serves 6, with leftovers

Pakistani weddings are grand celebrations lasting for several days. Tables are adorned with exotic curries, vegetable and rice dishes, and, at the center, a whole young lamb or goat. The meat may be spit-roasted or, more likely, cooked long and slow, braising in its own juices. My recipe was inspired by this grand tradition, but it uses a modest cut, lamb shoulder. Like any pot roast, it's easy to make, so don't wait for your daughter's marriage to prepare it. You can serve it as a main course for a family meal, or as a centerpiece for a multicourse Pakistani or Indian banquet, adding curries, vegetable side dishes, lentils, rice, pickles, and chutneys. The recipe calls for lots of fresh cilantro; once it has cooked for a long time, it takes on a wonderful mellow, herbaceous, and citrusy flavor.

Curry Rub

- 2 teaspoons Bruce's Curry Powder (recipe follows)
- 2 teaspoons ground cumin
- 2 teaspoons salt
- 2 teaspoons freshly ground black pepper
- 1 teaspoon ground coriander

- 1 3- to 4-pound boned, rolled, and tied lamb shoulder roast, trimmed of excess fat
- 2 tablespoons olive oil
- 3 cups thinly sliced onions
- 6 carrots, peeled and cut into ½-inch chunks

- 2 tablespoons finely chopped garlic
- 1 tablespoon minced fresh ginger
- 2 tablespoons Bruce's Curry Powder
- 2 tablespoons finely grated lime zest
- 3 tablespoons fresh lime juice
- 2 bunches fresh cilantro (about 8 ounces each), stems finely chopped, leaves coarsely chopped and kept separate
- 2 cups homemade lamb stock (see page 168) or canned low-sodium chicken broth
  Salt and freshly ground black pepper
  Cooked basmati rice

1. **Rub:** Combine all the ingredients in a small bowl and sprinkle over the lamb. Let sit for 1 hour at room temperature, or cover with plastic wrap and refrigerate overnight.

2. Preheat the oven to 325°F.

3. Heat the oil in a Dutch oven over medium-high heat. Add the lamb and brown on all

sides, about 10 minutes. Remove the lamb and set aside. Pour off all but 3 tablespoons of the fat. Reduce the heat to medium and add the onions and carrots. Cook, stirring, until the onions begin to soften, about 10 minutes. Stir in the garlic and ginger and cook for 1 minute more. Add the curry powder and stir until the vegetables are well coated. Add the lime zest, lime juice, cilantro stems, about half of the cilantro leaves, and the stock. Bring to a boil. Add the lamb, cover, and bake for 1½ hours, or until the meat is quite tender.

4 Transfer the pot to the stove top. Remove the lamb and degrease the surface of the sauce. The sauce should be soupy but intensely flavored; if it is too thin, bring to a boil and reduce until full-flavored. Stir in the remaining cilantro leaves and season with salt and pepper to taste. Cut the lamb into chunks or slices. Arrange over the rice on a platter, spoon plenty of sauce over the meat, and serve.

Alternative Cuts: Boneless goat shoulder or boneless leg of lamb. Also good with whole bone-in lamb or goat shanks or chunks of lamb or goat meat.

Cook's Note
- If you like a richer, thicker gravy, combine ½ cup plain whole-milk Greek yogurt, ¼ cup sour cream, and 2 tablespoons all-purpose flour in a small bowl. Whisk into the degreased sauce and gently heat until the sauce thickens.

Leftovers
- Turn into Lamb Biryani (page 527).

BRUCE'S CURRY POWDER

Makes a generous ½ cup

Start with whole spices and grind them in a spice grinder, a mortar with a pestle, or a clean coffee grinder.

2 teaspoons freshly ground cumin seeds	2 teaspoons freshly ground brown or yellow mustard seeds
2 tablespoons freshly ground coriander seeds	⅛ teaspoon ground cinnamon
1 tablespoon turmeric	3 tablespoons sweet Hungarian paprika
1 teaspoon freshly ground cardamom seeds	2 teaspoons cayenne pepper
⅛ teaspoon freshly ground cloves	1 teaspoon freshly ground fenugreek seeds (see Sources)
2 teaspoons freshly ground fennel seeds	

Combine all the ingredients in a small bowl. Store in a tightly sealed jar. (*The curry powder keeps for 1 to 2 months.*)

LAMB BIRYANI

Family Meal, Fit for Company

Serves 4 to 6

Calling this a biryani may upset devotees of authentic Indian cooking, because this recipe is not prepared like the traditional version. The dish is usually made from scratch by layering partially cooked basmati rice with cooked meat in a pot. The pot is then sealed and the ingredients slowly steamed until the rice is tender. But my recipe, in which the cooked lamb and rice are simply stirred together in a pot, is a very delicious way to use leftover curried meat to produce a quick and satisfying dish. The key is to have sufficient liquid to adequately cook the rice. My ratio is 1½ cups liquid for each 1 cup rice.

2 cups basmati rice

2 tablespoons ghee or butter (see Cook's Notes)

3 cups thinly sliced onions

2 cups ⅜-inch diced peeled carrots

1 tablespoon Bruce's Curry Powder (page 526)

½ teaspoon saffron threads

   Salt and freshly ground black pepper

3 cups liquid (leftover sauce from Pakistani Feast-Day Lamb [page 524] plus canned low-sodium chicken broth as needed)

1 cup diced dried apricots

1 cup raisins

2 cups diced lamb from Pakistani Feast-Day Lamb

½ cup roasted almonds

1 Place the rice in a strainer and wash well with cold water. Set aside.

2 Melt the ghee in a large Dutch oven over medium heat. Add the onions and carrots, cover, and cook until browned, stirring occasionally, about 15 minutes. Stir in the curry powder and saffron until the vegetables are well coated. Stir in the rice and season to taste with salt and pepper. Add the liquid, apricots, and raisins. Bring to a boil, reduce the heat to a simmer, cover, and cook for 15 minutes. Add the lamb, cover, and cook for 5 to 10 minutes more, or until the rice is tender. Season to taste with salt and pepper. Mound on a large platter, sprinkle with the almonds, and serve.

Cook's Notes

- Ghee is Indian clarified butter. It is cooked slightly longer than regular clarified butter, so the milk solids brown, adding a nutty flavor to the butter. It can be purchased in Indian markets (or see Sources).

- Instead of Pakistani Feast-Day Lamb, you can substitute leftover West Indian Goat Curry (page 513) or any braise or stew that yields 2 cups cooked meat and 3 cups sauce.

GRILL-BRAISED MOROCCAN LAMB SHANKS WITH HONEY GLAZE

Rewarms Well, Great Leftovers

Serves 4

Tagines, the stews of Morocco, are made in earthenware pots with cone-shaped lids that share the same name. Because the fuel supply was traditionally dear in this arid land, everything was made in the single pot, without browning or searing. The intense flavors come from long, slow cooking and the copious use of aromatic herbs and spices. Moroccan cooking often blends sweet flavors with savory, as in this dish, in which the cooked shanks are glazed with honey. In true Moroccan style, the stew and the lamb shanks are served over couscous. If you want to be thoroughly authentic, eat with your hands only. Because I love to eat these shanks in warm months, I have chosen to grill-braise them outdoors. See Cook's Note for the more traditional indoor method.

3 cups chopped onions

1 tablespoon chopped garlic

1 tablespoon sweet Hungarian paprika

1 teaspoon turmeric

1 teaspoon ground ginger

1 teaspoon cayenne pepper

½ teaspoon ground coriander

½ teaspoon ground cumin

1 teaspoon dried mint

   Salt and freshly ground black pepper

¼ cup finely chopped cilantro stems (reserve the leaves for garnish)

4 cups water

1 cup drained canned diced tomatoes

2 tablespoons fresh lemon juice, or more to taste

4 meaty lamb shanks (about 4 pounds total), trimmed of most external fat, each tied with 3–4 loops of butcher's twine

2 cups cooked chickpeas (freshly cooked or canned)

4 carrots, peeled and cut into 2-inch chunks

2 cups 1½-inch chunks peeled turnips

2 cups instant couscous

Honey Glaze

¼ cup honey

3 tablespoons braising liquid (from above)

1 teaspoon harissa (optional), store-bought or homemade (recipe follows)

2 teaspoons fresh lemon juice

1 teaspoon dried mint

Garnish

   Fresh cilantro leaves (from above)

   Harissa (optional)

1. Set up a charcoal or gas grill for indirect grilling (see page 11 for more on grilling).

2. Toss the onions and garlic with the spices, mint, 1 teaspoon salt, 1 teaspoon pepper, and the cilantro stems in a large Dutch oven until well combined. Stir in the water, tomatoes, and lemon juice, then add the shanks. Place the pot on the area of the grill without a fire. Cover the pot, close the grill lid, and cook for about 1 hour, until the meat is fork-tender. If not tender, continue to simmer, covered, checking every 15 minutes. It may take an additional 30 minutes to 1 hour. Transfer the shanks to a platter.

3. Add the chickpeas, carrots, and turnips to the pot and place over direct heat. Bring to a simmer and cook, uncovered, until the vegetables are tender, 15 to 20 minutes. Remove from the heat and degrease the surface. Taste the liquid. If it's too thin, remove the vegetables, return the pot to the heat, bring the liquid to a boil, and reduce to concentrate the flavors. Return the vegetables to the pot. Season to taste with salt, pepper, and lemon juice. (*The shanks and sauce can be cooled and refrigerated separately overnight; bring the shanks to room temperature, add to the sauce, and reheat over low heat on the stovetop.*)

4. Meanwhile, prepare the couscous according to the directions on the box and keep warm.

5. **Glaze:** Combine all the ingredients in a small saucepan. Heat over medium heat for 1 to 2 minutes, or until the mixture forms a light syrup. Brush the glaze over the shanks and grill them over direct medium heat, turning and basting them with the glaze, until the glaze bubbles and darkens with a few black spots, 5 to 7 minutes total; take care not to burn the glaze. Remove immediately.

6. To serve family style, mound the couscous in a large shallow serving bowl. Spoon over the vegetables and plenty of braising sauce. Remove the twine from the shanks, place on top, and scatter with the cilantro. Serve with harissa, if desired.

Alternative Cuts: Goat shanks, whole lamb or goat neck, or whole bone-in lamb or goat breast.

Cook's Note
- To braise these shanks indoors, follow the directions in step 2 for assembling the braising liquid. Add the shanks, cover, and cook in a 350°F oven for 1 to 2 hours, checking after 1 hour and every 15 minutes after that, or until the meat is fork-tender. Remove the shanks, add the chickpeas and vegetables, and cook on top of the stove for 15 to 20 minutes, or until the carrots and turnips are tender. You can serve as is or glaze the shanks under the broiler, 4 to 5 inches from the heat source, turning and basting them frequently, for 5 to 7 minutes, or until bubbly and darkened.

HARISSA (MOROCCAN SPICY RED PEPPER PASTE)

Makes about ¼ cup

Good canned or bottled varieties of harissa can be found in Middle Eastern specialty stores (see Sources). Because harissa can be very hot, a little goes a long way, but it keeps well in the refrigerator. I make my own and try to use a variety of ground or flaked spicy red peppers, such as Aleppo from Syria and Antep from Turkey. Or, use a combination of cayenne and crushed red pepper flakes. If you like harissa superhot, increase the amount of peppers to suit your taste.

2 tablespoons hot Hungarian paprika or ground California chile

2 teaspoons ground or flaked hot pepper of your choice (see headnote), or more to taste

½ teaspoon *each* ground cumin, ground coriander, ground fennel seeds, turmeric, and freshly ground black pepper

1 teaspoon salt

1 tablespoon red wine vinegar, or more if needed

2 tablespoons olive oil

Combine the spices and salt in a small bowl. Drizzle over the vinegar and stir to form a paste. If it is too dry, add more vinegar as needed. Taste and add more hot pepper if desired. Whisk in the oil and stir until smooth. (*Harissa is best made a day or two ahead so that the flavors can mellow. Store in a jar in the refrigerator for 2 to 3 weeks.*)

SAMI'S STUFFED LAMB BREAST

Cheap Eats, Fit for Company, Rewarms Well
Serves 8

My first experience with Iraqi food was at the house of Sami Zubaida, a great cook and professor of Middle Eastern politics at University of London, who had invited a dozen friends to dinner. When we sat down, two beautifully roasted stuffed breasts of lamb were delivered to the tables on a large platter. Stuffed with rice, nuts, and dried fruits, the lamb breasts had been braised, then roasted, and they had a burnished reddish-brown patina. They were accompanied by another platter, holding enormous carrots that were about 3 inches in diameter and had been hollowed out and filled with ground lamb.

I soon learned that Sami's family came from Baghdad's Jewish community, which has a long history and a well-developed culture, including its own style of cooking dating back many centuries. In the 1960s, as a result of one of the Arab-Israeli wars, Sami's family and the rest of the Iraqi Jewish community were thrown out with no warning, and Sami and many other displaced Iraqi Jews ended up in London.

This dish takes a little time to prepare. Although lamb breast is a humble cut, it's worthy of any special occasion.

Baghdad Basmati Rice Stuffing

- 1 cup ¼-inch diced peeled carrots
- 1 cup ¼-inch diced red onions
- 5 cups cooked basmati rice
- ½ teaspoon turmeric
- 2½ teaspoons Baharat (recipe follows)
- 1 teaspoon Aleppo pepper (see Sources), hot Hungarian paprika, or New Mexico chile powder
- ½ cup dried currants or raisins
- ½ cup dried apricots, cut into ½-inch dice
- 2 tablespoons chopped fresh mint
- ½ cup roasted almonds
- ½ cup shelled pistachios
- ½ cup thinly sliced scallions
- 4 tablespoons (½ stick) butter, melted
  Salt and freshly ground black pepper

- 2 large bone-in lamb breasts or 3 smaller lamb breasts (about 5 pounds total)
  Salt and freshly ground black pepper

Baghdad Braising Sauce

- 2 cups chopped onions
- 1 cup chopped peeled carrots
- 2 teaspoons Aleppo pepper, hot Hungarian paprika, or New Mexico chile powder
- 2 pinches of saffron threads
- 1 tablespoon Baharat (recipe follows)
- 1 cup homemade lamb stock (see page 168) or canned low-sodium chicken broth, or more if needed
- 1 cup peeled, halved, seeded, and diced vine-ripened tomatoes, or 1 cup canned diced tomatoes, drained
- 2 tablespoons tomato paste
  Salt and freshly ground black pepper

1 **Stuffing:** Bring a small pot of lightly salted water to a boil. Add the carrots and cook for 4 minutes. Add the red onions and cook for 1 minute more. Drain and add to a large bowl, along with all the remaining stuffing ingredients. Toss until the rice is coated with butter and everything is well mixed. Season to taste with salt and pepper. Set aside.

2 Lay a lamb breast fat side up on a cutting board. Remove any fell (papery membrane) by loosening one end and tearing it off, and trim away any excess external fat. With a sharp knife, cut a pocket between the rib bones and the meat along the length of each breast. The pocket should come to about ½ inch from the opposite side and the ends. Open up the pocket and fill it with half (or one third, if using 3 breasts) of the rice stuffing. Seal the pocket with small metal skewers. Repeat with the remaining breast(s). Season well with salt and pepper.

3 Preheat the oven to 350°F.

4 Heat roasting pan set over two burners over medium-high heat. Add the breasts, fat side down (no oil is needed), and brown for 3 to 5 minutes. Flip and brown the bone side for 3 to 5 minutes. Remove the lamb and set aside.

5 **Sauce:** Pour off all but 2 tablespoons of fat from the roasting pan and add the onions and carrots. Reduce the heat to medium and cook, stirring, until the vegetables begin to soften, about 5 minutes. Add the Aleppo pepper, saffron, and baharat and stir until the vegetables are well coated. Add the stock and bring to a boil, scraping up any browned bits from the bottom of the pan. Stir in the tomatoes and tomato paste until well mixed.

6 Return the lamb to the roasting pan on top of the sauce, fat side up. Cover the pan tightly with aluminum foil. Roast for 45 minutes, then flip the breasts over and check to make sure there is plenty of liquid in the pan, adding water or stock if needed. Reseal the pan with foil and roast for another 45 minutes, then flip over again so that the fat side is up. Reseal the pan, roast for 30 minutes more, then remove the foil. Spoon some sauce over the top of the lamb, adding more water or stock if needed, and roast for 30 minutes more (2½ hours total), until the meat is very tender and beginning to pull away from the bone. If it is not tender, continue to roast, checking the meat and liquid level every 20 minutes and adding more liquid if needed. When done, transfer the lamb to a warmed platter and cover loosely with aluminum foil.

7 Pour the sauce into a saucepan and degrease the surface. Taste the sauce, which should be full-flavored; if needed, boil it to concentrate the flavors. Season to taste with salt and pepper.

8   To serve, cut the breasts into 2-rib pieces and ladle over some of the sauce. Serve the extra sauce on the side.

Alternative Cuts: Boneless leg of lamb, lamb shoulder, or boneless breast of goat. Make only a half recipe of the stuffing. The cooking time and method are the same as for the lamb breast.

Cook's Notes

- Aleppo pepper (see Sources) has a sweet, raisiny flavor and is mildly spicy. Use more or less to suit your taste. Hungarian hot paprika or ground New Mexico chiles are acceptable substitutes.

- If you have extra rice stuffing after stuffing the breasts, bake it in a buttered casserole for 20 to 30 minutes and serve on the side.

Leftovers

- Make a stew of the leftovers: First remove the stuffing from the breast and transfer it to a casserole. Remove the meat from the bone, then combine the meat and sauce with cooked okra or green beans or roasted chunks of eggplant and heat until hot. Bake the rice at 350°F until warmed through and serve on the side.

BAHARAT

Makes about ½ cup

In Arabic, *baharat* means "spices," and the blend is used all over the Middle East, from Turkey to Iraq. There are many variations, depending on the country and family recipe. Baharat can be purchased from Middle Eastern specialty markets (or see Sources), but you can easily make your own. If possible, grind the spices from whole seeds.

2 tablespoons freshly ground black pepper

2 tablespoons ground coriander

2 tablespoons dried oregano (I use Greek)

1 tablespoon dried mint

1 tablespoon ground cumin

2 teaspoons ground fennel seeds

2 teaspoons ground brown mustard seeds or yellow dry mustard powder (I use Colman's)

1 teaspoon ground cinnamon

½ teaspoon freshly grated nutmeg

¼ teaspoon ground cloves

½ teaspoon ground allspice

Combine all the ingredients in a small bowl and mix well. Store in a tightly sealed jar. (*This will keep for 2 to 3 months.*)

DIAMOND LIL'S LAMB RIBLETS

Cheap Eats, Family Meal, Comfort Food
Serves 6 to 8

Sometimes recipes reflect the diversity of a family's history. This recipe came to me from Hiro Sone, chef/owner of Terra, my favorite restaurant in Napa Valley. Hiro, who is from Japan, is one of the most talented chefs I know. His wife, Lissa Doumani, is from a Lebanese family. Her grandmother, Diamond Lil, got her name because she loved to visit the gambling tables in Las Vegas. Her skills shone in the kitchen, however, and I spent time at her table both as a young boy and many years later over Thanksgiving meals. Every flavor I tasted was so exotic, and she always elevated the main ingredient's flavor to the maximum no matter how ordinary it may have been. This is Hiro's interpretation of Diamond Lil's recipe for a very humble cut, lamb riblets.

2 tablespoons olive oil

1 cup thinly sliced onions

Salt and freshly ground black pepper

2 tablespoons finely chopped garlic

1 teaspoon minced fresh ginger

½ teaspoon ground cumin

½ teaspoon turmeric

⅛ teaspoon ground cinnamon

2 large bone-in lamb breasts (4–5 pounds total), fell (papery membrane) removed, trimmed of excess fat, and cut into individual riblets

2 cups homemade lamb stock (see page 168) or canned low-sodium chicken broth

1 cup tomato puree

Fresh lemon juice

Garnish

½ cup plain whole-milk Greek yogurt mixed with 1 tablespoon fresh lemon juice

2 tablespoons toasted sesame seeds (see Step 3, page 569)

2 teaspoons sumac (optional; see Sources)

2 tablespoons chopped fresh cilantro

1 Preheat the oven to 350°F.

2 Heat the oil in a large Dutch oven over medium heat. Add the onions and salt and pepper to taste. Cover and cook, stirring occasionally, for 10 minutes, or until the onions are beginning to color. Stir in the garlic and ginger and cook for 1 minute more. Stir in the cumin, turmeric and cinnamon until the onions are well coated with the spices. Add the riblets, broth, tomato puree, and a good sprinkling of salt and pepper.

3 Cover the pot and place in the oven. Check the riblets after 1 hour to see if they are tender. If not, continue to cook, checking every 15 minutes.

4   Remove the ribs from the pot. Degrease the sauce and boil until the sauce becomes syrupy. Season to taste with salt, pepper, and lemon juice. Return the ribs to the sauce and rewarm.

5   Pile the ribs on a platter, pour over the sauce, and drizzle with the yogurt. Sprinkle with the sesame seeds, sumac (if using), and cilantro, and serve.

Alternative Cuts: Bone-in goat riblets or ½-inch-thick lamb or goat rib chops (cook rib chops for only about 20 minutes).

Cook's Note

- Hiro serves these riblets with a stew of eggplant and chickpeas and medallions of lamb tenderloin, but I like them with bulgur or rice and a side salad. You can also offer the riblets as finger food for a gathering around the TV or for a cocktail party. Be sure to provide lots of napkins.

LAMB RIBLETS WITH ASIAN TAMARIND GLAZE

Cheap Eats, Family Meal

Serves 4 to 6

I first encountered tamarind in Amsterdam long ago as a college student "doing Europe." Since my finances were starvingly modest, I sought out places that offered large portions at bargain prices, but I was also intent on trying new flavors and exotic cooking. Amsterdam's numerous Indonesian restaurants fit the bill perfectly. With four or five friends, I could order *Rijssafel,* a huge mound of rice accompanied by a dozen or more small dishes of various tamarind-flavored stews, pickles, vegetables, and glazed meats—all for a few guilders. More recently, after visiting Singapore, Vietnam, and China, countries that also use tamarind, I purchased some of the sour, fruity paste from my local Asian grocery store and began to experiment. Here tamarind flavors a delicious marinade, which is then turned into a glaze. Like pork spareribs, lamb breast becomes tender when roasted long and slow, and its ample fat keeps it succulent when cooked to well-done. Note that the riblets must marinate overnight.

Asian Tamarind Marinade
- ¼ cup tamarind paste (see Sources)
- ¼ cup water
- 2 tablespoons honey
- 1 teaspoon unsulfured molasses
- 2 tablespoons soy sauce
- 1 tablespoon Asian fish sauce
- 2 tablespoons minced fresh ginger

- 1 tablespoon minced garlic
- 1 tablespoon finely chopped scallions
- 2 teaspoons Asian toasted sesame oil
- 2 teaspoons Sriracha sauce, or more if needed

- 2–3 bone-in lamb breasts (4–5 pounds total), fell (papery membrane) removed, and trimmed of excess fat

1. **Marinade:** Combine the tamarind and water in a small bowl, then stir in the remaining ingredients. Taste and add more Sriracha to suit your taste, if desired. Place the lamb in a large zipper-lock bag, add the marinade, seal the bag, and turn and shake the bag so that all the pieces are coated with the marinade. Refrigerate overnight, turning the bag from time to time to redistribute the marinade.

2. Preheat the oven to 300°F.

3. Line a baking sheet or broiler pan with aluminum foil and place a rack in the pan. Remove the lamb from the marinade and set it on the rack, fat side up. Transfer the

marinade to a small saucepan. Roast the lamb for 1½ hours, or until the meat begins to pull away from the bone and is tender when tasted. While the meat is roasting, boil the marinade until it just turns syrupy enough to use as a glaze, 3 to 5 minutes.

4   When the meat is done, increase the oven temperature to 450°F. Baste the lamb with the glaze and roast until the glaze is bubbly and beginning to darken, about 10 minutes. Let the lamb rest for 10 minutes, loosely covered with aluminum foil. Cut the breasts into individual riblets. Serve any remaining glaze on the side as a dipping sauce.

Alternative Cuts: Lamb rib or shoulder chops; lamb kebabs; pork ribs or chops; goat breast; goat ribs and shoulder chops. Chops and kebabs take much less time: 7 to 10 minutes.

Cook's Notes
- You can also roast the lamb on a grill set up for indirect grilling (grill-roasting). Follow the directions for Grill-Roasted Cherry-Glazed St. Louis Ribs (page 395).
- Serve the riblets with Green Papaya Salad (page 271) and jasmine rice.

LAMB TONGUES ESCABECHE

Cheap Eats, Fit for Company
Serves 6 to 8

Escabeche — in which a tangy black sauce of vinegar, chopped vegetables, and olive oil is spooned over cooked food, such as fried fish, and allowed to sit, and then served at room temperature — is popular in many Spanish-speaking countries around the globe. This recipe comes from Ryan Farr, a San Francisco chef and self-taught butcher, a trade that many young culinarians are now pursuing. Trained as a chef, Ryan found that he really enjoyed the butcher's arts and began making sausages and tasty treats like pork rinds. He poaches the tongues in a full-flavored stock containing spices and vinegar, which gives the tongues a mild pickled taste. He then marinates them in a delicate mixture of sherry vinegar, cooked carrots, and shallots. While this recipe requires a few days to complete, it is well worth the effort.

2 pounds lamb tongues

1½ cups kosher salt (I use Diamond Crystal)

Poaching Liquid

3 quarts water

2 onions, halved

2 heads garlic, halved horizontally

2 carrots, peeled and halved

8 fresh thyme sprigs, tied in a bunch with butcher's twine

1 tablespoon black peppercorns

1 cup sherry vinegar

2 teaspoons salt

½ cup olive oil

1 cup thinly sliced peeled carrots

½ cup thinly sliced shallots

1 tablespoon chopped garlic

½ teaspoon chopped fresh thyme

1 bay leaf

½ teaspoon salt

½ teaspoon freshly ground black pepper

2 tablespoons fresh lemon juice

½ cup sherry vinegar

¼ cup water

¼ cup chopped fresh flat-leaf parsley

2 teaspoons finely grated lemon zest

1 Scrub the tongues under cold water until clean; pat dry. Place in a plastic storage container. Pack in the salt, cover, and refrigerate overnight.

2 **Poaching liquid:** The next day, combine all the poaching liquid ingredients in a large pot. Remove the tongues from the salt and rinse thoroughly. Add the tongues to the poaching liquid. Slowly bring the liquid to a low simmer, being careful not to let it come to a full boil. Simmer for 1½ hours, or until the tongues are very tender. Remove the tongues with a slotted spoon; transfer the liquid to a bowl or other container. When

the tongues are cool enough to handle, peel off the skin. Return the tongues to the poaching liquid and cool to room temperature, then cover and refrigerate overnight.

3 The following day, remove the tongues from the liquid; discard the liquid. Pat the tongues dry and cut in half lengthwise. Heat ¼ cup of the oil in a large skillet over medium-high heat. Sear the tongues, cut side down, until lightly browned, about 5 minutes; work in batches if necessary. Place the tongues in a casserole or shallow nonreactive pan.

4 Reduce the heat under the skillet to medium and add the remaining ¼ cup oil. Add the carrots, shallots, garlic, thyme, bay leaf, salt, and pepper and cook until the carrots are crisp-tender, about 10 minutes. Add the lemon juice, vinegar, and water. Bring to a simmer, then immediately pour over the tongues. Toss with the parsley and lemon zest. Cool to room temperature before serving. (*The tongues can be covered with plastic wrap and refrigerated overnight; bring to room temperature before serving.*)

Cook's Note
- Serve over sturdy salad greens, such as curly endive, frisée, or chicory, using some of the sauce to dress the greens. Or serve over boiled, chilled, and sliced potatoes, tossed with some of the sauce and garnished with hard-boiled eggs and chopped parsley or watercress.

LAMB TONGUES

Lamb tongues are appearing more frequently on restaurant menus — and with good reason. They have great flavor, they're very tender, and they're equally good warm or cold. I love them served over warm sliced potatoes or as a garnish to a potato salad.

Lamb tongues cook relatively quickly and have a delicate, faintly lamby flavor. They are an inexpensive cut, and it's worth searching for them. Look in Mexican and Middle Eastern markets, or, if you buy lamb at a farmers' market or directly from a producer, ask them to save you the tongues. The tongues freeze well, so you can buy several pounds.

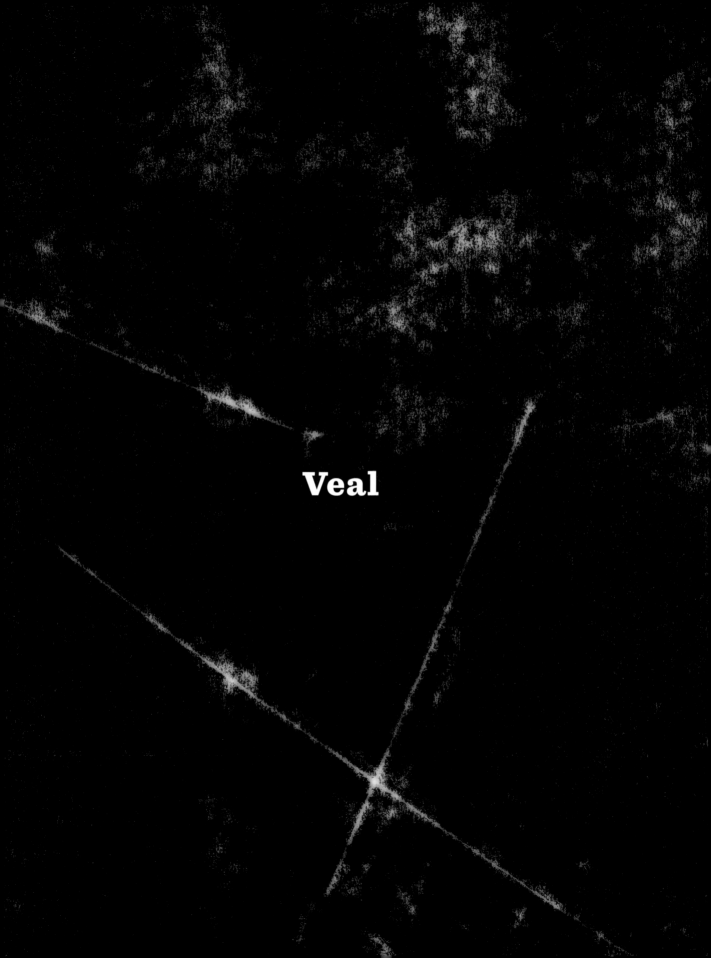

Veal

Veal

Rediscovering Veal

Veal has never been a significant part of the American red-meat diet (yes, veal is red meat). It reached its peak yearly consumption in 1944 — no doubt because of the wartime scarcity of beef — at about 8½ pounds per capita. Its consumption has declined ever since, with a scant ½ pound per person consumed as of 2004 (the most recent statistic). Most often, it is served in restaurants that offer veal scaloppine and osso buco or delicacies like sweetbreads and calf's liver. But for most Americans, it seldom if ever finds its way to the dinner table. It's not even sold in most mainstream supermarkets.

Veal has always been the most expensive red meat, but the reason for its decline in popularity has more to do with concerns about how it is raised. In the 1980s, photographs of veal calves raised in confined stalls first hit the news, and exposés about inhumane treatment changed our attitudes toward veal. Many Americans decided they would no longer eat veal, and several states passed laws prohibiting raising calves in confinement.

Changing Veal Choices

Traditional white veal (usually light pink) is from calves that have not been fed mother's milk but rather, a milk-replacement formula made from whey proteins and other milk by-products, vitamins, and minerals — but not iron, so that the meat stays pale. Because of shrinking demand, many of the traditional producers who raise formula-fed white veal have decided to switch from crates to group corrals, where five to seven calves are raised together in a corral inside a barn. The change is gradual, but as of this writing, two of the largest veal producers have switched to corrals, and many other producers are committed to changing by 2017.

Pasture-Raised Veal

A few producers have taken a different approach, returning to the old practice of raising calves out in the pasture, where they can feed on mother's milk and forage. Strauss Brands (the largest producer) calls the veal they raise this way "Free Raised" (the term is trademarked). They raise the heirloom French breed Limousin, but they don't say if the calves are fed solely on milk and grass, so their diet may be supplemented with grain. Veal calves that are allowed to graze produce meat with a distinct pink or rose color and a more beefy flavor than traditional white, formula-fed veal. Strauss veal can be purchased at Whole Foods Markets, and other pasture-raised veal can be found at farmers' markets or bought directly from the producers (visit www.eatwild.com for a list of local producers).

Veal from calves raised outdoors also goes by several other names: pasture-raised, range-fed, rose veal, or grass-fed veal. Usually these animals are raised without the use of antibiotics and they are fed a vegetarian diet. Giving hormones to any type of veal is not allowed. Pasture-raised veal calves go to the market at twenty-two to twenty-four weeks of age. Just as with beef or lamb, if the label or marketing materials say the veal is grass-fed, the producer must comply with all USDA requirements. In addition, veal labeled "USDA Certified Organic" must meet all the government requirements that certified beef or lamb must meet. Let me urge those of you who were once veal eaters to try pasture-raised veal. I think you'll enjoy its delightfully subtle beefy flavor.

Veal from calves raised on pasture is leaner, reddish gray to red in color, with fat that may have a yellowish tinge. The meat will have more depth of flavor than formula-fed veal. One caveat: Don't rely on color alone to determine if the veal is pasture-raised, because barn-raised calves whose diet is supplemented with grain will also have meat with a rosy color. Check with the producer to determine exactly how the calves were raised. Because the meat can be quite lean, take care not to overcook chops and roasts from pasture-raised animals when using dry heat; I recommend medium-rare to medium doneness.

Non–Formula-Fed Veal

This category might better be called "not-just-formula-fed." It includes calves raised in barns, or sometimes in pastures, that are fed grain, hay, and other foods in addition to milk or formula. Often these animals are allowed to grow to an older age (six to nine months) and to about 750 pounds. The meat will have a stronger beefy flavor.

Formula-Fed Veal

The majority of the veal that comes to market is raised indoors — in crates or sometimes in groups in corrals. These animals may be given low levels of antibiotics, both to ward off infection and to boost growth, but not hormones, which are for-

"NATURAL" AND "ALL-NATURAL" VEAL

You may come across the terms "natural" or "all natural" on veal labels. As with other red meats, these terms have no meaning unless they are qualified with how the animals are raised: no antibiotics, an all-vegetarian diet, not raised in confinement, etc. So if you see this term, ask for details.

If the label says "no hormones," remember that this does not distinguish the veal from that of other producers, because it is illegal to give hormones to any veal calves.

MY IDEAL VEAL

I buy pasture-raised veal, and the best comes from animals that have reached a sufficient age (about twenty-four weeks) to have meat with great flavor, yet are still young enough that it is very tender. I still remember the veal rib chop I got years ago from Jamie Nicoll's Summerfield Farms in Culpeper, Virginia. Nicoll believes that tra-ditional farming methods produce a supe-rior product, and he's always avoided meth-ods like confinement and drugs. The chop was cooked medium-rare and was succu-lent and tender, with a mild beef flavor.

Keep in mind that pasture-raised veal is seasonal. The calves should be raised when grass is at its very best—which is the time mother's milk will be at its best too.

bidden by federal regulations. They are fed a formula of milk by-products and other nutrients. The animals are sent to market at four to five months of age and will weigh about 450 pounds. The meat is bland-tasting and light pale pink, with creamy white fat.

"Bob" Veal

This meat comes from very young calves, those up to three weeks old and weigh-ing 150 pounds or less. Bob veal is inexpensive, but the cuts are very small, and the meat is very chewy and almost tasteless.

Veal Grades

Veal is slaughtered under state or USDA supervision, but as with beef and lamb, grading is optional and expensive. Veal grading is based on marbling. Good-quality grades for veal are Prime, Choice, and Good.

Many veal producers, especially farmers who raise the animals on pasture, choose to leave their veal ungraded. Most graded veal comes from formula-fed an-imals and most of it will be graded Choice. The small supply of Prime-grade veal usually is sold to high-end restaurants.

How to Buy Veal

Pasture-Raised Veal

- The meat should be slightly moist and rose to light reddish in color, with no blemishes.
- The fat may be slightly yellow, but it shouldn't have any brown edges.
- There should be no strong odor.

Formula-Fed Veal

- The meat should be slightly moist and pale to reddish pink in color, with no blemishes. Very dark meat indicates that it comes from a more mature calf (six to nine months old).
- The fat should be smooth and white to ivory in color, with no brown edges.
- There should be no strong odor or ammonia smell.
- Avoid wet, soft, or very pale meat, which may be from "bob" calves. Small cut sizes indicate tasteless bob veal as well.

Primal Cuts of Veal

Veal is divided into six primal cuts:

- Most cuts from the **shoulder** primal—which include the shoulder arm roast, blade roast and chops, and neck—are best cooked by moist heat.
- The **rib** primal produces my favorite chop, the rib chop, as well as the expensive and very special rib roast.
- From the **loin** primal come the T-bone chops, which are leaner than rib chops. Boneless loin can be cut into thin slices for very tender scaloppine.
- The **breast** primal, which has ample fat and great flavor, is by far my favorite cut for braising.
- The **foreleg** primal produces shanks. The **leg** primal yields shanks, leg roasts, and sirloin roasts. When sliced, veal shanks are called osso buco. The leg and sirloin are usually separated into individual muscle groups and sliced into thin cutlets. A whole leg cooked medium-rare to medium makes a spectacular roast, but you will need to special-order it.

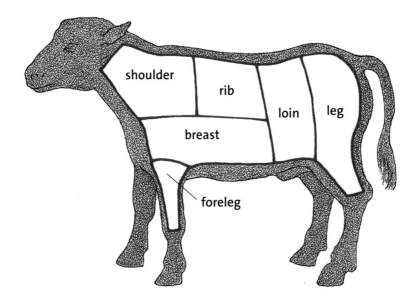

Veal will keep for 2 to 4 days in the refrigerator and for 2 to 4 months in the freezer.

Follow the guidelines for storing raw and cooked meat and for thawing meat on page 6.

Cooking Veal

Lean, tender cuts, such as chops, roasts, and cutlets, should be cooked with dry heat (grilling, roasting, frying). Pasture-raised veal is best cooked to medium-rare, while formula-fed veal, which has a milder taste, needs to be cooked to medium to develop more flavor. Because veal is lean, it's best not to cook it beyond medium.

With moist-heat cooking (braising and stewing), the meat is usually cooked to temperatures from 160°F to 190°F or more, at which point the collagen turns into gelatin. The best way to determine doneness is to see how easily a fork can penetrate the meat—or to taste it.

Veal Doneness

The following charts are based on what I believe give the best cooking results. They are lower than what the USDA recommends (see page 43 for more details). Err on the side of caution when cooking for those who are immunologically compromised or pregnant. My charts begin at medium-rare because I don't think rare veal is very good.

Use these temperatures for dry-heat methods such as roasting, grilling, and frying. Because carry-over heat will vary depending on the size of the piece of meat and the intensity of the heat source, consult the individual recipes to determine exactly at what internal temperature the meat should be removed from the heat source and follow the resting times given with the recipes.

Medium-Rare. Pasture-raised veal can be reliably cooked to this popular degree of doneness (formula-fed veal is best cooked to medium). The meat will be quite pink in the center, with no bloodred areas, and will have begun to turn grayish around the edges.

MEAT	REMOVE FROM HEAT	IDEAL TEMPERATURE (AFTER RESTING)	USDA RECOMMENDS
Veal chops	125°F to 130°F	130°F to 135°F	145°F
Veal roasts	120°F to 125°F	130°F to 135°F	145°F

Medium. The meat will be pink in the center and gray at the periphery. The texture will be quite firm, and the grain compact. Formula-fed veal should be cooked to this degree of doneness to develop its best flavor. This degree of doneness is also fine for marbled cuts of pasture-raised veal, such as the rack.

MEAT	REMOVE FROM HEAT	IDEAL TEMPERATURE (AFTER RESTING)	USDA RECOMMENDS
Veal chops	130°F to 135°F	140°F to 145°F	145°F
Veal roasts	130°F to 135°F	140°F to 145°F	145°F

Medium-Well. The meat will be almost uniformly gray, with a pinkish tint near the bone.

MEAT	REMOVE FROM HEAT	IDEAL TEMPERATURE (AFTER RESTING)	USDA RECOMMENDS
Veal chops	140°F to 145°F	150°F to 155°F	N/A*
Veal roasts	140°F to 150°F	150°F to 155°F	N/A*

* The USDA does not provide temperatures for this degree of doneness.

Veal Chops, Steaks, and Cutlets

Butchers tend to use the terms chops and steaks interchangeably for veal, which can lead to confusion. Most often, the term **veal chop** refers to 1- to 2-inch bone-in slices cut from the loin or rib primal. Thick slices from the shoulder or sirloin (with or without the bone) are often called **veal steaks** — examples are veal blade steaks or veal sirloin steaks — but some butchers may call these chops.

Rib chops and **loin chops** have great flavor and take well to marinades and herby rubs. My favorite is the rib chop, which has ample fat and yields succulent results even when cooked to medium doneness. Veal steaks cut from the **shoulder blade** or **forearm** can be chewy, but they're ideal when braised and can be used in any of my recipes for braised pork chops or braised beef steaks.

Veal **cutlets** are also called scallops, scaloppine (Italian), or *escalopes* (French). All these terms refer to boneless slices cut about ¼ inch thick and of varying diameters, from single muscles from the leg, sirloin, or loin. They are expensive, but usually a 3- to 4-ounce portion is adequate. Because cutlets are thin, they cook quickly and risk overcooking and drying out. To prevent this, recipes often call for coating them first in flour or bread crumbs, which protects the meat and provides a nice crust.

Many recipes call for pounding veal cutlets before cooking. This can overtenderize the veal and make it mushy, so I don't usually pound my veal. But if you're not sure how tender your cutlets are, fry up a small piece of meat and taste it. If it doesn't meet your standard for tenderness, pound the cutlets *gently*, taking care not to tear them.

Veal Chops, Steaks, and Cutlets at a Glance

From the Rib and Loin

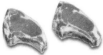

Rib chop, bone in. Look for chops 1¼ to 1½ inches thick. They have just enough fat to be tender and juicy. Very expensive.

Frenched rib chop, bone in. Look for chops 1¼ to 1½ inches thick. A more elegant presentation, with fewer pockets of fat. Even more expensive than unfrenched chops.

Loin chop, bone in (veal T-bone chop). Look for chops with a nice piece of the tenderloin section, 1¼ to 1½ inches thick. A little leaner than rib chops. Expensive.

From the Shoulder

Shoulder blade steak, bone in or boneless (shoulder chop, shoulder steak, blade chop). Look for steaks ¾ to 1 inch thick. They can be a bit chewy, but can be grilled to medium doneness without drying out. Best marinated. A good buy.

From the Leg

Sirloin steak, boneless (boneless veal sirloin chop). Ideal when marinated. Very lean, but can be grilled to medium-rare and still be juicy. When cut thin, can be used as cutlets.

Leg cutlets, boneless (veal scallops, scaloppine, *escalopes*). Cut from any single leg muscle or sirloin. Buy ½ to ¾ inch thick and pound to ⅛ to ¼ inch thickness, or buy ¼ inch thick. Very expensive.

THAI MARINATED VEAL CHOPS WITH CHILE-LEMONGRASS DIPPING SAUCE AND SKEWERED EGGPLANT

Fit for Company

Serves 4

These chops are seasoned twice: They take a brief turn in an Asian marinade seasoned with lemongrass, ginger, and garlic, which is also used to baste them as they grill. Then a spicy dipping sauce, served to guests in small bowls so that they can dip bites of meat and eggplant, provides another flavor punch.

If you can't find fresh lemongrass, you can replace it with an equal amount of grated lime zest.

Thai Lemongrass Marinade

- 1 tablespoon minced garlic
- 1 tablespoon minced fresh ginger
- 1 tablespoon finely chopped lemongrass (tender inner white leaves only) or 1 tablespoon finely grated lime zest
- 2 teaspoons seeded and finely chopped jalapeño chile
- 1 tablespoon finely chopped scallion greens (reserve white part for dipping sauce)
- 1 tablespoon Asian fish sauce
- 2 tablespoons soy sauce
- 1 teaspoon light brown sugar
- ¼ cup fresh lime juice
- ¼ cup peanut oil

- 4 1- to 1¼-inch-thick veal rib or T-bone loin chops (2–2½ pounds)
- 4 Japanese eggplants, cut into ¾-inch-thick ovals or rounds

Chile-Lemongrass Dipping Sauce

- 1 teaspoon minced garlic
- 1 tablespoon finely chopped lemongrass (tender inner white leaves only) or 1 tablespoon finely grated lime zest
- 2 tablespoons finely chopped scallion whites
- 2 tablespoons chopped fresh cilantro
- 1 tablespoon chopped fresh basil (I use Thai)
- 3 tablespoons fresh lime juice
- 1 teaspoon light brown sugar
- 3 tablespoons Asian fish sauce
- 1 tablespoon soy sauce
- 2 teaspoons Sriracha sauce, or more to taste, plus more for serving (see Cook's Note)

- 2 12-inch metal skewers

1 **Marinade:** Combine all the ingredients in a small bowl. Reserve ¼ cup for basting. Place the chops in a large zipper-lock bag and add the remaining marinade. Seal the bag, then turn and shake so that the chops are bathed in the marinade. Place the bag in a pan or bowl and marinate for 2 hours at room temperature.

2 Set up a charcoal or gas grill for direct grilling over medium-high heat (see page 11 for more on grilling).

3 Thread the eggplant slices onto two parallel skewers, pushing the skewers through the skin (this prevents them from slipping when you turn them). Set aside.

4 **Sauce:** Combine all the ingredients in a small bowl. Set aside. (*The sauce can be made up to 6 hours ahead, covered, and refrigerated.*)

5 Remove the chops from the marinade, shaking off the excess; discard the marinade. Place the chops on the grill and grill for 2 to 3 minutes. Baste the chops with the reserved marinade, turn, and grill for 2 to 3 minutes more. Baste again, turn, and grill for 2 minutes, then brush one last time and grill for 2 minutes more. Move the chops to a cooler part of the grill and cook until the internal temperature reaches 130°F on an instant-read thermometer, for medium. Remove the chops to a platter, cover loosely with aluminum foil, and let rest for 5 minutes.

6 Meanwhile, brush each eggplant skewer with marinade. Grill for 2 minutes, baste, turn, and grill for 2 minutes more, then baste again. Continue to baste and turn until the eggplant is quite soft to the touch and nicely browned, about 2 minutes. If they begin to burn, transfer the skewers to a cooler part of the grill to finish cooking.

7 Remove the eggplant from the skewers and arrange on the platter with the chops. Drizzle 2 tablespoons of the dipping sauce over the chops and eggplant and serve the remaining sauce on the side, along with Sriracha.

Alternative Cuts: Boneless veal sirloin chops, pork rib or loin chops, or goat rib chops.

Cook's Note
- If you don't have Sriracha, substitute ½ teaspoon Tabasco sauce plus 1½ teaspoons ketchup in the dip. Then add more Tabasco to the dipping sauce to suit your taste, or let guests add their own.

PAN-GRILLED VEAL CHOPS WITH TOMATO–BLUE CHEESE BUTTER AND CHERRY TOMATO SALAD

In a Hurry, Grass-Fed Veal, Fit for Company

Serves 4

Certain flavors have an affinity for each other: tomato and blue cheese, basil and tomato, blue cheese butter and grilled meat. With these combinations in mind, I came up with a couple of simple condiments that enhance veal chops, which can be somewhat bland. The tomato–blue cheese butter is ideal with grass-fed veal, but also goes well with the lighter formula-fed veal.

There are many types of blue cheeses, from milder Danish blues to the full-flavored and pungent Roquefort, and trying different varieties is a great way to experiment with this recipe. I like the blue cheese from Rogue Creamery in Oregon and often use a younger, milder one called Oregon Blue, but you may enjoy the stronger Rogue River Blue with veal as well. I also like making this butter with Stilton and Gorgonzola.

Cherry tomatoes remain sweet and flavorful long after other tomatoes have gone out of season, but if it's the middle of winter and you can find only tasteless ones, skip the salad. In the summer, substitute ripe heirloom tomatoes, cut into ½-inch dice, for the cherry tomatoes.

Tomato–Blue Cheese Butter

- 3½ ounces blue cheese (see headnote), diced
- 4 tablespoons (½ stick) butter, softened
- 1 tablespoon minced shallot
- 2 teaspoons coarsely ground black pepper
- 1 tablespoon tomato paste
- 1 teaspoon Aleppo pepper (see Sources) or ½ teaspoon cayenne pepper
- ½ teaspoon vodka (optional; see Cook's Notes)

- 4 1¼- to 1½-inch-thick veal rib or T-bone loin chops (2–2½ pounds total)
- 1 large garlic clove, cut in half
- Salt and freshly ground black pepper

Cherry Tomato Salad

- 1 cup halved cherry tomatoes or diced vine-ripened tomatoes
- 1 tablespoon finely chopped shallot or scallion
- 1 tablespoon extra-virgin olive oil
- 2 teaspoons sherry vinegar
- 6 fresh basil leaves, cut crosswise into thin shreds
- Salt and freshly ground black pepper

- 1 tablespoon olive oil

1. **Butter:** Pulse the blue cheese in a food processor until it has the texture of coarse meal. Add the remaining ingredients and process to form a homogenous paste. Spread a 12-x-8-inch sheet of plastic wrap on a work surface and scrape the butter onto the plastic wrap. Shape and roll the mixture into a log about 2 inches in diameter; seal the butter in the wrap. Refrigerate until firm, at least 1 hour, or until ready to use. (*You can make the butter up to a day ahead and refrigerate it. You can also freeze the butter for up to 2 months.*)

2. Rub the chops on both sides with the cut sides of the garlic. Discard the garlic. Season the chops with about ¼ teaspoon salt and ⅛ teaspoon pepper per side. Set aside.

3. No more than 30 minutes before you are ready to cook the veal chops, make the tomato salad (if made too far in advance, it will become watery): Toss the tomatoes, shallot, oil, vinegar, and basil together in a small bowl. Season to taste with salt and pepper. Set aside.

4. Heat a large cast-iron skillet or ridged grill pan over high heat. Brush the chops with the oil and add to the pan, making sure not to overcrowd the chops; if necessary, cook them in 2 batches. Sear for 2 to 3 minutes, or until nicely browned on the first side. Flip and sear the other side for 2 minutes. Reduce the heat to medium-high and cook for 3 minutes more per side, or until the internal temperature registers 125°F to 130°F on an instant-read thermometer for medium-rare or 130°F to 135°F for medium. Remove the chops to a warm platter and top each with a ¼-inch-thick pat of Tomato–Blue Cheese Butter. Let rest for 5 minutes, loosely covered with aluminum foil.

5. Smear the mostly melted butter over the chops, divide the tomato salad among the plates, and serve.

Alternative Cuts: Veal sirloin chops, boneless veal loin chops, or veal blade chops (blade chops should be cooked to medium doneness so that they are not chewy).

Cook's Notes
- The vodka in the Tomato–Blue Cheese Butter recipe enhances the flavors of the tomato and cheese. If you wish, leave it out.
- The butter makes enough for 8 to 12 veal chops. It is also excellent over grilled steaks and thick-cut pork chops.
- The veal chops can be grilled outdoors over a charcoal or gas grill. Follow the instructions for grilling veal chops in Thai Marinated Veal Chops (page 552).

VEAL CUTLETS WITH SCOTCH WHISKEY PAN SAUCE

In a Hurry, Fit for Company

Serves 4

The key to moist and tender veal cutlets is to cook them very quickly in hot fat so that they do not lose their juices. Don't overcrowd the pan; cook them in 2 batches and then rewarm them briefly once the pan sauce is finished. The sauce has a lovely undertone of smoke from the wee dram of scotch and the smoky Spanish paprika.

Once you master the simple technique in this basic recipe, you can vary the sauce to your heart's content. I have suggested two other sauces that work equally well; see page 561.

Spanish Tarragon Rub

Salt and freshly ground black pepper

1 garlic clove, minced

1 teaspoon chopped fresh thyme

1 teaspoon chopped fresh tarragon

1 teaspoon Spanish paprika (*pimentón de la Vera*; see Sources)

1¼ pounds ¼-inch-thick veal cutlets, cut from the leg or sirloin

Pan Sauce

2 tablespoons butter plus 1 tablespoon olive oil, or all olive oil, plus more as needed

½ pound mushrooms, sliced

1 tablespoon finely chopped shallot or scallion

Salt and freshly ground black pepper

½ cup scotch

½ cup dry white wine

1 cup homemade veal stock (see page 168) or canned low-sodium chicken broth

¼ cup heavy cream (optional)

A few drops of Tabasco or other hot sauce (optional)

1 tablespoon chopped fresh chervil or flat-leaf parsley

1 **Rub:** Mix together 1½ teaspoons salt, 1 teaspoon pepper, the garlic, thyme, tarragon, and paprika in a small bowl. Rub the mixture all over the veal cutlets.

2 Heat a large heavy skillet over medium-high heat and add half the butter and/or oil. Add 2 or 3 of the cutlets and cook until light brown, 1 to 2 minutes per side. Remove and set aside on a platter while you cook the remaining cutlets in batches, adding more butter and/or oil as needed (and removing them from the pan).

3   **Sauce:** Pour off all but 2 tablespoons of the fat from the pan. Add the mushrooms and shallot and sprinkle with salt and pepper to taste. Cook, stirring, until the mushrooms have exuded their liquid and begun to color lightly. Remove from the heat, carefully add the whiskey, and then ignite with a match or by slightly tipping the pan toward the flame. Return to the heat and shake the pan until the flames die down. Add the white wine and stock and bring to a boil, scraping up any browned bits from the bottom of the pan. Boil until the liquid begins to thicken. Add the cream (if using) and reduce until slightly thickened. Season to taste with salt and pepper and add the Tabasco (if using). Return the veal cutlets to the pan and cook for 1 minute to warm through.

4   Serve immediately, garnished with a sprinkling of chervil.

Alternative Cuts: Veal cutlets cut from the loin (which are even more expensive), bone-in or boneless veal chops cut ½ to ¾ inch thick (increase the cooking time to 3 minutes per side), or ¼-inch-thick pork cutlets from the loin or sirloin.

Cook's Note
- If you would like an extra hit of tarragon, garnish the veal with 2 teaspoons chopped fresh tarragon instead of chervil or parsley.

Other Pan Sauces for Veal Cutlets

FRESH FENNEL PAN SAUCE

1 medium fennel bulb, fronds removed and chopped for garnish, bulb trimmed and cut into ¼-inch dice

2 ounces dried coppa or prosciutto, finely chopped

2 teaspoons minced garlic

1 cup dry marsala

½ cup homemade veal stock (see page 168) or canned low-sodium chicken broth

Once the veal is cooked and set aside, add the diced fennel to the pan. Cook over medium heat for 5 minutes, stirring occasionally. Stir in the coppa and garlic and cook for 1 minute more. Pour in the marsala and bring to a boil, scraping up any browned bits from the bottom of the pan. Reduce to ½ cup. Add the stock and reduce until the sauce just starts to become syrupy. Return the veal to the pan and cook for 1 minute to rewarm. Serve garnished with the chopped fennel fronds.

SUMMER FRUIT PAN SAUCE

Summer fruits such as Mission figs, firm peaches, firm nectarines, firm apricots, or firm yellow-fleshed plums all work well. Cut figs in half through the stem and flower ends; cut peaches or nectarines into ½-inch-thick slices; quarter apricots or plums.

1 cup summer fruit (see headnote)

2 tablespoons butter (optional)

½ teaspoon light brown sugar

1 cup fruity white wine, such as Sauvignon Blanc or dry Riesling

Salt and freshly ground black pepper

Once the veal is cooked and set aside, add the fruit to the pan (if there is no fat in the pan, add 1 tablespoon of the butter). Sprinkle with the sugar and cook over medium-high heat for 1 minute. Gently turn over the fruit and cook until it just softens, about 1 minute more; don't overcook. Using a slotted spoon, remove the fruit from the pan and set aside, covered to keep warm. Add the white wine to the pan and bring to a boil, scraping up any browned bits from the bottom of the pan. Boil until the sauce just becomes syrupy. Reduce the heat to medium and stir in the remaining butter (if desired) to add richness and body to the sauce. Season to taste with salt and pepper. Return the veal to the pan and heat for 1 minute. Arrange the veal on a platter with the fruit on top, pour the sauce over all, and serve.

SICILIAN-STYLE INVOLTINI

In a Hurry, Fit for Company

Serves 4 to 6

Involtini are veal cutlets that are stuffed and rolled. They may be cooked slowly in a sauce or skewered and grilled. In this recipe, they are rolled in bread crumbs and baked until they are brown and crispy. I first had this Sicilian version of involtini while staying at COS Winery in southern Sicily, which is co-owned by Guisto Occhipinti. His sister, Angela, provides simple and delicious meals that go very well with the family's fine red wine. On the day she was cooking her involtini, I was, as usual, hanging out in the kitchen. This recipe, the result of my experimentation, is very close to what I tasted in Italy.

3 cups soft bread crumbs from day-old French or Italian bread	12 ¼-inch-thick veal cutlets (1¼–1½ pounds)
1½ cups freshly grated pecorino cheese or Parmigiano-Reggiano (about ⅓ pound)	12 scallions
1 tablespoon chopped fresh thyme	24 bay leaves (preferably fresh)
About ½ cup olive oil, plus more as needed	4 6-inch wooden skewers, soaked in water for 30 minutes
Salt and freshly ground black pepper	

1 Preheat the oven to 350°F.

2 Spread 1½ cups of the bread crumbs on a baking sheet and bake until nicely golden brown, stirring the crumbs occasionally, about 10 minutes. Remove from the oven and let cool. Increase the oven temperature to 425°F.

3 When the crumbs are cool, pulse them several times in a food processor until finely ground. Combine with ¾ cup of the cheese in a medium shallow bowl and set aside.

4 For the stuffing, place the remaining 1½ cups bread crumbs in a medium bowl. Stir in the remaining ¾ cup of the cheese and the thyme. Toss with ½ cup olive oil. Season to taste with salt and pepper. Set aside.

5 One at a time, place each veal cutlet between two sheets of plastic wrap and gently pound to a thickness of ⅛ inch. Lightly sprinkle on both sides with salt and pepper. Cut each cutlet into 2 equal pieces. Spread about 2 tablespoons of the stuffing on each cutlet half and roll up, starting from a long side. Set aside.

6 Trim the roots from each scallion and cut off enough of the green part to leave about a 4-inch piece of white. Set aside.

7　Brush each cutlet generously with some olive oil and roll in the toasted bread crumb mixture, pressing gently so that the crumbs adhere. When all the rolls are breaded, thread a bay leaf, then a veal roll crosswise, then a scallion, another veal roll, and finally another bay leaf onto a skewer. Repeat with the remaining ingredients. Generously oil a baking sheet and lay the skewers on it.

8　Bake for 10 minutes, or until the involtini turn golden. Brush with oil, turn over, and bake for 8 to 10 minutes more, or until golden brown and crisp. Remove from the skewers and discard the bay leaves. Serve 2 or 3 scallions and 4 to 6 rolls per person.

Alternative Cuts: Pork cutlets cut from the loin.

Cook's Notes

- Don't use store-bought toasted bread crumbs. They taste more like cardboard than bread.

- You can also grill the skewers. Don't bread them. Brush them with olive oil and sprinkle with salt, pepper, and chopped fresh thyme. Grill over medium-high heat, turning occasionally, for 6 to 8 minutes total.

Veal Roasts

The best veal roast for dry-heat roasting is the **rib roast** (also called rack of veal or veal standing rib roast). Considerably smaller than a beef rib roast, it is ideal for small elegant dinners. Delicious as it is, it can be difficult to find. Butchers who sell veal are more likely to cut the rib rack into chops, so you may have to special-order it.

Bone-in **loin roast** (sometimes called saddle of veal) is another great cut for roasting. Some butchers may offer roasts cut from the leg or sirloin. Both the **sirloin** and the **top round leg roast** are good for roasting. Be careful not to overcook them, because they can dry out.

Veal Roasts at a Glance

From the Rib

Frenched, rib roast, 6 ribs (rack of veal, standing rib roast). An elegant and delicious roast. Makes 6 generous portions, or remove the meat from the bones and slice to feed 8 people. Very expensive.

From the Leg

Sirloin roast, boneless (rolled and tied double sirloin roast). Easy to carve and tender.

From the Shoulder (Chuck)

Shoulder roast, boneless (veal chuck shoulder clod, veal shoulder arm roast, rolled veal shoulder roast). Can be roasted, but may be a bit chewy. Better used for pot roast. Also a good cut for stewing meat. Good buy. Look for a 4- to 6-pound roast, which will serve 8 or more.

Arm roast, bone in or boneless (veal clod roast). My favorite shoulder roast. Lots of rich flavor. Dry-roast or pot-roast. Good buy.

ROASTED HERB-MARINATED VEAL RACKS

Fit for Company, Fit for a Crowd

Serves 12

Although you may find a 7-bone veal rib roast, I recommend that you buy 6-bone roasts, because the meat near that last rib (closest to the shoulder) can be a bit tough. Each 6-bone rack can easily feed 6 people, with each person receiving a chop with the bone attached. If you want to stretch the roast a bit, you can remove the meat from the bones once it is cooked, cut it into thinner slices, and serve the bones separately to those who want them. Crisscrossing the bones of the two roasts makes for a dramatic presentation. I prefer veal roasted to an internal temperature of 125°F to 135°F, when it will be between medium-rare and medium and faintly pink.

Note that the roasts must be marinated overnight.

Fennel and Herb Marinade

- 4 garlic cloves, peeled
- 1 tablespoon chopped fennel fronds (see Cook's Note)
- 6 fresh sage leaves
- 2 teaspoons fresh thyme leaves
- 2 teaspoons fresh savory or rosemary leaves
- 2 tablespoons salt
- 2 teaspoons coarsely ground black pepper
- 3 tablespoons olive oil

- 2 6-bone racks of veal, chine bones removed, fat trimmed to ¼ inch, rib bones frenched (4–6 pounds each)
- Extra-virgin olive oil (optional)

1. **Marinade:** With the motor running, drop the garlic through the feed tube of a food processor. Stop the machine and scrape down the sides of the bowl. Add the remaining ingredients and process for 30 seconds, to form a wet paste. Smear the mixture all over the roasts. Wrap in plastic wrap, place in a baking pan or on a platter, and marinate in the refrigerator overnight.

2. Unwrap the roasts and lay them back to back in a roasting pan with the bones crisscrossed and pointing upward. Let stand at room temperature for 2 hours.

3. Preheat the oven to 450°F, with a rack in the lower third of the oven.

4. Roast the veal fat side up for 15 minutes. Reduce the oven temperature to 350°F and roast for 30 minutes more. Check the internal temperature with an instant-read ther-

mometer: it should read 125°F for medium-rare or 130°F for medium. If they are not ready, continue to check every 15 minutes until it reaches your preferred doneness. Remove the roasts from the oven, cover loosely with aluminum foil, and allow to rest for 15 to 20 minutes.

5   To serve, slice between the bones and serve a chop per person. Or remove each rack of bones by slicing between the rack and the meat, slice the meat about ½ inch thick and serve the bones separately. Drizzle the sliced meat with extra-virgin olive oil (if using).

Alternative Cuts: Two whole bone-in loins of veal (6 to 8 pounds).

Cook's Note

- I love to serve this roast with roasted fennel. Cut 6 fennel bulbs into 6 wedges each through the root end. (Save some fronds to use in the marinade.) Toss with plenty of olive oil and season with salt and pepper. Spread out in a baking pan and place in the oven when you turn it down to 350°F. Turn the fennel over after 15 minutes and check again after 15 minutes. The fennel is done when it is soft and the edges are becoming nice and browned. Roasted fennel is also a great side dish for roast pork.

Ground Veal

The meat marked "ground veal" at the butcher counter most likely comes from trimmings and cuts that are difficult to sell, such as the leg or flank. The best is made from meat cut from the chuck (shoulder). If your butcher grinds meat to order, ask for it — or grind it yourself at home. Aim for 15 percent fat for adequate moisture.

Because veal is richer in collagen than beef or pork, the ground meat tends to hold together better, and because of this binding quality, veal is often combined with beef and pork in recipes for meat loaf or meatballs. On its own, ground veal makes excellent meatballs, with a moist but firm texture. Its delicate taste goes well with a large range of spices and flavors, particularly Asian ingredients, such as soy sauce and ginger.

GRINDING MEAT AT HOME

Plan to grind meat the day that you purchase it so that it's at maximum freshness. If you want to be extra cautious, follow the advice of the food science writer Harold McGee. To kill surface bacteria, he brings a pot of water to a boil and blanches the large chunk of meat for 30 to 60 seconds. He immediately transfers the meat to an ice bath, then drains it and pats it dry. Otherwise, simply use freshly purchased meat directly from the refrigerator.

- To keep the fat firm and the meat cold during chopping, place the clean food processor bowl and the blade in the freezer for 30 minutes before you begin.
- Cut the meat into ¾-inch cubes. If you are not grinding the meat immediately, refrigerate it.
- Place no more than ¾ pound meat at a time in the food processor. Use the pulse switch in 2-second bursts to produce ⅛- to ¼-inch pieces of meat. Don't overprocess, or you'll end up with meat slurry.
- You can also use a meat grinder fitted with the ¼-inch plate.
- Use the ground meat immediately, or wrap it and freeze (see page 7) for up to 2 months.

VEAL YAKITORI PATTIES

In a Hurry, Fit for a Crowd

Serves 4

Yakitori restaurants are numerous and popular in Japan, and it's easy to see why. These tasty grilled skewered treats offer a variety of flavors, and they are inexpensive. The classic yakitori is made with diced or ground chicken, formed into meatballs, skewered, and slathered in a sweet soy glaze, not unlike teriyaki. Instead of chicken, I use ground veal, which has a little more flavor and a wonderful consistency, and instead of skewering meatballs, I form patties, which are much easier to grill. Serve them with grilled scallions and steamed rice, or shape them into burgers and serve on toasted buns (see Cook's Note).

Veal Patties

- 1¼ pounds ground veal
- 1 teaspoon minced garlic
- 2 teaspoons minced fresh ginger
- 2 tablespoons finely chopped scallion whites
- 1 teaspoon honey
- 1 tablespoon soy sauce
- 1 large egg, lightly beaten
- 2 teaspoons cornstarch
- ½ teaspoon freshly ground black pepper
- ½ teaspoon salt

- 2 tablespoons sesame seeds

Sweet Soy Glaze

- ¼ cup mirin (sweet rice wine) or sweet sherry
- ¼ cup soy sauce
- 1 tablespoon real maple syrup or honey
- 1 tablespoon dark brown sugar
- 2 teaspoons minced fresh ginger
- 2 tablespoons fresh lemon juice
- 1 teaspoon cornstarch mixed with 1 tablespoon cold water

- 16 scallions, trimmed to about 8 inches
  Cooked jasmine rice

1. **Patties:** Combine the ground veal with the remaining ingredients in a medium bowl. Squeeze and mix the mixture with your hands until well blended. Form into 8 equal patties, about ½ inch thick. Place on a plate, cover with plastic wrap, and refrigerate until you are ready to grill.

2. Set up a charcoal or gas grill for medium-high heat (see page 11 for more on grilling).

3. Toast the sesame seeds in a small dry skillet over medium heat, stirring occasionally, for 3 to 5 minutes, or until lightly golden and fragrant. Transfer to a small bowl and set aside.

4   **Glaze:** Combine all the ingredients except the cornstarch mixture in a small saucepan. Bring to a boil, then stir in the cornstarch mixture. Continue to boil, stirring, until lightly thickened, 15 to 30 seconds. Set aside.

5   Grill the patties for about 3 minutes per side, or until lightly browned. Brush with the glaze and turn over. Grill for 2 minutes more, then brush again, flip, and grill for 2 additional minutes, taking care not to scorch the glaze. Remove the patties from the grill. Cover to keep warm.

6   Place the scallions on the grill, brush them with the glaze, and grill until soft and slightly charred, about 5 minutes. Turn them frequently so as not to burn the glaze.

7   Right before serving, brush the patties and scallions on all sides with the glaze and then sprinkle with the toasted sesame seeds. Serve with rice.

Alternative Cuts: Ground pork (about 80% lean), a mixture of pork and veal, ground lamb (about 80% lean), or a mixture of lamb and veal.

Cook's Note

- To make burgers, shape the meat into 4 patties about the size of the buns. Grill until done to your liking, about 10 minutes total. Combine 2 tablespoons of the glaze with ½ cup mayonnaise and spread it over both halves of toasted sesame hamburger buns. Garnish with crispy iceberg lettuce, sliced vine-ripened tomatoes, and the grilled scallions.

Veal Stews and Other Braised Dishes

Because veal has a higher collagen content than beef, it yields good results when cooked with moist heat, producing pot roasts that hold together well, rather than falling apart or turning stringy, as some beef pot roasts can.

Any boneless roast cut from the **chuck (shoulder)** works well, but my favorite pot roast by far is the **veal breast**. This cut includes the veal equivalent of the brisket and some of the plate, or belly, area. It has ample fat, it is easy to stuff, and it is one of the kindest veal cuts on the pocketbook.

For veal stew, the most common and luxurious cut is the **shank**. It's usually sold crosscut into 2- to 3-inch rounds that are called osso buco. Because of its justifiable popularity, osso buco commands a higher price than other veal stewing cuts. If you can find a butcher who can sell you a whole shank, it makes for a spectacular presentation.

My favorite cut for stew, however, is the **cheek**, which may require a little searching and advance ordering, but it's well worth the effort. Veal breast cut into chunks, with or without the bones, produces glorious results when stewed. Breast tends to be fatty, though, so if you want a leaner stew, purchase meat from any area of the chuck. My top choice there is the tougher **neck** area, which has lots of connective tissue, but any chuck cut will do fine.

Avoid meat labeled "veal stew." Most likely it is cut from the lean and undesirable bottom round or eye of round, and you will be paying a premium for meat that will be dry, hard, and not very good.

Veal Braising Cuts at a Glance

From the Shoulder (Chuck)

Neck bone. Best cut for stew if you don't mind bones. A good buy.

Shoulder roast, boneless (veal chuck shoulder clod, veal shoulder arm roast, rolled veal shoulder roast). Can be roasted, but may be a bit chewy. Better used for pot roast. Also a good cut for stewing meat. Good buy. Look for a 4- to 6-pound roast, which will serve 8 or more.

Arm roast, bone in or boneless (veal clod roast). My favorite shoulder roast. Lots of rich flavor. Dry-roast or pot-roast. Good buy.

From the Front Leg and Hind Leg

Shank crosscuts (osso buco). Usually cut from the foreshank. Can be used for stew or braised for the classic Italian osso buco. Whole, it can be braised as pot roast. Expensive.

Hind shank. Meatier than foreshank. Treat as you would foreshank crosscuts (see above). A whole shank makes for an elegant presentation; it can be braised as pot roast. Expensive.

From the Breast

Veal breast, boneless. Sold whole or in pieces. Can be cooked as is or a pocket can be cut for filling with a savory stuffing before braising. A great way to feed a crowd inexpensively. Elegant enough for special occasions.

Whole veal breast, bone-in. Can weigh 10 to 12 pounds, depending on how large an animal it came from. Great cooked whole as a pot roast, or cut into ribs or chunks for stews. A pocket can also be cut and stuffed. My favorite braising cut. Great buy.

Breast riblets. Sold as whole riblets or cut into 2 pieces as veal "short ribs." Use in stews. An inexpensive cut.

POT-ROASTED VEAL ON A CLOUD

Comfort Food, Fit for Company, Fit for a Crowd
Serves 8

Every time I get together with Beth Setrakian, the conversation turns to food. Beth owns a cookie company called Beth's Community Kitchen, but the cookies she makes there are just a small example of her talents. One night over dinner, she waxed exuberant over some of her favorite dishes, including "veal pot roast on a cloud."

"What's that?" I asked. She replied that it was pot roast poking out of a bed of corn bread. Because I knew that Beth's corn bread on its own is very special, I was intrigued, and I immediately set a date to visit her. In addition to this most delicious pot roast, I was treated to her collard greens, black-eyed peas, hot rolls, roast beef, and coveted pecan pie.

Making the corn bread "cloud" is very simple: It's great on its own for a barbecue or any other occasion. You can also serve the pot roast "cloudless," with a side of mashed or roasted potatoes (see Cook's Note). The corn bread recipe comes from Beth's Texan mom, Lulee, who is still going strong at ninety.

3 tablespoons chopped fresh herbs (good choices are sage, thyme, winter savory, summer savory, tarragon, rosemary, dill, fennel, and/or basil; combine 2 or more)
Salt and freshly ground black pepper
1 3- to 4-pound boneless veal shoulder roast, such as shoulder clod, netted or tied
3 tablespoons olive oil
1 cup dry white wine
12 medium shallots, peeled
12 garlic cloves, peeled
4 celery stalks, cut into ½-inch-thick slices
⅓ pound pancetta, diced

2 cups homemade veal stock (see page 168) or canned low-sodium chicken broth, plus more if needed

Lulee's Corn Bread

1⅓ cups cornmeal
¾ cup all-purpose flour
1 tablespoon baking powder
½ teaspoon salt
1 large egg
1 cup whole milk
8 tablespoons (1 stick) butter, melted and still hot

1   Combine 1½ tablespoons of the chopped herbs with 2½ teaspoons salt and 1 teaspoon pepper in a small bowl. Brush the veal with some of the oil and sprinkle the herb mixture all over the roast. (*At this point, you can wrap the roast and refrigerate it overnight for more intense flavor.*)

2   Preheat the oven to 350°F.

3   You will need a 14-inch cast-iron skillet or a large roasting pan (11 x 15 inches) to cook the veal so that there is ample room to scatter the vegetables around the roast and spread out the corn bread "cloud." If you don't own a 14-inch skillet, brown the meat in a large skillet and then transfer it to a large roasting pan. Heat the remaining oil in the skillet over medium-high heat. Add the roast fat side down and brown all over, 7 to 10 minutes. Remove the roast and set aside.

4   Pour off any fat from the skillet and add the white wine. Scrape up any browned bits from the bottom of the pan. (Transfer the liquid to a roasting pan, if using.) Lay the roast in the pan and scatter the shallots, garlic, celery, and pancetta around it. Sprinkle lightly with salt and pepper to taste and pour in the stock.

5   Cover the pan tightly with aluminum foil and bake for 45 minutes. Turn the roast and stir the vegetables and pancetta. Add more stock to the pan if the liquid has evaporated. Reseal with the foil. Bake for 35 minutes more, then turn the roast again so it is fat side up, but leave off the foil. Bake for 30 minutes more, or until the internal temperature reaches 145°F on an instant-read thermometer; taste the meat, which should be tender. It's okay if most of the juices have evaporated, but don't let the vegetables and pancetta burn.

6   **Meanwhile, make the corn bread:** Combine the dry ingredients in a large bowl. In a medium bowl, whisk the egg. Add the milk and beat until well blended. Add the egg-milk mixture to the dry ingredients and mix well. Add the hot butter and beat until well blended.

7   Remove the roast from the oven and spoon the corn bread batter around the veal, covering the exposed area of the pan with the batter. Return to the oven and increase the oven temperature to 450°F. Bake for 20 minutes more, or until the corn bread is golden brown. Present the roast on the cloud to your guests so they can ooh and aah. Then pull the roast from the corn bread, remove any string or netting, and cut it into thick slices. Serve each guest a couple of slices of veal and spoon up some of the corn bread, roasted vegetables, and pancetta.

Alternative Cuts: Boneless veal breast, rolled and tied, or whole veal shank on the bone (cook for about 30 minutes longer).

Cook's Note
- If you choose to cook the roast without its corn bread cloud, cook the meat, covered, for 1½ to 2 hours, or until tender. Strain and degrease the juices. Serve the sliced meat with the juices and the roasted vegetables and pancetta.

NEW ORLEANS VEAL GRILLADES WITH CHEESY GRITS

Comfort Food, Rewarms Well, Great Leftovers
Serves 6

I first encountered grillades, a spicy veal version of braised steak, at the New Orleans restaurant Dooky Chase. Eating at the restaurant is like visiting the high temple of Creole cooking to pay homage to a master priestess. Now well into her eighties, Leah Chase still tends to her bubbling pots each day in her kitchen.

Soon after I met Leah, we became good friends. On one of my visits, she asked me and some Bay Area chef buddies if we had ever had a proper Creole breakfast. We had not. The next day, breakfast began around eleven o'clock and didn't end until near five. Who would have thought that braised thin sheets of veal served over grits could be so good? This is a substantial dish worthy of serving as a hearty dinner. It rewarms well and can be made a day or so ahead. If you want, serve the grillades with poached eggs nestled on top. Grillades are best made with rosy veal from pasture-raised calves, which has enough flavor to stand up to the spicy sauce.

Grillades Spice Rub

- 2 teaspoons Spanish paprika (*pimentón de la Vera*; see Sources) or sweet Hungarian paprika
- 1 teaspoon cayenne pepper
- 2 teaspoons dried thyme
- 2 teaspoons dried basil
- 2 teaspoons ground sage
- 2 teaspoons salt
- 1 teaspoon freshly ground black pepper

- 1 2½-pound boneless veal chuck roast, such as shoulder clod, cut into ¼-inch-thick slices
- ½ cup all-purpose flour
- 3 tablespoons peanut oil, or more if needed
- 3 cups finely chopped onions
- 1 cup finely chopped celery
- ¼ cup finely chopped green bell pepper
- ½ cup finely chopped red bell pepper
- ½ pound andouille sausage, cut into ½-inch dice
- 2 tablespoons chopped garlic
- 8 scallions, white and green parts separated and finely chopped
- 2 cups homemade beef, pork, or veal stock (see page 168) or canned low-sodium chicken broth
- 1 cup peeled and chopped vine-ripened tomatoes or diced canned tomatoes (I use Muir Glen)
- 2 teaspoons Worcestershire sauce
- ½ teaspoon dried thyme
- ½ teaspoon dried basil
  Salt and freshly ground black pepper
  Tabasco or other hot sauce
  Cheesy Grits (recipe follows)

1 **Rub:** Combine all the ingredients in a small bowl. Sprinkle generously over both sides of the sliced meat. If there is any leftover rub, save it to add to the sauce.

2 Spread the flour out in a pie tin or shallow bowl. Dredge each veal slice in the flour so that both sides are coated, shake off the excess, and place the slices on a platter or baking sheet.

3 Heat a large deep skillet or Dutch oven over medium-high heat and add the oil. Add the meat slices, in batches so that the pan is not overcrowded, and fry for 2 minutes per side, or until nicely browned. Remove the slices as they are done and set aside; add more oil if needed.

4 Reduce the heat to medium, add the onions and celery, and cook, stirring and scraping up any browned bits from the bottom of the pan, until softened. Cover and continue to cook until the vegetables are soft and beginning to color, stirring from time to time, about 10 minutes. Stir in the bell peppers and sausage and cook for 4 to 5 minutes more. Stir in the garlic and scallion whites. Set aside ¼ cup of the scallion greens and add the rest to the pan. Cook, stirring, for 1 minute. Add the stock, tomatoes, Worcestershire, thyme, basil, and any remaining spice rub. Stir, scraping up any browned bits from the bottom of the pan. Return the meat to the pan and bring to a boil. Reduce the heat to a simmer and cover the pan. Cook for 45 minutes. Taste the meat to see if it is tender. If not, continue to cook, checking every 15 minutes. (*At this point, you can cool the grillades and refrigerate overnight.*)

5 Degrease the surface of the sauce. Adjust the seasoning, adding salt, pepper, and/or Tabasco to suit your taste.

6 Spoon the grits into a large shallow bowl or onto a platter and top with the meat and sauce. Garnish with the reserved scallion greens.

Alternative Cuts: Slices cut from the leg (called veal round steak), veal sirloin, or veal rump, can be used for this recipe, but these leaner cuts can dry out easily, so you may want to treat them like veal cutlets and cook them in the sauce for only 3 to 5 minutes. (Cook the sauce separately for the full 45 minutes so that the flavors can adequately develop.) You can also make grillades with beef, choosing slices cut from the chuck, shoulder clod, rump, or top round. I also like grillades with pork slices cut from the Boston butt; treat as you would veal.

Cook's Note
- To serve with poached eggs, poach the eggs ahead of time and cool in cold water. Rewarm in hot water just before serving and garnish with grated cheddar cheese.

CHEESY GRITS

Serves 6 to 8

3 cups whole milk	½ cup half-and-half
3 cups water	2 cups finely sliced fresh chives or scallions
1 teaspoon salt	¼ cup chopped fresh flat-leaf parsley
1½ cups stone-ground grits (not instant)	1½ cups grated sharp cheddar cheese (I use Cabot Private Stock)
1 teaspoon Tabasco or other hot sauce	
2 large eggs, lightly beaten	

1 Preheat the oven to 350°F. Butter a 2-quart casserole.

2 Bring the milk and water to a boil in a 2- to 3-quart saucepan over medium heat. Add the salt. Pour the grits in slowly, stirring constantly and keeping the mixture gently boiling. Reduce the heat to a simmer and cook, stirring, for 30 to 40 minutes, or until the grits have thickened and are soft. Taste to make sure. Remove from the heat and cool for at least 10 minutes.

3 Stir the Tabasco, eggs, half-and-half, chives, parsley, and 1¼ cups of the cheese into the grits. Spoon the grits into the casserole and sprinkle with the remaining ¼ cup cheese. Bake for 35 to 45 minutes, until the top is puffed and a light golden brown.

VEAL BREAST STUFFED WITH MUSHROOMS, CHARD, AND PARMESAN

Fit for Company, Fit for a Crowd, Grass-Fed Veal, Cheap Eats, Rewarms Well

Serves 8, with leftovers

When it comes to feeding a large gathering for a special occasion without breaking the bank, stuffed veal breast is at the top of my list, and it ranks as one of my all-time favorite meat dishes, period. Why wouldn't it be delicious? This cut is made up of some of the tastiest areas of the animal, the brisket and the ribs, the veal equivalent of short ribs. Pasture-raised veal breast is particularly good, because it has ample fat, and its succulent meat has more flavor than formula-fed veal.

I like to use a whole bone-in breast, which makes a spectacular presentation. If you can't find it, purchase two of the rib sections, which should include 4 ribs. You can also buy a boneless veal breast. Breast of veal is an ideal dish to serve for a Hanukkah feast. If need be, the breast can be purchased from a kosher butcher. To make this recipe suitable for kosher cooking, omit the Parmigiano-Reggiano.

Veal breast is often sold with a pocket already cut into it; if you need to cut the pocket yourself, see Cook's Notes.

Cardamom-Paprika Rub

- 1 tablespoon salt
- 2 teaspoons freshly ground black pepper
- 1 tablespoon sweet Hungarian paprika
- 2 teaspoons chopped fresh sage
- 1 teaspoon ground cardamom

- 1 8- to 10-pound bone-in veal breast with a pocket cut for stuffing, two 4-rib boneless or bone-in breasts with a pocket cut for stuffing (6–8 pounds total; see Cook's Notes), or one 5- to 6-pound boneless veal breast with a pocket cut for stuffing

Mushroom and Chard Stuffing

- 1 ounce dried porcini mushrooms
- 2 cups boiling water
- 3 tablespoons olive oil
- 2 cups chopped onions
- 2 cups chopped leeks (white and pale green parts)
- 2 tablespoons minced garlic
  Salt and freshly ground black pepper
- 1 pound mushrooms, chopped
- 2 teaspoons chopped fresh sage
- 1 bunch chard, leaves stripped from stems (stems reserved for another purpose)
- 4 cups diced (½ inch) day-old bread (I use sourdough French bread)
- ½ cup freshly grated Parmigiano-Reggiano
- 2 large eggs, lightly beaten

Braising Liquid

- 2 cups chopped leeks (white and pale green parts)
- 1 cup chopped onions
- 2 cups peeled and diced carrots
- 1 cup diced celery

  Salt and freshly ground black pepper

- 1 teaspoon chopped fresh sage
- 2 teaspoons sweet Hungarian paprika
- 2 cups dry white wine
- 1 cup homemade veal stock (see page 168) or canned low-sodium chicken broth, or more as needed

1. **Rub:** Combine all the ingredients in a small bowl. Rub all the mixture over the veal breast(s) and set aside while you make the stuffing. (*For more flavor, wrap the veal in plastic wrap and refrigerate overnight.*)

2. **Stuffing:** Place the dried porcini in a small glass bowl and cover with the boiling water. Soak for at least 45 minutes, or up to several hours, until soft.

3. Remove the porcini from the liquid with a slotted spoon. Chop and set aside. Strain the soaking liquid, leaving behind any grit in the bottom of the bowl, and reserve.

4. Heat the oil in a large skillet over medium heat. Add the onions, leeks, and garlic and a pinch each of salt and pepper. Cover and cook, stirring, until the vegetables are soft, about 10 minutes. Add the fresh mushrooms, sage, and porcini. Cook, stirring, until the fresh mushrooms are soft and fragrant, about 5 minutes.

5. Meanwhile, bring a pot of salted water to a bowl. Add the chard and blanch for 5 minutes, or until wilted and tender. Drain, then cool, squeeze out as much liquid as you can, and chop.

6. Place the bread cubes in a large bowl and add the mushroom mixture, with any liquid in the pan, and the chard. Add the cheese and eggs and stir to moisten the bread, adding a little of the reserved porcini soaking liquid if necessary. (It should be moist enough to just hold together when mounded on a spoon.) Season to taste with salt and pepper.

7. Preheat the oven to 325°F.

8. Stuff the veal breast(s) with the stuffing. Do not pack too tightly because the stuffing will expand during cooking. (Place any excess stuffing in a buttered casserole dish and bake, covered, for 30 to 40 minutes.) Sew the pocket closed with twine or use small skewers to close it.

9. **Braising liquid:** Scatter the leeks, onions, carrots, and celery over the bottom of a roasting pan big enough to hold the veal. Sprinkle with some salt and pepper and the sage and paprika. Lay the veal bone side down on top of the vegetables. Pour in the

white wine, stock, and any remaining porcini soaking liquid. Cover the pan tightly with aluminum foil and roast for 2 hours. Remove the foil and ladle some of the juices over the veal. Continue to roast, uncovered, for 1 hour more, or until the veal is golden brown and tender, adding more stock if necessary. Transfer the veal breast to a carving board and cover loosely with aluminum foil while you make the sauce.

10 Pour the contents of the roasting pan into a large saucepan and degrease the surface. Strain the sauce and transfer the vegetables to a blender. Puree the vegetables, then whisk them back into the sauce. If it is too thin, boil briefly to reduce. Season to taste with salt and pepper.

11 To serve, slice the veal between the bones into thick slices, or cut boneless veal into ¾-inch slices. Moisten each slice with some sauce and pass the rest at the table.

Cook's Notes

- If your veal breast does not already have a pocket cut into it, lay the breast on a work surface with the thicker, long side facing you and the bone side down. Trim off as much external fat as you can. Insert a long sharp knife into the center of the side facing you and cut a pocket along the full length of the veal breast, leaving a 1- to 2-inch border on the 3 remaining sides. Run your hand around inside the pocket to make sure that no surfaces adhere to one another.

- The stuffing can be used to stuff any roast, such as a butterflied veal shoulder, boneless leg of lamb, or boneless leg of pork. For these cuts, reduce the recipe by half. The stuffing is also a great side dish. Toss with ½ cup melted butter and bake, uncovered, in a buttered baking dish for 30 to 40 minutes at 325°F.

Leftovers

- The veal rewarms well in the sauce. You can also eat the roast cold or use as a filling for sandwiches in place of cold meat loaf (see page 136).

PROVENÇAL-STYLE BRAISED VEAL BREAST RAGÙ

Rewarms Well

Serves 6

When it comes to choosing cuts for veal stew, I prefer ribs cut from a breast of veal, which have enough fat and collagen to turn tender and silky when fully cooked. My next choice is boneless veal breast. Otherwise, use any cut from the shoulder area and cut it into 2-inch cubes. Like so much of the cooking of Provence, this stew is full flavored and rustic, relying on some of the classic regional ingredients: olives, olive oil, anchovies, and tomatoes. I like to make the stew in the late summer or early fall, when vine-ripened tomatoes are at their peak. This dish calls out for a bottle of red wine, such as Gigondas, Vacqueyras, or Châteauneuf-du-Pape.

Salt and freshly ground black pepper

1 tablespoon chopped fresh thyme

1 tablespoon chopped fresh sage

4 pounds veal breast with bones, cut between the ribs and then each rib cut into 2 pieces (have the butcher do this), or 3 pounds boneless veal shoulder, cut into 2-inch cubes

2 tablespoons olive oil

2 cups thinly sliced onions

¼ cup chopped shallots

3 tablespoons minced garlic

3 anchovy fillets, minced

1 cup dry white wine

¼ cup Pernod or other anise-flavored liquor, such as anisette

1 tablespoon chopped fresh tarragon or 2 teaspoons dried

2 cups peeled and chopped vine-ripened tomatoes or canned diced tomatoes (I use Muir Glen)

1 cup homemade veal stock (see page 168) or canned low-sodium chicken broth

2 cups pearl onions, peeled (see Step 4, page 198)

1 cup green olives, such as picholine

2 tablespoons finely grated lemon zest

1 Preheat the oven to 325°F.

2 Combine 1 teaspoon salt, 1 teaspoon pepper, the thyme, and sage in a small bowl. Sprinkle all over the veal.

3 Heat the oil in a large Dutch oven over medium-high heat. Add the veal and brown all over, 7 to 10 minutes. (You may need to do this in batches.) Transfer to a bowl and set aside.

4   Reduce the heat to medium and add the onions, shallots, and garlic. Cover and cook, stirring and scraping up any browned bits from the bottom of the pot, until the vegetables are soft and fragrant, about 10 minutes. Stir in the anchovies and cook for 1 minute more. Pour in the white wine and Pernod and bring to a boil. Boil to reduce the liquid by half, continuing to scrape up any browned bits.

5   Add the tarragon, tomatoes, stock, and the meat, and any juices from the bowl. Cover and bake until the meat is tender, about 1½ hours. If not tender, continue to cook, checking every 30 minutes.

6   Add the pearl onions and olives and cook for 15 minutes more, or until the onions are tender. (*At this point, you can cool the ragù and refrigerate overnight.*)

7   Remove any fat from the surface of the sauce and taste the liquid. If it is too thin, remove the solids and boil down to a syrupy consistency, then add back the solids and warm for a minute or two. Stir in the lemon zest, and cook for 1 to 2 minutes more. Season to taste with salt and pepper. Serve in shallow bowls, warning guests about the olive pits.

Alternative Cuts: Cuts from the veal leg, such as top or bottom round; boneless veal shoulder; or osso buco (veal shanks cut into 2- to 3-inch rounds; increase the cooking time to 2 to 3 hours and use 4 pounds of shanks). A whole veal shank is good as well.

Cook's Note
- I like to serve this ragù with soft polenta, steamed couscous, brown rice, or orzo.

JEFF'S OSSO BUCO WITH ARTICHOKES

Fit for Company, Great Leftovers, Rewarms Well, Two-for-One

Serves 4, with leftovers

My talented friend Jeff Bergman likes to make this dish just as winter is turning the corner to spring. Tender baby artichokes are just right with veal. Crème fraîche adds richness, while lemon zest, parsley, and chives give the stew a bright, fresh finish.

3–4 pounds osso buco (veal shanks cut into 2-inch-thick rounds)	12 fresh flat-leaf parsley sprigs, plus 2 tablespoons finely chopped parsley
Salt and freshly ground black pepper	10 fresh thyme sprigs
2 tablespoons olive oil	2 bay leaves
2 carrots, peeled and cut into ¾-inch dice	About 4 cups homemade veal stock (see page 168) or canned low-sodium chicken broth
1 celery stalk, cut into ¾-inch dice	
4 large shallots, quartered	12 baby artichokes
1 leek, white and pale green parts, cut into ¾-inch-wide pieces	7 ounces crème fraîche or sour cream
6 garlic cloves, peeled	1½ teaspoons finely grated lemon zest
1 cup dry white wine	1 tablespoon finely snipped fresh chives

1 Preheat the oven to 325°F.

2 Sprinkle the osso buco with 2 teaspoons salt and 1 teaspoon pepper. Heat the oil in a large Dutch oven over medium-high heat. Place the veal in the pot and brown on all sides, 2 to 3 minutes per side. Remove to a platter and set aside.

3 Pour off all but 3 tablespoons of the fat from the pot and add the carrots, celery, shallots, leek, and garlic. Reduce the heat to medium and cook, scraping the browned bits from the bottom of the pot, until the vegetables have softened, about 5 minutes. Add the white wine, bring to a boil over medium-high heat, and cook for 2 to 3 minutes, scraping up any remaining browned bits from the bottom of the pot. Tie the parsley sprigs, thyme, and bay leaves into a bundle with twine and drop them into the pot.

4 Place the veal back in the pot and add enough stock to come halfway up the meat. Bring to a boil, cover tightly, and place in the oven. Cook, turning the osso buco every 30 minutes, and checking to make sure that the liquid is just simmering. After 1½ hours, check for tenderness. If the meat yields very easily to the tip of a knife, it is done; taste a bit to make sure. If not tender, continue to cook, checking every 30 minutes.

The cooking time may be as much as 2½ hours total. *(You can make the osso buco up to this point and refrigerate overnight.)*

5   Meanwhile, bring 2 quarts salted water to a boil. Cut the baby artichokes in half and check to see that there are no fuzzy chokes. If there are, carefully scoop them out with a grapefruit spoon or cut them out with the point of a paring knife. Drop the artichokes into the boiling water and cook until barely tender, 4 to 5 minutes. Drain, plunge into a bowl of ice water until cool, and then drain well and set aside.

6   When the veal shanks are tender, carefully transfer them to a large platter. Fish out the herb bundle and discard. Strain the braising liquid into a deep 3-quart saucepan, pressing down on the solids. (Save ½ cup vegetables if you want to make the ravioli; see Cook's Notes.) Bring the liquid to a boil over high heat. Reduce to about 2½ cups. Whisk in the crème fraîche. Bring back to a gentle simmer and reduce again, until the sauce lightly coats the back of a spoon, 10 to 15 minutes. Return the shanks to the pot.

7   Add the artichokes, lemon zest, and chopped parsley and season to taste with salt and pepper. Heat until the shanks and artichokes are warmed through, about 5 minutes. Season to taste with salt and pepper. Transfer the shanks and artichokes to a large shallow serving bowl and spoon the sauce over the top. Sprinkle with the chives.

Alternative Cuts: You can make this recipe as a pot roast using a 3- to 4-pound boneless veal shoulder roast, a veal 7-bone blade roast (the cooking time may be less than for shanks), or a 5- to 6-pound bone-in veal breast.

Cook's Notes

- Serve with a wide, flat noodle such as pappardelle, tossed with a little of the sauce, or serve with mashed potatoes.

- In place of the baby artichokes, you can use 3 large artichokes. Remove the outer leaves until you reach the pale green leaves, trim and peel the stems, and place in a bowl with the juice of 1 lemon until you need them. When ready to use, cut them into quarters and scoop out the chokes. Boil for 6 to 8 minutes and proceed with step 5.

- If you wish to make the Veal Shank Ravioli (page 588), save ½ cup of the smashed cooked vegetables from the cooking liquid, along with 1 cup diced meat and 2 tablespoons sauce.

VEAL SHANK RAVIOLI WITH BROWN BUTTER AND SAGE

Serves 6 (makes about 4 dozen ravioli)

1 cup diced leftover braised osso buco

½ cup smashed vegetables from Osso Buco braising liquid (page 585)

2 tablespoons or more leftover osso buco sauce

¼ cup freshly grated Parmigiano-Reggiano, plus more for serving

Salt and freshly ground black pepper

½ pound fresh pasta dough (homemade or store-bought), rolled into 18-inch-long sheets

8 tablespoons (1 stick) butter

¼ cup fresh sage leaves, cut crosswise into thin strips

1 Place the meat in a food processor and pulse until finely chopped. Combine with the vegetables in a medium bowl. Stir in the sauce and cheese. The mixture should be moist but not wet. Add more sauce if needed. Season to taste with salt and pepper. Cover with plastic wrap and refrigerate for at least 30 minutes, or as long as overnight.

2 Trim the pasta sheets to 3 inches wide. Mound teaspoons of the filling about ½ inch from the long side down one side of the pasta strip at about 1-inch intervals. Moisten the edge of the filled side of the pasta with a tiny bit of water, fold the unfilled side of the pasta over the filling, and press well all around the filling to seal, pressing out any air. Cut between the mounds of filling with a knife or ravioli cutting wheel. Put the ravioli on a floured baking sheet. Repeat with the remaining strips and filling.

3 Bring a large pot of salted water to a boil. Cook the ravioli until al dente, 3 to 5 minutes.

4 Meanwhile, heat the butter in a large skillet over medium heat until it begins to brown and smell nutty, about 5 minutes. Add the sage and cook, stirring, for 30 seconds, taking care not to burn the butter. Add the cooked ravioli and toss until well coated with the butter. Spoon onto warm plates and pass more cheese at the table.

Cook's Notes

- You can also serve the ravioli with Gary's Heirloom Tomato Sauce (page 316).

- You can also serve these ravioli with leftover sauce from the osso buco.

Veal Offal
(Calf's Liver, Tongue, and Sweetbreads)

Veal offal, despite the uninviting-sounding name, provides some of the finest gastronomic treats in the culinary world: choice morsels such as calf's liver, sweetbreads, tongue, calf's brains, and veal kidney. All have their fans.

It's sad that many of these have fallen out of favor, but today calf's liver and sweetbreads, at least, are gaining in popularity — and price — on the menus of expensive restaurants. However, veal tongue, when you can find it, is still reasonably priced.

Look for **calf's liver** that is light brown (not purple-brown), with no blemishes or dark brown edges. Remove any tough outer membranes and any veins or sinew. The liver should have a fresh but not strong odor.

Sweetbreads are the pancreas/heart glands, which are fairly uniform in shape, or the thymus glands, which are more irregular. Their very mild taste can easily be overpowered, so they are best paired with delicate flavors, such as mushrooms, cream, or a light, lemony vinaigrette. Rich, they are best enjoyed in small portions as a first course or lunch main course. Look for sweetbreads that are white or faintly gray with no blemishes, browned edges, or off colors. They should smell fresh, with very little odor at all.

When properly cooked, **veal tongue** is incredibly silky, with a very mild flavor. Look for tongue that is moist (never sticky), with no brown or reddish areas and no dark blemishes. It should smell very fresh.

CALF'S LIVER WITH FOUR LILIES AND SUN-DRIED TART CHERRIES

In a Hurry, Family Meal

Serves 4

Onions, shallots, leeks, and scallions are all members of the lily family. While onions are the classic accompaniment to calf's liver, shallots, leeks, and scallions are also delicious paired with it, contributing their own subtle nuances. Dried cherries and a little sherry vinegar add a gently tart flavor to counterbalance the sweetness of the onions.

Make sure to buy liver slices that are ⅜ to ½ inch thick so that you can nicely brown the exterior without overcooking the interior, which should remain lightly pink.

¼ cup sun-dried tart cherries

½ cup dry white wine

2 tablespoons sherry vinegar

6 ounces thick-cut bacon (4–6 strips), cut cross-wise into ½-inch-wide strips

2 cups thinly sliced onions

1 cup thinly sliced leeks (white and pale green parts)

½ cup thinly sliced shallots

Salt and freshly ground black pepper

½ cup thinly sliced scallion whites (reserve greens)

2 teaspoons chopped fresh sage

½ cup all-purpose flour

1½ pounds sliced calf's liver (about ½ inch thick slices), outer membranes and any veins and sinew removed

1 tablespoon butter, or more as needed

1 tablespoon olive oil, or more as needed

1 cup homemade beef or veal stock (see page 168) or canned low-sodium chicken broth

¼ cup thinly sliced scallion greens

1 Combine the cherries, white wine, and vinegar in a small saucepan and bring to a boil. Remove from the heat, cover, and set aside.

2 Heat a large heavy skillet over medium heat. Add the bacon and fry until nicely browned and just turning crisp. Remove with a slotted spoon and set aside. Leave about ¼ cup bacon fat in the pan. Add the onions, leeks, and shallots. Sprinkle with a little salt and pepper. Cover and cook until golden, stirring occasionally, 20 to 25 minutes.

3 Add the scallion whites and cook for 1 minute more. Pour in the cherries and all their liquid and cook until the liquid is reduced by half and becomes syrupy. Stir in the sage and reserved bacon and set aside.

4   Combine the flour with 2 teaspoons salt and 1 teaspoon pepper in a pie tin or shallow bowl. One at a time, dredge each slice of liver to coat on both sides, shaking off any excess, and lay the slices in a single layer on a plate.

5   Heat the butter and oil in a large, preferably nonstick, skillet over medium-high heat. Fry the liver slices in batches, for 2 to 3 minutes per side, or until nicely browned but the interior is pink when you cut into a slice to test. As the slices are done, transfer them to a platter. Add more butter and oil as needed.

6   Add the stock and scrape up any browned bits from the bottom of the pan. Reduce until the liquid just becomes syrupy, about 5 minutes. Add the "lily" mixture to the pan. Season to taste with salt and pepper. Add the liver and heat just to warm through, 1 to 2 minutes. Arrange the liver slices on the platter, spoon over the vegetables and sauce, garnish with the scallion greens, and serve.

Alternative Cuts: Beef liver or lamb's livers, which have a slightly stronger flavor. If you can find bison liver, it has great flavor. If liver isn't your thing, you can use veal or pork cutlets, cut ¼ inch thick.

Cook's Notes

- If dried cherries are too expensive, use the same amount of dried apricots, cut into ¼-inch strips, or use dried cranberries.

- Because the bacon is a major part of the flavoring for this dish, buy the best you can (see Sources).

OLIVE OIL–POACHED VEAL SWEETBREADS

Fit for Company

Serves 6 as a first course, 4 as a main course

Anyone who has cooked veal sweetbreads knows they take considerable advance preparation. The most finicky step is removing the tough membranes and then pressing the sweetbreads to make them firmer and easier to cut. My friend, the talented Italian chef Franco Dunn, has worked out a simpler method of slowly poaching the sweetbreads in olive oil. It not only cooks them to a perfect moist, firm, and creamy texture but eliminates peeling off the membranes, which become tender during poaching. The bonus is that you are left with the delicious flavored olive oil that can be used in future preparations of sweetbreads or for your favorite braised or sautéed veal dishes.

Because veal sweetbreads are rich, I recommend serving smaller portions as a first course at an elegant dinner party. On the other hand, if you're as crazy about these little morsels as I am, go ahead and serve them as a main course.

1 pound veal sweetbreads (2 whole pancreas/heart sweetbreads)	Olive oil for poaching
Salt and freshly ground black pepper	2 fresh thyme sprigs
	2 bay leaves

1   Place the sweetbreads in a medium bowl, cover with water, and refrigerate for 6 hours, changing the water 3 times to remove excess blood. Remove the sweetbreads from the water and pat dry.

2   Preheat the oven to 200°F.

3   Season the sweetbreads with a sprinkle of salt and pepper. Place in a small ovenproof saucepan or deep skillet, that is just large enough to hold them. Pour over the olive oil to completely cover them, and submerge the thyme and bay leaves in the oil. Place the pan in the oven. After 1 hour, begin checking the internal temperature of the sweetbreads; they are done when the temperature reaches 145°F to 150°F on an instant-read thermometer. If they're not yet there, continue to check every 10 minutes. Let the sweetbreads cool for 30 minutes in the oil.

4   Rmove the sweetbreads from the oil, letting the excess oil drain back into the pan. Trim off any loose pieces, tubes, ducts, cartilage, or bits of membrane from the sweetbreads. Strain the oil and reserve for another use.

5 Cut the sweetbreads into ½-inch-thick slices and gently rewarm in the reserved oil before serving.

Cook's Notes

- If you like your sweetbreads crisper, season the slices with a little salt and pepper, dip them in flour, and shake off the excess. Panfry in some of the reserved oil for 2 to 3 minutes per side, or until golden brown and beginning to crisp around the edges.

- If you want to use the poached sweetbreads at a later time (see the recipes that follow), wrap them in plastic wrap and refrigerate for up to 2 days. Place the cooking oil in a jar, seal, and refrigerate. The oil will congeal, so warm it at room temperature before using. It will keep for about 1 week. To rewarm the sweetbreads, combine with some of the oil in a small saucepan and heat over a very low flame for 5 minutes.

SWEETBREAD SALAD

Serves 4

2 teaspoons Dijon mustard	Salt and freshly ground black pepper
1½ tablespoons sherry vinegar	8 cups salad greens, such as friseé, mesclun,
2 teaspoons finely chopped shallot	or curly endive
1 teaspoon chopped fresh thyme	Olive Oil–Poached Veal Sweetbreads, sliced
2 tablespoons warm reserved sweetbread	and warmed
poaching oil (see above)	¼ cup finely chopped fresh chives or chervil
¼ cup extra-virgin olive oil	

1 Whisk together the mustard, vinegar, shallot, and thyme in a small bowl. Gradually whisk in the poaching oil and olive oil to form a smooth dressing. Season to taste with salt and pepper.

2 Divide the salad greens among four large chilled salad plates. Lay 2 or 3 slices of warm sweetbreads over each serving of greens and drizzle about 2 tablespoons of the dressing over each salad. Garnish with the chives.

CRISPY PANFRIED SWEETBREADS

In a Hurry, Fit for Company

Serves 4

First chilled until firm, the poached sweetbreads are sliced, dipped in flour, egg whites, and panko bread crumbs and panfried, which give them a lovely crisp coating. Serve them "saltimbocca" style with the prosciutto and sage sauce or with lemon wedges on lightly dressed salad greens or a bed of sautéed mushrooms.

Olive Oil–Poached Veal Sweetbreads (page 593), left whole and chilled
Salt and freshly ground black pepper
½ cup all-purpose flour
2 large egg whites, lightly beaten with 2 teaspoons water
¾ cup panko bread crumbs
3 tablespoons reserved sweetbread poaching oil, or more as needed
Lemon wedges (optional)

Saltimbocca Sauce (optional)
2 ounces thinly sliced prosciutto, cut into 2-x-¼-inch strips
12 fresh sage leaves, cut crosswise into ⅛-inch-wide strips
½ cup dry white wine
½ cup homemade veal stock (see page 168) or canned low-sodium chicken broth

1 Cut the sweetbreads into ⅜-inch-thick slices and sprinkle both sides with salt and pepper to taste. Place the flour, egg white mixture, and panko in separate pie tins or shallow bowls. Dip each sweetbread slice into the flour and shake off the excess, dip into the egg to coat completely, letting the excess drain, and then coat completely with the panko, pressing the crumbs into the sweetbreads to make them adhere. Put on a plate.

2 Heat ⅛ inch oil in a 10-inch nonstick skillet over medium heat. Working in batches, fry the slices until nicely browned on one side, about 2 minutes. Gently turn over and fry the other side for 1 or 2 minutes more, or until nicely browned and crisp, adding more oil if needed. Drain on paper towels. Transfer to a warm platter and serve with lemon wedges, or proceed with making the Saltimbocca Sauce.

3 **Sauce:** Pour off all but 2 tablespoons of the oil from the pan and add the prosciutto and sage. Cook, stirring, over medium heat until the sage just begins to crisp, about 1 minute. With a slotted spoon, transfer the prosciutto and sage to a small plate. Add the white wine to the pan and bring to a boil, scraping up any browned bits from the bottom of the pan. Boil the wine until it has almost evaporated. Add the stock and reduce until just turning syrupy.

4　Arrange the sweetbreads on four plates. Add the prosciutto and sage to the sauce, then spoon the sauce over the sweetbreads and serve.

Cook's Note

- Instead of serving the crispy sweetbreads with lemon wedges, drizzle a few drops of good aged balsamic vinegar over each slice.

Sources

Sustainable Meat and CSA Resources

American Grassfed Association *americangrassfed.org*

Eat Well Guide *eatwellguide.org*

Eat Wild *eatwild.com*

The Ethicurean *ethicurean.com*

Green Building Resource Guide *greenguide.com*

Local Harvest *localharvest.org*

Slow Food USA *slowfoodusa.org*

VanBuren's All Organic Grass Fed Beef *organicgrassfedbeef.com*

Meat Information Resources

American Humane Association *thehumanetouch.org*

American Lamb *lambcheckoff.com*

American Veal Association *americanveal.com*

Animal Welfare Approved *animalwelfareapproved.org*

The Boer & Meat Goat Information Center *boergoats.com*

Humane Farms Animal Care *certifiedhumane.org*

National Bison Association *bisoncentral.com*

National Cattlemen's Beef Association *beef.org*

National Pork Board *pork.org*

Sustainable Agriculture Research & Education *sare.org*

United States Department of Agriculture *usda.gov*

Specialty Meat Companies

Blackwing Quality Meats *blackwing.com*, 800-326-7874

Heritage Foods *heritagefoodsusa.com*, 718-389-0985

Nicky USA *nickyusa.com*

Niman Ranch *nimanranch.com*

Organic Prairie *organicprairie.com*, 877-662-6328

Preferred Meats *preferredmeats.com*, 800-397-6328

Beef

Alderspring Ranch Grass-Fed Beef *alderspring.com*

American Grass-Fed Beef *americangrassfedbeef.com*, 866-255-5002

Carman Ranch *carmanranch.com*, 541-263-0812

Coleman Natural Foods *colemannatural.com*, 800-442-8666

Country Natural Beef *countrynaturalbeef.com*, 541-473-3355

DeBragga *debragga.com*, 646-873-6555 (Wagu beef)

Grass-Fed Traditions *grassfedtraditions.com*

La Cense Beef *lacensebeef.com*, 866-442-2333

Lasater Grasslands Beef *lgbeef.com*, 866-454-2333

Laura's Lean Beef *laurasleanbeef.com*, 800-487-5326

Long Meadow Ranch *longmeadowranch.com*, 877-627-2645

Marin Grass-Fed Meat Company *maringrassfedmeat.com*, 415-381-1129

Marin Sun Farms *marinsunfarms.com*, 415-663-8997

Meadow View Farm *meadow-view-farm.com*, 802-626-3104

Meyer Natural Angus *meyernaturalangus.com*, 888-990-2333

Painted Hills Natural Beef *paintedhillsnaturalbeef.com*, 877-306-8247

Slanker's Grass-Fed Meat *texasgrassfedbeef.com*, 866-752-6537

Tallgrass Beef Company *tallgrassbeef.com*, 312-846-1361

U.S. Wellness Meats *grasslandbeef.com*, 877-383-0051

White Oak Pastures *whiteoakpastures.com*, 229-641-2081

Bison

Buffalo Hills Bison *buffalohillsbisonmeat.com*, 507-724-2833

Montana Bison Meat *montanabuffalomeat.com*, 800-495-0221

Pork

Becker Lane Organic Farm *beckerlaneorganic.com*, 563-875-2087

Berkridge Kurobuta *berkridge.com*, 712-707-5060

Cane Creek Farm *canecreekfarm.us*, 336-525-1744

Caw Caw Creek *cawcawcreek.com*, 803-255-0112

Eden Farms *betterpork.com*, 515-244-7675

Flying Pigs Farm *flyingpigsfarm.com*, 518-854-3844

Heritage Foods *heritagefoodsusa.com*, 718-389-0985

Sap Bush Hollow Farm *sapbush.com*, 518-234-2105

Tails & Trotters *tailsandtrotters.com*, 503-680-7697

Vande Rose Farms *vanderosefarms.com*, 866-522-4448

Bacon, Ham, Sausages, and Other Cured Meat

Aidells Sausage Company *aidells.com*, 877-243-3557 (andouille)

Benton's Smoky Mountain Country Hams *bentonscountryhams2.com*, 423-442-5003

Burgers' Smokehouse *smokehouse.com*, 800-345-5185

D'Artagnan *dartagnan.com*, 800-327-8246

Despaña Brand Foods *despanabrandfoods.com*, 888-779-8617

Early's *earlysgifts.com*, 800-523-2015

Edwards of Surry, Virginia *edwardsvaham.com*, 800-200-4267

Father's Country Hams *fatherscountryhams.com*, 877-525-4267

Finchville Farms *finchvillefarms.com*, 800-678-1521

Grateful Palate *gratefulpalate.com* 888-472-5283

Igourmet *igourmet.com*, 877-446-8763 (Jambon de Paris)

Johnston County Hams *countrycuredhams.com*, 800-543-4267

Jones Dairy Farm *jonesdairyfarm.com*, 800-563-1004 (partially cooked hams)

La Española Meats *laespanolameats.com*, 310-539-0455 (*semicurado chorizo*)

La Quercia *laquercia.us*, 515-981-1625 (speck)

Newsom's Country Hams *newsomscountryham.com*, 270-365-2482

Nueske's *nueskes.com*, 800-392-2266 (Westphalian ham)

Prime Smoked Meats *primesmoked.com*, 510-832-7167 (partially boned ham)

Salumi Artisan Cured Meats *salumicuredmeats.com*, 206-223-0817 (guanciale)

Scott Hams *scotthams.com*, 800-318-1353

Vande Rose Farms *vanderosefarms.com*, 866-522-4448 ("uncured" hams)

Wallace Edwards & Sons *virginiatraditions.com*, 800-222-4267 (fully cooked hams)

Lamb, Goat, and Veal

Cattail Creek Lamb *cattailcreeklamb.com*, 541-988-8505

D'Artagnan *dartagnan.com*, 800-327-8246

Dragonfly Cove Farm/Thyme for Goat *thymeforgoat.com*, 207-380-4014

Grande Premium Meats *elkusa.com*, 888-338-4581

Hearst Ranch *hearstranch.com*, 866-547-2624

Jamison Farm *jamisonfarm.com*, 800-237-5262

Lava Lake Lamb *lavalakelamb.com*, 888-528-5253

McCormack Ranch *mccormackranch.com*, 707-374-5236

Shepherd's Lamb *organiclamb.com*, 575-588-7792

Superior Farms *superiorfarms.com*

White Oak Pastures *whiteoakpastures.com*, 229-641-2081

Specialty Products, Herbs, Spices, and Ethnic Ingredients

Amazon *amazon.com* (specialty foods, herbs and spices, preserved lemons, dark treacle syrup, brown bean paste, Emergo beans, Gebhardt chili powder, ginger rice vinegar, masa harina, pomegranate molasses, pomegranate syrup, Chinese fermented black beans, La Tenuta Rocchetta olive oil, palm sugar, fresh kaffir lime leaves, tarbais beans)

Asian Food Grocer *asianfoodgrocer.com*, 888-482-2742 (Japanese ingredients, including dried shrimp)

Dean & Deluca *deandeluca.com* 800-221-7714 (specialty foods)

Frieda's *friedas.com*, 800-241-1771 (dried mushrooms, chiles, beans, Asian ingredients)

Global Palate *globalpalate.com* (*pimentón de la Vera, ras el hanout, baharat,* Aleppo pepper)

Kalustyan's *kalustyans.com*, 800-352-3451 (baharat, ghee, harissa, manioc flour, masa harina, dried chiles, dried mushrooms, olives, herbs, spices, dried kaffir lime leaves, tamarind paste)

King Arthur Flour *kingarthurflour.com*, 800-827-6836 (flours, maple sugar, malt syrup, maple syrup, vanilla)

La Tienda *tienda.com*, 800-710-4304 (*pimentón de la Vera,* piquillo peppers, Spanish chorizo, Marcona almonds, jamón)

Oregon Mushrooms *oregonmushrooms.com*, 800-682-0036 (fresh and dried mushrooms)

Pacific Rim Gourmet *pacificrimgourmet.com* (Chinese and Southeast Asian ingredients, including chili bean paste)

Penzeys Spices *penzeys.com*, 800-741-7787 (spices, herbs, and seasonings, including annatto seeds, fenugreek, sumac)

Phipps Country Store and Farm *phippscountry.com*, 650-879-1032 (heirloom beans)

Rancho Gordo *ranchogordo.com*, 707-259-1935 (heirloom beans)

Rogue Creamery *roguecreamery.com*, 866-396-4704 (Rogue River Blue, Oregon Blue, Oregonzola)

The Spanish Table *spanishtable.com*, (*pimentón de la Vera,* Spanish chorizo, jamón)

Vanns Spices *vannsspices.com*, 800-583-1693 (spices, including Espelette pepper)

Whole Spice *wholespice.com*, 707-778-1750 (herbs and spices, including herbes de Provence)

Zingerman's *zingermans.com*, 888-636-8162 (specialty foods, including fennel pollen)

Specialty Equipment, Hardwood Sawdust, Smokers and Wood-Fire Ovens, Jaccards, and Sausage-Making Supplies

Amazon *amazon.com* (Rösle tongs, Jaccards, water smokers, Big Green Egg, instant-read thermometers)

Butcher & Packer *butcher-packer.com*, 248-583-1250 (sausage-making supplies, including hardwood sawdust)

Cabela's *cabelas.com*, 800-237-4444 (sausage-making equipment)

California Butcher Supply, 800-662-6212 (sausage-making supplies)

Earthstone Ovens *earthstoneovens.com*, 800-840-4915 (wood-fired ovens)

Forno Bravo *fornobravo.com*, 800-407-5119 (wood-fired ovens)

Mugnaini *mugnaini.com*, 888-887-7206 (Italian wood- and gas-fired ovens)

Smokehouse, *smokehouseproducts.com*, 877-386-3871 (smokers)

The Sausage Maker, *sausagemaker.com*, 888-490-8525 (sausage-making supplies, including Insta Cure No. 1)

Acknowledgments

Without my editor, Rux Martin, who urged me for several years to take another look at the world of meat and meat cookery, this book would have never happened. Thank you, Rux, for your support, your ability to laugh when things got tough, and your uncanny vision to assemble a book whose beauty and clarity we are all truly proud of.

Many thanks to Anne-marie Ramo, for her great recipes and the splendid job she did helping write, compile and test all the recipes, as well as making sense of my scribbles.

To Roy Finamore, for his eloquent reworking of my prose and his help rendering complicated issues clear and precise.

To Luca Trovato, the photographer, and his wife, Rori Trovato, the food stylist, for bringing my recipes to life with scrumptious photographs.

Those photos could never have looked as appetizing if it were not for the superb quality of the meat generously supplied by my local specialty meat purveyors, Golden Gate Meat Company and Preferred Meats. Thank you to Jimi Offenback, the owner of Golden Gate, and Bala Kironde of Preferred Meats.

Thanks to the following for helping me understand how various livestock are raised and cared for and for explaining terms on meat labels: American Grassfed Association, Chris Calkins of the University of Nebraska, Cory Carman of Carman Ranch, Dave Carter of the National Bison Association, Davey Griffin of Texas A&M, Allan Nation of The Stockman Grass Farmer, Bill Niman of B N Ranch, Michael Pollan of the University of California, Jeff Savell of Texas A&M, John Simons, the Society of Concerned Scientists, and the United States Department of Agriculture.

For help on questions on butchery and meat cuts, I would like to thank Dave Barry, Sam Edwards, Marissa Guggiana, Ryan Farr, Tia Harrison, Kari Underly, and Liz Wunderlich. Thanks also to all the great meat organizations who supplied and allowed the use of photographs of meat cuts: Beef Checkoff, Certified Angus Beef, the American Lamb Board, and the National Pork Board.

Many fellow cooks, friends, cookbook writers, and inspired foodies contributed recipes, advice, and encouragement. Thanks to Michelle Aaron, Jeff Bergman, Carole

Bidnick, Leah Chase, Richard Crocker, Lissa Doumani, Diamond Lil Doumani, Franco Dunn, Kathy and Herb Eckhouse, Susan Friedland, Shannon Hayes, Carlos Hernandez, Jacob Kennedy, Kristine Kidd, Lars Kromark, Loni Kuhn, Karen Levin, Agustine Martinez, Pam Mazzola, Art Meyer, Nancy Oakes, Angela Occhipinti, Alex Padilla, James Peterson, Mai Pham, Beth Setrakian, David Shalleck, Marie Simmons, Richard Simon, Hiro Sone, Sarah Tenaglia, Elvia Vega, Jean-Michel Vallette, Dick Vennerbeck, Gary Wagner, Lisa Weiss, Cathy Whims, Faith Willinger, Priscilla Yee, Edy Young, and Sami Zubaida.

Beautiful books are the result of a well-orchestrated collaboration. Thanks to Jacinta Monniere for typing support and to Debbie Weiss Geline, Judith Sutton, and Shelley Berg for their careful copyediting and proofreading.

Thanks to George Restrepo for designing a beautiful and elegant book and to Eugenie Delaney for carrying it out.

Thanks also to the great team of professionals in the production crew, art director Melissa Lotfy, and production editor Rebecca Springer. Many thanks to Tim Mudie and Laney Whitt.

Recipes by Category

Freezes Well

Grass-Fed Beef and Veal

Great Meat Dishes of the World

Heirloom Pork

In a Hurry

Keeps Well

Index

An asterisk indicates a recipe for which the ingredient is an alternate cut.

hash cakes with poached eggs, 182–83
home-cured, 446
Insta Cure No. 1 in, 415
Irish, and vegetables with dill pickle–horseradish cream and Guinness-mustard sauce, 179–81
*tongue mousse, 426
cornichon butter, 258
Corsican Cuisine: Flavors of the Perfumed Isle (Meyer), 494
cottage ham/bacon (smoked Boston butt), 346, 348, 442
cottage pie, bison, 196–98
country ham, 355
with maple, tea, and cardamom glaze and sauce, 356–57
country-style beef ribs, 185, 186
country-style pork ribs, 393
all-pork cassoulet, 312–16
"cow-pooling," 30
Creole veal grillades with cheesy grits, 576–79
Crescimanno, Pierluigi, 294
cross-rib roast, 41, 94, 115, 120, 162, 170
with garlic-herb marinade, 119–20
cross-rib steak, 41, 128
crown roast of lamb, 491, 493
bulgur mint stuffing for, 492
cut for, 476, 477
crown roast of pork, 334
Cuban-style pork and rice, 368–70
culotte roast, 94, 115, 116
culotte steak, 47, 51, 62
CURED MEAT, 436–48
bacon, home-cured, 438–39
basic wet brine for, 437
beef tongue, pickled, 448
Boston butt, smoked (cottage ham/bacon), 442
corned beef and pastrami, home-cured, 446
ham, home-cured, 444–45
"ham," Dick Vennerbeck's overnight, 443

Insta Cure No. 1 in, 415
petit salé pork (brined pork), 447
pork loin, smoked (Canadian bacon), 441
CURRY:
goat, West Indian, 513–14
and Guinness–braised chuck steak, 163–64
paste, Caribbean, 513
powder, Bruce's, 526
rub, 524
Thai green, –marinated beef kebabs, 129–31
Thai red, glaze, 388–89
cutting boards, safety concerns and, 8

D

daikon radish, in pickled vegetables, 300–1
daube, Jeff's (Provençal beef stew), 190–92
Delmonico steak, 47, 50
Denver steak, 42, 46, 47, 50, 61, 128
dessert, Parmigiano-Reggiano and aged balsamico for, 110
deviled ham, Gammy Brown's, 364–65
dill pickle–horseradish cream, 181
direct grilling, 11–12
doneness, how to judge, 15
internal temperature and, 15–17
see also specific meats
Dooky Chase, New Orleans, 576
Doumani, Lissa, 537
DRESSINGS:
blue cheese, buttermilk, and scallion, 55
Russian, 136
Thai, 310
thousand island barbecue, 154
tomato-eggplant vinaigrette, 467–68
Dr Pepper glaze/sauce, 352
dry-curing, 436
dry-heat cooking methods, 10
see also grilling techniques

dry-salted fresh leg of pork, 342–43
duck livers:
Italian country terrine, 419–20
*smooth lamb liver pâté with Vin Santo, 421–23
dumplings:
egg, 189
pork and apple (pierogi), 305–7
spinach and ricotta, 108–9
Dunn, Franco, 419, 593
Duroc pigs, 236, 237–38

E

E. coli, 43
Eckhouse, Herb and Kathy, 342
egg(s):
dumplings, 189
poached, hash cakes with, 182–83
eggplant:
bell pepper, and tomato sauce, 506–7
skewered, 552–54
tomato vinaigrette, 467–68
English-cut short ribs, 185, 186
"enhanced" beef, 38
escabeche marinade, 541–42
escarole and white bean gratin, 109–10
Espelette pepper, spicy herb rub with, 274
eye-of-round steak, 48
eye-round roast, 115, 161

F

factory farming, 1, 3
beef and, 26–27
pork and, 236–37, 238, 239, 240–42
fats, 19
feijoada (Brazilian black bean stew), 193–95
FENNEL:
fresh, pan sauce, 561
and herb marinade, 565
and herb rub, 294
pork stew with butternut squash and, 371–73
roasted, 566

pork and, 240, 241

veal and, 546–47

hors d'oeuvres, *see* appetizers and hors d'oeuvres

horseradish–dill pickle cream, 181

Hungarian goulash, 187–89

I

Ibérico ham, 346–47

iceberg wedges with blue cheese, buttermilk, and scallion dressing, 55

INDIAN (FLAVORS AND CUISINE):

lamb biryani, 527

tandoori lamb shoulder chops, 472–73

indirect grilling, *see* grill-roasted or indirect grilled (meats)

ingredients, 19–20

Insta Cure No. 1, 415

internal temperature, doneness and, 8–9, 15–17

involtini, Sicilian-style, 562–63

IRAQI (FLAVORS AND CUISINE):

Baghdad basmati rice stuffing, 532–33

stuffed lamb breast, Sami's, 532–35

IRISH (FLAVORS AND CUISINE):

beef-cheek pie with stout, 222–24

corned beef and vegetables with dill pickle–horseradish cream and Guinness-mustard sauce, 179–81

Irish whiskey and cream pan sauce, pan-seared fillet steaks with, 86

ITALIAN (FLAVORS AND CUISINE):

beef fillet paillards with arugula, mushrooms, and Parmesan (steak tagliata), 84–85

braised oxtails with fried capers and sage leaves, 215–17

burger subs, 158–59

Calabrese burgers, 156–57

country terrine, 419–20

escarole and white bean gratin, 109–10

Florentine lamb pot roast with black olives, 522–23

Friuli-style braised beef cheeks, 220–21

grilled scallions wrapped in pork belly, 294–95

melt-in-your-mouth pork shoulder, 339–41

my Neapolitan cabbie's baked ziti with broccoli rabe and hot Italian sausage, 317–19

osso buco with artichokes, Jeff's, 585–88

Parmigiano-Reggiano and aged balsamico for dessert, 110

peposo alla fornacina (baker's peppery beef shanks), 218–19

pork tenderloin medallions with roasted pepper and cherry pepper pan sauce, 283–85

Rosa di Parma (whole beef fillet stuffed with prosciutto and Parmigiano-Reggiano), 106–10

sausage, sweet, 410

Sicilian lamb meatballs braised with eggplant, bell pepper, and tomatoes, 506–7

Sicilian-style involtini, 562–63

spinach and ricotta dumplings, 108–9

stinco (braised and roasted pork shanks), 385–87

veal shank ravioli with brown butter and sage, 588

wedding soup (Italian meatball soup), 140–42

J

Jaccard, 49

jalapeños chiles:

fire-roasted salsa, 259

Mexican pickled vegetables, 228–29

salsa verde, 260

Jamaican beef patties (spicy beef turnovers), 150–52

jambon de Paris, 347

Japanese-style veal yakitori patties, 569–70

jus, bacon and rosemary, 104

K

kale and garlic sausage, 412–13

KEBABS:

beef, 128–31; *see also* beef kebabs

lamb and goat, 496–502; *see also* goat kebabs; lamb kebabs

pork, 290–95; *see also* pork kebabs

Kentucky flavor brine, 251

khao soi (Thai goat and noodle soup), 517–18

Kobe beef, 34

Korean-style short ribs, 185

Kuhn, Loni, 508

Kurobuta (Berkshire) pigs, 236, 237

L

laab (Thai pork salad), 310–11

labels, reading, 5

LAMB, 449–542

buying, 456–57

commodity, 455

cooking and serving, 459–61

grades of, 457

grain-finished, 454

grass-fed or pasture-raised, 2–3, 454, 455; *see also* Grass-Fed Meat, 605

heirloom breeds of, 456

internal temperature and doneness of, 459–61

natural, 455

naturally raised, 455

primal cuts of, 458

storing, 458

USDA Certified Organic, 454, 455

shoulder roast/steak, 162
shoulder steak, 48, 50
SICILIAN (FLAVORS AND CUISINE):
  involtini, 562–63
  lamb meatballs braised with eggplant, bell pepper, and tomatoes, 506–7
SIDES:
  broccolini with pecan brown butter, 57
  cherry tomato salad, 555–57
  corn bread, Lulee's, 573–75
  egg dumplings, 189
  eggplant, skewered, 552–54
  escarole and white bean gratin, 109–10
  fennel, roasted, 566
  green papaya salad, 271
  grits, cheesy, 578–79
  iceberg wedges with blue cheese, buttermilk, and scallion dressing, 55
  potatoes, rosemary-scented, 479–81
  potatoes, twice-baked, with sour cream and Parmigiano filling, 56
  spinach and ricotta dumplings, 108–9
  white beans with sage, 489–90
  Yorkshire puddings, scallion and Parmesan, 105
  see also stuffings
sirloin primal, beef and bison, 41
sirloin roast, 118
  bison (recipe), 124
sirloin tip roast, 94, 115, 118, 120
sirloin tip steak, 41, 42, 47, 48, 49, 51
SKEWERS:
  beef kebabs, 128–31; see also beef kebabs
  eggplant, 552–54
  grilling mushrooms and onions on, 77
  lamb and goat kebabs, 496–502; see also goat kebabs; lamb kebabs

veal yakitori patties, 569–70
skirt steak, 37, 47, 51, 60, 61, 62, 95, 128
slaw, fennel, 482
sloppy Bruce sandwich, 173
smell, freshness of meat and, 5
smoked meat, 436
  Boston butt (cottage ham/bacon), 442
  cold-smoking, 439
  pork loin (Canadian bacon), 441
smoky bacon spice paste, 69
smoky bison cheeseburger, 154–55
smoky chile marinade, 398
soups:
  goat and noodle, Thai (khao soi), 517–18
  greens, fresh peas, and ham, 362–63
  Italian wedding (Italian meatball soup), 140–42
SOUTHEAST ASIAN (FLAVORS AND CUISINES):
  Malaysian marinated blade-end pork chops with green papaya salad, 268–71
  plum sambal, 263
  see also Thai (flavors and cuisine); Vietnamese (flavors and cuisine)
soy glaze, sweet, 569–70
SPANISH (FLAVORS AND CUISINE):
  adobo rub, 116
  braised bison or grass-fed beef brisket, 169–70
  chorizo, see chorizo, Spanish
  cocido from Castilla–La Mancha, 209–11
  flavor brine, 330
  pork burgers, 297–99
  pork stew with chorizo and paprika (carcamusas), 374–75
  roasted rack of pork with pan-roasted romesco sauce, 329–31
  spice pastes, 68, 320
  sweet pepper and chorizo butter, 59

spareribs, 392, 393
  baked, with lemon confit rub, 400–2
speck, 347
spice pastes, see pastes
spice rubs, see rubs, dry
spices, 20
  baharat, 144, 536
  curry powder, Bruce's, 526
  pickling, 445
spicy and smoky Mexican goat kebabs, 500–2
spicy beef turnovers (Jamaican beef patties), 150–52
spicy herb rub with Espelette pepper, 274
spicy Middle Eastern bison meatballs with cilantro-yogurt sauce, 138–39
spicy Thai peanut paste and sauce, 466
spinach:
  and Gorgonzola–stuffed flank steak, 121–23
  porcini stuffing, 99
  and ricotta dumplings, 108–9
  sautéed steak with "Rockefeller" pan sauce, 89
squash, winter:
  and beef brisket chili, Mexican, 199–201
  butternut, pork stew with fennel and, 371–73
standing rib roast, 42, 93
  with bacon and rosemary jus and Yorkshire puddings, 102–5
  with porcini-spinach stuffing, toasted peppercorn and whiskey sauce, and horseradish cream, 96–101
star anise:
  –flavored pork rillettes, 433
  and rosemary dry rub, 66
steak house experience:
  broccolini with pecan brown butter, 57
  grilled rib eye with flavored butter, 52–54
  iceberg wedges with blue cheese, buttermilk, and scallion dressing, 55

pork sausage, 411
red curry glaze, 388–89
thawing meat, 6–7
thermocouple digital
thermometers, 17
thermometers, 15–17
continuous-read, 15–16
how to use, 17
instant-read, 16–17
thousand island barbecue
dressing, 154
thyme:
and fennel–rubbed roast rack
of lamb, 483
fresh rosemary and, rub, 276
and sage rub, 378
tip roast/steak, 94, 161
tomatillos, in salsa verde, 260
TOMATO(ES):
blue cheese butter, 555–56
braised beef steak with
tequila, orange and, 165–
68
cherry, salad, 555–57
eggplant, and bell pepper
sauce, 506–7
eggplant vinaigrette, 467–68
fire-roasted salsa, 259
heirloom, sauce, Gary's, 316
olive garnish, 156–57
oven-roasted, 468
pan-roasted romesco sauce,
329–31
pico de gallo, 259
salsa verde, 326
tomato(es), sun-dried:
garlic oil, 264
grilled boneless pork chops
stuffed with fontina,
prosciutto and, 264–65
mayonnaise, 156
TONGUE(S):
lamb, 542
lamb, escabeche, 541–42
mousse, 426
veal, 589
see also beef tongue
top blade roast, 162, 170
top blade steak, 50
top loin, 40, 42
top loin roast, 93
top loin steak, 47, 50, 74

top round roast, 94, 120
top round steak, 47, 48, 51, 60–
61, 115, 128
top sirloin roast, 94, 115
top sirloin steak, 47, 51, 61, 62,
74, 128
tortas, Mexican, 302–4
touch, quality of meat and, 5
trichinosis, 247
tri-tip roast, 94, 115, 118
grill- or oven-roasted, with
Spanish adobo rub, 116–18
tri-tip steak, 47, 51, 61, 128
TURKISH (FLAVORS AND
CUISINE):
flavor brine, 252
pasta with bison sauce, 143–
44
pomegranate-glazed lamb
shoulder chops and
carrots, 519–21
spice paste, 465
turnovers, spicy beef (Jamaican
beef patties), 150–52
twice-baked potatoes with sour
cream and Parmigiano
filling, 56
two-step pan-broiled double-
thick steak, 82–83

U
Uniform Retail Meat Identity
Standards (URMIS), 49
USDA:
beef grades and, 38
grass-fed beef and, 28–29
grass-fed veal and, 546
ham's water content and, 345
USDA, internal temperatures
recommended by:
for beef, 43–46
for burgers, 153
for lamb and goat, 459–60
for pork, 248–49
for veal, 49–550
USDA Certified Organic:
beef, 30–31, 33
lamb, 454, 455
pork, 240, 241, 242
veal, 546
USDA "natural" labels:
for beef, 31–32

for ham, 348
for pork, 240, 241
for veal, 546
USDA "naturally raised" labels:
for beef, 32
for pork, 240, 241

V
Valette, Jean-Michel, 145
Valette family stuffed whole
cabbage, 145–49
VEAL, 543–96
"Bob," 547
buying, 547–48
changing choices for, 545–47
cooking, 549
formula-fed, 545, 546–47,
548
grades of, 547
internal temperature and
doneness of, 549–50
"natural" and "all-natural,"
546
nonformula-fed, 546
pasture-raised, 2–3, 545–46,
547; see also Grass-Fed
Meat, 605
primal cuts of, 548
storing, 549
VEAL, GROUND, 568–70
grinding meat at home, 568
*Italian burger subs, 158–59
*pork and apple dumplings
(pierogi), 305–7
*Spanish-style pork burgers,
297–99
*Valette family stuffed whole
cabbage, 145–49
yakitori patties, 569–70
VEAL CHOPS, 550–56
cuts of, 551
*mustard and savory–
marinated pork chops
with cornichon butter,
256–58
pan-grilled, with tomato–blue
cheese butter and cherry
tomato salad, 555–57
*sautéed goat T-bone loin
chops with pecorino
and toasted almonds,
474–75